MURDER
WHEREABOUTS

The good sense of the practitioner has
usually directed him to night and
privacy. Yet there have not been
wanting cases where this rule was
departed from with excellent effect.

Thomas de Quincey (1785–1859)
On Murder Considered as One of the Fine Arts

MURDER
WHEREABOUTS

J.H.H. Gaute and Robin Odell

Authors of
THE MURDERERS' WHO'S WHO
and
MURDER: 'WHATDUNIT'

HARRAP
LONDON

This book is dedicated to
Hale Lamont-Havers,
author, well-informed criminologist
and dear friend, with love and thanks
for all the help she has given us,
not only in the preparation of this work
but also of the other two books
of the trilogy.

First published in Great Britain 1986
by HARRAP Ltd
19-23 Ludgate Hill, London EC4M 7PD

© *J. H. H. Gaute and Robin Odell* 1986

ISBN 0 245-54258-2

Designed by Michael R. Carter

Printed and bound in Great Britain
by R. J. Acford, Chichester

CONTENTS

Preface

This is the third in the Gaute-Odell sequence of murder reference books. *The Murderers' Who's Who* and *Murder: 'Whatdunit'* analysed the subject by murderer and method. *Murder: Whereabouts* deals with the location of murder — not in the geographical sense, which would simply be a kind of gazetteer, but in terms of the characteristics which a place gives to murder. From the alleyway killings of Jack the Ripper to murder at London Zoo, the 'whereabouts' of murder are no less fascinating than 'whodunit' or 'whatdunit'.

The location of murder may be chosen deliberately by the perpetrator to afford him de Quincey's qualities of darkness and privacy or the place may be selected unwittingly by the victim — by the prostitute, for example, who lures her client into quiet seclusion. All the usual elements of chance and design play a part in the interaction between murderer and victim which result in possibilities for killing, concealment and disposal. What is certain is that, however well premeditated, murder cannot occur in a vacuum — fate or circumstance has to decree a place in which the deed can be enacted. *Murder: Whereabouts* includes fifty such locations which form the backdrop to murder.

Domestic murder being the most prevalent, the home is frequently the scene of the crime. George Orwell in his essay on the 'Decline of the English Murder' reconstructed the 'perfect murder' for the Sunday newspaper reader. The murderer would be 'a little man of the professional class' living in a suburban semi-detached house which permitted suspicious noises to permeate through the walls to the ears of neighbours.

Individual rooms in the home offer various possibilities for murder. The kitchen, for example, often proves to be the environment for domestic disputes which spill over into violence (facilitated by the availability of handy weapons such as knives). Dr Marvin Wolfgang, whose study of homicide patterns in Philadelphia is a milestone of criminal sociology, noted that 29 per cent of female offenders killed their victims in the kitchen.

The comfortable surroundings of the parlour or dining-room may soften the sinister moves of the murderer bent on poisoning his victim with food or drink, but it is the bedroom which proves to be the most dangerous room in the house.

The bedroom may turn into the locus for a crime of passion when sexual emotions or jealousies erupt into violence and, equally, it may become a place where a relative is slowly murdered by poison given under the guise of medication.

These places within the home are often chosen by the murderer to provide him with optimum protection and to make the killing easy by keeping the victim in familiar surroundings and by putting him at ease. Because murder is usually the last cause of death a family doctor looks for, the home often proves the best place for the murderer to commit domestic violence, and encourage its interpretation as accident, suicide or natural death.

The whereabouts of murder often depend on the murderer's special requirements — George Joseph Smith's insistence on his rented accommodation having a bathroom is well known. Cellars, attics, garages and gardens all have characteristics which may help the murderer in his tasks of commission and concealment. Some mass murderers have taken considerable trouble to convert their premises into specially equipped murder houses. Dr Marcel Petiot and H.H. Holmes fall into this class, as do John Christie and Henri Landru. Disposal by the elemental means of fire and water has long proved attractive, and the foul black smoke emitted from the chimneys of the residences of Petiot and Landru were sinister signals of elimination. The smell of decomposition is another legacy of foul play, especially where dismemberment and disposal are attempted indoors. Disposing of the victims is no easy task, as Dennis Nilsen learned to his cost.

Immersion in water to simulate drowning requires either the necessary apparatus or proximity to the element. In either case, the whereabouts of murder is important. Charlotte Corday had the good fortune to visit Marat while he was in the bath, so that her unsuspecting victim was immediately disadvantaged. The body pushed over the ship's side (or through a porthole) into the open sea seems a safe enough method of disposal, even bearing in mind — as James Camb discovered — that a murder charge can still be brought without a body being found. Unfortunately, as many would-be eliminators have found out, the sea has a habit of giving up its dead. The satisfaction gained by putting the victim out of sight and out of mind into the nearest river or stretch of water is often short-lived.

Indoors and outdoors, from Australia to Zimbabwe and from attic to zoo, every location has its opportunities for darkness and privacy so necessary to the commission of secret homicide. The anonymity provided by a hotel room in a crowded city with the chance to commit murder behind a locked door, and for the killer to melt away into some great metropolis, has been well practised. The loneliness of moor and mountain has also proved attractive, and the ease of access to remote places by motor car has added further dimensions to murderous planning.

Some murderers have gone to great lengths to transport their victims' bodies to locations at a distance from the crime scene. Mary Pearcey wheeled the remains of her fatal assault on a woman and child through several miles of London's streets in a perambulator before dumping them. Edgar Edwards similarly moved his victims across London in order to bury them in the garden of a house he had acquired. Sacks, trunks and boxes of all kinds have been used for the conveyance of corpses from one locus to another. In this the railways have played a significant part by carrying usually unaccompanied luggage from one place to another to 'await collection'.

Although *Murder: Whereabouts*, like its companion volumes *The Murderers' Who's Who* and *Murder: Whatdunit*, is addressed to a particular aspect of its subject, it also seeks perspectives on the wider issues affecting crime and punishment. Of particular concern is the balance of public interest between victim and murderer. Robert Songhurst, writing in *True Detective* magazine in September 1984, remarked that where it was at one time considered a wicked thing to deprive a person of his life, 'today every possible excuse is made for the murderer'. This is justified comment, for everything from pre-menstrual tension to so-called 'sexual addiction' has been used to argue the case for unavoidable provocation. Moreover, the victim may not simply be forgotten but may be 'faintly blamed for tempting the murderer off the path of virtue'. It is as if the criminal is no longer the murderer but the victim.

This is not an isolated view. J. D. Reed, reviewing Jack Olsen's book *Son* for MacLean's magazine, wrote in a similar vein. The subject of this psychobiography (as it has been described) is Fred Coe, a rapist from Spokane, Washington, who was sentenced to seventy-five years' imprisonment. The reviewer spoke of it as a case where the victims have walk-on parts while the wrongdoer is made into a symbol wherein his 'private ailments are seen as social ills'.

Nor are these views new. Arthur A. Carey, for many years a detective in the Homicide Bureau of the New York Police Department, wrote about 'A Philosophy of Murder' in 1929. He referred to the doubling of the US homicide rate over a twenty-year period, and grieved at the increase on the statute books of laws to safeguard the criminal. He spoke too of newly invented defences of murder — what he called *dementia Americana*.

Even in straightforward murder cases there is often a sense in which sympathy is directed away from the victim and focused on the killer, whose action is interpreted as in some way having been justifiably provoked.

Beth Fallon, an American journalist, took up the cause of the victim in the aftermath of John Lennon's murder in New York in 1980. She wrote in the *Baltimore Sun* that 'some instinct of revulsion' kept her away from Mark David Chapman's sentencing when he enjoyed 'his moment in the sun'. In her article she pointed out that Sirhan Sirhan, the Jordanian assassin of Robert Kennedy in 1968, who is serving a life sentence in California, was reported to be making travel plans in anticipation of his release from prison.

Life imprisonment in California normally means thirteen years maximum. Beth Fallon reminded her readers that Robert Kennedy, the victim of the assassin's bullets, will still be dead when his killer is released. Is it like a deal whereby 'I kill somebody and give eight years or twelve or seventeen years in exchange?' she questioned.

Colin Wilson, in his comprehensive book *A Criminal History of Mankind*, makes an examination of criminality or what he calls the 'flip-side' of the human capacity for creativity. He points out that the worst crimes are committed not by evil degenerates but by intelligent people who pursue a pragmatic solution to their problems. *Murder: Whereabouts* contains many examples; among whose number may be counted Ken Bianchi, Ted Bundy and Dennis Nilsen, all handsome, or at least pleasant-looking, intelligent men who could expect reasonable achievements in their lives. Instead, they showed what Wilson calls the criminal's distorted reflection of the human face, and between them they were responsible for at least forty-six murders.

The suggestion has been made that criminals are adults who go on behaving like children, in effect, because they cannot get their own way or succeed along the normal competitive routes. Certainly the number of killings committed because of a grudge against society seems to be increasing. Childhood rejection is a factor which psychologists have established as a common characteristic of serial killers. If not countered by other, kindlier, forces, rejection at an early age seems to inspire in some the childish desire for revenge in a form totally out of proportion to the original hurt. It appears that the command to loose vengeance on mankind often comes in the form of voices to the schizophrenic mind, as it did to David Berkowitz, Peter Sutcliffe and Joseph Kallinger. Some psychiatrists take the view that murder is the suicide of the self, however unconscious the realization may be. If the concept that every person who murders first wanted to kill himself is a correct one, it perhaps bears out the childish thesis of 'When I'm dead, you will be sorry.'

The criminal is not, as commonly supposed, a legacy of caveman ancestry. Although Lombroso's theories were debunked a long time ago, the idea of the criminal type is still attractive to the ordinary person in his attempts to explain some of the worst criminal excesses. As Colin Wilson points out, we are all capable of erring; it is just that the criminal goes further than most of us in embracing the wrong solution. In this sense, by recognizably going too far, the criminal provides the rest of us with a moment's insight into our own potential for error.

The history of violence is a record of society's instability. In Victorian England murder emerged from stuffy drawing-rooms and parlours as a reflection of domestic tension. Reviewing *Watson's Apology*, Beryl Bainbridge's account of the Rev. John Selby Watson's murder of his wife, John Mortimer wrote that there was no institution more likely to lead to violence than the Victorian suburban marriage.

American murders committed at the turn of the century by Robert Buchanan, Roland Molineux and Albert Patrick — respectively doctor, chemist and lawyer — all intelligent men with potential, suggest another kind of frustration. Arthur A. Carey in his book *On the Track of Murder* suggested it was their mediocrity which turned them into 'misplaced human units who killed to escape'.

In Germany between the two World Wars there was an upsurge of sex murders — Peter Kürten, Fritz Haarmann, Adolf Seefeld and Ludwig Tessnow, for example — whose feelings were of alienation and lack of purpose. But the modern crime explosion occurred in the USA against the background of social resentment which prevailed in the 1960s and of which Charles Manson was the chief exponent. Since then there has been a steady climb, both in the murder rate and in the brutality of individual crimes. Murder has become mass-murder, and mass-murder has become serial murder — it is, to use Colin Wilson's term, 'the collective nightmare of society'.

Adolphe Quételet, the father of modern statistics, wrote about murder in *Physique sociale* in 1869. His view that society contains within itself the germs of all future crimes is not a comforting doctrine to hold against the rising trends of violence. He added that society prepares in some degree to protect itself against the criminal, and Colin Wilson concludes on an optimistic note, believing that crime will always be outweighed by creativity and intelligence.

By structuring some of the scenes of crime, *Murder: Whereabouts* may be judged to have made a modest contribution to the debate. Certainly the environment in which murder takes place, whether it is victim-precipitated or decided by the killer, is no less important than other forensic questions.

Should the importance of location and its relationship to the criminal psyche be doubted, the background to the Manson killings provides sobering answers. In 1968 Charles Manson nursed ambitions to produce a record album, and talked to a producer about making a recording. He visited the producer in his home at 10050 Cielo Drive, Beverly Hills, California, but suffered disappointment when the talked-of record was not made. Exactly a year to the day, on 9 August 1969, Manson had his revenge on Hollywood society when his followers murdered Sharon Tate, then resident at 10050 Cielo Drive. Dr Thomas Noguchi, the former Los Angeles Medical Examiner, commenting on the incident, believed that neither the choice of day nor choice of house was coincidental. It was a matter of exacting symbolic revenge.

Of crime we hear more than enough, but what of its punishment? Most accounts come from the USA, where thirty-eight states have restored capital punishment. Press reports are usually concerned with last-minute stays of execution or with some hideous malfunction of the apparatus of death — the electric jolt that fails to work first time or the junkie murderer who no longer has a decent vein in which to put the final shot. Capital punishment has always been hedged around with ritual — the tolling bells and black flags have given way to death-cell press conferences and negotiations for film rights.

There has been a great deal of hand-wringing over the deterrent value of capital punishment, and majority public opinion is at variance with the facts. The return of the death penalty in the USA has not led to any reduction in the murder rate. Nevertheless, an opinion poll showed a majority of 84 per cent of Americans in favour of the death penalty. It is likely too that a public referendum in Britain would show a similar trend. We do know that the threat of capital punishment can have a curbing effect on violence. A generation ago, Alec de Antiquis, a member of the public and a family man with six children, tried to thwart the escape of three armed robbers in a London street. They shot him and left him dying in the gutter for his pains. His killers were brought to justice, and two of them, Charles Jenkins and Christopher Geraghty — both in their early twenties — were hanged. Superintendent Robert Fabian of Scotland Yard discussed the aftermath of the affair in his memoirs.

> For weeks after the hanging of Jenkins and Geraghty [he wrote] we began to find guns ... abandoned in parks under bushes, in dustbins, dropped through the floors of bombed houses, fished up by Thames River patrolmen in nets from the low-tide mud. The men of the underworld had decided to think twice about using guns in London. So whenever I think of Antiquis these days it is as one good life lost — but also as a thousand lives saved!

As Henry Schwarzschild of the American Civil Liberties Union has observed, most ordinary, law-abiding citizens, knowing that they would be deterred by the threat of capital punishment, assume that potential murderers would be also. But as we know only too well, domestic murder apart, today's killer is not blessed with the human attributes of compassion, decency and remorse, or, when it comes to it, fear of the law. He does not forget that society disapproves of murder — he simply does not care, or feels that he can override the accepted standards with his individual urges. The murderer's gut reaction is at the other end of the spectrum to the man-in-the-street, and the gap between them is so wide that neither hand-wringing nor reason is likely to bridge it.

We are left with an undercurrent of violence, especially in the form of international terrorism and inner-city aggression, that threatens to become a torrent, with the innocent and vulnerable as its victims. Justice is intended to be balanced, but all too often the balance favours the transgressor, who grabs self-seeking headlines and becomes the focus of attention as experts argue over his state of mind. Meanwhile his victims suffer their grief and nurse their injuries. Perhaps we have become unwitting accomplices to violence by too readily seeking to explain it and excuse it. Perhaps justice has become mesmerized by its procedural cleverness, and lost sight of its moral imperatives. After all, victims have rights too, and may we not have sheltered too long behind increasingly blurred definitions of responsibility and mitigation? Can we not say that the worst killers and terrorists, whose characters are flawed beyond comprehension and reason, have forfeited their right to humanity?

If the majority believes that properly convicted murders should be punished with death, whether prevailing statistics favour deterrence or not, should we not dispense with ritual and get on with it? Certainly society ought not to enact laws or penalties it is not prepared to enforce. Ultimately, the elemental strength of violence will not be ameliorated by making it an easy option for those who wish to oppose the accepted mores of civilized life.

J H H Gaute
Pyrford, Surrey

Robin Odell
Sonning Common
Oxfordshire

ACKNOWLEDGMENTS

The authors wish to thank their many friends and professional contacts who have furnished intelligence about books and documents relating to murder cases and crime reports. Particular thanks are expressed to Hale Lamont Havers, a friend and crime-writing associate over many years, to whom the present book is dedicated.

We are grateful to those who have willingly granted permission to use illustrations. If we have failed to trace any copyright-holders we offer our apologies.

We should also like to thank Susan Fennell, Richard Floyd, Dr Keiji Gotoh, Lorna Newman, Dr Artur Varatojo and S.M. Walton for their help in obtaining books and press cuttings.

The diligent work of our editor, Roy Minton, is gratefully acknowledged, as is the reassurance gained by knowing that the script has been scrutinized by so knowledgeable a crime historian as Richard Whittington-Egan.

Last, but by no means least, we again salute the perseverance of our wives during another lengthy excursion into crime.

NOTES

The numbers at the end of each entry refer to books included in the Bibliography. Readers may thereby follow up individual cases in more detail. The Bibliography stands in its own right as a comprehensive listing of non-fiction crime books. Place and year of publication are included where these are known in order to aid searches in the literature.

MURDER: WHEREABOUTS is a companion volume to THE MURDERERS' WHO'S WHO and MURDER: WHATDUNIT. As such it contains mostly new cases, although a number of old, familiar ones are included for the sake of completeness. These are designated by the abbreviations *MWW* and *mw*, indicating that they are more fully dealt with in THE MURDERERS' WHO'S WHO and MURDER: WHATDUNIT respectively.

The aim has been to compile three books which independently review the *Who*, *What* and *Where* of murder by means of different illustrative cases and which together provide a comprehensive collection of murders and their bibliographical sources.

PART ONE

SIX CONTINENTS OF MURDER

AFRICA

'Do Africans kill themselves and one another and in the same situations as Europeans and Americans?' was a question raised by Paul Bohannan in his highly respected sociological study *African Homicide and Suicide*.

The answer is not simple, but some crude comparisons provide useful clues. For example, the relationship between killer and victim recorded in homicide cases in Houston, Texas, and compared with similar information from a tribal district of Uganda, shows that the proportion of domestic killings is roughly similar. Allowance has to be made, of course, for the greater variety of sexual liaisons which prevail in the USA.

RELATIONSHIP BETWEEN KILLER AND VICTIM*

Victim's relationship to killer	% Uganda	% Houston
Husband/wife	37	12
Lover/paramour	2	22
Rival	5	–
In-Laws	8	4
Other relatives	8	8
Step relation	3	3
Neighbour	5	2
Friend/Acquaintance	–	32
Stranger	10	17
Unknown	20	–
Other	2	–
Total	**100**	**100**

*Based on information included in the surveys conducted by Bohannan (Biblio, 95) and by Henry P. Lundsgaarde (Biblio, 607) in the USA.

Murder is essentially a social relationship, and the pattern in Africa seems similar to that in the developed parts of the world, where a quarter of all murders are domestic in origin.

The weapons used to commit homicide form another basis for comparison between practices in tribal Africa and in America.

COMPARISON OF WEAPONS* USED TO COMMIT HOMICIDE

Weapon used	% Uganda	% Houston
Firearms	–	86
Knives	23	11
Clubs	21	–
Tools	17	2
Manual strangulation/beating	2	1
Miscellaneous	14	–
Unknown	23	–
Total	**100**	**100**

*Based on information included in the surveys conducted by Bohannan (Biblio, 95) and by Henry P. Lundsgaarde (Biblio, 607) in the USA.

It is well understood that the majority of murders in the USA are committed with firearms, and this pattern contrasts strongly with Africa, where guns are rarely used. When Africans kill it is usually with knife or club. It seems that neither Houstonians nor Africans have much use for poison. The former eschew the slow mechanics of poisoning in favour of the fast and remotely administered death delivered by a gun, while poison is used in Africa, but mostly in association with witchcraft or sorcery. In these instances it is administered in order to produce illness or madness, as part of a scheme to bewitch the victim and provoke him to take his own life.

Some forms of murder are either sanctioned by tribal law or at least regarded with a blind eye. In West Africa during the nineteenth century it was traditional for criminals to be executed by ritual sacrifice, and in the case of a thief the aggrieved victim often played the role of executioner. Adulterers were also fair targets for revenge killings. A case of true ritual sacrifice in this century was recorded by Benjamin Bennett in a chapter on native murders in his book *Up for Murder*. He cites the case of a ritual murder carried out by the Mtwara tribe in Southern Rhodesia (or what is now Zimbabwe). This tribe had a legendary 'Rain Goddess', selected from the young girls among its members, whose virginity was essential to the provision of rainfall.

In 1922 the country experienced a severe drought, and it was decided that the great spirit of the tribe was angry because the rain goddess had been deflowered. To lessen this anger and to ensure that the rains came, it was necessary to identify the culprit and kill him as a sacrificial offering to the gods. The elders of the tribe identified the chief's son as the seducer, and orders were given that the young man should be taken from his hut at night and conducted to the place of sacrifice. These instructions were duly carried out, and the supposed seducer of the rain goddess was burned to death in a sacrificial fire.

News of the killing reached the British authorities, and a chain of events began which brought the ideals of European justice into collision with tribal custom and belief. The Mtwara chief and several of his followers were charged with murder and brought to trial. In bizarre court proceedings which included the presence of the child rain goddess the chief was acquitted but six natives were convicted and sentenced to death. A recommendation to mercy had been made by the court, and this was heeded, so that the death sentences were not carried out. The rains which followed the ritual sacrifice brought floods in their wake and provoked native anger at the white man's meddling interference.

There have been a number of well-recorded cases of institutionalized killings, such as the so-called ritual murders in Basutoland (now Lesotho) in 1947–8, and the Mau Mau terrorist attacks which started in Kenya at about the same time. Both incidents had their roots in reactions to colonial rule. During the period 1940–58 there were over 130 ritual murders in Basutoland, a country in southern Africa which had been a British protectorate since 1868. The killings were described as ritualistic, and were related to the procurement of human tissue for magical purposes. A traditional Basuto belief was that human flesh possessed properties of protective medicine. Such material, known as *diretlo*, had formerly been collected from the bodies of enemies who fell in tribal battles. The advent of more peaceful times under British administrative rule made diretlo more difficult to obtain, so in the late 1940s some members of the ruling Basuto tribe instructed parties of their followers to select victims for the purpose of obtaining diretlo. Flesh and organs were cut from the live body, and the victim either died or was murdered at the end of it.

The reason for wanting to acquire diretlo in this way was to give the recipients protective medicine against the threat of insecurity to their personal status, in the climate of social change. The British Government, disturbed by the increased fashion for ritual murder, sent an anthropologist to Basutoland to investigate. The report by G.I. Jones published in 1951 contained a graphic account of one of the murders, which was preceded by the removal of numerous pieces of flesh, the tongue and the eyes as diretlo. As a result of recommendations that the people of Basutoland be given greater participation in the administration of their own affairs, the need for reassurance through protective medicine disappeared, and the sequence of murders stopped.

Murder for the acquisition of human organs is reported from various parts of Africa. Dr John Thompson, who headed Rhodesia's forensic science service from 1963 to 1977, quoted an instance in his book *Crime Scientist* which occurred in the Inyanga area. A herdsman made a gift of a parcel of meat to the foreman of his farm, who to his horror found that the otherwise acceptable offering contained two human fingers and an ear. Police discovered that the herdsman's hut was a human butcher's shop where strips of flesh hung from the roof, and dried organs lay about in profusion; buried near the hut were bones and a complete human skin. The herdsman admitted killing another African worker in order to obtain human organs which he could use as charms or sell as such to a witch-doctor. His primitive ambition served as no defence at his trial for murder, where he was convicted and sentenced to death.

Eight people were hanged in Swaziland in July 1981 after a period of four years during which the death sentence was suspended. The executions were carried out in order to curb an increase in ritual murders which had occurred in this kingdom of half a million people. The Prime Minister condemned medicine murders as a 'totally disgraceful and barbaric practice'.

A Swaziland police officer told the United Nations Conference on the Prevention of Crime meeting in 1980 in Venezuela that unless the state took steps to stop murder of all varieties, 'the people will take the law into their own hands and we will have chaos'.

Like the diretlo murders, the practice in Swaziland was to cut flesh from a still living body to make medicine or *muti*, which can be used to advance personal ambitions or to counteract the progress of rivals. Witch-doctors, fanning the flames of tribal beliefs, advise their clients to kill in order to obtain muti. Witnesses are reluctant to testify against witch-doctors, who have the fearful reputation of being able to kill their victims at a distance using black magic.

South Africa also has its problems over ritual murder, and a number of procurers of muti have been executed in the independent home-land of Venda. Among those executed was a deputy Cabinet Minister, while his son was in death row awaiting the outcome of an appeal. Doubts were aroused about the quality of the evidence which had secured some of these convictions. The testimony of eye-witnesses and self-confessed accomplices was judged to be unsatisfactory without the corroboration of 'real evidence'. Nevertheless, several persons have been hanged as murderers on the evidence of witch-doctors.

An inquiry by Mr Justice Strydom concluded that evidence gleaned from examination of the bodies of medicine-murder victims was not considered in any of the recent trials. Moreover, in four cases which resulted in the conviction of the accused there was no evidence of the existence of victims' bodies. Nineteen cases of ritual murder tried in Venda during the period 1982 to 1984 have resulted in eight hangings and four condemned men appealing against the verdicts.

Murder of a different kind was that practised by the Mau Mau terrorist movement in Kenya in the early 1950s. Kikuyu tribesmen formed themselves into a secret society and preached rebellion against the European settlers. Kikuyu, mainly young men and women, were initiated by oaths which had the purpose of distancing them from the colonial culture. A new fellowship grew up which resented the European influence and was prepared to carry out hitherto forbidden acts. Open rebellion broke out in October 1952 in a campaign of terror against the settlers, the government and any Kikuyu who remained loyal to the government. The first acts involved crop-burning and animal slaughter, but these violent attacks soon erupted into murder. Members of both Black and White communities were killed, and their bodies slashed and mutilated with panga knives. The British Government declared a state of emergency, and fears of political assassination mounted. In March 1953 Mau Mau terrorists ran wild at Lari, a township some twenty-five miles from Nairobi, torturing and killing men, women and children. The rebellion was suppressed by 1957, after 50,000 Mau Mau terrorists had been put into camps under military surveillance. Six years later the government of newly independent Kenya gave a free pardon to all outlawed terrorists, some of whom had committed horrendous acts of murder against settlers' families.

Africa is a vast continent supporting many different societies and cultures. There are no easy comparisons to be made between them,

Murder to procure human organs for magical purposes

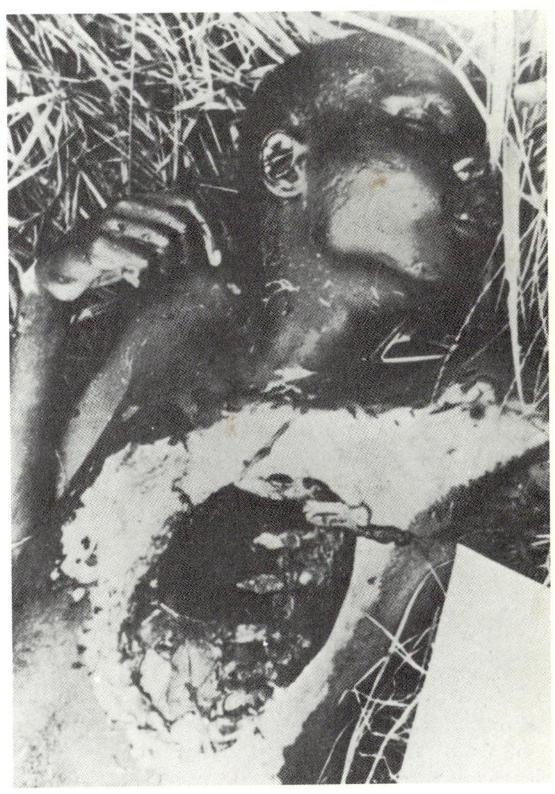

for while the result may be the same, murders committed in Arab, tribal or colonial Africa can have widely different motives. Some of the essential human appetites — greed, jealousy and revenge — might offer common themes, and disputes over possessions are always prevalent. An East African might kill most readily over a land dispute, while his brother on the west coast will more easily be motivated by some fancied affront. An Arab might kill his sister for being unchaste, and institutional murder can erupt, as instanced by the Mau Mau.

For the most part these crimes have gone unrecorded, only making news when colonial administrations tried to bend native custom to European laws. As Benjamin Bennett has pointed out, normal native customs rapidly became capital crimes under the white man's law. Faced with the dilemma of denying the demands of tribal custom or of flouting the European laws imposed on him, there was little doubt where the native would offer his obedience. The result is that only a handful of the murders committed ever came to light.

If the white man's law has been a dubious gift to Africa, the eruption of some of his own violent passions has been even less welcome. The majority of murders in Africa which have reached the headlines have been those committed in the colonies or former colonies where European newspaper traditions have given them distinction. The greatest wealth of reported murder cases has been in South Africa, where a number of remarkable stories have been documented. These have little to do with tribalism in the African sense, but a great deal to do with the traditions of murder imported by the European psyche. All the familiar motives and grisly expressions of violence are there — everything from jealousy and greed to murder by consent. Benjamin Bennett's books are a rich vein of information for these cases.

Baron Dieter von Schauroth was shot dead near Cape Town in 1961 by Marthinus Rossouw, his bodyguard. Rossouw admitted killing the farmer and diamond trader, but claimed that von Schauroth had given him a revolver and money with a request to kill him. The story was that the Baron had taken out large insurance policies to ensure the welfare of his family in the event of his death in the course of his illicit diamond trading. Rossouw carried

out the murder-by-consent, but this 'act of charity' towards his employer was rewarded with a conviction for straightforward murder and punishment by hanging.

Another rich man who added to the refinement of legal language was Ronald Cohen, a South African millionaire. He was charged with murdering his wife in Cape Town in 1970, but was judged to have committed the crime in a moment of intense rage when he lost all control. This was described in court as 'feral behaviour' induced by a catastrophic stimulus. Cohen was found to have acted without premeditation during a period of diminished responsibility. He thus avoided the death sentence and went to prison for twelve years.

Petrus Hauptfleisch committed the relatively rare act of matricide in 1924 in Richmond, Cape Province, a crime for which he was hanged. South Africa has also produced its share of female murderers, two of the most infamous being Daisy de Melker (1932) and Maria Groesbeek (1969). Both women used poison to dispose of their spouses, de Melker killing two husbands and also her son. Both women were convicted of murder and suffered the death penalty.

South Africa has had its share of unsolved and unusual murders. The killing of Arthur Kimber (see under TAXIS) in Maritzburg in 1931 remains on open file, and Huibrecht de Leeuw, the town clerk of Dewetsdorp (see under PUBLIC BUILDINGS), certainly adopted an extraordinary course when he blew up the city fathers in the town hall. Frederick Cox (see under SHOPS AND OFFICES) murdered his young cousin in Cape Town in 1924 in what he alleged was the first stage of a double death-pact. Another murderer with a mind-stretching motive was Robert Morton (see under NEXT DOOR) who killed his girl-friend in 1973 because he 'wanted to do something big'.

The incidence of murder in all its variety has contributed substantially to the rising spiral of executions in South Africa. Over a thousand criminals were executed during the fifteen-year period 1953–68, the hangman dispatching them at over one a week. The city of Pretoria has one of the highest murder rates in the world, recorded in 1959 as 13.9 cases of criminal homicide per hundred thousand of population.

Murder in Africa, as in other parts of the world, becomes ever more bizarre. In December 1984 reports from the island republic of Madagascar gave accounts of a massacre which left over a hundred dead literally at the hands of killers using Kung-fu methods. Victims had been killed without the use of weapons, and in some cases their heads were torn from their bodies and impaled on spikes in public squares. The killings were reportedly carried out by opponents of the government who went berserk after the authorities closed down many of the martial-arts clubs. The craze in Madagascar for Kung-fu spurred the government to take this action, as it was feared the martial-arts clubs were becoming powerful alternatives to the traditional secret societies. There was also the fear that Kung-fu exponents were providing back-up for the political opposition. In the event, the cure proved to be more violent than the problem.

Elsewhere in Africa, murder has become increasingly political in nature. When four leading members of the Malawi Congress Party were killed in a road accident in May 1983 rumours soon started, alleging that the deaths had been caused by hired assassins. One of the dead men was generally regarded as the likely successor to President Banda, and the deaths followed a number of fatal incidents involving political figures. Two Malawi men had been held in neighbouring Zimbabwe charged with murdering one of Dr Banda's opponents.

The painful collision of modern political power with tribal custom and religious aspiration has had an impact in other parts of Africa. In Ghana, on the west coast of the continent, three High Court judges were killed in 1982 as a prelude to the attempted coup against Flight-Lieutenant Rawlings's government. The coup failed, and in 1983 a top government official and three military personnel were tried on charges of murder and conspiracy. In the Sudan in August 1983 President Numeiri, alarmed at the rising crime-rate in his country — one killing every hour — imposed strict Islamic codes. Under Sharia law an offender's hand could be amputated if he was convicted of theft — a practice which quickly resulted in a 40 per cent reduction in this type of crime. (President Numeiri was deposed from office by a military coup early in 1985.)

Gone are the classic individual crimes committed in the former colonial territories, such as the unsolved murder of Lord Erroll in Kenya in 1941, the killing of Harriet Knowles in Ashanti in 1928 or the poisoning of Lieutenant Weiss in Algeria in 1890 (see under BARRACKS). In their place are political murders, spawned by power struggles fought in countries with fragile economies whose traditional cultures have been eroded by imported values. Individual murders still occur, and for the same centuries-old reasons that have always motivated the ultimate crime: elimination, gain, revenge, jealousy, lust and conviction.
(1, 60–73, 95, 295, 310, 424, 513, 620, 644, 929 MWW, mw)

ASIA

In his *Cameos of Indian Crime* H. Harvey, who spent thirty-five years in government service in India, surmised that the incentives to murder there were much the same as elsewhere. Doubtless that is correct, but the East has the distinction of giving the world at least three terms describing particular patterns of criminal behaviour — running amok, thuggery and assassination.

The Malay word *amok* means 'a furious charge', and at one time running amok might have been considered a purely Eastern phenomenon. The principal causes were thought to be religious hallucination resulting from a long period of asceticism and the desire to dispose of a few heretics for the sake of some religious ideal. More commonplace causes were rooted in jealousy and revenge, and the outcome was for a person to run madly about, indiscriminately attacking all-comers. Whatever the cause, running amok (or amuck) is a term that may aptly be used to describe some recent homicides in the West. James Huberty, for example, told his wife, 'I'm going hunting humans', before he shot and killed twenty-one people in a restaurant at San Ysidro, California, in July 1984.

Thuggery is certainly manifest in Western society. Taken from the Hindi word *thugna*, meaning 'to do evil', it was originally the name given to a brotherhood of robbers and murderers who were the scourge of India for centuries. The Thugs were devotees of Kali, the Goddess of Destruction, and their aim was to deliver up human sacrifices. Their *modus operandi* was to prey on travellers, whom they strangled and robbed.

The scourge of thuggery was stamped out by the British in India by 1840. No doubt leaders in many great cities round the world wish they could stamp out the vice of modern thuggery. The victims in many instances are travellers, but the strangulation cord of the original Thugs has given way to the knife and gun.

The word 'assassin' derives from *hashishin*, followers of the eleventh-century Moslem religious leader Hasan bin Sabah, who smoked hashish to give them the nerve to kill. Hasan was born in Persia, and led the Ismailis, a breakaway Moslem sect which disposed of rivals by killing them. Hasan's men smoked hashish in order to gain a 'glimpse of paradise' before dealing out death, and possibly being martyred in the process. The concept of assassination as practised in the West employed treachery and disguise in the manner of the *hashishin,* but for the most part avoided their drug-induced stimulation.

The British administrators of India listed connubial infidelity as a prime motive for murder, especially among the Hindus. The disparity in age between a typical husband and child-bride couple is an important factor. The custom of childhood betrothal precipitates a domestic scenario in which a girl reaching puberty at fourteen years is only half the age of her husband. By this time he has probably lost interest in her and she becomes simply a drudge, often living and working in the home of his parents.

When the girl meets a boy of her own age and interests, village gossip fuels the liaison and allows the husband to work up an indignant rage. Angered beyond all reason by the disobedience of his wife, he lies in wait for her to meet her boy-friend, when he pounces and kills the faithless girl. However strong the religious and social views on fidelity, this is still murder, and countless convictions have been handed out by Indian courts.

While the habit of marrying child-brides has to some extent been dulled by Western influences, the idea of profiting from the dowry system has not. Fifteen so-called dowry deaths were reported during a two-week period in New Delhi in 1983. These deaths were a mixture of murder and suicide. In some cases young women took their own lives as the result of continual harassment by their husbands' relatives, who were disappointed by dowries which failed to meet expectations. This perversion of a time-honoured custom led to a triple murder conviction in May 1983, when a husband, brother and mother-in-law were sentenced to death for killing a bride whose family did not meet their financial demands in respect of her dowry.

The traditional rivalry between Hindus and

Moslems in India, together with the political aspirations of the Sikhs, adds an explosive ingredient to deep-rooted prejudice. The desire for speedy justice and the vindication of their opinions runs strongly through the peoples of the sub-continent. If a man informs on another, or voices an insult, violence may quickly ensue. When this hair-trigger response is allied to political and religious extremism organized bloodshed is the result. It was against this background that in 1983 three judges of India's Supreme Court ruled in favour of retaining the death penalty.

Western influences have a great deal to answer for in loosening traditionally rigid social codes. The high rate of homicide in Sri Lanka, for example, is more prevalent among the Sinhalese than the Tamils, whose culture has been less subject to outside influences. The collision of cultures was evident in the Pope Murder Case at Pussellawa in 1941. C.A.G. Pope, Estate Superintendent, dismissed a worker who was secretary of the local union branch. When the man refused to leave the Superintendent had him charged with trespass. A few days later Pope was murdered when he was returning to his bungalow at night. His attackers were soon identified as estate-workers Weerasamy and Velaithen, who had been sufficiently injudicious as to make detailed inquiries about Pope's movements. They confessed to the crime, and the two men who showed their solidarity for a fellow-worker by committing a grudge murder were convicted and sentenced to death.

Maurice Collis, a Deputy Commissioner and District Magistrate in Burma in the late 1920s, relates in his autobiography, *Trials in Burma*, an incident which compared two sets of values. A young Englishman working in Rangoon lost a favourite pair of cuff-links and confronted his servant, one Ba Chit, with the accusation of theft. The servant, a known opium-addict, reacted violently by throwing himself out of the window and falling to his death thirty feet below.

The dead man's wife alleged that Ba Chit had been beaten and tortured, and that his murdered body had been thrown out of the window. To appease local opinion the Englishman was put on trial for murder. The medical testimony plainly showed that there was no evidence to support the suggestion of torture, and the charge was dismissed. The case was debated in the newspapers; the value of a pair of cuff-links was compared to a man's life. There was also much discussion of the standards a subject people should expect from their masters.

A sensational case which threw an unwelcome light on the morals of the colonial power was a lovers' conspiracy in Agra which ended in murder in 1911. Dr Henry Clark fell in love with another man's wife, and the couple decided to eliminate their unwanted spouses. Edward Fullam was poisoned with arsenic, and Clark hired four assassins to cut down his wife with swords. Sir Cecil Walsh, a judge and author of *Indian Village Crimes*, wrote a graphic account of the case which was illumined by love-letters exchanged by the murderers. Not only did Clark hire natives to carry out his dirty work but his lover, pregnant with his child, turned King's Evidence. To native eyes there must have seemed no end to the duplicity, but the law did not hesitate to find the pair guilty.

Countries that did not experience British colonial influence have less accessible criminal records, at least for English readers. But a few trends and highlights reach the international press, and both Indonesia and China made news in 1984 on account of their crackdown against crime. Death squads in Indonesia were reported in June to have disposed of up to ten thousand criminals in the previous year. Bullet-riddled bodies found dumped in the countryside and washed up by the Indian Ocean caused a political rumpus. But the reduction in crime rate met with approval in crime-ridden West Java, where the activities of the death squads were welcomed.

The People's Republic of China also adopted a stern policy in dealing with its murderers and rapists. A Hong Kong newspaper reported a total of 40,000 murders in China over a three-and-a-half year period, with only 8,000 convictions. Following the first three months of new measures — consisting of public humiliation and execution of convicted murderers — the crime-rate dropped by 40 per cent. Death posters are a regular feature in Chinese cities, and the names of those executed are underlined in red, and often accompanied by photographs of their dead bodies. Most of those executed are men in their twenties convicted of murder, burglary or rape.

As the cities of Asia — especially of south-east Asia — grow in prosperity and acquire influence in big business so the scope for intrigue and greed increases, with the menace of violence waiting in the wings. The discovery of the strangled corpse of a Malaysian banker in April 1984 in a banana plantation in the New Territories, a few miles from the Chinese border, sparked off a sensation in banking and property circles. A murder charge was brought against a Malay, and three days before he was due to appear on trial in Hong Kong a highly respected English lawyer, Richard Wimbush, was found dead in the swimming-pool at his luxurious flat — he had a 55lb manhole cover tied around his neck. The first reaction was that he had committed suicide, but later it was rumoured that he had been murdered in order to prevent him passing on vital information to the police.

The Japanese police have a reputation for being tough. Certainly the crime-rate in Tokyo has gone down, while in most comparable cities the rate has risen. Japan retains the death penalty for seventeen offences, including besides murder, arson and death resulting from rape and robbery. However, there has only been one execution a year since 1979, and reversals of two long-standing convictions have thrown a spotlight on the legal system. In July 1983 Sakae Menda was found innocent of murder after spending thirty-three years awaiting execution, and in March 1984 another man was similarly released. Shigeyoshi Taniguchi had spent a record thirty-four years on Death Row. Sadamichi Hirasawa, though, remains the most talked about Japanese murderer (see under BANKS). He has been in prison since 1948.

In an age of international travel Charles Sobhraj, Vietnamese by birth but cosmopolitan by nature, came to epitomize the jet-setting criminal. He used the world's airways to travel from one crime scene to another. Asia was his patch, and he flitted between India, Nepal, Pakistan, Hong Kong and Thailand, leaving behind him a trail of robberies and unexplained deaths. He felt too crowded in Europe, and preferred the openness of the East. But it was the Indian press which drew attention to his activities and helped eventually to bring him to justice. (For a full account see under FARMS AND FIELDS.)
(189, 438, 931, 979, 980)

The cities of Charles Sobhraj's eastern travels

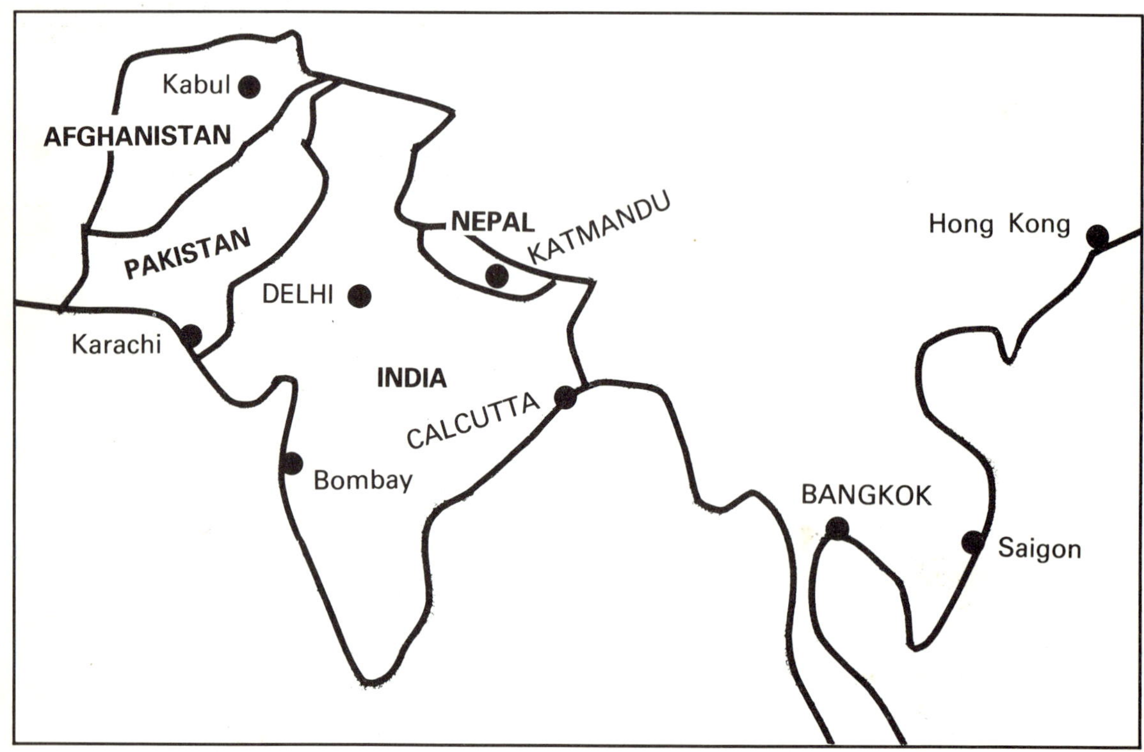

AUSTRALASIA

'Blow for blow, bullet for bullet, Australia in her short history can claim a variety of crimes as baffling, bizarre and brutal as any in the world.' This was the way author Alan Sharpe opened the introduction to his book *Australian Crimes* published in 1979. Australian crime literature is not extensive, but the last decade has seen a number of famous cases appear in print which certainly bear out Alan Sharpe's contention.

In many eyes Ned Kelly, the notorious bushranger who became a cult figure after his execution, symbolizes the Australian criminal to the world. Unlike many of his type, Ned Kelly had not been transported from England to serve in a penal settlement, although his father had. Kelly senior was transported to Australia in 1842, and served for seven years in convict gangs in Van Diemen's Land (Tasmania). When he was released from servitude he lapsed into a life of lawlessness, mainly cattle-thieving, and developed a hatred for the police. Ned was born into this climate of antagonism to law and order, and soon followed in his father's footsteps.

The Kelly gang was the most notorious of the bushranger gangs, whose particular skills were a close knowledge of their territories. They knew the terrain intimately, and their activities and hideaways were protected by friends. The gangs roamed almost at will, and the stretched resources of the police were not up to the task of bringing them to book. In the 1870s there were about fifty police officers to patrol an area of 11,000 square miles. The north-east part of New South Wales was known as Kelly country. It was here at Stringybark Creek in October 1878 that Ned Kelly shot and killed Constable Thomas Lonigan, the crime for which he was eventually executed.

Bank robberies followed during the next two years, and a police informer was also murdered. On 27 June 1880 Kelly and three of his gang were located by police at Glenrowan. Reinforcements were called for, and fifty officers surrounded the rebels, who prepared for the eventual gun-fight by donning armour made from scrap iron and cooking-pots. All

Ned Kelly, dressed to kill

three of Kelly's followers perished, and Ned himself was taken prisoner. He was tried for murder at Melbourne, and after passing sentence of death Mr Justice Barry said, 'May the Lord have mercy on your soul,' to which Kelly replied, 'Yes, I will meet you there.'

Ned Kelly was hanged on 1 November 1880, and Mr Justice Barry died two weeks later.

Subsequently Kelly has been turned into a figure of romance and legend. The folklore has been perpetuated in films and books, and something of his macho style is reflected in the lines of the ballad: 'Ned Kelly terrified them all and put their blood to shame.'

The bushrangers were probably the direct result of England's policy of transporting its criminals to the colonies. As the felons completed their sentences, so they were released, to be absorbed in a rugged society and to mingle with entrepreneurs who travelled to Australia and New Zealand out of a sense of opportunity. They were men like Frank Butler (see under MOUNTAINS), who deserted from the Royal Navy, and Alfred Lester and George Nichols (see under RIVERS AND LAKES), who had criminal records in England.

So great was the crime in Sydney in the 1820s that a contemporary observer remarked, 'There is more immorality in Sydney than in any English town of the same size.' As crime increased, so the punishments increased in severity. Convicts worked in chain-gangs in stockades where military law applied. The worst offenders were sent to Norfolk Island and Pentridge, where the regimes were so repressive that 'the heart of a man was taken from him and he was given the heart of a beast'.

The more inventive criminal minds contrived to escape from these penal settlements, and those who breached the walls were swallowed up by the vastness of the bush. Another incentive to escape was the lure of riches. Henry White, who worked for over thirty years in the penal settlements, wrote about the stirring times of the 1850s in his book *Crimes and Criminals*. 'The discovery of the goldfields caused the worst class of convicts to immigrate from Van Diemen's Land and Norfolk Island to these shores,' he said, adding, 'The result was that bushranging, horse-stealing, murders and in fact the whole catalogue of the most heinous crimes quickly prevailed ...'

Robbing the gold escorts became a favourite pastime, and those responsible were not always transportees. Thomas Griffin, who robbed and killed the Clermont gold escort in 1867 (see under CAMPS AND CARAVANS), was a magistrate and former Chief Constable of Brisbane. Transportation ceased in 1864 and a steady improvement came about in the incidence of crime. Penal reform in many cases was slow to filter through from the Motherland, but in some instances the colonies were ahead of their time. Public execution ceased in New South Wales in 1853 (1868 in England), and Queensland abolished capital punishment as early as 1922.

In the post-transportation years the wild, bushranging days waned and Australian crime settled down to the domestic pattern of murder so familiar in Europe. Indeed, credit (if credit it is) must go to Frederick Deeming for importing his particular *modus operandi* from England. Having murdered his wife and four

children in Liverpool in 1891, he set out for Australia, where the following year he murdered his second wife in Melbourne. His method — which led to detection by the resultant disagreeable odour — was to cement his victims under the fireplace. Having murdered in two continents, Deeming shared with Ned Kelly the distinction of having his head examined after execution for traces of likely anthropoid ancestry.

Australian murders certainly match up to crimes committed elsewhere when it comes to the bizarre. 'The Man they Couldn't Hang' predated England's similarly famous incident on the scaffold by eighty years. Joseph Samuels was a transported convict who arrived in New South Wales in 1801. He completed his sentence and promptly went back to a life of crime. In May 1803 he killed a police officer following a house burglary, and in due course was convicted of murder. Hanging at that time was carried out by standing the condemned man in a cart, which was then moved forward, leaving him dangling at the rope's end. This procedure was followed at the execution of Samuels, but instead of being suspended in the air he fell to the ground when the rope broke. The hangman repeated the exercise, but at the second attempt Samuels again fell to the ground when the fixed end of the rope unravelled. The condemned man was prepared for a third attempt, after first being revived. Incredibly, the rope snapped again, and under pressure from the crowd and cries of 'Will of God', the execution was called off.

Like John Lee, who also survived attempts to hang him at Exeter Prison in 1885, Joseph Samuels was reprieved. His sentence was commuted to life imprisonment, and he died in 1806 in an ill-fated escape from the penal settlement at Kings Town. It seemed that Divine Providence had granted only a temporary reprieve in his case, whereas John Lee of Babbacombe died a free man at the age of sixty-eight. A film about his life was made in Australia in 1917; and it is possible that 'The Man they Couldn't Hang' in England read about the fate of his fellow-sufferer in the *Sydney Gazette*.

It is inevitable that Australian crime should have many historical links with England, but Alan Sharpe's contention that the continent has its own unique murders is certainly borne out by the Shark Arm Case (see under BEACHES). Sharpe in his *Crimes That Shocked Australia* noted that 'crime cases provide a unique opportunity to examine the aberrations of human nature'. This indeed is part of the fascination for those who follow the progress of the big murder stories in newspapers and books.

'The Mad Dentist of Wynyard Square', as Louis Bertrand was dubbed in 1865 (see under PARLOURS), provided a wealth of fascinating detail for the student of human nature, as did the unsolved murders of three members of the Gatton family in 1898 (see under WOODS AND FORESTS). In modern times the unsolved Bogle-Chandler case continues to inspire speculation. A recent theory is that Dr Bogle — acknowledged as an outstanding scientist — was involved in work with a high-security rating which drew him into the web of an international conspiracy and precipitated his death.

New Zealand's murders generally lack that element of frontier wildness which stamped many of Australia's crimes. Although Treadwell's book of *Notable New Zealand Trials* contains several cases involving Maoris demonstrating, as he put it, 'the baneful effect of western habits on simple native minds', the murders described are not particularly exotic. The same is true for Dudley Dyne's *Famous New Zealand Murders*, but a number of the cases are powerful examples of the criminal mind at work.

New Zealand has had its share of gunmen, such as William Bayly, whose trial in Auckland in 1934 was distinguished for the part played by forensic science. In 1941 Eric Graham, killer of six and an expert marksman, eluded a police manhunt for two weeks before being fatally wounded. Both Bayly and Graham quarrelled with their neighbours and their violence was almost domestic in character.

Robert Butler, an out-of-work ex-gaolbird with a string of aliases, was charged with murdering three members of the Dewar family in their beds. The fire brigade was called to quell a blaze at a house in Cumberland Street, Dunedin, in the early hours of 14 March 1880. Inside the house, in the bedroom, firemen found the bodies of James Dewar and his wife who had been axed to death; their child was also dead. Sent for trial, Butler distinguished himself by conducting his own defence with

surprising eloquence. He told the judge, 'Whilst the adage says "The man who is his own counsel has a fool for a client", I can only say that there is another which says, "Thrice armed is he who has his quarrel just".' Having addressed the jury for six hours, he won a verdict of not guilty. Butler was later sent to prison for eighteen years, following conviction for arson, and in 1905 the law exacted a kind of retribution by hanging him for a murder committed in Queensland.

While Butler's cunning ability was in a class of its own, it is New Zealand's female murderers who have captured the world's headlines. The activities of Minnie Dean (see under GARDENS), the baby farmer from Invercargill, predated those of Britain's Amelia Dyer by several years. Minnie at least had the distinction of being the only woman to be legally hanged in New Zealand.

The murder committed by the two schoolgirls Pauline Parker and Juliet Hulme is the most provocative because of its uniqueness. These two teenagers murdered Parker's mother because they saw her as a threat to their special relationship. On 22 June 1954 Mrs Parker was battered to death with a brick in a stocking. The girls' special relationship had homosexual overtones, and they expressed themselves with extraordinary arrogance and deceit. They acted together, exercising a kind of combined paranoia which the French call *folie à deux* or shared madness. They were likened to Leopold and Loeb, the teenagers who killed a youth in Chicago in 1924 in an act which was given Nietzschean characteristics and described by some as an 'intellectual murder'.

A searching account of the Parker and Hulme case has been written in the form of a 'documentary novel' called *Obsession*, by Tom Gurr and H.H. Cox. The girls' arrogance was prodigious, and comes over powerfully in some lines of verse written by Pauline Parker and entitled *The Ones that I Worship*. She speaks of 'two beautiful daughters' who are the 'most glorious beings in creation', and goes on:

> The outstanding genius of this pair
> Is understood by few, they are so rare.
> Compared with these two every man is a fool.
> The world is most honoured that they should
> deign to rule.

The same high opinion of his intellectual capabilities was expressed by Peter Sutcliffe, the Yorkshire Ripper (see under ALLEY-WAYS), in the notice he displayed in the cab window of his truck:

> In this truck is a man whose latent genius if unleashed would rock the nation, whose dynamic energy would overpower those around him. Better let him sleep?

Australia and New Zealand have had their share of controversial cases which have brought justice into question. Darryl Beamish, the deaf mute convicted of murdering a young woman in Western Australia (see under NEXT DOOR) after another man had confessed to the crime, had his appeal heard in five courts. Finally, in 1971, he was released from prison on parole twelve years after his initial arrest.

Arthur Alan Thomas served nine years in prison before receiving an official pardon in 1980 and $NZ 1,000,000 compensation from the New Zealand government. He was convicted of double murder in 1971 after Jeanette and Harvey Crewe had been found shot dead with a .22 gun at their farm at Pukekwa; their bodies were retrieved from the Waikato River. Collection and test firing of .22 rifles in the neighbourhood led police to Thomas, who farmed within a few miles of Pukekwa. He was convicted on firearms evidence which purported to show that a cartridge case found at the crime-scene matched the characteristics of his rifle. This evidence was widely regarded as inconclusive at the time, but nevertheless Thomas was found guilty and sentenced to life imprisonment.

A public outcry ensued and there were demands for a retrial which were pressed home by writer Terry Bell in a publication called *Bitter Hill*, and subsequently the public disquiet was argued at length by David Yallop in *Beyond Reasonable Doubt?* In due course a Royal Commission concluded that Thomas's arrest and prosecution were unjustified and that an innocent man had been convicted by false evidence planted at the scene of the crime. This bore out the simple statement made by his wife in 1972 requesting a new trial: 'Arthur knows he is innocent. And I know he is innocent.' Finally, the wronged man was returned to his family and the murders of Jeanette and Harvey Crewe were re-entered on the list of unsolved crimes.

The growth of organized crime in Australia during the last twenty years appears to have reached almost epidemic proportions. The deteriorating position of law and order led Mr Justice Moffitt, president of the New South Wales Court of Appeal, to make a public statement in May 1983. He warned about corruption and said that no group, professional or political, was free from the likelihood of infection. The judge's remarks followed an interim report published by the Royal Commission set up to investigate crime and corruption which stated, 'Organized crime is unchecked, out of control ... to overcome it is one of the challenges of this decade.'

One of those who did challenge it, with apparently fatal consequences, was Mrs Juanita Nielsen. This 38-year-old heiress to a family retail business espoused the cause of those living in the older residential areas of Kings Cross, the Sydney suburb, who felt threatened by the developers. Juanita Nielsen ran a community newspaper, called *Now,* in which she campaigned against the developers who, she alleged, used strong-arm tactics to dispossess people of their property.

On 4 July 1975 she kept a business appointment in the morning, and was later seen in a car with two men. She has not been seen since, and the only clue to her disappearance was the discovery of her handbag on the F4 freeway, some 55 kilometres west of Sydney. In 1977, on the second anniversary of her disappearance, her father offered a reward of $50,000 for information leading to the conviction of those responsible for her murder. Others also thought that she had been murdered, her body in all probability being buried in the concrete of one of the new motorways. In 1981 two men were convicted of conspiring with persons unknown to abduct her.

Another scandal involving drugs, murder and corruption occurred in 1977 in a most unlikely setting. Griffith is a small farming town in New South Wales which burst into the news when local politician Don Mackay campaigned against its development as a drugs centre. Marijuana was being grown in the district in industrial quantities which were harvested at night to avoid the prying attentions of the law. After a successful police raid by the New South Wales drug squad which resulted in five arrests, Don Mackay disappeared.

In 1983 the bodies of two Italians were pulled out of the Murrumbidgee river, some twenty miles from Griffith. These murder victims had been mutilated after being shot and stabbed. Following the murders a group of local citizens was formed to fight the growing of marijuana, and all the violence and corruption which it brings in its wake. The marijuana barons are said to be Italians who farm ground bought with the proceeds of kidnapping in Italy. They live in ostentatious ranches which are known locally as the 'grass castles'.

The scale of the problem is considerable, and corruption at senior levels is alleged. Mr Justice Woodward's Royal Commission Report in 1981 on drug-trafficking and corruption concluded that Don Mackay had been murdered by a hired killer. Meanwhile Griffith has a 'Concerned Citizens Group', and the Royal Commission, after collecting evidence for three years, has compiled a list of forty-two names (as yet only code names) of individuals associated with organized crime. These cover every activity from drug-peddling to large-scale tax evasion, with a number of witnesses suffering mysterious deaths or simply disappearing.

(1, 57, 65, 162, 236, 246, 261, 286, 287, 316, 343, 368, 389, 390, 519, 590, 617, 724, 853, 854, 870, 945, 996, 1029, 1032, 1051, MWW)

EUROPE

'Crime, like apples or cheese, has a different flavour in every country. The seeds or ingredients may appear identical, but not the finished product ... the whole method and psychology of crime — and consequently, of its detection and solution — bears a distinct national trademark.' Thus wrote David Rowan in the preface to his *Famous European Crimes*, and he went on to talk of the French *crime passionel*, the use of long knives in Italy and the resort to physical brutality in Germany.

An early taste for these distinctions permeates the pages of *The Black Register or Revelations of Crime Selected from the Criminal Records of All Nations*, published in London in 1852. The Marquise de Brinvilliers and Madame Lafarge are marshalled here together with many lesser known villains, some of them dignified by the title of Abbot, Duke or Count. The Duc de Praslin (see under MANSIONS, RANCHES AND VILLAS) thought he could be exonerated from suspicion of murder simply because he was a Peer of France, and the Marquise de Brinvilliers had to be broken by torture to confess her crimes. The permissible foul play of the aristocracy eventually gave way to the fair play of the people, and in few places was this better organized than in France. The first criminal law was introduced to Europe by the Romans, where it was developed empirially by the English into one system and by the French, with mathematical precision, into another. The Code Napoléon, developed during the nineteenth century, embodied the ideals of Civil Law or legislation by statute, as opposed to the Common Law evolved in England. The French Code d'Instruction Criminelle was adopted by many European countries, whereas the Common Law approach to criminal justice gained influence in North America and the former British colonial territories.

Scottish law differs from that of England in numerous respects. There is no coroner system, but each county appoints a Procurator Fiscal, attached to the Sheriff's Court, who is responsible for the preliminary questioning of witnesses when a crime or suspicious death is investigated. This is a similar role to that of the *juge d'instruction*, or examining magistrate, in France. Scottish juries consist of fifteen members, and in addition to the usual verdicts of 'guilty' or 'not guilty' they may return a verdict of 'not proven'. Madeleine Smith in 1857 was one of the best known recipients of this verdict, which is often said to mean, 'Go away and don't do it again!'

Documentary accounts of European crimes in English are probably biased towards the French. Two volumes of Albert Bataille's records have appeared under the editorship of Philip A. Wilkins: *Inside the French Courts* and *Dramas of the French Courts*. A fascination with the methods of the French police has resulted in numerous books on the subject. The same cannot be said for other European countries, whose murders appear largely in collections such as Horace Wyndham's *Crime on the Continent* and *With Detectives Around the World* by Frank Longworth. Individual murderers such as Peter Kürten, Dr Marcel Petiot and Henri Landru have merited detailed studies as murderers commanding international interest.

Commenting on the impression he may have created that the French are a particularly criminal nation, Rayner Heppenstall in his book *Bluebeard and After* wrote, 'As a matter of statistical fact, they are, on average, rather more than twice as murderous as ourselves, not only in bright rooms and dark lanes but in their cars on the roads.' Taking up a similar theme in his *Famous European Crimes*, David Rowan spoke of the influence of France's geographical position, the volatile temperament of the people and the country's generous attitude towards refugees and foreign visitors. The delights of Paris and the French countryside have long been an attraction for tourists from all nations, some of whom, regrettably, end up as missing persons, or worse, as murder victims. Many of these cases remain unsolved, and in his book *They Were Murdered in France* Harry J. Greenwall suggested that the French police were perhaps lacking in real aptitude for criminal investigation despite the success of their fictional counterparts.

Fifteen British visitors met mysterious ends in France during the period 1920 to 1955

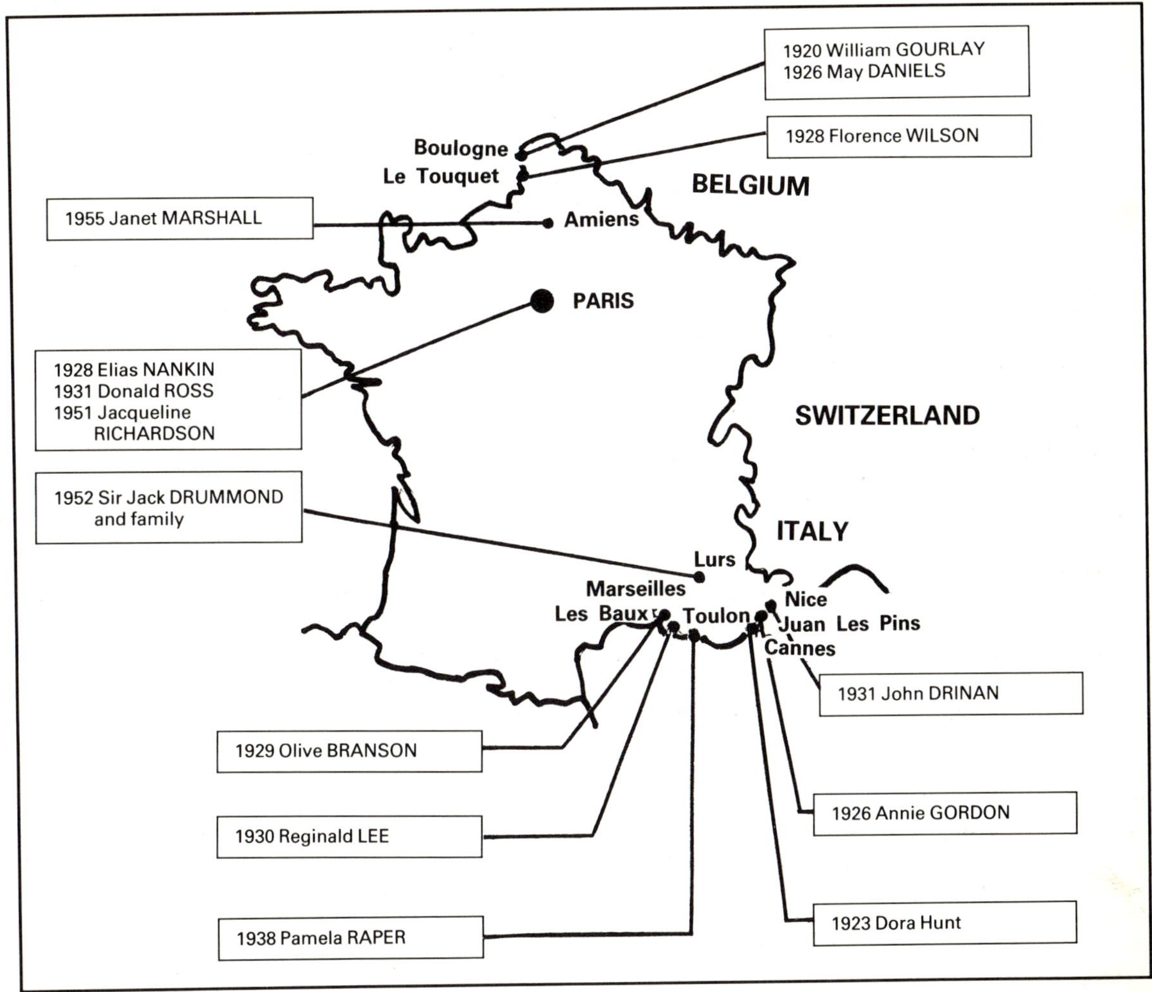

Foreigners murdered in France: mostly unsolved cases

(discounting the war years). Eleven of these were acknowledged as murders occurring in a variety of circumstances. Some created large headlines at the time, such as the stabbing to death in 1928 of Florence Aline Wilson near Le Touquet (see under GOLF COURSES). In 1938 Pamela Raper, a young painter and sculptress, was pulled out of the sea near Toulon; despite her having sustained a fractured skull, and being dead before she entered the sea, an official verdict was given of accidental death. Probably the best known foreign tourists to be murdered in France were Sir Jack Drummond and his wife and daughter. Their deaths in 1952 in a field near Lurs inspired international interest and several books.

An elderly farmer, Gaston Dominici, was convicted of the murders, a verdict which was described as having been contrived 'to please the English'. Maître René Floriot in his book *When Justice Falters* examined the sources for error which existed in the law and wrote forcibly that 'Doubt should always lead to acquittal.' He dealt with the Dominici case under the heading 'The law is led astray by the defendant', and maintained that the police were too ready to hear the old man's confession. Dominici, aged seventy-six and grandfather to twenty-one children, declared himself innocent of the charge of murder, but said he was prepared to accuse himself in order 'to save the honour of my grandchildren'. Although sentenced to death, the old man was reprieved by the President of the Republic and had long before then withdrawn his confession.

Perhaps it is the 'mentality of the French criminal, whose originality is so often something to marvel at', as Sidney Theodore Felstead put it in his introduction to René Cassellari's *Dramas of French Crime*, which outwits the detective system. Not that this was a view shared by Major Arthur Griffiths, who was at pains in his work *Mysteries of Police and Crime* to defend the French police against their critics. Certainly there has been no shortage of thinking and resourceful men in the detective service. Indeed, Eugène-François Vidocq, the former convict who became head of the Sûreté in 1811, is credited with organizing the first regular detective force.

Gustave Macé, the detective who brought Pierre Voirbo to justice in 1869 and succeeded Vidocq at the Sûreté, contributed his own insight to the craft by observing in his book *My First Crime* that 'murderers generally commit themselves by having taken too many or too few precautions. They rarely know how to preserve the exact medium to make things appear normal.' It was the tradition of careful observation which led to French successes in forensic science, first with Alphonse Bertillon and later with Edmond Locard. Vidocq's 'Brigade de Sûreté', as his detectives were known, solved fifteen murders in 1817, the first full year of their operations.

Monsieur Claude, who became Chief of Police during the reign of Napoleon III, counted the arrest of Jean-Baptiste Troppmann among his successes. That was in 1869, the year this accident-prone detective had his wallet stolen by pickpockets for at least the second time. It was the year too in which the Bonaparte dynasty began to crumble, assisted, so it was said, by the uproar caused by Troppmann's activities. By the same token, the flight of Louis-Philippe in 1848 in face of revolution was thought to have been precipitated by the murder of the Duchesse de Praslin.

Two French ladies who gave violence rather than received it were Jeanne-Marguerite Steinheil and Henriette Caillaux. Their stories were told by Rayner Heppenstall in his book *A Little Pattern of French Crime,* in which he set out a number of criminal cases, murder included, which occurred during the period known as 'La Belle Epoque' (1880 to 1914). The trial of Jeanne-Marguerite Steinheil for the murder of her husband and mother created a major

scandal in 1909. Mme Steinheil, who entertained the literary and artistic talent of Paris in her salon, was popularly supposed to have contrived the murders with the aid of a mysterious lover whose royal origins were speculated on in the newspapers. In the event, with the evidence piled high against her, Mme Steinheil wept copiously and the jury could not bring itself to find her guilty. Five years later Henriette Caillaux, in another famous case — directed more by patriotism and passion than by due process — was also acquitted (see under SHOPS AND OFFICES).

Two women in a previous age had shown a certain entrepreneurial spirit in responding to the needs of the time. The reign of Louis XIV in seventeenth-century France was a period of corruption when rivals might be bought or simply eliminated. Marie-Madeleine, Marquise de Brinvilliers, and Catherine Montvoisin (known as La Voisin) peddled arsenic with such devastating effect that it became known as *poudre de succession*, or inheritance powder.

Brinvilliers murdered countless patients at the Paris public hospital and then set about poisoning her father, brothers and daughter. She was tried and condemned in 1676, her body being publicly burned. La Voisin followed in her footsteps, dealing in arsenic with all who wished to secure some advantage by eliminating a relative or enemy. This period came to be called 'The Age of Arsenic', and in 1679 the King set up La Chambre Ardente (Chamber of Poisons) to investigate the crime-ridden state of the country. In the three years of its existence the Chamber ordered nearly four hundred arrests and had thirty-six convicted poisoners executed. In 1682 the King forbade apothecaries to sell arsenic, and priests at Notre-Dame Cathedral reported difficulty in keeping up with the confessions of self-accused poisoners. La Voisin was condemned to death and was burnt at the stake in 1680 at the Place de Grève.

France is the home of two distinctive forms of crime and punishment: the *crime passionel* and the guillotine. The first is still in evidence but the second was abandoned in 1981, although there have been demands for its reappearance. A Gaullist deputy proposed a Bill in 1984 to restore capital punishment, following a series of nine murders of elderly women in Montmartre. Extra police were drafted into the area after a spate of killing in which women living alone had been robbed, tortured and murdered in their apartments. Politicians called for strong measures to counter the rising tide of violence and one national newspaper carried the headline 'France is Afraid.'

By any standard, the curtailment of life by murder is brutal, but modern trends in France have shifted from the understandable emotion of the *crime passionel* to more ugly expressions of violence. For example, two doctors in a hospital at Poitiers were alleged in 1984 to have killed a randomly selected patient. Their motive appeared to be one of seeking revenge by placing blame for the death on a senior colleague with whom they were in dispute. An extraordinary example of brutality came to light in November 1984 when Jean-Pierre Leymarie, a smallholder who scratched a meagre living in Brive, was convicted of murdering seven of his children at birth and sentenced to eight years' imprisonment. His wife bore twelve children between 1970 and 1983, the first two of which were wanted as a family, three died of natural causes and seven were killed — put down, like unwanted domestic animals. Leymarie delivered the children himself, cut the umbilical cord and suffocated them. The bodies were buried in the garden and created no pangs of conscience.

France has a rich criminal history with many classic murder cases in its archives. Landru, the 'Bluebeard' of the First World War years, was a name as synonymous with murder in France as was Crippen in England. Pierre Lacenaire appealed to the public with his poetry, but the credo of hatred for society which he announced in 1835 encouraged a powerful addiction in modern times for individuals like Charles Manson and others. Joseph Vacher took Jack the Ripper's techniques out into the French countryside and murdered eleven times during the 1890s. Jean-Baptiste Troppmann, the mother's boy who was ill-treated by his father, took his revenge against society by murdering a family of six in 1869, and Martin Dumollard, aided and abetted by his wife, took his toll of innocent life purely for gain between 1849 and 1861. Eugen Weidmann, a cold-blooded killer of modern times, achieved the distinction in 1939 of being the last convicted murderer to be publicly guillotined in France.

A number of the more startling murders in France have been committed by women usu-

ally cast in the role of poisoner, such as Marie Lafarge and Hélène Jegado, the latter entering the ranks of mass murder with her twenty-three victims. Mary Hartman in her book *Victorian Murderesses* catalogued the emergence of female self-expression from claustrophobic nineteenth-century domesticity. Henriette Caillaux tested the new-found freedom when she was acquitted of murdering the editor of *Le Figaro* in 1914. Denise Labbé, on the other hand, also a modern woman, demonstrated her willingness to be enslaved by male domination when she murdered her young daughter as a ritual sacrifice for her lover in 1954. Jeanne Weiss (see under BARRACKS) also came under the spell of male domination and attempted to murder her husband in 1890. She added to her guilt by being foolish enough to record her plans in letters sent to her lover.

As in England, a number of doctors convinced themselves that they could get away with murder. Dr Edmé Castaing, a young Parisian doctor, committed the first murder with morphine in 1823 and Dr Edmond de la Pommerais used the drug digitalis to murder for gain in the 1860s. Dr Marcel Petiot murdered on a mass scale, eliminating twenty-seven war refugees who passed through his Paris consulting-rooms in the 1940s, while Dr Pierre Bougrat murdered his victim in Marseilles in 1925 under the guise of treating him for syphilis (see under CONSULTING-ROOMS). Dr Eustachy, faced with a powerful rival, attempted to eliminate him by doctoring some game birds with atropine (see DINING-ROOMS AND RESTAURANTS). Like murderous physicians elsewhere, French doctors proved to be strong on method but weak on administration.

France has produced a number of master crooks who have taken robbery and murder in their stride. Emile Buisson began his criminal career as a bank robber in the 1930s and continued his activities throughout the German occupation of his country. In February 1941 he robbed a Paris bank of nearly four million francs and shot dead a messenger while escaping. In 1943 he was arrested by the Gestapo and sentenced to hard labour for life, but managed to escape from custody. Buisson's criminal career came to an end in 1950 after a nationwide manhunt. The man who was thought to have committed twenty murders and a hundred robberies went to the guillotine in 1956. The story of his remarkable career was told by Roger Borniche, the Sûreté officer who tracked him down, in a book called *Flic Story*.

Jacques Mesrine was another master criminal who grew up during the German occupation and graduated to robbery and murder via delinquency. When arrested in 1973 he claimed to have killed thirty-nine people. Like Buisson, he was a prison escape specialist and in a busy career fought and talked his way out of tight situations in Algeria, Canada and the USA. He was acquitted of a murder charge in Canada in 1972 although he served ten years in prison for a kidnapping. Mesrine's exploits in North America earned him the title of 'international criminal' and his activities in his own country made him France's 'Public Enemy No.1'. While in La Santé prison in Paris he wrote a book called *The Death Instinct* which contained detailed descriptions of murders he claimed to have committed, although the bodies were never found. The man whom the Paris underworld regarded as a loner who killed too easily died in a hail of police bullets in a Paris street in 1979. His career was documented in a book called simply *Mesrine* by Carey Schofield.

Edgar Zemour, known to his associates as 'Dapper Eddie', and self-styled Napoleon of French crime, was killed by a hired assassin in Miami in 1983. He had been a member of the Z gang which ruled the Paris underworld during the 1960s and '70s and cornered a lucrative slice of the garment trade. Their fringe activities included vice, gambling and protection. Violence dogged Zemour's footsteps and two of his brothers were murdered in France. 'Dapper Eddie' went to live in the USA in 1975 although he made frequent business trips to Europe. He once boasted that he had made crime pay, but it was his supposed ambition to oppose Mafia gambling interests in the Caribbean which led to his downfall.

Spain acquired a bad reputation in 1984 on account of the murders of three tourists in separate incidents on the Costa del Sol. In reality, though, the Iberian countries have low murder rates and in 1959 Madrid had 1.5 criminal homicides per 100,000 of population. In Portugal the total number of violent crimes has declined since 1980 although the propor-

tion of murders has risen. Spain's most sensational murder in recent times was the double killing of the Marqués and Marquesa del Urquijo in 1980 by their son-in-law, Rafael Escobedo (see under BEDROOMS).

Greece has also had its share of foreign visitors who have succumbed to murderous encounters. The most celebrated are the Dilessi Murders which caused a political storm in 1870. In April of that year Lord and Lady Muncaster were travelling in Bœotia with a party of friends, mostly English aristocrats. On 11 April the party was kidnapped by brigands who descended from the mountains and held its members to ransom. Lord and Lady Muncaster, together with the children and servants, were released, while the remaining four adults were held as hostages. Ten days after the kidnapping the four hostages were murdered. Shock waves went through Victorian England, although it was well understood that banditry was rife in Greece and a number of other European countries at the time. Romilly Jenkins in his account of the incident, *The Dilessi Murders*, remarked that organized brigandage was 'directed and exploited by political managers'. The bands of brigands which roamed the mountains of Greece were manipulated and used as mercenaries by ambitious politicians to terrorize the electorate.

A hundred years later, another visitor to Greece at a time of political upheaval was to meet murder on the way. Ann Chapman, a 25-year-old British journalist, travelled to Greece in 1971 to write some articles for a travel firm. She stayed at the Pine Hill Hotel in the resort town of Kavouri with friends and colleagues. On 18 October her body — strangled, battered and bound — was found less than two hundred yards from the hotel. A 37-year-old Greek, Nikolaos Moundis, a former prison guard, was charged with murder. He had a reputation in the district as a 'Peeping Tom' and had been convicted for indecent assault. In April 1973 Moundis (who denied any guilt) was found guilty of attempted rape and manslaughter. He was sentenced to life imprisonment.

All this occurred during the rule of the Greek Colonels and there have been subsequent suspicions that Ann Chapman's murder was politically motivated and that Moundis was framed. Chapman herself had let it be known that she was on to a 'big story', and it was suggested that she had become a victim in the aftermath of a plan to free Alexandros Panagoulis, who had been imprisoned for allegedly plotting to murder the Prime Minister. Secret American intelligence documents also came to light, together with a letter claiming to know the real identity of Ann Chapman's killer. Despite the considerable speculation and an investigation of the case initiated by the European Parliament (not to mention death threats received by some of those contesting the evidence), the official verdict remains.

Kidnapping, banditry and terrorism have long been strong themes in the Italian crime scene. In Campania, the region of which Naples is the chief city, there is one murder every day and a crime of some description is committed every minute. The members of one farming family in Calabria have been victims of kidnapping on six separate occasions.

The crime capital of Italy is Palermo, the Sicilian city which is the centre of Mafia activities. There were 150 murders in the city in 1982 as organized crime — thought to be declining in the 1960s — reasserted itself. The dead were mostly victims of gang warfare and the struggle to control the drugs and construction interests. The killings are often public and the victims include police officers and magistrates. Apart from the numerous murders, there are also as many persons reported missing — the victims of so-called 'white murders' — who are thought to end up buried in the concrete foundations of some of Palermo's construction projects. Building, tourist development and drugs represent big business interests, and the Sicilian Mafia is thought to supply 30 per cent of the heroin demands in the USA.

Historically, it was the Italians who perfected the poison arts during the Middle Ages and their use became something of a mania. Politicians and princes hired exponents of the art as medieval hit-men to eliminate their rivals. C.J.S. Thompson in his *Poison Mysteries in History, Romance and Crime* devoted a chapter to the Italian school of poisoners. Few were more business-like than John of Ragusa, who in 1543 issued a sliding scale of charges for his services. He was prepared to poison the King of Spain for 150 ducats and the Pope for a hundred (plus travelling expenses, of course).

In a note which set the trend for later hired assassins he wrote, 'The farther the journey, the more eminent the man, the more it is necessary to reward the toil and hardships undertaken ....'

The power of poison was fully exploited by the Borgias who came to Italy from Spain in 1455. Pope Alexander VI was a Borgia, and father of the celebrated Cesare and Lucrezia. He died in 1503 after drinking poisoned wine; his son Cesare was ill at the time, recovering from a poison attack, only to die four years later in battle. It was Lucrezia Borgia whose name was to become synonymous with poison, although historians differ in their interpretation of the facts. The kindly view is that she was unfairly blamed for the crimes of her brother.

Setting a trend for organized crime in a later age, Sicily in the seventeenth century became one of the centres for the poison trade. Palermo was the birthplace of Teofania di Adamo, and it was there that she began her murderous career before moving to Naples. 'Aqua Toffana' — whose main ingredient was arsenic — was her special brew, which she peddled under the guise of cosmetic preparations. Two Popes are included in the six hundred people that her skills are said to have poisoned. At the age of seventy she was accused of countless crimes to which she readily confessed when tortured. She was judicially strangled in 1709.

Plots to kill the Pope are by no means confined to the Middle Ages. In May 1981 an attempt was made to kill Pope John Paul II by a lone gunman in the environs of the Vatican. The Pope recovered from his wounds, and Mehmet Ali Agca, a Turkish member of a right-wing group motivated by anti-Western, extreme Islamic ideas, was arrested. Agca was later gaoled for life, amid rising speculation that he had not acted alone. In 1984 a press report appeared stating that the French counter-espionage service had received a tip-off in 1981 that an attempt was to be made on the Pope's life. Agca later named several accomplices who are awaiting trial for conspiracy.

In June 1984 an account appeared of the alleged murder of Pope John Paul I in 1978. David Yallop in his book *In God's Name* maintained that the Pope (who reigned for only thirty-three days) was poisoned with digitalis. He called for the Pope's body to be exhumed for post-mortem examination in order to establish the true cause of death, which at the time was stated as a heart attack. The reason, he said, for the wish to murder the Pope was the latter's proposed action that would have affected the Italian Masonic Lodge P2, which came to prominence at the time the Banco Ambrosiano collapsed in 1982. In June of that year the bank's president, Roberto Calvi, was found hanged under Blackfriars Bridge in London. This incident, and the convoluted story which led up to it, is exhaustively dealt with by Rupert Cornwall in his book *God's Banker*, and by Larry Gurwin in *The Calvi Affair*.

A number of Italian murders have reached into high places, and that of Wilma Montesi in 1953 (see under BEACHES) certainly rocked the government. The disappearance of Jeannette May and Gabriella Guerin from Sarnano in 1980, and the subsequent discovery of their bodies later that year (see under MOUNTAINS), also aroused controversy. Official views that the deaths were accidental began to waver as the evidence mounted indicating a bungled kidnap attempt followed by murder. The trial of Countess Tarnowska (see under MANSIONS, RANCHES AND VILLAS) attracted many spectators including a number of European aristocrats who came to see the 'Russian Vampire' answer a charge of conspiring to murder. The case had all the elements of the celebrated trials of Steinheil and Caillaux except that for Tarnowska the verdict was different.

On the theme of national characteristics in certain types of crime, David Rowan referred to the German tendency towards physical brutality. Certainly, sex murderers have dominated the crime headlines in Germany, led by Peter Kürten, 'the Düsseldorf Vampire'. In her book, *The Monster of Düsseldorf*, Margaret Seaton Wagner quotes Kürten's own appreciation of his motives: 'If I had had the means of doing so, I would have killed whole masses of people — brought about catastrophes ... the sex urge was always strong in me ... but it was increased by the deeds in themselves. That was why I had to go out again and again to look for another victim.'

Germany suffered an epidemic of sex murders during the inter-war years. Fritz Haarmann committed twenty-seven or more murders between 1918 and 1924, preying on young refugees and inflicting his perverted sexual practices on their tortured bodies before killing them and selling the corpses for meat. Equally disgusting were the practices of Karl Denke, who let rooms in his house at Münsterberg in Silesia. He operated during the same period as Haarmann and in sympathy with his fellow pervert's motives. In December 1924 a resident in the house at Münsterberg whose room was above Denke's accommodation heard screams rising from below and went to investigate. He stumbled across a youth with injuries to the head who claimed Denke had attacked him with an axe.

Karl Denke was arrested and a search of his rooms produced the identity papers of twelve young travelling workers together with numerous items of clothing. In various receptacles and pots in the house were found pickled flesh, fat and bones constituting the remains of thirty human beings of both sexes. A ledger was also discovered in which, with great thoroughness, Denke had entered the names and weight of each victim along with the date of his murder. The first entry was made in 1921. Shortly after being arrested Denke committed suicide. Not a great deal is known about his personal life although, like Haarmann, he was probably homosexual.

Another inter-war years sex murderer was Adolf Seefeld. He was an itinerant odd-job man who wandered about the countryside looking for work and potential victims for his lusts. He had spent twenty-three years of his life in prison, and when he was arrested was charged with over thirty murders and innumerable sex crimes. He murdered his victims in the seclusion of forests, usually carefully arranging their bodies in sleeping poses. Like Denke, he kept records and his notebooks contained secret annotations which were thought to correspond to each murder he had committed.

At the age of sixty-five Seefeld received twelve sentences of death and was beheaded in 1936 during the rise of the Nazi State. Seefeld, whose origins were pure Aryan, presented the Nazis with a minor problem in explaining his criminality. The press referred to him as a 'devil incarnate' who 'was able to commit his crimes only because of the silly humanitarianism of the old liberalistic system'. The prosecutor at his trial pursued a similar line and the court in passing judgment proclaimed the sentences to be 'for the entire world the strongest justifica-

DEUTSCHE DEMOKRATISCHE REPUBLIK

Die Echtheit der vorstehenden Unterschrift wird hiermit beglaubigt.
Schwerin, den 8. Juli 1981
I. A.

Sterbeurkunde

Standesamt Schwerin(Meckl) Nr. 370/1936

Adolf Seefeld---

wohnhaft in ohne festen Wohnsitz---

ist am 23. Mai 1936--- um 04 Uhr 15 Minuten

in Schwerin(Meckl)--- verstorben.

Der Verstorbene war geboren am 66 Jahre alt, geboren

in Potsdam.---

und war nicht verheiratet

Schwerin(Meckl), den 30. Juni 1981

Geburtsstandesamt und Nr.

Reg.-Nr. 815055

Gesehen

zur Beglaubigung der vorstehenden Unterschrift
des/der Frau Buchien
Berlin, den 16. Juli 1981

**Ministerium
für Auswärtige Angelegenheiten**
der Deutschen Demokratischen Republik

— Heer —

Bestell-Nr. 220 10 VV Spremberg (87/11) 7849 Ag 310/78/DDR/4553

Adolf Seefeld's execution certificate

tion for National Socialist legislation for the protection of race and people'.

As well as confessing to a large number of murders in addition to those for which he was charged, Seefeld claimed to have killed his victims with a special poison he had concocted which it was impossible to trace. Press reports of the case in 1936 mentioned rather ominously that he had passed on the secrets to the Gestapo.

Other sex murderers included Ludwig Tessnow, who killed four children at Rügen in 1901; Werner Boost, the so-called 'Düsseldorf Doubles' killer, who sought out courting couples in their cars; and Heinrich Pommerencke, who claimed ten victims and earned the name 'The Beast of the Black Forest'. The investigation of Tessnow's crimes produced a breakthrough in forensic science when Dr Paul Uhlenhuth developed the precipitin test for differentiating between human and animal blood. No such advance could be claimed for Boost and Pommerencke, who received life sentences for their crimes in 1959 and 1960 respectively.

Germany has also produced its share of murderers motivated by the more common urges of gain, elimination and jealousy. Karl Hau, a bright young lawyer, murdered his mother-in-law at Baden-Baden for gain in 1901 (see under STREETS), and two blazing car incidents were contrived to consume the evidence of murder. In 1929 Erich Tetzner picked up a hitch-hiker and set his car on fire near Regensburg. Like Tessnow before him, his crime prompted an advance in forensic science with Dr Richard Kockel's studies of the effects of burning on the human body. Dr Richard Müller, bent on eliminating his wife, chose the blazing car method at Otterbach in 1954. (See under CARS for full story.)

The literature of German murder cases

published in English is fairly sparse, although a few well-known cases have found their way into books dealing with international crime. An outstanding collection is Anselm Ritter von Feuerbach's *Narratives of Remarkable Criminal Trials,* covering the period 1800–25, which contains among other stories a full account of the crimes of Anna Maria Zwanziger, the notorious poisoner. His description of the poisoner's mind has seldom been bettered:

> But no means of acquiring independence presented itself to her within the pale of social order, till at length she discovered the secret of hidden power, by the exercise of which she might not only emancipate herself from restraint, but also rule unseen and uncontrolled. This secret power was poison.

Von Feuerbach served for a number of years as President of the Central Criminal Court of one of the Bavarian provinces. He won a worthy reputation as a judge, and his extensive writings are distinguished by his perception and knowledge of the criminal law. Another useful collection of German cases is contained in *Continental Crimes* by von Sonnenberg and Trettin, who were senior officers in the Kriminalpolizei of Berlin in the early 1900s. The foreword of this book was contributed by English crime writer George Dilnot, who thought the German system of justice was altogether too lenient.

The German-speaking countries have produced a number of distinguished scientists and jurists who have contributed significant developments in the fields of criminology and crime investigation. Germany, with the quality of its science between the two world wars, pioneered many forensic advances, but it was Austria which engendered a better understanding of the psychology of the sex criminal. Professor Krafft-Ebing of the University of Vienna was an outstanding authority on the psychology of sexual deviation. It was Austria, too, which produced the founder of modern criminology in Dr Hans Gross, a lawyer with a liking for scientific method.

Austria has also generated a number of notable murders, including those of Martha Marek, who poisoned four victims in 1932 with thallium. Lainz Zoo in 1929 was the unlikely location for one of Austria's more controversial murders for which Gustav Bauer was acquitted but later committed suicide. (For the full story see under ZOOS.) Lieutenant Adolph Hofrichter provided Vienna with a sensation in 1909 by attempting to poison his rival army officers (see under BARRACKS) and a bogus count, Henri de Tourville, threw his English wife off a mountain top in the Austrian Tyrol in 1876. Although de Tourville escaped to England, the Austrian authorities had him extradited to stand trial at Bötzen for murder (see under MOUNTAINS).

Scandinavia has one of the lowest murder rates in Europe, the city of Oslo in Norway, for example, recording 0.2 criminal homicides per hundred thousand of the population in 1959. Nevertheless, the occasional noteworthy crime emerges, such as the poisoned chocolate case in 1949 which resulted in Carsten Brekke's conviction for attempted murder (see under MURDER BY POST). Scandinavia's greatest trial for mass murder took place at Trondheim in 1982 when Arnfinn Nesset, a nursing-home attendant, was convicted of charges of murdering twenty-one patients (see under HOSPITALS, NURSING-HOMES AND SICK-ROOMS).

The Low Countries, principally Belgium and the Netherlands, have contributed their share of murder cases to Europe's crime catalogue. Marie van der Linden claimed twenty-seven victims with arsenic and was tried for mass murder in The Hague in 1885. Marie Becker was another mass murderer who was convicted at Liège in 1936 of eleven killings using poison administered under the guise of medical treatment (see under HOSPITALS, NURSING-HOMES AND SICK-ROOMS).

Russia and East Europe present major difficulties in gleaning accounts of murder cases. It may reasonably be supposed that Russians murder one another with much the same frequency and for the same reasons as their European neighbours of different political persuasion. At least, that is probably true as far as individual murders are concerned — the political arena is another matter entirely.

Maxim Gorky wrote that cruelty is as much a central feature of a Russian's character as humour is of the English. Further insights are provided by A.T. Vassilyev, the last Chief of Police under the Tsars, in his book *The*

Ochrana. His translator commented that the Russian 'does not in his heart respect the law', and quotes the jurist B. Kistayakovsky, who said, 'Our public consciousness has never allowed the ideal of the person with legal rights to emerge.' Colin Wilson has also written about the origins of violence, and in his *Order of Assassins* refers to Dostoevsky whose plots are essentially about cruel personalities.

Probably the best known Russian murder is that in which Grigori Rasputin was the victim. The incident is as famous for the monk's influence over Tsar Nicholas II and Tsarina Alexandra as for the man's obvious durability. At the home of Prince Yussopov on 16 December (O.S.) 1916 he was fed 'enough potassium cyanide to kill a monastery of monks', as it was later described. When this failed to have the desired effect, he was shot in the back and left for dead. When, two hours later, he proved to be still alive, he was shot again and bludgeoned for good measure before being thrown into the icy waters of the river Neva, where he eventually perished. The Chief of Police, A.T. Vassilyev, investigated the murder of Rasputin, which he described as a 'prelude to those melancholy events that were destined to occur within an ever-widening sphere and to lead to the collapse of the Russian Empire'.

Britain has an extensive crime literature at the pinnacle of which stands the *Notable British Trials* series published by William Hodge with several of them edited by William Roughead, the Scottish lawyer and criminologist. Roughead, as might be expected of a stylish writer, had the gift of perception, and he well understood what he termed the 'peculiar alchemy' of murder. It lies in the mean streets and dark alleys of towns, in the bright parlours of private dwellings, in the silence of the countryside, in the darkened forest and on the lonely moor and in all that myriad of places which permit circumstances of human passion and privacy to combine in violence.

Many other writers have catalogued the murder trail and detailed its locations: Ivan Butler's *Murderers' England* and *Murderers' London* have particularly focused on the geographical locus of murder. Countless others have woven the significance of place into their narratives of individual murders, and there are many lesser known records of regional

significance. *Crime and Murder in Victorian Leicestershire* by Michael Tanner and *Murderous Yorkshire* by Barry Shaw are examples. In a Royal Commission Report on murder in England and Wales published in 1905 Sir John Macdonell described the crime as 'an incident in miserable lives in which disputes, quarrels, angry words and blows are common ....' He thus put murder into its predominantly domestic setting, for more than half the homicides committed involve the murderer and victim in some kind of family relationship.

In 1979 Professor Terence Morris and Louis Blom-Cooper published an analysis entitled *Murder in England and Wales since 1957* which reviewed the trends over a twenty-year period. The authors confirmed the continuing domestic nature of murder and noted that up to two-thirds of all persons indicted had a personal relationship of some kind with the victim. The most frequently used method was stabbing, which in 1977 accounted for 38 per cent of all murders. Firearms used during the period at most accounted for 11 per cent of the murders. Tennyson Jesse's remark, made in 1948, that 'In England it is in normal times easier for a camel to enter the eye of a needle than for a man to buy a gun' reflected the state of play at the time. Nevertheless, within a few years Derek Bentley was hanged for being involved in the murder of a police officer though a younger man Christopher Craig actually fired the fatal shot. Resort to firearms — often unloaded and used to menace — has grown in the 1980s. In 1981 the criminal statistics for England and Wales showed an increase of 20 per cent during the previous year in the number of offences involving firearms.

An interesting feature has been the increasing involvement of women in homicide investigations. The number almost doubled between 1969 and 1977, and reduced willingness to accept violence as passive victims is one factor suggested to account for this. Increased mobility and attainment of equality are also likely to be relevant. A sidelight on female involvement in crime was that an English court in 1981 accepted a defence plea based on pre-menstrual tension (PMT) from a woman who had killed her lover. The subject was reviewed at length by Susan Edwards in her book *Women on Trial*, published in 1984.

A more disturbing tendency which was

highlighted in the British press in 1982 was the increase of murder among elderly people. A report on geriatric murder was presented at a British Medical Association symposium by Professor Bernard Knight, an internationally recognized forensic pathologist. Most murder incidents involve individuals in the 16 to 30 age group, but the trend towards greater longevity probably drew more old people into the web. Professor Knight cited a case in which a couple in their seventies, whom neighbours claimed had never spoken an ill word to each other, resorted to violence in which the woman battered her husband to death. In another case an octogenarian husband killed his wife with a hammer in a horrific attack apparently prompted by jealousy. Changes in the brain brought about by senility which release years of inhibition and pent-up feelings were possible causes of this behaviour.

The progress of murder in England has been well charted, and the literature is vast. The quintessential commentator on the murder scene is Thomas De Quincey, whose *Murder Considered as One of the Fine Arts*, written in 1827, sets out the intellectual basis for proper consideration of the subject. For a man who could claim, 'I never attempted any murder in my life except in the year 1801, upon the body of a tom cat', De Quincey had the insights which otherwise come from experience. The particular murderer to whom he addressed his attentions was John Williams, who killed the Marr and Williamson families in 1811 in London's Ratcliff Highway (see under SHOPS AND OFFICES). Referring to Williams's murderous mind, De Quincey wrote, 'the tiger's heart was masked by the most insinuating and snaky refinement'.

This was a description which also applied to the individual who was England's best-known murderer — Jack the Ripper. The five murders committed in 1888 in the foggy, gas-lit streets of London's East End may fairly claim to have won worldwide fame as a story of mystery and horror. Whether in France as L'éventreur or in Spain as Jack el Destripador, the world ranking of the Ripper is unchallenged. The literature on Jack the Ripper has grown to such proportions as to necessitate its own bibliography, yet despite all the words and analysis, the East End killer retains that most precious gift of the murderer — his anonymity.

There is a strong tendency towards poison among British murderers, typified perhaps by Major Armstrong, whom C.P. Snow described as 'the supreme expression of English middle-class gentility'. Practitioners of the poison arts include several doctors: William Palmer (1856), Edward Pritchard (1865), George Henry Lamson (1882) and Neill Cream (1892) as well as small businessmen such as George Chapman (1903) and Frederick Seddon (1912). But it is a female poisoner, Mary Ann Cotton (1873), who gains the distinction of being Britain's greatest mass murderer, although Dennis Nilsen (see under MURDER HOUSES) runs her close.

An interesting feature of British murders is the transatlantic connection. Dr Crippen, whose name became a household word in England in 1910, highlighted this connection when he was overtaken in his escape across the Atlantic by Inspector Dew (alerted by a wireless message from Crippen's liner, and travelling in a faster ship). Dr Cream was born in Glasgow, studied medicine in Canada and practised it in the USA; but when it came to murder he crossed to England in 1891. Florence Maybrick, an Alabama girl, married an English businessman whom she poisoned in Liverpool at their home in 1889. She returned to the USA after she was released from prison in 1904. Chung Yi Miao, a young lawyer, married a wealthy Chinese girl in New York and brought her to England where he killed her during their honeymoon in 1928 and was duly hanged.

It was not surprising that the stationing of US troops in England during the Second World War should trail murder in its wake. August Sangret, a French-Canadian soldier, murdered a young woman on Hankley Common near Godalming in 1942 and Gustav Hulten, aided by his eighteen-year-old English girl-friend, murdered a London taxi-driver in 1944 (see under TAXIS). USAF Master-Sergeant Marcus Marymont poisoned his wife with arsenic and was found guilty by a US General Court Martial in 1958. He was sentenced to life imprisonment to be served at Fort Leavenworth, but both Sangret and Hulten were hanged in Britain.

The press has endowed some of Britain's murders with titles which in many cases have become better known than the murderers themselves: Brides in the Bath (George Joseph

Smith), Acid Bath Murderer (John George Haigh), the Black Panther (Donald Neilson), Murder in the Red Barn (William Corder), the Green Bicycle Case (unsolved) and the Hammersmith Nudes Murders (unsolved). Perhaps the best known trio of murderers were those who emerged in the immediate post-war years and whose names leapt out from the front pages of the newspapers: Neville Heath (1946), John Haigh (1949) and John Christie (1953).

There are also a number of first-time occurrences, such as the world's first murder on a train committed in 1864 by Franz Müller (see under RAILWAY MURDERS) and what was probably recognizable as a sex murder, when William Baker killed Fanny Adams in 1867 (see under FARMS AND FIELDS). The Stratton brothers were the first murderers to be convicted using the Henry fingerprint system, in 1905, and Major Armstrong in 1922 was the first — and so far the only — solicitor to be hanged for murder. There are also some significant last occurrences. The last public execution in Scotland was that of Dr Pritchard in 1865 and in England of Michael Barrett, convicted of causing explosions, in 1868. The last woman to be hanged in England was Ruth Ellis in 1955, and the last hangings of any kind were those of Peter Allen and Gwynne Evans in 1964. The death penalty was abolished in England and Wales under the Abolition of the Death Penalty Act of 1964.

The murder rate in Britain remains lower than that of most countries in Western Europe. In 1980 the rate for England and Wales was eight homicides per million, but nearly double that in Scotland, which had fifteen per million. The trends of violence, as evidenced elsewhere, are towards terrorist or gangland-inspired killings — what Dorothy Dunbar called 'the era of booze and bullets'.
(97, 140, 141, 165, 198, 229, 258, 274, 289, 324, 359, 382, 383, 392, 417, 434, 435, 436, 482, 483, 501, 504, 526, 598, 623, 694, 772, 842, 928, 963, 965, 968, 969, 970, 1009, 1010, 1024, 1045, 1052)

NORTH AMERICA

The United States of America does not top the poll for the world's highest murder rate — that unenviable record belongs to Mexico — but murder in the USA is subjected to greater publicity, drama and analysis. Since 1975 over 20,000 citizens have been killed each year in acts of criminal violence, and homicide ranks as the fourth highest cause of death for men aged between twenty-five and forty-four.

Both in quality and in quantity, murder in America has unique features. The New World has given us the milestones of murder in modern times — political assassinations, stranger-to-stranger killings, serial murders, sado-masochistic murder and drug-induced killings, all accentuated by public agonizing over the death penalty and definitions of insanity. As the rhetoric continues, so the statistics mount, and for many of the victims there is not even the dignity of proper identification. At any one time some five thousand unidentified corpses lie in mortuaries all over the USA; they share the distinction of being victims of unknown killers.

The greatest majority of murders are committed with firearms. 'The gun is far and away

The Top Ten US murder states

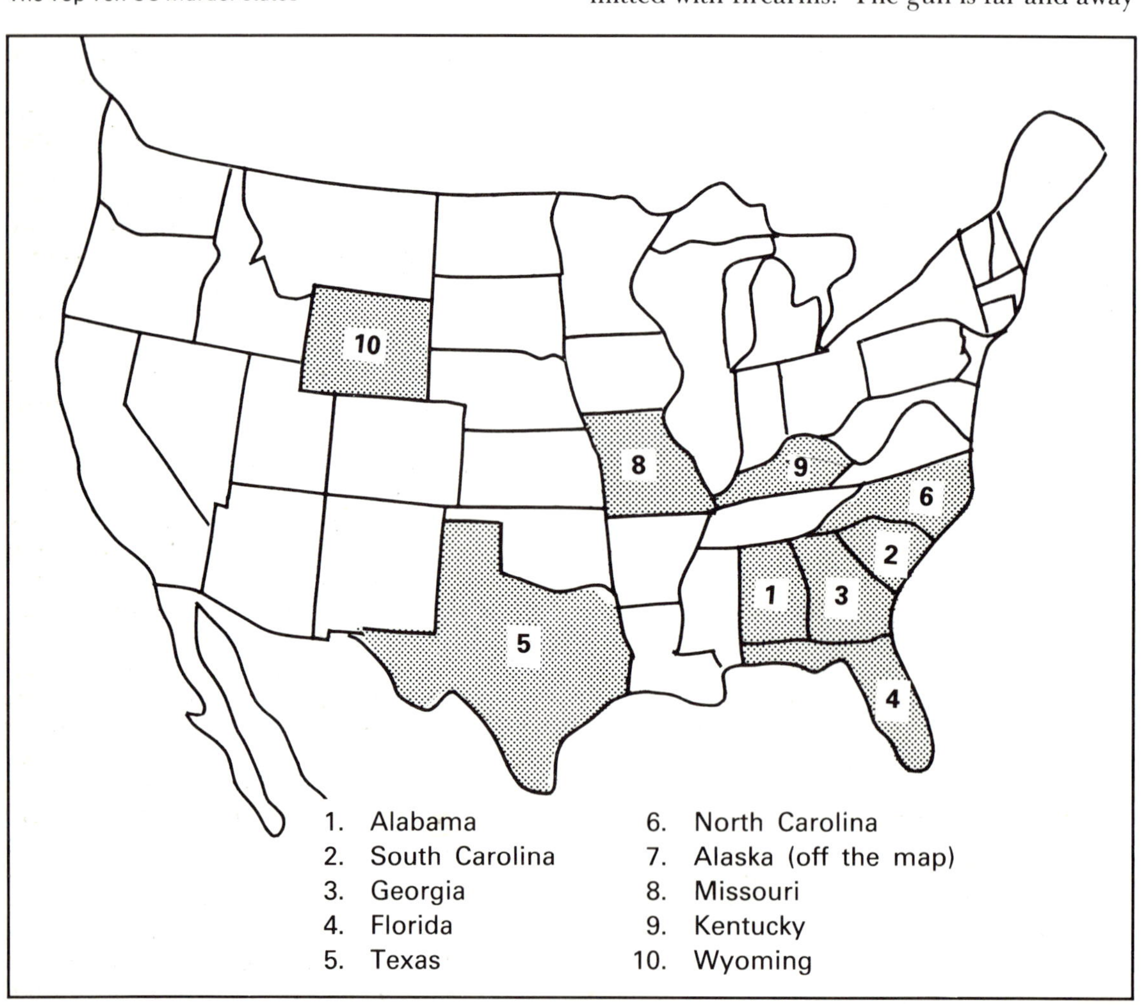

1.	Alabama	6.	North Carolina
2.	South Carolina	7.	Alaska (off the map)
3.	Georgia	8.	Missouri
4.	Florida	9.	Kentucky
5.	Texas	10.	Wyoming

our top murder utensil,' wrote John Godwin in *Murder USA,* and about 68 per cent of all homicides are carried out using guns. When John Hinckley junior fired a Saturday Night Special at President Reagan in March 1981, wounding him in the chest, there were renewed cries for gun-control in some quarters, in spite of the fact that the victim, the eighth US President to be the target of an assassination attempt, had during his election campaign promised to weaken current gun-control laws.

The National Rifle Association remains a powerful exponent of every American's right under the constitution to bear arms. Selling slogans like 'Buy a gun and get a bang out of life' exacerbate fear and excitement which encourage Americans in the prevailing climate of violence to purchase firearms. Over 55 million handguns are in private ownership, and sales in the 1980s are running at three million a year.

Gun-control laws vary from state to state. New York and Washington DC have strict rules while in Florida a seventeen-year-old with a driver's licence can buy a gun, and in New Mexico there are no controls at all. Guns are transported across state boundaries with impunity — John Hinckley bought his handgun in Dallas and took it to Washington DC, and Mark David Chapman — who killed pop-star John Lennon in New York in 1980 — bought his weapon in Hawaii. Some of those who have campaigned for tighter gun-control have ended up as victims of shooting. Ironically, Robert Kennedy warned about the dangers of growing gun ownership only five days before he was struck down by an assassin's bullet.

In Los Angeles, following a record number of assaults against teachers in the city's high schools and pitched battles in playgrounds, parents started to train their children to handle guns. In 1980 there were 192 youth gang murders in Los Angeles, and four thirteen-year-old children faced trial for murder. The school-children sent to gun clubs to learn how to use firearms for self-defence only added to the dangers of accidental death. Each year two hundred American children die as the result of gun accidents.

In New York City many of the older inhabitants are enrolling in self-defence courses. In the borough of Queens, many elderly residents are afraid to go out without protection. A 63-year-old woman who had lived in Queens for thirty years, and felt it necessary to put bars on all her windows and security devices on her doors, said, 'The criminals are running free while I am a prisoner.' She signed up for a thirty-dollar course on 'Shotgun Orientation.' 'People are scared and mad,' remarked one gun-range owner. The proprietor of a gun shop in Nashville, Tennessee, boosted his sales of firearms after he placed a Valentine's Day advertisement in *The Tennessean:* 'For a lasting gift of love, insure her with a Colt,' he appealed to men looking for presents.

Those who are not in favour of proposals to limit ownership of firearms argue that it is not guns which kill but people using them. This is irrefutable — if somewhat irrelevant, for the victims are just as dead. The frontier spirit has been blamed for the continuous and rising pattern of violence in America. A demonstration of that outlook resulted in a death from shooting in Rock Springs, Wyoming, in 1979. The city's public safety director (sheriff), who was also a well-known fast-draw expert, shot dead a young man outside the Silver Dollar saloon. The victim was a police undercover agent who was gathering evidence on corruption in Rock Springs. The sheriff was tried for murder, and if anyone doubted that it was possible for a man to draw and fire his gun faster than an opponent holding a cocked weapon could pull the trigger, an expert demonstrated the fact in court. The expert also testified that it was well established in gun-fighting technique for two armed men to engage each other's eyes in locked vision. It was understood that the slightest hand movement would result in shooting. The sheriff was cleared of the charge of premeditated murder, while the man he shot went to the modern equivalent of Boot Hill.

The transition of the Wild West gun-carrying habit and vigilante temperament to the streets of American cities struck a sympathetic public chord in the film *Deathwatch.* It surfaced in reality in New York's subway in January 1985. Bernhard Goetz became a folk hero overnight when, fearing that he was about to be mugged by four coloured men who approached him on a subway train, he drew a gun and shot each of them. Goetz had been mugged in 1981 and applied unsuccessfully for a firearms permit in New York; he was reported to have said, 'The city doesn't care what happens to you.' Eventually he acquired a gun in Florida, and his use of it required him to answer a charge of attempted murder. Initial public reaction was to dub him the 'subway vigilante', and there was a strong feeling of support for a citizen who had shown that he was prepared to fight back. 'The city should thank him for his help and start fighting the crime that is destroying this city,' wrote one newspaper correspondent. The subway system alone is the setting for 12,000 crimes reported annually, and the killing rate in the city as a whole has steadily risen to 1800 a year.*

Writing in *The Murdered and the Missing* of the forty years served in the New York Police Department by Captain John Stein, Armstrong Livingston referred to the increase in murder rate during the prohibition era to 500 killings a year. 'The majority of these,' he wrote, 'were fortunately cases of racketeers killing each other; frequently a murder would be committed, the murderer's identity would be known, the police would fare forth to bring him in and they would find his dead body where the first man's friends had left it. These gangsters were doing their best to purify the city ....' Times have changed drastically and in the second half of the twentieth century we have entered what writer John Godwin calls the age of multiple slayings. In *Murder USA*, published in 1978, he listed twenty-one multiple killers, headed by Dean Corll, the Houston mass murderer who claimed twenty-seven victims in the early 1970s. Since then this score has been overtaken by John Wayne Gacy (1979) with thirty-two, Ted Bundy (1979, see under CAMPUS) with thirty-four and Henry Lee Lucas (1983) who at one time claimed an incredible 300, or more, victims.

David Berkowitz, who terrorized New York City with his Son of Sam killings in 1976/77, heralded the onset of stranger-to-stranger killings. In the great majority of murders there is some relationship between killer and victim. This is often domestic and provides the root cause for an act of violence; the existence of a relationship also helps the police to investigate crime. Speaking of the Christmas murder spree in 1981 which left New York City with

over twenty victims, psychiatrist Dr Gary Emery was reported as saying, 'There are more family parties around the holidays, get-togethers with friends, and the people who kill each other are usually friends and relatives.' Motives for this sort of killing lie in human emotions which, while they may exceed normal limits, are still understandable, such as rage, jealousy and sexual passion. But the increase in stranger-to-stranger killings is sinister, for the only motive appears to be killing for its own sake.

Even worse is the trend towards stranger-to-stranger killings on a mass scale. Ted Bundy and Henry Lee Lucas have been called 'serial murderers' — men who kill not for gain or passion but for pleasure. They are human predators, roaming the concrete jungle for opportunities to kill. They kill at random and keep on the move, using the country's vast road network. Henry Lee Lucas, a 47-year-old drifter, claimed to have killed 360 people between 1975 and 1983. He has been convicted of murder in three states and faces indictments in five others. Lucas told police, 'Once I've done it, I just forget it.' He claimed to have killed his first victim when he was thirteen; by the time he was twenty-four he had stabbed his mother to death. He gave details of 200 murders he had committed in every state of the Union except Hawaii and Alaska. He wandered the highways, picking up hitch-hikers, mainly women and children, whom he stabbed or strangled. Sexual abuse, necrophilia and mutilation were also part of his stock in trade. He may, in addition, have accounted for another 100 victims, making him the most prolific murderer in history (but see Pedro Lopez under SOUTH AMERICA).

Dr Jack Levin, a sociologist at Northeastern University, has described the serial killer as a 'psychopath who is into his work. This is fun for this person.' This type of murderer has an urge to control others and frequently preys on vulnerable members of society such as children, prostitutes or homosexuals. Dr William Eckert, Director of the Milton Helpern International Center for the Forensic Sciences at Wichita, Kansas, described the serial murderers as 'Hunters of Death.' The FBI's Behavioral Science Unit at Quantico, Virginia, has interviewed thirty-eight such killers to establish some common features in their personalities which will enable police to seek out the thirty

---

*In January 1986 a New York court cleared Bernhard Goetz of the charges of attempted murder and assault.

or forty serial murderers currently at large. One characteristic which they share is a background of unhappy childhood often accompanied by rejection or abuse. (See Ken Bianchi under HILLSIDES.) Usually these killers deal out death with their hands, and torture, molestation and mutilation are part of their repertoire.

The 'Green River Killer' who has murdered thirteen young women in the Seattle area since 1982 remains at large but Randall Woodfield, perpetrator of a string of robberies, assaults and murders, was convicted in 1981. Woodfield, a handsome young athlete who played football for the Green Bay Packers, patrolled the inter-state highway 1–5, which runs for eight hundred miles down the Pacific coast from British Columbia to Mexico. Andy Stack in his book *The 1–5 Killer* described how Randy Woodfield wearing a false beard and with a band-aid over his nose terrorized, abused and murdered his way through the months of 1981. A series of forty-four offences — including robbery, attempted kidnapping and sodomy, in addition to murder — was attributed to him. Following conviction he was sentenced to life imprisonment plus one hundred and twenty-five years.

The police suspected that Woodfield was guilty of many more murders than the handful of which he was accused. In 1981 over 6,000 murder cases remained unsolved throughout the USA and the situation is hardly likely to improve with many police departments below strength. The Los Angeles Police Department, for instance, even at full strength, still has only the same number of officers it had ten years ago, when killings were half the rate they are today.

Los Angeles is the scene of six killings a day on average; on a really bad day the city's mortuaries cannot cope. From 398 criminal homicides in 1952 for a population of two million, the rate rose to 830 murders out of a population of three million in 1983. When thousands of visitors journeyed to Los Angeles for the Olympic Games in 1984 the police put out leaflets warning them to avoid poorly lit streets or car parks, and to guard their luggage at all times. They did not warn them — nor could they have done — about Daniel Lee Young. Before the Games started 21-year-old Young mowed down fifty-four people strolling in the evening sunlight in Westwood, killing a fifteen-year-old girl and leaving three others critically injured. His motive, he explained, was a grudge against the police because he had been placed on probation following conviction for burglary. Charged with murder, Young was reported to have said he hoped a policeman was in the crowd when he drove into it. Another grim statistic is the killing toll of police officers — 372 were killed throughout the USA during 1972–74 and the numbers are rising.

Ramsey Clark, a former Attorney General, in his book *Crime in America* talked about murder being principally a family affair. He wrote, 'If you are afraid of being murdered, there is more safety in deserting your family and having no friends than in additional police who rarely have the opportunity to prevent friends and relatives from murdering each other.' He is probably right, which is why elderly New Yorkers are spending money on courses learning how to defend themselves.

The fact is that potential danger lurks in even the most innocent encounters, as Sandy Fawkes, a London journalist, recounted in her book *Killing Time*. During a visit to the USA in 1974 she met a man calling himself Daryl Golden in the bar of a hotel in Atlanta, Georgia. He was tall and handsome and they were mutually attracted to the extent that they spent the next six days and nights together. The man's real name was Paul John Knowles, a multiple killer and rapist who the previous day had murdered a man and his daughter in Milledgeville. By the time he met Sandy Fawkes in November, Knowles had averaged one murder a week for the past four months. During the time they spent together Knowles had hinted at being a mass murderer, and told his companion that he had made tapes which she, a journalist, could use to write a book about him. He said the tapes — which contained 'thoughts about life and death' — were in the safe-keeping of his lawyer in Miami with instructions that they were not to be heard until after his death.

Knowles shared the serial murderer's characteristics: an unhappy childhood and lack of sexual accomplishment. He had been brought up in foster homes and dreamed of fame and fortune. His first killing was accidental but it gave him both a sense of power and of extracting his revenge on society, although he said of his victims, 'I never wanted to hurt them.'

Despite his attractive qualities, Sandy Fawkes

sensed something powerfully evil in Knowles. When he stopped the car in which they were travelling and pulled a gun she made a dash for safety and broke the spell. Knowles killed two men, one of whom was a police officer, before he was arrested. Fawkes realized she had experienced a flirtation with death in the company of a mass murderer who had told her, 'I am going to be killed ... within a year I shall be dead. I am going to be killed by someone.' His prophecy proved an accurate one, for while in police custody he tried to seize an officer's gun and was shot dead by an FBI agent.

Analysing her experience in *Killing Time*, Fawkes asked, 'Can a personality change overnight? Do some personalities have a physiological San Andreas fault built into them so that when the time comes they will split asunder and wreak havoc around them?' The answers may lie in Paul John Knowles's tapes which were heard in court in 1975 but the judge ruled that their contents must never be disclosed.

The capital punishment issue has continued to tax the American conscience. Like all the other milestones of violence it can be delineated by statistics. According to Watt Espy, Head of the Capital Punishment Research Project at the University of Alabama, writing in Doug Magee's book *Slow Coming Dark,* there have been 11,334 legal executions in the USA since 1622. In that year one Daniel Frank was hanged for theft in Virginia. In 1967 the US Supreme Court halted all executions while an investigation was carried out into the validity of capital punishment. By a five to four majority the Supreme Court ruled against the death penalty in 1972, but in 1976, by a seven to two majority, found capital punishment appropriate in murder cases. National opinion polls indicated a three to one majority in favour of the death penalty. Neither homicide nor its punishment has a federal definition but depends on state laws. Thirty-seven out of fifty individual states have the death penalty on their statute books, but the methods of exercising it are all different.

Gary Gilmore, the double murderer immortalized by Norman Mailer in his *Executioner's Song,* demanded of the state authorities in Utah that they carry out the sentence of death passed on him. He was the first to test the new freedom when he went before a firing squad in

1977. After Gilmore came Jesse Bishop, who perished in the gas chamber at Carson City, Nevada, in October 1979. He too demanded that sentence be carried out. He refused to appeal and despised the 'Monday morning do-gooders' (as he termed campaigners) for the American Civil Liberties Union (ACLU).

In May 1979 John Spenkelink was the first convicted murderer executed against his wishes since the US Supreme Court relaxed its moratorium. Charlie Brooks was the first to be executed by lethal injection of drugs. Demonstrators outside the prison at Huntsville, Texas, in December 1982 chanted their approval — 'Let's bring back the hangman's noose' and 'Kill 'em in plain view.' The first woman to be executed in the USA for twenty-two years was Velma Barfield, a 52-year-old grandmother. She had been convicted of poisoning her fiancé with arsenic, and admitted killing three other persons, including her mother. In November 1984 at Raleigh, North Carolina, wearing pink pyjamas and with her hair carefully curled the night before, she was injected with sodium thiopental to induce sleep, following by procuronium bromide to relax the chest muscles and arrest her breathing.

Velma Barfield, who became a born again Christian while awaiting trial, drew attention to the plight of women condemned to death in the USA. Of the total of 1,350 condemned awaiting execution in Death Row cells throughout the country in 1984, eighteen were women. The youngest was a nineteen-year-old girl convicted of the murder of her former boy-friend, and the eldest a 56-year-old convicted of six murders and twenty-three counts of attempted murder. Between them these eighteen women had killed twenty-four people, including four children, two husbands and one policeman, who had been variously shot, poisoned, stabbed, axed and mown down by motor vehicles. In 1981 the FBI reported that one in eight persons arrested for homicide was a woman. The ratio of murderesses executed since 1930 is 120 to 1. A Tufts University professor commenting on this anomaly said, 'If you're a woman you won't get the death sentence. If you do get the death sentence, you won't get executed.' There is also a reluctance to send women to prison — the ratio of men to women incarcerated is 20 to 1.

The executions themselves provide many horror stories. Alpha Otis Stephens survived a two-minute 2,000 volt shock in the electric chair at Jackson, Georgia, in December 1984. A second jolt was needed to finish him off. In the same month, Robert Lee Willie was electrocuted at Angola, Louisiana, in a chair which had been wired up by his father, who had previously been an inmate. Willie told a reporter before he was executed, 'Electric chair don't worry me, man, I have a lot of pride. I don't run from nothing.' A relative of the teenage girl he had raped and murdered said he was happy 'to see the smoke fly off' Willie's body. Steven Judy, killer of four, threatened the lives of his trial judge and jury if they did not sentence him to die. He was granted his wish in the electric chair at Indiana State Prison in August 1981. ACLU demonstrators outside the prison bore placards aloft carrying the question, 'Why do we kill people who kill people to show that killing is wrong?'

The poignancy of the whole business of death was brought into sharp focus by *Newsweek* magazine in a Special Report entitled *To Die or Not to Die* in October 1983. The magazine devoted twenty-four pages to the subject of capital punishment, highlighted by the eleventh-hour reprieve granted to James David Autry in Texas. The 26-year-old Autry, who had been convicted of a double killing in Port Arthur in April 1980, was dramatically reprieved while he lay strapped to a prison gurney waiting to receive a lethal injection. The crowd outside the prison which had been chanting, 'Kill him! Kill him!' changed the cry to 'Bullshit!' when the reprieve was announced.

Many Americans are frustrated by the weight of consideration given to the killer and the lack of concern shown to the victim and his family. Beth Fallon, writing in the *Baltimore Sun* in the wake of the twenty years to life sentence passed on Mark Chapman, killer of pop star John Lennon, spoke of her realization that 'another killer, crazed or sane, may very well walk the streets again in our lifetime'. She referred to reports that Sirhan Sirhan, the Jordanian who killed Robert Kennedy in 1968 and was serving a life sentence in California, was making plans to travel to Libya when he was released. Life imprisonment in California usually means a maximum of thirteen years; it seems like a trade arrangement, commented Beth Fallon, whereby 'I kill somebody and give eight years or twelve or seventeen in exchange!'

The citizens of Lovelock, Nevada, disappointed at the way the legal system seemed to protect known killers, decided to pay for justice out of their own pockets. Gerald Armond Gallego, already under sentence of death in California for committing two murders, was wanted for trial in Lovelock on charges of murdering four girls. Sheriff's deputies spirited him out of California (where there have been no executions for seventeen years) and took him across the state line into Nevada where, according to one commentator, 'He'll get his just deserts.' As Lovelock could not afford the trial costs of $60,000, US citizens, both local and nationwide, subscribed to a trial fund. Contributions poured in, often accompanied by notes such as 'Hang him by his toes' and 'Kill him good.'

American attitudes towards crime and punishment were taxed in 1982 when a verdict of not guilty by reason of insanity was reached at the trial of John Hinckley, the man who had attempted to assassinate President Ronald Reagan. Outrage was expressed by public and officialdom alike; it was a licence for the 'crazies of the world' to do what they liked, said the Treasury Secretary. Hinckley was the first would-be assassin to plead insanity successfully since 1835, when Richard Lawrence was found not guilty by reason of insanity after he had tried to shoot President Andrew Jackson. More recent assassins, including Sirhan Sirhan and James Earl Ray, were found guilty as charged.

The Hinckley verdict raised questions about personal responsibility and many felt that justice had not been done. The insanity defence is pleaded in less than 2 per cent of felony cases and the failure rate is high — approximately 75 per cent. The outcome is that successful pleas result in a great deal of publicity. Britain's M'Naghten Rules dating back to Victorian times have been widely adopted by the English-speaking countries including the USA, excepting the state of New Hampshire which rejected them in 1869 in favour of its own rule. The Durham Rule brought in by the District of Columbia in 1954 and the Model Penal Code proposed by the American Law Institute in 1972 were attempts to refine criminal responsibility. The concept of 'substantial capacity' was interposed between mental disease and its causation of crime. Consequently, criminal responsibility did not exist if as a result of mental disease or defect an individual lacked 'substantial capacity either to appreciate the criminality of his conduct or to conform his conduct to the requirements of the law'.

This still leaves much that is open to interpretation, and the result is that the differences between legal and psychiatric definitions of insanity are battled out in court. The evidence of opposing experts frequently borders on opinion, and the burden on jurors, men and women of ordinary ability to understand such testimony and to weigh its value is onerous. Powerful evidence was presented at the trial of Jack Ruby, killer of Lee Harvey Oswald, President John F. Kennedy's assassin in 1963. Ruby pleaded not guilty by reason of insanity, and his defence argued that he suffered from epilepsy and had acted on impulse. The jury nevertheless found him guilty as charged.

Herbert Mullin, the California mass murderer of the early 1970s, was a schizophrenic who heard voices which commanded him to kill, but the jury would not bring in an insanity verdict. David Berkowitz (Son of Sam, 1976–7) killer of six in New York, was another schizophrenic commanded to kill by voices. He pleaded guilty and was sentenced to a long prison term. As the human psyche is analysed to determine the cases which tip behaviour into criminality, so the discussion becomes more esoteric and real understanding as elusive as ever. 'Sexual addiction' emerged in 1984 as an explanation of excessive sexual behaviour. If rape and sex killing can be attributed to sexual addiction, and be considered as acts over which the perpetrator has no control, it is conceivable that such behaviour may be judged legally unaccountable.

Among the numerous attempts to analyse the mainsprings of murder in America are two especially notable studies. *Patterns in Criminal Homicide* by Dr Marvin Wolfgang, published in 1958, analysed over 500 homicides which occurred in Philadelphia during the period 1948–52. The author looked more closely than hitherto at the relationship between victim and murderer and especially at the concept of victim-precipitated homicide. Wolfgang's book was a unique study which highlighted many significant associations between the various elements of crime. He showed, for example,

that the age group 20–24 years contained the highest number of offenders, that there is a relationship between race and sex of offenders and the method used to inflict death, and that homicide is significantly related to days of the week and hours of the day.

The decline of family life, lack of religious observance and the deprivations of poverty are among the reasons popularly suggested from time to time to account for the rising murder rate in the USA. The first two may be contributory factors but the idea that poverty breeds murder is not readily substantiated. Homicide is one of the ten principal causes of death in Texas, which is hardly an impoverished state. Of the 1264 homicides committed in Texas in 1969, over 300 occurred in Houston. This inspired Henry P. Lundsgaarde to write his cultural analysis of Houston homicide patterns, *Murder in Space City*, published in 1977. He wanted to find out why people killed each other in this prosperous city with a world-wide reputation for space and medical technology.

The Rev. Billy Graham's description of Houston as 'the murder capital of the United States' was incorrect as Miami held the title at the time. Nevertheless, Houston has one of the highest per capita homicide rates in the USA, and has produced at least two celebrated murder cases over the years. Dean Corll, the mass murderer of the 1970s, was an electrician in Houston and Dr John Hill, a plastic surgeon in the city, was indicted with causing the death of his wife in 1969 in 'murder by omission'. Both cases left their scars.

Houston proved to be no different from Philadelphia nearly twenty years earlier in that the majority of murders occur at weekends, peaking between the hours of 6.0 p.m. and 2.0 a.m. on Saturday night and Sunday morning. May, August, September and October turned out to be the most dangerous months in Houston, and the 27th day of every month attracted the most killings. The reason for the high rate of murder at the weekend is not difficult to discern, for that is the time when people socialize the most, but the significance of the 27th day of the month is a mystery. Aside from the part which population density plays — a person living in a US city with a population of more than 250,000 inhabitants has a three to ten times greater chance of being a crime victim than a person in a rural area —

the reason for Houston's high homicide rate may be related to the provisions of Texas law.

Considerable scope is afforded to Texas citizens to respond to threats as provocation from others. Before 1974 it was regarded as justifiable for a husband to kill his wife or her lover in the matter of adultery. Since then the lists of acts which constitute justifiable — and therefore non-criminal — homicide has grown. It includes killing in the performance of a public duty, killing to prevent a person's escape from custody, the necessary use of force to avoid harm, self-defence, defence of the person, defence of a third person, protection of life or health, protection of one's property, protection of a third person's property, as well as law enforcement. It is noted too that Houston grand juries fail to indict a significant proportion of homicidal offenders. This might be interpreted as demonstrating a lenient view of culpability regarding some forms of killing.

Not all murders in America are of the multiple and perverted kind. Many single homicides result from the time-honoured eruption of passion into violence which is the essence of the classical murder. Buddy Jacobson (see under APARTMENTS AND PENTHOUSES) was convicted in 1980 for murdering his rival in an emotional triangle and Dorothy Stratten, the Centrefold model, was killed by her boy friend in 1980 in a fit of jealous rage (see under BEDROOMS for full story).

There are also numerous murder cases which contain unusual or distinguishing features of the kind that have always signposted expressions of violence and created new dimensions of human behaviour. Dr Jeffrey MacDonald killed his wife and two daughters by multiple stabbing in a Mansonesque incident at Fort Bragg in 1970. The ex-Green Beret doctor, described as an 'individual trying to be superman', gave vent to a fit of rage which released tremendous violence (see under BARRACKS for full story). Ronald De Feo who said of himself, 'I'm a secret agent for God', destroyed his family in their house at Amityville, Long Island, in 1974, thus inspiring the Amityville horror story (see under MURDER HOUSES). G. Daniel Walker, an escaped convict, set up his victim in an isolated ranch in 1973 (see under MANSIONS, RANCHES AND VILLAS) and Dale Pierre and friends inflicted robbery, rape, torture and

murder on the occupants of a Hi-Fi shop in 1974 (see under SHOPS AND OFFICES). These and many other murders included under their various location headings illustrate the diversified nature of murder in America.

The quest for understanding goes on and the weight of attention given to the mentality of the murderer is occasionally offset by a look at the victims of violence. Calvin Trillin, a columnist on *The New Yorker*, brought together in a volume called *Killings* a collection of sixteen incidents of violent death which he had reported between 1969 and 1982. They illustrate, as the author puts it, how 'Murders unsettle communities, revealing to the keen eye what lies just below the surface.' The seeming inevitability of violence was illustrated in a feud between two families which began in 1964 at Casa Blanca, California. A member of the Ahumada family was badly beaten up and, contrary to the conventional practice of settling disputes within the community, police were called in. Two members of the Lozanos family were convicted of assault and sent to prison. Thus were the seeds of confrontation and violence sown. One man was killed in 1976, three in 1978 and three more in 1980, with numerous others seriously injured. All concerned seem convinced that violence is now endemic in Casa Blanca.

Murder as the tool of organized crime — apart from that of Albert Anastasia, whom Fate placed in a Manhattan barber's chair in 1957 (see under ARMCHAIR MURDERS) — does not feature in this review of murder by location. While the cases cited are unique in their incidents, they do have one common aspect which is that they were the work of individuals and not of organizations. Discussion of organized crime is a subject in its own right and is left to others; full accounts are to be found in *Crime in America* by Estes Kefauver and *Crime Inc.* by Martin Short.

Just across the border from the USA lies Canada, which indulges in a similar life-style to its neighbour but, proportionally, suffers only one-fifth of the homicide rate. In a world ranking of homicide rates per 100,000 of population in 1959, Montreal came fifth, below Washington DC; Sydney, Australia; and Wellington, New Zealand. Comparing two cities of similar population size, Philadelphia and Toronto, and looking at the number of homicides in 1973 gives 430 for the American city and 45 for the Canadian.

One of the distinguishing features of murder in Toronto is the number of unsolved cases. In 1983 seven major cases were outstanding. One concerned an incident in which Philip Rimmington, the Metro Deputy Planning Commissioner, was shot dead while he was walking to his car. The 42-year-old executive was killed in the basement car park below the high-rise apartment block in which he lived in Balliol Street. Early on the morning of 10 February 1983 he was shot with a .22 calibre semi-automatic Colt Woodman. A man was seen emerging from a basement fire exit after the noise of the shot alerted residents. A description was issued but no trace of the man could be found. Rimmington owned three handguns, all of which were missing, and one of them was a Colt Woodman. The possibility is that he was shot with his own gun. Robbery was not thought to be the motive and the case remains a mystery.

Other unsolved Toronto murders include the killing of an eighty-year-old widow in her apartment in Bloor Street, the stabbing to death of an elderly man who was sleeping in his car to protect it from vandals, and the killing of a teacher in the bathroom of his apartment. A nationwide murder hunt was set up in February 1983 for a man thought to have assaulted and killed nine-year-old Sharin' Morningstar Keenan. Her body was found inside the refrigerator of a lodging-house in Brunswick Avenue. These and two other unsolved murders claimed solitary victims, unlike the contemporary pattern in the USA where cases of multicide are so prevalent.

An exception was the sensational series of child deaths which occurred in Toronto's Hospital for Sick Children. (See under HOSPITALS, NURSING-HOMES AND SICKROOMS.) A Royal Commission investigating the mysterious deaths of thirty-six infants in the hospital concluded in January 1985 that at least eight and possibly twenty-three of the deaths were murders, which so far remain unsolved. The causal agent was thought to be digoxin, administered as an overdose to some of the babies who had been prescribed that particular drug. The motive for killing such defenceless victims is difficult to comprehend but there is no denying the ingenuity of the method. In his book *Coroner to the Stars* Dr

Thomas Noguchi, the former Los Angeles Medical Examiner, quoted a case of multiple hospital killings where the murderer introduced fatal quantities of insulin into his victims' bodies by injecting the drug through the tubing of an intravenous drip. This method left no unaccounted-for needle-marks and posed a new dimension for hospital security.

The pioneering character of Canada in the nineteenth century produced a number of well-documented killings such as the Lucan Murders in 1880. Five members of the Donnelly family were murdered by a gang at their farm in Lucan, Ontario, in what was thought to be a violent feud. A local cover-up ensured that the murderers never came to justice. In the last decade of that century Frederick Benwell travelled from England full of hope and bent on becoming a farmer. Unfortunately, he encountered one of nature's marauders, Reginald Birchall, who fleeced him and shot him dead. Justice was visited on Birchall who suffered at the hands of a clumsy hangman.

Canada's vast northern remoteness has lent special qualities to a number of murders. A teenage Eskimo, Aligoomiak, ran amok on Herschel Island in 1922 and was brought to book by the Mounties in an epic story of adventure and danger (see under REMOTE PLACES). In a totally different story, the lure of the wild tempted three Americans to the Gaspé Peninsula in 1953, and cost them their lives. Wilbert Coffin was hanged for murdering the Americans in a case which provoked a great deal of controversy at the time (see also under REMOTE PLACES).

Canada has had its share of exceptional murder cases, and none more so than that of Steven Truscott. Sentence of death passed on a fourteen-year-old boy convicted of rape and murder in 1959 shocked the Canadian public and created a lasting controversy. (In the event, the sentence was commuted to life imprisonment, and Truscott was released from prison in 1969, starting life under a new name.) Albert Guay contrived the first civil aviation disaster known to have been caused by a bomb in 1949 which killed twenty-three passengers (including his wife) when their jet airliner exploded in mid-air after take-off from Quebec. This crime was bettered six years later in the USA by John Graham. (Both cases are recounted under AIRCRAFT.) The

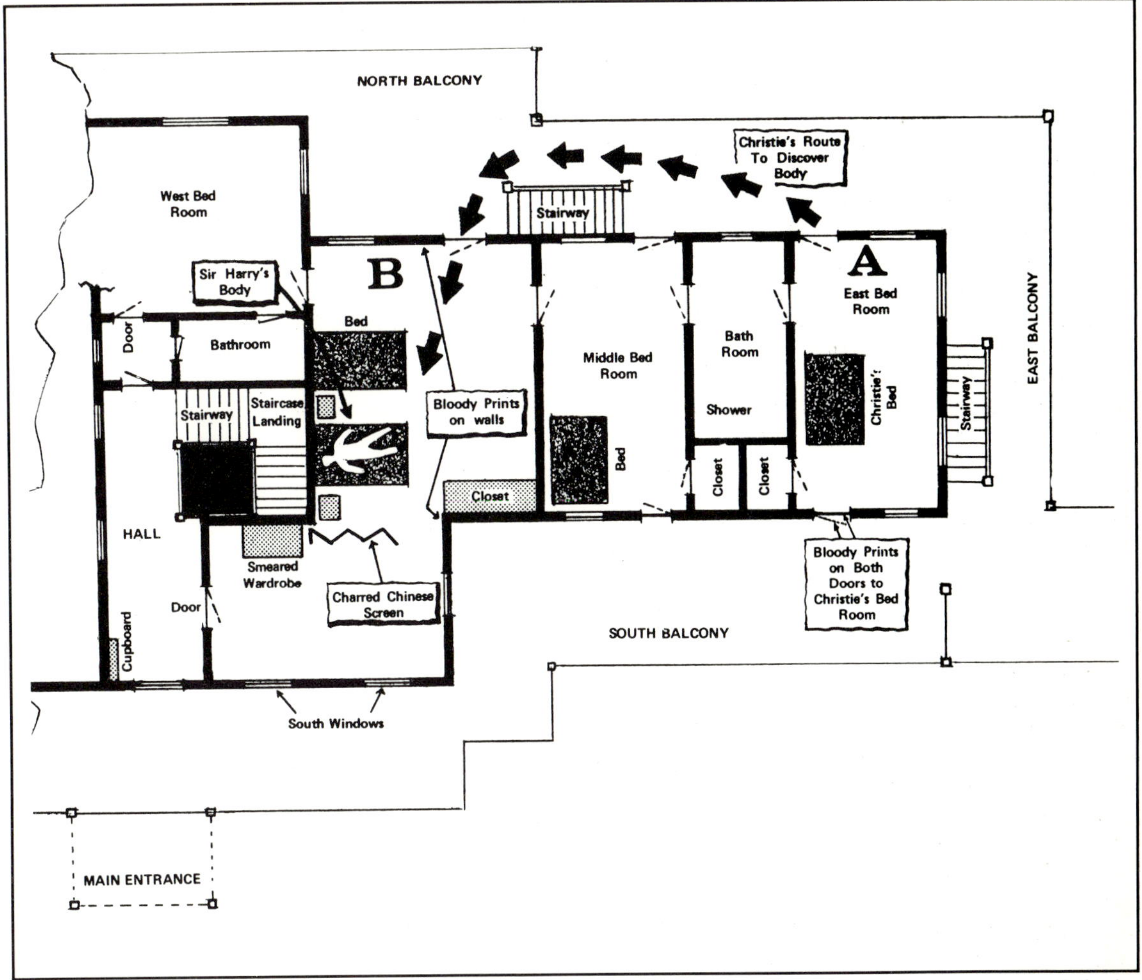

Plan of the second floor of 'Westbourne', showing the room in which Sir Harry Oakes' body was discovered

conviction of Peter Demeter in 1974 for the murder of his wife came after the longest trial in Canadian criminal history (see under GARAGES). The proceedings contained all the sensational elements of a crime thriller: a secretly tape-recorded conversation, false confession, death of a witness and alleged contracts to kill set against a background of the criminal underworld. Demeter served ten years in prison and soon after his release on parole in 1983 was charged with arson and 'counselling' to commit murder.

Probably the best-known murder in the Caribbean was the killing of Sir Harry Oakes, an American-born millionaire who was found dead in his home at Nassau in the Bahamas. He died mysteriously during a stormy night in 1943, and his battered, partially burned corpse was discovered lying on his bed. Feathers had been scattered over the body, adding to the intrigue of this unsolved murder. The significance of this act might be explained by the native superstition in which removal of feathers from the bed of a dying person is supposed to ease death. The deliberate scattering of feathers over the body might therefore signify a wish to prolong the pain of death, if credence is given to the view that the victim had incurred the wrath of local people. A number of books have been written about the Oakes case, and the theory of a murder conspiracy has been advocated.

The Caribbean islands form part of many people's idea of paradise — sun-drenched beaches bordered by sparkling blue sea and shaded by tall palm-trees. Yet even these havens of peace and tranquillity have been habitually penetrated by violence. Spanish interests in South America and the Caribbean islands — the so-called Spanish Main — attracted pirates and plunderers from other nations, especially Britain. One of the most famous was Henry Morgan, who was aided and abetted by the Governor of Jamaica in the 1660s. Sir Henry Morgan, as the pirate later became, returned to the West Indies in 1674 as Deputy Governor, the champion of law and order with a mandate to eradicate piracy.

In modern times piracy has enjoyed something of a renaissance in the Caribbean and elsewhere on the world's oceans. In 1982 Michael Crocker, an Englishman pursuing sea adventure in the Caribbean paradise, was murdered on board his yacht off Port of Spain, Trinidad (see under BOATS). Criminal entrepreneurs have set themselves up to prey on those seeking adventure and pleasure, whom they regard (often erroneously) as the idle, pleasure-seeking rich. Feelings of resentment lay behind the murder of Sir Richard Sharples, Governor of Bermuda, in 1973. He was shot dead in the grounds of Government House (see under ISLANDS) by two men who wanted to express their anti-colonialism.

Other murders which have disturbed the tranquillity of the Caribbean include Dr Dalip Singh's murder of his wife in Port of Spain, Trinidad, in 1954 (see under BEACHES) and the violence brought to the same island by Michael X, otherwise known as Abdul Malik or Michael de Freitas. He was imprisoned in England for preaching his extreme racism, and having been made unwelcome in that country, returned to Trinidad, where he headed a small group of Black Muslim supporters. His delusions of grandeur soon evaporated into sordid violence for which he eventually paid the price (see under GARDENS). *(54, 108, 144, 174, 175, 218, 230, 250, 267, 277, 282, 328, 342, 388, 391, 404, 515, 517, 520, 527, 528, 546, 557, 564, 565, 585, 607, 620, 629, 630, 631, 651, 661, 669, 674, 701–704, 705, 713, 735–740, 747, 752, 763–767, 768, 771, 787–795, 808, 858, 860–863, 867, 868, 881, 897–899, 915, 917, 930, 933, 948, 976, 989, 997, 1035)*

SOUTH AMERICA

The fourth largest continent on earth conjures up thoughts of a violent past exemplified by the Spanish Conquest and of an equally violent modern history directed by military dictatorship. Francisco Pizarro, the Spanish adventurer, perhaps set the tone and sowed the seeds of future revolution by his treachery towards the Incas. The conquistadores executed Atahualpa, the Inca, during their conquest of Peru in 1530 and subsequently fell out among themselves. In the course of the ensuing rebellion Pizarro was murdered.

In more prosaic terms, South America conjures up notions of being both a haven and also a repository for criminals. Rumours of Martin Bormann's exile to Paraguay have never been substantiated, but another Nazi war criminal, Adolf Eichmann, instrumental in the extermination of six million Jews, was kidnapped by Israeli agents in Buenos Aires in 1959. For years the Nazi-hunters searched for Josef Mengele, the concentration camp doctor, in South America. Remains purporting to be those of the 'Angel of Death' were found in Brazil in June 1985. Representing the other side of the coin was the legendary 'Papillon', who escaped from the French penal colony on Devil's Island, which is off the coast of French Guiana.

Criminologically speaking, South America can claim two firsts: Colombia, Nicaragua and Mexico* are reported to have the highest crime-rates in the world, and Argentina can claim the first conviction of a murderer by means of fingerprint evidence. In 1892 a double murder occurred in Necochea on the outskirts of Buenos Aires. Francesca Rojas accused a neighbour of murdering her two sons and of wounding her in the throat. Bloody fingerprints were found on a door at the crime scene; these were cut out and sent to police headquarters at La Plata. The Bureau of Anthropometric Identification at La Plata was headed by Juan Vucetich, an immigrant from Central Europe, who for the previous twelve

months had been specializing in identification by fingerprints. He had formulated a ten-finger classification system based on the work of Sir Francis Galton. By comparing the bloody fingerprints with impressions taken from Francesca Rojas and her accused neighbour Vucetich had no hesitation in naming the mother as the murderer of her own children. Faced with this accusation Rojas confessed, and was eventually punished by imprisonment for the murder of her two sons.

Vucetich received scant recognition of his work by his adopted country but published his work *Conferencia sobre el Sistema Dactyloscópico* in La Plata in 1901. His claim to have used fingerprints for criminal identification in September 1891, thus predating Scotland Yard's use of fingerprints by several years, is well substantiated. In 1909 Juan Vucetich was honoured by Argentina with the title 'Perito Identificator', acknowledging him as 'skilled in identification'. His system of fingerprint classification is still used in some South American countries, but elsewhere has been rejected in favour of the system devised in 1901 by Sir Edward Henry.

Mexico's reputation for murder has certainly been enhanced by accounts of some of its crimes which have reached the newspapers. The Gonzales sisters (see under BROTHELS), for example, were reputed to have killed more than eighty victims during the early 1960s and José Alfredo del Valle killed three and wounded fourteen others in an explosion at a Mexican airport. On 9 May 1953 an explosion occurred at Mazatlán while baggage was being loaded on a flight bound for California. Remains of a timing device and traces of dynamite were found among the wreckage. The piece of baggage thought to have contained the bomb had been consigned at Culiacán with the intention that it should be loaded on a direct flight to La Paz in California. At this point Fate intervened, for the direct flight was fully loaded and the baggage was put instead on an indirect flight which called at Mazatlán.

Some time after the explosion a man was arrested at La Paz after he had failed in an

We take Mexico and Central America as part of Latin America, and so linguistically and culturally to be aligned with South America.

attempt to take his own life. Questioned by police, José Alfredo del Valle confessed to causing the explosion at Mazatlán in an elaborate insurance fraud which involved faking his own death in an air disaster, thereby entitling his widow to a large sum in compensation. When del Valle learned that his bomb had been put on another aircraft, the route of which thwarted his plans for a mid-flight explosion, he travelled to California where he attempted suicide.

Del Valle claimed to have been influenced by an aircraft bomb incident which had occurred in the previous year. On 24 September 1952 a bomb exploded on a Mexican Airlines aircraft on an internal flight. The pilot brought the aircraft down safely and there were no casualties. Two men, Emilio Arellano and Paco Sierra, had tried to operate an insurance swindle which if the mid-air explosion had destroyed the aircraft would have netted them insurance on seven of the victims. Del Valle, like the two men whose scheme he had adopted, was sentenced to thirty years' imprisonment. He later succeeded in committing suicide.

Individual South American murder cases are not normally reported in English sources unless they contain some compelling feature. One such arrest which occurred in Ecuador is rated as that of the world's worst mass murder. Pedro Alonzo Lopez confessed to murdering over three hundred times — an incredible admission which earned him the title 'Monster of the Andes'. In April 1980 he was arrested in the town of Ambato, Ecuador, high up in the mountains, after he had picked up a young girl in the market.

Lopez showed the police fifty-three graves of girls aged between eight and twelve years whom he had raped and strangled. He said that he had killed a hundred girls in Ecuador and as many again in both Colombia and Peru. Born of a prostitute in Colombia, he was reported as saying, 'I lost my innocence at the age of eight, so I decided to do the same to as many young girls as I could.' Lopez was charged with murder in Ecuador, and was punished with a life sentence. Ecuador abandoned the death penalty in 1897; elsewhere in South America conviction of murder would have resulted in execution.

A teenage youth who killed a homosexual lawyer in Valparaiso, Chile, in 1962 was convicted and sentenced to ten years' imprisonment. The case of Manuel Garcés (see under SHOPS AND OFFICES) was taken up by Professor Christopher Jackson, who visited the seventeen-year-old while he was awaiting trial, and later wrote a book called simply *Manuel*, which showed the life of a boy born in the slums and reared on petty crime which degenerated into violence.

Another academic who pursued a violent incident with a view to solving a mystery was John Treherne in his book *The Galapagos Affair*. The Galápagos Islands, situated on the Equator in the Pacific Ocean some six hundred miles from the coast of Ecuador, are technically part of South America. One of these islands (then normally uninhabited) provided the background in the late 1920s for an extraordinary story in which a handful of people inspired by high ideals came face to face with the harsher realities of human behaviour. (See under ISLANDS for a full account.)

Apart from a few distinctive cases of murder such as those mentioned which have been published in the English language, most reporting of South American affairs centres on political violence. In Argentina, for example, torture and repression during the 1970s — the so-called 'dirty war' — led to the disappearance of between ten and thirty thousand people. A planned campaign of terror was used to eliminate subversion and destroy support for opposition groups. The police set up death squads to deal with those singled out as subversives, and the scale of operations had echoes of Nazi Germany about it. Sixty secret camps were used as detention and torture centres, and it was alleged that one was set aside to process pregnant women and nursing mothers. Lethal injection followed by cremation was the preferred method of disposal, and it was reported that a 'blood pact' existed to strengthen the bonds of secrecy. High-ranking officers in the regime were personally involved in acts of execution, thus ensuring their total commitment. Relatives of the 'Disappeared Ones' paraded in the streets of Buenos Aires, demanding information and protesting at the loss of their loved ones. Argentina attracted widespread condemnation over this episode, and criminal proceedings followed the replacement of the military regime by a civilian government in 1983.

A similar pattern of corruption and repression was repeated in other South and Central American countries. In Guatemala in 1982 General Romeo Lucas García began an assassination campaign to rid his country of guerrillas. No section of the community was spared, and wholesale killing became the order of the day. General Efrain Rios Montt came to power with a plan to beat the guerrillas and check the assassinations. He used the armed forces to comb out the guerrillas from among the mountain communities, with the result that thousands of Guatemalans were displaced from their homes and the killing continued unabated. Guatemala's bishops described the killings as the highest in their country's history. 'Not even the lives of old people, pregnant women or innocent children were respected,' they said.

The struggle between right-wing governments and revolutionary guerrilla movements has led to numerous politically inspired murders. In Nicaragua in April 1983 the Salvadorean guerrilla leader Aña Maria was found in her house at Managua with her throat cut. The Nicaraguan government claimed that America's CIA had initiated the killing. In neighbouring El Salvador, Boris King Montes, the teenage son of the peasant union leader, was alleged to have been murdered in October 1984. His father claimed that the boy had been killed by right-wing death squads and dumped on a road outside the capital. A note on the body supposedly instructed Montes to stop working for the union. There was no trace of the body or of any real evidence of a murder having been committed, which created an embarrassing situation for the USA, whose embassy had put out a communiqué condemning the murder.

Human rights is a controversial issue in South America, both for those who suffer their infringement and also for those who investigate them. Four reporters and four photographers on a human rights inquiry in Peru were killed in January 1983. They were stoned and hacked to death in the remote Andean town of Ayacucho. An official inquiry concluded that Indian villagers had killed the men, mistaking them for rebels who had been terrorizing their community. Three Indians were tried for the murders in 1984 (thirteen others were tried *in absentia*), amid mounting national concern over the way human rights were trampled on in the government's conduct of its anti-guerrilla campaign.

The prospect of rich pickings from industrial development in the Greater Carajás region of Brazil sparked off a spate of violence and murder during 1984. It was reported that landowners were using terror tactics to buy out peasant farmers and smallholders so that they could resell the land for high profits to the internationally financed project-developers. Twenty-eight murders had occurred during a bitter campaign of reprisals. Whole villages had been burned down in incidents where it was alleged that the police had been bribed by the landowners. Evicted farmers retaliated violently, and the Brazilian government was faced with a sensitive issue in respect of its image to the outside world.

Murder in Latin America is ever bizarre, and Mexico contributed an amazing figure to the statistics of crime in 1964. In a village comprising less than 2,000 inhabitants, all Mayan Indians, the homicide rate was reported as over twenty times greater than that of Houston, Texas.

(93, 485, 555, 620, 684, 946)

FIFTY PLACES OF
MURDER

AIRCRAFT

'When the plane left the ground, a load came off my shoulders.'
John Gilbert Graham

The advent of flight, like the emergence of travel by rail and automobile (see under RAILWAY MURDERS and CARS) almost inevitably brought with it scope for the destructive mind. The idea of dynamiting an aircraft out of the sky as a means of eliminating a particular individual or of making a political point dawned on the world in 1937. On 6 May the pride of Germany, the airship *Hindenburg*, exploded at her moorings at Lakehurst, New Jersey after completing a transatlantic journey from Frankfurt.

Thirteen passengers, twenty-two crew members and one ground crew died in the fireball, which was recorded for posterity by shocked cameramen waiting to film the disembarkation. For long hailed as a mysterious accident, the loss of the giant airship may have been due to an act of sabotage. In his book *The Hindenburg*, published in 1972, Michael Mooney suggested that a bomb had been placed in one of the gas cells by Eric Spehl, a crewman who died in the blast. The reason for this act was to express disaffection with the Nazi regime in Germany.

This first spectacular case of aerial sabotage set the scene for an era of violence against civil aircraft deferred only by the onset of the Second World War. Hostilities had barely ceased before the first hijacking occurred in 1947. In July three Chinese took over a Cathay Pacific Airlines flight after it took off from Macao. Threatened at gun-point, one of the crew struggled with the Chinese, and in the process the pilot was shot dead. The plane crashed, and Wong Yu, one of the pirates, was the only survivor. His intention had been to direct the pilot to make a forced landing, when he and his accomplices would rob the passengers. This attempt at aerial robbery ended in Wong's confession and execution for committing murder.

Hijacking aircraft for political or terrorist motives reached a peak in the 1960s, when alarming numbers of commercial planes were taken over at gun-point and their passengers held to ransom. The success of the hijackers stimulated technology to perfect the security screening of air baggage, thus greatly reducing the possibility of firearms or explosives being carried on board civil aircraft. Before this routine security checking had been established two murderously inclined individuals, in separate incidents, had dynamited aircraft out of the sky with high loss of life, in order to collect insurance money on a single passenger. Albert Guay disposed of his wife in this way, and he was followed by John Gilbert Graham, who eliminated his mother in an aircraft explosion.

On 9 September 1949 a DC–3 of Quebec Airways took off with twenty-three passengers from Quebec. Five minutes later the aircraft exploded above the forest of Sault-au-Cochon and everyone on board was killed. An examination of the wreckage indicated that an explosive device might have been detonated in the baggage compartment. Moreover, eye-witnesses on the ground confirmed that the aircraft's engines continued to run after the explosion, thus ruling out a mechanical fault.

A check of the baggage manifest showed that a parcel containing a religious statue weighing 28 lb had been put on board at Quebec. The parcel was addressed to a man at St Baie Comeau — neither the man nor the address existed. The freight-handler at the airport remembered that the parcel had been given to him by a fat, middle-aged woman who had arrived by taxi. Patient questioning by the police led them to the taxi driver who had driven this woman to the airport, and he was able to recall the address from which he had picked her up. The woman was Marguerite Pitre, whose lover was Albert Guay, a jeweller in Seven Islands. A passenger by the name of Guay was listed among the fatalities in the air crash — she was Guay's wife, Rita.

Albert Guay was arrested on 23 September and the full story of the callous murder of his wife, together with twenty-two other persons, emerged. Guay appeared to be a man who needed several lovers, but lacked the guile to separate his affairs. Marguerite Pitre had been his lover for several years, and Rita Guay more or less acquiesced. But when Guay acquired a second mistress his wife took exception, and in order to solve the accommodation problem Guay installed his two lovers in the same flat. It was a recipe for disaster, and in the course of the emotional tangle which followed Guay decided to eliminate his wife.

Guay enlisted Pitre's help, and also that of her crippled brother, Généreux Ruest, who had a knowledge of explosives. He insured his wife for $10,000 and he and his five-year-old daughter went to the airport to see her off. Marguerite Pitre carried out the next part of the plan, arriving at the airport by taxi to have a parcel put in the freight hold of the same aircraft. The parcel contained a bomb consisting of several pounds of dynamite wired up to a timing mechanism, the product of Ruest's handicraft.

Albert Guay was tried for murder in February 1950, and was convicted by overwhelming evidence. He was hanged in January 1951, a fate later shared by both Pitre and Ruest. Public sympathy for Pitre, who was plainly under Guay's domination, evaporated when her willingness to go along with a plan involving mass destruction became evident.

When United Airlines flight 629 lifted off the runway at Stapleton Airport, Denver, on 1 November 1955 the DC–6B was ten minutes from catastrophe. The aircraft exploded in mid-air, killing all forty-four passengers and crew members. The wreckage was spread over a wide area, but there was sufficient evidence for investigators to be sure that the crash had been caused by a detonation of explosive deliberately placed on board. The source of the explosion was No.4 baggage compartment, which had contained the luggage of passengers boarding the inter-city flight at Denver.

One of these passengers was Mrs Daisy King, a wealthy woman with relatives in Denver. Her son, John Gilbert Graham, married with two children, had seen his mother off on her fateful journey to visit her daughter in Alaska, and had taken out $37,500 worth of insurance policies on her life (which he had neglected to sign). He had told his wife that he had put a 'Christmas package' in his mother's suitcase. His gift proved to be a time-bomb consisting of 14 lb of dynamite and an alarm-clock detonating mechanism.

Graham had been put into an orphanage by his widowed mother, and he stayed in institutions until he was eight years old. When his mother remarried in 1940 to wealthy rancher John Earl King she reclaimed her son, and lavished on him all those things he had been denied in the orphanage. He became what the newspapers later called a 'pampered misfit' and, far from expressing gratitude to his mother, developed a smouldering hatred for her. He played truant from school and began to pursue petty criminal activities. In 1951 he forged a number of cheques, and only escaped charges because his mother repaid the money. He also perpetrated a number of insurance frauds.

Graham confessed to his crime, and showed no remorse for having sent forty-three people to their deaths in addition to his mother. His main concern seemed to be that he had been neglected as a child. 'Can't you just see Mother when all those shells began to go off in the plane?' he said, referring to the shotgun cartridges his mother was carrying with the intention of doing some hunting in Alaska.

He subsequently withdrew his confession, but the jury — which tried him only for the murder of his mother — found little difficulty in bringing in a guilty verdict. Before going to the gas chamber in January 1957 Graham made a further confession and told prison officials, 'When the plane left the ground a load came off my shoulders. I watched her go off for the last time, and I felt freer than I have ever felt before in my life.'
(376, 397, 620, 682, 765, MWW, mw)

ALLEYWAYS

'Two little whores, shivering with fright,
Seek a cosy doorway in the middle of the night.
Jack's knife flashes, then there's but one,
And the last one's the ripest for Jack's idea of fun.'

Anon (1888)

'The fronts of the houses, as was common in Old Edinburgh architecture, were broken at intervals by alleys — locally termed 'closes' — leading to back tenements, yards and waste land behind the street. Dismal and malodorous by day, they were at night both dark and dangerous, being illuminated by scanty oil lamps and unpatrolled by any regular police.' Thus did William Roughead, the celebrated Scottish criminologist, describe the West Port area of Edinburgh which spawned the menace of Burke and Hare, the infamous body-snatchers, whose murder victims ended up in the City's medical schools.

Alleyways, always potentially 'dark and dangerous', lie in the very midst of the teeming populations of most great cities. They provide those pockets of seclusion so vital to the craft of robber and murderer, and nowhere have they been better exploited than in London's East End by Jack the Ripper. The anonymous murderer's horrific predations on the area's prostitutes in 1888 shook England to its roots. Jack the Ripper used Whitechapel's network of dingy alleys and yards to their maximum potential. His victims unwittingly cooperated in their destruction by leading him into the darkest and quietest corners in order, as they thought, to pursue their time-honoured profession. Cloaked by darkness and completely insensitive to danger, they fell easily to the Ripper's knife, and became ready material for his sadistic mutilations.

The advantages to the Ripper of those alleyways of death lay not only in the confidence with which the victims selected them but also in his own unerring geography of escape. Even with the whole of London teetering on the brink of hysteria, and with the East End swamped by police, he still managed to kill, mutilate and escape with ease. Above all else, Jack the Ripper demonstrated what (happily for the sake of law enforcement) many murderers have forgotten: that an important part of the planning is to plot the escape route from the scene of crime. No murderer better exemplifies the premium which Thomas de Quincey put on the location of murder when he wrote, 'The good practitioner has usually directed him to night and privacy.'

Jack the Ripper had both admirers and imitators, and for a decade or more after his exploits in London in 1888 stories emerged from America, Argentina, South Africa and Australia of sightings and copycat murders. One of the most successful imitators in modern times was Peter Sutcliffe, whose activities eighty-seven years later provided such powerful associations that he was soon dubbed 'The Yorkshire Ripper'. But despite his tally of thirteen victims, Sutcliffe failed to line up to that most important Ripper attribute — anonymity — when he was caught off guard and brought to justice. Nevertheless, during his reign of terror — which lasted from 1975 to 1980 — he showed a masterful appreciation of the most favourable murder locations.

This modern sex killer, as befitted the social times, did his prowling in a car. He roamed the red-light districts of the Yorkshire towns, picking up women whom he savagely dispatched with blows from a hammer. Although his victims were mostly prostitutes, his net was cast widely enough to ensnare other women. Exceptionally, one victim was strangled but all were subjected to frenzied stabbing and slashing knife wounds which in some instances resulted in disembowelment. He also attacked numerous other women who, mercifully, escaped with their lives. His choice of murder locations was effective. He exploited the prostitutes' haunts in the Yorkshire towns, purring about the dimly lit streets in his car and spiriting his victims off to some dark corner for his fiendish work. The Yorkshire Ripper took risks, but had a knack for finding enough cover — often within yards of a busy street — to dispatch his victim and make off.

He also had luck, as on the night in January 1978 that he murdered Helen Rytka in Huddersfield. He drove her to a deserted timber yard under a railway arch and stopped the car. They climbed into the back, where he attacked the girl with a hammer and she fell out of the open door and lay semi-conscious on the ground. Realizing that there were two taxi-drivers approaching from some forty yards distance he lay on top of the girl and went through the pretence of sex with her until the two men walked away. He then finished her off and repeatedly stabbed her before hiding her body under a pile of wood.

Sutcliffe also took a risk with his next killing

One of the Yorkshire Ripper's alleyway killing grounds

on 16 May 1978, when he attacked Vera Millward in the car-park at Manchester Royal Infirmary. The area was well lit, and a man attending the hospital was convinced that he heard a cry of 'Help' shouted out three times. Next morning the woman's battered and mutilated body was found by a gardener lying on a heap of refuse in a corner of the car-park.

But the Yorkshire Ripper's luck eventually ran out on 2 January 1981. That night Sergeant Robert Ring and PC Robert Hyde were on a routine car patrol in Sheffield. Driving along Melbourne Avenue, they spotted a car parked in the darkened driveway of one of the premises, and decided to investigate. The vehicle's occupants were a man who gave his name as Peter Williams and a young coloured woman. The Sergeant thought the girl was a prostitute. 'Who's she?' he asked the driver. 'My girl friend,' came the reply. 'What's her name?' 'I don't know. I haven't known her all that long.' 'Who are you trying to kid?' said the Sergeant, adding, 'I haven't fallen off the Christmas tree.' A radio call was put through to the police national computer with a request to check the vehicle's registration number. Within minutes the answer came back that the number was registered to a car of a different make. Close inspection of the number plate showed that it was fastened by means of adhesive tape.

Before being taken in for questioning the driver was allowed to walk a few yards up the street to relieve himself. He and his companion were then driven to Hammerton Road Police Station. The following day, on returning to the scene, Sergeant Ring found a hammer and a knife hidden behind an oil storage tank in a house farther down Melbourne Avenue where the man now known as Peter Sutcliffe had ostensibly gone to urinate.

The five-year search for the 'Yorkshire Ripper' had ended. Thirteen women had been murdered, and the police, taunted by letters

---

THE YORKSHIRE RIPPER'S VICTIMS AND MURDER LOCATIONS

Victim	Date	Location
Wilma McCANN	October 1975	LEEDS: Body found on a playing-field in the Chapeltown area
Emily JACKSON	January 1976	LEEDS: Cul-de-sac between two derelict houses in Chapeltown
Irene RICHARDSON	February 1977	LEEDS: Behind a sports pavilion in Roundhay Park
Patricia ATKINSON	April 1977	BRADFORD: Murdered in her flat a short distance from Sutcliffe's home
Jayne MACDONALD	June 1977	LEEDS: Body found by the wall of a children's adventure playground in Chapeltown
Jean JORDAN	October 1977	MANCHESTER: Murdered on a path between cemetery and allotments in Princess Road
Yvonne PEARSON	January 1978	BRADFORD: Victim's body found under upturned furniture on waste ground in Arthington Street
Helen RYTKA	January 1978	HUDDERSFIELD: Murdered in a timber yard near the Leeds to Manchester railway line
Vera MILLWARD	May 1978	MANCHESTER: Body found in the car-park of the city's Royal Infirmary
Josephine WHITAKER	April 1979	HALIFAX: Murdered in Savile Park
Barbara LEACH	September 1979	BRADFORD: Found in an alleyway near Back Ash Grove
Marguerite WALLS	August 1980	LEEDS: Body found in the wooded grounds of a house at Farsley
Jacqueline HILL	November 1980	LEEDS: Murdered on waste ground near a shopping-centre car-park

and a tape-recording, checked 5.2 million car registrations, interviewed 250,000 individuals and wrote down 32,000 statements in the course of their frustrating inquiries which cost £4 millions. Apart from the tantalizing letters and recordings, what was so galling was that Sutcliffe had been questioned several times by the police, and succeeded in avoiding all suspicion. The newspapers had a heyday with headlines like 'Nine Times Police let The Ripper Go Free.'

What became known as 'The Gun Alley Murder' came to light in Australia in 1921 because the murderer lost his nerve. On 31 December of that year the naked body of thirteen-year-old Alma Tirtsche was found by a patrolling policeman in a cul-de-sac, her flowing red hair spilling out over the ground. The spot was near Gun Alley in Melbourne's Eastern Arcades, a colourful area bustling with market stalls and sideshows which attracted men in search of drink, tattoos or prostitutes.

The pathologist, Dr Crawford Mollison, said that the girl had been strangled, and that her body had been washed and dried before being placed where it was found. The conclusion was that she had been killed elsewhere, and the trail led to a sleazy wine bar frequented by petty crooks whose owner, Colin Ross, was said to have entertained the girl in his shop the evening before she was murdered. In his eagerness to answer police questions, Ross came out with details about the dead girl's clothing which had not at that time been published. A witness came forward who claimed to have seen Ross behaving furtively, and struggling with an awkward bundle in Gun Alley.

On the strength of mounting suspicion, the police raided Ross's house, which was situated in another part of the city, and recovered some blankets which they thought had come from his shop. The view was formed that Ross had sexually assaulted and strangled the girl in the parlour of his shop, which was separated from the wine bar by a beaded curtain. He then washed the body of the dead girl to remove all traces of evidence and, covering it with a blanket, carried it out into the street heading for the cul-de-sac off Gun Alley. His intention was to drop the corpse through an iron grating and conceal it in the drain beneath, but at that very moment a policeman patrolling the area approached and shone his torch into Gun Alley. Had he ventured into the alley itself he would

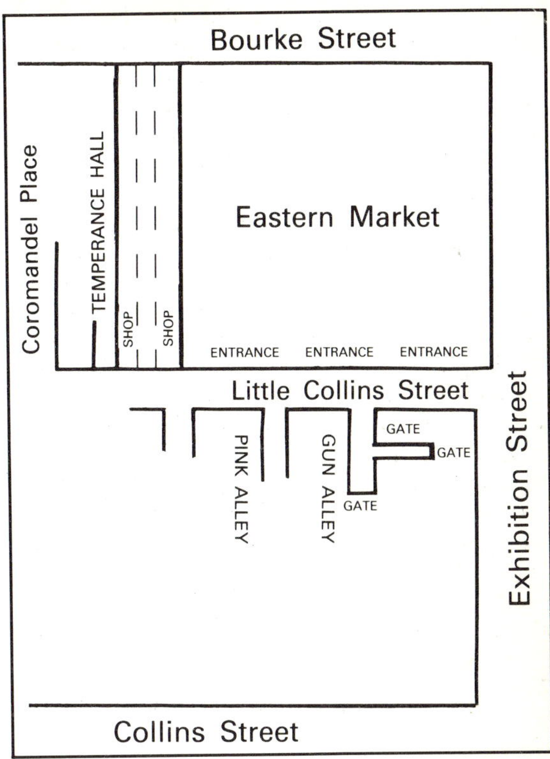

The Gun Alley Murder in Melbourne, Australia

probably have spotted Ross cowering in the shadows of the cul-de-sac with his victim. As the policeman's footsteps receded, the murderer lost his nerve. Clutching the blanket, he left the body sprawling on the cobblestones and hastily retreated to the safety of his wine bar.

Colin Ross was charged with murder, and apart from the testimony of the eye-witness who had seen him in the company of the girl in suspicious circumstances, damning evidence was found on the blanket. Several long strands of red hair were retrieved which matched perfectly with Alma's head hair. This evidence was presented at Ross's trial, and played a major part in securing his conviction. The Gun Alley murderer was sentenced to death and hanged at Melbourne Gaol.

Alleys were conceived as short-cuts for the convenient use of town and city dwellers to connect their journeys between the streets of great cities for social and trading purposes. At the same time these badly illuminated short-cuts offered a marvellously safe environment for the ill-doer. Those who strayed into their dark seclusion at night offered themselves as victims of assault or worse. Seconds were all that was necessary for robbery and murder to be effected, and for the perpetrator with a knowledge of his territory to emerge from the shadows and be swallowed up by the vibrant life of busy streets. No matter how well the architects and planners improve the design of buildings and dwellings, there will always be corners which provide dim seclusion from the surrounding bustle. For example, elevators in the high-rise buildings of many inner-city areas have been alleyways of their own, holding fear for many who depend on them. Thus, there will always be scope for cunning minds to prey on their fellows and, as the Yorkshire Ripper showed, there are always those who are willing to accept the risks of stepping into the shadows.

(109, 134, 206, 208, 244, 247, 275, 536, 641, 658, 711, 716, 819, 896, 907, 1050, MWW, mw)

APARTMENTS AND PENTHOUSES

'I am very lonesome tonight.'
Carl Otto Wanderer (1920)

The apartment and the stairway giving access to it are part of what sociologist Marvin Wolfgang calls the 'personal microcosm' which binds both victim and murderer. They are also part of the concrete jungle, providing high-density living quarters with energy-efficient insulation and smoothly gliding elevators. Despite their close proximity, individual apartments can be remote, sound-proof islands of existence which conceal secret homicide.

Thousands of inner-city dwellers are obliged to live in apartment blocks, and their passions and violence naturally spill over into their environment. Others choose to live in penthouses or exclusive apartments in order to be accessible to the city's heart. They reach their apartments by elevators which all too frequently become traps for innocent tenants closeted with would-be robbers or assassins. Stairways, entrances and passages — often shadowy places even in daylight — become ill-lit alleys in the sky when night closes.

Because of their high degree of isolation, apartments are often impersonal places where the neighbours neither hear nor see anything that is happening next door. This appeared to be the case regarding Number 155, East 84th Street on the fashionable East Upper Side of Manhattan. The property was owned by Howard Buddy Jacobson, a horse-trainer turned property-dealer and modelling agent. He lived in apartment 7D, and for a while his girl-friend Melanie Cain, a rising nineteen-year-old model and cover girl, lived with him. Early in August 1978, Melanie had moved across the hallway to apartment 7C to live with Jack Tupper.

One of Melanie's reasons for moving was to escape Buddy Jacobson's obsessiveness, and she planned to take a lease on a new apartment several blocks distant to get away from him. On Sunday 6 August she left Tupper asleep in bed when she went off to sign the new lease. When she returned soon after midday he had disappeared. She saw signs indicating that violence had taken place — there was blood on the elevator in the hallway, and also wet patches on the carpet. She knocked up Buddy Jacobson, who said he knew nothing of Tupper's whereabouts. At about 4.30 that afternoon a fire was reported on an area of waste ground in the Bronx. Two fire-trucks from Ash Loop answered the call, which turned out to be a rubbish fire; not an unusual occurrence in the dilapidated borough. The focus of the fire amid the usual debris of cans and paper was a wooden crate. It was padlocked, but a smoke-grimed human leg protruded from the smouldering wood. Jack Tupper had been found. When the police arrived on the scene two one-gallon wine jugs stinking of gasoline were found among the garbage.

The man who reported the fire was a New York bus-driver who was driving his family through the Bronx when he spotted two tricycles which had been dumped on a piece of waste land. Thinking they might be worth retrieving, he turned the car round and drove back, only to see two men standing near the tricycles. The men appeared somewhat furtive, and ran off to a near-by car — a yellow Cadillac with the registration number 777GHH. Thinking he had been beaten to possession of the tricycles, he drove away, gaining a clear view of one of the men, whom he later identified as Buddy Jacobson. When he realized that the tricycles had not been taken to the Cadillac he went back to the site again, which was then on fire.

The autopsy on Tupper's body showed that

he had been bludgeoned, shot and stabbed. His head had been a particular target for several savage blows which had fractured the skull. The police put out a call for the yellow Cadillac, which was spotted by an alert patrol on Bruckner Expressway. When the car was stopped a dishevelled Buddy Jacobson emerged; his jeans appeared to be spattered with blood. His passenger was Salvatore Prainito. Both men were arrested.

What emerged during the next few months was a convoluted love triangle with a background of glossy modelling, harassment and drug-dealing. Jacobson, who was in his late forties, was an eccentric individual who affected a more or less permanently unkempt appearance. He chose not to wear socks or underwear, and was described as a 'phonoholic'. Nevertheless, he had attractive qualities which drew beautiful young women, including Melanie Cain, to his modelling agency. The other side of Jacobson's character was a dark mixture of jealousy and fantasy which eventually alienated Melanie, whom he subjected to considerable harassment when she tried to withdraw from the relationship.

Jack Tupper, a charmingly attractive man, worked at the fringe of success and became involved in New York's drug-smuggling world. He sold second-hand computers, and purchased a half-share in a bar which brought him into contact with Buddy Jacobson and his social circle, including Melanie. The triangle was thus complete until the shattering events of 6 August.

Buddy Jacobson's tale was that Melanie and Tupper were, as he put it, 'hanging out with trouble', and that Tupper was killed in a fight between rival drug gangs. The violence took place in the hallway of his apartment house, hence the blood on the carpet and elevator. Melanie sought his help, and Tupper, either dead or dying, was dragged into Jacobson's own apartment, number 7D. He did not think it wise for the murdered body of a drug-smuggler to be found in his building, so he elicited help from Sal Prainito to put the dead man in a crate and dispose of it.

Jacobson and Prainito were charged with second-degree murder. The trial began on 30 January 1980 and the exhibits in court included the charred wooden crate, two wine jugs and a hammer found in the boot of the yellow Cadillac which the prosecution claimed was the murder weapon. The proceedings made big headlines in the New York newspapers, but few larger than when Buddy Jacobson escaped from detention between verdict and sentence.

Prainito was found Not Guilty but Buddy (once again in custody) was convicted. On 25 May Buddy escaped again, this time from Brooklyn House of Detention, with the help of a bogus lawyer and on 3 June was sentenced *in absentia* to a minimum of twenty-five years' imprisonment. He was located in California where he was arrested on 9 June and returned to New York. Later he was transferred to Clinton prison near the Canadian border from which in 1981 he made an abortive attempt to escape.

Hallways and stairs in apartment blocks are places of transition, and because of their closeness to home, inspire feelings of security which may be misplaced. They may be chosen as sites for murder precisely for this reason and because their shadows provide concealment. Heroes are not expected to become villains, but such was the fate of Carl Otto Wanderer. A man of German extraction, he had a liking for soldiering and fought in the Mexican War and then volunteered for the US Expeditionary Force heading for France to fight the Germans in the First World War. He returned from the war in 1919 with the rank of second lieutenant, and Chicago welcomed him home as a hero.

In October 1919 he married twenty-year-old Ruth Johnson and they lived in her mother's apartment at 4732 North Campbell Avenue until they could afford a place of their own. On 21 June 1920 they entered the darkened hall of the apartment block on their return home from a cinema. Ruth reached out for the light switch when she was startled to hear a man's voice say, 'Don't turn on the light.' The darkness was then rent by gun-flashes and a fusillade of shots which resulted in Ruth slumping to the floor next to a stranger whom Carl shot repeatedly with his service revolver.

Ruth, who was seven months pregnant, had received two gunshot wounds from which she later died. 'The Ragged Stranger', as the newspapers called him, was a down-and-out with $3.80 in his pockets; he had been hit four times by bullets from Carl's gun and died immediately. Chicago mourned with Wanderer, the war hero who had tried to stave off a murderous attack on his young wife.

Both weapons used in the incident were .45 Colt service automatics. This fact triggered off the curiosity of Walter Howey, Editor of *The Herald Examiner*. It seemed reasonable, he believed, that an ex-officer should be in the habit of carrying his service weapon, but what was a down-and-out doing with one? After all, 'The Ragged Stranger' was almost penniless, yet possessed a weapon which would have fetched him at least $10.

The manufacturer's numbers on both guns were checked. Wanderer's was an army issue weapon, the other was part of a consignment ordered by a Chicago sports shop in 1913. Its sale was traced to a man who said he had sold it to his brother-in-law, Fred Wanderer, who was Carl's cousin. Questioned about the gun, Fred said he had lent it to Carl early on the evening of the shooting. His reasons for not reporting this information were obscure, but the police lost no time in talking to Carl.

While he was held at police headquarters, Carl's apartment was searched and photographs were found of him posing with different girls. Torn fragments of a draft of a letter written by him to one of them two weeks before his wife's death read, 'Sweetheart: I am very lonesome tonight. I am thinking of you ... I am longing to have you close to me ....' The recipient of these endearments was a sixteen-year-old girl to whom Wanderer had proposed marriage. It was evident that war heroes had no shortage of female admirers, and he later admitted courting several women at the same time.

Wanderer confessed to both killings. His scheme was to use a hold-up man who was told that he would be equipped with a pistol and instructions to leap out on Wanderer and his wife at a predetermined time and place. The plan allowed for him to fell the gunman with a punch in order to re-establish the hero in the eyes of his wife. He found a down-and-out ex-serviceman, Al Watson, who agreed to carry out the plan for an immediate cash payment of five dollars with the promise of five more on completing the mission. Thus was the poor 'Ragged Stranger' duped by a war hero turned villain.

Wanderer was tried for the murder of his wife, and to the general astonishment of the public, given a sentence of twenty years in prison. Furious at the jury's leniency, *The Herald Examiner* campaigned for Wanderer to stand trial for murdering the stranger. This was supported by public demands and following a second murder trial he was convicted and sentenced to death.

One of the reasons that Wanderer gave for killing his wife was that he was a secret homosexual and felt threatened by her pregnancy. After giving a rendering of 'Old Pal, Why Don't you Answer Me?' he was hanged on 19 March 1921 at Chicago's Cook County Jail.

The isolation of the luxury apartment was fully exploited by Archibald Thompson Hall, who planned murder and robbery from within (see also MANSIONS, RANCHES AND VILLAS). From his position of trust as a butler he came and went about his criminal business without exciting undue attention. Hall was a confidence trickster whose smooth manners and smart appearance earned him positions as butler in wealthy homes. Roy, as he liked to be called, had received no training for the profession but relied on his plausible style and quick wits. He could turn on an educated accent and adopt an appropriately servile demeanour when occasion demanded. His numerous terms of imprisonment for theft and house-breaking had trained him in the art of criminal duplicity.

He first worked as a butler in a house in Mayfair and could include employment with Lady Hudson, Sir Charles Clore and the Lord Mayor of London in his *curriculum vitae*. Hall did not impress all his titled employers and one said, 'He was a flashy dresser with many frilled shirts.' When he was released from one of his periodic spells of imprisonment in 1977 he made for Scotland where he worked as a butler for a few months until his criminal record caught up with him. Then he travelled south to London where in November he secured a position as butler to ex-M.P. Walter Scott-Elliot, in his Knightsbridge apartment. Scott-Elliot was an elderly retired business-man who lived with his second wife Dorothy in an Aladdin's Cave of antiques and treasures. They were a couple of considerable wealth with houses in France and Italy, and their home glittered with gold and silver ware, porcelain and paintings. Mrs Scott-Elliot was badly affected by arthritis and her husband took regular medication. Roy Hall, thief and trickster, whom fate had elected as a butler to this frail, wealthy couple, thought he had found his crock of gold.

Hall decided to rob the Scott-Elliots, and he

enlisted the help of Mary Coggle, his former mistress, and Michael Kitto, a petty thief and homosexual. Their plan was that Kitto should break into the apartment to simulate an ordinary burglary and protect the sinister butler who could remain on the inside. The plot went wrong from the beginning. On 8 December 1977, while Hall was conducting his accomplice on a reconnaissance tour round the house, he entered Mrs Scott-Elliot's bedroom in the belief that she was resident for a few days in a nursing-home. To their surprise they found her awake in bed and no doubt not pleased at the intrusion. Hall's response was to stifle any scream or complaint she might have made by smothering her with a pillow. When Mr Scott-Elliot called out from his room asking what the trouble was, Hall told him that his wife had been having a nightmare, but that she was now sleeping. In fact she was dead.

Such was the old man's trust in his butler that the following day he allowed himself to be sent out to his club for lunch, having been told that his wife had gone shopping. Hall and his confederates now hatched a new plan. They hired a car in order to drive north to Cumbria where Hall had rented a cottage near Newton Arlosh. Mrs Scott-Elliot's body, wrapped in a deerskin rug and blanket, was hidden in the boot of the car. Mary Coggle dressed in some of the dead woman's clothes so that when Mr Scott-Elliot was dosed with drugs he would believe she was his wife. The befuddled old man was pushed into the car, and with Kitto driving the four sped along the motorway with their murder victim's body as their main luggage.

From the cottage in Cumbria the party drove to Scotland where they intended to dispose of the body. Hall voiced the opinion that in Scotland there was a chance of obtaining a Not Proven verdict if they ended up in court. They stopped at Lanark to buy a fork and spade to facilitate their grisly work, but in the event elected to dump the body into the cold waters of a stream running in remote countryside near Loch Earn. This task completed, with Mr Scott-Elliot half-drugged and sleeping in the car, they drove back to Cumbria. 'The old man didn't know which day of the week it was,' Hall said later.

Mr Scott-Elliot was left in the charge of Mary Coggle while Hall and Kitto drove to London. They ransacked the Knightsbridge apartment,

filling the car boot with silverware, paintings, china and rare coins. Once again they headed north, breaking the journey to exchange some of their booty for cash. Picking up Mr Scott-Elliot and Mary Coggle, they drove to a bleak spot in Inverness-shire, where on 14 December Mr Scott-Elliot was ordered out of the car. The old soldier who had survived the battles of the First World War fought hard against his assailants, but as he lay insensible from partial strangulation they finished him off with blows from the spade they had bought earlier. His body was put into a shallow grave.

The thieves now quarrelled among themselves. Mary Coggle had taken a fancy to Mrs Scott-Elliot's mink coat and wanted to keep it. Hall argued that it was too incriminating and should be burned. When Mary became hysterical in her refusal to part with the coat the two men asphyxiated her with a plastic bag. Her body was thrown into a stream running under the Glasgow to Carlisle Road.

Hall and Kitto sold some further items of booty and, flush with money, spent Christmas and New Year with Hall's relatives. His brother Donald, recently released from prison, took an unhealthy interest in the source of the visitors' wealth. He was invited to travel with them to the cottage in Cumbria where his curiosity was satisfied; Donald Hall was chloroformed and drowned in the bath. The following day his body was put into the car, and again a journey to Scotland was indicated by Hall. The error which was to lead to their capture had already been made — they had changed the car's number-plates. When Hall and Kitto pulled in to a hotel in North Berwick the astute proprietor wondered if his two guests who had arrived without luggage would be able to pay their bill. He decided to telephone the police, who checked out the car registration and discovered that it belonged to a make of car different from the one standing in the hotel car park. Soon after officers arrived to question the two guests Donald Hall's body was found in the boot of their car.

Roy Hall told the full story to the police and admitted an earlier murder — that of David Wright, whom he had killed in 1977 following an argument over stolen jewellery. 'It's not every day that somebody admits five murders to you,' he told the detectives. Hall tried to take his life with an overdose of drugs, but survived to face trial in Edinburgh. Both he and Kitto were sentenced to life imprisonment. They were returned to England to face additional charges of murder and manslaughter. Kitto was sentenced to life with a minimum of fifteen years and Roy Hall, the so-called 'Monster Butler', to imprisonment which the judge recommended should be for the rest of his natural life.

(196, 395, 404, 604, 660, 981)

ARMCHAIR MURDERS

'Beware of the red armchair.'
Alain Bernardy de Sigoyer (1944)

Twenty-five-year-old Marquise Jeanne de Sigoyer visited her estranged husband's Paris house on 28 March 1944 to demand an alimony settlement. Irène Lebeau, the Marquise's former maid and now her husband's lover, was present when Alain de Sigoyer received his wife and invited her into the library, where she sat in a solidly built, red plush upholstered armchair. The initial conversation was good-natured, and he asked her, jokingly, if she was the mistress of a mutual friend. She replied, 'I won't tell you.' Smilingly, he produced a piece of cord from his pocket and said, 'Suppose I strangle you for that?' He walked behind the chair, and the Marquise, entering into the spirit of this play-acting, allowed him to put the cord loosely around her neck. Abruptly the mood changed as Sigoyer viciously tightened the cord and put his knee against the back of the chair to strengthen his strangulation hold. His wife put her hands to her neck to fight off the noose, but her husband's powerful pull against the unyielding chair-back was too much for her. Her struggles ebbed until she sat lifeless in the red armchair.

Alain Bernardy de Sigoyer, like fellow-countryman Dr Marcel Petiot — whose crime had been discovered less than two weeks previously — had a pedigree of violence. The forty-year-old self-styled Marquis, who modelled his appearance on Emperor Napoleon III, was an utter phoney who had several times been convicted of fraud. He was suspected of murder before the war, and there were rumours that his residence, dubbed 'The Red House', was used to torture robbery victims. In 1938 he was certified insane and committed to an asylum in Clermont, from which he escaped

after four months. He then went into hiding until 1940, when he appeared in German-occupied Paris to make a fortune as a black marketeer.

When Paris was liberated in August 1944 de Sigoyer was denounced as a collaborator and thrown into Fresnes Prison. No progress had been made by the police in their search for his wife, who had been reported missing since March. While in prison he wrote a letter to Irène Lebeau which contained veiled threats such as, 'Beware of the red armchair', which were intended to intimidate her into continued silence over the manner of his wife's death. As all correspondence was censored by the prison authorities this letter sparked off a new line of inquiry, and a police search of de Sigoyer's wine cellar revealed a pit in the floor which contained his wife's body. Irène Lebeau now came forward to state that she had been present when de Sigoyer murdered his wife, adding that he had threatened her to make her remain silent.

De Sigoyer was tried for murder in Paris in December 1946, and the infamous red armchair occupied a prominent place in court as a murder exhibit. Irène, charged as an accomplice, repeated her story, giving a graphic account of how de Sigoyer had engaged his wife in pleasant conversation before killing her. The accused, who had promised 'sensational revelations', countered with the claim that the two women had quarrelled over him and in the ensuing argument Irène shot his wife dead. He challenged the court to look for the bullet in her body.

The judge ordered the corpse to be X-rayed, and while the results were awaited de Sigoyer's defence counsel tried to prove that it would have been impossible to strangle a person seated in the red armchair as Irène had claimed. A practical demonstration was arranged for the court with a volunteer in the chair to test the claim that the chair-back was too low to permit strangulation in the manner described. The prosecution contended that it was merely a matter of technique. When the result of the X-ray examination of the murder victim's body was known — no traces of a bullet were found — de Sigoyer's defence crumbled badly. He was found guilty, and Irène was acquitted.

The devious Marquis even managed to cause a delay at the guillotine by declaring that he had fresh evidence. The magistrate who had examined de Sigoyer when he was first charged was rushed to the scaffold to be informed, 'You never inspired me with confidence. It is your fault that I have been sentenced to death.' The very last word lay with the executioner, who signalled the release of the blade which parted de Sigoyer's head from his body.

The chair as a place of murder has several attractions; chief of these is that the intended victim is lulled into a false sense of security and remains entirely unsuspecting of violence. The armchair especially is a place of comfort and safety, and for these reasons completely disarms the incumbent. Other types of chair — as used by the barber or dentist — while not, in the second case, sought after as positions of comfort, are nevertheless places to receive professional consideration. When these are

adapted to the violence of murder it is the seated person's head-back attitude which makes the throat so vulnerable.

At least one of America's gangland murders amply demonstrated the disadvantages of the barber's chair. Albert Anastasia, 'Lord High Executioner' of 'Murder Inc.' in New York, stepped into the basement barber shop of the Park Sheraton Hotel on 25 October 1957 and ordered 'a quick haircut'. With his head back against the chair-rest, he waited for the scissors and comb, but died from multiple gunshot wounds through the body as two men appeared behind him with automatic pistols. Discarding their weapons as they fled, the gunmen melted into New York's busy streets and were never apprehended.

'I was playing cards with my husband when he dared me to kill him as he wanted to die. I picked up the mallet ... I then hit him with the mallet.' Thus did Alma Rattenbury in one of several erratic statements claim to have struck her husband as he sat in his chair by the

Albert Anastasia: murdered in the barber's chair

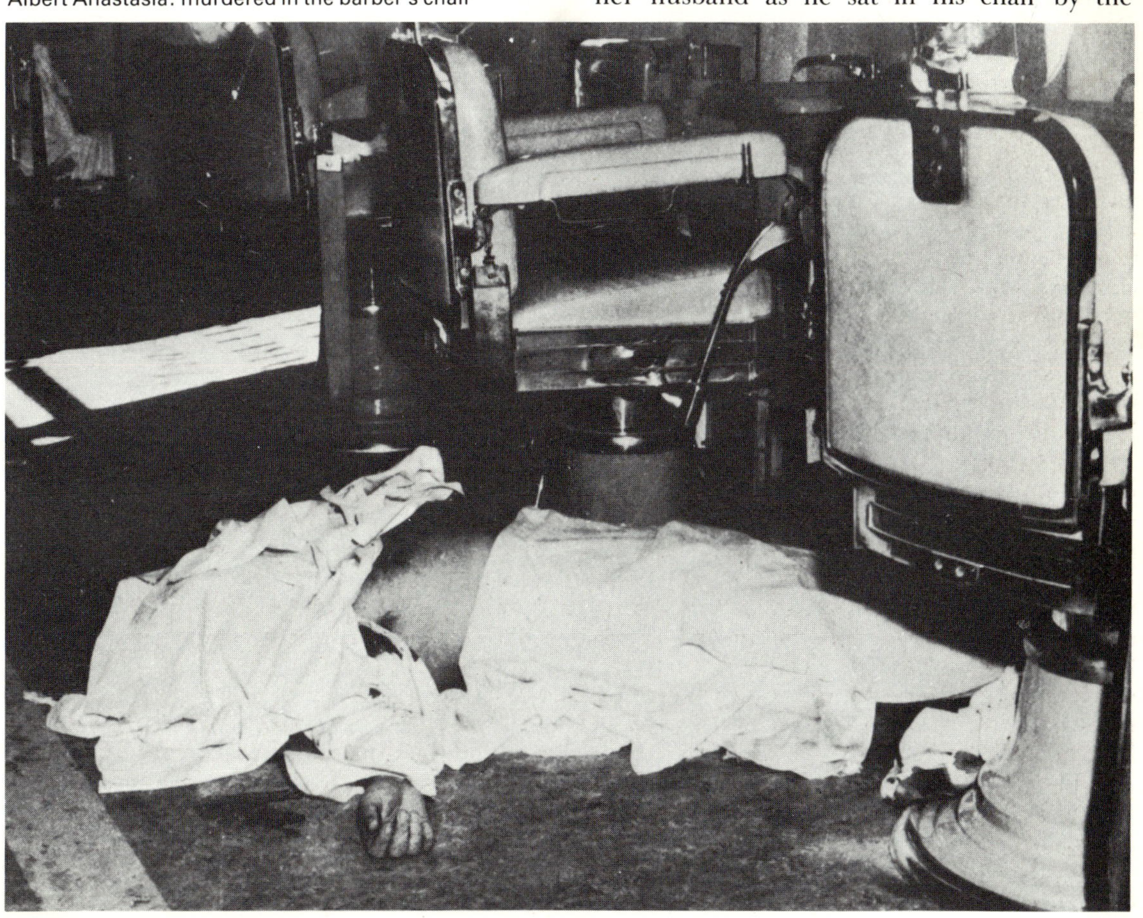

drawing-room fire. This famous English murder which occurred in the quiet environs of Bournemouth in 1935 was a sensation at the time because of the relationship between 31-year-old Alma and her jealous teenage lover, George Stoner. It has been much written about since, and vividly illustrates the danger of armchair complacency on the part of the weak member of a *ménage à trois*. All that elderly, retired Francis Rattenbury wanted was a quiet life, but he got in the way of the passions aroused between his sexually obsessive wife and her immature lover. The youth provided the weapon — a mallet — and the victim obliged by offering himself as a sitting target. Stoner eventually claimed the burden of guilt and was convicted of murder, while Alma Rattenbury was acquitted. She committed suicide almost immediately, and his sentence was commuted to life imprisonment in one of those fickle turns of fate that often characterize such crimes.

While Rattenbury was completely unsuspecting and probably asleep when his killer struck, General Emile Deisser was wide awake and impatient in his barber's chair. The elderly Belgian army officer was in the habit of being shaved regularly by a barber who called at his house in Rue Royale, Brussels. On a January evening in 1956 he told his barber to 'get on with it', but the man who stood behind him was preparing not a razor but a noose which he quickly slipped over the General's neck.

In the ensuing struggle the chair turned over and the two men collapsed on the floor. Slowly one of the heaving bodies grew limp and the murderer, his work done, stepped back, only to be confronted by the startled face of his victim's sister-in-law. He ignored her while he moved the body and Madame Louise Marcette, an alert old lady, rushed to the telephone to put a call through to the police. Realizing the danger, the murderer pulled out the telephone wire before the call was completed and strangled the old woman with the cord. He then pursued the only other occupant of the house, housekeeper Marie Foulon, and bludgeoned her to death. He was now free to ransack the premises.

The police eventually located the source of the half-completed emergency call made by Madame Marcette and arrived at the house in Rue Royale to find the triple murder. The fact that the house had not been forcibly entered suggested that the murderer had been known to his victims. Unidentified fingerprints were found, and the police set about eliminating from their inquiries the list of people known to the Deisser household. In the course of this investigation one of those questioned asked if the police had interviewed Jean-Marie Lefèbre. This came as a surprise, for the name was not even on the list of interviewees. Further inquiries revealed that Lefèbre was a hairdresser who had been employed for several weeks as the General's barber, and who called regularly at the house in Rue Royale. Lefèbre was questioned, and it was soon established that his fingerprints matched those found at the scene of the crime. Moreover, he was known to have debts, but recently had been in possession of various sums of money. Pressed for answers by the police, Lefèbre broke down and confessed to the three murders.

Anxious to make a strong case, the Belgian police decided to stage a reconstruction of the crime at the Deisser residence in Rue Royale. So great was public feeling that a crowd of five thousand gathered outside, and when Lefèbre arrived in a police car pandemonium broke loose. It was only with difficulty that officers prevented the mob from seizing their prisoner. Despite the chaos, the reconstruction was carried out and detectives were able to check every detail of Lefèbre's statement in the rooms where the murders had been committed.

A plea of diminished responsibility was entered by Lefèbre's defence at his trial, but the prosecution showed clearly how he had cunningly exploited the confidence of an elderly man whom he had savagely attacked at the moment he was least expecting any danger. His motive was robbery, and he had ruthlessly killed two others who might have acted as witnesses against him. Jean-Marie Lefèbre was found guilty and sentenced to death, a penalty which was later commuted to imprisonment.

Another advantage to the intending murderer of seating his victim comfortably is that he can make his attack from the most cowardly position of all — from behind. What might be called 'The Sweeney Todd Position' was certainly used by the three murderers of Filippo Caruso, who had every reason not to want to look him in the eye. Caruso, a successful fruit merchant, was reported missing in Chicago on 2 May 1885. As a routine matter police asked his brother to view an unidentified body which had been shipped in a trunk from Chicago to Pittsburgh on 30 April. The body in the trunk had been bound hand and foot, and death had resulted from strangulation — Filippo Caruso had been found.

The railway baggage attendant at Chicago recalled that the man who shipped the trunk had a mole on his chin. This feature was emphasized in a full description circulated to all Police Departments, and came to the notice of Thomas Byrnes of the New York Police. Byrnes had a reputation as a detective who never forgot a face, and his amazing recollection of criminal physiognomy led him to believe that the man his Chicago colleagues were looking for was Agostino Gelardi, a thief who plied his trade in New York and elsewhere.

Gelardi was picked up in New York and sent to Chicago, where he was immediately identified as the man who had shipped the trunk containing Caruso's body. A witness also identified him as the person he had seen manhandling a trunk down the stairs of an apartment building in Tilden Avenue. Two Italians who shared Gelardi's apartment, Agrazio Silvestri and Giovanni Azari, were questioned and accusations and counter-accusations began to fly thick and fast.

It became evident that Gelardi, Silvestri and Azari had been boyhood friends of Caruso in Italy. After Caruso went to America and established himself in the fruit trade, he sent home for his three friends to come and join him in the New World. Far from expressing their gratitude, the three so-called friends plotted to kill their wealthy benefactor.

When Caruso called on them at their apartment on Tilden Avenue they decided to shave each other in a chair which had been set up for the purpose. One of the plotters was shaved first, and when it came to Caruso's turn he was carefully seated and given a clean shave with all the professional flourishes which included placing hot towels over his face. This was the signal for their cowardly attack on a friend whom they had placed completely at ease. Caruso was entirely at their mercy when a noose was placed over his head and he was strangled.

The money Caruso had on him was divided up by the three murderers and his body was put in the trunk for dispatch to Pittsburgh. That done, the three Italians went into hiding, but Gelardi had reckoned without the tell-tale mole on his face, and certainly had not given a thought to the brilliant memory of Thomas Byrnes.

The three Italians were brought to trial in July 1885, and all were found guilty. The trio were hanged a few weeks later, each reportedly refusing to have the traditional shave beforehand. The electric chair might have been a more fitting punishment for their particular crime, but they were five years too soon.

Mr Justice Simon Kuper, a Transvaal Supreme Court Judge, literally made himself a sitting target when he sat reading in the study of his house in Sixth Street, Lower Houghton, Johannesburg. On the evening of 8 March 1963 he sat in a chair near the window in the company of his wife and daughter. Suddenly the tranquillity of this scene was shattered by the sound of a shot and the crash of splintering glass. Judge Kuper slumped in his chair with a bullet-wound in his head.

Still conscious, the judge was rushed to hospital. In the ambulance he spoke in slurred tones to the doctor, and tried to write down a message. He uttered a word beginning with 'p' which could have been 'police', and he also managed to write down the same initial letter. He underwent emergency surgery but died several days later.

The police were baffled by the murder, and it was assumed that Judge Kuper (who was a staunch Zionist) had been murdered by someone who bore him a grudge. Criminal case files were searched for possible leads, but to no avail. The fatal shot had been fired from outside the house, and the gunman had been careful enough to retrieve the spent cartridge case. At least, it was never found, and neither was the murder weapon. The killer had chosen his moment well, for his victim was a motionless target in a well-lit room. Judge Kuper's death remains one of South Africa's unsolved murders.

(64, 523, 526, 611, 703, 809, 832)

ATTICS

'... every time a different pretty girl, and the funny thing was that the lady always paid the bill.'
Budapest waiter on Bela Kiss (1916)

The attic tends to be one of the least visited parts of the house. The spaces under the roof are traditionally dark, dusty areas for storing the unwanted and half-forgotten lumber of living. Lack of easy access, combined with few reasons for entering it, give the attic an air of secrecy, a characteristic occasionally exploited by the murderer.

Having committed his act of violence, the murderer is faced with the problem of how and where to dispose of the body. Fifteen-year-old Harold Jones, for example — who held the remarkable record for one so young of being twice tried for murder — hid the body of one of his victims in the attic of his home in 1921. He foolishly neglected to wipe clean the bloody marks which he left around the ceiling entry to the attic, and his crime was quickly discovered.

A celebrated attic belonged to a house in the sleepy Hungarian village of Czinkota, near Budapest, which was raided by police in May 1916. Their task was to commandeer any secret hoards of petrol which they could find in private hands. The engines of the Great War were consuming vast quantities of fuel, and petrol was sought from civilian sources to augment military supplies.

A police detail visited the inn at Czinkota, and the inn-keeper volunteered the information that the tinsmith's house on the hill might be worth investigating. The two-storey house belonged to Bela Kiss, a man with a somewhat sinister reputation, who had been called up for military service in the spring of 1914. Kiss worked as a tinsmith in premises attached to the house and, if rumour could be believed, practised black magic as well as metalcraft.

He had answered the call to the colours reluctantly, and before he left had heavily fortified his house with iron bars at the windows and padlocks on the doors. This was how the police found his house in May 1916, and thinking that such heavy security must be to hide something valuable — like petrol-supplies — forced one of the doors with a crowbar. The living-room and bedrooms were furnished quite normally and contained nothing unusual, but the attic was thought worthy of inspection. The officer who climbed up into the attic gave a whoop of joy when he saw seven large metal casks each capable of holding a hundred gallons. They were supported on trestles and lined up against one of the walls. Surely they contained a secret fuel-supply?

With the aid of his sergeant, the policeman hauled one of the casks to the centre of the attic space to inspect it more closely. It had been carefully sealed by the tinsmith's art, and considerable effort with an axe and saw was necessary to prise the lid open. Excitement gave way to disappointment when the two men found that the contents of the cask were not petrol or even wine but simply old clothes. Horror intervened as the clothes were pulled out to reveal the naked body of a woman coiled up in the cask. The corpse was well preserved, and the neck bore the clear impression of the strangler's noose; the body was trussed up like a chicken to fit into the confines of the cask.

The policemen sent for a senior officer and some reinforcements in order to examine the remaining casks. Their worst fears were realized when each one was opened to reveal similar contents to the first. Seven young women, not immediately identifiable, had been strangled and sealed up in the casks. Their hermetically sealed coffins had lain in the tinsmith's dusty attic for at least two years like so many heirlooms. Eventual identification of the murder victims showed that one was the daughter of the village inn-keeper who went missing from her home in November 1913. Another came from the village, four from Budapest and the last from Vienna.

Close scrutiny of the house and its surroundings turned up ten more bodies buried in the garden and several others in a neighbouring wood. In all twenty-four victims were attributed to the murderous activities of the tinsmith. By putting his skills to use in sealing seven of his victims in metal casks he had at least overcome the messy problem of disposal which haunted other murderers. Moreover, his choice of the attic as a last resting-place would have succeeded but for the unforeseen demands of war creating a fuel shortage.

A search of the bureau in Kiss's house

provided a few significant clues. Over a hundred pawn tickets were found relating to items of jewellery and articles of female clothing, and it became evident that he lured his victims to his house by means of advertisements placed in the newspapers. Using the name of Hofmann, he posed as a matrimonial agent seeking to match ladies and gentlemen of good character and position. He also offered to foretell the fortunes and future of any young woman who cared to visit him. Photographs of Kiss found in the bureau enabled the police to further their inquiries about his activities. Several expensive restaurants in Budapest knew him as a customer, and it was observed that he invariably had a different female companion who usually paid the bill.

The task of tracking down Bela Kiss proved more difficult. The War Office confirmed his army number and regiment, and the records showed that he had apparently died of fever while serving in Serbia. The police decided to check this information at the hospital itself, the records of which clearly entered the death of Bela Kiss and gave his correct personal details. It was only when one of the nursing staff remarked that the patient was 'such a nice lad' that the police became suspicious. Kiss was thirty-five and had a swarthy complexion, whereas the 'nice lad' was eighteen and fair with blue eyes.

It transpired that Kiss had indeed been ill, and had used his admission to hospital to exchange identity discs with a wounded soldier who later died. Thus Kiss was born again with the name of Mackavee and returned to his military duties. He was subsequently thought to have been killed on the battlefield, but in 1919 there was a report that he had been seen in the centre of Budapest. In 1924 there was a story that he had joined and deserted from the French Foreign Legion using the name of Hofmann, and in 1932 an American detective believed he saw him in New York. The homicidal tinsmith was never found.

Most murderers usually distance themselves from the scene of their crimes, but a few have opted to stay close by concealing themselves in the attic. The 'Spiderman of Denver' earned his nickname by indulging in this strange behaviour. Theodore Coneys, a 59-year-old vagrant, gained entry into the house of Philip Peters, an elderly Denver citizen, in September 1941. The intruder's original objective was

theft, but once inside the house he decided to go up into the attic, where he hid himself with a supply of food.

When Mr Peters left the house for any reason Coneys descended from his lofty perch to shave and take a bath. On 17 October 1941, at a time when Mrs Peters was in hospital and thinking that the coast was clear, he came down into the kitchen where he disturbed the old man who was taking a nap. Snatching up a poker, Coneys killed him, and instead of taking flight returned to his attic. Neighbours worried at the non-appearance of Mr Peters called the police, who were puzzled to find the old man lying dead in the kitchen with all the doors of the house locked from the inside. After Mrs Peters returned from hospital and resumed living in the house, she thought she heard noises in the roof, and rumours developed that the place was haunted by her husband's ghost. She left the house, and police kept the premises under surveillance. Their vigilance was rewarded on 30 July 1942, when Coneys was seen disappearing into the attic after one of his periodic sorties. Thus was the 'Spiderman of Denver' caught after ten months of living in an attic. He was sentenced to life imprisonment for the murder he had committed.

Another murderer who chose to live over his crimes was Raymond Armanasco. In October 1950 he killed his wife and five of their six children in their home in Perth, Australia. A caller at the house stumbled on a scene of carnage in which each victim had suffered a cut throat. Armanasco, a milk roundsman, appeared to have taken flight, and the sole survivor of the family was his favourite child, nine-year-old Elsie Rose, whom he had taken to friends on the eve of the killings. He remarked at the time that his marriage was finished. A blood-stained hammer and razors were found in the house and it appeared that the victims had been knocked unconscious before having their throats cut. Nothing had been disturbed in the house, and the killings appeared to have been an object in themselves.

While police officers were in the house examining the scene some flakes of plaster floated down from the ceiling, which appeared to be bulging over their heads. They quickly realized that someone was lurking in the roof, and Armanasco was hauled down from the attic where he had gone into hiding equipped with food and blankets. He had been moving about in the roof-space to eavesdrop on the detectives' conversations below when he put a foot wrong and drew attention to his place of concealment. Raymond Armanasco was convicted of murder and sentenced to life imprisonment.

(93, 200, 598, 788, 868, 905)

BANKS

'Money I want. And money I must have.'
Herbert Glasson (1893)

Murder in the course of bank robbery is a class of violence which belongs principally to the world of the gangster. An early exponent, who combined the advantages of the motor car and the handgun, was French anarchist Jules Joseph Bonnot. On 25 March 1912 he and several companions crouched by the side of the road leading out of Paris to Montgéron. They waited for the noise of an approaching car.

The Marquis de Rouget had recently taken delivery of a new 40 h.p. De Dion, and on this day it was being driven by his chauffeur, who had a representative of the manufacturer as his passenger. Suddenly a man stepped out into the road and signalled the driver to stop. As the car drew up several men leapt out, shots were fired and the occupants of the De Dion slumped dead in their seats. The lifeless bodies were thrown into the ditch and Jules Bonnot, wanted anarchist and an ex-racing driver, slipped behind the steering-wheel and drove towards Chantilly.

Bonnot stopped the car outside the Société Générale bank in Chantilly and kept the engine running while four members of his gang ran into the bank brandishing guns. They opened fire immediately, hitting several bank staff. In the ensuing chaos they emptied the counter clerk's cash drawers and made for the waiting car. With Bonnot still at the wheel the De Dion roared off, bearing the gang to safety and leaving two dead bank employees in their wake.

Despite intensive police activity, Bonnot

Jules Bonnot practised robbery with violence and died under a hail of police bullets

remained at large until 20 April when he was cornered in a garage at Choisy-le-Roi. The place was put under siege by six hundred armed police and military personnel. In a shoot-out lasting six hours Bonnot was finally shot dead. He had left a written note which read: 'I am famous now.' Twenty-one members of his gang were eventually rounded up and brought to trial.

Jules Bonnot blazed a trail for others in what became a peculiarly French tradition of robbery with violence. Emile Buisson went to the guillotine in 1956 to end a career which included two bank murders, and in November 1979 Jacques Mesrine, declared Public Enemy Number One and a man who had committed bank robbery and murder in two continents, died in a hail of bullets when he was trapped in a police ambush. The pattern of violence involving stolen cars, reckless use of firearms and bank robbery to finance a criminal career was also enthusiastically pursued in America in the 1930s by Bonnie Parker and Clyde Barrow.

Bank robbery was easier in the days before strict security measures were introduced, but armed bank hold-ups continue to find favour with groups seeking to acquire funds for political or terrorist ends. In the Paris area in 1966 there were but six bank robberies. By 1973 there were two a day, and such attacks have increased to a rate of ten a day.

Most bank killings have associations with the underworld that make them rather uninteresting as murders, but there are exceptions. Herbert Glasson, for example, was prepared to mete out violence to obtain money, and went to pieces when his demands were questioned by people who knew him and were trying to divert him from catastrophe.

The City Bank of Sydney had a branch in the small farming town of Carcoar in New South Wales. The bank, one of two in the town, was a two-storey brick building which contained the bank itself and also living accommodation for the manager and his family. Until 25 September 1893 the manager was John Phillips, but on that day he was due to take up a new appointment at another branch.

Phillips — who was married with two children — had arranged for his sister-in-law and her friend to come to Carcoar and stay with his wife until he was able to move his family. On 23 September he met the Sydney train and escorted home Susan Stoddart, his wife's sister,

and Fanny Cavanagh, her friend. John and Anne Phillips spent a convivial evening with their guests, and in due course retired to their rooms for the night. The family and guests slept on the first floor, and the only servant in the house, Agnes McVicar, slept in the basement.

In the early hours of the following morning Mrs Phillips heard sounds of an intruder downstairs. She woke her husband, who armed himself with the bank's revolver before going quietly down the stairs. Anne Phillips lighted the way with a candle. As they reached the foot of the stairs they could see a masked intruder in the dining-room. When he spotted them he turned, brandishing an axe, and struck out at John Phillips, who collapsed on the floor.

Fearful for her children's safety, Anne Phillips turned and ran back up the stairs shouting, 'Murder.' The intruder pursued her into the bedroom and wounded her in the face. Awakened by the commotion, Susan Stoddart and Fanny Cavanagh rushed to protect the children. Fanny snatched up the three-year-old, and was confronted by the axeman, who felled her with a single blow. The masked man, addressing Anne Phillips, said, 'Money I want. And money I must have. Give me the safe keys.' She complied with his demand and he went downstairs to the bank.

The frightened women and terrified children huddled together, and were joined by Agnes McVicar who had come up from her room in the basement. The intruder soon came storming back, saying that the keys did not fit the safe. This was not surprising, for the keys belonged to the bank in the other town to which John Phillips had been appointed manager; the keys of the Carcoar bank were in the pocket of the new manager, who at that moment was sleeping peacefully in his hotel room. Exasperated and running out of time, the intruder rushed out of the house, leaving the safe intact.

Agnes McVicar and Susan Stoddart raised the alarm with a neighbour, and help was quickly on the scene. The injured Anne Phillips was cradling the body of her mortally wounded husband, and her friend Fanny Cavanagh lay, already dead, in one of the bedrooms. Angry citizens mounted an immediate search for the murderous intruder, and within hours had narrowed their quest to the near-by township of Cowra. The fleeing man had shed his bloodstained clothing and taken refuge in the town's barber shop, where he was arrested. The people of Carcoar were horrified to learn that the murderer was one of their own number, a local business-man from a respected family. Twenty-five-year-old Herbert Edwin Glasson ran a butcher's shop in the town and was a popular man in the district. He was regarded as something of a black sheep, but since he had recently married the hope was that he would curb his wild ways. Certainly no-one in their wildest imagination had him pegged as a violent criminal.

When he was arrested Glasson said simply, 'I did not do it ... I am mad.' The same feeling was expressed in a letter to his wife which he was carrying in his pocket. 'I am going mad,' he wrote, 'and felt it coming on for some time. I came to myself today ... I had on a black suit of clothes all covered in blood. What I have done I have no idea .... Better for me to be dead than you to have a mad husband.'

The inquest on the deaths at the bank established that Glasson had arrived at Carcoar on the same train as the late John Phillips's guests. Glasson had been picked out at an identity parade by Susan Stoddart, and Anne Phillips confirmed that she had recognized him at the time of the shooting. She said that her husband had tried to reason with him. It appeared that Glasson had ample motive for wanting to rob a bank as he was in considerable financial trouble. He had been asked by the bank to reduce his overdraft, and the man he employed to run his butcher's shop had not been paid for three months.

The main question at the murder trial held at Bathurst in October 1893 was whether or not Glasson was sane. His wife testified that several weeks before the killings at Carcoar he had suffered severe sunstroke and thought he was going mad. There was also a history of insanity in his family. Considerable medical evidence was heard at the trial and the judge advised the jury not to let 'the subtleties of the law of mania affect them'. They took note of this advice and returned a guilty verdict; Glasson was sentenced to death. As a measure of their sympathy for her ordeal, the citizens of Carcoar put on record their appreciation of Anne Phillips's devotion to her husband.

Probably the best-known bank murders are those attributed to the Japanese artist Sadamichi Hirasawa. Bank employees fell easy

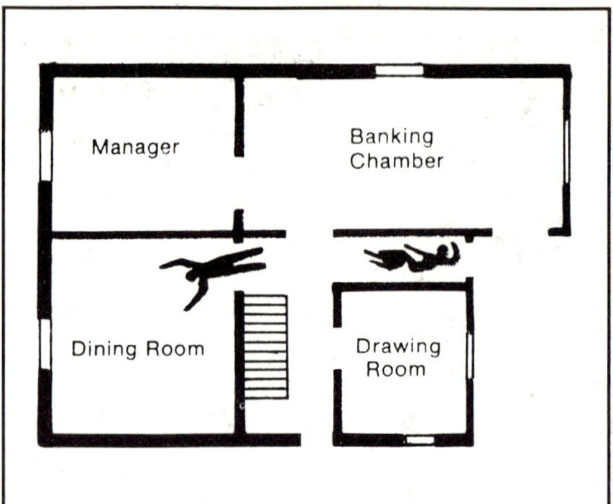

Plan of the ground floor of the City Bank, Carcoar, Australia

victims to the compulsive poisoner who committed robbery almost as an afterthought. The Shiinamachi branch of the Imperial Bank of Tokyo is situated in a busy shopping area near the Meiji Gardens. On 26 January 1948, just before the bank closed for business at 3.0 p.m. a man wearing an armband which identified him as a member of the Tokyo Metropolitan Disinfectant Corps appeared at the main entrance. He presented his business card to the Acting Manager, and 'Dr Jiro Yamaguchi' was admitted to the bank.

'Dr Yamaguchi' explained that there was an outbreak of dysentery in the district and he had been instructed to distribute preventive medicine. His orders came from GHQ of the American Occupying Forces. Sixteen employees of the bank, including cleaners as well as counter staff, dutifully lined up to comply with instructions. The doctor gave each employee a pill and took one himself. Then, having assembled a number of small cups, he dispensed into each a quantity of liquid medicine which he transferred by means of a dropper from a bottle he had brought with him. He explained that they could add a little water if they wished before swallowing the medicine.

Within seconds of drinking the liquid the bank employees collapsed where they stood. Ten died immediately, two lingered for a while before succumbing and four survived after hospital treatment. The mass killing had been swiftly committed using cyanide, and stepping over the prostrate bodies, the 'doctor' ransack-

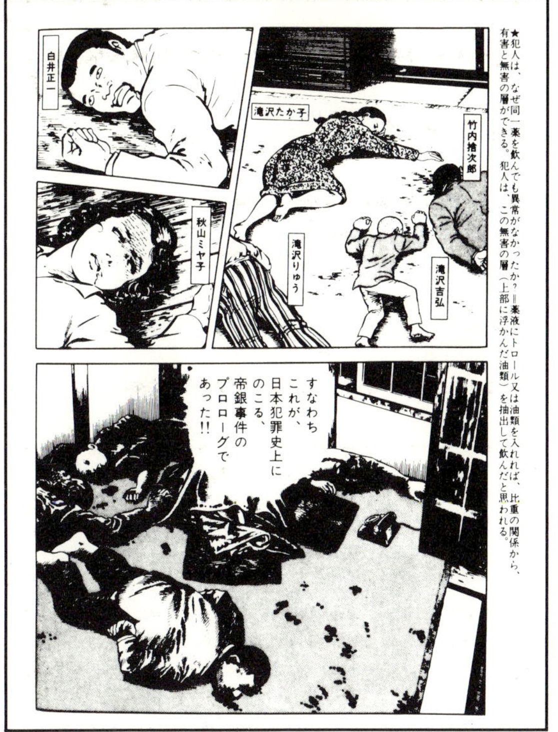

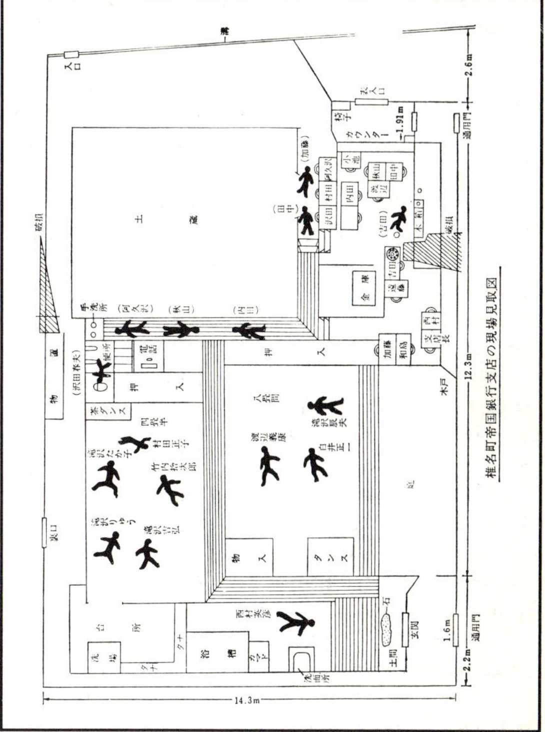

The Tokyo bank murder

ed the bank, escaping with 164,000 yen in cash and 17,000 yen in cheques.

The police discovered that 'Dr Yamaguchi' had carried out a murder rehearsal on 19 January when he 'immunized' staff at the Mitsubishi Bank. There were no ill effects on this occasion, but no doubt he felt that he had perfected the method. It also emerged that the staff of the Yasuda Bank had been 'immunized' the previous October by 'Dr Shigeru Matsui'. Again there were no ill effects.

The Japanese custom of using exchanges of visiting cards for almost any business encounter gave detectives a possible lead. They had no luck with Dr Yamaguchi's card, for that name is one of the most common in Japan, but by good fortune Dr Shigeru Matsui reported to the police he had read about the bank murders and wanted to help. It was possible that the murderer had met Dr Matsui at some time and, following the ritual exchange of cards, had inadvertently used Dr Matsui's at one of his murder rehearsals. If this reasoning was correct, it meant that the murderer's card was among the ninety-six which Dr Matsui handed over to the police.

By a process of elimination detectives narrowed their search down to one man, Sada-michi Hirasawa, an artist whom Dr Matsui had met two months before the bank murders. Survivors of the poisoning described the murderer as middle-aged with greying hair, whose face was distinguished by a mole on the left cheek and a scar under his chin. Hirasawa, aged fifty, matched this description, and a search of his accommodation turned up a medical bag and clothing, including a pair of red rubber boots similar to those worn by the murderer.

Hirasawa was arrested and made a confession. He was tried for murder in December 1948, when he pleaded partial insanity due to damage of the brain resulting from an anti-rabies injection he had been given in 1925. This, he claimed, had led to a general deterioration of his faculties, including his painting skills. During the trial Hirasawa withdrew his earlier confession, saying it had been obtained as the result of subjecting him to torture and hypnosis. He was found guilty and sentenced to hang.

His lawyers successfully appealed against the

death sentence, arguing that it violated Japanese law which protected citizens from participating in their own destruction. The thesis was that hanging was self-strangulation, which required the victim's weight to produce death. The Supreme Court rejected an appeal against conviction in 1955 and Hirasawa, now nearing his nineties, remains in prison. His appeals number seventeen and he occupies a cell-cum-studio in Sendai Prison where he paints pictures for exhibition in public galleries. He has also written his autobiography.

Hirasawa probably holds the world record for the length of time spent on Death Row. A 'Save Hirasawa Committee', which includes lawyers, MPs, writers and artists, claims that he is the innocent victim of a cover-up. Collusion is alleged between the Japanese and American governments to hide wartime atrocities. The real bank murderer is said to be an ex-Japanese officer who served in Manchuria with a secret unit called the Manchu 731 company. One of the tasks of this unit was to infiltrate enemy lines and poison the leaders with untraceable toxins. Cyanide was one of the agents used by these assassination squads. It was also alleged that during Japan's wartime occupation of China human guinea-pigs were used in experiments to test the use of chemical agents.

At the end of the war those involved in this work were released by the occupation authorities in exchange for the documents relating to their researches. The circumstances of the bank murders were said to have led the police to conclude that the man they were looking for was someone with a background in the military medical service. This line of inquiry was also pursued by the press, and progress was halted by official intervention. Members of the wartime assassination unit were under house arrest in order that the US Occupation Forces could learn from them. By co-operating in this way they would escape punishment as war criminals. This plan would have been jeopardized if it were made public that the bank murderer was a former officer of this special unit. Hence, according to his supporters, Sadamichi Hirasawa, an innocent man, was wrongly convicted.

(97, 165, 842, 854, mw)

BARRACKS

'I had resolved to poison a number of staff officers.'

Lieutenant Adolph Hofrichter (1912)

The disciplined atmosphere of the military barracks might suggest that crime is less likely to occur there than in civilian life. Nevertheless, the provost authorities exist to investigate breaches of discipline and transgressions of both military and civil law. Murder is not a common occurrence in military circles, and it might therefore be supposed that investigators are less experienced than are their civilian counterparts. This fact has been borne out in a number of investigations, although the co-operation between the military and civil authorities is usually good.

The fact that military establishments are relatively closed communities with their own rules and regulations creates possibilities for the inventive criminal mind. The idea of committing a crime in the outside world and then retreating to the security of the barracks, ostensibly beyond the arm of the law, is an attractive one. Many have tried it and failed. Dale Pierre, for example, the US airman who committed the Hi-Fi shop murders in Utah in 1974, retired afterwards to the USAF Hill Field base with the hope of finding safety in numbers (see under SHOPS AND OFFICES). Lieutenant Samuel Epes, who disposed of an unwanted wife in 1955 at Fort Jackson, South Carolina, reported her missing to the civil police. He no doubt hoped to draw attention away from the military base where he had buried her corpse in a foxhole in the manœuvres area. As in the case of Dale Pierre, civil and military authorities combined effectively to bring the murderer to justice.

Sexual rivalry can occur among military colleagues, with all the potential for violence which overheated emotions can generate. Frederick Emmett-Dunne and Reginald Watters were both regular army sergeants serving with the British occupation forces in Germany after the Second World War. They were based at the REME Technical Training College at Duisburg, where the two men were thought by their fellow NCOs to be on friendly terms. Like many British servicemen at that time, Watters had married a German girl.

Rumours eventually began to circulate in the Sergeants' Mess that Emmett-Dunne was seeing Watters's wife. The knowledge that Watters was an obsessive, jealous personality suggested that an explosive confrontation might occur between the two men.

On 30 November 1953 Sergeant Watters was reported missing from duty. A search party found his body dangling from a rope in the stair well of Block No.3, Glamorgan Barracks. He had apparently committed suicide, and an Army court of enquiry returned such a verdict.

Rumour persisted that the truth of the matter lay elsewhere, and in due course, the case of Watters's death was reopened. In the meantime Emmett-Dunne had been posted back to England, where he married his dead colleague's widow. Sergeant Watters's body was exhumed, and a further post-mortem examination concluded that he had died not by hanging but from a karate-type blow to the throat.

Frederick Emmett-Dunne was arrested and returned to Germany to face trial at Düsseldorf in 1955. His story was that Watters had confronted him with accusations regarding his friendship with his wife, and had threatened him with a loaded revolver. Feeling himself in danger, Emmett-Dunne said he struck out with his hand, intending to stun the other man and thereby head off his threat.

When he realized that Watters was dead, Emmett-Dunne sought the help of his half-brother (who was also stationed at Duisburg) to make the death look like suicide. His contention therefore was that Watters had died accidentally while he was trying to defend himself. The heavy-handed sergeant was nevertheless found guilty of murder and, there being no capital punishment in Germany, he was sentenced to life imprisonment.

In some ways the military establishment intensifies rather than lessens the emotions, and high on the list of stimuli to violence is professional jealousy. The very concept of privilege and rank inspires healthy competition, but also stirs darker feelings. Lieutenant Hubert Chevis probably fell victim to a jealous motive when he was poisoned in his quarters at Aldershot in 1931 with a meal of doctored partridge. His murder remains unsolved, although a telegram sent to his father reading, 'Hooray, hooray, hooray' demonstrated jubilation at the death of the young officer.

Professional jealousy certainly lay behind a strange incident which occurred in Austria in 1909. As Christmas approached, several Austrian army staff officers received an unexpected gift. Each received a package through the mail containing a druggist's pillbox filled with capsules and a circular letter declaring that the contents were a 'nerve strengthening remedy' which was 'absolutely harmless' and promising results that 'will be startling'.

The results were indeed startling, and precipitated a national sensation. Most recipients of this unsolicited gift consigned it to the waste-paper basket, but one officer was tempted. While writing letters in his quarters Captain Richard Mader decided to try the tonic remedy. Within seconds of swallowing a capsule he collapsed, and died inside a few minutes.

When the dead captain's body was found the first conclusion was that he had died suddenly of natural causes. But when a fellow-officer mentioned that Mader and some of his companions had received boxes of capsules in the mail, the investigation was widened. The interest taken in the incident by Emperor Franz-Josef, who demanded daily progress reports, added to the investigators' efforts. Analysis of the remaining capsules showed that each contained a massive dose of potassium cyanide, and traces of the lethal poison were found in the dead man's body.

It was ascertained that twelve officers recently promoted to appointments on the General Staff had been sent boxes of capsules. Only Captain Mader had sampled the so-called remedy, which according to the accompanying letter had been sent by 'Charles Francis, Box 5, Post Office, No.6 District, Vienna'.

Captain Mader was a popular officer not thought to have any enemies and it was believed that his death might have been part of an anarchist plot to strike at the military establishment. But suspicion began to narrow when it was realized that all the recipients of poisoned capsules had graduated from War College at about the same time. The theory that the culprit might be found among the officer corps was strengthened by the argument that a civilian would have been unlikely to know the names and garrison addresses of such a select group of officers. As the view hardened that the sender of the capsules might be a disgruntled officer, so suspicion began to

Lieutenant Adolph Hofrichter had fatal designs on promotion

focus on Lieutenant Adolph Hofrichter of the 14th Infantry Regiment based at Linz.

Twenty-eight-year-old Hofrichter had done well at War College and was known to be ambitious, but he had not been among those selected for a permanent staff appointment. He lived in married quarters at Linz, where a search of his rooms revealed a number of empty capsules which he explained were used to adminster worm mixture to his dog. It was also discovered that Hofrichter had bought a quantity of pill-boxes identical to those used to send the cyanide capsules. One week after the murder of Captain Mader the young lieutenant was arrested and taken under military guard to Vienna. His garrison commander, General Weigl, told newspaper reporters that he was fully convinced of Hofrichter's innocence of any charge of murder.

Public opinion was generally in Hofrichter's favour, and the view was that the charge was trumped up. There was also disquiet when it was learned that he would be tried not by the civil courts but by court martial, the proceedings of which would be conducted in secret. A preliminary investigation lasting three months was completed in February 1912, and all the evidence was repeated in detail at the court martial, which lasted six months.

The prosecution case was largely circumstantial. The claim was made that Hofrichter deliberately plotted the deaths of his recently appointed comrades with the object of stepping into the shoes of one of them. It was shown that he had been in Vienna at the time the packages of capsules were dispatched through the mail. The handwriting on the accompanying note was said to resemble his, and the fact that he was an amateur photographer made it possible for him to have access to cyanide.

Hofrichter protested his complete innocence, and a strong point in his favour was that he could not be linked to any known purchases of potassium cyanide, and no trace of poison was found either on his person or in his quarters. But fate worked against him as the court martial proceeded, for unsavoury news of his private life began to emerge. It appeared that the young lieutenant whom fellow-officers regarded as an ambitious professional soldier spent a great deal of his off-duty hours in unseemly debauchery. Using the fictitious name of Dr Haller, he preyed on young women, stupefying them with drugs before forcing his attentions on them. A girl who had answered Dr Haller's advertisement for a governess identified Hofrichter as her would-be employer.

Support for Hofrichter now fell away, and his loyal wife was devastated by the revelation that her husband was a Dr Jekyll and Mr Hyde figure. Hofrichter contemplated suicide, and in a letter to his wife asked her to smuggle 'a small quantity of hyoscyamine or atropine' into his prison cell in a bunch of flowers. This communication was intercepted and all of the prisoner's privileges were withdrawn.

At the end of April Hofrichter changed his plea to one of guilty. He wrote a confession in which he stated: 'I am the sender of the poison letters. In order to regain a position on the General Staff, I had resolved to poison a number of staff officers by sending them these pills.' Despite his admission of guilt, he still refused to say how he came by the poison, and to add to his misery his wife was arrested on the grounds that she had given false evidence on her husband's behalf.

The court martial accepted the guilty plea, and in consideration of the doctors' opinion that Hofrichter was 'morally abnormal', sentence of death was passed with the recommendation that it be commuted to long imprisonment. At this point Hofrichter withdrew his confession but his action had no effect on the outcome, for the Emperor demanded his expulsion from the army and directed that he undergo twenty years of rigorous imprisonment.

Where a military base on foreign soil tends to become a close-knit community, wives living in married quarters form a small minority. In consequence they find themselves in great social demand, with the attendant danger of sparking off relationships that arouse sexual passion and jealousy.

Jeanne Daniloff Weiss was the illegitimate child of a Russian émigrée. She was brought up by her grandmother in Nice, on the French Riviera. In 1886, at the age of eighteen, she married a young army officer, Lieutenant Weiss. Shortly afterwards he was posted to an army unit based at Ain-Fezza, near Oran in Algeria. During the next three years Jeanne bore her husband two children, and impressed her friends as an admirable wife and mother.

This blissful pattern was disrupted in 1889 when Jeanne met Félix Roques, a French engineer working on the West Algerian railways. This apparently staid woman fell madly in love with Roques, becoming his mistress and slave. Lieutenant Weiss, alarmed at his wife's errant behaviour, took her and the children to Nice for a holiday in the hope of breaking the spell. Jeanne was pregnant with Roques's child.

On returning to Algeria Jeanne and Félix Roques discussed their future plans. Elopement was ruled out, leaving elimination of Lieutenant Weiss as the only course of action which would allow the lovers to marry. So completely was Jeanne controlled by Roques that in order to ensure that she carried out the plan he made her sign a statement written in his pocket-book: 'I swear that I will murder my husband, that I may belong to you alone — Jeanne.' Only rarely can murderous intent have been so clearly expressed in such an incriminating form.

Roques meanwhile travelled to Madrid on an engineering project, leaving Jeanne to carry out the agreed plan. But she now had second thoughts: 'What I am about to do is very ugly,' she wrote in a letter to her lover. He replied, brushing aside her misgivings and virtually instructing her to get on with it. 'It is agreed, Félix, you shall be obeyed .... Crimes against the law don't bother me at all. It is only crimes against Nature that revolt me,' she answered plaintively. But still she hesitated, causing Roques to write to her, saying, 'You promised to obey me. I implore you to obey me.'

Finally, in October 1890, Lieutenant Weiss was taken ill as his wife began systematically to poison his food. As his condition deteriorated and he was racked with fever, convulsions and vomiting, some of his army friends grew suspicious of his loving and attentive wife who so carefully washed his food receptacles. Suspicion was fuelled by the post-mistress at Ain-Fezza, who had been in the habit of reading the correspondence which passed between Mme Weiss and Félix Roques.

A letter sent by Jeanne on 9 October was intercepted, and gave the game away. She referred to her husband's 'sheer vitality and instinct of self-preservation' and said, 'I am afraid, afraid that I haven't got enough of the remedy left and that I shan't be able to bring it off. Couldn't you send me some by parcel post to the railway station of Ain-Fezza?' Lieutenant de Guerry, a friend of the sick officer, was given this letter and immediately went to the authorities. Jeanne Weiss was confronted, and admitted that Félix Roques was her lover. 'I tried to pacify him,' she said, 'by pretending that I was poisoning my husband.' Large quantities of Fowler's Solution, prussic acid and corrosive sublimate were found in the house, and she unsuccessfully tried to poison herself before being taken into custody.

Roques was arrested in Madrid, where Jeanne's letters were found in his apartment. These provided eloquent testimony of the lovers' plot, as did the documents already drawn up for their intended marriage. On 20 October Roques shot himself in the Spanish gaol where he was being held, leaving Jeanne to face the music on her own. She was tried in May 1891 for attempted murder. Her husband, recovering from the attempt on his life, gave evidence. He told the court, 'I do not and I never will forgive her ... I only wish never to hear her name again.'

The jury found Jeanne Weiss guilty and she was sentenced to twenty-five years' penal servitude. Spectators at the trial applauded the verdict, but she denied them final satisfaction by taking her own life. When she was returned to her cell at the conclusion of the trial on 29 May 1891 she put her handkerchief into her mouth, and died a violent death from absorbing the strychnine which she had sewn into the seam. 'I am happy. Adieu.' were her last words. She left her body to the 'service of science'.

Domestic violence of a certain kind will spill over whatever the circumstances. But when the locus is army married quarters, the ensuing legal proceedings may be complex. This proved to be the outcome when, in the early hours of 17 February 1970, Military Police HQ at Fort Bragg received an emergency telephone call from one of the base doctors. Captain Jeffrey MacDonald said simply, 'Stabbing .... Hurry!' Within minutes MPs were at the doctor's quarters in Castle Drive, Corregidor Courts. Inside the house they were confronted by a scene of carnage — Colette MacDonald lay on the floor of the master bedroom in a welter of blood with her husband lying beside her, and their two children lay dead in their blood-spattered bedrooms.

Dr MacDonald had several superficial wounds and a partially collapsed lung; his wife and two daughters had been savagely clubbed and stabbed to death. He told MPs that four 'acid heads' wearing hippie clothing had attacked his family. One of them, a woman, had said, 'Acid is groovy — kill the pigs.' The word PIG had been daubed in blood on the bedhead. The brutal killings echoed the Manson murders committed in California a year earlier. Like Sharon Tate, who met her death on that occasion, Colette MacDonald was pregnant.

Jeffrey MacDonald had an impeccable background as a scholar, and soon after he qualified as a doctor enlisted in the army and volunteered for the Green Berets. He was disappointed at not being posted to Vietnam, but made the best of being sent to the USA's largest military base at Fort Bragg, North Carolina. The story of the Green Beret doctor

The murder scene at the MacDonald home

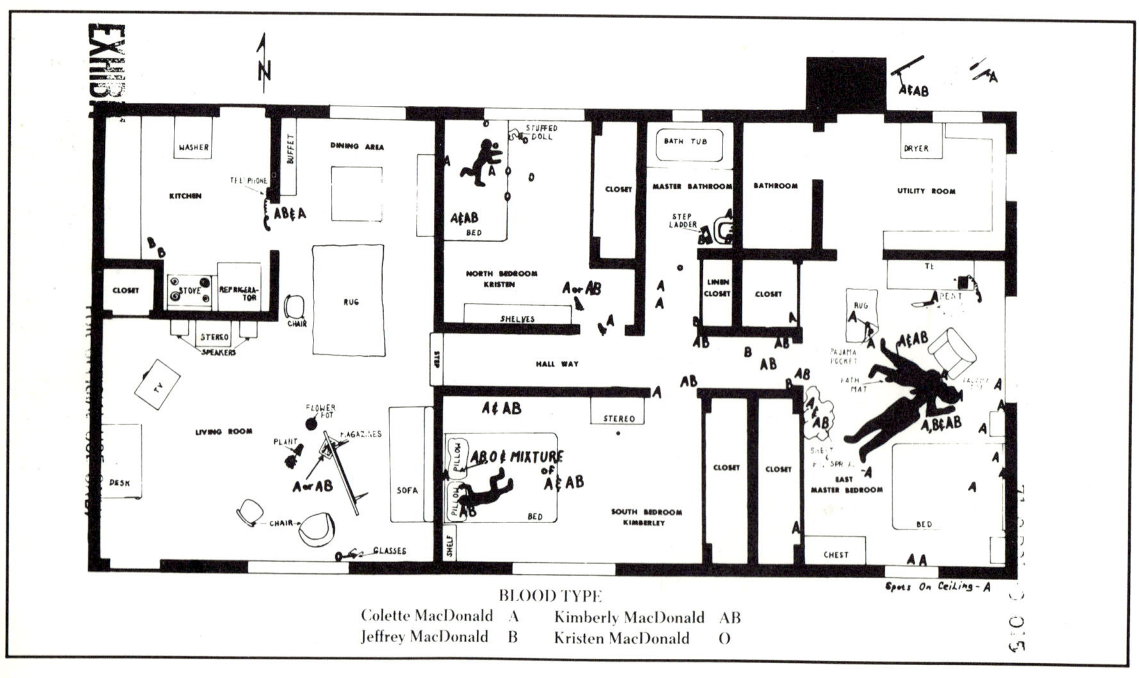

BLOOD TYPE
| Colette MacDonald | A | Kimberly MacDonald | AB |
| Jeffrey MacDonald | B | Kristen MacDonald | O |

whose family was killed by drug-crazed attackers made large headlines; but MacDonald became the prime suspect.

Observers thought it significant that despite the violence there were so few signs of disorder in the house, especially as four intruders were involved. The idea began to form that MacDonald had killed his wife and children and made the scene conform to a Manson, hippie-style attack. The investigation which followed was flawed from the start, when evidence was inadvertently destroyed at the crime scene, and vital clues were lost in the laboratory. After four months' investigation, the military authorities dropped all charges against MacDonald due to insufficient evidence. The Green Beret officer took an honourable discharge from the Service and went back to private practice. He also revelled in the publicity which the case had attracted, and made several appearances on television.

Despite the army's dismissal of charges, others had their private doubts. One of these was MacDonald's father-in-law, previously a staunch supporter but increasingly suspicious of inconsistencies in his son-in-law's statements. In June 1972 army investigators, in a report to the Justice Department, stated that the evidence pointed to Dr MacDonald's guilt. In January 1974 the Justice Department sent the papers back to the army's Criminal Investigation Division for further inquiries to be made. MacDonald was called to testify before a Grand Jury in January 1975, as a result of which he was indicted on three counts of murder. He appealed, and a ruling was given that his constitutional rights had been violated by virtue of delays and negligence in the judiciary process and the indictment was dismissed.

The chief participant in this drama heard the news of the judge's ruling while he was holidaying in Hawaii with his girl-friend. By this time he was Director of Emergencies at St Mary's Hospital, Long Beach, California, where he was highly respected. But if he had grown complacent about his safety from the law, he had reckoned without its persistence. In June 1977 the Supreme Court decided to reconsider the MacDonald affair, and hearings began in the following year. Finally, in June 1979, nine and half years after the murders committed in his Fort Bragg home, Jeffrey MacDonald was brought to trial at Raleigh, North Carolina.

Attempts by the defence to show a video-tape taken while MacDonald was under hypnosis were rejected by the judge. The film depicted him describing what happened when the four intruders entered his house. Commenting on the film, a psychiatrist had said, 'If he's guilty, he deserves an Academy Award.' MacDonald wept in court when he testified, and some of the jury wept with him when he denied harming his wife and children. But under cross-examination he proved hostile and sarcastic. The forensic evidence came in for some strong criticism because of earlier omissions, but two aspects went against the accused man. Firstly, in view of the terrible wounds inflicted on the victims — Colette MacDonald had been stabbed nine times in the neck, and seven times through the chest with a knife, twenty-one times in the chest with an ice pick, six clubbing blows to the head and both arms broken — MacDonald himself was strangely unharmed. Secondly, it turned out that each member of the family had a different blood-group. This meant that the location and type of every bloodstain at the crime scene could be accurately logged. It was shown that some of the victims had been attacked in rooms other than those in which they were found dead, in contradiction of Dr MacDonald's account of events.

The jury believed that MacDonald had worked himself into a rage with his wife which spilled over into brutal violence. One of the psychiatric assessments of his personality was that he was 'an individual striving constantly to be superman'. Jeffrey MacDonald was found guilty of second-degree murder regarding the deaths of his wife and eldest daughter and of first-degree murder in respect of his youngest daughter. The reason for this was the belief that he had killed the two-year-old girl out of calculation in order to support his story of a hippie attack. Dr MacDonald was sentenced to three terms of life imprisonment.

The MacDonald murders were the subject of a celebrated TV documentary which was shown on both sides of the Atlantic.
(151, 317, 384, 483, 489, 492, 510, 662, 811, 1045, MWW)

BARS, CLUBS AND THEATRES

'Posterity, I am sure, will justify me.'
John Wilkes Booth (1865)

Bars, clubs and theatres are places of relaxation where people meet for entertainment and conversation over a drink. Occasionally the drinking may become heavy, and innocuous argument flares into trouble. Argument, sharpened by alcohol, quickly spills over into violence. Fights in bars which end with the death of one of the participants often lead to defence pleas of manslaughter rather than murder. The distinction is one of guilty intent, as Antonio Mancini — nicknamed 'Babe' — discovered to his cost.

Mancini was manager of the Palm Beach Club in Wardour Street, Soho. At the end of April 1941, following a fight in the club, he was obliged to bar two men from the premises. A few days later, on 1 May, a fight broke out in the Billiard Club, which was situated in the same building. Among the thirty or forty men playing billiards was one of the customers whom Mancini had ejected from his club. This man seemed to be the focus of the brawl, and he was defending himself with help from Harry Distleman, a friend who was also known as 'Scarface'.

After the brawl Distleman and his friend went to Charing Cross Hospital to have their cuts and bruises treated. Long after midnight they decided to return to the Billiards Club, where they encountered Antonio Mancini, who had been attracted to the place by the original rumpus. This encounter immediately led to another scuffle during which Distleman collapsed, claiming that Mancini had stabbed him. According to witnesses Mancini went wild, chasing the other man round the billiard tables, slashing him with a knife. By this time Distleman had staggered out into the street, where he fell dead to the ground.

Mancini was charged with murder. He denied stabbing Distleman, although he admitted injuring his friend; he claimed that the two men had threatened him, and that he acted in self-defence. The jury at his trial rejected the idea of manslaughter and found him guilty of murder. Both the Court of Criminal Appeal and the House of Lords upheld this verdict, and Mancini was duly hanged for his crime.

Clubs are also places of assignation, and Ruth Ellis's tragic slide towards impassioned provocation began at the Court Club in Mayfair. What began as escapism finished in disaster when Ruth met David Blakely, a racing-car driver. The couple embarked on an emotional merry-go-round which lasted for eighteen months. On 10 April 1955 Ruth Ellis, her nerves stretched tight by jealousy and rejection, shot Blakely dead outside the Magdala public house in Hampstead.

Another type of assignation is one that is far from random. It is the sure knowledge that his intended victim will be in a certain place at a particular time which determines the murderer's plan. At 8.30 p.m. on 14 April 1865, Good Friday, President Abraham Lincoln, with his wife and two guests, was escorted to Box Number 7 at Ford's Theatre, Washington D.C., to watch a performance of the comedy *Our American Cousin*. Earlier that day John Wilkes Booth, a handsome man of twenty-six and a promising actor, walked into the theatre to collect his mail. He learned that the Presidential Box had been reserved for that evening, and this knowledge determined his plan of action. At 9.30 p.m. that evening Booth walked unchallenged to the door of the Presidential Box — the guards were relieving their boredom in a near-by bar. He opened the door and shot President Lincoln in the back of the head. Fighting off all efforts to restrain him, Booth leapt eleven feet on to the theatre's stage. He fell awkwardly, breaking his leg in the process, but with the theatre in total confusion limped his way to a waiting horse and escaped the scene of assassination.

At the same time that the President fell to Booth's bullet a fellow-conspirator, Lewis Paine, made an unsuccessful attempt to stab to death the Secretary of State, William H. Seward. A third conspirator, George Atzerodt, charged with the task of killing Vice-President Andrew Johnson, got drunk and failed to carry out his part of the plan. President Lincoln died the day after the shooting. Booth, hampered by his injured leg, sought refuge with various friends but was constantly harried by searching soldiers. Eventually he holed up in a barn in Virginia where he was found on 26 April. Although surrounded, he defiantly refused to surrender and was mortally wounded by Sergeant Boston Corbett, whose claim that he had fired

President Abraham Lincoln — a sitting target

on orders from the Almighty won him a place in legend and history.

Booth was consumed by political allegiance to the South, and with the help of a handful of conspirators his original plan was to kidnap the President and spirit him away to Richmond, where he would be used as a political bargaining counter to turn the tide of the Civil War. But the war outpaced Booth's plans, and when General Lee surrendered to Grant the conspirators' thoughts turned to more desperate measures and to assassination. When he learned that President Lincoln's programme placed him in Ford's Theatre on Good Friday at 8.30 p.m. and that he would be seated for the duration of the play with his back to the door of the box, Booth knew that he had been given a unique opportunity to carry out his murder plan. In a letter written to the *National Intelligencer* on the afternoon of the assassination Booth stated, 'Many will blame me for what I am about to do, but posterity, I am sure, will justify me.'

All too often bars and cinemas become the background to murder resulting from robbery. The murder sprees which Walter Kelbach and Myron Lance unleashed on Salt Lake City in December 1966 started and finished in a bar. The pair of ex-convicts dosed themselves with drugs and alcohol, and on 17 December terrorized á filling-station attendant. They refused to pay their bill, and then abducted the teenage attendant to a remote spot in the desert, where he was sexually assaulted and killed. The following night the murderous pair repeated the exercise, leaving another corpse in their wake.

On 21 December Kelbach and Lance hired a cab and killed the driver. They then drove to Lolly's Tavern near Salt Lake City airport where they threatened the customers with guns, indiscriminately killing one of them. They stole $300 from the bartender before firing at the remaining four customers. Two died immediately, but the bartender, although wounded, managed to grab a gun from behind the bar and fired back at his assailants.

The two murderers were caught within hours at a police road-block. They were convicted at their trial but were saved from execution by the US Supreme Court ruling in 1967 abolishing capital punishment. Kelbach and Lance were committed instead to Utah State Penitentiary, and in 1972 appeared on a NCB television programme where they amply demonstrated their philosophy of complete disregard for human life.

Robbery with violence is no stranger to the cinema where audience takings kept on the premises might suggest rich pickings to the unscrupulous. John Stockwell, the nineteen-year-old attendant at the Eastern Palace Cinema in Bow Road, London, devised a get-rich-quick scheme. Early on the morning of 7 August 1934 Stockwell appeared in the manager's office and floored Dudley Hoard with an axe. He took £90 from the safe and made his escape. Dudley Hoard was found collapsed behind the upper circle by the cinema cleaners when they came on duty. The manager was beyond assistance and died from his wounds in hospital. Stockwell laid an intricate plan intended to cover his tracks. First he put the stolen money into a suitcase which he left at Aldgate East Station. Then he took a train to Lowestoft, whence he sent a letter to an address with the clear intention that it should be delivered into the hands of the police. This duly occurred. The letter declared that he had run away because he thought the police might believe he was connected with the 'London cinema affair'. Officers visited the Lowestoft address from which Stockwell had sent this letter, but by then the schemer was about to launch the next stage of his plan.

Stockwell had decided that he would disappear by faking his suicide. Accordingly he went to the beach at Great Yarmouth where he stripped off his clothes and left them in a forlorn heap together with his watch and Post Office Savings Book. Wearing a new suit, he signed into the Metropole Hotel using the name of Smith and, with his flair for writing letters, informed the Lowestoft police, 'I am going to drown myself....'

Young Stockwell, alias Smith, probably thought he had done really well covering his tracks and making the police look foolish. However, he had already made a fatal mistake. When signing the hotel register he gave an address in Luton, which he wrote as situated in Hertfordshire rather than in Bedfordshire. The hotel manager thought this was rather strange, and coupling the incident with other suspicions about his guest, called the police. John Stockwell, who proved too clever for his own good, was convicted of the cinema murder and went to the scaffold in November 1934.

An anonymous tip-off provided the police with an answer to the Cameo Cinema Murders in 1949 at Liverpool. At about 9.30 p.m. on 19 March the box-office cashier heard six shots in rapid succession coming from the direction of the manager's office. She rushed along to the office and was nearly knocked over by a masked gunman who made his escape down the emergency staircase. In the office she found Leonard Thomas, the manager, and John Catterall, his assistant, dying from gunshot wounds. They had been counting the evening's takings, which had been stolen by the intruder. Oblivious to the violence enacted a short distance from where they were sitting, the cinema audience continued to view the screened entertainment.

The police inquiry was faltering when an anonymous letter was received offering information in return for a guarantee of protection. Acceptance of this condition was published in *The Liverpool Echo* and the outcome was that George Kelly and Charles Connolly, both in their mid-twenties and members of Liverpool's fraternity of small-time gangsters, were arrested. They were both charged with murder, Connolly being accused of aiding and abetting Kelly by keeping watch outside the cinema.

After a trial lasting thirteen days, the jury could not agree on its verdict, and a re-trial was

ordered. This took place in 1950 when Kelly was convicted. He was hanged on 28 March. No evidence was offered against Connolly on the murder charge, but he pleaded guilty to conspiracy to rob, for which he received a prison sentence.
(243, 864, 865)

BASEMENTS, CAVES AND CELLARS

'In the unheard music I hear his command to kill ....'
Joe Kallinger (1975)

Below-ground locations provide the murderer with two attractive qualities — darkness and privacy. The desire to reach some dark recess in which to commit murder or to conceal the *corpus delicti* runs deep in criminal minds. Dr Hawley Harvey Crippen, the so-called 'cellar murderer' of 39 Hilldrop Crescent, and Louis Voisin, the Belgian butcher of Regent's Park, are two of the best-known exponents of this. Equally well known are mass murderers Dr Marcel Petiot and H.H. Holmes (see under MURDER HOUSES), who used the basements of their respective houses in Paris and Chicago as murder factories.

Caves have primeval and legendary significance as refuges and bolt-holes for the pursued, and also as bases for robbers and smugglers. According to the *The Newgate Calendar*, Sawney Beane, 'The Maneater of Midlothian', preyed on travellers along the Scottish coast from his cave near Galloway. From this lair, during the reign of James I of Scotland, legend has it that Sawney Beane waylaid, robbed and murdered over a thousand victims. His cave, a system of underground passages, again according to legend, was the setting for an orgy of cannibalism in which his wife and children also indulged. But there is no real certainty that the family ever existed.

Caves also provide ready-made graves, and there is always a chance that a body hidden in a rocky tomb will remain undiscovered. Eugene Aram, a celebrated eighteenth-century murderer, hid his victim in a Yorkshire cave where it remained for fourteen years before being found. Aram ran a school at Knaresborough for which he received esteem while maintaining a secret life of crime.

In due course Aram's greed took control, and with the help of Richard Houseman he plotted to rob a local tradesman who had acquired a large dowry from his wife. On 7 February 1744 Aram and Houseman waylaid Daniel Clark, killed him with a pick-axe and robbed him of £200. They bundled up their victim's body and hid it in near-by St Robert's cave, where but for a trick of fate it would have stayed hidden for a very long while.

Aram fled from the scene of his crime, deserting his job and family, to live first in Nottingham and then in London. In 1758 a body thought to be that of the long-missing Daniel Clark was found at Knaresborough. Thinking that his secret had been uncovered, Houseman made an immediate confession to murder and implicated Aram in the crime. The remains which had triggered off this admission proved not to be those of Clark, for when Houseman led officials to St Robert's Cave the body of his victim — now reduced to a skeleton — lay where he and Aram had left it fourteen years previously.

Aram, who had been recognized by chance in the streets of Kings Lynn, was arrested and quickly brought to trial. Houseman became a witness for the Crown and Aram, confined in York Castle, wrote poetry and prepared his defence. He claimed that the skeleton found in the cave might have been the bones of a religious martyr or saint. The trial jury paid scant attention to this argument and found Aram guilty. On the eve of his execution in August 1759 the condemned man cut his wrists, and the next day was dragged half dead to the scaffold to be finished off by the hangman. Eugene Aram became a figure of much fable and romance, and his skull was displayed in the museum of the Royal College of Surgeons as an object of anatomical curiosity. He was a scholar of some note, and his peers were perplexed that such a man could turn to murder. In his biography of Aram, Lord Lytton described his crime as belonging to 'those startling paradoxes which the poetry of all countries, and especially of our own, has always delighted to contemplate and examine'.

The story of another Eugen also merited a footnote in criminal history. Eugen Weidmann achieved the distinction of being the subject of the last public execution in France in 1939. He had been convicted of robbery and murder, on

Eugene Aram batters his victim to death at Knaresborough

one occasion using tactics reminiscent of the infamous Landru. He used a newspaper advertisement for a nurse-companion to lure Jeannine Keller, a Strasbourg girl, to Paris. With promises of a job on the Riviera, he drove her south to Barbizon on the edge of the Forest of Fontainebleau. He walked her to an isolated spot in the woods where he strangled her and hid the body in one of the caves for which the region is noted.

Cellars, with their underground, tomb-like character, are possibly the most fitting locations for murder. Those who use them perhaps do so out of some primitive urge to retreat from the reality of daylight in order to indulge in secret pursuits. One such individual was Joe Kallinger, a Philadelphia shoemaker, whose obsession led him to dig a cellar under one of his properties. Certainly, when his mind turned to violence his instinct was to go underground. Joseph Kallinger believed he could correct his behaviour by fitting wedges

in his shoes. By this means he thought he could adjust the angle of his feet to harmonize with the functioning of his brain. The power of his orthopaedic experiments was such that he believed he could solve not only his own problems but also those of the world. This turned out to be the lesser of Kallinger's delusions.

Kallinger's early behaviour was simply eccentric, such as filling his house with junk — second-hand electrical parts from old TV sets and vacuum cleaners which he thought would come in useful. Then in 1967 he moved his wife and six children to a new home in East Sterner Street. By this time he had taken on the management of his father's shoemaking business, and appeared to be making a good living. However, this was also the time when he began to hallucinate, receiving commands from both God and the Devil.

Fearing that he was being spied on, and that he was under threat, Kallinger turned his house into something of a fortress, putting bars over the windows and maintaining a nightly vigil to ward off intruders. He called his home 'Joe Kallinger's Castle'.

In 1969 Kallinger bought another house in near-by East Hagert Street. This was to be his own secret refuge — an extension to his castle. With help from his children he dug a twenty-foot hole in the basement as his personal retreat. It was here in 1972 that he tortured his children by burning them, acts for which he was sent to hospital. Psychiatric opinion at the time was that he was probably suffering from paranoid schizophrenia and belonged in hospital. Instead he was put on probation and returned to his family.

During the early 1970s Joe Kallinger had regular hallucinations. He believed God had ordered him to destroy mankind: 'to kill with a butcher's knife every man, woman and child and infant on the face of the earth'. For this purpose he enrolled his twelve-year-old son Michael. During 1973 and 1974 father and son committed several robberies, and theft soon turned to murder. On 7 July 1974 they abducted a boy from a recreation centre in Philadelphia and took him to a disused factory where he was sexually mutilated and murdered. On 28 July Kallinger took his fourteen-year-old son Joey, ostensibly for adventure, to the flooded basement of some derelict buildings. With Michael in attendance, Kallinger drowned his own son, and later reported him missing.

The fact that Kallinger had taken out life insurance on his young son totalling $69,000 led the police to the firm conclusion that he had murdered the boy. They were unable to press home a charge, though, and Kallinger and Michael continued with their criminal acts. After a series of four break-ins, where they meted out terror but desisted from killing, they entered a house in Leonia, New Jersey, on 8 January 1975 when nemesis finally caught up with Joe Kallinger.

They tied up the occupants of the house while they roamed about and discussed what to do. Finally, Kallinger took down to the basement a 22-year-old nurse who had unexpectedly called on a friend in the house. He ordered her to perform an unspeakable mutilation on one of the captive men. When she refused he killed her in a frenzy of stabbing.

When the Kallingers fled from the house Joe discarded his blood-stained shirt and tie. These were found by an alert resident who promptly reported the discovery to the police. Within nine days Kallinger and his son were under arrest. They were charged with kidnapping, robbery and assault and Joe, eventually, with murder. Both were identified by some of those they had assaulted, and Michael was sent to an institution for the rehabilitation of delinquents.

Joe Kallinger was tried for burglary and robbery in September 1975, and despite defence pleas that he did not know right from wrong, was convicted. Psychiatric evidence was given that he was schizophrenic and paranoid and might have been pushed over into a psychotic state by the effects of glue sniffing. Joe testified that he had communicated directly with God, a claim which added little support to his cause. The judge called him 'an evil man ... utterly vile and depraved' and sentenced him to a minimum of thirty years' imprisonment.

While awaiting trial for the murder of the nurse in Leonia, Kallinger became obsessed with religion and added dreams of the Devil to his other fantasies. At his trial in 1976 he had convulsions in court, foamed at the mouth and chanted in an incomprehensible language. His counsel described him as 'totally crazy', and defence psychiatrists said he was psychotic. Prosecution experts believed that he was an anti-social personality, although not psychotic — in other words, that he was not mentally ill in a legal sense. The jury, in finding Kallinger guilty, agreed with the prosecution's views. He was sentenced to a minimum of forty-two years' imprisonment.

While in prison awaiting trial Kallinger was visited by Flora Rheta Schreiber, a professor at John Jay College of Criminal Justice in New York. She wrote a compelling book about Joe Kallinger called *The Shoemaker* which probed his early life and plotted his degeneration into psychosis. A watershed in the mental life of this adopted child was the sexual abuse he received at the hands of his parents. They led him to believe that he had been castrated so that he would be able to avoid the iniquities of sex. This response from his adoptive parents is held by some to have filled the boy with hostility and vindictiveness which were the seeds of his later murderous and sadistic acts.

Louise Peete's ideas for concealing her crimes did not include digging out an entirely new cellar. Her inclination was to extend the cellar that already existed in order to provide a place for the interment of one of her victims. She married three times between 1903 and 1915 and was three times divorced. That in itself was not so remarkable, but each husband committed suicide, one at least in circumstances which caused questions to be asked of the widow.

In 1920 Louise Peete, aged thirty-five and with a reputation for being an incorrigible liar, arrived in Los Angeles. There she rented accommodation in a large house in South Catalina Street owned by Jacob C. Denton, a wealthy widower. The neighbours thought that there was more to the relationship than that of tenant and landlord, but on 30 May Denton disappeared. Louise Peete stayed on in the house and assumed the role of owner. She sold some of the house contents, charged purchases to Denton's account and signed documents and cheques as 'Mrs J.C. Denton'. She held parties for her friends, sub-let the rooms and took in boarders. When Denton's relatives made inquiries as to his whereabouts they were told that he had gone into hiding. This was supported by a fantastic tale which Louise had dreamed up. She said that the old man had quarrelled with a woman who was 'Spanish-looking' and had drawn a knife. There was a struggle, as a result of which

Denton lost part of his arm due to a knife-wound. Because of the humiliating circumstances in which he had sustained the injury Denton had gone into hiding and authorized Louise to act for him. She said he laid his good hand on hers when she signed cheques for him, thus making the signature legal!

Visitors to the house were impressed by an extension to the cellar which Louise had ordered to be built. This, she explained, was to accommodate some of Denton's personal effects. A large quantity of earth heaped up on the cellar floor also excited attention, but this was to be used on the garden, said Louise. Denton's continued disappearance, in addition to the strange happenings in his house, led to a police investigation. In September 1920 the missing man's body was found in the cellar — he had been shot in the back of the neck. Louise Peete was tried for his murder and sentenced to life imprisonment. She regained her freedom on parole in 1939 and was put under the care of Arthur and Margaret Logan who had visited her while she was in prison.

The Logans were an elderly couple who lived at Pacific Palisades. They took Louise Peete into their home and she immediately set out to repay their kindness by fleecing them of their money. She tried to secure a half-share in their property by means of a joint lease, and sought to dispatch Mr Logan to a psychiatric hospital.

Louise was leading a double life at this time, for unknown to the Logans she had remarried in 1944. Her husband, elderly Lee Judson, had no inkling of her past history and seemed content to live in a hotel and be visited occasionally by his wife. On 30 May Margaret Logan disappeared, and in the following month Louise succeeded in committing Arthur Logan to a hospital for the insane where he died a few months later. A familiar pattern was now repeated. Louise Peete took over the Logans' house, signing cheques and selling furniture as she saw fit. She also moved her husband into their new home. Again, following the previous sequence of events in Los Angeles, the police grew suspicious about Mrs Logan's disappearance and made inquiries at Pacific Palisades. The house lacked a cellar but the missing woman's body was found buried in the garden — she too had been shot in the back of the neck.

For the second time in her sixty-one years

Louise Peete was charged with murder. Poor Lee Judson, shocked by the revelation of his wife's criminal history, committed suicide. Thus all four of Louise's husbands had been driven to self-destruction. Found guilty of murder and sentenced to death, Louise waited for the appeals that would keep her out of the gas chamber. Twice her execution was postponed, but finally, on 11 April 1947, she died in San Quentin's gas chamber, the second woman in Californian history to be so executed. She told the prison officials, 'There will be no screaming or hysterics,' and she was true to her word.

(1, 56, 84, 126, 209, 226, 233, 234, 269, 279, 334, 382, 409, 435, 464, 465, 502, 619, 714, 733, 762, 787, 843, MWW)

BATHROOMS

'The damned snakes didn't work. I'm going to drown her.'

Robert James (1935)

Of all the rooms in a house, the bathroom and kitchen are the best equipped to meet the requirements of murder. The bathtub itself provides a convenient vessel for drowning the victim, with the possibility of contriving an appearance of accidental death. Moreover, the bather, relaxed both physically and mentally by the warm soapy embrace of the water, least expects violence. The victim's very nakedness adds to his vulnerability, as does his sitting or lying position — it is certainly not a situation offering much advantage in trying to fight off an attacker.

The bath as an instrument with which to effect murder cannot be mentioned without reference to George Joseph Smith, the 'Brides in the Bath' murderer who was hanged at Maidstone in 1915 for the murder of three wives by drowning them in their bath. It is perhaps worth noting the simplicity of his method, which was adopted by Terrence Milligan and Robert James whose stories are told later in this article. Smith's technique was dramatically outlined by the great pathologist Sir Bernard Spilsbury in notes made by Sir William Willcox: 'right hand on head of woman. Left forearm of assailant beneath both knees. Left forearm of assailant suddenly raised while right hand is pressed down on

George Joseph Smith — The Brides in the Bath Murderer

head of woman. Then the trunk of body slides down towards the foot end of the bath, the head being submerged in water.' He might have said 'Voilà!' Once the victim is off guard and lying within the rounded, water-filled confines of the traditional bathtub, the murderer's task is simple. The victim's flesh might squeak against the porcelain, but swift movement disarms a struggle and the noise of quick drowning is minimal.

Apart from the activities of G. J. Smith, probably the most famous murder in the bath was that of Jean-Paul Marat, the French Revolutionary, in July 1793. Charlotte Corday, a 25-year-old supporter of the Girondins, the right-wing republican party ousted by Robespierre, came to Paris intent on murder. Her targets were either Robespierre himself or Jean-Paul Marat, a member of the National Assembly and idol of the working classes.

Corday gained admittance to Marat's apart-ment, where he was taking a bath in a tub fitted with a cover through which his head and shoulders protruded. This arrangement, as Alan Brock neatly described it in his *Casebook of Crime*, 'preserved the propriety of the interview, but, by ensuring the immobility of the bather, must have materially assisted her in the delivery of the stroke with the table knife that ended his life'. Charlotte Corday stabbed Marat through the heart, his lifeblood drained into the bath water and she herself was seized, to be put to the guillotine four days later.

The bath has also been used to simulate accidental drowning following murder procured by other means. Kenneth Barlow, the insulin poisoner, tried this procedure on his wife in their home at Bradford in 1957. Another advantage of the bath with its connection of a waste pipe to the house drains is that it provides a useful sluice for the murderer who chooses to dismember his victim. Fred Thorn, New York City's 'Jigsaw Murderer' of 1897, and his accomplice Augusta Nack, lured their victim to an empty house where they first shot him and then, having put his body in the bath, cut his throat. The corpse was dismembered and the parcelled-up portions were thrown into New York harbour. The blood and detritus of dismemberment were flushed out of the bath and, so the murderers believed, into the drains. Regrettably for them, the house was not connected to a main drainage system, and the bathwater merely flowed into a soakaway beside the house which quickly overflowed with bloody water. This crimson pool attracted attention, and the murderous pair were brought to account. Ironically, perhaps, their victim, a masseur by the name of Willie Guldensuppe, worked in one of New York's Turkish baths.

One of G. J. Smith's heirs was a young Canadian, Terrence Milligan, who had a high IQ of 135 but failed to lie convincingly. Police were called to his apartment in Toronto on the evening of 11 June 1967 after he had reported the death of his wife. When officers arrived at the apartment off Eglinton Avenue in the eastern part of the city, they found nineteen-year-old Jane Milligan dead in the bath. She was sitting with her back to the taps in about twelve inches of water. A mains radio with a lead trailing to an electric socket in the living-room lay immersed in the water beside her.

Milligan seemed remarkably calm about the

sudden death of the young wife to whom he had been married less than a year. Much was made of his wife's dangerous habit of placing the radio on a precarious position on the edge of the bath. It was curious, to say the least, that the instrument had been set up with an extension lead running into the living-room when it could have been operated more easily using its normal lead from an outlet in the bathroom itself. If this looked contrived, the fact that Milligan stood to gain $30,000 from a double indemnity insurance policy on his wife's life certainly fuelled suspicion. Added to this was a neighbour's statement that the couple frequently quarrelled and had a noisy row on the day of the accident — a day on which the neighbour also heard the unmistakable bathroom noise of wet flesh squeaking against the side of the bath.

Whatever the suspicions of the police amounted to, they were nullified by the pathologist's report which stated that Jane Milligan had died of asphyxia probably due to electrocution. Milligan's light-hearted behaviour raised a few eyebrows, and when some of his workmates were questioned it appeared that on numerous occasions he had referred to his wife's dangerous habit of taking the radio into the bathroom. Although the body had been buried, the major organs had been preserved, and medical examination of these suggested that drowning, not electrocution, was the real cause of death. Furthermore, hitherto unmentioned bruises to the face and body came to light.

The police decided to search Milligan's belongings at his uncle's farm on Prince Edward Island, which he had visited after his wife's death. There they found a copy of *The Doomsters* by Ross MacDonald, which was a story of a person killed when a mains radio was thrown into the bathtub. At the inquest on Jane Milligan's death on 27 July 1967 a verdict was returned of 'Homicide at the hands of her husband.' Terrence Milligan was arrested and charged with non-capital murder.

Experiments at police headquarters on the bathtub removed from the Milligan apartment proved that the radio could not be balanced on the edge of the bath. Moreover, a policewoman volunteer sat with her back to the taps, and in twelve inches of water demonstrated that accidental drowning was not possible. At Milligan's trial in May 1968 it was shown that he

drowned his wife and simulated accidental death by electrocution by throwing the radio into the water. When he was first questioned by the police Milligan said he touched his wife when he found her to see if she was still alive. The detective remarked that he must have received an electric shock, but Milligan replied that he must have first switched off the current by pulling out the plug. With a callousness reminiscent of George Joseph Smith, Milligan told a cemetery official with whom he was negotiating for his wife's burial plot, 'It is probably better than she deserves.' Milligan was convicted of non-capital murder and sentenced to life imprisonment.

Another murderer who resorted to the bathroom was Robert James, whose real name was James Lisemba, and who achieved notoriety as much for the murder method that failed as for the one which succeeded. His wife Mary has been described as the victim of one of America's most bizarre murders. On 5 August 1935 Robert James, at that time a successful barber's shop proprietor in Los Angeles, telephoned the police from his home at La Canada to say that he had found his pregnant wife dead in the garden of their bungalow.

Officers at the scene saw 25-year-old Mary James lying face down in a shallow lily pond — apparently drowned in six inches of water. The medical examiner noticed that the woman's left leg was grotesquely swollen. An insect bite was postulated as a cause, and it was supposed that she had become dizzy and fallen headlong into the pond. It was concluded that her death was accidental.

Several weeks later Robert James received a modest pay-out from the insurance company for his wife's accident, and there matters might have rested but for an impetuous act which drew attention to himself. He accosted a woman in the street outside his barber's shop and made a lewd suggestion which she reported to the police. James was fined for his uncivil behaviour, but he stimulated the interest of the police who began discreet inquiries into his background.

James's past proved to be somewhat colourful. He was born in Alabama and worked as a cotton boiler before taking up barbering. He married in 1921, but his wife left him, claiming that he tortured her. His second marriage ended in divorce, and the third in disaster when his wife Winona, allegedly suffering dizzy spells following a car accident, was found drowned in the bathtub. James prepared his murderous path by insuring his victims, and in Winona's case collected $14,000. His fourth wife, Helen, was more astute. She told him, 'I don't believe in insurance. People who have it always die of something strange.' James was a sado-masochist who liked to be whipped by his partners, but also enjoyed inflicting pain on them. Helen wisely separated from him.

During their inquiries detectives came across Charles Hope, who had worked as a barber for James. A search of Hope's apartment revealed a receipt from one Snake Joe Houtenbrink of Long Beach for the sale of two rattlesnakes in July 1935. Snake Joe recalled making the sale of the two snakes named Lethal and Lightnin' for 75 cents per pound. He also remembered Hope returning them within two weeks muttering that they didn't work, and buying them back at half price!

When interviewed by the police Hope readily told his sordid tale of murder, although he was quick to absolve himself. He said that James had offered him $100 to find a pair of snakes, as he wanted them to bite the wife of a friend who was proving a nuisance to her husband. After two false starts, Hope turned up at La Canada with Lethal and Lightnin' and James passed him off as a doctor. Mary James prepared dinner, and during the meal 'Dr. Hope referred to her pregnancy and commented that she did not look well. He advised her not to have the baby; 'It could kill you,' he said. Alarmed by this observation and displaying frightening gullibility, Mary agreed to have an abortion there and then!

She swallowed a bottle of whisky, the anaesthetic prescribed by the 'doctor', and once she had collapsed in a drunken state the two men stripped her and put the body on the kitchen table. A box containing the two rattlesnakes was brought in and the lid pushed back sufficiently to insert Mary's foot. James and his henchman then retired to the garage to have a few drinks and await developments. Checks were made on the victim periodically, and although her leg was badly swollen from several bites, she was still alive. Commenting, 'The damned snakes didn't work,' James announced, 'I'm going to drown her.' He helped her down from the kitchen table and, recovering now from her alcoholic stupor, she complained that she didn't hurt where she

expected. She hobbled about on her painfully swollen leg while her indulgent husband filled the bath, telling her that the water would relieve her pain.

Once she was sitting in the water-filled bath James, after the style perfected by the 'Brides in the Bath' murderer, pulled her legs up out of the bath so that she slid down under the water and quickly drowned. He removed her dripping body, which he carefully dried and dressed in her normal clothes. Then with Hope's help he carried her to the garden and arranged the corpse so that she appeared to have sprawled face down into the lily pond.

Armed with Hope's account of murder at La Canada, the police went in search of James, and found him in a motel room where his latest lover was busily whipping him. His trial for murder was distinguished by the testimony of Charles Hope, who turned State's Evidence, and by the sinister presence of Lethal and Lightnin'. Hope was sentenced to life imprisonment and James was given the death sentence. For four years he remained in San Quentin, where he was nicknamed 'Rattlesnake', while various appeals were heard. He languished for a further three years in Los Angeles County Jail, where on 1 May 1942, all legal appeals exhausted, he was the last man to be legally hanged in California. Subsequent executions were carried out in the gas chamber.

The advent of polythene sheeting made the task of dismemberment somewhat easier for the murderer, and the resultant segments could be readily bagged up for disposal. Prior to the widespread use of plastic, the murderer intent on cutting up his victim could always make use of the bath to minimize the inevitable mess. This was the procedure adopted by James Joseph Keenan when he disposed of his wife in their Lanarkshire home in 1969.

On 24 March 1969, a railway permanent-way inspector found a parcel on the Aberdeen to Edinburgh track just outside Edinburgh. He reported it to a railway patrolman, suggesting that the package possibly contained a dead cat. Consternation followed when the parcel was found to contain a female human leg still encased in a nylon stocking. The same day the other leg was found in a parcel spotted lying in a river at Balerno, a village some four miles away. The pathologist who examined these grim relics judged that the victim of violence was a well-nourished woman aged between thirty and forty, and probably a brunette.

A massive inquiry was begun to identify the victim by checking all missing or unaccounted-for women. At that time 668 women were on missing-persons lists throughout the UK. A painstaking process of elimination was started, and all au pair girls, students, army wives and hospital patients in the area were also checked. Parallel inquiries were conducted on the pieces of blanket, string and other materials used to wrap the legs. Senior police officers appealed through press and television for anyone with information or suspicions about a missing neighbour or acquaintance to come forward.

On 26 March 35-year-old James Joseph Keenan — known to his workmates as 'Tarzan' on account of his body-building activities — reported that his wife was missing from their home in Lanark. Twenty-nine-year-old Elizabeth Keenan had left home some six days previously following a domestic disagreement. Their fourteen-month-old baby was being looked after by his mother-in-law, who knew that her daughter had left home. The incident had the appearance of a fairly ordinary domestic tiff, and beyond appealing to Mrs Keenan to report her whereabouts to the police for the purpose of eliminating her from their murder inquiry, the authorities did not immediately take any other action.

As a follow-up to the elimination routine, detectives asked Keenan if they could have a pair of his wife's shoes. He raised no objections, and murder-hunt detectives became excited when forensic scientists reported that the shoes fitted the amputated limbs. More specimens of Mrs Keenan's shoes were requested, and while asking for these it was decided to show her mother-in-law a piece of the blanket which had been used as wrapping for the legs. She recognized it immediately.

On 30 April, in a copse about a mile from Keenan's home, a headless torso wrapped in a blanket was found by some tinkers. The abdomen bore an abdominal scar consistent with an operation that Elizabeth Keenan was known to have undergone. Finally, matching of fingerprints made from the withered hands of the torso with impressions taken from the house confirmed the identification. Keenan's house was examined, and the bathroom came under special scrutiny. There was powerful evidence of cleaning powder having been used extensively on the bath and washbasin, and the U-bend in the waste outlet from the bath gave a positive reaction to a test for blood, as did the panel in front of the bath.

By now James Keenan had been arrested and charged with murder. He made a statement in which he said he killed his wife with an axe following a quarrel. He cut the body up in the bath with a hacksaw, and wrapped the four portions in bits torn from a blanket. With the sawn-up segments of his wife's corpse lying in the boot of his car, he drove his child to his mother-in-law's house before embarking on a journey to distribute the parcels around the countryside. Keenan showed police officers where he had left the head in a heavily wooded area near Carnwath — it was still readily identifiable.

James Keenan pleaded guilty at his trial for murder, and was sentenced to life imprisonment. In this case, as in so many murder stories, there was a touch of irony. The spark which ignited the quarrel leading to Elizabeth Keenan's murder by her husband was a disagreement over their baby's bath routine. *(1, 22, 29, 37, 55, 96, 104, 120, 126, 222, 235, 246, 365, 397, 398, 440, 530, 549, 618, 680, 697, 703, 770, 792, 1036, MWW)*

BEACHES

'If one wants to get away with murder one has to jolly well keep one's wits about one. It's the same way with suicide.'

Starr Faithfull (1931)

A number of murderers have entertained the idea that the sea will work in their favour by sweeping up their victims from a deserted beach to swallow them in its depths. Unfortunately, the fickle nature of tides often prevents the sea acting in this way, and a body may appear to have been carried away only to be cast up at another spot. Perversely, beaches are the places where the sea often gives up its dead, the murdered among them.

Sandy beaches also provide convenient material for burial. Unlike digging a hole in earth, sand has no distinctive sub-soil to give away a grave's location, and the effects of wind and tide cover up the surface disturbance. The problem with this otherwise perfect medium for secret burial is that once the body has been put into the hole and covered over, there is always a great deal of spoil left over. Not that this bothered William A. Hightower, murderer of a priest in San Francisco in 1921. He made such a good job of burying his victim on Salada Beach that the authorities could not find the missing man's grave without help from his murderer. Hightower marked the grave with a scarf so that he could triumphantly reveal its location to the police 'because of my civic duty', as he put it.

A secluded beach at night also offers the intending murderer that degree of seclusion which he looks for to commit his act and cloak his escape. The same attractions of darkness and seclusion makes beaches suitable places for casual sex, and in seaside towns may be included in a prostitute's beat for those reasons. Nineteen-year-old Beatrice Vera Aanhuizen lived in Woodstock near Cape Town, and on 18 March 1933 finished up on a beach near the Grand Parade as a murder victim.

She was seen in the company of two men at about 10.50 p.m. in the vicinity of Grand Parade, and next morning her body was found less than fifty yards from the esplanade. The upper part of her body was covered with a mound of sand from which her legs protruded in a grotesque fashion. The position in which the corpse was found was reflected in the newspaper headlines of 'Beach Pyramid Murder'.

The girl's clothing had been badly torn, and the medical examiner determined from bruises around the neck that she had been strangled. She was probably still conscious when the sand was heaped over her. Her wrist-watch had stopped at 11.30 — a mere forty minutes after she had last been seen alive — and her handbag was missing. Footmarks in the sand had been virtually washed away by the encroaching sea, but sufficient remained to indicate that a violent struggle had taken place some eight or more yards from the spot where the body was found.

The murderer's reason for building a sand pyramid over his victim probably stemmed from a wish to conceal the body. The fact that the legs protruded may have been due to haste, and fear that he would be interrupted. It was thought that burial under sand was in any case an afterthought following failure of the tide to sweep the body out to sea. The men seen with the dead prostitute in Grand Parade were traced and interviewed, but no arrest was made. A suggestion that the murderer was a sailor from a Portuguese naval ship docked in Cape Town Harbour also came to nothing. The murder remains unsolved, and apart from highlighting the vulnerability of prostitutes also shows that sand and sea are unreliable elements for the disposal of a body.

So-called beach murders are usually cases in which the victim has been killed elsewhere and subsequently dumped on a beach in the hope that the sea will remove it. This was certainly the thinking which led to Wilma Montesi's body being carried to an Italian beach. Unfortunately for those involved in her death, the tides merely cast her up on another part of the coastline, to precipitate one of the greatest post-war scandals.

Geography of the Montesi scandal

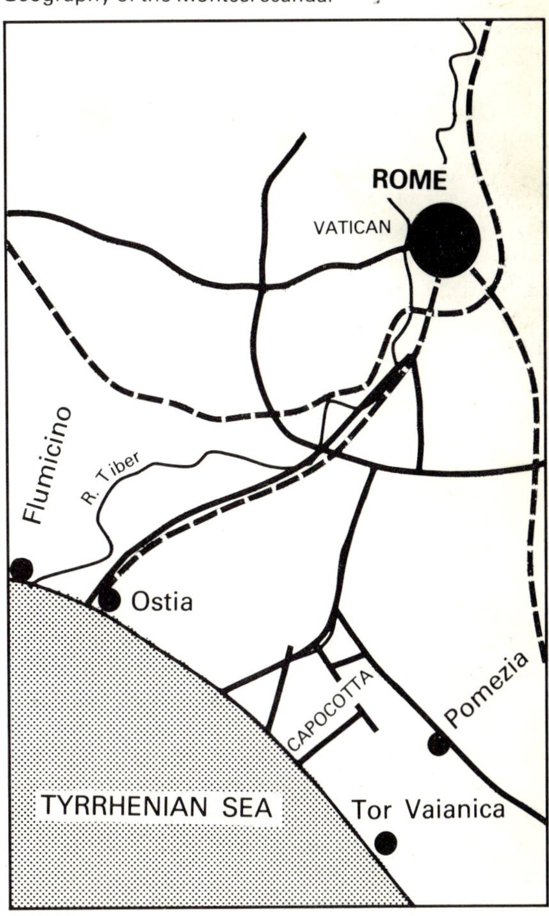

Wilma Montesi, the 21-year-old daughter of an Italian carpenter, left her parents' home on 9 April 1953 bound for the lido at Ostia. She disappeared for thirty-six hours until her dead body was found on the beach at Tor Vaianica, fifteen miles south of Rome. Clad only in her slip, she lay half in and half out of the water with the waves gently lapping around her face.

The immediate official reaction was that she had fainted while paddling at Ostia and drowned, her body being carried down the coast to the spot where it was found. The fact that her outer clothes were missing was not judged serious, but her lack of a suspender belt struck a curious note. An official explanaton was that this garment had simply been washed from her body by the action of the sea. Another account — and one which carried the first whiff of the scandal to come — appeared in a newspaper report of the girl's death which said the missing suspender belt had been brought to Rome headquarters by carrier pigeons, which in Italian are called *piccioni viaggiatori*. The Foreign Minister of the day was one Attilio Piccioni. The dead girl's parents discounted the suicide theory of their daughter's death, saying that she was a well-balanced girl who was to be married to a police officer. The police then decided on accidental death, despite the fact that Wilma Montesi was known to be a strong swimmer. Wilma was duly buried, and her tombstone recorded that she was a 'pure creature of rare beauty'.

A few months later, in January 1954, the newspaper *Attualità* published a story by Silvano Muto in which it was stated that Wilma Montesi had taken part in a sex party in Rome where she died from taking drugs. No names were mentioned, but it was reported that some of the prominent socialites at the party had dumped the dead girl's body on the beach.

Public uproar followed publication of this story, and there were demands for the case to be reopened. Silvano Muto was charged with spreading false and alarming news likely to prejudice public order, and was instructed to appear before a tribunal. Now the real storm broke. The charge of experimenting with drugs at a sex party was repeated, and Muto offered to produce witnesses who would testify how Wilma Montesi died. The party had taken place at a hunting-lodge called Capocotta, which was located near the coast about three miles north of Tor Vaianica. The lodge was used by a shooting syndicate whose secretary was Ugo Montagna, a Sicilian with the title Marquis of San Bartolomeo.

Two young actresses, one of whom was recovering from barbiturate poisoning, gave evidence at the tribunal. It was alleged that Ugo Montagna and Piero Piccioni (son of the Foreign Minister) had conspired in a cover-up of Montesi's death. There were also allegations tying in the head of Rome's Security Police with the conspiracy.

The immediate effects of these allegations (apart from a field day for newspaper reporters) were the resignations of Foreign Minister Piccioni and the head of the Security Police. Ugo Montagna sued Silvano Muto for libel, and in a further sensational development it was alleged that one of the actresses who testified at the tribunal had written to her landlady divulging the name of Wilma Montesi's murderer. The recipient of this letter after reading its contents had as requested returned it to the sender. The letter was eventually found in a postal sorting-office and rushed to the tribunal where it was read out — Piero Piccioni was named as the murderer.

Two years later, in 1957, Piccioni, a 35-year-old jazz musician, was tried for the culpable homicide of Wilma Montesi. Ugo Montagna and Rome's Chief of Police were charged with complicity. The trial took place not in Rome (the scene of so much sensation) but in Venice, where the risk of public demonstration was thought to be less likely.

Much of the evidence was medical, and the experts disagreed on virtually everything. There were arguments about how long the body had been in the water, whether the girl was pregnant or not and whether there were traces of drugs. The three principal experts settled one each for murder, accident and suicide. The only points of agreement that finally emerged were that the dead girl had drowned, and that she was a virgin.

Many witnesses were paraded through the court, and there were some undignified scuffles in the dock. In the end Piero Piccioni produced an alibi for the night in question, and this was corroborated by reliable witnesses. The Public Prosecutor settled for a statement in which he declared that Wilma Montesi had gone to the beach at Ostia with a man, but there was no evidence to show that he was Piccioni. After retiring for seven hours, the three judges acquitted Piccioni and dropped the charges against the other two accused.

The dead girl on the beach had created a political upheaval and a scandal of national proportions, but despite all the furore, her parents were not granted the assurance of knowing how she had died.

A girl on another beach in an earlier age created a similar scandal. Starr Faithfull, an intriguing girl with a reputation for unusual sexual appetites, met a mysterious death at the age of twenty-five in New York in 1931. She took her name from her stepfather, Stanley E. Faithfull, a retired chemist who married her mother and settled in New York's Greenwich Village in the early 1920s.

Starr was seduced at the tender age of eleven by a distant relative who assisted his advances with the use of ether. The girl became an ether addict, and in her teens was regarded as a singularly erotic sexual partner. She developed masochistic tendencies, and kept a diary containing the initials of her lovers, against which she recorded their performance ratings.

On the insistence of her parents Starr sought psychiatric treatment, but this appeared to have little effect on her behaviour. Her reputation for being a teaser and driving her lovers out of their wits grew steadily after a hotel incident in which she was found being given a beating by an angry and frustrated ship's cook she had picked up in a bar.

She made two trips to England, and on board the transatlantic liner *Franconia* made a passionate and embarrassing bid for the affections of the ship's surgeon. On 29 May 1931 she boarded the liner at New York in pursuit of her prey, but the surgeon decided to make himself unavailable. Not to be thwarted, Starr hid on board the vessel until after she sailed, only to be discovered and put ashore from a tug after creating a furious scene.

The following day she wrote to her surgeon threatening to commit suicide. This was followed by a letter of apology, and in a third letter, written on 4 June, she said, 'If one wants to get away with murder one has to jolly well keep one's wits about one. It's the same way with suicide. If I don't watch out I will wake up in a psychopathic ward, but I intend to watch out and accomplish my end this time. No ether, allonal or window jumping. I don't want to be maimed. I want oblivion. If there is an after life it would be a dirty trick — but I'm sure fifty million priests ARE wrong. That is one of the things one *knows*.' She disappeared on the same day, and on 8 June her body was washed up on Long Beach. She was presumed to have drowned, but her body was bruised and there was evidence of sex having taken place prior to death.

The discovery of Starr's body made a sensational story in itself, but when the cremation ceremony was rudely interrupted by officials demanding the body for a further post-mortem, the newspapers had a field day. It was thought at first that she had committed suicide by throwing herself in the sea — she was seen on board the *Mauretania* on 5 June. After the second autopsy thoughts turned to murder, and the District Attorney went so far as to claim knowledge of who had killed her, and boasted of making arrests within thirty-six hours.

The fact that two grains of veronal were found in Starr's body, and that her lungs were filled with sand, added weight to the murder theory. It was suggested that she had been murdered in a fit of violence by a lover whom she had teased beyond endurance. Perhaps under the influence of drugs she had been forcibly held under water at Long Beach until she drowned. This was borne out by the ingested sand, and also by the severe bruising to the upper part of her body.

Her stepfather, Stanley E. Faithfull, rejected the notion of suicide, and firmly proclaimed that Starr had been murdered. He gradually leaked information to the press about her childhood molestation by a relative, and quoted intimate details of Starr's love-life from her 'Mein Book', as she called her diary. Writing about the case in *The Aspirin Age*, Morris Markey, a reporter for the *New Yorker*, posed the question of why, if this unpremeditated murder occurred on Friday night, the body had not been discovered by the crowds of trippers who swarmed to Long Beach at the weekend. He also supplied the answer. The murderer owed his prolonged getaway time to the movement of the tides. As Markey pointed out, the bodies of bathers drowned close inshore often drift out to sea and are not borne back again for several days.

That the sea often inconveniently gives up its dead was demonstrated by Australia's famous Shark Arm case in 1935, in which the tattooed forearm of a murder victim was disgorged by a captive shark in an aquarium. A less dramatic but equally forceful demonstration of the sea's unreliability as far as the disposal of corpses is concerned occurred in April 1954, when the body of an unidentified woman was washed up at Godinot Bay, about thirty-five miles from Port of Spain on the island of Trinidad. The body was that of a blonde white woman aged between twenty-five and thirty-five. She had been strangled and bundled up in a jute sack weighted with sand. A medallion and charm bracelet were found in the sack, and the body was taken to San Fernando for post-mortem examination.

Death had been caused by strangulation, but doctors were horrified to note that the jugular vein had been cut in order to drain off the blood, and a six-inch incision had been made in the abdomen so that the body could be eviscerated. While the body was under examination Dr Singh, a Port of Spain physician, turned up unannounced. He borrowed some text-books from the pathologist, but there was a feeling that this was not his true purpose.

When this slightly strange occurrence was reported to the police detectives investigating the murder decided to question Dr Singh. Dr Dalip Lutchmie Persad Singh was the son of Hindu parents in Trinidad. He had studied in Scotland and returned home with a German girl whom he married. Inge was a qualified optician, with a practice which included Trinidad, and several other Caribbean islands. Dr Singh himself had a medical practice in Port of Spain.

Dr Singh told detectives that he last saw his wife on 6 April when she walked out on him. He indicated that this was fairly commonplace as his wife suffered occasional depression, and he had not felt the need to report her missing. When he heard that a body had been washed ashore he visited the mortuary at San Fernando to see it for himself. He had not at that time recognized the corpse as his wife, but the detectives confirmed the identification, and the doctor said the medallion and charm bracelet belonged to Inge.

Sufficient circumstantial evidence built up to throw suspicion on Singh, and he was charged with murdering his wife. An anonymous pencilled note sent to the police proclaiming, 'I sorry for Dr Singh he is not guilty', and written on notepaper of a distinctive kind used only by the doctor merely hardened the attitudes against him.

At his trial in November 1954 Dr Singh's fiercely jealous nature was revealed. He had tried to hire a private detective three weeks before the murder to shadow his wife, whom he believed to be committing adultery with a man in St Vincent. He met his wife at the airport on 6 April, and Singh's houseboy testified that the doctor and his wife quarrelled that evening. There was a heated argument, and later the doctor's car was heard being driven out of the garage and returning in the small hours of the morning. Singh made some perfunctory excuse for his wife's absence at breakfast.

Apparently at the beginning of April Dr Singh had borrowed a book on surgery from a doctor colleague which gave a detailed description of removing the viscera from a body. It was presumed that the body washed up at Godinot Bay had been eviscerated in order to prevent it floating. This, coupled with the sand packed around the corpse in the jute sack, should have ensured its sinking to the bottom of the ocean. But the sea has a habit of giving up its dead, as Dr Singh discovered to his cost. He was found guilty of murder, and suffered execution on 28 June 1955.
(64, 193, 207, 299, 570, 873, 1055)

BEDROOMS

'Sometimes Playmates get killed.'
Paul Snider (1980)

If the parlour is the forum of a home's domestic affairs, the bedroom is the centre of its passions. It is a place both for rest and for the pursuit of love. But when the quiet, orderly rhythm of domesticity is overturned by stronger passions the bedroom can become a place of violence and murder.

The symbolic significance of the bedroom as the place of sexual fulfilment often concentrates the erupting forces of violence. In July 1983 Vicki Morgan, a 31-year-old former model, was found dead in her Los Angeles apartment. She had created a sensation by lodging a palimony claim of $11 million against Alfred Bloomingdale, the department store magnate whose mistress she had been for twelve years. The claim was rejected in court, but revelations continued about sex parties with top U.S. government officials, and Vicki Morgan was negotiating book and television rights for the story of her life. Her partially clad body was found sprawled across the bed in her apartment — a baseball bat lay near by, testifying to the beating which had ended her life. In September 1984, Marvin Pancoast received a sentence of twenty-five years to life for killing Vicki Morgan.

The bedroom is also used as a place of safe retreat. It is a haven for sleep, yet it is the sleeping state which places a person at the peak of vulnerability. This is a condition which many murderers have exploited to full advantage in order to eliminate their victims without fear of confrontation or resistance.

In December 1982 Muriel McCullough, a former beauty queen, was convicted of the contract killing of her husband. She hired the services of James Collingwood to murder her wealthy industrialist husband at their home in Ailsworth near Peterborough in what came to be called the 'Kiss of Death' case. On the evening of the murder Mrs McCullough telephoned home to make sure her husband was alone. Later the hired killer entered the house and shot the victim dead while he lay asleep. Mrs McCullough's motive was one of the oldest in the history of crime — elimination.

Rafael Escobedo, a 29-year-old playboy, entertained the same notion in respect of his millionaire parents-in-law, the Marqués and Marquesa del Urquijo. They disapproved of his marriage to their daughter, and cut off the couple financially. In August 1980 the Urquijos were found dead in the beds at their luxurious house in the Somosauguas suburb of Madrid. The Marqués had a bullet in his brain and his wife was shot twice in the throat. Intriguing aspects of the incident highlighted the knowledge and stealth of the killer. The dogs in the house were undisturbed, a living-in maid slept through the whole affair and the burglar alarm had been deactivated. The fact that nothing was stolen strengthened the theory that the deaths had been due to a plan of elimination. Rafael Escobedo came under suspicion, and when ammunition was found in his possession which firearms experts said matched bullets found at the murder scene, he confessed.

Spanish newspapers called Escobedo's trial 'The murder case of the century.' He retracted his earlier confession, which he said had been made under duress, and to the embarrassment of the police the vital ballistics evidence disappeared before the trial began. Nevertheless, Escobedo was convicted of murder and sentenced to fifty-three years' imprisonment.

The murderous attack made on Joseph Yablonski in 1969 was planned to take full advantage of the victim's helplessness while he was asleep. He was a man marked down for assassination by hired killers who proposed to carry out their work at least risk to themselves. They waited until their victim and his family had settled down for the night in their darkened house before striking.

In 1969 Joseph Yablonski, a long-serving officer of the US Union of Mine Workers (UMW), stood against W.A. (Tony) Boyle, the incumbent president, in the campaign to elect a new Union President. Disillusionment with the existing leadership had grown following a mining tragedy the previous year in West Virginia in which seventy-eight men lost their lives. Yablonski represented a new force which many miners wanted in order to bring change to their Union's affairs.

A bitterly fought election campaign was won by Tony Boyle on 9 December, but there were immediate allegations of voting irregularities and misappropriation of funds. Yablonski accused Boyle of embezzling millions of dollars from the UMW to finance his campaign, and of using more than five hundred union employees as election workers.

The advent of Christmas broke up the dispute, and the contestants retired to their homes and families to enjoy the festive spirit. Joseph Yablonski lived with his wife Margaret and 25-year-old daughter Charlotte in Clarksville, Pennsylvania. Their house was a hundred years old, three-storey, fieldstone property overlooking Bridge Street. It was set in spacious grounds, and the nearest neighbour was some four hundred yards distant.

On 29 December three men met in a bar in Clarksville to discuss a proposed murder. They considered a contract for $5,000 to kill a labour leader called Yablonski. Late the following evening the trio drank a few beers before driving up to the Yablonski house. They waited for the lights to go out, and consumed more beer to allow time for the occupants to settle down to sleep. The plan was to enter the house and kill Joseph Yablonski. If anyone else got in the way he was to be eliminated — the job called for no witnesses. About 1.15 a.m. the three men approached the house. They cut the telephone wires and disabled the family's cars. An entry was forced, and having first removed their shoes, the intruders padded quietly along to the bedrooms, guns in hands.

After several days' silence from their parents, the married sons became worried, and on 5 January 1970 an appalling discovery was made. Joseph Yablonski, his wife and daughter were all found dead in their bedrooms from gunshot wounds in the head. Coming so quickly after the UMW election, the deaths were seen as a continuation of the bitter aftermath of the campaign.

On 7 January police picked up a man named Aubron Wayne Martin following a routine complaint about his behaviour. He was un-cooperative and known to have a criminal record. His 'Personal Telephone Directory' contained numbers for 'Paul' and 'Claude'. These led to Paul Gilly and Claude Vealey, who were questioned by FBI agents. On 20 January Vealey admitted, 'Me, Martin and Gilly, all three of us went in the house.' He gave a full account of three murders, and confessed to reloading Martin's .38 revolver and shooting Joseph Yablonski. He was 'gurgling', he said. 'I wanted to make sure he died.' The three men named as the Yablonski killers were tried separately. Vealey in his evidence said that he and Martin refused to go in the house unless Gilly went too; then, as he put it, 'All three of us would be equally guilty.' Vealey pleaded guilty to all three murder charges.

At Martin's trial in November 1971 the evidence showed that Gilly recruited the con-tract killers, who had practised for their mission by shooting at targets set up in the basement of his house. The prosecutor de-scribed Gilly as 'the captain of the ship', and referred scathingly to Martin as 'a baby-faced killer' and Vealey as 'have gun, will travel'. Martin was convicted of first-degree murder, as was Gilly as his trial in February 1972. Juries in both cases recommended the death sentence.

As the result of an intensive FBI investiga-tion, three murder charges were brought against UMW officials for complicity in the Yablonski murders. In March 1972 Tony Boyle was convicted on thirteen counts of embezzling Union funds. He was sentenced to two five-year terms of imprisonment, fined $130,000 and ordered to repay nearly $50,000 to the Union treasury. In May a Washington court overturned Boyle's 1969 election win on the grounds that he had perpetrated a massive fraud.

Finally, in September 1973, the probe into the power struggle among the UMW leader-ship led to Boyle's arrest on a charge of conspiring to murder. He was tried in March 1974, four years after the Yablonski killings. It was alleged that he had said to his confeder-ates, 'We are in a fight. Yablonski ought to be killed or done away with.' This 'act of vengean-ce', as it was called, resulted in Boyle's convic-tion for first-degree murder.

The seclusion and intimacy of the bedroom provide a frequent backdrop for the enact-ment of jealous passion leading to violence. Jean Harris, for example, drove for five hours to confront her lover in his bedroom before killing him. Paul Snider chose the bedroom as the location for the jealous destruction of his wife and the termination of his own life. Dorothy Ruth Hoogstraten, a beautiful eight-een-year-old girl with a nice nature and few pretensions, worked as a waitress in a Dairy Queen restaurant in Vancouver. She lived with her mother, and was training to be a secretary. In 1978 suave, 24-year-old hustler and pimp Paul Snider was a customer at the Dairy Queen, where he spotted Dorothy and began to date her.

Snider, a sleazy entrepreneur with expensive tastes, saw in this young woman possibilities for exploitation. He remarked to a friend at the time, 'That girl could make me a lot of money.' He dazzled Dorothy with visits to night clubs and expensive restaurants, and tried to talk her into posing nude for *Playboy* magazine. The girl succumbed to his persuasion, and her mother reluctantly gave permission. In August 1978 the couple flew to Los Angeles for photo tests, and within a year Dorothy's natural talents had made her a centrefold Playmate-of-the-Month.

The new Playmate changed her name to Dorothy Stratten and began to climb the ladder of success in the film and TV world. Snider's hunch had paid off, and he became her business manager and then, in June 1979, her husband. In 1980 Dorothy was chosen by *Playboy* magazine as Playmate-of-the-year and she really began to go places, with high earning potential and moving in exclusive Beverly Hills social circles.

Snider did not have the talent or appeal to match his wife, and he grew resentful of her success. It was clear that the former waitress was destined for a considerable career, and was even spoken of as a successor to Marilyn Monroe. The couple argued frequently, and they separated. Snider stayed in their Los Angeles bungalow and Dorothy went to New York to make a film. When she returned she asked Snider for a divorce, as she had fallen in love with film director Peter Bogdanovitch. Her husband proved difficult; he bullied and cajoled, and hired a private detective to track her movements.

Paul Snider asked Dorothy to visit him at the bungalow on 14 August 1980 to discuss the divorce. She arrived at midday, and when Snider's current girl-friend let herself into the house she found the bedroom door closed and discreetly left, believing that the couple were perhaps making it up. Several hours later a doctor who shared the bungalow accommodation with Snider returned home. He knocked on the bedroom door, and when there was no answer walked in.

Dorothy Stratten lay naked and dead sprawled on the bed. Her face had been torn away by a shotgun blast and Snider lay on the floor, also dead from a shotgun wound. It seemed clear that Snider murdered his wife because he was convinced he was going to lose a valuable asset. Indeed, he had bought a 12-bore shotgun shortly before, and had remarked to a photographer acquaintance, 'Sometimes Playmates get killed.'

Having killed Dorothy out of jealousy in the cruellest possible way by destroying her beauty, he turned the gun on himself.

Dorothy Stratten, who died six months short of her twenty-first birthday, was genuinely mourned by the many friends she had made in Hollywood. Two years after her death she

Israel Lipski hides under the bed on which Miriam Angel lays dead

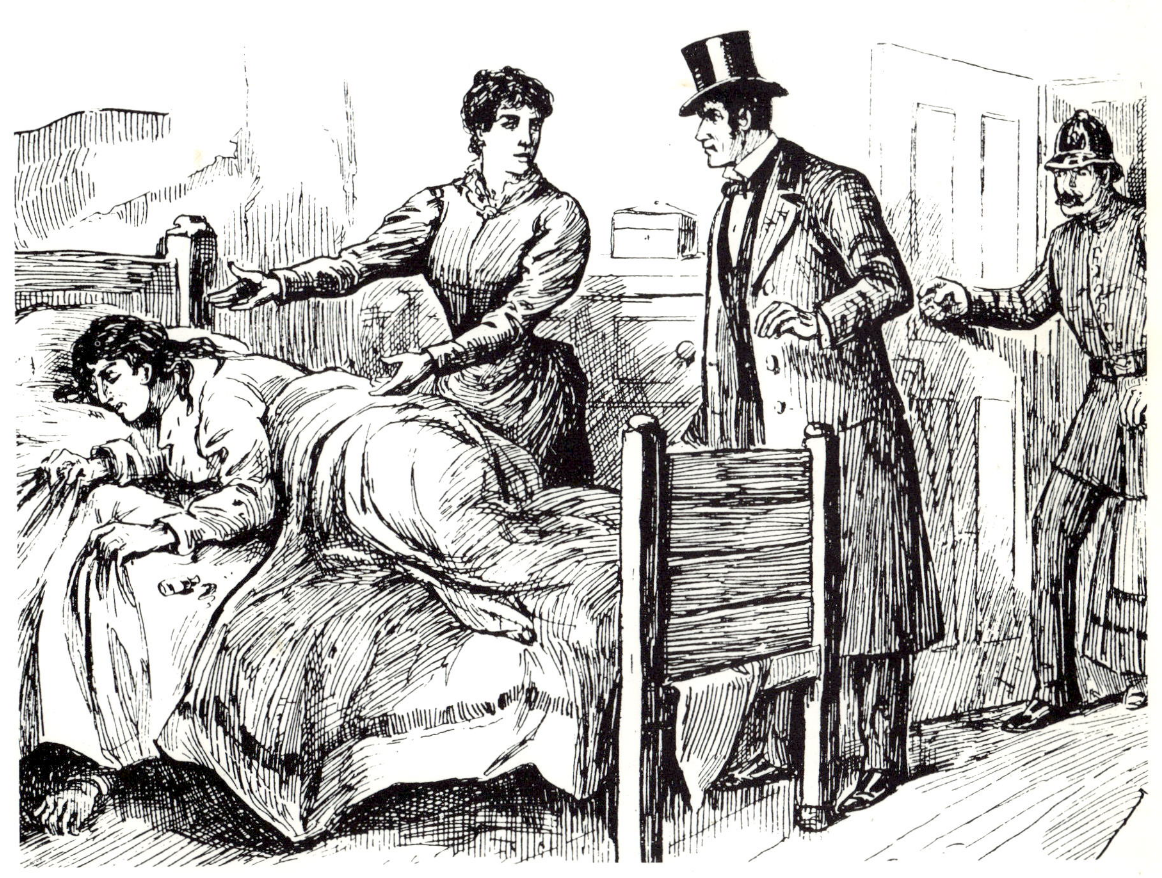

became something of a legend, and the subject of several films and a book.

A surge of 'sudden passion' on looking through a window at a woman in bed was the motive attributed to Israel Lipski in the killing of Miriam Angel. Lipski, aged twenty-two, lived alone in the attic at 16 Batty Street in London's East End. He was a tenant in a three-storey house which provided accommodation for fifteen persons, all Polish Jews.

On 28 June 1887 a relative called at the house to visit Miriam Angel, a young married woman who occupied a room on the second floor. The girl, who was six months pregnant, was found lying on her bed. She was dead, and the yellow froth exuding from her mouth was later proved to be nitric acid. A doctor was called, and a search made of the room to locate the container of the corrosive poison. When the bed was moved Israel Lipski was found lying insensible beneath it — he too had marks of corrosive poisoning around his mouth, but he was revived.

Lipski alleged that two workmen had murdered Miriam Angel and then attacked him, leaving him for dead. He was not believed, and he was charged with murder. Although the dead woman had been covered with a blanket, the position of the body suggested a sexual assault, and there were hints that the murderer had committed necrophilia.

Lipski was tried before Mr Justice James Fitzjames Stephen in July 1887. The judge summed up against the accused, and spoke of the influence of temptation when the victim was viewed through the window of her room, which was accessible from the stairs used by other tenants. Israel Lipski was found guilty, and he made a full confession the day before he was hanged at Newgate Prison.

The case was a curious one which exercised Victorian commentators on the position of Jewish immigrants in the capital city of England. There was a widely held view that Lipski was innocent, and much debate about the judge's summing up. One of the most unusual features of the case was the use of nitric acid as a poison to procure murder.

Fire was the method used to destroy Mickey Hughes, whose favourite pastime was provoking his wife. He frequently argued with his wife Francine, and was in the habit of hitting her while their three children looked on. They quarrelled on 9 March 1977, and the argu-

ment was about Francine's school classes. Mickey beat her and tore up her books. For good measure, he made her burn the remains in the garden incinerator.

Having vented his spleen, Hughes retired to bed, leaving Francine to give the children their supper. After they had eaten she told them to get ready to go out. While they waited obediently at the car, Francine took a can of gasoline and emptied it on the floor around the bed on which her husband lay sleeping. With the house in flames, she drove to the police station in the near-by town of Mason. She was hysterical. 'I did it! I did it!', she shouted. The screw cap of the gasoline container was still in her hand.

By the time the police and fire department had arrived at 1079 Grove Street, Dansville, Michigan, Mickey Hughes was dead. Francine was charged with first-degree murder. The prosecution case at her trial was simple. It was claimed that she had set the house on fire, using gasoline to fuel the flames, and burned her husband to death. Moreover, she had confessed her crime by going straight to the police.

The defence argued that Francine had been provoked beyond endurance over a long period of ill-treatment by her husband. The children said their father beat her up about once a week, and her friends testified that she was frequently seen with bruises and cuts on her face. The police had been called to the house earlier on the day of the fire during the course of the Hughes' bitter argument. Mickey Hughes told his wife, 'If you ever call the police again, I'm going to kill you.'

The incident with her books was too much for Francine. She brooded over what had happened and heard a voice telling her, 'Do it! Do it!' Finally she snapped, and acting under irresistible impulse, killed her husband. the defence argued that the act was not premeditated but was carried out while she was temporarily insane. The jury thought so too, and acquitted her of the murder charge. (28, 304, 328, 673, 667, 895, 949, *mw*)

BOATS

'This is the axe that done it.'
Thomas Mead Chambers Bram (1896)

Like trains in motion, boats at sea provide a closed environment for murder. Victim and murderer are trapped together in a kind of space capsule which is a closed community with limited places to hide and few escape routes. Emotions are heightened and actions dramatized in cramped quarters presided over by the captain, whose authority may be seriously challenged only by the crime of mutiny.

The explosive nature of resentment against the captain's authority at sea was illustrated by the *Veronica* mutineers in 1902. Five murders resulted, and the bodies of the captain and first officer were thrown overboard. Another celebrated murder at sea was that of actress Gay Gibson, who disappeared from her cabin on the *Durban Castle* in 1947. With its sexual overtones, this was the sort of murder which might have happened anywhere, but James Camb, a ship's steward, saw his opportunity and believed that the cabin porthole with the ocean racing beneath provided a convenient way to dispose of his victim's body. Like the *Veronica* mutineers, he was to find that this apparent attraction of murder at sea in no way prevented the law from convicting him. The body may be an encumbrance to the murderer but its absence is no obstacle to justice.

Piracy is a time-honoured scourge of the sea, and in recent times has taken on new criminal dimensions. The boarding of Michael Crocker's yacht off Port of Spain in 1982 which ended in his murder by a lone assailant was an example of the resurgence of piracy in the Caribbean. Press reports have mentioned the loss of many lives in the area as the result of organized crime squabbles. Boats smuggling consignments of drugs fall prey to pirates operating from well-armed, high-powered motor launches, and fortunes exchange hands in encounters where loss of life is incidental. Marine archaeological expeditions and pleasure yachtsmen have also found themselves innocent targets of this modern pirate menace.

Michael Crocker and his American-born wife, Tricia, sold their business in England to realize a dream of sailing around the world in their 33-foot yacht *Nyn*. They reached the

The *Nyn* moored on the river Thames

Caribbean in early 1982, and took on board two friends, David and Christine Drake. Unable to find a place in the crowded marina at Port of Spain in Trinidad, they moored just outside the harbour in the Gulf of Paria.

At about 11.00 p.m. on 30 January 1982 Tricia and Mike Crocker were awakened by the sound of scuffling. They leapt out of bed and saw David Drake staggering about with blood streaming from his neck; he was supported by his wife Christine, and behind them was a bearded intruder brandishing a knife. The man demanded money, and Christine gave him all she had. He threatened to finish off David Drake if they went near him, and he then ordered the two women to tie up Michael Crocker. As instructed, they tied his hands and feet, and during the pleading and arguing that ensued the intruder cut off a piece of spare rope and made a noose around Crocker's neck. Tricia's shouts for help were drowned by the noise of the generators on near-by boats.

What happened next was blurred in the memories of those who took part. The women pleaded with the intruder to release the rope around Crocker's neck. His reply was, 'He'll have to die.' At some stage Tricia jumped overboard to swim for help, and then the assailant — with Crocker lying limp on the deck — made off in a dinghy. David and Christine Drake also leapt overboard, and swam a quarter of a mile to the shore to seek assistance. When help arrived Michael Crocker was found to be dead and David Drake was sent to hospital, where he later recovered from his wounds.

The dinghy used by the murderer had been

stolen from the Guyanese vessel *Haladi*, which was anchored in the harbour waiting to off-load a cargo of rice. Police inquiries elicited from the captain that he had sacked one of his seamen, 29-year-old Allan Henry, for taking the ship's dinghy without permission. The captain told Henry he must pay for the missing dinghy, and when he refused dismissed him and instructed the man to return to Guyana.

Allan Henry was arrested in Guyana on 4 February and put in an identification line-up attended by the Drakes. They had no hesitation in picking him out as the intruder who had boarded the *Nyn*. He denied being on board the Crockers' boat, but the dead man's watch was found among his possessions.

Henry was extradited to Trinidad, where he stood trial for murder. His defence claimed the evidence was circumstantial, and suggested that the police identification parade was improperly conducted. The most damning evidence was the accused man's possession of Crocker's watch. His explanation that he had bought it from a 'Rasta' at Trinidad Airport on his way home to Guyana did not impress the jury, which found him guilty. He was sentenced to death, and remains in Death Row on an island which has not carried out capital punishment since 1976.

As a location for murder inspired by the familiarly domestic motive of jealousy, boats at sea have their disadvantages. Once he has committed his act, there is nowhere for the murderer to go except overboard or by absconding at the next port of call. Earl Leo Battice became caught up in a *ménage à trois* at sea, and after he had killed found there was no escape, even with the help of his captain.

The 12,000-ton schooner *Kingsway* was berthed at Port Amboy, New Jersey, in July 1926, loading cargo for her crossing to the African west coast. It was to prove an ill-fated journey. Captain Chase sailed with Frederick Mortimer, a veteran first mate, and a crew of mixed nationalities, including winchman Waldemar Karl Badke. Captain Chase was taken ill during the first leg of the journey, and was put ashore at Pensacola in Florida. His place was taken by Captain F.E. Lawry — much to the disappointment of Mortimer, who had ambitions of being given his first command. The voyage resumed, and at the next port of call, San Juan in Puerto Rico, the ship's cook absconded. His place in the galley was taken by

Earl Leo Battice, who insisted that his wife Lucia accompanied him. Captain Lawry agreed, for no better reason than his knowledge that he could not sail without a cook. The *Kingsway's* crew now contained all the characters whose emotions were to determine the outcome of a dramatic voyage.

From the start the crew resented Captain Lawry, whom they regarded as an interloper out of sympathy for the first mate who had been overlooked for the captaincy. But the real trouble began when the new cook's wife took a fancy to the well-muscled Badke. Within the limited confines of the ship this liaison was bound to lead to disaster. At first Earl Battice confronted Badke, but the big German easily resisted his threats. Then he threatened to kill Lucia if she did not break off the relationship, and when this failed he appealed to Captain Lawry.

The already unpopular captain ordered Badke to desist, and told him to stay clear of the galley. These instructions were contemptuously disobeyed, and Badke carried on with Lucia in front of the sniggering crew and her humiliated husband. On the surface Battice appeared to have been bested and to have swallowed his pride, but underneath he was simmering with rage.

On 4 February 1927 Battice asked to borrow Captain Lawry's flashlight. His intention was to surprise Badke and Lucia in the galley storeroom. He successfully interrupted their love-making in the dark, and in the ensuing scuffle Badke fled from the scene. Attracted by the noise, the crew found Lucia lying among sacks of potatoes. She was still alive, but had severe knife wounds in her throat and body. Battice was arrested by the captain and put in irons. He offered no protest, and Lucia died from her wounds six days later.

The murder victim's body was buried at sea and Captain Lawry's attempt to put Battice ashore was prevented by the authorities, who told him he must return to the USA with his captive. The ship acquired a new cook in the form of a West African called Cedgo, whose presence was to add another dimension to the strange journey of the *Kingsway*. Battice meanwhile saw his chance to escape at Accra and made off for the interior, although he was promptly recaptured and returned to the ship, no doubt to Captain Lawry's considerable disappointment.

During the voyage across the Atlantic several of the crew were taken ill. Grumbles became complaints and these were quickly turned into accusations of poisoning directed at Cedgo, chiefly by Badke. When the first mate, Mortimer, was taken ill and died the gloom which settled over the *Kingsway* was complete. His body was taken from the seemingly accursed ship and buried in Barbados. It was later shown that the sailors had not been poisoned at all but were suffering the effects of scurvy.

On 20 August 1927 Captain Lawry brought his vessel into New York and handed the manacled Battice over to the police with his account of murder at sea. The one-time cook was convicted of second-degree murder and sentenced to ten years in prison.

One mode of escape for the murderer at sea is to take over the ship, thus compounding his felony with mutiny and conspiracy. This was the crime which occurred aboard the Boston schooner *Fairy* in 1820, and which provided one of those strange coincidences which enliven the study of crime. The event in itself was unremarkable save for the lack of a reasonable motive.

The *Fairy* was scheduled to sail to Europe with a cargo of timber under Captain Edward Selfridge, Thomas Paine Jenkins the mate, and four seamen. The tone of the voyage was set from the start when Jenkins had a row on the quayside with Charles Marchant, one of the crew. Marchant's resentment at being made to obey orders infected the other crew members. Soon after the vessel sailed, Marchant began to complain about the length of time he was made to stay at the helm, and seamen Sylvester Colson and John Hughes complained that their watches were too long.

During the night of 24 August 1820, after they had been at sea for only four days, Colson and Hughes were on deck together after Captain Selfridge had retired below. On the completion of his duty Hughes went below to call Marchant and Jenkins for the next watch. Marchant was at the helm when he settled down to sleep, and was still there, accompanied by Colson, when he next went on deck. In answer to his question as to the whereabouts of the mate, Marchant told him casually that both the mate and the captain had been killed and thrown overboard.

Hughes was aghast when he saw blood on Marchant's clothes and observed the violence

in the captain's cabin. There was no doubting the turn of events when Marchant and Colson began to prepare the ship for scuttling. They cut away the anchor, smashed the water casks and destroyed everything on deck. Ship's papers were also destroyed, and the late Captain Selfridge's effects were divided between them.

On 29 August the coast of Nova Scotia was sighted and the ship's boat was swung out ready for action. Marchant and Colson stowed their booty in trunks which were put into the boat and then they hacked holes in the *Fairy's* hull so that she would take on water and sink. As they pulled ashore a story was invented which all four men were supposed to use when they were questioned.

They landed at Cape Breton near Louisburg and the ringleaders related their story to the captain of an American vessel that was in harbour with a request to take them to Halifax. John Murray, who up to this point could do little apart from obeying the mutineers, found a way of detaching himself from their surveillance and spoke to Captain Hook. Having been informed about the real situation, Captain Hook lost no time in taking action. He arrested Marchant and notified the police, who promptly sent out a search party to retrieve Colson.

In due time Colson and Marchant were returned to Boston, where in November 1826 they were charged with revolt, piracy and murder. The two men were tried separately, but in each case the jury returned guilty verdicts and sentences of death were meted out. The motive which drove these two men to their crimes at sea was obscure. The prospects of gain were small, whereas the penalties for murdering the ship's captain and mate out of a sense of provocation were high.

Marchant committed suicide in his cell and Colson met his death at the hands of the hangman. The final indignity came with the handing over of his corpse to Dr John White Webster for the purpose of experimentation. Boston's *Columbian Sentinel* on 3 February 1827 reported that Colson's body was submitted to a powerful Galvanic battery by means of large pins inserted through the skin; 'The exhibition was, to us, astonishing; and gave a good test of the powerful effects of Galvanic experiments ... the leg was much agitated at every contact, and more than once thrown forward with

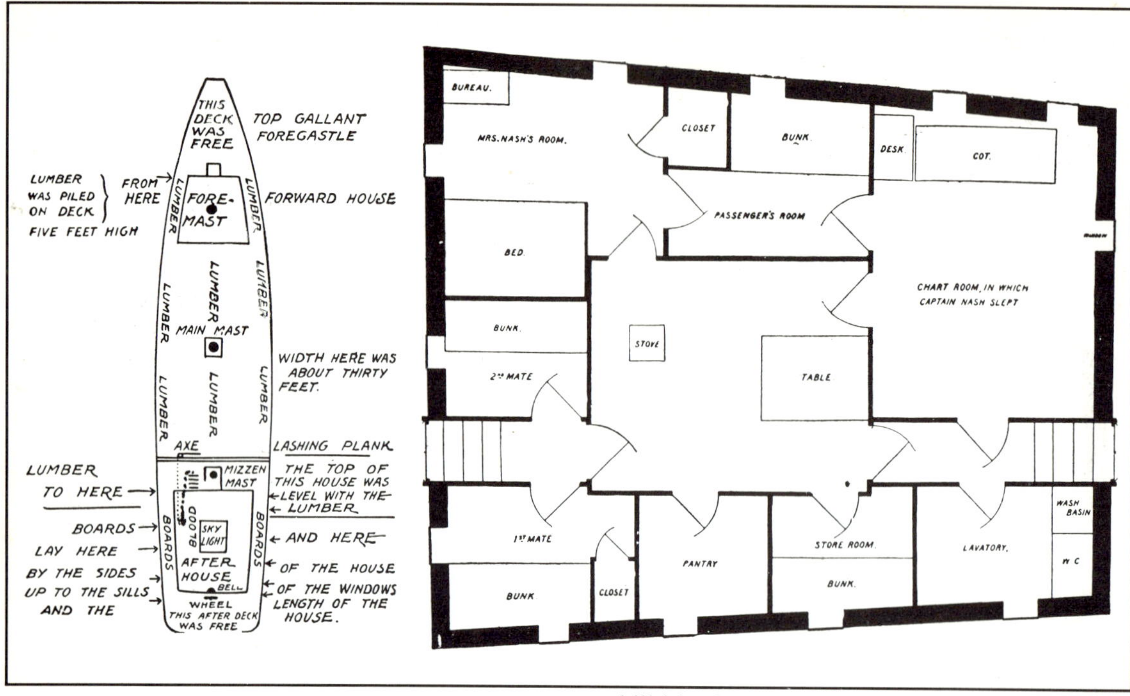

Deck plans of the *Herbert Fuller*

force and the toes moved briskly.' Whatever Dr Webster may have learned from this experiment, it did little to assist his own criminal ambitions when he murdered fellow-academic Dr George Parkman in 1850. Like Colson, he too felt the hangman's noose about his neck.

Murderous violence struck the crew of the *Herbert Fuller*, a sailing-vessel carrying a cargo of timber, when she was ten days out of Boston bound for Argentina. On the storm-tossed night of 13 July 1896, Lester Monks, the only passenger on board, thought he heard screams rising above the sound of the wind. Cautiously he made his way to the chartroom, where he discovered a scene of carnage. Captain Charles I. Nash lay on the floor, his life ebbing away, and his wife Laura lay dead on her bunk, where she had been hacked to pieces.

Monks raised the alarm and fetched the first mate, Thomas Mead Chambers Bram, who was reluctant at first to believe Monks's claim that the captain had been murdered. Bram's behaviour was strange from the start, for he refused to rouse the second mate, August Blomberg, on the grounds that he was leading the crew in mutiny. At this point Bram broke down sobbing, claiming that the crew planned to kill him because he had been hard on them. Shortly after this extraordinary episode it was discovered that Blomberg was also dead — his battered body with the head crushed was lying on his bunk.

Bram, now in command of the ship, found an axe lying on the deck and exclaimed excitedly, 'This is the axe that did it!' Despite attempts to stop him, he threw the blood-stained weapon overboard, chanting, 'This is the axe that done it. This is the axe that done it.' Bram's next move was to attempt to throw the bodies overboard. This was effectively resisted and, bereft of any authority, he could only acquiesce when his crew members turned the *Herbert Fuller* about and headed back to the mainland.

During the six days that it took to reach port, Bram attempted to pin the blame for the murders on a crewman called Charley Brown. Almost any accusation had credence at that time on the terror-filled boat, and Brown was put into irons. But the crewman was not prepared to be turned into a scapegoat — he told his fellow-sailors that while he was at the ship's helm on the night of the murders he saw Bram in the chartroom and heard the Captain's wife screaming. He had kept quiet about this, he explained, for fear of what Bram might do next. Before port was reached, Bram was accused of murder by the crew and chained to the mast.

Thomas Bram was tried for murder at Boston in December 1896. Former crew members testified that he had talked about seizing a ship after killing all the officers on board, so that he could commandeer the cargo and sell it for his own gain. He had also bragged about looting ships on which he had served. Bram's notions to be a pirate were well-substantiated, and vivid testimony as to his behaviour on the *Herbert Fuller* was sufficient to gain his conviction for murder. He was sentenced to be hanged.

Appeals were lodged and, on account of technical errors in the trial procedure, a retrial was ordered. This took place in March 1898 and Bram was again found guilty, although on this occasion he was sentenced to life imprisonment. The cause of the former first mate of the *Herbert Fuller* was championed by the thriller writer Mary Roberts Rhinehart, who believed him to be an innocent man. She wrote a mystery story called *The After House* in which murders of a ship's captain and his wife were committed by a character named 'Charley Jones'. This story was published in 1914, the author claiming that it was a protest against the conviction of Thomas Bram. She subsequently persuaded President Woodrow Wilson of the validity of her claim, and he was instrumental in pardoning Bram in 1919.

Two years previously, the *Herbert Fuller*, sailing under a new name, was torpedoed in the Mediterranean in a First World War naval action. History does not relate what happened to Charley Brown, whom Bram had accused of murder, but whom a Boston Grand Jury refused to indict. Bram became a successful business-man, and talked freely about the murders to anyone who would listen.

Violence at sea overtook the cruising vessel *Bluebelle* in the Caribbean in 1961. Captain Julian Harvey was rescued from the ship's dinghy on 13 November; the body of one of his passengers, a seven-year-old girl, lay in the bottom of the boat. Harvey appeared to be the sole survivor of the *Bluebelle*, which he said had caught fire and sunk fifty miles from Nassau in the Bahamas. His wife perished together with his passengers, Mr and Mrs Arthur Dupperrault and their three children.

A few days after Harvey was rescued, another survivor from the *Bluebelle* was found at sea supported on a raft. This was eleven-year-old Terry Jo Dupperrault, who claimed that Harvey had killed her parents and the other passengers, leaving her to fend for herself on the sinking ship.

Captain Harvey was given news of the girl's rescue while he was attending a Coast Guard inquiry into the loss of his vessel. He returned to his motel room in Miami, where he killed himself by opening his veins. It was discovered that Harvey had taken out a double-indemnity insurance policy on his wife worth $20,000 shortly before they sailed from Fort Lauderdale, Florida. The woman who perished on the *Bluebelle* was his second wife, his first having died in 1949 as the result of a mysterious car crash from which Harvey emerged without a scratch. Julian Harvey joined his second wife in a watery grave when his wish to be buried at sea was honoured by the prison authorities. *(1, 60, 167, 254, 369, 414, 486, 492, 561, 784, 868, 871, 887, 1040, MWW)*

BROTHELS

'It is no crime to kill a whore.'
Anon (1836)

As a profession prostitutes are particularly vulnerable to the predations of the sadistic murderer. The activities of Jack the Ripper in the last century and the Yorkshire Ripper in this show all too clearly what easy victims these women can be (see under ALLEYWAYS).

Murders of prostitutes usually occur in the alleys and dark corners of large cities — places where they take their customers for quiet anonymity. Only rarely do prostitutes fall victim to murder in brothels. Organized prostitution forsakes the grime of the street and offers service with a degree of comfort in a private room. There may be a madam directing negotiations, and more often than not other people, both prostitutes and clients, on the premises. The scope for murder is diminished, but occasionally passion, and frequently jealousy, precipitates fatal violence.

Julia Bulette was the popular madam in Virginia City's chief brothel in the 1860s. Catering for the demands of coal-miners, her parlour with its six girls was a place of ceaseless activity. As the most popular girl in town Julia led the Fourth of July parade, and her murder in January 1867 was treated as a local catastrophe. She was found dead from strangulation in a manner described at the time as 'foully murdered, and stiff and cold in her clotted gore'.

A huge crowd attended her funeral, and it was rumoured that upright matrons lurked behind closed shutters for fear that they would see their menfolk paying their respects to a fallen woman. Julia had been robbed, and several months after the murder a man was charged. To considerable public satisfaction John Millain, her convicted murderer, was hanged in April 1868.

Brothels in those times often had their rooms fitted with sliding panels so that hands could reach out and steal from a client's clothes while he was otherwise engaged. These 'panel-houses' gave brothels an even worse name than they enjoyed for their main activities, and vengeful passions were aroused.

Violence certainly overtook Helen Jewett, a beautiful young woman aged twenty-three, who had been turned out of her adopted home because of her promiscuity. She quickly slipped into what writers of the time called the *demi-monde* of New York in the 1830s. She was undoubtedly a forward lady, and maintained a considerable correspondence network with her lovers.

In 1834 she met by chance encounter in a Broadway theatre Richard P. Robinson, a man about town who worked as a clerk in the city. The two were drawn together in a stormy relationship. Robinson, who was described as a frequenter of 'every *maison de plaisir* in the city', merely added Helen to his string of girl-friends. Helen, despite her background as a lady of easy virtue, wanted more. She grew jealous of his other attachments, and on one occasion followed him from his office to a lodging house where she surprised him with one of his girl-friends. The two women fought like cats, and a bitter row followed.

Robinson decided to keep his distance from the volatile Helen but she pursued him with letters begging him to return to her. He relented, but toyed with her feelings by sending her anonymous letters chiding her about her morals. After another major quarrel he swore that he would never see her again. A year passed, and then in October 1835 they met again by chance and Helen learned that he was contemplating marriage to another

woman. She tried to coax him back to her embraces, and sought to strengthen her claims by taunting him about a rumour that he had poisoned a former girl-friend who died mysteriously. When she threatened to reveal his background to his intended bride tragedy was not far away.

In the spring of 1836 Robinson's marriage plans fell in ruins when his bride-to-be learned of his murky past. Whether or not Helen was responsible was not known, but she certainly carried the blame. She wrote to Robinson trying to patch up their various quarrels: 'Come and see me and tell me how we may renew the sweetness of our earlier acquaintance ....' He responded with an unsigned letter which advised her, 'Keep quiet until I come on Saturday night ....' Some time between 9 and 10 p.m. on 11 April 1836 Mrs Townsend, the proprietress of 41 Thomas Street, admitted Robinson into her house, whose occupants included Helen among its numerous *filles de joie*. The couple disappeared into Helen's room, and about 11 p.m. sent down for a bottle of champagne. About 2 p.m. when the house was quiet, the girl in the room opposite Helen's heard a thud followed by a moan. She peeped out of her door and saw a cloaked figure disappearing down the stairs. As this was not an unusual occurrence in Mrs Townsend's establishment, the girl returned to her bed and her partner.

At about 3 p.m. Mrs Townsend was awakened by a latecomer's knock to be let into the house. The proprietress decided to make a quick inspection of the premises and noted that the rear door was open. Moving upstairs, she found Helen's door on the latch, and when she pushed it open was overwhelmed by the thick black smoke issuing from the room. The alarm was raised and Helen was found lying on the floor near her bed. Her head was split open with a gaping wound, and her body was badly burned in places. It was plain that she had been murdered.

The murderer had obviously escaped through the back yard leaving his cloak behind as he scaled one fence, and a bloody hatchet when he climbed another. Robinson was immediately suspected. He had after all been admitted to the house by Mrs Townsend when he requested to see Helen. Police went to his lodgings in Dey Street to find him apparently sound asleep. When told about the murder he said, 'This is a bad business.' The verdict of the Coroner's court was unequivocal: 'It is the opinion of the jury, from the evidence submitted before them, that Helen Jewett came to her death by a blow or blows, inflicted on the head with a hatchet, by the hand of Richard P. Robinson.'

Robinson's trial for murder began in June 1836. The bloodstained axe was identified as a tool normally kept at the premises where he was employed as a clerk. The cloak found near the scene of the crime was of a type known as a Spanish cloak, and one that Robinson habitually wore. Despite his denials the garment was identified as his by a lady who had repaired it for him. His defence was based on a dubious alibi provided by a grocer who claimed that Robinson was at his shop until a late hour on the night of the murder. To the amazement of the court, the jury brought in a 'not guilty' verdict. Robinson accepted his freedom and went to Texas, where he later died. Allegations that the jury had been bribed were not substantiated. Officially, therefore, the murder of Helen Jewett, of whom the *New York Herald* said, 'She has seduced by her beauty and blandishments more young men than any known in the police records', remained unsolved. Few had any doubts that Robinson was the murderer, and one of his friends remarked, 'It is no crime to kill a whore.'

Mexican police investigating the disappearance of sixteen-year-old Maria Hernandez uncovered a trail which exposed the country's

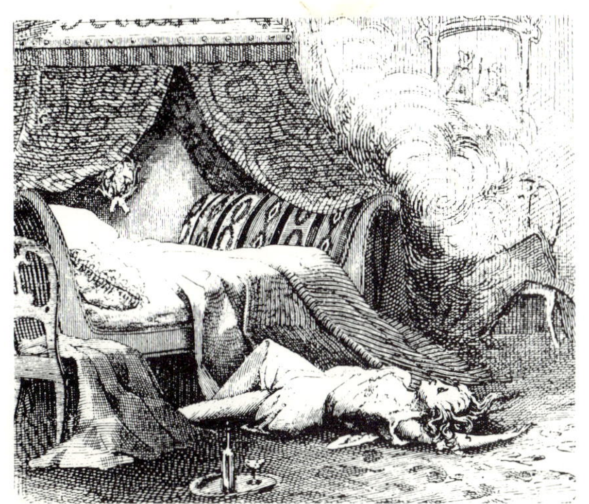

Helen Jewett lies murdered in her boudoir

worst mass murder. The young girl was the latest in a series of disappearances from the west coast province of Guadalajara. Maria was reported missing in December 1963 after she had gone to San Juan de los Lagos to meet a woman who had promised her a job as a maid. From her description, police thought this woman was the same person they suspected of enrolling young women to serve in brothels. She was traced to a house of ill-repute in San Juan de los Lagos where police surveillance was maintained. In due course Josefina Gutierrez was arrested, and her answers under interrogation proved valuable. She worked as a talent scout for the Gonzales sisters, who ran various brothels, including a remote establishment near the town of San Francisco del Rincon called Rancho El Ángel.

It appeared that Delfina and Maria de Jesus Gonzales had caught wind of the police investigation, for when officers arrived at Rancho El Ángel the place was under the charge of a 28-year-old prostitute. Approached by unmade roads, surrounded by a tall fence and with its entrance guarded, Rancho El Ángel proved to be something of a fortress. The prostitute guardian gave full co-operation to the police, who found thirteen girls, Maria Hernandez among them, locked up in various rooms.

Maria described how she had been forced into a brothel in San Juan de los Lagos, where she had been crudely initiated and later taken to Rancho El Ángel. The Gonzales sisters consistently ill-treated their girls until their spirit was broken. Some of them were suffering from venereal disease, and girls who became pregnant were beaten until they aborted. Drugs were also administered to keep the inmates subdued. Not surprisingly, many girls did not survive this treatment, and in any case those who faltered were simply killed.

The grounds of Rancho El Ángel were carefully dug, and the remains of eighty women and infants were discovered. The remains of eleven male corpses were also uncovered. A sideline of the brothel's proprietresses was to lure migratory workers returning from America into the embraces of their girls, and then kill them for their fat pay-packets.

Delfina and Maria de Jesus Gonzales had enjoyed connivance and protection at a high level, and once they were prised out of hiding a major inquiry was started. The deadly sisters

were convicted of murder and given forty-year prison sentences. The money which they had accumulated as ill-gotten gains was distributed among the relatives of their victims.
(207, 868, 915, 1028)

CAMPS AND CARAVANS

'It will be while the men are in camp.'
Thomas John Griffin (1867)

Camps and caravans make possible the 'ambush' murder. Lacking the security of permanent buildings, tents and mobile homes set in the isolation of scenic countryside can provide the robber with opportunity and the murderer with temptation.

Such an opportunity overtook three white brothers and their black companion, recent escapees from prison, who were roaming the back roads of Georgia bent on robbery. Travelling in a stolen car on 14 May 1973 along dusty roads near Donalsonville in Seminole County, they spotted a mobile home parked in a clearing approached by a dirt track among the cornfields.

George Dungee, the black member of the foursome, was left in the car ready for a quick getaway, while Carl and Billy Issacs and their half-brother, Wayne Coleman, approached the trailer belonging to Jerry and Mary Alday. To their surprise they found the door open and the trailer unoccupied. They began to turn over its contents, but when they saw a jeep approaching down the dirt road they panicked and, realizing that the jeep and its two occupants blocked the escape path to their own car, the burglars decided on confrontation. They held up Jerry Alday and his father Ned at gun-point and forced them into the trailer. Once inside, they robbed the two men of their personal possessions — money and rings — before deciding what to do next. The burglars realized that the Aldays could identify them. 'Tie them up,' said Carl. 'Let's blow 'em away.' suggested Wayne. Jerry Alday and his father were led away into one of the trailer's bedrooms and made to lie on the beds. While they lay helpless under the power of their captors, father and son were shot dead through the back of the head.

Hardly had the noise of the shots subsided when a tractor rolled up at the trailer driven by Jimmy Alday, who had been working in the near-by fields. He too was directed into the trailer at gun-point, where he was robbed and shot dead. As events unfolded, it seemed that the Alday family had a destiny with death, for the next one to arrive at the trailer was Mary, Jerry's wife, in her blue Chevrolet. She too was confronted by gunmen who forced her into the trailer. Closely following on this a pick-up arrived bearing Jerry's brother Shugie, and his uncle Aubrey. Apprehended at gun-point, they were led into the trailer's bedroom and dispatched with bullets next to their already dead relatives.

Surrounded by five dead members of her family, Mary was raped by Carl Issacs and then blindfolded before being abducted in the car driven by George Dungee. Followed by the others riding in the Alday car, Dungee headed north. They soon pulled off into some woods where Mary was again raped by Carl Issacs before being shot dead by Dungee. The four killers then made off in the stolen Alday car.

Exactly a week later, the four men were captured. The carnage in the trailer led to threats of a lynching party, but normal justice had its way. Billy Issacs, aged sixteen, agreed to testify as a prosecution witness in order to avoid a death sentence. He faced his brother Carl in court, and his evidence was shattering. Carl Issacs was convicted of murder in the first degree. Wayne Coleman and George Dungee were tried separately, and like Carl ended up with death sentences. Billy was sentenced to life imprisonment, and his three companions were put into Death Row cells. 'Too evil to be called animals' was the headline summing-up of a magazine report of the case.

An ambush of a different kind was masterminded by Thomas John Griffin in a celebrated Australian murder case. Griffin, aged thirty-five, an Irishman decorated in the Crimean War, arrived in Australia in 1856. He had taken advantage of a free passage offered to ex-soldiers to start a new life in the Antipodes. Griffin began well by marrying a girl he met on board ship, and when the couple reached Melbourne they set up a boarding house. But Griffin tired of this unexciting occupation and deserted it — and his wife too — in favour of the outdoor life. He enlisted in the New South Wales police, and by 1861 was Chief Constable at Brisbane.

The popular Irishman mixed well with the

right people and counted the Governor among his social circle. In 1863 Griffin was appointed Gold Commissioner and Chief Magistrate at Clermont. This was the peak of his attainments, for his popularity waned when he turned out to be an unfair and tyrannical magistrate. Following public complaints about his lack of fairness and inefficiency, Griffin was transferred to Rockhampton as Gold Commissioner in 1867.

These were the days of Australia's gold rush, and the mining district of Queensland attracted a considerable influx of prospectors. Clermont, some hundred miles west of the Mackenzie river, was one of the prospecting centres. The job of the Gold Commissioner was to buy the precious metal from the miners. On 27 October 1867, Griffin set out from Rockhampton with an armed police escort consisting of troopers John Power and Patrick Cahill carrying £4,000 in notes and coin. Their journey to Clermont was about two hundred miles, and they had to cross the Mackenzie river.

They reached the river crossing on 5 November and camped at a bush hotel run by a man called Bedford. At this point Griffin decided to return to Rockhampton with Bedford, leaving his two troopers to continue with their ten canvas bags of cash to Clermont. Having completed the last stage of his return trip by train, Griffin reached Rockhampton on 7 November. The next day the Gold Commissioner rushed into the office of the police inspector and asked if it was true that the gold escort had been killed. The dramatic news that Power and Cahill had been found dead in the bush was confirmed later the same day. Griffin dismissed the police theory of a daylight ambush by bushrangers, saying, 'It will never be done that way. If it is ever attempted it will be while the men are in camp — and coming on for daylight, when the man left on watch is likely to go to sleep.' Thus did Griffin sow the first seeds of suspicion against himself. First reports of the deaths stated that the two troopers had been poisoned, but again, Griffin dismissed this contemptuously. 'They are not poisoned; it's all a trumped-up yarn — a false report; they are shot, you'll see if they aren't.'

A small party was assembled to visit the scene of crime, and Griffin volunteered to drive the trap. He drove so recklessly that the doctor in the party ordered him to step down

as he would have them all killed. Once they reached the bodies of the dead men in scrubland several hundred yards from Bedford's hotel, it was plain that each trooper had been shot through the head. Shortly afterwards Griffin was arrested on suspicion of murder. He did not know that the numbers of the notes in the consignment of cash carried by the escort had been recorded, and with the careless bravado which he had shown throughout, he had on his arrival at Rockhampton on 7 November bought a round of drinks for his friends in the Commercial Hotel, for which he paid with a £1 note. This note was part of the consignment which he had stolen in order to pay off a debt, and later hidden in a tree stump.

Strong circumstantial evidence was brought against Griffin at his trial for murder in Rockhampton. The jury convicted him, and after the judge had passed sentence of death Griffin made a long, rambling speech protesting his innocence and referring to his war service. While in the condemned cell he tried to persuade the warders to aid his escape, or at least to get him some poison to finish his own life, in return for telling them the whereabouts of the money stolen from the gold escort. Asked if he had anything to confess while he stood on the scaffold, Griffin impatiently declined, telling the hangman, 'Go on. I am ready.'

An extraordinary sequel to the termination of Griffin's criminal career was the fear of the authorities that an attempt would be made to remove the head from his body after its interment. In order to prevent this another corpse was buried in the same grave on top of Griffin's coffin. Despite this precaution, Griffin's head was removed and the skull was displayed as a grisly trophy in the surgery of the doctor whose life Griffin had jeopardized by his dangerous driving.

Pleasure-seeking campers pitching their tents in quiet countryside have been unknowingly cast in the role of victims. Sir Jack Drummond, on holiday in Southern France with his wife and daughter in August 1952, parked his estate car on land adjoining a farm. When night fell the family undressed and made ready for bed, unaware that they were being observed by elderly Gaston Dominici, owner of near-by Grand'Terre farm. When Sir Jack realized that his family was being watched he remonstrated with the farmer, who shot him. Dominici then shot and bludgeoned Lady Drummond and her daughter, leaving their bodies close to the camp site. The alarm was raised early the following morning by one of Dominici's sons who found the dead girl's body.

The residents of Grand'Terre farm were under strong suspicion, and after prolonged interrogation one of the sons declared that his patriarchal father had committed the killings. Eventually Gaston Dominici confessed, saying that he had watched Lady Drummond undress and made advances to her when her husband intervened and a struggle ensued in which the Englishman was shot. After protracted criminal proceedings the 75-year-old farmer was found guilty of murder and sentenced to life imprisonment. An octogenarian, he died in 1960, having by that time been released from prison.

A camp site that was to become famous in headlines all round the world was located at Ayers Rock, the famous landmark in the central Australian desert. On 16 August 1980 Michael and Lindy Chamberlain set up their ridged-top tent near the perimeter fence of the camp site at Ayers Rock. The couple had driven there from their home in Mount Isa with their two sons aged six and four, and 9-week-old daughter Azaria. The Chamberlains pitched their tent about sixty feet from the camp site's barbecue area and just across the road from the ridge on which visitors perched to observe the changing colours on Ayers Rock at sunrise.

The following evening, after a day spent rambling and sight-seeing, the Chamberlains prepared to settle the children for the night. Baby Azaria lay in her carry-cot in the tent, the flap of which was unzipped. Lindy was preparing food in the barbecue area when she thought she heard a noise from the tent. She went over to investigate and in the darkness saw a dingo in the vicinity of the tent. She looked inside — Azaria was missing, and the infant's blankets had been scattered. 'The dingo's got my baby,' she shouted.

A search was made of the area, and as the news spread, three hundred campers with flashlights combed the area, but to no avail — Baby Azaria was missing. Dingoes had been seen around the camp site, and despite warnings to the contrary, visitors encouraged the

scavengers by feeding them. The distraught Chamberlain family packed up their gear and moved into a motel. They made a statement to the police, and on 18 August two dingoes and two dogs were shot by police and rangers in the Ayers Rock camp site. Michael and Lindy Chamberlain came to terms with their loss, supported by their membership of the Seventh Day Adventist Church. Michael said, 'My faith has allowed me to accept this tragic incident. I don't think they will find any sign of our little Azaria.'

Eight days after the disappearance of the baby, a tourist walking along the west side of Ayers Rock found a bundle of bloodstained clothing. Azaria's jumpsuit and singlet were discovered some three miles from the camp site where she went missing, and about twenty yards from a dingo lair. The jumpsuit was bloodstained around the collar, and the singlet had been turned inside out — there was no sign of the matinée jacket that had been wrapped around the infant when she was put into her cot. Strangely, in view of the suggestion that the baby had been carried off by a dingo, there were no hairs or saliva traces on the clothes, nor the pulled threads which might be expected to result from her being dragged through the scrub.

The whereabouts of the child's body remained a mystery and examination of the stomach contents of several dingoes shot dead near the camp site proved negative for human remains. Curiosity regarding the incident mounted, and theories of dingo behaviour abounded. The bereaved couple continued to declare their belief in God, but public opinion began to believe there was more to the story than a dingo carrying off a child — for the first time there was talk of murder.

The first inquest took place in December 1980. Expert witnesses gave evidence regarding the condition of Baby Azaria's clothes, which it was thought had been buried before being placed where they were found. The undamaged state of the clothing was a major factor in considering foul play. A report was given of experiments carried out at Adelaide Zoo which included feeding a goat kid wrapped in infant's clothes to a dingo. Animal hairs by the hundred rubbed off on to the clothes, whereas there were none on Azaria's garments. The Coroner's verdict was that the child met her death when attacked by a dingo and that afterwards her body was disposed of by an unknown method by a person or persons, name unknown.

Within a month of the conclusion of the inquest a new, secret investigation was begun. In the meantime the Chamberlains had received death threats and drew further attention to themselves by appearing in a TV re-enactment of events on the night Azaria disappeared. Subsequently Lindy was critical of the police, who, she said, ignored clues and failed to follow up a number of lines of investigation. The Australian authorities had asked Professor James Cameron, the British forensic scientist, to examine the missing baby's clothing. A new inquest was ordered which began in Alice Springs in December 1981. New forensic evidence was presented and key testimony concerned the discovery of foetal blood (found in babies up to six months old) on the carpet and on one of the seats of the Chamberlains' car. Professor Cameron told the inquest that tiny cuts in the neck of the child's jumpsuit had probably been made with a pair of scissors.

The weight of the experts' evidence went against the dingo theory. There was a complete absence of any signs of dragging on the clothing which would be expected if the baby had been carried through scrubland in the jaws of a dingo. Furthermore, there were no grip marks or saliva traces on the fabric. Dingoes, like dogs, perspire through their mouths and saliva deposits would almost certainly be transferred to any garment carried in the mouth. Specialized examination of the jumpsuit revealed bloody imprints, indicating that the clothed body of the baby had been held by hands stained with its blood. A prima facie case was argued that Azaria was killed in the Chamberlains' car; that the clothed corpse was buried and later dug up, when the clothes were removed and placed at a spot some distance from the camp-site. Lindy Chamberlain was committed for trial on a charge of murdering her baby and Michael was charged with being an accessory after the fact.

Lindy Chamberlain was pregnant when she appeared in the Darwin Supreme Court on trial for murder in September 1982. The prosecutor stated the charge bluntly. 'I put it to you,' he said to Mrs Chamberlain, 'that you sat in the front passenger's seat ... that you held the baby in front of you and that you cut its throat.' She answered simply, 'No.' The story of a dingo seizing the baby was described as 'a fanciful invention'. Much of the trial was taken up with the forensic evidence which had been introduced at the inquest.

The jury were unanimous in finding the couple guilty as charged. Lindy Chamberlain was imprisoned with hard labour for life and Michael was given a suspended sentence of eighteen months' hard labour. Two weeks after being found guilty, Lindy Chamberlain gave birth to a baby girl in prison — the infant was named Kahlia. Her appeal against conviction was heard in April 1983 and rejected. Many aspects of the 'Dingo Baby Case', as it became known, continued to be shrouded in mystery. Lindy Chamberlain maintained her denials throughout the long period of accusation. The child's body was never recovered, and the exact manner of its death still remains a complete mystery.*
(286, 289, 333, 418, 459, 550, 725, 859, 1054)

CAMPUS

'The kids messed up my career.'
Robert Wickes (1983)

Schools and colleges have the reputation of peaceful havens affording a tranquil background for studious pursuits. But many campuses are also closed, often stuffy, places in which professional rivalry can lead to violence. No one illustrated this better than Professor John White Webster, a respected academic at Massachusetts Medical College, who borrowed money from fellow-teacher Dr George Parkman. Non-payment of the loan was greeted with remarks about professional conduct which kindled the fires of resentment. In November 1849 Parkman's persistent demands for repayment were rewarded by Webster clubbing him to death.

Even the sanctity of the headmaster's study has been breached by the murderer bent on

*Since this account was written, using the information available at the time, further evidence has come to light which resulted in Lindy Chamberlain's release from prison and increasing pressure to reopen the investigation. In February 1986, Northern Territories authorities announced the discovery of a baby's tattered jacket near Ayers Rock, close to the spot where Mrs Chamberlain said her child was taken away by a dingo. The Territories' Attorney-General said that she would not return to gaol.

eliminating his victim. Dr George Henry Lamson, hoping to acquire his brother-in-law's money, visited the young man at Blenheim House School, Wimbledon, in 1881. Lamson and eighteen-year-old Percy John took sherry with the headmaster, and the visitor produced cut slices of Dundee cake from a bag he was carrying. A slice that had been carefully spiked with aconitine was given to young Percy, who became ill and subsequently died. Lamson murdered for greed, and made preparations to administer poison to his victim in surroundings which he knew would inspire confidence and well-being. Then he carried out his act of murder right under the nose of the headmaster.

In modern times schools have become places where innocents have been slaughtered to satisfy a murderer's crazed feelings of resentment. In May 1983 a deranged teacher held eighteen students hostage at Brentwood Junior High School, Long Island. Armed with a .22 rifle, 24-year-old Robert Wickes (who had been dismissed from the school the previous week), wounded the headmaster and a boy while a local radio station played his record requests. He told the radio station that the kids 'messed up my career' and he threatened to 'paint the road with carnage'. After a ten-hour siege Wickes — who it transpired had made death threats against a number of top US government officials — finally shot himself.

A similar incident occurred a month later in West Germany when Karol Chawa, a 34-year-old Czech-trained psychologist, stormed into a school armed with two pistols. On 3 June 1983 he burst into a classroom at the Freiherr-vom-Stern comprehensive school at Epstein and began firing indiscriminately. He killed two thirteen-year-old girls, a boy of twelve and a teacher before police officers arrived at the scene. One policeman was shot dead before Chawa ended it all by killing himself.

Charles Whitman, a University of Texas student on the Austin campus, became a mass murderer in August 1966. He had been acting strangely for some time, and was known to suffer severe headaches and to give vent to violent temper. On 31 July he killed his wife and mother, leaving behind a note which read simply, 'Life is not worth living.' Heavily armed and well-provisioned, he climbed to the top of the campus's 300-foot-high tower, killing three people on the way. The ex-Marine marksman then began picking off targets below, killing sixteen and wounding thirty, before a fusillade of police bullets ended his private vendetta.

Schools and colleges are places where young people are subject to sexual exploitation, especially in the explicit society of modern times. In 1982 Michael Davies, a 34-year-old headmaster of a school in Kent, was married with four children. He could not resist the temptation to seduce a fourteen-year-old girl to whom he gave private tuition in physics. Davies was already involved with another woman who believed she was going to elope with him. His plan to solve the dilemma was to murder the older woman and run away with the fourteen-year-old. Anxious not to leave his family in any financial difficulty, Davies doubled his life insurance, which was payable to his wife in the event of an accident. He then staged a fake drowning on the Kent coast, and his teenage lover telephoned the police, saying 'My boyfriend has drowned.' Later he met the woman who wanted to be his mistress and killed her. Her body was buried in Challock Forest and her clothes disposed of. Davies lost his nerve at this point and gave himself up. He was convicted of murder and sentenced to life imprisonment.

Young women students just by being on their campuses have provided easy prey for a number of psychopathic murderers such as Ed Kemper. His favourite pastime during the early 1970s was to linger near the Santa Cruz campus of the University of California. He picked up girls thumbing lifts from passing motorists, and many of them never lived to tell the tale. It was estimated that he had given lifts to some 150 girls, and when eventually captured in 1975 he was convicted on eight counts of first-degree murder.

John Norman Collins, the so-called Michigan co-ed killer, murdered seven girls who were studying at Eastern Michigan University. He killed over a two-year period, the last being in July 1969. The victim on this occasion had been seen with Collins, and several students had heard the 22-year-old student drop strong hints that he was the co-ed killer. He was convicted, and given a life sentence.

The master campus killer was Theodore (Ted) Bundy, a man who has excited considerable attention since his capture in 1979. Young women students began disappearing in the

Seattle area of Washington State at the beginning of 1974. The first was Lynda Ann Healy, a 21-year-old student at the State University, who went missing from her rented accommodation on 1 February — ominously, the bedclothes in her room were stained with blood. Thereafter girls were reported missing in the area at the rate of about one a month until April 1975.

In the middle of this sequence, in July 1974, a young woman at a picnic by Lake Sammamich in Washington State was approached by a handsome man who asked her to help him with his boat. She declined, but heard him introduce himself as 'Ted' to another girl to whom he made a similar request. On 7 September the bodies of two of the missing girls were found on a hillside a few miles from the lake. The girls had been strangled and bludgeoned to death.

The following month remains of two women were found a hundred and thirty miles from Lake Sammamich. One of these was unidentified, but the other was recognizable as one of the girls who had earlier been reported missing. There were stories from several girl students about a man called 'Ted' who had tried to pick them up. The disappearances continued, but in October 1974 the hunting-ground had switched from Washington to Utah. On 8 November Carol DaRonch was approached by a man in a shopping centre in Salt Lake City. By posing as a plain-clothes police officer he persuaded the girl to get into his Volkswagen car. He drove to a quiet street where he started to assault her, but luckily she broke free and escaped. Police began to receive reports that 'Ted' might be Theodore Bundy, a psychology student at Seattle.

In January 1975 the disappearances switched to Colorado, where three young women were reported missing during the first four months of the year. Then, on 16 August, Ted Bundy was arrested in Salt Lake City after a chase by an alert police officer who was suspicious of the man's Volkswagen car. At the time Bundy was taking a law course in Salt Lake City. A search of his room produced nothing incriminating, but hair found in his car matched that of one of the girls who disappeared in Utah in October 1974, and whose bludgeoned body was found ten days later. He was duly charged with her murder.

In January 1977 Bundy was extradited to Colorado and continued to study law in prison while the authorities built up a case for a pre-trial hearing. On 7 June he escaped, only to be caught eight days later. Using all his guile and legal knowledge, he produced a string of motions to delay the hearing. On 30 December 1977 he escaped again, and this time arrived by a roundabout route in Tallahassee, Florida, where as Chris Hagen he took a room close to Florida State University's student accommodation.

Two blocks away from Bundy's room was the University sorority house. There on 15 January 1978 he attacked two girls in their rooms, sexually abusing them and leaving them dead by strangulation. He also attacked two other girls in the sorority house and another woman in a near-by apartment block before going to ground as 'Chris Hagen'. He remained at liberty until 14 February 1978, when he was caught driving a stolen car. He was charged with theft, and identified as Ted Bundy. Teeth impressions taken from the reluctant prisoner proved to be identical to bite-marks made by the killer on the body of one of the sorority house victims. Ted Bundy's private reign of terror thus came to an end after he had attacked or killed over twenty women in three states. The police thought the real total might have been nearer forty.

Bundy was tried at Miami and pleaded not guilty, although he had confided to a detective at the time of his arrest, 'Sometimes I feel like a vampire.' He was sentenced to death following three convictions for murder, which in practice meant isolation on Death Row in a Florida maximum security prison.

Bundy fascinated all those with whom he came in contact, not least the police, for he was far from the stereotype sex killer. He was a good-looking young man, intelligent and with a bright future. As a criminal type he provided a wealth of material for commentators on criminological matters. In 1980 Ann Rule, a former policewoman turned crime reporter, published *The Stranger Beside Me*. She had known Bundy for ten years after they met at a Seattle Crisis Clinic where they were both volunteers. They corresponded while the book was being written, and the author concluded that 'Ted Bundy fits no pattern at all; you could not look at his record and say: " 'See, it was inevitable that he would turn out like this.' "

Bundy told the authors of *The Only Living Witness* that an 'entity' or malignant force resided within him which gradually took over his conscious mind and led him to sexual assault and rape. The quest to discover the original cause which excites a person to commit mass murder has long been pursued: that such a personality trait can be identified has been the hope of generations of criminologists. Bundy, an unusually intelligent man for a sex murderer, perhaps offered promising material, but the nearest one can get is that he experienced an identity crisis when he learned that he was illegitimate. Bundy himself blamed his behaviour on his genes, which in its sweeping generality is probably correct.

Like Richard Speck, who killed eight girls in a Chicago nurses' hostel in 1966, Ted Bundy found the students in the sorority house temptingly vulnerable to the opportunist killer; teachers are also at risk. When Raymond Gunn, a convicted rapist, walked past the one-room school at Gareth, near Maryville, Missouri, USA, he noticed the nineteen-year-old girl who was the teacher-in-charge. On 16 December 1930 he lay in wait for her after lessons had finished for the day. After the last pupil had left, with rape in his mind Gunn crept into the schoolroom where the teacher was cleaning out the fire grate, and attacked her with a club. The girl fought back with a spirited defence, but was soon overpowered and clubbed to death.

Gunn had been deterred from rape by the

TED BUNDY'S DIARY OF DEATHS, DISAPPEARANCES AND ASSAULTS FEBRUARY 1974 TO FEBRUARY 1978

Date	Place	Victim	Event
1 Feb 1974	Seattle, Washington	Lynda Ann Healy	Disappeared; body found in mountains 20 miles away in March 1975
12 Mar 1974	Olympia, Washington	Donna Gail Manson	Disappeared; never found
17 Apr 1974	Ellensburg, Wash.	Susan Rancourt	Disappeared; body found in March 1975
6 May 1974	Corvallis, Oregon	Roberta Kathleen Parks	Disappeared; body found in March 1975
1 June 1974	Burien, Washington	Brenda Ball	Disappeared; body found in March 1975
11 June 1974	Seattle, Washington	Georgann Hawkins	Disappeared; never found
14 July 1974	Lake Sammamish	Janice Ott *and* Denise Naslund	Disappeared; bodies found four miles from lake in September 1974
2 Aug 1974	Vancouver, Wash.	Carol Valenzuela	Disappeared; body found in October 1974
2 Oct 1974	Holladay, Utah	Nancy Wilcox	Disappeared; never found
18 Oct 1974	Midvale, Utah	Melissa Smith	Disappeared; body found on 28 Oct 1974
31 October 1974	Lehi, Utah	Laura Aime	Disappeared; body found in November 1974
8 Nov 1974	Bountiful, Utah	Debra Kent	Disappeared; never found
8 Nov 1974	Salt Lake City, Utah	Carol DaRonch	Attacked but survived
7 Jan 1975	Farmington, Utah	Nancy Baird	Disappeared; never found
12 Jan 1975	Snowmass, Colorado	Caryn Campbell	Disappeared; body found in February 1975
15 Mar 1975	Vail, Colorado	Julie Cunningham	Disappeared; never found
6 Apr 1975	Grand Junction, Col.	Denise Oliverson	Disappeared; never found

16 Aug 1975 Ted Bundy was arrested in Salt Lake City and remained in custody until 30 December 1977 when he escaped

Date	Place	Victim	Event
15 Jan 1978	Tallahassee, Florida	Lisa Levy *and* Margaret Bowman	Killed in sorority house attack
15 Jan 1978	Tallahassee, Florida	Kathy Kleiner *and* Karen Chandler	Survived attack in sorority house
15 Jan 1978	Tallahassee, Florida	Cheryl Thomas	Survived attack in her apartment
9 Feb 1978	Lake City, Florida	Kimberly Leach	Disappeared; body found in April 1978

14 Feb 1978 Ted Bundy was arrested near Pensacola Airport in a stolen car

girl's fierce resistance and by sounds of someone approaching the school. He therefore abandoned the scene, but the consequences of his attack were quickly discovered. A hue and cry was raised, and Gunn, who had a bad reputation in the neighbourhood, was immediately suspected. He was arrested within two days of the crime. His clothing was bloodstained, and his shoe-prints matched the impressions left in the soil outside the schoolroom. He made a ready confession, which he later said was the result of being subjected to third degree.

Gunn was taken to St Joseph for safe-keeping and to protect him from a hostile crowd which throbbed with talk of lynching. As an added precaution, the Missouri National Guard was called out to keep the crowd at bay. The murder trial was fixed for 12 January 1931, but Gunn never made it. When he was driven up to the Maryville Courthouse with a sheriff's escort, he was seized by the mob, who eluded both the law officers and the National Guard.

The mob put their prisoner in chains and, having beaten him up, took him to the school where the young teacher had been murdered. There he was made to repeat his confession, and he was told that his punishment was to be burned. He was hauled on to the roof of the school building and tied down. Gasoline poured into the schoolroom and ignited completed a public act of violence which claimed Raymond Gunn as America's five-thousandth recorded lynch victim. He perished within two and a half hours of being snatched from the steps of the court, and the Sheriff explained that he was unwilling to turn out the National Guard in case an innocent member of the public was hurt.

The school has become one of the main locations for urban violence, and the gangland attacks prevalent in the streets of the inner cities have spilled over into playground and campus. In a 1974 survey of 775 American schools, the US Senate Subcommittee on Juvenile Delinquency reported that 355 student deaths had occurred. Firearms featured prominently in the assaults, which also included thousands of incidents of wounding of both students and teachers. The Report referred to schools as the new 'combat zones' of urban violence. *(1, 2, 54, 83, 127, 128, 135, 234, 262, 337, 482, 527, 676, 692, 733, 818, 901, 904, 912, 933, 958, MWW)*

CARS

'A woman was knocked down and fatally injured ... the car did not stop.'
James Ronald Robertson (1950)

Like trains, the great advantage of motor cars for the criminal is mobility combined with scope for concealment and accident. With transport at his command and a road network before him the criminal could easily put distance between himself and his crime. It was inevitable, therefore, that the increased use of the car in everyday life would open up new vistas of opportunity for the criminal population (see under RAILWAY MURDERS).

The car inaugurated the possibility of hit-and-run, and a whole strategy of mobile murder and terror was developed in America in the 1920s and '30s by the organized crime syndicates. Bonnie and Clyde made motorized bank robbery fashionable, and helped to establish a trend in which gun and car symbolized criminal power. When their Ford V-8 was ambushed by police in Louisiana in 1934 and riddled with bullets, twelve handguns, three automatic rifles, one shotgun and three thousand pounds of ammunition were found in the trunk.

Despite being mass-produced, cars have individual characteristics which opened up vehicle examination as a specialized category of forensic science. This was evident as early as 1930 in the case of the famous 'Blazing Car Murder' in which the body of an unidentified man was burned. A vehicle expert who examined the charred wreck of the car was able to say in court that the carburettor had been tampered with. This helped to send Alfred Arthur Rouse to the scaffold.

A year earlier Erich Tetzner had capitalized on the explosive potential of the petrol-driven vehicle in a blazing-car incident in Germany. This was murder dressed up to look like accident, which is one of the classic uses of the car as a murderer's weapon. Immolation was probably the intended fate of Evelyn Foster, whose car was found ablaze on a Northumbrian moor in 1931. She survived the immediate conflagration, but died later from her injuries in a case which has never been officially solved.

A variation on the theme of murder made to

look like accident was devised by G. Edward Grammer for the elimination of his wife. The two officers in a police patrol car cruising along Belair Road on the outskirts of Baltimore about 10.30 p.m. on 19 August 1952 were startled to see a car careering down the hill towards them, apparently out of control. The vehicle narrowly missed the patrol car, swerved off the road, hit a telegraph pole and overturned. The woman driver was dragged clear and rushed to hospital, but was found to be dead on arrival.

Dorothy Grammer, aged thirty-three and mother of three children, had died of severe head wounds which included deep lacerations. Her husband, 35-year-old G. Edward Grammer, office manager for a mining company, was located and informed of his wife's death. He told police that he last saw his wife when she drove him to the railway station to board a train for New York. Grammer went into shock, and was taken into his physician's care.

Meanwhile pathologists examining the body of his dead wife were dubious about her injuries. The lacerations to the head were of a type that might have been caused by flying glass, yet the windscreen of the car was not shattered, and the side windows were wound down. Moreover the body was hardly bruised, which was surprising, bearing in mind that the car had turned over. The conclusion was that Mrs Grammer was dead before the car crashed so dramatically in Belair Road. Murder was an obvious possibility, and this was borne out by an examination of the car, which showed that the accelerator had been jammed with a pebble.

An inquiry into G. Edward Grammer's background showed him to be well regarded by his employers, and he was a regular attender at his local Methodist church. It also became clear that his job permitted association with a number of young women office employees. He had become infatuated with a 28-year-old Canadian woman with whom he had stayed in a hotel on Lake Michigan. They corresponded and spoke of marriage, which Grammer knew was impossible unless he divorced his wife.

As part of a carefully prepared plan, Grammer bought his wife a new car in the spring of 1952 to mark their wedding anniversary. She was thrilled with her gift, but perhaps a little disappointed when her husband insisted she took it back to the garage to have the new accelerator checked, which he claimed was sticking. The garage mechanic looked into the complaint and recorded on his job sheet that the accelerator was working properly.

When Grammer was confronted with the irregularities concerning his wife's death some ten days after the crash he spoke about a quarrel. He said that they had had an argument while she was driving him to the station. She accused him of loving his job more than he loved her, and goaded to rage, he stopped the car and got out. He saw a piece of pipe lying in the road and returned with it to the car, where he hit her on the head. His rage vented, he claimed to have left the scene and walked to the railway station to catch his train.

At his trial for murder Grammer asked to be tried not by a jury but by a judge alone. The case for premeditated murder was amply made out, and the prosecutor remarked on the coincidence that the pebble found jamming the accelerator in an open position was the same as the gravel on Grammer's front drive. The wife-murderer was sent to the electric chair after Judge Herman M. Mosel spent several hours in private deliberation considering the verdict.

Faking a car accident to cover up murder in a way which will convince experienced investigators is not an easy proposition, even when it is planned in advance. When police officers were called to the scene of a car crash on the evening of 2 March 1967 they were struck by the inconsistency between the slight damage to the car and the severe injuries sustained by one of the occupants.

Police found a red Mini with its front end resting against a tree in beech woods near the village of Nettlebed in Oxfordshire. The vehicle had only minimal damage — principally a broken headlamp — despite its collision with a tree, and the windscreen had not even shattered. The interior of the car was heavily bloodstained on the driver's side but the circumstances suggested nothing more than minor injuries to the occupants, who had been taken to Reading before the police arrived. It was therefore a matter of some surprise when it was learned that the woman travelling in the car, Mrs June Cook, had died in hospital of severe head injuries.

Raymond Cook told detectives that he and his wife had been driving home after dinner at

The mini car used to make a murder look like an accident

Pangbourne when he felt sick and asked his wife to drive. She took the wheel, and he remembered being dazzled by oncoming headlights before feeling the impact of a collision. He thought they were travelling at between 30 and 40 m.p.h. at the time.

A more detailed examination of the car and the scene of the crash heightened the mystery. The car's ignition and lights had been switched off and the hand-brake pulled on. The amount of blood inside the car and the severity of the dead woman's injuries suggested that she must have hit the windscreen at least. When forensic investigators appeared on the scene, mystery changed to suspicion of foul play. The speed of the vehicle at the time it hit the tree was estimated at no more than 10 m.p.h. More significantly, a human bloodstain was found on the road about seventy-five yards from the spot where the car came to rest.

The conclusion of the post-mortem examination on June Cook was that the injuries to her skull (which exposed the brain) had been caused by a blunt instrument. Tiny fragments of bone among leaves lying on the ground between the bloodstain in the road and the car helped to turn the inquiry into a murder investigation.

Police now began to probe Raymond Cook's background. June, his wife for eight years, was a teacher who had been previously married. She was a strong character, used to expressing herself and earning more than her husband. Cook, who had worked as a draughtsman, was a soft, easy-going personality never known to express strong opinions. In June 1966 Cook took a job as a student nurse at Borocourt

Mental Hospital near Nettlebed. There he met 23-year-old Kim Newall, also a student nurse.

Raymond Cook and Kim Newall fell for each other, and their liaison became a regular source of gossip among the hospital staff. In August, Cook made a public declaration of his love for Kim, and two months later she was dismissed from her post on account of the embarrassment which their relationship caused at the hospital. About this time Cook left his wife and went to live with Kim Newall.

In view of the changed circumstances, June Cook made a new will, leaving her assets of over £10,000 to her children. In January 1967, with the prospect of reconciliation in the air, she altered her will, on this occasion in favour of her husband. At the time Raymond Cook was attempting to support Kim Newall, who was pregnant, and he was stretched both financially and emotionally.

The detectives' picture of a fairly straightforward love triangle was clouded by another man who came on the scene. On the night of June Cook's death a blue car, registration number 7711 FM, was seen parked in the woods near the red Mini. The same car was also seen entering Reading from the Nettlebed direction. A man was driving, and he had a female passenger who was giving him directions. The man proved to be Eric Jones, who ran a plant-hire firm in Wales, and the woman was Kim Newall.

After extensive questioning it emerged that Cook, Jones and Newall were each known to the other. Eric Jones, a former acquaintance of Newall, had been asked to arrange an abortion for her. A conspiracy to arrange a fatal accident for Mrs Cook also emerged from this liaison. The trio staged a rehearsal for a plan whereby their victim was to be drowned when her car accidentally ran into the river at a spot near Woodley in Berkshire. The scenario was abandoned in favour of the fake car accident at Nettlebed.

On the fateful night Jones lay in wait in his car on the quiet road and flagged down Cook, who by prior arrangement drove past with his wife between 9.30 and 10.00 p.m. Jones asked for the loan of a foot-pump, saying his car had a flat tyre. On the pretence of giving him a lift into Reading, Cook invited Jones into his car. Then the violence began. Jones hit Mrs Cook with his fist and then with a car jack which was handed to him by Raymond Cook. The two men contrived to put the car into gear and it rolled, probably more gently than they wished, into a tree to feign an accident.

Cook, Jones and Newall were tried for murder at Oxford in June 1967. All three received sentences of life imprisonment.

With their flammable cargoes of petrol, cars can be turned into veritable bombs when triggered either by accident or by design. The drama of the flaming car disintegrating in a sensational explosion is an almost essential ingredient of most television thrillers, and the car bomb is a weapon all too frequently used by terrorist groups. The car bomb designed for individual homicide is fortunately less com-mon, but Arthur D. Payne, a successful lawyer from Amarillo, Texas, saw its possibilities. He lived in a comfortable house with his wife and three children, and life seemed serene. On 27 June 1930 he decided to walk from his home to the office, and left the car free for his wife to use.

Later that morning Mrs Payne backed the car off the drive and set off to the grocery store. She had with her their nine-year-old son, Arthur D. junior. They had travelled only a short distance when the car began to emit smoke. Mrs Payne's reaction was to accelerate in order to clear it. About half a mile from the Paynes' home the car disintegrated in a tremendous explosion. Both occupants were hurled into the air. The boy was badly injured, and although his life was saved he was crip-

Arthur D. Payne wired the family car with explosives

pled. His mother was beyond all aid, and was pronounced dead.

It was evident that a quantity of high explosive had been planted in the car and detonated by a time fuse. The police were baffled, but the editor of the *Amarillo News*, Gene Howe, had no doubts. He reported his belief that Mrs Payne had been murdered, and declared that if the police could not find a lead he would take action himself. Payne thanked Howe for his concern, and offered to put up $5,000 reward for anyone who could solve the mystery. The crusading editor recruited the services of one B. MacDonald, a well-known investigative reporter from the *Kansas City Star*.

MacDonald soon discovered that an overwhelming number of Amarillo citizens believed Payne killed his wife, although this view was not substantiated by any proof. The reporter continued his probe into Payne's background, and gleaned several pieces of information which heightened his suspicions. He found out that the attorney had heavily insured his wife and children, naming himself as the beneficiary, and also that his secretaries did not stay long at his office; four women had come and gone in less than twelve months.

MacDonald interviewed Payne and discussed some of these matters. He thought the normally smooth lawyer was distinctly edgy. When he got to the subject of secretaries his reporter's 'nose' told him that Payne was floundering. On hearing Verona Thompson described by her former employer as a 'rather commonplace woman, not particularly good-looking', MacDonald resolved to interview the lady. She turned out to be a beautiful woman of twenty-five who had been Payne's lover for several months. She said that he had remarked to her that he would get rid of his wife in order to marry her.

When he was arrested Payne said, 'Well, gentlemen, I hope you know what you are doing.' Confronted with the information about his extramarital activities acquired by the newspaper probe, he broke down and made a full confession — so full, indeed, that it ran to 60,000 words. He admitted trying to poison his wife, and also attempting to kill her with a shotgun rigged to simulate an accident. When these methods failed he decided to use dynamite.

A murder trial jury lost no time in finding Arthur D. Payne guilty, and he joined the ranks of that small band of convicted murderers who were once lawyers. However, he cheated the executioner by using one of his explosive devices to blow himself up in his cell two days before he was due to be electrocuted. The blast was sufficient to blow out one of the cell walls, but no one apart from the inmate was injured. His last wish was that the song *Home Sweet Home* should be played at his funeral.

Driven at an unsuspecting victim, a car can easily deliver fatal injuries: the fragile human frame is no match for the motorized blunt instrument. Most hit-and-run deaths are accidental, although there are exceptions. One such was perpetrated by Charles Arthur Mortimer in 1935. His pastime was to roam about the Hampshire lanes, colliding with girls riding bicycles. His aim was to fell his victims so that he could attack them with his hands. He went too far when he caused a youngster to topple to her death from a railway bridge, a murder for which he was later convicted.

Only rarely has the car been deliberately used as the prime implement of murder. A taxi driver motoring along Prospecthill Road, Glasgow, in the early hours of 28 July 1950 saw a bundle in the road which he thought at first glance had probably fallen from a passing truck. It was only when he stopped to give the object a closer examination that he realized it was a badly mangled female body.

When the police arrived on the scene their first thought was that the woman was a hit-and-run victim. Experienced officers noticed that blood and tissue had been ground into the road surface over a considerable area around the body. Moreover, there were no signs of broken glass or dislodged mud particles usually found at a hit-and-run scene as the result of impact.

A terrible catalogue of injuries was noted at the post-mortem examination, including a bruise on the head which might have been sustained before death. Earlier views that this was a hit-and-run case gave way to the idea of murder by motor-car. It appeared that the woman had been knocked unconscious and then repeatedly run over by a vehicle whose driver had executed several figures-of-eight in order to crush the life out of his victim.

The offending car, a black Austin, was quickly discovered in a side-street where it appeared to have been abandoned. Its underside was heavily smeared with blood, and its last-known driver was James Ronald Robertson, a serving police officer. He was arrested and charged with the murder of Catherine McCluskey, an unmarried mother of two children.

Robertson's story was that while out on patrol he had noticed the car in a back street. He checked police records and found that it had been stolen, but instead of reporting his discovery he decided to take the car for his own use. He bought another set of registration plates, and acquired forged documents. Robertson admitted meeting Catherine McCluskey in the summer of 1949, when he had been called to a disturbance at her Gorbals home. They became friendly, and he fathered her second child. McCluskey would not identify the child's father in order to protect his marriage, but let it be known he was a police officer.

On the night of 27 July 1950 Robertson said he had trouble with the car. He absented himself from his night duty from 11.00 p.m. to 1.00 a.m. in order to deal with it, telling his colleague that he had to repair the exhaust. In his official log Robertson reported an incident timed at 12.50 a.m. when, 'a woman was knocked down and fatally injured .... The car did not stop and was last seen driving city-wards.'

Confronted with the accusation of murder, Robertson broke down and made a statement. He said that he had decided to abandon the car, as he knew his false ownership would be discovered. While driving down Cavendish Street he saw McCluskey and stopped. She asked him for a lift, but he was anxious to return to duty and refused, despite her threats to raise a fuss. He drove on, but then relented and decided to go back. Putting the car into reverse, he pressed hard on the accelerator and sped rapidly backward, and to his horror realized he had knocked the girl over. He claimed that her body lay under the rear wheels and was jammed against the underside of the car. He struggled to free her, and when this failed he drove backward and forward in panic until finally the obstruction was shifted.

Police Constable Robertson was tried for murder in Glasgow in November 1950. He went into the witness box and, against the advice he had been given, refused to admit his relationship with the dead woman. He took

this action to spare his wife and family, but his lies were revealed under devastating cross-examination. Despite his insistence that the woman's death was 'an absolute accident', Robertson was convicted and sentenced to death.

The use of cars as status symbols or expressions of a driver's personality has given scope to designers to produce ever more distinctive and flamboyant models. In an unusual case a yellow Jaguar convertible was given to the victim to mark her out for murder. The murderer was obsessed by the trappings of the macho killer — guns, cars and physical fitness — but the story began in a house in El Sereno, Los Angeles.

While he watched television and refreshed himself with a beer in the living-room Henry Stockton was too absorbed to realize that intruders had entered his unlocked house. In the early hours of 11 December 1966 a neighbour smelled smoke and called the fire department to 2723 Ballard Street. Henry Stockton was found dead, staring blankly at the equally blank TV set. He had three bullet wounds in the head and two in the chest. There were no signs of a struggle, and he seemed to have been caught completely off guard.

Stockton, who was in his late twenties, worked as a stock clerk in the mail-order department of a large store. He had been remarried to Sandra, whom he had first married in 1960 and divorced early in 1966. Sandra Stockton was Henry's beneficiary, and stood to gain about $75,000 from insurance pay-outs.

Police discovered that Sandra had bought a .22 calibre pistol in the summer of 1966. Their inquiries also led them to Alan Palliko, a former police officer, with whom Sandra had become friendly at the Auto Club where she worked. A complex chain of events unfolded before a murder charge could be brought in the matter of Henry Stockton's death.

Palliko, who predicted that he would make his first million by the time he was thirty-five, married Katherine Drummond in 1964. He was fascinated by body-building and guns. He also neglected his wife, and his philandering put their marriage under strain. At the time when their respective marriages were on the rocks, Palliko met Sandra Stockton and they were attracted to each other.

About a year later, in August 1965, Palliko's wife Katherine was severely injured in a hit-and-run incident and suffered a broken pelvis. A few months later, to complete her misery, Katherine was attacked by Alan in her car. Late one night he appeared in the road when Katherine was driving away from a meeting and made her brake sharply. He had been drinking heavily. He got into the car and proceeded to beat her with his fists before attempting to strangle her. 'I'm going to kill you,' he told her. She screamed and struggled, and when passers-by stopped he released his grip and made off into the darkness.

Katherine was treated in hospital for bruises and lacerations. Palliko was arrested and charged with wife-beating although, against the advice of the police, Katherine later dropped the charge. By this time Palliko's all-consuming love of guns meant that he always carried a weapon wherever he went, and told an acquaintance, 'Every citizen and his sister is going to be packing a gun; on the street, in a holster.' By September 1966 Katherine was aware of Palliko's adultery with Sandra Stockton, and made it clear she wanted a divorce.

In October 1967 Palliko became the owner of The Grand Duke bar in Burbank, and later moved near by into a luxury apartment house called the Castillian. He changed his apartment almost as frequently as he changed his girl-friends, but appeared to settle down after meeting Judy Davis, an attractive instructor at a Burbank swimming pool. They married in March 1968, and Judy managed Palliko's second bar, The Grand Duchess at Sunland. The marriage was already full of tension when, on 18 April, Palliko leased a yellow Jaguar motor-car for Judy's use. Two days later his bride of six weeks died a violent death in her sleek new motor.

Judy Palliko was shot at the wheel of her stationary car in a parking lot opposite the Castillian apartment. She had been viciously beaten over the head with the butt of a gun and shot twice; she died in hospital. Palliko had told his former wife Katherine, 'I'm going to have to do something that I don't want to do, but I have no choice.' And to a friend whom he employed in one of his bars he made an admission of murder. He asked his friend if he was ever curious how he came by his money. 'Do you remember Sandra Stockton?' he inquired. 'I killed her husband.' Alan Palliko was arrested in The Grand Duke on 30 April 1968 and charged with the murder of Henry Stockton and Judy Palliko. A search of his apartment turned up a veritable arsenal of guns, including a .38 under his pillow.

The trial of Palliko and Sandra Stockton began in November 1968 in the Los Angeles Supreme Court, and lasted for thirteen weeks. The evidence was mainly circumstantial, but the prosecution argued strongly that the accused had conspired to murder Henry Stockton for his money. Sandra had taken out a double indemnity policy on her husband sixteen days before he was killed. A large part of the insurance pay-out found its way into Palliko's hands.

Palliko had insured his intended wife before they were married, and, it was suggested, had set her up for murder. The purpose behind leasing the distinctive yellow Jaguar convertible was to mark Judy for her killer when she parked the car. Palliko denied killing his wife, claiming that the crime had been committed in order to get at him. The fact that Palliko had asked four women to marry him in the space of six months strengthened the idea that romance was not his only intention. Despite the lack of physical evidence, the well-argued prosecution by Vincent Bugliosi persuaded the jury. Palliko and Sandra Stockton together were convicted of murdering Judy and of the attempted murder of his former wife.

Alan Palliko, the would-be millionaire, was sentenced to death and Sandra Stockton received a sentence of life imprisonment. Palliko made three attempts to escape from prison, and in 1972 his death sentence was commuted to life imprisonment.

The blazing car continues to be a popular way of attempting to conceal murder, even though the pioneers of the method in the 1930s were not entirely successful in avoiding detection. On 18 February 1954 Dr Richard Müller, a dentist with a practice in Otterbach, West Germany, returned home late. He was accompanied by ambulance attendants and his hands, which had been burned, were covered in bandages. In a state of distress he told his sons that their mother had been burned to death in the family car.

Richard and Gertrud Müller had taken the car out that evening to drive round to a few farms to find a home help. When returning home after nightfall along the darkened country roads Frau Müller spotted a hedgehog in the beam of the car's headlights. She thought it would be fun to pick it up and take it back to their sons. Müller stopped the car just outside the village of Birotshof and walked back along the road to retrieve the hedgehog. As he bent down he heard a noise, and looking back to the car saw it enveloped in a mass of flame.

He ran to the blazing vehicle, but the intense heat prevented him pulling his wife clear. It was fifteen minutes before the fire brigade arrived, and by the time the flames had been quenched all that was left of Gertrud Müller was her charred body. Several aspects of the incident worried the police, and the following day Dr Richard Müller was arrested and charged with murder.

Inquiries showed that although he had been married twenty years Müller was something of a philanderer, and had had several affairs. The most recent of these involved the young woman who was the receptionist at his dental surgery. Frau Müller had found a note from this woman containing various endearments, which the dentist had been indiscreet enough to leave in his coat pocket. Frau Müller implored the girl to leave her husband alone and to allow the situation to cool off. The receptionist broke off the relationship and went to work in England. The police view was that Müller had decided to murder his wife to leave him free to marry his mistress.

Müller was tried for murder at Kaiserslaütern in November 1955. He pleaded not guilty. The prosecution showed that he had bought a new heater for the car, and also four gallons of petrol which he kept in cans stowed in the boot. The contention was that having made an excuse to drive in the country with his wife, he stopped on a deserted stretch of road so close to some kerbside trees that it was impossible to open the passenger door. With his wife trapped in the car, he stunned her and pulled her over into the driving seat. All that remained was to put the newly purchased car heater under her legs to simulate an accidental fire source and to douse the interior of the car with petrol. One empty can was found next to the body and another on the back seat — a single match consigned his wife to a fiery end.

Müller repeated the story he had told earlier, and he created a sensation by attempting suicide midway through the trial. This resulted in a few days' delay, but the proceedings continued, and the accused man was convicted on largely circumstantial evidence. He received a prison sentence of six years, which some considered remarkably light, while others thought the trial proceeded with undue haste after the suicide attempt.
(1, 2, 22, 106, 126, 133, 152, 346, 421, 478, 520, 650, 702, 703, 717, 730, 937, 1006, MWW)

CASTLES AND PALACES

'Tell us who did it. I shall be blamed.'
Peter Grupen (1921)

Castles and palaces, no less than humbler abodes, have featured in the annals of crime. Indeed, in the days of the early Roman Emperors, such as Nero, murder was almost endemic in the Imperial palaces. This was also true of fifteenth-century Rome and of other Italian cities during the period of dominance by the Borgia family. It was the age of princely power, when murder was used simply to eliminate rivals.

Castles were built as fortresses to repel assault from outside the walls. Similarly, the palatial residences of princes were protected from the external threat of the hired assassin by armed palace guards. Murder from within was not so easily diverted. Poison was a widely used weapon which could be subtly administered under the noses of even the most vigilant servants and guards. Moreover, as the administration of poison required guile rather than strength, it was a method which allowed women to play the power game. Locusta used her talents to good effect on behalf of the Emperor Nero, and Toffana, the infamous poisoner of seventeenth-century Naples, included two Popes in her tally of victims.

The remoteness of castles from other dwellings, and their self-containment, lends secrecy to what goes on inside. Access to and from the outside world is easily controlled, and unwelcome curiosity can be stilled. Privacy is thus easily maintained, and even official questioning may be overcome by the use of rank. These were considerations which Countess Erzsébet Báthory used to the full in order to satisfy her lust for murder.

Erzsébet (or Elizabeth) Báthory was born in

Erzsébet Báthory: Hungary's Blood Countess

1560 in Transylvanian Hungary, a region steeped in sorcery and magic. She was a beautiful girl, born into a family noted for its eccentricity, not to mention madness and cruelty. The beauty was to become a beast, and when she died Erzsébet Báthory's notebook recorded the names of six hundred and ten girls she is thought to have tortured and murdered. She was fascinated by her own appearance to the point of narcissism — she spent long hours looking into mirrors and fussing over her complexion. She was a lesbian, and although she married, preferred the company of women. She suffered frequent headaches, and was thought to be epileptic like other members of her family; her uncle, the King of Poland, died of the disease.

In 1575, barely fifteen years old, she married Ferencz Nádasdy, who distinguished himself as a soldier fighting for the Hungarian cause against the Turks. Now a countess, she lived at Csejthe Castle in what is now Czechoslovakia. With her husband away for long periods during his military campaigns Erzsébet was left to her own devices. She became obsessed with her appearance, and was constantly trying out new potions and remedies to cure her real or imaginary ills. She bore four children, and when Ferencz died at the age of forty-nine she truly became mistress of Csejthe Castle. She was always attended by Jó Ilona, a former wet nurse, and Dorkó, a servant with a passion for cruelty.

Rumour quickly gained ground that Countess Báthory was responsible for the disappearance of many young girls from the region. There were stories of mass murder, and the legend grew that Erzsébet bathed in the blood of virgins to improve the whiteness of her skin. Indeed, in Vienna, which she visited two or three times a year, she was known as 'Die Blutgräfin' (Blood Countess). What became evident was that this beautiful woman was a sadist who indulged in torture and horrific excesses, ending in countless murders.

Her sinister pair of servants, Jó Ilona and Dorkó, used the influence of the Countess's name to lure peasant girls to Csejthe Castle. As the widow of a respected nobleman Erzsébet had little difficulty at first in disposing of the bodies of her victims — the girls were simply spoken of as dying of unknown causes at the castle. The chaplain of the parish had his suspicions, however, and recorded the frequent burials which on one occasion included nine in a single day.

News of Countess Báthory's excesses eventually reached the ears of King Mathias of Hungary, who ordered an investigation. The official dispatched to Csejthe Castle caught the Countess literally red-handed with two dead girls and one dying of torture. An attempt to hush up the affair to protect the reputation of Hungary's ruling class did not succeed. A murder trial was held at Bisce in 1611. Although Erzsébet did not appear, her accomplices gave ample testimony of their mistress's sadistic behaviour.

Jó Ilona confessed to killing fifty girls, and related that the Countess tore the flesh from the living bodies of her victims with pincers before cutting their veins to wallow in the blood. The servant said that often there was so much blood swilling around the floor of her mistress's bedroom that it was necessary to throw down fire ashes to soak it up. A whole industry of death and destruction was set up, with numerous individuals paid by the Countess to procure victims and then dispose of their tortured bodies. As many as five girls a week might be murdered when Erzsébet's sadism reached its peak. Sometimes they would be brought to her bedroom, where she would fly at their naked bodies, biting the flesh in uncontrollable frenzy.

The court condemned Jó Ilona and Dorkó to death, and they were burned at the stake first, having their fingers pulled off in cruel yet ironic justice. The greatest irony was that their mistress, although sentenced to death, was not executed but condemned to perpetual imprisonment. Erzsébet Báthory, on account of the nation's respect for her late husband, was allowed to live. She was confined to a single room in Csjethe Castle, whose thick walls had deadened the screams of her many murder victims. The windows of her room were sealed and the door too was bricked up, allowing just a slit for food to be passed in. Scaffolds placed at the extremities of the castle informed the world that its sole occupant was condemned to death. There in her own torture chamber with only bats for companions, Erzsébet Báthory died in 1614 after three and a half years' seclusion.

A small group of family members and servants provided both victims and murderer in an incident which provided Germany after the First World War with a sensational trial. The death of a beautiful heiress and undertones of unusual sexual relationships and greed were essential ingredients of events at Kleppelsdorf Castle in 1921. The Castle stands in spacious grounds near the river Bober at Lähn, in what was once German Silesia but is now Poland, and was bought at the turn of the century by a Berlin business-man who dreamed of founding a dynasty. The dream collapsed when his wife died during childbirth and he himself died at the end of the First World War.

At the age of fourteen Dorothea Rohrbeck inherited the castle, and with it the ill-fortune which had beset her family. In 1921 Dorothea was living at Kleppelsdorf with her governess, Fräulein Zahn, and her grandmother, Frau Eckhardt. Also staying in the castle during the early part of the year was Dorothea's twelve-year-old cousin Ursula, a precocious child and not well disposed to her host. Ursula's step-father, Peter Grupen, a veteran of Verdun and a post-war speculator, completed the family group. Ursula's mother had mysteriously dis-

appeared several months previously, leaving Grupen to look after her daughter. On 21 February 1921, a cold wintry day, the family gathered in the dining-room for the midday meal. Dorothea and Ursula were late, and a maid was sent to fetch them. Screams echoed round the castle walls when the maid found the two girls lying in a pool of blood on the floor of their room. Dorothea was dead, and though Ursula was still breathing she died without speaking, despite Grupen urging her to 'Tell us who did it. I shall be blamed.'

A revolver was found near the bodies which Grupen admitted was his. Unwisely (for the police had not yet been called) Grupen decided to move Ursula's body. Underneath he found a note addressed 'To Grannie'; its brief message read, 'I shot Dörte [Dorothea] first and then myself. Now you won't have to worry about Dörte any more .... Your unhappy Ursel.' The police doctor was sceptical about the suicide theory of the girls' deaths. Dorothea had been shot twice and Ursula once, but none of the wounds had the close-range appearance of suicidal injuries. Moreover, the spent cartridge cases were scattered about the room and, most significant of all, the revolver's safety catch was on. The doctor remarked, 'I should not be surprised if this was the "little mistake" that every murderer makes sooner or later.'

Suspicion focused on Grupen, who it was learned had an unnatural hold over his step-daughter. It was rumoured that she was his love slave, and that he controlled her by hypnosis. Servants at the castle also made it known that Grupen had pursued Dorothea, the beautiful young heiress, but that she had spurned his advances. Peter Grupen was charged with double murder and sent for trial at Hirschberg in December 1921.

A Svengali-like picture was painted of Grupen at his trial. He was shown to be over-sexed, and to have been intimate with servants and relatives, both young and old. A horrified court heard that Ursula had gonorrhoea, which in all probability had been contracted from her step-father. Several witnesses testified that Dorothea was frightened of him, and that he had tried to kill her during a boating trip at Hamburg. There was considerable suspicion over his missing wife, who before her disappearance had given him power of attorney and transferred a large mortgage to him. She too had left a note written to Dorothea, 'to say goodbye again before I leave for America'.

Handwriting experts testified in court that the writing on Ursula's suicide note was definitely her own. The question being asked was whether the girl had been directed to write the note while under hypnotic influence. The handwriting experts did not believe this was the case, but the prosecution produced a trump card in the form of elderly Dr Moll from Berlin, who was considered to be the foremost expert on hypnosis.

The old man's evidence filled a day of the court's time. He declared that Grupen was unquestionably a dominant personality and he had no doubt that both his wife and his stepdaughter had been the subjects of sexual bondage. The mixture of sex and suggestion which Grupen dealt in was strong enough to influence children and to sap the will-power of adults. The doctor believed that once under this influence, people could readily be directed to carry out such actions as writing letters.

Hypnosis was a popular pursuit in post-war Germany and in Berlin séances and mediums provided fashionable entertainment. The trial of Peter Grupen was dominated, if not obsessed, by the subject, and the jury took only two hours to bring in a guilty verdict. The convicted man declared that the verdict was a miscarriage of justice, but this claim did not spare him from execution in January 1922.

Suborning servants is a ploy that has been used down the centuries to place the assassin close to his target. In Roman times the imperial food taster or physician was often persuaded or threatened with menaces to drop his vigilance. In modern times political disaffection and revolutionary fervour have provided a means of eroding loyalty. The need to fight the enemy planted within has given rise to a whole technology of security to protect the world's rich, famous and powerful figures.

All was quiet in the Barompiman Palace early on the morning of 9 June 1946, save for the servants bustling about preparing breakfast. Ananda Mahidol, King of Siam (now Thailand), slept peacefully under the mosquito netting covering the royal bed. He had suffered a mild stomach upset the previous day, and his brother looked in on him at 0900 hours but did not disturb him.

The royal bedchamber was guarded outside by four men, and only members of the royal family and personal servants had access. King Ananda had been visited at six o'clock by his mother, and at about half-past eight he was up in his dressing-gown, although he declined the breakfast offered him by Butr Pathamasirind, his page. Butr's relief, Mai Chit, was also in the palace, and it was he who shouted out, 'The King's shot himself' when the noise of a single shot reverberated around the building at about nine-twenty.

Pandemonium ensued as everyone rushed to the King's bedside. Ananda lay on his bed dead from a bullet wound in the head just above the left eye. A .45 Colt automatic pistol lay close to his left hand. The weapon was removed by a servant and priority was given to washing the King's body and cooling it with ice and by means of electric fans to slow decomposition, which would otherwise be rapid in the hot climate. Because the dead King was a divine being, the police were not allowed to examine his body. They were permitted to see the gun — which by this time was covered with innumerable fingerprints. It was ascertained, however, that only one shot had been fired from the weapon. The bullet was not found, but a servant produced the spent cartridge case.

Among the officers and courtiers swarming about the Palace was the late king's Chief Minister, Pridi Banomyong. He declared simply, 'The King is a suicide.' After the royal corpse had been washed and prepared doctors were allowed to make an examination. They found a wound at the back of the head which, because it was smaller than the one over the eye, they took to be an entry wound, and concluded that the King had been shot through the back of the head. Assassination and murder were now talked about, and wild accusations were made — Pridi's name was one of several mentioned.

A public inquiry was set up which in due course reported that the King's death was not an accident, but there was insufficient evidence to prove either murder or suicide.

Meanwhile in 1948, following a bloodless coup, Marshal Pibul Songgram took over the country. Pridi, who had been branded as King Ananda's assassin, fled. The new regime, anxious to clear up the mystery of the King's death, asked Professor Keith Simpson, the distinguished pathologist, to review the forensic evidence. For a start, it was felt that the

King (who was trained in the use of firearms) would have been unlikely to have shot himself accidentally. That left suicide or murder.

Professor Simpson thought the position of the body ruled out suicide, and the King had never hinted at being depressed or suicidal. More importantly, the gun lay by the dead King's left hand, and he was known to have been right-handed. The Professor concluded that there was strong evidence in favour of murder.

In August 1948 Butr Pathamasirind and Mai Chit, together with a third royal servant, were put on trial for murder. The proceedings dragged on for nearly three years, during which time two defence counsel were murdered and two were charged with treason. The trial finally ended in May 1951 with the conclusion that King Ananda had been murdered. All three accused were executed.
(394, 743, 871)

CHURCHES AND CEMETERIES

'Murders are expected ... in saloons and other vile places; but when the church is the chosen place, we are horrified at such a state of society.'
The Pacific (1895)

To choose holy ground on which to violate the commandment 'Thou shalt not kill' in an act of premeditated murder is perhaps the ultimate profanity. History shows, however, that the compelling urge to eliminate a rival does not necessarily stop at the church steps.

The actual murder of Thomas à Becket in Canterbury Cathedral in 1170 and the postulated murder of Pope John Paul I in the Vatican in 1978 suggest that the quest for power and domination stops at nothing. Violence in this context is no stranger to the Vatican. For reasons of political expediency Cesare Borgia had his sister's husband, Alfonso, murdered in August 1500. The Duke had been injured by hired assassins in Rome, and when these wounds proved less than fatal he was strangled in his room inside the Papal palace.

Churches or holy places, like many other locations of murder, are visited by violence simply because that is where the victim is to be found. But aside from fatal incidents which

have helped to determine the course of history, there are many instances of more commonplace murders committed on consecrated ground. For the most part they have been committed not for elimination but for lust.

Probably the most celebrated case is that of San Francisco's 'Demon in the Belfry' in 1898. Theodore Durrant, a young medical student, was Sunday School superintendent at the Emanuel Baptist Church on 23rd Street. He used his position of trust to lure two young women to their deaths. On 3 April 1895 he strangled Blanche Lamont and dragged her body up to the belfry, where it remained hidden for over a week. On 12 April Durrant strangled Minnie Williams and mutilated her body, which he left lying in the deserted church. That same evening he attended a Christian Endeavour meeting with his usual amiable and carefree manner.

The next day women decorating the Emanuel Baptist Church for Easter discovered Minnie's body. When the police were called and conducted a thorough search of the premises the other girl's body was found in the belfry. The 'Crime of the Century', as the press called it, was soon accounted for. The finger of suspicion was immediately pointed at Durrant by various parishioners who believed him to be a seducer.

Theodore Durrant was virtually tried and convicted by the newspapers. He was found guilty and sentenced to death, the penalty being carried out on 7 January 1898. A stream of confessions to the murders emerged after Durrant's execution — no doubt these were the usual indulgences of the lunatic fringe. Durrant's acts of frenzy captured the headlines in America and also in Europe, but he was by no means the first murderer in the belfry.

Worshippers at Warren Avenue Baptist Church in Boston, Massachusetts, thought their sexton was 'not quite right'. They were accustomed to seeing him in the church belfry on Sundays summoning the faithful to service, but 26-year-old William Piper's antics in the rear pews were thought to be somewhat unorthodox. He developed the habit of reading novels during church services, and, it was thought by some, he also swigged from a whisky bottle. Piper's unorthodox behaviour took a turn for the worse in 1873, when it became known that he made a habit of embarrassing teenage churchgoers by making suggestive remarks to them. At about this time too a series of brutal sexual attacks were made on young women in the Boston area.

On 5 December 1873 the naked body of a local girl was stumbled over by a walker in woods on the outskirts of the city. The girl was dead from head injuries, and the shadowy figure of a man was observed running away from the scene. During the following months two other girls were sexually assaulted and murdered in the same vicinity. On 23 May 1875 churchgoers arriving at Warren Avenue Baptish Church doubtless had the savagery of the recent killings in their thoughts and prayers. The familiar figure of Sexton Piper could be seen standing near the door — he appeared to be holding a heavy stick. When the service was over Piper spoke to five-year-old Mabel Young and invited her up to the belfry to see his pigeons.

The eager child followed the sexton, and once they had reached the belfry he began to hit her with his stick. Sufficient time had elapsed for the adults accompanying the child to realize that she was missing and they returned to the church. Hearing noises in the belfry, they began to climb the stairs. Aware that he was about to be caught red-handed, Piper threw the unconscious form of his victim to the floor and made his exit to the ground by jumping out of a window. Quickly recovering his feet, he nonchalantly re-entered the church. By this time the search party had reached the belfry and discovered the dying child. Poor Mabel Young expired without identifying her attacker, and Piper no doubt thought he was in the clear. But then the stick which he had been seen holding was found — it was thick with the murdered child's blood, and he was roundly accused.

At first Piper protested his innocence, although at his trial he admitted to drinking heavily on the day the girl was attacked. He was convicted of murder, and prior to his execution in 1876 the 'Monster of the Belfry', as he became known, confessed to killing the three other girls.

Cemeteries have a special place in the history of murder on account of the activities of Burke and Hare in Edinburgh's graveyards in the 1820s. The 'Resurrection Men', as they and others like them were known, merely wanted to line their pockets by supplying the needs of the medical schools for corpses on which to

Thomas Piper abducts his five-year-old victim into the church tower and then escapes by leaping from a window

practise dissection and teach anatomy. Fear of body-snatching led to the erection of high-railed fences round cemeteries to protect the graves from theft.

Exhumation might be considered a legalized form of body-snatching. It is certainly an aspect of forensic pathology which has brought unwelcome publicity to many cemeteries that have received the mortal remains of murder victims. The need to check on suspicion of poisoning has been the usual reason for ordering the exhumation of a body. There is a group which wants Napoleon's tomb to be opened so that the body of the long-dead Emperor may be tested for arsenic to prove the theory that he was poisoned while exiled on St Helena (see under ISLANDS).

Murder may also occur among the tombstones, and, like the belfry murders, lust is usually the motive. Linda Peacock, aged fifteen, was a keen horsewoman and spent most of the day on 6 August 1967 with her ponies at a farm close to her home at Biggar in Scotland. A friend gave her a lift back to Biggar at about 8.00 p.m., and she was seen walking in the village main street with another girl. When Linda did not return home by late evening the police were called in. A search was mounted for her the next morning, and anxiety for her safety turned to horror when her body was found in St Mary's Cemetery. The time of the attack was fixed at about 10.20 p.m. when three witnesses heard screams. The attack had occurred in a quiet part of the graveyard, and the spot was well shielded by a large yew-tree.

Near the cemetery was a school for problem

boys, which not surprisingly became a focal point for police inquiries. Several witnesses who had passed the cemetery late on the evening of Linda's disappearance had noticed a young couple near the gate. One witness commented to her husband as they drove past that it was strange for a couple to go courting in a graveyard. While the boys at the school were being patiently questioned senior detectives were considering how to proceed with one of the clues they possessed. The attacker had bitten the girl on the breast, leaving some clear impressions of his teeth. They were advised that it would be possible to use these marks to identify the murderer. Impressions would need to be taken of the teeth of any suspects and comparisons made with the marks left on the dead girl.

In the meantime officers at the school had found a boy who admitted telling a lie to cover for a fellow pupil. He said that seventeen-year-old Gordon Hay had been missing from school until about 10.30 p.m. on 6 August when he burst into the dormitory in a disturbed and dishevelled state. He had quickly washed and changed into his pyjamas before the duty teacher arrived to signal lights out.

Gordon Hay was interviewed and maintained that he had returned to school by 10 p.m. He also denied knowing Linda Peacock. The youth agreed to have a dental impression taken and the necessary arrangements were made for a case that was to make forensic dental history. In order to be completely objective, Hay was not identified as a suspect in the murder inquiry; together with twenty-eight pupils and staff from his school he went to Glasgow Dental Hospital and teeth impressions were taken from them all. A dental expert compared all the impressions with the bite mark on the dead girl and eliminated all save four which included Hay. A further close examination of the youth's teeth enabled the dentist to confirm the presence of some highly distinguishing characteristics in the form of pits in the canine teeth. These corresponded exactly with the teeth impressions made on the dead girl's body by her attacker.

Gordon Hay was arrested and sent for trial. The dental evidence was critical and the expert witness spent a whole day in the witness box explaining his evidence. The judge in his summing up spoke of forensic dentistry as a 'relatively new science' and maintained that the

law should keep pace with technical achievements. On 7 March 1967 Hay was found guilty. As he was under the age of eighteen he was ordered to be detained during Her Majesty's pleasure.

Another graveyard murderer was Gerald Thompson. On a wet Sunday evening in June 1935 he stopped his car at a bus stop near Peoria, Illinois, and asked the lone girl standing there if she would like a lift. Mildred Hallmark, cautious on account of a number of assaults which had occurred recently in the district, nevertheless accepted. Thompson drove to Springdale Cemetery near Peoria and parked inside its grounds. Mildred Hallmark resisted Thompson's advances, but her attempts to escape from the car were thwarted because the practised rapist had wired the door handles so that they were electrified from the car battery. He raped the girl and killed her, dumping her body in the cemetery before driving off into the night. The following morning an elderly cemetery employee found the dead girl. The skin tissue found under her fingernails testified to the fight she had put up, and it appeared that she had also used a fountain pen to ward off her attacker's assault.

The police began their inquiry by interviewing known sex offenders, and received a number of wild if fanciful accounts from excited young women. A number of possible suspects were questioned, but no arrests were made until an anonymous tip-off focused attention on Gerald Thompson, a 25-year-old toolmaker. Thompson worked in the same factory as the dead girl's father, and he had made an ostentatious contribution to the collection made at the works to send flowers to the funeral. After a lengthy period of questioning Thompson confessed to being the killer, and he was charged with first-degree murder. He described how he had cut his victim's clothes with a pair of scissors and raped her. There were traces of blood on his clothing and also of mercurochrome, which he had used to treat the cuts and scratches on his face.

Thompson lived with his grandmother, and among his possessions was a diary containing the names and addresses of sixteen girls he had raped between November 1934 and June 1935. There were also hundreds of obscene photographs taken by his special method. His technique was to force his victims to pose naked with him in the glare of his car head-lights while a self-timing camera clicked away. He secured the girls' silence by threatening to blackmail them with the photographs. He once boasted to a friend that he had arranged a rape a week for over a year, but when rape turned to murder someone broke the silence and named him.

There was strong public feeling against Thompson, and threats of lynching were in the air. He had to be spirited away before the trial so that anger could cool. He was eventually tried in Peoria and found guilty. The arch-rapist who had used electricity to imprison his victims died in the electric chair on 15 October 1935.
(103, 253, 265, 379, 697, 795, 836, MWW, mw)

CONSULTING-ROOMS

'I did it all for France.'
Dr Marcel Petiot (1944)

Most doctors when their minds have turned to murder have committed the act at home, usually with poison administered to a relative. Only rarely do they breach professional eti-quette by using their consulting-rooms for such base purposes. There are exceptions, one of whom was the sinister Dr Marcel Petiot, who murdered twenty-seven war refugees in 1944. His house at 21 rue Lesueur contained a sound-proofed chamber next to his consulting--room. Its only fittings were a door with no handle on the inside, a single, naked electric light bulb in the ceiling and eight metal rings fixed to one wall. The opposite wall was fitted with a magnifying spy-glass which permitted a viewer outside to observe the wall with the rings. The purpose of this room was never fully established, but it was supposed Dr Petiot tied his victims to the rings and watched them through the spy-glass at some stage during the murder process.

Consulting-rooms are ideally suited to the requirements of murder, especially if the victim is cast in the role of patient seeking treatment. The handy hypodermic syringe and selection of drugs make the administration of a fatal dose potentially easy. As always, it is disposal of the body which is the problem. Dr Petiot had to rely on a basement furnace and quicklime pits for the destruction of his vic-tims' remains. A well-equipped consulting-room offers scope for dismemberment, but with the exception of Dr Buck Ruxton and Dr Hawley Harvey Crippen few medical murder-ers have elected to practise their surgical skills on their victims.

With poison being a favoured murder weapon, simulation of death by natural causes removes the necessity to dispose of the corpse. A steady nerve is a prerequisite for this approach and in 1933 Dr Alice Wynekoop demonstrated how easily panic can set in. Having administered a fatal chloroform anaes-thetic to her daughter-in-law in her Chicago consulting-room, she lost her head and shot her already dead victim in the chest. This act of panic served to undermine the story that her patient had died accidentally while undergoing examination.

Dr Pierre Bougrat made use of his consult-ing-room at 37 rue Senac in Marseilles to murder his victim, but found it impossible to dispose of the body. On 14 March 1925 an old friend from his army days, Jacques Rumèbe, visited him for an injection of mercuric chlor-ide, part of a course of treatment for syphilis. About midday Bougrat told Henri and Augus-tine Prevost, the couple who managed his household affairs, that he would be out for the rest of the day. Their instructions were not to answer the telephone, and on no account were they to go into the consulting-room.

The Prevosts, curious at all the mystery, took a peek through the keyhole in the surgery door. Henri thought he could see the legs of a person lying on the examination couch, and on the floor he saw a brief-case which he recog-nized as Rumèbe's. The doctor returned about midnight, but no mention was made of what was in the consulting-room.

A couple of days later Mme Rumèbe called at 37 rue Senac, inquiring about her husband who had gone missing. Bougrat offered no information, other than to confirm that he had treated his patient. Mme Rumèbe was distres-sed because her husband had been carrying 20,000 francs worth of wages money which he had collected from the bank for his firm. There was a suspicion that he had stolen the money and then absconded.

At this point Dr Bougrat had another unexpected visitor in the form of Andrea Meilhan, a former prostitute who had lived with him for a while during the previous year.

He had married the daughter of a professor at the Marseilles Medical School in 1919, and his father-in-law had set him up in practice. Despite the advantages of a potentially prosperous practice and influential family backing, Bougrat opted for the sleazy life. Bored by his wife's incessant dinner parties, he took to absenting himself in favour of other pursuits. These usually led him to the red-light area of Marseilles, where he encountered Andrea, whom he met on a regular basis.

Mme Bougrat, not surprisingly, found her husband's behaviour unacceptable, and in 1924 divorced him. The doctor was so infatuated with Andrea that he bought off her protector for 8,800 francs and installed her at 37 rue Senac, after his wife and child had left. By this time the once prosperous medical practice was declining and Bougrat simply did not have the money to fulfil the wild promises he had made. The novelty soon wore off for Andrea, and after a few months she walked out, taking some of her lover's jewellery with her. Nevertheless, when she turned up on Bougrat's doorstep in April 1925 imploring him to take her back, he forgave her transgressions and she moved in with him.

This incident prevented Bougrat from carrying out a vital part of his plan. The smell which arose in his house was a daily reminder of this omission. He told the Prevosts that the smell was caused by a dead rat, and when neighbours complained he was forced to call in the City Sanitation Department to spray the premises with formalin.

At the end of May police arrived and arrested the doctor in connection with cheques he had issued without the funds to honour them. His finances were in such a perilous position that his father had to meet his debts and bail him out of prison. While Bougrat was behind bars the police decided to investigate his apartment. They were immediately overwhelmed by the smell when admitted by Andrea, who gave the now customary 'dead rat' explanation. In the consulting-room officers found two new passports which convinced them that the doctor and his companion planned to flee the country.

With Bougrat released from prison on the fraud charge the police conducted a thorough search of his premises. The source of the all-pervading smell seemed to be a long cupboard recessed in a wall of the consulting-room

Dr Bougrat's victim is discovered

high up under the ceiling. The cupboard had been papered over to match the pattern on the wall so that it was well concealed. When the double doors of the cupboard were opened the room was filled with the stench of decay arising from the putrefying body of Jacques Rumèbe.

Bougrat denied killing his former friend and claimed 'he committed suicide in this room'. His story was that Rumèbe came to him for treatment following a beating-up when he was robbed of the wages money he was carrying. He asked the doctor to help him retrieve the stolen money, which amounted to 25,000 francs. Bougrat left the house, and on returning found Rumèbe lying semi-conscious in his consulting-room. He claimed that his friend had injected himself with a fatal dose of mercuric cyanide. Fearing that the police would suspect him of theft, and with a dead man on his hands, Bougrat decided to keep quiet and to hide the corpse until he could dispose of it properly. Thus Rumèbe's body ended up in the cupboard in the consulting-room and the unexpected arrival of Andrea prevented his carrying out his disposal plan.

Needles to say, none of this impressed the

police, and Dr Bougrat was brought to trial for murder and theft. Evidence given by the Prevosts of what they had seen through the key-hole proved damaging, and Andrea's testimony was not favourable. Bougrat was found guilty and sentenced to hard labour for life on Devil's Island. He landed there in 1927, but the following year escaped to Venezuela. After various escapades — including an incident in which he impressed the Venezuelans with his medical skills — he was allowed to stay. He married an Italian nurse, practised medicine and died in 1962 at the age of seventy-five, a free man and one who was respected by the community in which he worked.

Because the consulting-room is the medical man's place of work, it is also the place where he can fall victim. This was the fate of Dr Harvey Burdell, a wealthy American dentist. His consulting-room was on the first floor of the mansion he owned at 31 Bond Street, New York City, the other rooms of which he sublet to various tenants. At the age of forty-six Dr Burdell had gained considerable wealth from his dental practice, but in the process had also acquired an unsavoury reputation as a sly swindler.

On 29 January 1857 several people observed the tall, bearded figure of the dentist enter his house at about 10.45 p.m. Shortly afterwards a cry, sounding like 'Murd ...' was emitted from the house, and heard by both a passer-by and

Dr Harvey Burdell done to death in his own consulting-room

by a neighbour. Dr Burdell's body was found the next morning lying on the floor of his consulting-room — he had been stabbed twelve times, and strangled for good measure.

From an examination of the murder scene it appeared that the victim had been taken by surprise while sitting at his desk. He was stabbed in the shoulder and appeared to have struggled with his assailant, who managed to strike him a blow in the neck which cut the carotid artery. Further knife thrusts penetrated the heart and abdomen. There was blood everywhere — on the desk and chair, splashed on the walls and other furniture as the victim and attacker lurched about the room, and finally on the carpet as the mortally wounded dentist's life ebbed away.

As there were no signs that the house had been forcibly entered, suspicion focused on the other residents at 31 Bond Street. Strangely, while several persons outside the house had heard a cry, none of those within had heard a sound. The chief suspect was Mrs Emma Cunningham, who had an arrangement with Burdell whereby she sublet rooms to boarders. At the time of the murders there were two boarders — John J. Eckel, a dealer in hides and animal fats, who lived on the third floor, and George Snodgrass, the slightly effeminate son of a church minister.

Despite the lack of evidence (except for the fact that her left-handedness was said to match that of Burdell's murderer), Mrs Cunningham was charged with involvement in the crime. Eckel and Snodgrass were similarly charged. At this point Mrs Cunningham lodged a claim for part of the dead man's estate, claiming that they had been secretly married. As the result of the coroner's inquiry, all three were charged with murder and sent for trial.

Emma Cunningham was the first to face a trial jury, and the weak prosecution against her collapsed when she let it be known that she was pregnant. The jury brought in a not guilty verdict, and the charges against Eckel and Snodgrass were also dropped. Emma continued to press her claim to Burdell's estate, but doubts as to the validity of her condition were aroused by her refusal to permit a doctor to examine her. She denied the examination on the grounds of old-fashioned modesty, but it was being strongly rumoured that she was not pregnant at all.

Rumour stimulated police surveillance, and

it was learned that she had given $1,000 to an unmarried girl for her infant child. Vigilant police burst in on Emma at the very moment she was taking possession of the child. Now it had been proved that she had lied about being pregnant it was thought that she was more likely to be a murderess. While she could not be charged twice with the same crime, she was charged with fraud, although this was subsequently dropped.

Eckel and Snodgrass had wisely removed themselves from the public eye and Emma, completely undaunted, rented her impostor child to P. T. Barnum for $25 a week so that 'The Bogus Burdell Baby', as it was described, could be viewed as a curiosity. While Mrs Cunningham prospered, the contents of the murdered man's house were sold by auction. The street outside was thronged with people as the doctor's furniture and dental apparatus went to the highest bidders — one of the first items to go was the blood-soaked carpet from the consulting-room.

This murder, which caused such a sensation in New York in the 1850s, remains unsolved. Dr Burdell was known to be in debt, and it was thought that one of his creditors had killed him. A man named Lewis, executed in New Jersey for another murder, claimed to be Burdell's murderer, but this was never proved. *(103, 145, 282, 298, 386, 397, 628, 704, 734, 735, 787, 868, MWW, mw)*

DOCTORS AND DENTISTS WHO HAVE FEATURED IN MURDER CASES

Accused	Year	Victim	Weapon		Location
Louis BERTRAND	1865	Lover's husband	Gun	Parlour	Sydney, Australia
Morris BOLBER	1932	Immigrants	Bludgeon	Various	Philadelphia, USA
Pierre BOUGRAT	1925	Friend	Poison	Consulting-room	Marseilles, France
Robert BUCHANAN	1892	Wife	Poison	Parlour	New York City, USA
Edmé CASTAING	1832	Acquaintance	Poison	Inn	Paris, France
Robert CLEMENTS	1945	Wife	Poison	Sick-room	Southport, England
Carl COPPOLINO	1967	Wife	Poison	Parlour	Florida, USA
Thomas Neill CREAM	1892	Prostitutes	Poison	Bedroom	London, England
Hawley Harvey CRIPPEN	1910	Wife	Poison	Parlour	London, England
Philip CROSS	1887	Wife	Poison	Parlour	County Cork, Ireland
Edmond De La POMMERAIS	1863	Mistress	Poison	Parlour	Paris, France
Geza De KAPLANY	1962	Wife	Acid	Apartment	California, USA
Etienne DESCHAMPS	1889	Young girl	Poison	Bedroom	New Orleans, USA
Bernard FINCH (with Carole Tregoff)	1958	Wife	Gun	House driveway	California, USA
Thomas GRAVES	1892	Widow	Poison	Parlour	Colorado, USA
John HILL	1969	Wife	Poison	Sick-room	Houston, Texas
Bennett Clarke HYDE*	1910	Patients	Poison	Sick-room	Kansas City, USA
William KING	1859	Wife	Poison	Sick-room	Coburg, Canada
George Henry LAMSON	1881	Brother-in-law	Poison	School	Wimbledon, England
Jeffrey MACDONALD	1970	Wife and daughters	Knife	Army married quarters	Fort Bragg, USA
William PALMER	1855	Friend	Poison	Inn	Rugeley, England
Marcel PETIOT	1944	War refugees	?	Consulting-room	Paris, France
Edward PRITCHARD	1865	Wife and mother-in-law	Poison	Parlour	Glasgow, Scotland
Buck RUXTON	1935	Wife and maid	Various	Parlour	Lancaster, England
Samuel SHEPPARD	1954	Wife	Bludgeon	Bedroom	Ohio, USA
Thomas SMETHURST	1859	Mistress	Poison	Sick-room	Richmond, England
Arthur Warren WAITE	1916	Relatives	Poison	Sick-room	New York City, USA
Walter WILKINS	1919	Wife	Bludgeon	House driveway	Long Island, USA
Alice WYNEKOOP	1933	Daughter-in-law	Poison and Gun	Consulting-room	Chicago, Illinois, USA

*See under Murder by post.

DINING-ROOMS AND RESTAURANTS

'But, alas! The cruel spoiler came ....'
Lucretia Chapman (1831)

Dining-rooms are places where the poisoned cup or adulterated food may be set before the unsuspecting victim. The chance of death being immediately attributed to food-poisoning rather than to premeditated murder is high. Murderers have gone to considerable lengths to ensure that their special brands of culinary arts are directed to their victims. Buttered scones, slices of cake, flesh, fowl, wine, milk and soup have all been used as media for poison.

Poor Lieutenant Hubert Chevis sat down to a meal of poisoned partridge (see under BARRACKS) and died of strychnine poisoning in 1931. This was a technique which had been used many years earlier by Dr Eustachy, who practised medicine in the southern French town of Pertuis, where he was also a member of the council. All was serene until a younger doctor arrived in the town and set up a rival practice. The new man, Dr Tournatoire, attracted a number of Eustachy's patients, and, worse still, opposed him as a candidate for election to the council.

Eustachy's reaction to these sudden reverses was to attack his rival in the newspapers with ill-considered language. In November 1884 Dr Tournatoire sued for libel and won his action with costs. Several weeks later he received an unsolicited gift of half a dozen thrushes ready for the table, ostensibly sent by a grateful patient. The doctor's wife decided to eat one of the birds for her lunch-time meal. She was soon stricken with pain, and suffered hallucinations which led her to think she was going mad.

Dr Tournatoire decided to examine the remaining birds for suspected poison, and the use of chemical tests identified the presence of atropine. In view of the history of animosity between the town's two doctors, it was not long before Eustachy's name was linked with the sending of the thrushes. It was found that he had recently ordered a quantity of atropine from his pharmacist and won some game birds, including a dozen thrushes, in a lottery. Confronted with the accusation, Eustachy admitted sending the birds to Tournatoire, explaining that it was merely a practical joke. It was certainly a dangerous prank, for the thrushes had been filled with sufficient atropine to kill several people.

Eustachy was charged with attempted murder and sent for trial. He withdrew his confession, but it did him little good. The presence of atropine in the poisoned birds was confirmed by chemical evidence which included the first recorded use of microphotography in a court — enlarged pictures were shown of the crystals of atropine. Eustachy was convicted and sentenced to eight years' hard labour. His remaining patients thus had no alternative but to go over to the rival he had tried so ineffectually to eliminate.

Soup and broth are excellent vehicles for the poisoner's craft. The poison is easily stirred in, and the soup masks any unwelcome taste. An added advantage for the murderously inclined is that even the chronically poisoned victim continues to seek nourishment that is traditionally provided by soup, and hence there is no difficulty in maintaining the dose until death results. Mary Blandy souped up her father's gruel with arsenic under the instructions of her lover, and secured the old man's demise at his home in Henley-on-Thames in 1746. She was hanged for murder, and her lover was thwarted in his attempts to gain a handsome dowry.

Lucretia Chapman was also tempted by her lover to spice the soup with arsenic — in this case, to poison her husband. On 19 May 1831 a young man appeared at the Chapman home in Andalusia, Pennsylvania, asking for accommodation for the night. Lucretia, a hard-working mother and schoolteacher, was captivated by the visitor, who introduced himself as Don Lino Amalia Expos y Mina, a scion of a noble Mexican family. He explained that he had fallen on hard times after being sent to Europe to finish his schooling.

Lucretia was so impressed that she agreed Mina could stay for three years and learn English under her tuition. The couple spent more and more time closeted together in a relationship which completely excluded William Chapman. Lucretia and Mina became lovers, and her husband became a candidate for elimination. In June 1831 William Chapman fell ill after dining on pork. His doctor prescribed chicken soup to aid his recuperation, but the poor man's health failed completely and he died. Twelve days later Lucretia and Mina were secretly married in New York City, but their previously close relationship changed. Mina took his new wife's horse and wagon together with much of her savings to go in pursuit of mythical relatives, whom he claimed would bequeath him large sums of money.

The inquiry into William Chapman's death soon pointed to foul play, which was proved when his exhumed body was shown to contain arsenic. Mina fell into the hands of the Boston police after he had committed fraud in that city and he and Lucretia were charged with murder. The couple were tried separately — Lucretia's case being heard first. After a sensational trial at Doylestown in 1832 she was found not guilty, despite damning evidence given by a servant and neighbours. It was proved that she had bought a chicken from a neighbouring farmer expressly to make soup and the home help claimed that Lucretia had taken the soup into the dining-room, where Mina 'seasoned' it.

At his trial Mina took a generally light-hearted view of the proceedings and attempted to sidetrack the court by discussing his grand origins in Mexico and Cuba. When his delaying tactics failed he made a confession, claiming not only that Lucretia had seduced him but that she had bought the poison and administered it to her husband. The jury saw through the 'cruel spoiler', as Lucretia had come to call him, and Mina was convicted of murder and later hanged.

Another exponent of the poisoned culinary arts was Tillie Mitkiewitz. She lived in the Polish community in Chicago, and after twenty-six years of marriage, mostly spent slaving for an indolent husband, discovered that she had acquired the gift of prophecy. Like her fellow East European, the 'Great Billik' (see under NEXT DOOR), this was a talent which she developed for gain. Tillie forecast the imminent demise of her husband, and when John Mitkiewitz died ten days later in January 1914 her Polish immigrant neighbours, steeped in superstitious beliefs, marvelled at her powers of precognition. While they stood in awe Tillie collected the insurance money on her late husband.

Within a month Tillie had remarried, and John Ruskowski soon fell victim to her fatal predictions. In April 1920 she predicted the death of her third husband, Frank Kutczyk. She was so sure of her forecast that she bought a coffin and stored it in the basement to save time when her prophecy was fulfilled.

Husband number four was Anton Klimek, a brewery worker. This healthy man was soon talking of feeling weak, and especially complained of numbness in the legs. He spoke warmly of his wife's attention to his ills. 'Tillie is doing what she can to help me,' he told his brother. Anton's condition did not improve, and in October 1920 his brother called a doctor to give him a thorough examination. With little hesitation the doctor diagnosed poisoning and had his patient admitted to hospital, where his diagnosis was confirmed.

Tests proved that the poisonous agent was arsenic, and suspicion immediately fell on Tillie, whom Anton had suspected of doctoring his food. Tillie's neighbours talked freely when prompted by the police, and information about the sad deaths of her three previous husbands came to light; the phenomenon of her predictive abilities was especially significant. The prophetess was arrested, and confessed to poisoning Anton, although she steadfastly denied killing her previous husbands. She let it be known that her method was to stir rat poison into the stew which was one of her favourite dishes. Tillie Klimek was tried for murder in March 1922, when her confession, reinforced by the discovery of arsenic in the bodies of her exhumed husbands, led to her conviction. She was sentenced to life imprisonment after squeezing every drop of publicity she could out of her notoriety.

The 'Polish Borgia', as she was called in the newspapers, died in prison aged seventy-one. Tillie was suspected of procuring the deaths of several of her children and relatives in addition to her unfortunate husbands. She was also alleged to have helped a cousin dispose of her unwanted husband, no doubt by providing a lethal recipe for stew.

Doctored milk left on the victim's doorstep was the means used to murder elderly Walter Lewis Samples. He lived a quiet bachelor life in his bungalow in a comfortable residential area of Memphis, Tennessee. A retired engineer, he had travelled the world and fought in the Spanish-American War. He spent his time working for the Veterans' Association and managing the various properties which he owned.

On 21 February 1941 Samples telephoned his doctor asking him to call urgently. The doctor found Samples in agony from stomach pains and being tended by a woman considerably younger than himself. Before being rushed to hospital he said that he had been taken ill two days earlier after breakfast. He had cooked bacon and eggs and drunk two glasses of milk. He remarked that the bottle of milk which he had picked up from the front door of the bungalow was not from his usual supplier but from another Memphis dairy. Samples nevertheless drank the milk, and when his stomach pains became unbearable he called for the doctor. The sick man died shortly after being admitted to hospital.

The doctor had taken an opened bottle of milk from the refrigerator in the bungalow and thought he detected the odour of phosphorus. He sealed the bottle and gave it to Samples's female companion with instructions to take it to the police. An autopsy confirmed that the dead man had been poisoned with phosphorus and traces of the poison were found in the milk left in the bottle. A review of the procedure used at the dairy bottling plant ruled out the accidental introduction of poison. As it was thought unlikely that Samples would have committed suicide, his death was investigated as murder on the basis that someone who wanted him dead had adulterated his milk with phosphorus.

The woman found in the bungalow when the doctor called was quickly ruled out of the inquiry. She was a widow whose financial affairs Samples had sorted out, and in return she helped him with his work for the Veterans' Association. While she denied a close relationship with Samples, a search of his bungalow revealed that he had been leading a double life full of passion. Many photographs were found, some bearing tender endearments, together with a number of ardent love letters. The senders in many cases were recognized by the police as respected Memphis women. It seemed that the retired engineer had been leading a far from quiet life.

It was clear that there were many possible motives for Samples's death — a lover seeking the return of incriminating letters or a husband pursuing revenge. Some of the women were visited by detectives and discreetly questioned. It was clear that Samples had a compelling influence over many of them — one said, 'Whenever he wanted me, I went to him.'

The breakthrough in the police inquiry came by chance. In view of the dead man's extensive property dealings detectives decided to search through court records to see if he had been involved in litigation. His name came up in reference to a dispute with a man named LeRoy House who lived in the neighbouring state of Mississippi. House's wife answered the description of a woman neighbours had seen at Samples's house, but who had so far been unidentified. She admitted having an affair with Samples in 1925 but said she broke it off when she married LeRoy House. A search of the couple's home turned up several milk bottles belonging to the same Memphis dairy which supplied Samples. Mrs House was found to be carrying a will signed by Samples which named her as his sole beneficiary. LeRoy House claimed no knowledge of this.

The signature on the will was proved to be a forgery, and the Houses were charged with murder. At this point LeRoy House confessed that he had poisoned the milk left on Samples's doorstep and absolved his wife of any blame. The pair were tried in June 1941, when LeRoy House withdrew his confession. The jury nevertheless found them both guilty of murder and they were sentenced to twenty years' imprisonment.

Following an appeal a new trial was granted in 1943, when Mrs House created a sensation by declaring, 'My husband is innocent. I did it alone and he's trying to protect me.' Her conviction and sentence were confirmed and the charge against her husband was dismissed.

Despite their often intimate surroundings, restaurants do not offer the same opportunities as the domestic dining-room to tamper with the food. Restaurant murders tend therefore to be more violent, and locations are chosen because the murderer knows of his victim's intention to dine in a particular place. This has been a favourite *modus operandi* for gangland murders. Dutch Schultz and three of his bodyguards were gunned down by rival crime syndicate members in the Palace Chophouse, Newark, New Jersey, in October 1935.

Restaurants also feature as locations for murder committed in the furtherance of theft. The Green Parrot Restaurant in New York

City was the scene of such an incident on 12 July 1942 when the proprietor, Max Geller, was shot dead by a robber. The customers present at the time had been too concerned for their own safety to be able to give the police any useful descriptions of the gunman.

Confirmation of the shooting was provided by the green parrot which was kept behind the bar when it repeated the cry 'Robber! Robber!', thought to be an imitation of Geller's last words. The police inquiry was stalemated until a detective on the case learned that one of the green parrot's tricks was to pick up a customer's name and keep repeating it. Acting on the hunch that the parrot's apparent cry of 'Robber' might have been 'Robert', all known customers of that name were questioned. This line of inquiry reached Robert Butler, a local resident and customer of the restaurant, who proved to be the killer. He was convicted on a parrot's evidence, so to speak, in February 1944, and was sentenced to a term of imprisonment in Sing Sing.

The perpetrator of America's worst one-day massacre, surpassing Charles Whitman's killing of sixteen persons at the University of Texas in 1966, was James Huberty. Following the loss of his job and a row with his wife, in 1984 Huberty chose a McDonald's hamburger restaurant as the location for his revenge against mankind.

He walked into the restaurant at San Ysidro near San Diego, California, carrying three guns, one of which was a high-powered automatic rifle. Shouting, 'I've killed a thousand. I'll kill a thousand more', he opened fire indiscriminately, killing twenty men, women and children immediately, with one more dying later of wounds.

Police surrounded the restaurant, mindful that Huberty held hostages inside the building. After a siege lasting an hour and a half, a police marksman sighted Huberty as a clear target and killed him with a single shot.
(1, 309, 337, 384, 506, 683, 764, 927, mw)

FARMS AND FIELDS

'Killed a young girl — it was fine and hot.'

William Baker (1867)

Farms are ideal locations for murders, at least from the perpetrator's point of view. The mixture of open field, stock pens and out-buildings offers plenty of scope for criminal ingenuity. Ploughed fields provide tempting burial grounds for victims' corpses, and animals, especially pigs, have their uses as consumers of human remains.

Farms are places where people disappear, frequently without trace, as the late un-lamented Belle Gunness proved. Fourteen men went missing from her farm at Laporte in Indiana in the early 1900s. Their bodies were eventually discovered in 1908 when the farm burned down, but by then Belle herself had vanished and was never seen again.

By contrast, the Hosein brothers and Michael Onufrejczyk were all convicted of murder down on the farm in the absence of their victims' bodies. Arthur and Nizamodeen Hosein were presumed to have killed their kidnap victim in 1969 and to have fed her body to the pigs at Rooks Farm at Stocking Pelham, Hertfordshire. Onufrejczyk, an ex-Polish soldier turned farmer, was convicted in 1955 of murdering his partner at their farm at Cefu Hendre in Wales. Again, no body was found.

Another farm murderer in Wales was Thomas Harries, who might have escaped detection but for a clever ruse on the part of the police. Convinced that Harries had buried the bodies of his adopted aunt and uncle on their farm in Carmarthenshire, they tied cotton threads across the gate posts at the entrances to all the fields. Next they made a great commotion to make Harries believe they had found something and then retired. Anxious to learn if his secret had been discovered, Harries bided his time to make an inspection of the field containing the grave. As soon as he passed through the entrance he broke the cotton thread and led the police to the burial place of his victims. Harries was convicted of murder in 1954.

The foolishness of involving weak characters in an otherwise perfect murder plot was demonstrated by Charles Fielding when he came under the spell of Lottie Freeman. She was an attractive single woman who ran a farm in Cumberland County, Maine. She had many admirers and eventually accepted William Sanborn's proposal of marriage. The couple settled down on the farm and had three children, but then rumours began to spread that Lottie was secretly dating other men.

During the summer of 1910 Sanborn mysteriously disappeared. Lottie did not appear to be too distressed — she said merely that he had abandoned his responsibilities. In 1925 Lottie married again, having obtained a divorce on the grounds of her first husband's desertion. During the intervening period two of her hired farmhands had gone missing. This did not excite much attention at the time, as itinerant farm workers often left their employment without giving notice. But when Lottie's second husband, Alphonse Cote, disappeared in 1924 questions were asked. 'I simply thought that he was going deer-hunting,' Lottie told the police. She claimed that he had taken $200 of her money, and she assumed he had gone to Canada where he had family connections. She pressed the sheriff to post a notice offering a reward for information as to Cote's whereabouts, 'to stop the gossips in this town talking about me', as she put it.

Rumour hardened into suspicion when Cote's brother reported to the police that Lottie had written to a member of the family offering sympathy over Alphonse's disappearance but referring to his 'bad temper' which 'has carried him to ruin'. Alphonse was regarded as a most placid man, protested his brother, who hinted that Lottie had probably disposed of him. Lottie gave nothing away when she was more closely questioned, but investigators at the farm discovered a heap of ashes near the barn which contained fragments of clothing. Evidence from numerous witnesses confirmed that Lottie had entertained various admirers in the farmhouse, and shots had been heard by neighbours on the night that Alphonse Cote disappeared.

Sensing that the answer to the disappearance lay close to the farm, the police pressed Lottie's son, Ralph Sanborn, for answers. Eventually he confessed that his mother and one of her lovers planned the murder of Cote. Charles Fielding, a friend of Lottie's half-sister, was staying at the farm. He shot Cote in the back and Ralph was ordered to help him bury the body at night in a field scheduled for ploughing. After the plough passed over the field all evidence of the grave was destroyed.

Confronted with this allegation, Fielding made a full confession. He claimed that Lottie had promised him the earth if he would eliminate her husband. She denied everything, but a thorough search of the freshly ploughed field turned up the body of Alphonse Cote.

The disposal plan had been a good one, but the mistake was to involve her son. Lottie died before she could be tried for murder, but Fielding was sentenced to life imprisonment.

Fields are often the hunting-grounds of sex murderers who prowl lonely country lanes and tracks in the hope of encountering a solitary female who can be marked down as a victim. An incident which created a sensation in its day, and in due course added a new expression to the English language, was the brutal murder of eight-year-old Fanny Adams in a field at Alton in 1867. On 24 August in the early afternoon Fanny, her younger sister Elizabeth and a friend, Minnie Warner, left their homes in Tan House Lane to play in the fields. Their favourite spot was in Flood Meadow, less than half a mile away, which led down to a stretch of the river Wey shallow enough to paddle in.

At about 5.00 p.m. Minnie and Elizabeth returned home without Fanny. They explained to their parents that they had met William Baker, a local solicitor's clerk, who offered Fanny a halfpenny to go with him to The Hollow, a country road leading to the near-by village of Shalden. He also gave Minnie three halfpence to take Elizabeth home. Clutching their money, they had played together for the greater part of the afternoon before returning.

Mrs Adams and a neighbour immediately went in search of Fanny, but had only gone a short distance when they met 29-year-old William Baker. They questioned him and he admitted giving money to the children, although he denied knowing anything about Fanny. Reassured by his answers — he was, after all, a respectable solicitor's clerk — the two women gave up their search, assuming that the child had gone off on her own to play and would soon be home.

When Fanny had not returned by 7.00 p.m. a proper search was mounted. In the hopfield at the top of The Hollow they found the child's horribly mutilated body. The head had been severed, and the eyes and an ear were missing. The torso had been dismembered and disembowelled, with the remains strewn about. As the last person known to have seen the dead girl, Baker immediately came under suspicion. He was saved from the wrath of Fanny's father — armed with a shotgun — and of the angry townsfolk, by being arrested. Two small knives, one of them bloodstained, were found

William Baker: the charmer at work in the fields around Alton, Hampshire

in Baker's possession, and there were traces of blood on his clothes. Most damning of all was the discovery of his diary in the desk he used at the solicitor's office. The entry recorded against Saturday 24 August read, 'Killed a young girl — it was fine and hot.' He later claimed to have been drunk when he wrote this, and in any case it was shorthand for 'A young girl was killed on a fine hot day.'

William Baker was tried for murder at Winchester in December 1867 in an atmosphere of great enmity. He protested his innocence of the charge, claiming that his knives were too small to be used for mutilation, and that the children had lied about him. In his defence it was stated that he had been depressed and suicidal after a broken love affair, and experienced severe headaches and nose-bleeds due to overwork. It was also plain that a strong streak of insanity ran through his family. Despite these claims the jury was not inclined to mercy, and found him guilty. Baker was executed on Christmas Eve at Winchester before a crowd of five thousand.

Poor Fanny's name became the subject of black humour in the Royal Navy, whose sailors' dislike of newly introduced tinned rations found an outlet by referring to them as 'sweet Fanny Adams', implying that the tins contained the remains of Fanny Adams. The expression was later taken to mean 'nothing' and was further corrupted by subsequent generations of servicemen to 'sweet FA'.

The marauding sex murderer of the modern age is exemplified by Harvey Carignan, who planned his killings with the aid of maps, on which he carefully marked remote areas which suited his purpose. When 47-year-old Harvey Louis Carignan was arrested in Minneapolis in September 1974 he had already spent more than half his life in prison. He had graduated from juvenile delinquency to burglary, and finally to rape and murder.

While serving in the US Army and based at Anchorage in Alaska he narrowly escaped execution following a conviction for murder in 1949. He admitted attempting rape, but at first denied committing murder. He was convicted on the basis of his confession, which was subsequently challenged in the US Supreme Court, with the result that the death sentence was commuted to fifteen years' imprisonment. Carignan was released on parole in 1960 but remained at liberty for only four months before being convicted of burglary, first in Duluth, Minnesota, and then in Seattle, Washington. He used his time in prison to study journalism, sociology and psychology. As events subsequently turned out, he probably included geography, or at least map-reading, in his studies.

In 1969 Carignan married his first wife. They were soon divorced, and in 1972 he married again. This relationship lasted little longer than the first. His behaviour was characterized by frequent 'rages', and long periods away from home in the car. He drove many thousands of miles, and frequently crossed the US border into Canada.

Carignan ran a filling-station in 1973, and hit on the idea of advertising for assistance by placing want-ads in the *Seattle Times*. On 1 May his advertisement attracted fifteen-year-old Kathy Miller, who replied and promptly disappeared. Her school books were found a few days later twenty-six miles away in a parking lot at Everett, but the girl remained missing. Carignan was questioned by police — he admitted setting up an appointment to interview the girl, but nothing more. Kathy's body was found several weeks later in a field near Everett.

The police were unable to pin any firm evidence on Carignan, but in response to the pressure he deserted his business and moved to Denver and Minneapolis. He met Eileen Hunley, whom he may have seen as the third Mrs Carignan — she disappeared from her home in August 1974. In the following months several girls in the Minneapolis area were unfortunate to hitch lifts with a balding man in his forties who raped and assaulted them.

An alarming pattern developed where girls were picked up and driven to some remote area — usually a field reached by a deserted road — and then attacked. The assaults were sexual, sadistic and vicious. Four girls who had sustained blows to the head inflicted with a hammer survived their injuries and recounted the horror of the attack. On 24 September 1974 two alert Minneapolis police officers spotted a man answering the attacker's description and arrested him as he was about to enter his car. Harvey Carignan pleaded his innocence, but several of the girls he had attacked identified him. That the police had secured their quarry was made virtually certain when the tyres on Carignan's car were found to match impressions made in the soil alongside the corpse of a young woman found in a cornfield some forty miles from Minneapolis.

A search of Carignan's accommodation and of his car produced a large number of road maps of Washington, Kansas, Wisconsin, Oregon, Minnesota and other states. The maps had been marked with red circles drawn over remote country areas. Some of these circles (of which there were 181), coincided with known assaults on young women. The body of Kathy Miller, who had answered one of Carignan's want-ads in 1973, was found at a marked location, and there were other similar comparisons.

In February 1975 Harvey Carignan was tried for the attempted murder of a girl he had assaulted and left for dead in a field near Minneapolis. Still partially paralysed from her injuries, the girl gave damning evidence in court. Carignan testified, and when asked why he had stopped to pick up the girl, he replied, 'God told me to.' He said that he talked to God 'quite frequently', and had been instructed to 'kill and humiliate' four women. Of the girl he had tried to murder he said, 'I was sorry I didn't kill her ... because I was supposed to.'

The defence psychiatrist said that Carignan was mentally ill: 'He believes he is an ambassador of God and his mission is to kill certain young women.' Prosecution psychiatrists diagnosed him as a paranoid schizophrenic, but did not agree that he lacked control over what he did. The jury found him guilty of aggravated sodomy and attempted murder.

Further trials ensued, and Carignan was convicted on several charges of sexual assault and on two counts of murder. His accumulated sentences ran to over a hundred years plus life. Like the Yorkshire Ripper and Son of Sam, Harvey Carignan claimed to have heard voices instructing him to kill. But 'Harv the Hammer', as he became known in prison, also said that God appeared to him in person with slippers on his feet and a hood over his head.

Murderers usually confine their activities to a particular locale, city or country. Apart from terrorist killings, murder on an international scale is not a common occurrence. But there are exceptions, and Charles Sobhraj, born in Japanese-occupied Saigon in 1944, is one. His mother was the Vietnamese mistress of an Indian tailor; she married a French officer in 1948 and moved to France. Her young son was rejected by both his natural father and his stepfather. In 1953 the nine-year-old boy was legally adopted, but his stepfather refused to give him his name. Hotchand Bhawanni Gurmukh Sobhraj at the age of fifteen had his name recorded as Charles Sobhraj. Not that it mattered a great deal, for as his life unfolded he found it convenient to use a variety of aliases.

Young Charles was always in trouble as a teenager, and caused his stepfather — who was invalided home from Indo-China with shell-shock — a great deal of aggravation. He absconded from boarding-school to Paris, where he developed a taste for robbery which in 1964 earned him a three-year prison sentence. While in prison he honed his body and mind in tune with karate philosophy. 'There are people who are weak from the moment they leave their mother's breast. They are condemned. I believe I am in the category of the strong,' he wrote.

In 1969 Charles Sobhraj acquired much-prized French citizenship and married Hélène, a twenty-year-old butcher's daughter. One of the less attractive benefits of his new citizenship was to be conscripted in the French army. He was called up in 1970, but served only a few weeks before being discharged on medical grounds. This point in his life marked a steady slide into full-time criminal activity. He got heavily into debt, gambled recklessly and even stole from his sister. When his father visited Paris in 1970 he warned Hélène, 'You are married to a Number One crook ... my son is a destructor.'

He now embarked on a succession of travels in the East, invariably leaving behind a trail of unpaid bills. Charles established himself in Bombay for a while, where he set up shady car sales, importing stolen prestige cars from Europe by way of Iran. He frequently left Hélène with their infant while he travelled alone to Hong Kong and elsewhere 'on business'.

In October 1971 Charles and his gang robbed the jewellery shop beneath the Ashoka Hotel in Delhi. He escaped to Teheran, leaving Hélène and the stolen gems behind, only to be arrested when he returned to Delhi. He evaded the police by skipping bail, ending up in Afghanistan, where the following year he was arrested for debt. Again Charles escaped from custody, and during the next two years embroiled his half-brother, André, in thefts from tourists in Greece and Turkey. 'I use psychology like stupid people use guns,' he

boasted to his young companion when they were arrested in Greece. He amply demonstrated this by escaping from a Greek prison leaving André to face the music, which in this case amounted to a sentence of eighteen years' hard labour.

Europe proved too hazardous for Charles, and his Oriental instincts drew him back to the East, where the pickings were easy and the police less alert. By the time he arrived in Delhi in May 1975 Hélène had left him, and he encountered a young Canadian girl, Marie Andrée Leclerc, whom he took as a lover. By August the couple were set up in Bangkok, a city in which Charles could give full rein to his talents. He posed as a gem dealer, using the name Alain Gautier, and involved Marie in thefts from tourists. They took a fifth-floor apartment at Kanit House in the centre of Bangkok, which became a sort of transit camp for young travellers to the East whom Charles proposed to rob.

In October 1975 Jennie Bolliver, a 23-year-old Californian drop-out, arrived in Bangkok on her way to Katmandu. She encountered Charles, who took her back to Kanit House and offered her hospitality. The next day her body was found on the beach at Pattaya. At first it was thought that she had accidentally drowned, but later it was shown she had been forcibly held under water.

People came and went from Kanit House, with Charles acting as mine host and Marie working as chief cook and bottle-washer. Some of the visitors mysteriously fell ill after taking meals with Charles, and never really responded to the special medicine which he insisted they take to cure their 'Bangkok Belly'. 'This is Bangkok,' he said in explanation. 'I can't help it if people get sick. I'm trying to help them.'

In November 1975 Vitali Hakim, a Turkish entrepreneur, arrived in Bangkok hoping to deal in gems. He met Charles Sobhraj and was invited back to Kanit House. On 29 November the burnt remains of Hakim were found in a field near the Siam Country Club at Pattaya. He had been bludgeoned to death, and his body set alight with the aid of petrol. In December Charles went to Hong Kong 'on business', using his alias Alain Dupuis. There he met Dutchman Henricus Bintanja and his girl-friend Cornelia Hemker, and persuaded them to visit him in Bangkok. The couple duly turned up at Kanit House at about the same time that a French woman, Charmayne Carrou, arrived looking for Vitali Hakim, her Turkish boy-friend. Charmayne's body was found in a tidal creek near Pattaya — she was presumed to have drowned. On 18 December Thai newspapers reported the discovery of two partly burned bodies in a roadside ditch some thirty miles south of Bangkok. Henricus Bintanja and his girl-friend had been strangled.

Charles and his partner in crime, a young Indian called Ajay Chowdhury, moved to Katmandu for Christmas — Marie tagged along. Their travels were financed by stolen travellers cheques and credit cards; borders were crossed using stolen passports with new photographs pasted in. In Katmandu Charles

ran into an itinerant North American couple — Laddie DuParr, a Canadian, and Annabella Tremont, an American. On 22 December DuParr's burnt corpse was found in a field a short distance from the city, and the next day the blackened corpse of his girl-friend was discovered in another field. It was known that the dead couple had been in contact with Charles, who was masquerading as Henricus Bintanja. He talked his way through police questioning and made a hasty exit from Nepal by road to India.

In Calcutta a young Jew, Avoni Jacobs, who was studying Eastern religion, had the misfortune to encounter Charles Sobhraj. Jacobs was found dead in his room — he had been drugged and strangled. With eight deaths in his wake and the police of several countries searching for him, Charles returned to Bangkok. There, thanks to the efforts of a Dutch

Thai police uncover a victim of violence in the Sobhraj case

Embassy official investigating the deaths of Bintanja and Hemker, he was traced to Kanit House. Charles's apartment was raided in March 1976, and he was arrested. He passed himself off as an American visitor and slipped through the fingers of the police, whom it was later alleged he had bribed.

In the apartment of Kanit House were found fifteen kilos of proprietary drugs, mostly barbiturates, together with a number of used hypodermic syringes. There were also many documents — used airline tickets, hotel bills, car rental agreements and driving licences belonging to twenty different people. Most significant was the discovery of personal effects belonging to some of the dead young people who had encountered Charles Sobhraj.

The most wanted man in Asia travelled to Paris via Karachi and looked up Hélène, his former wife, and other friends and acquaintances. Then, it was back East when in June 1976 *Asia Week* magazine carried an article about murders in Bangkok and the search being made by Thai police for Alain Gautier and his female companion. Warrants were issued for their arrest, and Interpol was alerted.

Undaunted, Charles and Marie turned up in India, where with the help of some new confederates a jewel robbery was planned in Delhi. This venture fell through, and with dwindling funds it became necessary to rob a young Frenchman staying at the Ranjit Hotel. Jean-Luc Solomon was found drugged and dying in his room following a meal taken with Sobhraj. Moving to the Vikram Hotel, the conspirators planned multiple thefts against a party of visiting French people. It proved disastrous.

Ingratiating himself with the visitors who were making a tour of Asia, Charles, the experienced traveller, warned them against the perils of stomach upsets. He persuaded twenty members of the party to swallow pills which he offered them to combat the evils of dysentery. The pills were produced late in the evening, in the expectation that the travellers would retire for the night. Once in their rooms they would collapse as a result of taking Charles's powerful hypnotic potion and become easy prey for his band of thieves. Despite Charles's dramatic yawns, the party decided to stay up late, and drama ensued when one after another they began collapsing and falling

about in the hotel lounge. Eyes fastened on Charles. There were accusations of 'Poison!' and strong hands held him captive until the arrival of the police.

Charles Sobhraj was arrested, protesting outraged innocence, and his companions — who had fled when the rumpus developed — were quickly rounded up. Marie-Andrée Leclerc made a long statement in which she cast herself as subordinate to Sobhraj in every way. He led and she, who had neither money nor valid passport, followed. Charles admitted several cases of drugging but denied charges of killing people. If there had been any deaths they must be attributed to Ajay Chowdhury was his explanation.

The Indian Press ran stories about the 'International Killers' in prison at Delhi and the teleprinters were kept busy with police messages to and from Bangkok. When he appeared before the magistrates Charles absolved Marie of any guilt. 'She is a victim of love,' he explained. 'She should not be accused of anything else.' They waited a year in prison before their trial date came up, and it was another ten months before a verdict was announced. After hearing the evidence regarding the death of Jean-Luc Solomon in Delhi the judge acquitted Marie and sentenced Charles Sobhraj to seven years' hard labour for culpable homicide not amounting to murder.

In 1982 Sobhraj and Leclerc were tried for the murder of Avoni Jacobs, the young Jewish student killed in Calcutta, and sentenced to life imprisonment. The authorities in Thailand and Nepal still have outstanding charges of murders against Sobhraj. The man whom Richard Neville, one of the authors of *Bad Blood*, interviewed in a Delhi jail in 1977 and described as 'a brilliant psychopath', told an Indian court, 'I am my own judge and I judge myself innocent.'
(27, 140, 157, 227, 316, 375, 397, 453, 709, 783, 810, 899, 931, 957, 986, MWW)

GARAGES

'You'll see, they're going to get rid of me.'

Christine Demeter (1973)

Perhaps the most famous garage murder is that of Vivian Messiter in Southampton in

1929. The incident produced large headlines at the time, and included many of the elements which turn garages into murder locations. Messiter was an oil-company representative who used a lock-up garage in Grove Street to accommodate his company car, and to store drums of oil. The garage was in a quiet area close to Messiter's lodgings. The premises contained the usual clutter to be found in a garage, including various tools.

A confrontation took place between Messiter and William Podmore, a local agent who was operating a swindle. In the heat of the argument Podmore snatched up a hammer and battered his accuser to death, in an act of violence which led to his conviction for murder. The noise of the struggle was confined to the garage, and the murderer locked up behind him and fled from the scene. It was several weeks before Messiter's body was found.

Garages are often self-contained buildings separated from the rest of the owner's property, to provide seclusion for car maintenance work or workshop activities, where any noise causes least disturbance. This seclusion offers scope for secrecy, and persons intending suicide often retreat to the garage. There they can fatally poison themselves by running the car engine in a closed space without fear of attracting attention. By the same token, a murderer can lie in wait for his victim, safe in the knowledge that the sound of violence will not attract attention.

This was the fate which awaited Christine Demeter in the garage of her luxury home at Mississauga in Ontario, Canada. On 18 July 1973 her husband Peter drove their house guests into Toronto in her Mercedes to do some shopping; Christine and her three-year old daughter Andrea stayed at home. The shopping party returned at about 9.45 p.m., and Peter operated the remote-controlled door to the double garage. As the door slowly lifted a pool of blood glistened in the car

Christine Demeter lies dead in the garage of her home in Mississauga, Ontario, Canada

headlights, and then the outstretched body of Christine came into view. She lay face down next to Peter's Cadillac, which was spattered with blood. Her head had been brutally crushed with a heavy weapon. Inside the house, and oblivious of the drama unfolding in the garage, Andrea sat quietly watching TV.

Mississauga had not often been visited by violent death, but in the space of a few weeks a female student was raped and murdered within a mile of the Demeters' home and another girl had been reported missing. It was natural that people should link the three incidents, but as events developed it became clear that Christine Demeter's death was in a class of its own.

Peter Demeter came from a well-regarded Hungarian family whose home in Budapest was destroyed when the Russians drove the Nazi occupiers out of the city in 1944. After several attempts to cross the border with Austria, Demeter finally escaped to Vienna in 1954 and applied for political asylum at the US Embassy. He arrived in Toronto in 1956 with only eight dollars to his name, and virtually no English. He worked hard at whatever jobs he could find, and made enough money to afford several trips to Vienna during the next ten years. His fortunes improved when he obtained a real estate licence and began to sell houses, mostly to fellow-Hungarians. In 1962 he registered Eden Gardens Limited, a property development company, and began to acquire some of life's luxuries.

One of the reasons for his frequent visits to Vienna was to see his Austrian girl-friend, with whom he had an indecisive relationship. During one of the cool periods he met Christine, another Austrian girl, who at the time was engaged to a film producer. Peter swept her off to Canada, where she fulfilled a promising modelling career, and in November 1967 they were married at Toronto Town Hall.

At the beginning of 1973 Peter's business began to boom. They had already moved into a 150-year-old former farmhouse set in two acres of land at Dundas Crescent in Mississauga. Now he was able to buy Christine a Mercedes, and in February they took a holiday in Acapulco. But their marriage was far from secure, and friends and acquaintances alike had noticed the strains, particularly Peter's often belligerent behaviour. Moreover, Peter had been in touch with his former Austrian

girl-friend, and a secret trip was planned to Montreal. When Christine found out about this she was furious, and the further discovery in Peter's business files of letters which had passed between him and his girl-friend merely added fuel to the flames.

In June Christine consulted her attorney about getting a divorce, and she told a friend that her marriage had been sheer hell, adding, 'You'll see, they're going to get rid of me.'

When Peter returned from his trip to Montreal they discussed a divorce settlement. On 18 July Christine died violently at a time when Peter was in the company of friends some twenty miles away. No evidence of sexual attack was found at the autopsy, and death was the result of seven massive blows to the head. The weapon was not found, and murder during the course of robbery was ruled out as the contents of the house had not been disturbed in any way. The killer had done his work quickly, and silently enough to avoid disturbing the child watching TV inside the house. The residence itself was the last but one house in a cul-de-sac, and was well shielded by the dense foliage of numerous trees and bushes.

A possible solution to the crime emerged during the preliminary hearing when Csaba Szilagyi, a close friend of Peter's, made a statement regarding a conversation with Peter Demeter which took place in Vienna. Peter had mentioned in a roundabout way and then more directly that he wanted to get rid of his wife. Various methods were discussed, ranging from shooting in the course of a break-in to accidental electrocution in the swimming-pool, and he wanted Csaba to do it. Csaba later told a trial court that he came to Canada in 1969 to prevent the murder of Christine Demeter.

Two days after Christine was murdered, Csaba made a statement to the police, and on the day of her funeral he spoke to Peter Demeter, who was unaware that his friend was wired up for electronic surveillance. The tape was eventually heard in court. Reacting to Csaba's reference to a police request that he should take a lie detector test, Peter advised him strongly against it. 'You are the only one who knows,' he said.

Peter Demeter was tried for the non-capital offence of procuring his wife's murder. The court in London, Ontario, sat through the longest trial in Canadian history, and listened to evidence given by a bizarre set of witnesses, which included numerous members of the Hungarian underworld and the self-confessed murderer of two women in Mississauga who denied any implication in the death of Christine Demeter. In the intricate tangle of their relationships it seemed that both Christine and Peter had discussed with mutual friends the possibility of eliminating each other.

The jury in this extraordinary case at length concluded on 4 December 1974 that Peter Demeter was guilty as charged. His appeal was turned down, and he was sentenced to life imprisonment.

A well-equipped garage workshop provided Jerry Brudos with all the facilities he needed to further his murderous impulse. When Linda Slawson, a door-to-door encyclopedia saleswoman, called at the Brudos residence in Portland, Oregon, on 26 January 1968 she was given a warm welcome. 'I'm really interested in buying encyclopedias,' Jerry Brudos told her. He invited her down to his workshop, explaining, 'There's some company upstairs.' With his mother looking after his two children in the absence of his wife, he clubbed the girl to death. After playing about with her body he cut off one of her feet complete with shoe and put it in the freezer. At dead of night he drove out to St John's Bridge at Portland and dumped his victim's corpse into the Willamette river. Brudos returned home to his family, and Linda Slawson entered the ranks of the missing.

During the next few months three more young women disappeared in the Portland area. On 26 November 1968 Jan Witney, a student, vanished without trace, although her empty car was found in a parking lot, and on 27 March 1969 another student, Karen Sprinker, failed to turn up for a lunch appointment with her mother. On 23 April 1969 Linda Salee, an office worker, missed her date with her boy-friend. All three girls were reported as missing persons.

On 10 May a man fishing in the Long Tom river, a tributary of the Willamette, hooked the body of Linda Salee. The girl had been strangled, and her body weighted with part of a car's transmission. Two days later another body was discovered about fifty feet from the first. This was Karen Sprinker, who in addition to being strangled had been sexually mutilated.

Police inquiries concentrated on Oregon State University, and among the many girl students interviewed one spoke of a tall, heavily built freckle-faced man who had hung about the campus looking for dates. This description, especially the reference to freckles, matched an account given to the police of a man who had attacked a fifteen-year-old girl on 22 April. The university student was asked to inform the police if this man contacted her again. The call came on 25 May, reporting that the man had asked for a date. The girl stalled him, and when he arrived he was intercepted by police officers. Twenty-eight-year-old Jerry Brudos was taken for questioning, but there was insufficient evidence on which to detain him. Once he was free Jerry Brudos promptly disappeared with his family, but he was tailed and subsequently arrested.

During the second bout of questioning Brudos poured out a story of bizarre sexual behaviour leading to rape, murder, mutilation and necrophilia. A search of his home produced a box containing forty pairs of women's shoes hidden in the attic, but it was the garage, a building separate from the house, which proved to be the centre of his activities. The garage-workshop had a hook in the ceiling from which he suspended the bodies of his victims when he toyed with them after death. He was a shoe and undergarment fetishist, and had accumulated a vast collection of articles with which he dressed his victims' dead bodies before photographing them. Glossy prints provided ample testimony of the sinister world he enjoyed in the privacy of his garage.

On 27 June 1969 Brudos pleaded guilty to murder, dropping an earlier plea of not guilty by reason of insanity. Seven doctors had found him sane despite his being diagnosed as having a sexual deviation — fetishism personality disorder — when he was aged seventeen. He had also been discharged from the US army after only eight months' service because of his obsessions. All his life Brudos had been dominated by his mother, for whom he developed a strong hatred which eventually spilled over into hatred for all women. Although he made perverse sexual demands on his wife, he did not ill-treat her. She recognized that his behaviour was odd, and spoke of the severe migraines he suffered after they moved from Portland to 3123 Center Street, Salem, where he frequently locked himself away in the garage.

Jerry Brudos was sentenced to three consecutive terms of life imprisonment and, by a cruel twist of irony, his long-suffering wife was charged with murder in July 1969, in that she had aided and abetted her husband. This stemmed from neighbourhood malice, and although she had to face the ordeal of a trial Darcie Brudos was acquitted.

(2, 126, 305, 491, 505, 750, 815, 898, 1053, *MWW*)

GARDENS

'A lady, country resident, wants infant to adopt.'

Minnie Dean (1895)

Secret burial of the dead seems a foolproof solution to the problem of disposing of the murder victim's body, but there are unforeseen difficulties. It is difficult to keep a grave hidden, as disturbance of soil and vegetation leaves a scar in the ground, and it is never possible to return all the soil to the original hole. Sand is in fact one of the few materials which lend themselves to secret burial (see BEACHES). There is usually no difference in colour between the surface and sub-surface material, and surplus sand can be dispersed without being noticeable.

Despite the disadvantages, garden burial which puts the victim out of sight and out of mind proves too great an attraction for some murderers. The convenience is easy to understand — after all, domestic murder in a house with a garden attached is to have all mod. con. But apart from the noise of digging which might attract the attention of neighbours, a disconcerting pitfall is that decomposition of a corpse under the soil can fertilize plants growing above. To the perceptive detective luxuriant growth in the garden of a murder suspect gives grounds for thinking about secret burial.

Minnie Dean, an Edinburgh minister's daughter, emigrated to New Zealand in 1868. She married Charles Dean, and in 1886 they moved into a small timber house at East Winton, about nineteen miles from Invercargill on South Island. Although the Deans had a 22-acre site, their house, called 'The Larches', was a humble affair with three rooms and a lean-to. Nevertheless the garden was well kept

up, and Minnie liked to boast about her lovely dahlias and chrysanthemums.

Despite the lack of proper accommodation, Minnie decided to advertise her services as a baby-farmer. This was a pursuit which was to be highlighted in England in 1896 by the dreadful Amelia Dyer, who murdered several of the babies which she took into care. But Minnie Dean's activities came to light as early as 1889, when an adopted child in her care died, and again in 1891 when another infant perished under her keeping. In both cases doctors decided that death was due to natural causes, but there was apprehension about Minnie Dean's arrangements. She had ten children in her small house. Three slept with her, four slept in boxes in her room, one in the kitchen and one in the lean-to with her husband.

These revelations led the Commissioner of Police for the Colony to condemn the practice of baby-farming in his Annual Report of 1893. Aware that the authorities were keeping a watchful eye on her, Minnie resorted to disguising her name in the advertisements which she placed in the New Zealand *Times Herald*. In April 1895 the following notice appeared: 'A lady, country resident, wants infant to adopt. Comfortable home, address "Mater", Herald Office.' The police checked the entry and found that it had been placed by Miss Cameron, 'The Larches', East Winton. Miss Cameron turned out to be Minnie Dean, and the going rate for taking on a child was £10.

The following month an alert railway guard in the region noticed that a woman he had seen on the train nursing an infant left the carriage without the child. He notified the police of what he thought was a suspicious occurrence. The woman proved to be Minnie Dean, who had taken into her care a month-old girl, handed over, together with £4, by the infant's grandmother, Mrs Hornsby. This lady had no hesitation in identifying Minnie Dean when she confronted her, but the baby-farmer denied all knowledge of having taken a child and then abandoning it.

When some of the missing baby's clothing was found at 'The Larches' the discovery was sufficient to warrant the arrest of Minnie Dean and her husband. While standing outside the house discussing the course of their inquiries, one officer among a group of detectives noticed an unusually wet patch of soil in one of the flower beds. Pulling up the flowers, he uncovered a shallow grave containing two small bodies. The skeleton of a third child was found in another part of the garden. The two corpses discovered in the flower garden were identified as Eva Hornsby and Dorothy Edith Carter.

Traces of morphia were found in one of the bodies, and it was thought that the child had probably been killed with poison. Bottles containing laudanum and chloroform were discovered in Minnie Dean's bedroom. Local people said that Minnie would never let her husband work in the garden, especially the flower beds which were her pride and joy. Charles Dean knew nothing of what was going on, and he was eventually discharged.

Minnie Dean was tried for murder at Invercargill, and despite her plea of not guilty, the evidence told against her and she was convicted. On 12 August 1895 she attained the dubious distinction of being the first and last woman to be hanged in New Zealand. Asked at the scaffold if she had anything to say she replied, 'No, I have nothing to say, except that I am innocent', adding for the benefit of the hangman, 'Oh God, let me not suffer.'

In another case, in another continent, it was the vegetable patch rather than the flower garden which attracted attention. The Fire Brigade was called on 19 February 1972 to deal with a blazing house in Christina Gardens, Port of Spain, Trinidad. Once the fire was brought under control police arrived on the scene to examine the ruins of what had been the rented home of Black Power leader Michael X, otherwise known as Abdul Malik. An alert police officer casting his eye over the garden thought that a bed of lettuce looked uncharacteristically 'tall and yellow'. The bed was probed with a long pole, and it was quickly discovered that the lettuce plants were growing over a grave. A man's body was exhumed — it was partially mummified due to the depth of burial.

Two days later another grave was discovered in the garden, and this time a woman's body was brought to light. Professor Keith Simpson was flown from London to carry out a pathological examination of the bodies, which were identified by dental and fingerprint evidence as Joe Skerrit and Gail Benson, both followers of Abdul Malik. The woman's body had been slashed and stabbed; soil in the air passages and the stomach showed that she had been buried alive. Skerrit had been slashed and finally battered to death with a heavy object.

Three of Malik's followers were rounded up and charged with murder, but the Black Power leader had disappeared to Guyana. He was spotted in that country carrying a briefcase and cutlass, heading for Brazil, arrested and deported to Trinidad on 1 March 1972 to face murder charges.

Abdul Malik (born as Michael de Freitas in Trinidad in 1933), spent a major part of his life in England, where he attempted to set up a Black Power movement. He changed his name to Abdul Malik in 1963, following his conversion to the Muslim faith, and two years later adopted the name Michael X. He was greatly influenced by the American Black Power leader Malcolm X, who visited Britain in 1965.

Abdul Malik, already an influential force in London's immigrant community, founded the Racial Advancement and Action Society (RAAS) in 1965. He moved in smart London circles, and fascinated the media, which wrote extensively about him, and also some of the celebrities of the time, who helped to fund his activities. He made speeches at Oxford and Cambridge Universities, and generally conducted himself as a person of influence.

Malik's extreme racialism — which advocated, among other things, that any white man seen with a black girl should be killed — quickly led to confrontation with the law. In 1967 he was imprisoned for twelve months under the provisions of the Race Relations Act after a tour of the Midlands and the North of England. In one of his speeches he declared, 'Fear of the white monkeys is nothing. We should feel this in our hearts. We can deal with them ... killing is a strange thing. Before I killed for the first time I wondered if I would have a conscience. But I slept well. And now I am no longer afraid.'

In 1970 Malik was charged with robbery, and it was plain that his London activities were under close scrutiny. In December 1970 he resigned all his Black Power appointments, including the chairmanship of RAAS, and having been refused permission to settle in Jamaica, returned with his wife and children to Trinidad. He moved into a large four-bedroom house at 24–26 Christina Gardens, La Chance, Port of Spain. The house, which was set in one and a half acres of land, became the base for Malik's commune.

Having courted political and religious groups in Trinidad and been rebuffed, Malik (who had once called himself 'the best known black man in the world'), gathered around him a small band of Black Muslim followers. These included Hakim Jamal, a forty-year-old American, and his lover, English-born Gail Benson, a girl with an upper-class background. Joe Skerrit, Malik's cousin, was the group's handyman, Stanley Abbott, an ex-Borstal boy and associate during Malik's activities in London, was a willing henchman, as were Edward Chadee and Steven Yeates.

According to another of Malik's followers who later became a prosecution witness, the Black Power leader decided on 1 January 1972 that Gail Benson would have to be killed because she was causing Hakim Jamal mental distress. Abbott and Yeates were given instructions to dig a pit in the garden. Next morning Gail Benson was dragged into the pit by Abbott, who muffled her screams while she was hacked to death with a cutlass wielded by Yeates. She was left dying, and was buried

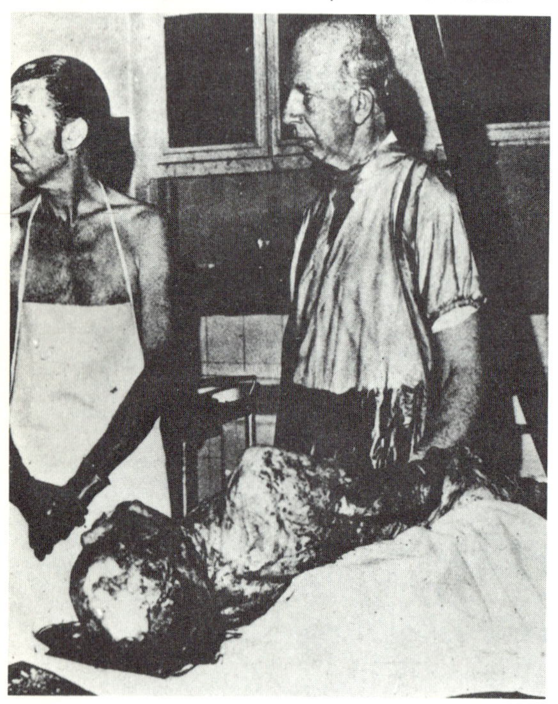

One of Michael X's victims in the post-mortem room

alive when the pit was filled in by Chadee and others.

On 8 February Joe Skerrit was killed by Malik because he had refused to take part in an armed hold-up. Again a pit had been dug in the garden ready to receive the body, and Malik attacked his victim with a cutlass, and eventually bludgeoned him to death with a large stone. Two days later Steven Yeates was drowned at San Souci when Malik's party got into difficulties while bathing. After this the commune broke up and Malik fled to Guyana.

Charged with the murder of Joe Skerrit, Malik was tried in Trinidad in August 1972, protesting, 'Violence is not my way.' Abbott was charged with him, and both men faced overwhelming prosecution evidence. Malik was found guilty of murder, and Abbott — who also faced a charge of murder in respect of Gail Benson — guilty of manslaughter. Malik appealed unsuccessfully, and was executed on 16 May 1975. Abbott and Chadee were tried for the murder of Gail Benson in July 1973. Both were convicted and sentenced to death. Chadee was reprieved, but Abbott went to the gallows on 27 April 1979. Thus of Malik's small commune two were murdered, one drowned accidentally and two died by judicial hanging.

Apart from the attractions of secret burial, gardens offer other possibilities for disposal of victims. They are places where bonfires might excite nothing more than the irritation of neighbours on wash-day. Dennis Nilsen (see under MURDER HOUSES) made good use of this facility in burning up the remains of some of his victims.

The use of chemicals and fertilizers in the garden are also matters of routine. Warren Lincoln, a retired Chicago lawyer, was a keen gardener and user of fertilizer in hs garden at Aurora, Illinois. He retired early only to find that his intended haven of peace was spoiled by his nagging wife Lena, who brought her brother to live with them.

When his wife and brother-in-law disappeared Lincoln told the neighbours that Lena had left him for another man, and that he had thrown his brother-in-law out of the house. Indeed he had, for the fertilizer which he had so diligently applied to his garden contained a considerable amount of human ash. Lincoln had killed both of them and burnt their entire remains save for the heads, which were planted in flower boxes on the porch. The garden-loving attorney was convicted of murder and sentenced to life imprisonment. He died in gaol in 1941.

Gardening has many attractions, but for Tony Costa, a part-time carpenter in the hippie resort of Provincetown, Cape Cod, horticulture meant growing marijuana. An addict himself, he believed that he could cash in on the drug scene by growing the plant in the wooded garden of his home. Tony's place soon became a popular stop on the youthful drug trail.

In January 1969 police were alerted when two girls on holiday in the area from Rhode Island were reported missing. They had been seen in Costa's company, but then he had disappeared from the locale. Questioning of neighbours and acquaintances soon brought to light the existence of Tony's marijuana plot. The garden was dug up, and the bodies of the missing girls were discovered in shallow graves. Both had been sexually assaulted and mutilated. Corpses of two other missing girls were also found. Costa at first denied the killings but eventually admitted his guilt. He was convicted on two counts of murder and sentenced to two terms of life imprisonment. In May 1974 he hanged himself in his prison cell.
(213, 261, 852, 871)

GOLF COURSES

'So I hit her with the tee iron.'
Michael Queripel (1955)

It is said that 'lightning never strikes twice,' but murder did strike twice at Potter's Bar Golf Course, although not on the same tee. The seventh and seventeenth fairways on the course proved unlucky holes for two murder victims in the space of seven years.

In May 1948 two enterprising schoolboys looking for lost golf balls saw a human arm protruding from the weeds surrounding a pond at the seventh green. The police dragged the pond, and retrieved various pieces of a dismembered corpse. Decomposition was so far advanced that identification by usual means was impossible; the pathologist estimated that the body had been immersed in the pond for close on six months. Careful

measurement of the bones and examination of the skull sutures enabled some characteristics of the remains to be determined. They were of a left-handed male aged between forty and forty-five, whose height was about 5ft 2 inches. The files were sifted of forty-eight men who had been reported as missing during the previous twelve months and who fitted this general description. This list was narrowed down to two, and finally to one: Albert Welsh, aged forty-four, a railway linesman who had been reported missing on 18 November 1947.

Identification was confirmed by superimposing a photograph of Welsh's head and face on a photograph of the skull recovered from the pond.* The two pictures matched, and convinced a Coroner's Court that Albert Welsh's remains were those found on the golf course. It was known that when Welsh left his home near the golf course he had written a note to his wife: 'I have gone for a walk. Shan't be in for tea — Albert.'

Somewhere along that walk Welsh met his murderer, who dealt him some massive blows to the head. The skull found with his remains testified to the savagery of the attack. The murderer then crudely dismembered the body for disposal in the pond at the seventh green.

Murder struck again at Potter's Bar Golf Course on 29 April 1955. That evening Elizabeth Currell took her dog for a walk on the golf course, as she had done nearly every evening for four years. When she failed to return home, and then the dog turned up alone, her husband went to the police to report her missing. An immediate search of the golf course was begun, and at dawn Mrs Currell's body was found in rough grass near the seventeenth tee. She had been savagely beaten about the head with the heavy iron tee-marker which lay close by.

The dead woman's clothing had been tampered with, and sexual assault was the likely motive. The fact that intercourse had not taken place indicated that the assailant had been disturbed. The tee-marker bore a bloody impression of a palm-print which became the focal point for murder inquiry detectives. House-to-house checks were made and officers called at local factories, shops and offices, all to no avail. Eventually it was decided to take

*Photo-imposition was first used successfully in the Ruxton Case in 1935.

palm-prints of the entire male population of Potter's Bar and district. Nearly nine thousand impressions had been collected when painstaking comparisons produced a match with the 4605th palm-print. The person who had made the bloody impression on the tee-marker was Michael Queripel, a junior clerk who worked for the Potter's Bar Urban District Council.

Queripel told the police that he had found the body on the golf course but did not inform them because he did not think he would be believed. In due course he confessed to hitting and strangling the woman he found walking on the golf course. He wrote a statement for the police in which he said, 'I had a migraine attack when I got home from work. I always go for a walk when I get them .... I saw her walking towards me with her dog .... I waited until she was out of sight behind the trees. I walked over to the green and waited ....' He hit her on the jaw, and then tried to strangle her. She struggled, so he hit her with a piece of wood which broke in two, 'So I hit her with the tee iron', he explained.

At his trial Queripel pleaded guilty to murder, and as he was not yet eighteen years old he was sentenced to be detained during Her Majesty's pleasure.

Murder on the thirteenth tee with the body hidden in the clubhouse was the unwelcome news which greeted members of the golf club in Grahamstown, South Africa, in 1907. Nine-year-old Edith Pinnock was sent by her mother to do some shopping on 8 October and never returned home. The girl walked the one and a half miles from her home in Craddock Road, Grahamstown, to South's Stores. She left the shop at about 12.40 p.m. carrying some tins of 'Loyalty' brand meat and other groceries. When last seen she was walking home near the golf course.

When the child had not returned by 3.00 p.m. her mother raised the alarm and called the police. The golf clubhouse was searched, and the caretaker, Thomas Andrew Kerr, was questioned. He said he had been in town on business, returning to the clubhouse around 11 a.m. He had been seen arriving in a taxi, and at 11.30 a.m. two golfers saw him at the 13th hole. Kerr's story was that he went back to town in the afternoon, where he stayed drinking until about 8.00 p.m. Mrs Pinnock, hysterical with anxiety over her missing daughter, accused Kerr of knowing something about her disappearance. She later apologized for this remark.

Jabez South, the owner of the store from which Edith had bought her groceries, made his contribution to the search by employing the services of a clairvoyant. The conclusion was that the missing child's body would be found in the clubhouse cellar. The stench which arose from the cellar when the door was opened presaged what was to be found in the darkness below. Edith Pinnock's decomposing body was found in a sack which had previously contained mineral ash used on the putting greens. A post-mortem examination established that the child had been raped, and killed by a heavy blow to the head.

Suspicious fingers were pointed at Kerr, and his bedroom at the clubhouse was found to be reeking of iodoform, a mild antiseptic fluid, which he said he used to bathe his feet but which the police began to think had been used to counteract the smell of the decomposing body. Suspicions hardened when two tins of 'Loyalty' brand meat were found in the club's garbage and the head of a golf club was discoverd hidden under the window of Kerr's bedroom. Kerr denied any responsibility for the girl's disappearance, and said he had not noticed any smell emanating from the cellar. Other users of the clubhouse confirmed that they had not seen Kerr acting suspiciously, nor had they detected a smell. Nevertheless, the circumstantial evidence was strong, and Kerr was duly charged with murder and rape.

The jury could not agree on a verdict at the trial and Kerr was discharged, only to be immediately rearrested on the same charges. There was no legal precedent in South Africa for a man discharged in a court of law to be charged a second time with the same offence. Nevertheless, an appeal judge ruled that the previous acquittal verdict on a charge of murder did not rule out proceedings on a charge of rape.

Kerr was therefore tried a second time, and in fairness to the prisoner, the venue was changed to Cape Town. The case against him was that he had raped and murdered the girl at the 13th green on the golf course and hidden her body in a sack. Kerr maintained that the witnesses falsely accused him and said that he was merely doing some weeding at the 13th hole. His defence counsel argued that at the time the murder was alleged to have been

Investigating an unsolved murder at Le Touquet

committed (between 12.55 and 1.20 p.m.) Kerr was on his way to Grahamstown to visit his brother-in-law. The jury distrusted the circumstantial evidence, and again Kerr was acquitted of the charges. He left the court a free man, and the mystery of what happened on the golf course remains unsolved.

'Murder on the Golf Links' was the headline announcing the mysterious death of Florence Aline Wilson at Le Touquet in May 1928. She had been staying with her husband in a rented house near the golf course at the French coastal resort. On the day of her disappearance this 25-year-old grand-daughter of an English industrialist had taken tea with her husband and friends at the golf-course clubhouse. Afterwards, when the others decided to play golf, she announced her intention to walk over to the casino. They all agreed to meet about one and a half hours later, and Florence made for the path through the woods which linked the golf course and the casino.

She never returned. An all-night search mounted by the police and friends eventually located her body at dawn the next day. Still wearing several pieces of expensive jewellery, her raped and strangled body was found lying in the woods. Robbery did not appear to be the

motive, and disturbance of the ground around the body suggested that a fierce struggle had taken place. Several suspects were questioned by the police, but the death of the Englishwoman remained a mystery.

Two years went by and then in July 1930 a sixteen-year-old youth was arrested at Le Touquet after being identified by a woman who had been assaulted. During the course of questioning, it was alleged that this youth had admitted several attacks on women in the area, including the killing of Mrs Wilson. Despite the fact that he would only have been aged fourteen years at the time, the lad was sent for trial. He denied making a confession, and was acquitted of the charge on account of weak prosecution.

There the matter rested until 1933 when new evidence came to light regarding Mrs Wilson's death. An anonymous letter was received by the French police in which it was claimed that a man who had recently drowned at near-by Etaples was the murderer. For the first time it was revealed that a letter had been found near the body at the crime scene five years earlier. The text of this had never been released, but it was supposed to have involved an intermediary (the likely murderer) who was acting for another person who regularly passed letters to Florence Wilson.

Speculation that she was an agent of the

British Secret Service working in France and operating a 'post-box' was never substantiated. Allegations in 1934 of police corruption in the Le Touquet area and of gangland killings involving senior police officers only added to the mystery, which remains unsolved.
(1, 359, 361, 487, 642, 773, MWW)

HILLSIDES

'This is the day I kill someone ....'
Penny Bjorkland (1959)

August Sangret, a French-Canadian soldier who murdered a girl on Hankley Common in Surrey in 1942, was said to have had Red Indian blood in his veins. Following his ancestral instinct to bury the body of a conquered enemy on high ground, he dragged his victim's corpse to a rise where he put it in a shallow grave.

The instincts which lead a murderer to kill or dispose of his victim on a hillside might be thought deep-seated, bearing in mind the risks of discovery that accompany such a high profile. Courting danger by such actions is part of the deliberate attention-seeking which motivates some murderers. Eighteen-year-old Penny Bjorkland, for instance, went out into the hills near her home in the role of huntress, and having found and killed her quarry, busily advertised the fact. When Penny woke up on the morning of 1 February 1959 in her home in California she said to herself, 'This is the day I kill someone. If I meet anyone, that will be IT.' She took up a US army issue .38 revolver which she had stolen from a friend and a box of cartridges and set out for the near-by hills.

In a hilly area near Daly City she saw a parked pick-up truck. The driver, 27-year-old August Norry, was a landscape gardener. His reason for being in that particular spot was that he intended dumping some grass trimmings. As he sat in the driver's cab he was utterly unaware that death stalked him in the form of a blonde, freckle-faced teenager. Penny Bjorkland appeared at the cab window and emptied her revolver into the driver. She reloaded the gun and again fired it until all the bullets were expended. She put eighteen shots into her victim, pulled his body out of the vehicle and drove it some distance from the scene before abandoning it. Penny Bjorkland

then went home and sat down to dinner with her family. Norry's body was found the next day, and the investigation of his death focused immediately on the firearms evidence. The bullets which had killed him were from practice ammunition called 'wadcutters', and a discarded box of unused cartridges was found at the crime scene. The bullets were of a particular type having three cannelures or grease rings round the circumference. These were traced to a Connecticut manufacturer, and were of a type sold to target-shooting enthusiasts who liked to make up their own ammunition. The amount of powder in the unused cartridges was higher than normal and indicated that the user favoured the so-called 'hot load'. Police inquiries eventually led to a man who said he had sold a box of fifty hand-made cartridges of this type to Penny Bjorkland for $3. She explained that she already had a revolver and wanted the ammunition for target practice.

On 15 April Penny was interviewed by the police at her home, and the following day she confessed to the shooting. The remainder of the specially made cartridges were retrieved from the drains in the street near her home, and the revolver was found similarly disposed of at a place en route to the office where she worked in San Francisco. On the day after the hillside shooting Penny Bjorkland had sent anonymous handwritten letters to some of the San Francisco newspapers claiming that a friend had committed the murder; she mentioned the registration number of the dead man's pick-up truck as proof of her claim. At the office she had told workmates, 'I'm the blonde they're looking for in the Daly City murder.' Her friends laughed at her grim sense of humour.

Penny was indicted for murder and referred for psychiatric examination. Like Ronald De-Feo (see under MURDER HOUSES), she hated her family, especially her mother, and since the age of thirteen she had dreamed recurrently of killing someone in order to strike back at them. She was emotionally disturbed, drank excessively and sometimes slept for long periods; twenty-four hours during the course of a weekend was not unknown. Despite this erratic behaviour she caused no problems at her work-place. On 6 May Penny pleaded guilty, and her fate rested on the psychiatrists' reports. All but one of the seven experts thought that while emotionally unstable she was legally sane. The defence psychiatrist argued that she was a paranoid schizophrenic. Having pleaded guilty to 'wilful, wanton murder', Penny Bjorkland was sentenced to life imprisonment. Her victim, whom she had met once before, was to all intents and purposes a stranger. He was the prey who fell to the hunter in the hills.

A mysterious series of killings in Hollywood and Los Angeles in the late 1970s earned the murderer the title of 'The Hillside Strangler'. The first victim was Yolanda Washington, a Hollywood prostitute whose nude body was found on a hillside at Forest Lawn on 17 October 1977. She had been strangled. During November eight other women were murdered in the Los Angeles area. The killings had a number of common features: the victims were all strangled, all had been tied up before death, all were found on hillside locations, and in each case there was evidence of sexual intercourse involving two men, one of whom was a non-secretor.*

The significance of the hillside locations was that the murderer did not merely dump his victims — he carefully arranged them. The corpses were positioned in what the newspapers called 'a sexually meaningful way', and on a prominent site which would eventually attract the gaze of passers-by.

This murder ritual came to an end in January following the killing of two girls in Bellingham, Washington state. Karen Mandie, a 22-year-old student, took a job as 'housesitter' in the Edgemoor residence of wealthy owners who were away in Europe. Security was in the hands of an agency, and because the house alarm system had failed Karen, who also worked at a local department store, was hired to live in on the evening of 11 January. The girl picked up fellow-student Diane Wilder for company and drove to the Edgemoor house. When Karen, a normally reliable person, failed to check in on time for her department-store job she and her companion were reported missing. The police put out an alert for her car, which had also disappeared, and a member of the public responded quickly, having spotted the vehicle parked in a Bellingham street. The car contained the bodies of Karen and Diane, who had both been strangled. The 'Hillside Strangler' appeared to have struck again, except that he had not found time to display the bodies in ritualistic fashion.

The police had already established that Karen Mandie had been hired by the security agency's supervisor, Ken Bianchi. He denied knowing Karen, but a note of her telephone number was found at his home, and a scarf belonging to Diane was discovered in his truck. Ken Bianchi, security supervisor and a member of the Sheriff's Reserve (a sort of Special Constabulary), was arrested for murder. Bianchi was questioned many times by different psychiatrists. At a sanity hearing in October 1979 he wept when the murders were discussed and said, 'I can't find the words to express the sorrow for what I have done.' He spoke of another person within himself who was a voyeur and loved watching death. Under hypnosis he talked of this other personality, whom he called 'Steve' and described as the murderer. His own guilt, he said, was in not preventing the killings.

There was no doubt that Bianchi had committed the killings, for he related details of the murders known only to the police. But as the probing questioning continued, Bianchi's account became more complex, and he referred to yet another personality within himself called 'Billy'. He also implicated his cousin, Angelo Buono, in the killings, whom the police thought might be the second individual which their semen tests on the dead girl's bodies had suggested they look for.

Dr Donald T. Lunde, the distinguished psychiatrist, testified that Bianchi had suffered dissociative reaction since childhood, and that this bordered on psychosis which took the form of unconscious repressed hostility to women. Expert opinions varied as to Bianchi's true state of mind. He impressed some psychiatrists who examined him as a genuine multiple personality, his alter ego appearing when he was questioned under hypnosis. Others saw him simply as a malingerer who feigned hypnosis and was intent on proving insanity in order to escape the death penalty.

It was known that Bianchi had seen the film *The Three Faces of Eve*, which was described as the equivalent of a course in faking multiple personality. Evidence was also available which

---

*Eighty-six per cent of the population are termed 'secretors' because their blood-group characteristics are also present in their saliva and other body fluids. The remaining 14 per cent are non-secretors.

clearly showed his interest in psychology. A number of text-books on various aspects of the subject were found at his home. He had tried to set up a counselling service, practising transactional analysis therapy on the basis of bogus medical degrees and certificates. It was also alleged that he and Buono had at one time operated a ring of teenage prostitutes.

There was insufficient evidence against Buono to bring charges, and the key element in the case was the decision about Bianchi's mental state. If he was found insane, he would not be allowed to testify against Buono. As the psychiatric arguments continued back and forth, the police made an interesting discovery. 'Steve Walker', Bianchi's alter ego, was not just a random product of his imagination but a real person. Thomas Steven Walker was a graduate student whose academic record Bianchi had stolen, even to the extent of substituting his own name on the other man's records, and so falsely claiming his scholastic achievements. As this undermined the multiple personality theory, Bianchi pleaded guilty to the charges and agreed to testify against Buono as part of a deal which would save him from the death sentence. In November 1981 judgment was given that Ken Bianchi had faked hypnosis and multiple personality. He was sentenced to life imprisonment.

Angelo Buono was sent for trial, and Bianchi gave evidence against him. In January 1984, after the longest criminal trial in US history, Buono was convicted of one of the hillside murders and sentenced to life imprisonment. He aided Bianchi, the plausible sexual psychopath, in snuffing out the lives of ten girls, using a combination of strangulation, lethal gas, electrocution and torture. Bianchi's gratification from killing was complete when he prominently exhibited his victim's bodies on a convenient hillside for the passing world to observe.
(1, 36, 226, 576, 835, 844, MWW)

HOSPITALS, NURSING-HOMES AND SICK-ROOMS

'Sister knows best.'
Jane Toppan (1901)

Like the doctor's consulting-room, these are places where the sick, the elderly and the infirm put their trust in those who have a responsibility to care for them. It is a sinister thought that murder can stalk such innocent victims at the very moment when they are least able to defend themselves.

It seems almost unthinkable that a place of healing so respected as the Hospital for Sick Children in Toronto should contain the elements of violence which led to its being called the 'Kill or Cure Hospital'. Such proved to be the case when in March 1981 police were called in to investigate a series of infant deaths which had occurred during the previous nine months. In that period, from 1 July 1980 to March 1981, baby deaths at the hospital had increased by more than six times compared to similar periods.

Thirty-four children (the figure was later increased) aged between nine days and eighteen months had died — seven of them, it was thought, from deliberately administered overdoses of the heart drug digoxin, which caused death through cardiac arrest. Twenty-four of these deaths occurred between the hours of 1 a.m. and 5 a.m., and the high rate of mortality stopped after the police were called in. Many of the dead babies had been prescribed digoxin, but traces found later in their bodies were judged to be well above the normally accepted dosage.

A hearing into four of the deaths in May 1982 cleared a member of the hospital nursing staff who had been under suspicion. The judge nevertheless concluded that some person unknown had administered digoxin and killed five of the babies. There were technical problems regarding the analysis required for digoxin, and the evidence was conflicting. The drug was difficult to analyse in human tissue because the level in the blood tended to increase naturally after death, thus clouding the picture for the analyst.

In January 1985 a previously confidential report compiled by the Center for Disease Control in Atlanta was made public at a Royal Commission inquiry into the mysterious hospital deaths. The report acknowledged that eighteen out of the thirty-six babies treated in the cardiac wards between June 1980 and March 1981 may have been caused by digoxin poisoning. The case of the infant deaths remains unsolved.

Hospitals are busy places, with medical staff coming and going on their different duty rosters and a changing population of visitors. It is easy for an intending murderer to gain admittance without being observed. This was how Peter Griffiths slipped into the children's ward of the Queen's Park Hospital, Blackburn, upon the night of 14 May 1948. He seized a four-year-old girl from her cot and took her out into the hospital grounds, where he committed sexual assault and murder. Fingerprint impressions left at the crime-scene led to one of Britain's greatest manhunts. The entire male population of Blackburn was fingerprinted, with the result that Griffiths, a young ex-serviceman, was eventually identified as the murderer.

Nursing-homes, in the days when they were less strictly controlled, provided employment for nursing staff with mediocre professional qualifications and questionable vocation. The type of patient was often elderly, wealthy and demanding. Extra attention could be commanded by giving money and gifts to the staff, which was a short step to the manipulation of the patient's life for greater gain.

Dorothea Waddingham, a self-styled 'nurse', was an example of the avaricious angel of mercy. She ran a nursing-home for 'Aged and Chronic Cases' at Nottingham. In 1935 she murdered two women who were in her care after securing their property in a will. Fatal injections of morphine hastened the demise of her patients. The treatment was easily given without need of secrecy in the nursing environment. But for a clumsy attempt to ensure the cremation of one of her victims Waddingham might have succeeded.

Another nurse of doubtful qualifications was Amy Archer-Gilligan, who also ran a nursing-home. The Archer Home for Elderly People in Windsor, Connecticut, registered forty-eight deaths during the period 1911–16. The frequency of undertakers' visits to the home made local tongues wag, but then a high death-rate would be expected in a home devoted to the care of the sick and the elderly.

The home was founded in 1907 by James H. Archer and his wife Amy, and by 1910 they had twenty patients in their care. Just as the enterprise seemed to be prospering James Archer died, leaving his widow to run the home on her own. Amy married Michael W. Gilligan in 1913, but four months later the unfortunate man died after a short illness, leaving Amy a widow for the second time.

On 30 May 1914 another death occurred in the Archer Home. Franklin R. Andrews had been enjoying good health until dinner that evening, when he complained of feeling unwell and went to bed early. At 11 p.m. 'Nurse' Gilligan phoned his sister telling her that Andrews was ill. Before the night was out he was dead. Amy had called Dr H.F. King to the sick-room, and he issued a death certificate giving gastric ulcers as the cause of death. Again the tongues wagged and fingers were pointed at Amy Gilligan, but Dr King rallied to her support, pouring cold water on any suggestion of wrongdoing.

Despite the doctor's reassurances the citizens of Windsor remained unconvinced, and a number of them went to see the editor of the *Hartford Courant* to tell him of their suspicions. Inquiries were intensified, and women detectives were infiltrated into Mrs Gilligan's establishment to see what they could find. Meanwhile it was discovered that Amy had obtained a loan from the late Mr Andrews which she had not repaid.

The police remained indecisive until 8 May 1916, when they swooped on the Archer Home and arrested Amy. Great excitement ensued in the press as news of the forty-eight deaths — over six times greater than the normal rate for nursing-homes — was reported. The arrangement for admission to the Archer Home was that each client paid between $1,000 and $1,500, depending on age and financial background, which gave an entitlement of care for life. Obviously, the shorter the client's stay, the greater the profit to the Home.

Amy Gilligan denied everything, and friends came to her support, claiming her to be a devoted nurse and hard worker for the Church. But mere suspicion turned into firm evidence following exhumation of the bodies of the late Messrs Andrews and Gilligan — both contained arsenic. It was also discovered that Amy had regularly bought large quantities of arsenical rat poison from a local druggist. She bought over 1lb in 1914 alone. Further exhumations brought similar revelations of arsenical poisoning.

In June 1917 Amy Archer-Gilligan faced trial at Hartford charged with five murders. A formidable array of circumstantial evidence was ranged against her, but as is customary in poison cases, no-one could testify that she had been seen administering fatal doses to her clients. Judge Gardiner Greene told the jury that wilful poisoning could not conceivably be rated anything but premeditated and heinous murder, for which a first-degree verdict must be returned.

Amy was duly found guilty and sentenced to death. An appeal was heard, and a new trial was granted. This took place at Middletown, Connecticut, in June 1919 when alienists (forerunners of modern psychiatrists) testified regarding her mental condition. The arguments raged back and forth, and in the end (perhaps overwhelmed by the whole procedure) Amy pleaded guilty to murdering Franklin Andrews. She was imprisoned for life at Wethersfield, and later moved to an asylum where she died in 1928 aged fifty-nine.

The ease with which medical treatment can be abused over a long period without creating suspicion was demonstrated by Arnfinn Nesset, the 46-year-old manager of an old people's nursing-home in the Norwegian village of Orkdale. During the three years that he had been running the home an unusually large number of inmates died. Between 1977 and 1980 thirty elderly persons aged between sixty-seven and ninety-four passed away. While the number was high, some of the deceased were extremely elderly, and death was the naturally expected outcome.

What finally threw suspicion on to Nesset was the discovery in his office of a large amount of the drug curacit. This is a hospital drug used in small doses to relax the muscles of patients undergoing surgery. Nesset had sufficient of the substance to kill two hundred people. His claim that he had obtained it in order to put down his dog collapsed when it was found that he did not own a dog.

Nesset was arrested in March 1981, and promptly admitted killing twenty-seven people, a confession which he subsequently withdrew. Doctors who examined him found him sane and fit to stand trial. Proceedings against him began in Trondheim in October 1982, in what proved to be Scandinavia's greatest trial for mass murder. Nesset pleaded not guilty to the charge of murdering twenty-eight old persons by injecting curacit into their veins. Witnesses were called who remembered seeing him giving injections in the nursing-home, although they did not know which drugs he was using.

Curacit kills slowly and painfully, yet the defence argued that the motive was one of carrying out euthanasia, or mercy killing. Motive was difficult to establish, but it was thought that Nesset might have been misappropriating small sums of money from those patients under his care. Whatever the reason, the jury rejected the idea of mercy killing and found him guilty on twenty-one counts of murder. He was sentenced to twenty-one years' imprisonment, the maximum permitted under Norwegian law.

The sick-room at home, where a relative is nursed by members of the family or by a paid nursing attendant, has provided a frequent scenario for murder. The sick-room with its regime of medical treatment provides scope for the poisoner to overdo the dose or to administer a fatal agent using food as a vehicle. Major Herbert Rowse Armstrong successfully disposed of his already sick wife by giving her arsenic in her food. She died at their home in Cusop, Hay-on-Wye, in 1921 of what the doctor thought was gastritis. Armstrong was eventually found out because he was foolish enough to attempt to kill a fellow-solicitor, but the murder he committed in his wife's sick-room demonstrated the ease of the method and the lack of suspicion it creates. Poisoning is always a secret business, but adminstered to an already sick person under the guise of medical treatment or masked by food the murderer reduces the risk of detection.

The temptations of the sick-room appealed to Anna Marie Hahn, who when she emigrated to America in 1929 first put her singing-voice to use in the beer gardens of Cincinnati's German district. She married and started a bakery business entertaining the drinkers in the 'Over the River' district in her spare time. Anna was especially popular with the old men, whom she realized were well off and looking for companionship. She quickly decided that her talents would be put to better use in the role of nurse-companion.

She deserted her husband in 1932 — he was suffering from a mysterious illness at the time — and moved in with one of her elderly gentlemen. The latter died on 6 May and left his property to Anna. Three other men died during the next four years following Anna's ministrations, and on each occasion she was named as beneficiary.

Suspicion arose over her hasty transfer of

funds in respect of the death of elderly George Obendorfer, and a post-mortem was ordered. Arsenic was found in the old man's body, and enough of the poison was discovered in Anna's home 'to kill half of Cincinnati'. Arsenic was also present in the exhumed bodies of four more men who had experienced Anna's companionship.

When she was questioned Anna said, 'I love to make old people comfy .... I have been like an angel of mercy to them.' The jury at her trial in June 1938 did not hold the same view, and found her guilty of murder with no recommendation to mercy. She was sentenced to death in the electric chair. Anna was said to have given a farewell party in her cell for press reporters, telling them, 'The least I could do was to throw a bash for you.' Anna Hahn became the first woman to be executed in the electric chair in the state of Ohio.

Another predator of the sick-room was Marie Petitjean Becker, a 56-year-old widow who busied herself nursing sick, elderly people to whom she gave herbal tea to improve their strength. The fact that those she ministered to eventually died — ostensibly of natural causes — did not pass unnoticed. In October 1936 a citizen of Liège in Belgium, the seat of Marie Becker's activities, sent an anonymous letter to the police authority inviting their interest in her.

Even a cursory glance at the records was sufficient to show that in the space of a few months four women had died in Liège, all of whom had been attended by Marie Becker. The lady in question was interviewed by the police, to whom she expressed considerable irritation that her humanitarian motives should be so badly misinterpreted. The police backed off, although they took the precaution of exhuming a few bodies, but with inconclusive results. The next move was to investigate Mrs Becker's background.

It appeared that her husband, Charles Becker — a carpenter by trade, and by all accounts in good health — died suddenly from a wasting illness. The widow then became closely associated with the Castadet family, and it was rumoured that she fancied Paul Castadet, a serving policeman, as her next husband. At any rate, in February 1933 Mme Castadet became ill with symptoms remarkably similar to those of the late M. Becker. Marie was in constant attendance at the sick woman's bed-side, plying her with cups full of health-giving herbal tea. Mme Castadet died on 23 March, and her husband rejected whatever designs Marie Becker may have had on him.

In October 1934 Marie befriended Lambert Beyer, a prosperous middle-aged landowner, who unfortunately soon had to take to his bed through illness. He told his anxious friends, 'Don't worry ... Marie takes good care of me.' He died several days later. A procession of Marie's patients followed him to their graves up to the autumn of 1936, when the anonymous letter-writer alerted the police.

When Marie was taken in for questioning a second time she was searched, and 15 grams of digitalis were found in her handbag. She claimed that she used the drug to treat herself for a heart complaint. The amount she carried was rather large, bearing in mind that 2 grams of the drug is a fatal dose. Marie's apartment was searched, and it proved to be a virtual store-room of women's clothing and jewellery. Bodies of some of her more recent patients were exhumed, and traces of digitalis were found in them.

It appeared that Marie Becker had made a profitable living quietly poisoning her patients under the guise of helping them back to health. She was tried for murder in July 1937, and a great deal of evidence was taken up by medical matters. The fatal effects of digitalis were not well understood, for the drug has been little used for murder. Nevertheless, the jury was sufficiently convinced of her guilt to convict her in eleven cases of murder. She was sentenced to death, but this was later commuted to life imprisonment.

One of America's better-known bogus nurses who took to murder was Jane Toppan. 'You're looking terrible. Let me give you a tonic,' she said to a visitor to her house. Brushing aside protestations with the words, 'Sister knows best', she administered a medicine glass of her tonic mixture. Within hours the recipient was dead, like so many of Jane Toppan's patients.

The future mass murderess was an adopted child. She was given a home by the Toppan family of Lowell, Massachusetts, whom she impressed with her religious application and progress at school. After being jilted and attempting suicide, young Jane announced that she had decided to take up nursing. In 1882 she enrolled for a nursing course at a hospital in Cambridge, and quickly came to the notice of her tutors by virtue of her eagerness to learn. It was also observed that she appeared to have more than the normal interest in post-mortem work.

This early promise came to nothing when Jane was dismissed following the unexpected deaths of two patients whom she had been tending. She applied for the position of head nurse at another hospital, and was successful in obtaining the post. But when it was discovered that her claims to be qualified were invalid she was dismissed. At this point Jane decided to forgo the rigours of formal training and elected instead to look after the sick and the elderly in their own homes and in her own way.

At the age of twenty-six Jane became a private nurse and worked for many New England families. She was regarded as a caring person, and won wide admiration. Of course, she lost patients at times, but since she moved about from home to home, only she knew what the tally was. In 1901 she tended the Davis family in Cataumet, and by the time the summer was over the whole family had perished. First she nursed Mattie Davis, then a married daughter from Chicago, and finally Mr Davis. Each died from a strange sickness with distressing symptoms which failed to respond to Jane's tonic medicine. Alone in the house with the second married daughter (whose husband, Captain Gibbs, was away at sea), Jane offered sympathy and tonic; 'It will do you good,' she said, proffering the glass. The following day the surviving member of the Davis family died and Jane hurried off to her next nursing assignment.

When Captain Gibbs returned to an empty home and learned what had happened he lost no time in seeking an exhumation order for his wife's body. Doctors determined that his wife had died of morphine poisoning. This vexed the family doctor, who admitted that his patients' symptoms were similar to those of morphine poisoning but maintained the tell-tale pin-pointing of the pupils in the eyes which always accompanied such poisoning was not present.

By the time the police had been informed of the suspicion against Jane Toppan and sent a detective to Lowell to question her, another of her patients had died and she had moved on to a family in Amherst. It was there that she was apprehended, later to be charged with murder. 'I have a clear conscience,' she said. 'I wouldn't kill a chicken.' While she was awaiting trial many prosperous New England families campaigned for her, and subscribed to her defence fund.

Meanwhile graves were being opened up throughout the state, and time after time pathologists found morphine in 'Nurse' Toppan's deceased patients. Detectives pursuing the source of her drugs eventually tracked down a pharmacist who had regularly supplied her with morphine on doctors' prescriptions. These prescriptions, it turned out, had been cunningly forged by Jane Toppan.

While in gaol awaiting trial 'Nurse' Toppan made a confession in which she named thirty-one of her victims: 'Yes, I killed them .... I killed Mattie. Then I killed Annie .... Oh, I killed so many of them.' Her technique was to poison her victims with a mixture of morphine and atropine, the latter counteracting the familiar pin-pointing of the pupils so indicative of morphine poisoning. This was a trick she had probably learnt from another morphine poisoner, Dr Robert Buchanan, a New York physician who murdered his wife in 1892. This angel of the sick-room tended her patients at their bedsides, feeding them with nourishment doctored with ever-increasing doses of her deadly mixture. Her victims suffered from painful breathing and convulsions until they died.

'Everybody trusted me,' said Jane Toppan. 'It was so easy. I felt strange when I watched them die. I was all excited and my blood seemed to sweep madly through my veins. It was the only pleasure I had ... I had to do it. They hadn't done anything to me and I gained nothing from their deaths except the excitement of watching them die. I couldn't resist doing it.' Her confessions said all; to the horror of those present at her trial she added, 'This is my ambition — to have killed more people — more helpless people — than any man or woman has ever killed.' A plea of not guilty by reason of insanity was agreed between the opposing lawyers on condition that Jane Toppan would never be paroled.

The defence admitted she had murdered eleven people, while she herself confessed to thirty-one. The real figure was put at nearer a hundred, and Ellery Sedgwick, editor of the *Atlantic Monthly* — who had enjoyed the benefit of being nursed by Jane Toppan and survived — wrote of her 'Without the slightest doubt, she outranks both Bluebeard and Jack the Ripper.' In June 1902 the nurse everyone trusted unto death was sent to the State Hospital at Taunton, where she died in 1938 at the age of eighty-one.

Jealousy is one of the most time-honoured motives for murder, and can trigger off what might be called the situation killing. Mrs Rattan Bai Jain's situation was that she disapproved of the lusting gaze which her husband directed towards her female employees. In a country teeming with people India would seem to be the last place to need a fertility clinic, but Mr and Mrs Jain decided to establish one in New Delhi.

Mrs Jain administered a mixture of psychological therapy and physical manipulation to her often wealthy clients, who felt their childlessness was a matter of shame. Mr Jain looked after the advertising for the clinic, and when his wife was not making demands on him spent his time among the young female assistants. This was a situation which roused Rattan Bai Jain to jealous fury, and her outbursts were well known to the staff.

In May 1954 three of the assistants were taken ill at the clinic and collapsed when they reached their homes. It was thought at first that they were suffering from snake-bite poisoning; one died immediately, and the other two went into coma. The police made inquiries at the clinic where they worked, and Mrs Jain, showing no sympathy at all for the plight of her girls, simply abused their character. She said they were lazy, incompetent and sex-mad. Detectives at the hospital bedside noted that each of the sick girls referred to some sweets which Mrs Jain had given them. Autopsies on the three dead girls confirmed that they had died of arsenical poisoning.

Mrs Jain had taken flight, but she was duly caught and, despite her attempts to shift the blame, purchases of arsenic were clearly attributed to her. Employees at the clinic said that they had been instructed by her not to talk to Mr Jain, and when rumours gained currency that he was having affairs with some of her girls Mrs Jain's jealousy reached murderous proportions. She doctored some sweets with arsenic and offered them to the three girls she regarded as her husband's seducers. Mrs Rattan Bai Jain was convicted of murder and

sentenced to death. She was the first woman to be hanged in the then new Republic of India.

The midwife, whose calling is to usher in new life, is not a person on whom the suspicion of murder often falls. Yet even this respected profession has its deviants, and about the turn of the century two Hungarian villages came into prominence through the activities of Susanna Olah.

The villages of Tiszakurt and Nagyrev lie about sixty miles from Budapest in one of Hungary's wine-growing areas. These small communities were peopled by peasant farmers who made a meagre living out of backbreaking toil. Communications with these outlying villages were non-existent for large parts of the year, especially during the winter snows and spring floods. The villagers were thus frequently isolated from the outside world.

In 1905 a young midwife came to prominence in Nagyrev. She not only practised as a midwife, delivering the farmers' wives of their offspring, but also carried out abortions when requested. Abortion was against the law, and the other midwives in the area refused to consider it. In a poor peasant community, however, the desire not to overburden the family economy with too many children was an ever-present problem. Susanna Olah, with her willingness to perform abortions, quickly became a sought-after and influential figure.

With no doctor practising locally, Susanna was the person everyone turned to for all medical matters. The minor functionary in the district who issued death certificates was the village bell-ringer, who was also her son-in-law. Although she was several times charged with performing illegal operations, she was never convicted. Bolstered by her own success, and by the esteem in which she was held by the villagers, Susanna hit on the idea of controlling births not by abortion but by poisoning the newly born infants. The instrument to be used was arsenic leached out of fly-papers. She reasoned that a small increase in the infant mortality rate would go virtually unobserved.

When Susanna Olah's fellow-midwives died mysteriously her influence increased still further, and so too did people's fear of her. The death of her own husband caused the men of the two villages to warn their women-folk against consorting with Aunt Susanna, as she had become known. Susanna's reaction was to create a virtual sisterhood of all the women, who banded together to demand sexual equality, freedom to deny sex to their husbands and to take lovers if they wished. The tight-knit family structure began to break down in the face of this rebellion, and Susanna offered her women an easy way to eliminate an unwanted spouse — arsenic poisoning. She sold bottles of arsenic mixture, and unwanted husbands dropped like flies.

The Great War caused sufficient administrative confusion for the epidemic of death in Nagyrev and Tiszakurt to go largely unnoticed. Then, after twenty years of having everything running her way, trouble loomed for Susanna Olah. In 1929 the Pastor of Tiszakurt confronted one of his parishioners over mounting rumours that she had poisoned two elderly members of her family. The rumours were strongly denied over cups of tea, but after the Pastor had been taken violently ill more probing questions were asked, and this time by the police. Inevitably, Susanna Olah's name featured prominently in the inquiries, and several women made full confessions. The trail of poisonings which had begun with infants had been extended at Aunt Susanna's suggestion to eliminate any unwanted person. Seeing everything collapsing about her, Susanna determined not to be questioned about her activities, and hanged herself.

In 1931 thirty-one women from the two villages were tried for the arsenic poisonings. Five of them committed suicide, several were sentenced to death and the remainder served varying sentences in prison. The total number of deaths procured in Nagyrev and Tiszakurt by Susanna's influence is not known for sure, but probably ran to over a hundred.
(110, 186, 300, 337, 346, 376, 460, 486, 579, 718, 868, 875, 881, 1028, 1033, MWW)

HOTELS, INNS AND BOARDING-HOUSES

'I took up a flat iron from the wall of the beer cellar and hit her with it.'
Jack Hewett (1922)

Hotels and inns provide many of the familiar comforts of home, and offer relative anonymity for those who seek it. They are places of assignation or of chance encounter where people may affect poses with little fear of discovery. Hotels have long been places for what used to be called 'illicit liaison'. Their neutrality is such that few questions are asked, provided the register is signed and the bill paid. What occurs within the privacy of its rooms is a matter only for the temporary occupants, and perhaps also for the room maid.

Many murders have started or finished in a hotel, and there have been many narrow escapes in between. London journalist Sandy Fawkes, by the pure lottery of chance, met a handsome American in a hotel bar in Atlanta, Georgia, in 1974. The couple were mutually attracted to each other, and spent the next six days and nights together. Later she discovered that her companion was Paul John Knowles, a rapist and murderer of eighteen persons. He did not harm her, and much of her fright was retrospective.

Neville Heath used hotels as part of his murder technique. He posed as an Army officer to book a room in a London hotel, in which he savagely killed and mutilated a woman in June 1946. He switched Services, posing as an Air Force officer, when he met a girl at a hotel in Bournemouth the following month and lured her to a brutal death. Hotel staff tend to accept people at face value, and a charmer like Heath easily carried off his bogus identity and used it to impress his victims.

Sidney Harry Fox was a poseur of a different kind. He used an Air Force officer's rank to which he was not entitled in order to gain plausibility. He left a trail of debts behind him, and ended up in 1929 murdering his mother in a Margate hotel for her insurance money.

The ever-changing clientele of a hotel creates many chance encounters of strangers, usually with inconsequential results. Occasionally strangers do not always merely pass in the night but decide to linger, sometimes with disastrous results. The venue for one such encounter was the Brown Palace Hotel in Denver, Colorado. This hotel was a fashionable meeting place for the city's politicians and visiting business-men. In 1911 its rooms separately housed three people whose lives were destined to meet in tragedy. During the early part of the year local banker and business-man John W. Springer rented a suite on the sixth floor of the hotel for the use of his wife Isabelle.

John Springer married Isabelle after his first

wife died, leaving him with a young family to bring up. His new wife, a divorcée with a reputation for fast living and Bohemian pursuits (which included posing in the nude), did not meet with the approval of Springer's father-in-law. The wealthy cattleman, commenting that Isabelle was not a suitable person to take care of his grandchildren, withdrew the powerful backing which he had given to Springer's enterprises.

Undaunted, Springer first installed his wife at his ranch outside town, and then when she did not settle there, rented the suite at the Brown Palace Hotel. From her base on the sixth floor, Isabelle threw lavish parties attended by all kinds of men friends, frequently in the absence of her husband. A resident at the hotel who found himself invited up to the sixth floor was Sylvester Louis von Phul, a well-known adventurer and balloonist. He met Isabelle, and a passionate romance ensued during the next few months. The couple exchanged letters, and they conducted their affair before the very nose of John Springer.

Then the third personality of the eventual ménage arrived at the Brown Palace Hotel. He was Frank Harold Henwood, representative for a gas company which planned to build a plant in Denver. He met John Springer, the local banker, and the two men became firm friends. In the course of their friendship Henwood was introduced to Isabelle, and the three often wined and dined together. Springer was keenly interested in Henwood's project, and the latter was strongly smitten by Isabelle. In no time at all he became her lover, and it was common knowledge that they had spent a night together during Springer's absence on business.

At this point Henwood became aware of Isabelle's affair with von Phul and persuaded her to reject the balloonist. She mentioned that von Phul had some 'silly little letters' of hers which he might threaten to use to expose their affair to her husband. She asked Henwood to retrieve them for her. Thus were the three central characters drawn together. Henwood composed a letter for Isabelle to send von Phul. It advised him not to communicate in any way: 'Everything is finally and fully off ....' At the same time von Phul, realizing there was a rival to deal with, wrote to Isabelle telling her to 'have nothing to do with that doublecrosser ... just show him where he gets off or I will'.

On 23 May, during one of his periodic visits to Denver, von Phul met Henwood for the first time while they were both staying at the Brown Palace Hotel. Henwood said, 'I'm the party referred to in that letter,' and von Phul suggested that they went up to his room to discuss the matter. In the privacy of his rival's room Henwood asked von Phul to return the letters. Tempers flared and von Phul hit the other man, knocking him to the floor, and drew a gun. He told him to get out and to leave Isabelle alone. Thoroughly humiliated, Henwood left.

Von Phul then went up to Isabelle's room and upbraided her for getting involved with Henwood. With mounting rage he struck her in the face. Fearful of what might happen, Isabelle took the first opportunity to advise Henwood to drop his request for the return of her letters. He went to the police and told them about von Phul's behaviour, but there was no inclination on their part to become involved in a minor brawl. Before joining Isabelle and her husband at the theatre that evening, Henwood bought a .38 revolver.

At about 11.15 p.m., after the theatre performance had finished, Henwood returned to the Brown Palace Hotel. He went into the crowded bar and ordered a drink. Fifteen minutes later, von Phul appeared in the bar and stood next to Henwood. Words were exchanged and von Phul dealt Henwood a punch which sent him reeling to the floor. With his antagonist standing over him, and bested for a second time, Henwood drew his gun and emptied it at von Phul. The bullets sprayed around the bar, felling von Phul and wounding two other men who were unlucky enough to be in the line of fire. Henwood stood up and quietly waited for the police to take him away.

Von Phul died in hospital during the following day without making any reference to Isabelle Springer as the cause of the rivalry between him and Henwood. One of the men injured in the bar-room shooting incident also died, and Henwood was charged with double murder. He expressed regret that an innocent bystander had been killed, but said he was glad that von Phul was dead. Isabelle, meanwhile, had fled to Chicago, where she stayed under an assumed name.

On 12 June 1912 Henwood was tried for murder — not for that of von Phul, but for killing the man in the bar, whose name was Copeland. This strange decision sparked off a legal controversy, for it was considered that conviction on this charge depended entirely on proving that von Phul had been murdered. Isabelle appeared for the defence and the whole story, including the attempt to retrieve the letters, came out in court. Adding fuel to an already controversial case, the judge advised the jury that there was no possible verdict of manslaughter. Accordingly, Henwood was found guilty of second-degree murder.

In an extraordinary statement made from the dock before sentence was passed, Henwood castigated the judge for his bias and said, 'Now I am ready for your unjust sentence.' This was life imprisonment, but he spent the next few months living in prison in some style while appeals were fought on his behalf. In the meantime, the von Phul murder charge was dropped, which led his defence to the view that since the Copeland case depended on the other charge, if he was innocent of one, he must be innocent of the other. Henwood secured a new trial in 1913 when John Springer testified on his behalf. It was widely believed that Henwood would be acquitted, but to the court's astonishment a verdict of guilty of murder in the first degree was brought in. Amid considerable uproar, Henwood was sentenced to death. This was later commuted to life imprisonment, and he died in 1929 at Colorado State Penitentiary.

Murders by hotel staff are fortunately uncommon, despite the temptations sometimes put in their path by overbearing and arrogant guests. Robbery was the motive which led an eighteen-year-old pantry boy, Henry Jacoby, to the room of a guest in one of London's West End hotels in 1922. The lad panicked when his entry into a room he thought was unoccupied disturbed an elderly lady in bed. He hit her with a hammer he was carrying to lend courage to his enterprise, and killed her in a tragic accident which cost him his life on the scaffold.

The way in which people come and go in a hotel with scant notice taken of their movements or identity was demonstrated by an unsolved murder in New York City. Emmeline Reynolds, an attractive woman in her early twenties, checked into the Grand Hotel at 31st Street and Broadway on 15 August 1898. It was just before noon on a humid day. The desk clerk noted that his hotel's guest was stylishly dressed and wore expensive jewellery. She signed the register 'E. Maxwell and wife: Brooklyn' and explained, 'My husband will be here this evening.' 'Mrs Maxwell' was assigned Room Number 84 on the fourth floor. Shortly afterwards she took lunch in the hotel dining-room and then went out.

Later the same afternoon she returned to the hotel in the company of a man aged about thirty who wore a blue suit and a straw hat. This man (presumed to be Mr Maxwell), escorted his companion to Room No.84. They ordered a bottle of champagne about 6.30 p.m. and then left the hotel together — 'Mrs Maxwell' was expensively dressed and adorned with much jewellery. The couple returned to their room at about 11.30 and the man was seen leaving at 2.30 when he came down the elevator and walked through the lobby.

When the chambermaid used her pass-key to enter Room No.84 at 9.45 a.m. she found 'Mrs Maxwell' lying face down and fully clothed on the floor. A dark bloodstain on the carpet originated from a severe wound in the head. Near-by lay a fourteen-inch-long piece of lead pipe which had been strengthened with a piece of iron rod pushed inside. One end was covered in blood. The dead woman's ears were swollen where her earrings had been wrenched off, and her handbag (which was locked by a patent fastener) had been ripped open with a knife.

The murder victim was identified as Emmeline 'Dolly' Reynolds, the unmarried daughter of a successful builder. She lived in New York in a house set up for her by Maurice B. Wendham, a wealthy broker, who was her admirer. Dolly had come to New York to make her name on the stage, but, discouraged by her lack of ability, had resorted to selling books. She termed herself 'Mrs' Reynolds, and her 'sugar daddy' kept her in jewellery and rent money.

There were several curious aspects to the murder in Room No.84, and one of these was a cheque for $13,000 found in the dead woman's dress. This was made out to Emma Reynolds and signed 'Dudley Gideon'. It was endorsed on the back by S.J. Kennedy, who proved to be Dolly's dentist. It appears that Dr Kennedy became enamoured of Dolly when she attended his surgery, and he drew her into the excitement of betting on horse races. Dolly had told her mother how Kennedy was going to put $500 of her money on a 'sure thing' which would win her $4,000.

Kennedy, a mild man who had never even been seen in Dolly's company, was arrested and charged with murder. He was identified in a line-up as the man seen leaving the Grand Hotel in the early hours of the morning. His clothes were examined for bloodstains but none were found, although a mark on his underclothes was said to have been made by the murder weapon (fashioned from a piece of lead pipe) hanging down inside his trousers. Dr Kennedy proclaimed his innocence throughout, and maintained that at the material time he was at home with his family on Staten Island.

Maurice B. Wendham also had an alibi for the night of the murder, claiming that he was at a party in New Jersey. One theory had it that Wendham tired of his mistress and devised a complicated scheme to buy her off with a worthless cheque. The signatory, Dudley Gideon, did not exist, and the endorsement by Kennedy was to embarrass her and prevent recrimination. The man seen in the hotel with Dolly was Wendham's agent, and when he left, a burglar, operating quite independently, entered Room No.84 and murdered its occupant for her jewellery.

This far-fetched theory did little to comfort Dr Kennedy, who stood trial for murder on three occasions. He was found guilty, and sentenced to death at the first trial. At the second, in February 1901, his defence produced witnesses who supported his alibi, and there was a hung jury. The third trial in May 1901 produced doubt in the minds of the hotel staff, who were now uncertain about identifying Kennedy as the man they had seen with Dolly Reynolds. Dr Sam Kennedy was released on bail, and seven years later the charges against him were dismissed. The murder of Dolly Reynolds remains unsolved.

Inns customarily have a little more bonhomie associated with their business than do hotels, and more of their customers are known to the innkeeper. This was certainly the case with George Chapman, who murdered his first wife in 1897 after using her money to buy a public house, and then twice married barmaids whom he poisoned with antimony. Murder at the Monument Tavern and Prince of Wales was Chapman's style, but it seems that none of his customers had cause to complain about the beer.

The intimate atmosphere of the public house has also inspired fiery passions, as in the case of Jean Pierre Vaquier, who fell for the landlady of the Blue Anchor at Byfleet in Surrey. He became part of a *ménage à trois* at the inn in 1924, and his feelings drove him to eliminate mine host with a draught of strychnine secreted in the landlord's bromo salts.

A different type of compulsion motivated teenager Jack Hewett when he selected the landlady of the Crown and Anchor as a murder victim. Sarah Blake, a 55-year-old widow, kept the rather run-down public house at Gallows Tree Common in Oxfordshire. Early on the morning of 4 March 1922 a neighbour called by to honour a prior arrangement to look after the place while Mrs Blake was away for the day. The landlady did not answer the knock on her door — her dead body, the head smashed, was found lying in a pool of blood on the kitchen floor. Blood spattered on the ceiling and on furniture testified to the ferocity of the attack. Blood had also been transferred to other rooms, and robbery as a motive was ruled out when it was established that various sums of money in the public house remained untouched.

Sir Bernard Spilsbury, the great pathologist, was called in to carry out a post-mortem. He found more than sixty bruises and injuries on the dead woman's face, neck and arms; the skull was fractured in four places, and there was a deep stab-wound in the neck. A thick iron bar lay beside the body, but the knife used in the attack was missing.

Police inquiries revealed that trade in the Crown and Anchor during the evening prior to the murder was not exactly brisk. Two men tried the pub door at about 7.40 p.m. but, finding it locked, walked on to another local tavern. It appeared that only two customers were served at the pub that night. One of these was fifteen-year-old Jack Hewett, who lived with his mother and stepfather a short distance away.

Hewett told the police that he had gone to the pub after he had his tea and Mrs Blake served him with ginger beer. He returned later to fetch some beer for his mother, but by then the place was closed and in darkness. The only other drinker was another local man who ordered a glass of beer which he finished quickly and then left. Mrs Blake had been seen alive at 6.30 p.m., and it was the pathologist's opinion that she had been murdered soon afterwards.

On 14 March the missing knife was found in a hedge near the Crown and Anchor. It was bloodstained, and bore head hair similar to that of Mrs Blake. On 17 March a man detained in Reading for a minor offence admitted to committing the murder. Robert Shepperd's confession turned out to be a piece of exhibitionism, but it did not lead the police astray for long. On 4 April detectives took a statement from Jack Hewett in which he said, 'I cannot remember what happened for a few minutes, but I took up a flat iron from the wall of the beer cellar and hit her with it ... I'm very sorry it happened, and don't know what made me do it.'

Hewett was tried for murder at Oxford in June 1922. The evidence against him appeared overwhelming in view of two separate confessions which he had made, but he withdrew these in court, claiming that he had been led on by the police. He was nevertheless found guilty, and sentenced to be detained during His Majesty's pleasure. The only hint of motive to emerge from the incident was that three days before the murder a villager had heard Mrs Blake admonish the youth over some unknown misdemeanour. Hewett himself when he was arrested told the police, 'I wish I had never seen the pictures. They are the cause of this.' The 'pictures' was the current term for the cinema, and the Hewett case has been referred to as an early example of the alleged connection between violence depicted on film or TV screen and murder in reality.

One or two notorious medical murderers have selected inns as locations for their crimes. In 1855 Dr William Palmer lodged his victim in the Talbot Arms Hotel at Rugeley, conveniently situated opposite the doctor's home. John Parsons Cook was deprived of both his horse-race winnings and his life by the scheming doctor who entered the history books as England's most vilified poisoner.

Another doctor who merited an entry in the record books was Edmé Castaing, a 27-year-old French physician. He holds the dubious distinction of being the first physician to use the drug morphine for murder. The young doctor enjoyed an extravagant way of life which he found difficult to maintain through shortage of funds. One of his patients was Hippolyte Ballet, a man of considerable wealth and property, who lived at Saint-Cloud outside Paris.

This man of property had a brother, Auguste, whom the doctor befriended. It appeared that Hippolyte had excluded his younger brother from his will — a problem for which Castaing offered a solution. He proposed to steal Hippolyte's will and destroy it, with the effect that Auguste would inherit when his brother died. For this service Castaing would be rewarded with a substantial fee. The will was duly disposed of and Hippolyte died mysteriously from the effects of an unknown poison.

Dr Castaing now turned his attention to Auguste whom he invited for a ride out into the country in his horse and carriage. They set out on 29 May 1823 and stopped at the Blackamoor's Head near Saint-Cloud, where Castaing asked the innkeeper to bring some mulled wine for his friend. The wine duly arrived and Auguste's host declined the innkeeper's offer of sugar, saying that he had brought some with him. He sugared the wine which Auguste found very bitter to his taste, with the result that he felt ill. Castaing decided it would be necessary for them to stay overnight at the inn to allow his friend to recover.

Castaing was up and about very early the following morning and drove off to Paris. When he returned to the inn he gave Auguste some milk, but the poor man was obviously worse and his vomiting and diarrhoea continued unabated. The sick man wanted a doctor brought in from Paris, but Castaing sent for the local physician who prescribed a sedative which he left with Castaing to administer. Within a short time Auguste lost consciousness and breathed his last.

The local doctor, alarmed that Castaing had thrown away the sick man's vomit, informed the Mayor of Saint-Cloud of his suspicions. A post-mortem ordered by Auguste's relatives indicated that he had died of morphine poisoning. Castaing, who was the chief beneficiary of the dead man's will, was also the chief suspect.

Dr Castaing was tried for murder at the Paris Assize Court in November 1823. It was proved that he had at one time asked a lawyer's advice regarding the validity of a will made in favour of a doctor, and it was known that he was fascinated with poisons. His sudden dash into Paris while his friend lay prostrated with illness was to a pharmacy, where he bought some morphine acetate. He gave his full name, and explained that he wanted the substance to kill rats for experimental purposes. A string of medical men testified about the properties of this little-known drug, but there were few doubts that Castaing had used it to commit murder.

Despite his claims of innocence, Dr Castaing was found guilty of murdering Auguste Ballet, but was acquitted of a similar charge regarding Hippolyte. He was sentenced to death.

Boarding-houses form a class of accommodation which, unlike hotels and inns, cater for people who stay in residence for fairly long periods. Families and groups of lodgers find themselves sharing facilities in the same premises with a closeness of contact bordering on intimacy. Nicolaas Lotz, a factory hand at Talana in Natal, South Africa, found himself in such a situation. He stayed at Vann's lodging-house in the town, where he shared a room with another young man. The next room was occupied by Henry Russel and his wife Cornelia and their three-year-old daughter. Lotz, whose childhood had been spent in an orphanage, found that he coveted his neighbour's wife. At first he fantasized to his room-mate about being in love with Corrie Russel, but the attraction proved to be mutual, and soon a friendship grew up.

Friendship developed into an affair, and Corrie would signal to Lotz next door so that he could join her when her husband was out. Henry Russel suspected nothing more than neighbourliness in his wife's friendship with Lotz, at least until she asked him for a divorce. He said he would only entertain the idea providing he had custody of their daughter. Despite her feelings for Lotz, Corrie was not prepared to forsake her child, and after discussing the position, Lotz decided that he should leave the district.

The thwarted lover bought a train ticket to Cape Town, and on the morning of 15 June 1955 visited Corrie to say his farewell. She sobbed and begged him to stay, and he left the highly charged emotional atmosphere to think the matter over. He returned to his own room with the intention of killing himself, but decided first on a further meeting with Corrie. Occupants of the lodging-house heard one shot boom out, followed by several more. When neighbours rushed to the Russels' room they found Corrie sprawled out on the veranda with Lotz standing in the room holding a revolver. 'I've shot Corrie,' he told them, 'I have committed murder .... I have shot a woman.'

Lotz was tried for murder at Ladysmith in November 1955. His defence was that he had fired the fatal shots during a mental blackout, and claimed to have suffered from amnesia since 1942 following a sports injury. A psychiatrist testified that Lotz was a hysterical personality who suffered from anxiety neurosis. Learned debates ensued about 'patchy amnesia' and it was suggested that Lotz began to dissociate from reality when, according to his account, he raised the gun to his own head with a view to taking his life. The defence notion was that when he fired the shots at Corrie Russel he was unaware of what he was doing.

The jury was not convinced by the amnesia plea and brought in a verdict of guilty. The fact that Lotz had bought a train ticket to Cape Town supported his statement that he had tried to withdraw from the emotional tangle, and was sufficient grounds for a recommendation to mercy. Sentence of death was commuted to life imprisonment.

Boarding-house life means the comings and goings of individual tenants are almost certain to be observed by someone. Such observation led to the downfall of New York's parcel murderer. In July 1927 brown-paper parcels began appearing in the Brooklyn area of the city. The first was noticed by a policeman patrolling the Battery Park district who spotted a bundle protruding from a subway ventilator. The second, also discovered by a police officer, lay in a Brooklyn churchyard, and another was found a few blocks away by a theatre manager checking his premises. The contents of the parcels proved rather gruesome — they consisted of dismembered portions of a human body.

Several more parcels were found in various parts of Brooklyn and Manhattan, and the combined contents constituted two headless female bodies. The only clue available was the brown wrapping-paper which came from a well-known grocery chain store, and one piece in particular which bore a column of pencilled numbers adding up to 204.

While the police began the task of tracing the origin of the writing a missing-persons report was filed by Alfred Bennett, a Brooklyn resident. His wife had disappeared after she left home to visit a near-by boarding-house at 28 Prospect Place. One of the Bennett children had seen their mother enter No.28, which she had recently sold to elderly Miss Sarah Brownell. It appeared that the purpose of Mrs Bennett's visit was to collect rent money which was owing. It was a mission from which she never returned.

Armed with this information, police officers called at the boarding-house, and were admitted by a man who said his name was Ludwig Lee. He was of Norwegian origin, and worked as an odd-job man. He claimed to have been a tenant in Miss Brownell's boarding-house for several years, but could not help regarding her present whereabouts. Questioned about Mrs Bennett's visit, Lee confirmed that she had called at the house to complain about some leaking water-pipes.

During the interrogation of Lee the keen nostrils of the detectives picked up the unmistakably cloying smell of decomposition. A search of the basement revealed various parts of a human body including Mrs Bennett's head, together with a large axe which had obviously been recently cleaned. Another tenant at 28 Prospect Place, Christian Jensen, worked as a clerk at the Brooklyn branch of Atlantic and Pacific grocery stores, and said he had given Lee a great deal of wrapping paper because he wanted to parcel up some gifts. Jensen identified the writing on one of the pieces of wrapping-paper as his, and recalled Lee's considerable consternation when he tried the door to the basement and found it locked, with Lee on the other side.

Doctors pieced together Lee's grim gifts, and reassembled the bodies of Mrs Bennett and Miss Brownell. Lee vociferously denied killing the women, but Sarah Brownell's savings book with deposits amounting to $4,000 was found in his room. Moreover, the odd-job man had been seen leaving 28 Prospect Place on 10 July 1927 carrying a parcel, and it was known that he had repeated his parcel delivery.

Confronted by Jensen, the grocery clerk who had befriended him, Lee broke down and confessed to murder. His story was that he had killed Miss Brownell with his axe in order to rob her of her savings and Mrs Bennett had stumbled across him red-handed in the act of hacking his victim to pieces. He therefore killed Mrs Bennett in order to eliminate a witness. With regard to his method of disposing of the bodies Lee admitted, 'It was a lot of work doing all that running around.' Ludwig Lee, the odd job killer, was convicted of murder and suffered execution in the electric chair in 1928.

(1, 18, 62, 158, 268, 309, 398, 410, 444, 633, 733, 788, 794, 927, 1032, MWW)

ISLANDS

'Only Germans on the island and all enemies.'

Margret Wittmer (1934)

The idyllic peace of the tropical island, where nature is usually bountiful and the climate generous, conjures up the idea of the palm-fringed paradise that people dream about. The Caribbean islands fall readily into this category, but even paradise has its ugly side and violence can erupt as suddenly as a tropical storm.

A tropical storm blew in the Bahamas on the July night in 1943 when Sir Harry Oakes was battered to death. He met a violent end somewhere on the island and his body was unceremoniously dumped on the bed in his house at Nassau. This remains one of the Caribbean's most famous unsolved murders. Less mysterious were Michael X's three murders in Trinidad in 1972 (see under GARDENS) and Dr Dalip Singh's elimination of his wife on the same island in 1954 (see under BEACHES).

Bermuda also has been visited by violence, and there were echoes of Michael X's influence during an outburst of violence on the island in 1973. The Governor of Bermuda, Sir Richard Sharples, decided to walk his dog Horsa following a dinner party at Government House on 10 March. Lady Sharples, who was unwell, had retired for the night when Sir Richard stepped out on to the terrace with his aide-de-camp, Captain Hugh Sayer, in attendance.

At about 11.30 p.m. four shots rang out and the police constable on duty in the house found the Governor and his ADC sprawled dead on the terrace, with Sir Richard's Great Dane lying dead a short distance away. The alarm was raised and the house and garden surrounded by police, but the assailant had got clean away. Local residents saw two men running from the scene. Examination of the area revealed powder-traces on the stone balustrade of the terrace at Government House, indicating that the gunman had lain in wait in the garden below and fired up at the two men walking above.

The police immediately associated this double killing with the murder of George Duckett, the Police Commissioner, who had been shot dead at his house only a month before. These three killings triggered off a year of violence in Bermuda in which two shop-owners were shot dead in Hamilton on 6 April. They had been bound hand and foot and shot at close range. A series of random shootings and robberies followed, and a man on a motor cycle fired through the windows of Police Headquarters on 5 May. On 25 September the Bank of Bermuda was robbed by an armed man, and a year after the Police Commissioner had been killed shots were fired at his home.

The police had obtained a description of a man seen running away from the shooting in the Hamilton shop. He was identified as Larry Winfield Tacklyn, a local man, who was quickly arrested. Similarly keen observation enabled a witness at the bank robbery to identify a fleeing man as Erskine Durrant Burrows. The same man was identified as the armed robber in another incident. Although he had gone into hiding, a search of Burrows's accommodation furnished evidence which linked him to a number of the shooting incidents. A pair of wire-cutters was matched forensically to the cut ends of severed telephone cables at the home of the murdered Police Commissioner.

Burrows was seen in Hamilton on 18 October 1973. Although armed with a sawn-off shotgun, he was overpowered and taken into police custody to join Tacklyn. Witnesses, previously feeling intimidated, now came forward with incriminating evidence. It appeared that Tacklyn and Burrows had discussed their part in the various murders on the island, and they had admitted to the killings at Government House.

The two men were thought to have some sympathy for the aims of the Black Power movement, whose one-time exponent in the Caribbean, Michael X, was hanged for murder a few months earlier. Burrows made a confession in which he said he shot the Governor to draw attention to the iniquities of the colonial system. Tacklyn and Burrows were hanged following their conviction for murder.

Murder on an island has the effect of confining the investigation to a relatively small territory, which should work to the advantage of the police and the detriment of the fleeing murderer. Seaports and airports are confined areas, which in theory makes them easy to control. In practice, as centuries of smugglers have proved, it is a simple matter to put a boat ashore at night to embark or disembark goods and passengers. If Sir Harry Oakes's murderers arrived on Nassau by boat after nightfall, as is supposed, and left the same way, they demonstrated the ease of the method.

It may be part of the insular mentality to combine sluggish police work with a tendency to close ranks if the questions come too close to home. That too may have been part of the

John Laurie: Murder on high

Bahamas murder mystery. It is also true that in a small island community the comings and goings of strangers are readily observed. This was a factor of which John Watson Laurie took too little account when he selected an island location for murder.

Laurie, a 25-year-old pattern-maker from Glasgow, bumped into an acquaintance in Rothesay in the summer of 1889. Laurie mentioned that he was travelling to the Isle of Arran with an Englishman he had met, by the name of Edwin Rose. The steamer *Ivanhoe* picked up passengers at Rothesay on 12 July. Among them were Edwin Rose, a London clerk on holiday in Scotland, and Laurie, who was using the name John Annandale.

The travellers landed at Brodick on Arran, and Annandale invited Rose to share his lodgings at Invercloy village. They befriended two other young men, and the four spent their time walking and boating. During the course of these few days one of his newly found friends took Rose on one side and warned him about Annandale, of whom he had formed an unfavourable impression. In particular he advised the Londoner against making a proposed climb of Goatfell (2866 ft) with Annandale.

On 15 July Rose and Annandale stood on the pier and waved goodbye to their holiday acquaintances as the steamer bound for Rothesay left the island. The next day, when the landlady at Annandale's lodgings knocked on his door, she found that her guests had disappeared with their bags, although a few scattered belongings were left behind. She assumed they had done a bunk to avoid paying the rent.

When Edwin Rose did not return to London at the end of his holiday on 18 July his brother grew alarmed. On 27 July he arrived on the Isle of Arran with the police. The local information was that Rose had gone up to Goatfell on the 15th in the company of Annandale, who was seen leaving the island

The Isle of Arran and murder on Goatfell

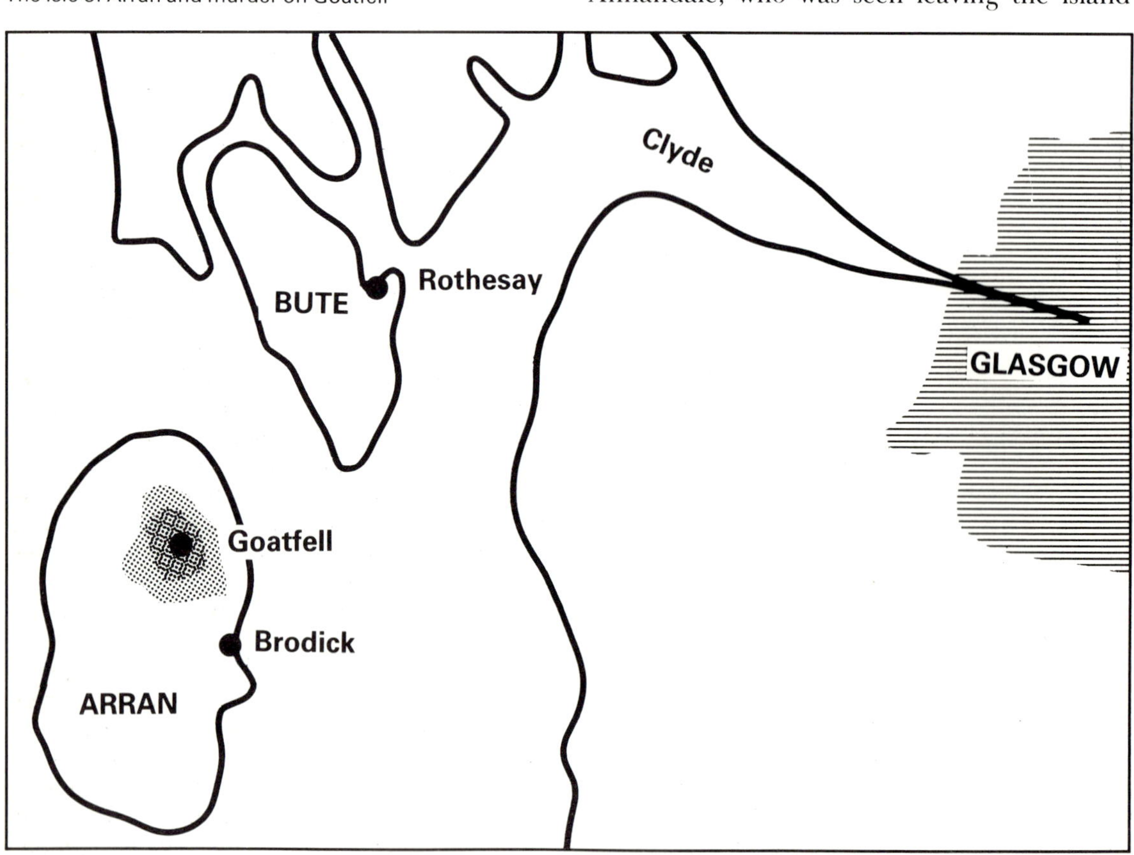

early the next morning. A search was organized in which two hundred islanders and visitors took part. On 4 August a group of searchers high up on the craggy east side of Goatfell at a spot called Coire-na-fuhren saw a human arm beneath a pile of rocks. After pulling away nearly a hundredweight of rocks and stones, the searchers discovered a man's body lying in a cavity beneath. Edwin Rose had been found — he had been bludgeoned to death. His pockets were empty, and his cap, walking-stick and other possessions were strewn about the rocks.

The police now began to trace Annandale's movements. He had been seen in the company of Rose by several people fell-walking as they began their climb to Goatfell on 15 July. Later that evening a shepherd saw a solitary exhausted-looking man descend from the summit. The next morning Annandale, carrying two bags, was seen on the pier at Brodick waiting to board the 7 a.m. steamer to Greenock.

On 31 July, by pure chance, John Laurie alias Annandale met the acquaintance in Rothesay with whom he had discussed his impending trip to the Isle of Arran in the company of an Englishman. He appeared to be flustered by inquiries about his companion in the light of newspaper reports of his disappearance. When the news broke that Rose's body had been found on Goatfell, Laurie's acquaintance went straight to the police.

Alerted to the danger he was in, Laurie collected his wages from the Glasgow firm which employed him, sold his tools and moved to Liverpool. A large-scale hunt was set up and the newspapers carried detailed reports of 'The Arran Murder'. In the classic mould of the murderer who must advertise, Laurie wrote to the newspapers: 'I smile when I read that my arrest is hourly expected.' On 3 September an alert policeman at Ferniegair spotted Laurie about to board a train. The wanted man took to his heels, and was eventually cornered in a wood some three miles away. He tried unsuccessfully to cut his throat with a razor, and was placed under arrest.

John Laurie was tried for murder at Edinburgh in November 1889. He had admitted being on the Isle of Arran with Rose and said, 'I robbed the man but I did not murder him.' His defence counsel argued that the dead man's injuries were consistent with having fallen. The prosecution countered this with skilfully presented medical evidence, added to which were Laurie's use of an alias, his possession of some of the dead man's belongings and his furtive behaviour. It was also known that Laurie was highly familiar with the terrain on the island. The jury found him guilty on a majority verdict and he was sentenced to death. Sentence was commuted to life imprisonment after a medical commission judged him to be of unsound mind. In 1893 he escaped from Peterhead prison but was recaptured and finished his days in Perth Criminal Asylum, where he died in 1930.

The idea of the island paradise as an escape from the worst aspects of civilization and human behaviour has appealed to many adventurous spirits. This was the aim of a German couple who set out to turn the dream into reality. Unfortunately, the reality proved disappointing, for ill-feeling and suspicious death intervened.

The Galápagos Islands, situated on the Equator some six hundred miles off Ecuador's Pacific coast, were made famous by Charles Darwin's *Voyage of the Beagle* in 1839. Another book, William Beebe's *Galápagos: World's End*, published in 1924, described the islands' giant tortoises and other animals. It was to these islands that Friedrich Ritter and Dore Koerwin travelled in 1929.

Dr Friedrich Ritter, aged forty-three, who had worked at the Hydrotherapeutic Institute of the University of Berlin, was a devotee of the philosopher Friedrich Nietzsche. He dreamed of a 'great ideal of solitude' and of a remote island Garden of Eden where he could settle as a sort of latter-day Robinson Crusoe. His companion in this enterprise was Dore Strauch Koerwin, another man's wife. The couple had been lovers in Berlin for two years, and, having arranged for Ritter's wife to act as housekeeper to Dore's schoolteacher husband, they pursued their castaway ideals on the other side of the world.

They chose to live on Floreana, one of the smaller islands, which was unoccupied save for an assortment of cattle, wild pigs and goats, and some donkeys. There had been earlier settlers, but the last, a group of Norwegians, had given up the struggle in 1926. Their legacy was a corrugated iron building and a small pier at Post Office Bay. Friedrich and Dore assembled their stores and equipment and chose an island site on which to build their

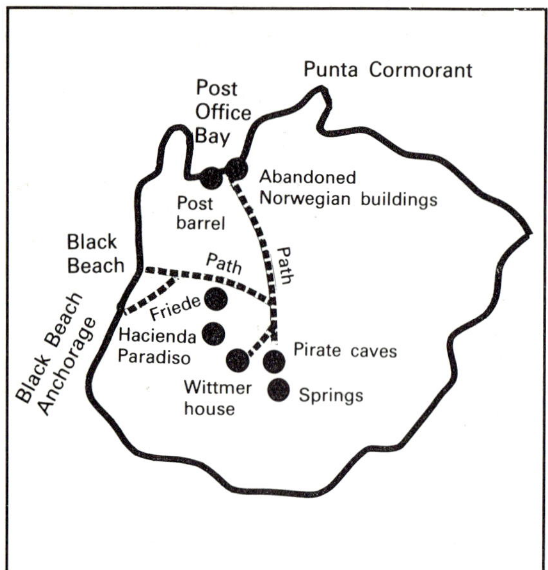

Floreana, the Galápagos island where a dream turned into a tragedy

home, which they named 'Friede' (Peace). They planted a garden and organized a water supply, but life on the tropical island was less idyllic, and rather more like unremitting hard labour.

Ritter, whose favourite book was Nietzsche's *Thus Spake Zarathustra*, planned to write up his own philosophical ideas with help from Dore, his soul-mate. She hero-worshipped her philosopher, but the reality was that they quarrelled over trivia. They received visitors occasionally from passing boats, and stories reached the newspapers idealizing the life of the voluntary castaways, who were described as Adam and Eve.

In August 1932 another German couple arrived on Floreana. Heinz and Margret Wittmer had sold up in Cologne, determined to escape the difficulties in Germany and start a new life; they had one son, and Margret was pregnant. The Wittmers set up their home on another part of the island, some two miles from 'Friede'. More visitors arrived on Floreana in October — they too were German. Baroness Eloise Wagner-Bosquet, a flamboyant, domineering character, was accompanied by her lover, Robert Philippson, and another man, Rudolf Lorenz.

The Baroness and her entourage set up home at a place she called 'Hacienda Paradiso' midway between 'Friede' and the Wittmers'

home. Dr Ritter did not welcome these intruders to his island paradise, and relations were strained from the beginning. The Baroness regarded herself as the uncrowned queen of the island, and expected the others to pay homage. She had plans — announced in an Ecuadorian newspaper — to build a hotel on Floreana to attract an American millionaire clientele. Incensed at the idea of the island becoming a kind of Miami, Ritter wrote to the Governor of the Galápagos complaining about the Baroness's megalomania and asking him 'to put this crazy woman under observation in a sanatorium'.

Relations between the three groups on the island became severely strained, with allegations of purloined stores and tampered mail, directed mostly at the Baroness. While Philippson was tactfully referred to by the others as her husband, it did not pass without comment that he contributed little to the daily travail. It was poor Lorenz, a weakly, tubercular individual, who was directed to a life of ceaseless toil. He feared the Baroness, and sought refuge occasionally with the Wittmers.

Suddenly, on 25 March 1934, the Baroness declared that she and Philippson were taking passage to Tahiti on a visiting yacht. Lorenz was the bearer of the joyous tidings that his tormentor had left, and he and Dr Ritter sorted through the Baroness's possessions, most of which had been left behind at the 'Hacienda Paradiso'. In July Lorenz also left the island in a boat sailed by a Norwegian, Trygve Nuggerud. It had long been understood that Lorenz wanted to leave, and they were said to be bound for Guayaquil on the coast of Ecuador. On 19 November 1934 the mummified bodies of the two men were found beside their boat on uninhabited Marchena Island. They had been dead many weeks, supposedly from thirst and starvation after being shipwrecked. Subsequently stories circulated that they had quarrelled, with one killing the other over an alleged treasure.

On 21 November 1934, when questions were being asked in Europe about the disappearance of the Baroness and Philippson, Dr Ritter died of food poisoning. The offending meal was bad chicken — a strange menu for a vegetarian. With her idyll — or perhaps ordeal — over, Dore returned to Germany to tell the story of her life in Paradise. In this she had some competition when Margret Wittmer turned up to give her account. Margret returned to Floreana to live out her chosen existence; her husband died there in 1963.

Floreana's missing residents — Baroness Eloise Wagner-Bosquet and Robert Philippson — were never seen again. Dr Ritter had written to an Ecuadorian newspaper accusing Heinz Wittmer of murdering them. This allegation was investigated by the Governor of the Galápagos, who was inclined to accept Wittmer's innocence. The persons with the most likely motives for eliminating the Baroness were Lorenz, whom she had mistreated, and Ritter himself, who could see her destroying his dream. It is possible that they combined forces to murder her and her companion and to dispose of the bodies. There was speculation that when Lorenz left Floreana by boat he had the bodies on board, and committed them to the sea for the sharks to destroy. The mystery remains unsolved, but a fitting epitaph for this island drama was provided by Margret Wittmer: 'Only Germans on the island and all enemies.'

Napoleon Bonaparte, vanquished at Waterloo in 1815, was exiled by the English to the island of St Helena in the South Atlantic. With a handful of servants and former courtiers who volunteered to share his exile, Napoleon remained on this remote island until his death on 4 May 1821.

St Helena, situated in the middle of the South Atlantic 700 miles from the nearest land, 4,000 miles from England and 1,700 miles from Cape Town, ruled out escape. There were rumours of Napoleonic forces gathering in the USA and Mexico intent on freeing the exile if they could mount a plan to overcome the 3,000-strong British garrison.

But the real danger — or so it was later imagined — came from within. In 1959 Sten Forshufud, a Swedish Napoleonic scholar, concluded from his studies of eye-witness accounts of Napoleon's last days that the former Emperor had died of arsenical poisoning (rather than gastric cancer, as commonly supposed). The description of Napoleon's illness bore all the hallmarks of poisoning, and theory was given reality after analysis of specimens of hair showed that the amount of arsenic present was thirteen times greater than normal. Locks cut from the Emperor's hair and given to various individuals as gifts during his lifetime were traced, and where possible subjected to

analysis. All the results told the same story — Napoleon had ingested regular amounts of arsenic.

Critics of the murder theory argued that the poison had been acquired by some innocent route through the environment. But why was it so selective, was the counter-argument of those who favoured the idea of the deliberate administration of poison. By a process of elimination, Major-General Count Charles-Tristan de Montholon was singled out as Napoleon's murderer. He was one of those who chose exile with him in St Helena, and his rank gave him a position of trust in the former Emperor's household.

The thesis was developed that Montholon was used by the Bourbon royal family in Paris, who feared the influence of Napoleon even from such a remote place of exile. The chief manipulator was identified as Count d'Artois, who would succeed as King when his elder brother, Louis XVIII, died.

Montholon, despite receiving a legacy of over a million francs from Napoleon, was bankrupt within eight years of returning to Paris. He died in Paris in 1853 after spending six years in prison for his part in a military coup aimed at conveying France to Napoleon's nephew Louis, the future Napoleon III. This followed the disgrace and death of Count D'Artois, who as King Charles X was ousted from his throne in 1830 and the expulsion of his successor, Louis-Philippe (the 'Citizen King') in 1848.

If Montholon had in fact been sent to St Helena for the purpose of murdering Napoleon, he may be said to have carried out his master's bidding well. On that remote island there was no escape for either victim or murderer. It is recorded that Napoleon had his suspicions of being poisoned, but it took 138 years for that suspicion to be given any substance.

(94, 228, 456, 457, 461, 564, 584, 705, 731, 799, 916, 946, 954, 988)

KITCHENS

'I prepared the copper with water to boil the body.'

Kate Webster (1879)

Next to BEDROOMS and PARLOURS the kitchen is probably the most dangerous room in the house from the point of view of domestic murder. As the centre of a great deal of family activity, the kitchen is often the place where arguments fester and tempers flare up. It is a dangerous environment when passions are roused because of the availability of knives, which all too easily become murder weapons.

The kitchen in most households is essentially the woman's domain, and it is the place where many women who are motivated to murder commit the act — usually by stabbing their victims. Dr Marvin Wolfgang in his sociological analysis of homicide in Philadelphia ranked the kitchen as third in the hierarchy of places in the home where murder is committed. His survey of nearly six hundred cases showed that women used the kitchen to kill more often than any other place.

Kate Webster, the servant who murdered her mistress in 1879, was one murderess who made full use of the opportunities afforded by her kitchen. In the confession which she made on the eve of execution she related how she dealt with the body after strangling her victim:

> I determined to do away with the body as best I could. I chopped the head from the body with the assistance of a razor which I used to cut through the flesh afterwards. I also used the meat saw and the carving knife to cut the body up with. I prepared the copper with water to boil the body to prevent identity; and as soon as I succeeded in cutting it up I placed it in the copper and boiled it. I opened the stomach with the carving knife, and burned up as much of the parts as I could.

Kate Webster showed how the culinary arts could be applied to more sinister ends, but in common with many murderers, she underestimated the task of disposing of the corpse. The presence of a fire and of a water-supply in the kitchen assisted her endeavours, but she still found it a tremendous labour. She commented in her confession that her flagging determination was maintained by the Devil.

The killing of Dr John Bradford in the kitchen of his own home was described by the press as 'The Frying Pan Murder'. Police were called in to 208 Dubber Road, Melbourne, Florida, by his wife Priscilla Bradford on 28 March 1980. The 53-year-old optometrist lay

in a pool of blood on the floor of the kitchen; he had been battered to death. Two of Priscilla's friends, Joyce Lisa Cummings and Janice Gould, were in the house, standing about in wet swimming costumes. They claimed to have been in the pool when the commotion began in the house. Eden Elaine, Priscilla's daughter by a previous marriage, was also present.

Priscilla explained to the police that a domestic quarrel had erupted and her husband had attacked her with such violence that she was forced to desperate defence. She admitted striking the blows which killed him, and she had been aided by Cummings and Gould, who had come in from the swimming-pool. This story was regarded with some suspicion from the start, and the indecent haste with which the dead man's funeral was carried out prompted a detailed background investigation.

In the first place, no one who knew him believed John Bradford to be a violent man. Indeed, his first wife — to whom he had been married for over twenty-five years — said he had never struck her. On the contrary, it was Bradford himself who feared assault. He had told his attorney that he thought his wife was trying to poison him, and a month before he died he told employees of a car-rental firm where he was doing business, 'I think they plan to kill me.' 'They' were Priscilla and her friends, Cummings and Gould. John Bradford had married Priscilla in 1976, and she assisted him in his successful optical business, which included a laboratory with several employees. The relationship between John and Priscilla became increasingly strained as her identification with women's liberation ideas became more fanatical. When she filled the house with her friends (including Cummings and Gould, who also worked in his laboratory) life became impossible. Priscilla told him that her love was for her friends and not for him, and in any case they were all man-haters.

After he had been attacked late one night at the laboratory, and survived what he thought to be a poisoning attempt, John Bradford filed divorce proceedings. Eventually his step-daughter, ashamed at what had happened, was coaxed by the police to tell the full story. She said that Priscilla had planned the murder with the help of Cummings and Gould. The idea was to ambush their victim in the kitchen, beat him to death and make it look like self-defence. This scenario was hatched in a Burger King Restaurant after other methods — poisoning with orange juice laced with amphetamines, luring him out into the country and shooting him and cutting the brake hoses on his car — had either failed or been rejected.

On the day of the murder Priscilla had her henchwomen slap and punch her to produce bruises on her body to substantiate her claim of having been attacked. Eden Elaine was to stand in the shower with the water running so that she would be unable to hear her stepfather's screams. Cummings and Gould were dressed in swimming costumes so that they could easily wash off the ambush victim's blood. Thus prepared, they waited in the kitchen for John Bradford to arrive. When he appeared at the house Priscilla smilingly led him into the trap. He was felled, and bludgeoned to death with a variety of weapons, which included two apothecary's jars, a heavy metal bottle-capper, a cast-iron frying-pan, a wooden stool and some golf clubs. When Eden Elaine emerged from the shower Priscilla handed her the bottle-capper and said, 'Keep hitting him — anywhere.' The ferocity of the attack was indicated by the fact that the frying pan was broken into several pieces.

Priscilla and companions oozed defiance from their prison custody, and even tried to arrange the contract killing of a laboratory employee whose testimony would harm them. There was abundant evidence of Priscilla's determination to commit murder, and motive was supplied by Joyce Cummings, who remarked, 'All we wanted was an all-female Lab.' At her trial in August 1980 Priscilla Bradford pleaded guilty to murder, saying that she did not want to hear her daughter testify against her in court. She was convicted, as were her two companions, and all three were sentenced to life imprisonment.

When Mathilde Ladestock's husband came home from work he found a hatchet lying in the hearth and she told him, 'You must do it today.' Just Ladestock, an uncouth Russian, was completely dominated by Mathilde, and the subject of her remark was her one-time friend, Frau Röchling, whom she wished to have murdered.

Frau Röchling, a woman in her early sixties, was caretaker at a tenement in Brückenstrasse, in one of Berlin's poorer areas. Frau Ladestock lived with Just and her son in the same tenement. The two women's friendly relationship began to go sour at about the time Mathilde stored some of Frau Röchling's furniture in her two-room apartment. This was done to help the older woman, but there were undoubted advantages for Mathilde, who possessed virtually no furniture of her own. Not surprisingly, the older woman wanted to keep an eye on her possessions, and made frequent visits to her friend's flat.

Just objected to Frau Röchling's frequent visits and when there was a suggestion that her belongings were being ill-used she quickly became a nuisance and the object of hatred. Frau Röchling went missing on 19 February 1923 and shortly afterwards Just and Mathilde Ladestock were seen closing down her apartment, and they themselves moved to a basement flat in Reichenbergerstrasse.

On 6 February an engineer at Mühlendamm Lock on the Spree saw an unusual-looking package floating in the debris by the weir. When he retrieved the bundle he found a human torso wrapped in pieces of shawl and a curtain. The remains, which were minus head and limbs, had evidently been dismembered with a saw and subsequently boiled. In order to identify the torso the police decided to display the material in which it had been wrapped at police headquarters in the hope that a member of the public would recognize them. As a result, a woman who lived in Brückenstrasse came forward to report that the caretaker was missing, and that she recognized the material as curtains from Frau Röchling's apartment. Suspicion of Frau Ladestock's part in the furniture drama soon came to light and a search of Mathilde's vacated apartment revealed human blood splashes on the wallpaper, and also on a kitchen knife and apron.

When questioned about her missing friend Mathilde Ladestock said she would soon turn up again. Confronted by witnesses' statements, she could not deny that practically the entire contents of her flat had been Frau Röchling's possessions. Moreover, her young child was wearing clothes made of the same material as that found wrapped round the human torso recovered from Mühlendamm Lock. Mathilde's husband was made of weaker stuff, for he soon confessed to committing murder at the instigation of his strong-minded partner. Just said that the quarrel between the two women over the furniture came to a head when Frau Röchling made an accusation of theft and threatened to fetch the police. Mathilde, pregnant with his child, goaded him to drown the old woman when he went fishing. He refused such incitement until one day when he returned home drunk Mathilde whispered to him, 'If you love me you must do it today!' and placed a hatchet beside him on the sofa. She plied him with more liquor, and when by accident or design Frau Röchling appeared at the apartment he felled her with some mighty swings from the axe.

'You can trust me. I'll soon get rid of the body,' said Mathilde encouragingly. With her usual careful planning, she had laid out a saw and knife in the kitchen ready to cut up the body. With her child sleeping in the next room Mathilde helped Just to dismember the body and parcel it up into five packages. Their toil took several hours and neighbours later said they thought they heard sawing noises during the early hours of the morning. Mathilde herself took the bundles of the victim's remains down to the river at Waisenbrücke and threw them into the murky waters. Unfortunately, the out-of-sight-out-of-mind principle backfired due to the curiosity of the lock-keeper farther downstream.

Just and Mathilde Ladestock were twice tried for murder. They were found guilty of murder at the first trial, a verdict which was later quashed on account of a legal technicality. At the second trial Just was judged mentally deficient and sentenced to six years' penal servitude, and Mathilde was convicted of attempted murder and sentenced to nine years' imprisonment. It came out in court that before she finally persuaded Just to murder Frau Röchling she had tried to poison her with an overdose of aspirin tablets.

The kitchen in many houses has its own access at the side or rear, and although it is less common today, it was once the practice for tradesmen, hawkers and other callers to appear at the kitchen door to conduct their business with the occupier. This arrangement provides the opportunity for a miscreant to reconnoitre the prospects for crime. This is what happened at Water Royd House on 12 May 1847. James Wraith, an elderly retired farmer, and his wife were preparing their midday meal when an Irish hawker approached their house. Wraith — reputedly a wealthy man — had bought Water Royd House, near Mirfield in Yorkshire, in which to live in comfort in his old age. Mrs Wraith was laying the table and James had gone down to the cellar to draw himself a mug of beer; their servant Caroline Ellis was busy in the kitchen. It was a thundery day, and menace was in the air when Patrick Reid knocked on the door.

Caroline answered the door, and admitted Reid to the kitchen, where he asked if the household wanted to buy any of his wares. Before the servant had a chance to answer Reid delved into his bag and produced a soldering iron with which he bludgeoned the girl to the floor. Turning quickly, he noticed Mr Wraith emerging from the cellar, and struck him so forcibly on the head that the soldering-iron broke in two. Disturbed by the noise, Mrs Wraith ran into the kitchen to be confronted by the intruder. Weaponless, Reid searched for an implement and his eyes fell on the kitchen poker. Snatching this up, he belaboured Mrs Wraith with such fury that the poker was bent.

Patrick Reid was in the process of stealing a watch and jewellery from his victims when he was interrupted by the appearance in the house of another Irish hawker. This was Michael McCabe, who was innocently plying his trade in the district. Closing the door on the carnage in the kitchen, Reid tried to pass himself off as the occupier of the house and declined McCabe's offer of articles for sale. With the unexpected caller gone Reid ransacked the house and ensured the destruction of his victims by cutting their throats with a razor. That done, he locked the house and threw the key and the soldering iron down a well.

The alarm was raised at about 1.30 p.m. when a relative visited Water Royd House but found it locked up. Blood issuing from under the back door which led into the kitchen was sufficient to turn consternation into sensation. The horror of what had happened to the Wraiths was only too apparent when the police entered the house.

After he left Water Royd House, Michael McCabe made his way to Roberttown where he spoke to a dealer. News of the murder at Mirfield had spread by then and McCabe told the dealer that he had called at the house earlier in the day. As a result McCabe's conversation was reported to the police and he was quickly taken in for questioning. He told his story and gave a full description of Reid who was arrested at a near-by gipsy encampment. Both Reid and McCabe were charged with murder and committed for trial. McCabe turned Queen's Evidence at the trial in July 1847 at York Assizes. Reid pleaded not guilty to the charge of murder of James Wraith, and owing to the sophisticated eloquence of the prosecutor, a confused jury acquitted him. Later that year both men were tried for murders of the two women. Despite McCabe's pleas of innocence and evidence that he and Reid were unknown to each other before the crime, they were judged to be in it together and both were convicted.

In the condemned cell McCabe pleaded with Reid to tell the authorities that he was innocent. Reid made a statement to his solicitor completely absolving McCabe, whose sentence was commuted to transportation for life. This was scarcely justice for an innocent man, but at least he avoided the gallows. Reid went to the scaffold at York on 8 January 1848 and before he was hanged in front of 40,000 spectators took full responsibility for the murders at Water Royd House and again absolved McCabe.

(1, 293, 326, 593, 598, 685, 857, 969, 1037, MWW)

LANES AND BYWAYS

'I was in a kind of rage.'
Leslie Stone (1937)

Lanes and byways are the places where people meet what Shelley described as 'Murder on the way'. The morning stroller or workbound walker may chance upon a murder scene; the courting couple may stumble across the murder victim; so too may the delivery roundsman. For the murderer the lane wending its quiet way through the countryside, the path that is off the beaten track and which use has turned into a short cut, and the lovers' lane are all convenient places of privacy. There violence can be exercised with scope for concealing the body and for escaping unnoticed.

It was a young couple walking down Lovers' Lane, an offshoot of De Russey's Lane in New Brunswick, New Jersey, on the morning of 16 September 1922 who discovered the murders of the Minister and the Choir Singer. They found the bodies of Rev. Edward Hall, a local pastor, and Mrs Eleanor Mills, a member of his church choir, lying with their throats cut among the crab-apple trees. This famous case remains officially unsolved, as does the murder discovered by a police constable on early-morning patrol in Eltham on 26 April 1871. He saw a woman on her knees in Kidbrooke Lane, a well-known Lovers' Lane, and at first thought she was drunk. As he walked closer he realized that she was reeling from a terrible injury to the head through which her brains were protruding. 'Let me die,' she moaned.

Help was summoned, and the dying woman was put into a cab and rushed away for medical attention. Doctors found that she had sustained a dozen axe wounds to the head and face. She had been brutally disfigured, and was not immediately identifiable. The state of her hands suggested that she worked as a domestic servant, and the discovery that she was two months pregnant indicated a possible reason for the attack.

While the fatally wounded girl lay in Guy's Hospital, police examined the scene of the crime. There was a large pool of blood which identified the location of the attack, and there were numerous footmarks, including some widely spaced tracks indicating a person running in the general direction of near-by Morden College. A search of the college grounds turned up a bloodstained hammer of the type which combined a hammer head and an axe blade. News of the terrible attack in Kidbrooke Lane stimulated horror and curiosity. Some twenty thousand people were estimated to have visited the crime-scene during the weekend following the attack.

The victim was identified on 30 April — the day she died — as seventeen-year-old Jane Clouson, parlourmaid in the house of Ebenezer Pook, a Greenwich printer. Inquiries showed that Jane had been dismissed from Mr Pook's service twelve days before she was attacked. She had not gone to stay with relatives but with a friend who found lodgings for her. Her landlady reported that when Jane left the house at 6.40 p.m. on 25 April she said her intention was to meet Edmund, the Pooks' twenty-year-old son.

Edmund Pook, who worked in his father's printing business, adopted an arrogant line when interviewed by the police. Regarding

Jane Clouson he said, 'I know nothing of her,' but added, 'She was a dirty young woman ....' He claimed an alibi for the night in question, but when he was asked to produce the shirt he had worn the garment proved to be blood-stained on one cuff. An explanation given for this was that he suffered fits and had bitten his tongue, making it bleed. Edmund Pook was nevertheless charged with murder.

The police accumulated a considerable amount of evidence, and many witnesses came forward to make statements. Jane's cousin revealed that the dead girl had told her not to be surprised if she went missing for a while, as she might go away with Edmund, who had given her strict instructions to keep silent about the plan. A Deptford ironmonger identified Edmund as a customer who had entered his shop on the day before the attack to purchase an axe. He thought the items available were too expensive and said he would try elsewhere. The murder weapon was bought at another shop in Deptford High Street, but the proprietor was unable to identify the purchaser.

A man who lived in Kidbrooke Lane stated that he saw Edmund Pook and a young woman walking in a cornfield towards Lovers' Lane at about 7.00 p.m. Another man returning home from work claimed to have seen a man and a girl struggling; the girl was crying, 'Let me go!' A local coachman also saw a couple in the lane and he heard the girl scream, after which the man ran off in the direction of Morden College. A woman who ran a confectionery shop on Royal Hill reported that Edmund Pook had come into her shop on the evening of 25 April looking hot and bothered. He asked for a brush to clean his clothes, and explained that he had run from Lewisham Road. This statement was confirmed by the assistant who was in the shop at the time.

Edmund Pook was tried for murder in July 1871, and public hostility towards him was so great that no jurors from Kent or Surrey were selected. Pook's defence was in the hands of Henry Pook, a Greenwich solicitor, but not a relative. Henry Pook's dubious conduct of his client's affairs had caused a considerable stir even before the trial, and he had managed to create a climate of confusion in which it was difficult for justice to work. After a reiteration of all the previous evidence, the trial judge declared it to be circumstantial, and Pook was

acquitted. The trial was a shambles, as some of the prosecution witnesses plainly committed perjury and parts of the police evidence were badly prepared. Pook's alibi had not been properly checked, and useful clues had been overlooked.

The man responsible for Jane Clouson's pregnancy was not proved as Edmund Pook. But local opinion was firm in its belief that the young master had seduced the parlourmaid, rejected her when he learned she was pregnant and, when she pestered him to marry her, lured her to Lovers' Lane where he savagely killed her. There was anger in Greenwich that he had been found not guilty. Far from counting his good fortune and seeking to return to a quiet life, Edmund Pook allowed his advisers to campaign to clear his name. His father wrote to *The Times* claiming a police conspiracy to convict his son, and demanded an inquiry. In this quest he was aided by solicitor Henry Pook, who issued writs against those who continued to speak of Edmund's guilt. Pook was charged with using insulting and indecent language to the police. It became difficult for anyone to probe into the case, and Henry Pook won a victory which could only be called hollow, as most people believed Edmund to be guilty. This Victorian *cause célèbre* is an early example of the way in which the victim of murder is so often relegated from the scene, while every attention is devoted to the murderer or suspect.

A milk roundsman was the discoverer of a Lovers' Lane murder in Washington DC in 1937. He was working his round near Eastern Avenue when he heard moaning noises from a near-by lane. His investigation of the noise led him to a young woman lying on the ground and bleeding profusely from a head wound. Milkman Thomas C. Boss ran for help, and the injured woman was taken to hospital, where she spoke disjointedly to the police about her attacker. 'He beat me terribly,' was all she could say before dying.

The dead woman was identified as Blanche Landis. She had sustained a fractured jaw and other injuries, and died from loss of blood. At the murder-scene detectives found a man's sock filled with sand and stones; it was heavily bloodstained. It became known that Blanche had separated from her husband, although it was understood that the couple had remained on good terms. James L. Landis, an officer with the Washington fire service, was told of his wife's death. In answer to questions regarding his whereabouts at the estimated time of the assault he claimed to have been on duty until 1.00 a.m. and his colleagues said they had seen him drinking coffee in the firehouse at 4.00 a.m. A routine check of Landis's locker turned up a solitary sock which a detective thought looked similar to the one found at the scene of the crime. Visual comparison soon proved the socks to be a pair. Confronted with this discovery, Landis lost his earlier composure, and after intense questioning made a statement.

He said that after completing his shift in the early hours of the morning — and despite the rule that he was not supposed to leave the premises — he went to his wife's home. They took the car and drove around for a while. He claimed that his wife seemed nervous about his attitude, and without warning jumped from the moving car. This, he alleged, was how she sustained her injuries. Realizing that she was badly hurt, he panicked and decided to leave her where she was and return to the firehouse, from which he was absent without permission.

James Landis stuck to this story when he was tried for murder, but the jury did not believe him. Medical evidence that the dead woman's injuries had been caused by repeated blows to the head helped to convict him; he was found guilty of second-degree murder, and sentenced to life imprisonment.

Yet another Lovers' Lane murder was that which claimed attractive Ruby Anne Keen as its victim. She was a factory worker in her early twenties who attracted many admirers. Among them was Leslie Stone, who was perhaps her most regular boy-friend. Their respective families at Leighton Buzzard in Bedfordshire assumed that the couple would marry in due course. But when Stone joined the Army in 1932 the prospect of marriage faded, and their separation was heightened when the young soldier was posted to Hong Kong. They exchanged letters for a while, but after about twelve months the correspondence had dropped to a trickle.

During the time that Stone was out of the country Ruby, a vivacious young woman, naturally enjoyed the company of other admirers. She became particularly attracted to a young police constable to whom she became engaged in 1936. Towards the end of that year Leslie Stone was discharged from the Army and made his way home to Leighton Buzzard. He soon realized that Ruby had acquired another boy-friend during his absence, yet he fondly believed that after three years he could pick up with her affections where he had left off.

In April 1937 Stone met Ruby in the Golden Bell public house and tried to date her. She was noncommittal but he ran into her in the same pub about a week later on 11 April, when they had a few drinks. A few drinks 'for old time's sake' developed into something of a carousing session, and the pair moved on to the Cross Keys and thence to the Stag Hotel. Customers in the Stag overheard Stone earnestly trying to persuade Ruby to throw over her policeman boy-friend and marry him instead. At about 10 p.m., after he had consumed several pints of beer and as many 'chasers', Stone escorted Ruby from the Stag and the couple made their way past the girl's home to a well-known lovers' lane on the outskirts of town called The Firs. A couple walking through The Firs at about 10.30 p.m. saw Ruby in the arms of a man wearing a dark suit who was later erroneously assumed to be her policeman boy-friend.

Early next morning a railwayman on his way to work came across the dead body of Ruby Keen. Her clothes had been pulled off and the marks in the soil near the body indicated that the girl had fought hard to ward off her attacker before being strangled with her own scarf. She had not, however, been sexually assaulted. Scotland Yard detectives were quickly called in to investigate the crime, and with them Sir Bernard Spilsbury, the pathologist. Their attention focused on the footprints round the body, which, disappointingly, had been so scuffed about in the course of the assault as to prove useless as clues. Fortunately, the murderer had left other indications of his presence in the shape of two knee marks where he had knelt down on the sandy soil when he strangled the girl. Casts were made of these marks, which showed a clear impression of the trouser material worn by the killer.

It did not take the police long to learn about the dead girl's boy-friends. Her policeman fiancé was quickly eliminated from the investigation, and Leslie Stone was detained for questioning. He had reported to the local police on the day that the body was found in order to clear his name, as he explained at the time. Now the officers wanted to see his shoes and trousers. He produced a pair of dark blue trousers which had been so heavily brushed at the knees that the nap of the material had been worn away.

When subjected to a microscopic examination the trousers were found to have specks of sandy soil adhering to them — soil which proved identical to that at the spot where Ruby Keen had been murdered. And, to clinch a case made famous by linking trace evidence between murderer and victim, a fibre found on the suit of Stone's jacket proved to have come from the cream silk underslip worn by his victim. On 24 April Leslie Stone was charged with murder. He was tried at the Old Bailey, where the scientific evidence was powerful enough to make him change his plea. He admitted in the dock that he had quarrelled with Ruby Keen, and claimed that she had provoked his anger by striking him. He grabbed her scarf and pulled her to the ground. Still holding the scarf round her neck, he said, 'I think I knotted it ... I was in a kind of rage.' Stone said he thought she was only stunned, and he walked away believing she would recover. The prosecution believed that he was only deterred from committing rape by the realization that she was dead.

While out of the courtroom considering their verdict the jury asked the judge for clarification on a point that was bothering them. The question was: 'If as the result of an intention to commit rape a girl is killed — although there is no intention to kill her — is a man guilty of murder?' The judge answered, 'Yes, undoubtedly,' and the jury returned a guilty verdict. Leslie Stone was hanged on 13 August 1937, his appeal against sentence having been dismissed. Ruby Keen's policeman fiancé, whose only crime was to have been innocently associated with a murder victim, was asked to resign from the police force.

Death lurked in a quiet Welsh country lane for an unsuspecting farmer doing nothing more provocative than leading a horse to his friend's farm. Edward Nicholas farmed at Penypare, Llantarnam, in Monmouthshire. He bought a horse in the early summer of 1954, and on 12 June set out in a cattle truck with his friend, Granville George Jenkins, to collect the animal from St Bride's Wentloog. The horse was a spirited young animal, and defied all force and cajolery to enter the truck, which in any case was ill equipped for its purpose. The men decided to take advantage of a loading ramp offered by a local farmer.

The plan was that Jenkins would walk the horse about a mile through the country lanes to the farm, with Nicholas following in the truck. Nicholas delayed his departure in order to give his companion a head-start. He had not travelled far when he saw the horse in a lather heading towards him down a lane called Belt Road. The farmer imagined that his friend had encountered some difficulty with the horse, as a result of which the animal had bolted.

Nicholas walked down the lane calling out Jenkins's name. He received no answer, but after about ten minutes came across a neatly folded raincoat and canvas hold-all lying on the verge of the road. Neither article appeared to belong to his companion. Walking on a little farther, he noticed an area of flattened grass by the roadside which looked as if a scuffle had taken place. Turning his attention to the opposite side of the lane, Nicholas looked into the ditch and saw Jenkins lying there in the weed-choked water. He tried to haul him out, and saw several deep cuts on his head; he also realized that his friend was dead.

When the police arrived the body was retrieved and the full extent of the injuries realized. Jenkins had sustained thirty-two knife wounds, one of which had severed his carotid artery. Defensive wounds on his hands and arms testified to the ferocity of the attack to which he had been subjected. Clinging to the legs of the body was a water-sodden jacket, the pocket of which contained a National Insurance card made out in the name of 'T. Gass'. The policeman who found this recognized the name immediately. Taher Gass was known locally as the 'Crazy Somali' on account of his mad behaviour.

Gass was presumably the owner of the discarded raincoat and hold-all and a tea-cosy found near the crime scene was also thought to belong to him. At least one of the reasons why local people regarded him as crazy was that he often wore a tea-cosy in place of a hat. The Somali was known to live rough when he was unable to find lodgings. A large-scale search was now mounted in order to find him for questioning. Taher Gass was quickly located by detectives visiting some of his favourite haunts, but as soon as he spotted the police he took to his heels. The area which ran along the Bristol Channel was drained by a network of deep ditches to deal with tidal flooding. Gass took flight with several police in pursuit across this difficult terrain and eventually he was cornered. Once at bay he produced a knife and threatened his pursuers, but was soon disarmed and arrested. His only comment was, 'Me no kill nobody.'

An intensive search of the district had produced a large machete which doctors were confident had inflicted the wounds on the murdered man. Moreover, blood of the same group as Jenkins's was found on the suspect's clothing. Taher Gass was tried at Monmouthshire Assizes where his plea of diminished responsibility was accepted. He had a history of treatment for mental instability and the judge ordered him to be sent to Broadmoor Hospital. In 1955 the 'Crazy Somali' who dealt out death in a quiet country lane was returned to his own country.

(54, 138, 186, 373, 450, 544, 692, 736, 884, 914, 925, MWW, mw)

MANSIONS, RANCHES AND VILLAS

'My only guilt is that I have been connected with men of bad character.'
Countess Maria Tarnowska (1910)

The notion that wealthy and titled persons who live in grand surroundings are above suspicion of murder has always been a myth, and was amply demonstrated as such by the Duc de Praslin. Early on a summer's morning in 1847 he surveyed the blood-letting which had occurred in his wife's bedroom at his fashionable Paris mansion in rue Faubourg Saint-Honoré. Her dead body lay on the floor in her blood-spattered room. She had been stabbed and bludgeoned, and her throat was cut. He declined to answer the deferential questions put to him with the pompous remark, 'I am a peer of France. I do not give explanations to police officers.'

His attitude served only to harden suspicion, and the knowledge that he had neglected his wife for years in favour of his children's governess perhaps made the police press their

Discovering the body of the Duchesse de Praslin

inquiries. The Duke's own room contained bloody remnants of his involvement in the violence inflicted on his wife. That his was the hand which ended her life seemed proved when the bell-pull from her room — by which she might have summoned aid — was found hidden in his clothes. The law of France would not permit a man of his standing to be arrested without the consent of the Court of Peers. While this was being sought as an inevitable step towards proving his guilt, the Duc de Praslin poisoned himself. In so doing he precipitated a scandal in French society, and showed quite clearly that high rank was no insurance against committing base deeds.

The London home of the Earl of Lucan in fashionable Belgravia was the scene of murder in November 1974 when his children's nanny was battered to death in the basement. The assailant was identified as her husband by Lady Lucan, who was also attacked but sustained only minor injuries. She was the intended victim, but Lord Lucan killed the nanny by mistake. A warrant for his arrest was taken out, but despite extensive searches and several alleged sightings he remains numbered among the missing.

Countess Maria Tarnowska was not so fortunate with her escape plans after being party to a murder committed in an Italian villa. The Countess was a beautiful, deadly female of the human species who lured several men to destruction. Born in St Petersburg in 1878, she married Count Vassili Tarnowski when she was aged sixteen, against her parents' wishes and following an elopement. Thereafter she flitted about the aristocratic mansions and villas of Europe preying on the rich and foolish.

She lived with Count Vassili in Kiev, where the lustre of their elopement quickly wore off and the Count sought the embraces of a

Countess Maria Tarnowska — the Russian Vampire

mistress. Maria retaliated by taking several lovers, one of whom was Captain Alex Bozevsky, an officer in the Imperial Guard. The Captain's demands proved excessive even for Maria, and she decided to dispense with him. She arranged for Bozevsky to visit her in St Petersburg, where she received him seductively in her bedroom in the knowledge that her husband would soon arrive. When Count Tarnowski turned up he found his wife in the arms of the other man, whom he promptly shot when Maria claimed that he had assaulted her.

At this point her plan began to go awry. In the first place, Bozevsky was not dead, although he eventually succumbed following the attentions of Maria's physician, Dr Vladimir Stahl. Count Tarnowski was charged with the murder, and banking on his being exiled to Siberia, Maria schemed to acquire his property. She was aided in this by Dr Stahl and by a married lawyer, Donat Prilukoff, who became one of her pawns. The plot collapsed when Count Tarnowski was acquitted of murder; he divorced Maria, and threw her out of his house.

Maria launched herself on Dr Stahl, whom she used unashamedly to finance her extravagant life-style. His reward came in the form of sexual favours at the same time that Maria was having an affair with Prilukoff. Sucked dry like a fly in a spider's web, Dr Stahl ended his misery by shooting himself. Donat Prilukoff now found himself the centre of attention, and Maria persuaded him to embezzle money from a company he represented in order to finance her activities. Abandoning his wife and children, Prilukoff accompanied Maria on her travels around Europe. In Paris he attempted to escape her clutches, but he remained ensnared in her web ready to be activated in another bold plan.

In Moscow she met a former acquaintance, Count Paul Kamarowsky, a rich widower and member of an influential family. He became infatuated with Maria and wanted to marry her, but through the Count she met twenty-year-old Nicolas Naumoff and immediately took him as a lover. All the participants in the drama that was to come were by now drawn into her web of intrigue with its strong elements of sex and sadism.

Not wishing to play the part of the old fool, Kamarowsky withdrew his financial support when Maria became besotted with Naumoff. While the young man amused her, he had no money, so Maria returned to Kamarowsky and persuaded him to take out a large life insurance naming her as the sole beneficiary. Then she told Naumoff and Prilukoff she wanted them to murder Kamarowsky for her.

Naumoff responded at once by travelling to Italy, where Count Kamarowsky was on holiday in Venice. Prilukoff at first refused to co-operate, but such was Maria's guile that she induced him to go to Venice and arrange for detectives to be present when Naumoff carried out the murder plan. On 3 September 1907 the quiet of Kamarowsky's villa on the Campo Santa Maria del Giglio was shattered when Naumoff burst in and shot the Count dead in his bedroom.

Naumoff was quickly arrested, and confessed the whole story. Maria was apprehended in Vienna and Prilukoff in Trieste. The trio were tried in Venice in March 1910. Each blamed the other, and, devious to the last, Maria the arch-schemer excused her behaviour by saying, 'My only guilt is that I have been connected with men of bad character.' The trial attracted huge numbers of spectators, including many members of Europe's titled families. The newspapers were provided with a feast of entertainment by the evidence of sexual intrigue, inflamed passion and the sheer bravado of Maria Tarnowska. She was called a 'Russian Vampire' and a 'Sphinx'; a French paper described her as 'distinguished by an aristocratic elegance, and throws around her the sparks of a cultivated mind and a voice of soft caress.'

The sparks had finally ignited a conflagration which consumed Maria and all her works. She was found guilty of aiding Naumoff, and was sentenced to eight years' imprisonment. Prilukoff received ten years in prison, and Naumoff, the murderer, only three years on the grounds that he had been the tool of others. Maria spent her days in the Italian women's prison at Trani overlooking the Adriatic. There she wrote verses, some of which found their way into French publications. She was released in 1912 and ended up in Paris, where the former scheming temptress died in obscurity in 1923.

The ranks of the titled and well-to-do have certainly produced their murderers and also their victims. The owners of large houses sometimes become easy prey for resentful or villainous servants. Elderly Lord William Russell was murdered in his London home in 1840 by his valet. François Courvoisier disliked carrying out his master's orders, and decided to rob him. For the sake of stealing a few pieces of silver he cut the old man's throat. He confessed readily enough, and was subsequently executed at Newgate. His victim paid the price, as other wealthy house-owners have done, of employing poorly vetted servants and putting them into positions of trust. Tyranny is always easier to practise when the climate is one of confidence. This was the basis from which Archibald Thompson Hall, the murderous butler, worked. (See under APARTMENTS AND PENTHOUSES.)

Provoking the already resentful servant is also a prescription for murder, as Mme Marie Riel discovered to her cost. This middle-aged French widow lived at No.13 Park Lane, London, and counted General Lord Lucan among her friends. The General, of Crimean War fame, was then in his seventies, and he lived in near-by South Street. Madame Riel had two servants, a maid and a cook, to look after her and her daughter Julie, an actress, who also lived in London.

In November 1871, following the loss of her cook, Madame Riel hired a 29-year-old Belgian, Marguerite Diblanc, as her replacement. She joined Eliza Watts to complete the domestic staff at 13 Park Lane. Mistress and cook frequently argued, but as she did not understand French, Eliza Watts (who was the only witness to these encounters) did not know what was said. In March 1872 Julie Riel dismissed Marguerite Diblanc from her job. There was an argument over the cook's entitlement to wages, and it was decided that she should work out a month's notice. Shortly after this episode Julie Riel left for an acting engagement in Paris, leaving behind a rather tense household.

During her daughter's absence Madame Riel had a further altercation with her cook, but apart from realizing that a quarrel was a quarrel in any language Eliza Watts was no wiser as to what matters were at issue. On 7 April, just before lunch-time, Mme Riel dressed to go out, indicating that she intended walking the dog in Green Park. She had not returned by 4.00 p.m. when a visitor arrived by invitation to take tea with her. The visitor waited for three hours and then left.

The two servants sat together attempting to discuss their mistress's absence by sign language. Marguerite several times asked Eliza to go out and buy some beer — it was no secret that the cook liked her drink. Eventually Eliza obliged, and had some difficulty in getting Marguerite to answer the door when she returned. At about 8.00 p.m. Marguerite went out, saying she would be back about ten. Eliza waited up until midnight, but when neither her mistress nor the cook returned she went to bed.

The following morning Eliza awoke to find she was still the sole occupant of the house. The first caller was Julie Riel who was surprised to learn that her mother was not at home. Eliza was sent round to Lord Lucan's house in South Street, but Mme Riel was not to be found there. A search of 13 Park Lane soon disclosed that the pantry was locked. When it was opened Mme Riel's body was found lying in a heap on the floor.

A local doctor was called to examine her, and he pronounced her dead. She had bruises on her face, and there were rope-marks on her neck. Cinders and dust in the dead woman's hair and clothing indicated that she had lain in the cellar at some stage after she had been murdered. Eighty pounds in notes and coins were missing from the house, but the main question concerned the whereabouts of Marguerite Diblanc. It was thought that she might have taken the Paris train from Victoria, and the Parisian police were asked to trace her. It was discovered that Marguerite used lodgings at 192 rue St Denis. Although the landlady at this address claimed to know nothing, a letter addressed to her was found which made it clear that she and Diblanc were in contact with each other. Posted in London and dated 6 April 1872, the letter advised, 'I will try to leave for America ....' Before she could put her plans for flight into effect Marguerite Diblanc was arrested at a friend's house in Paris. She admitted killing her mistress for reasons of resentment; not for robbery, she told the detectives.

After some difficulties regarding extradition, Diblanc was returned to England on 29 April to face charges of murder. A magistrates' court committed her for trial at the Old Bailey on 12 June. The British press was not particu-

Marguerite Diblanc: the truculent servant who murdered her mistress

larly well disposed to the Continental servant accused of murdering her mistress. She was described as 'short in stature, stout, thick-necked and of coarse, muscular type ....' Particular attention was drawn to her hands, which 'are those of a man'. Obviously, as far as the press was concerned, she was quite capable of committing a violent act.

In her statement made to the French police at the time of her arrest Diblanc related how the argument with Mme Riel began in the kitchen. She was told to get out of the house, but she said she would not go until she had been properly paid. After some unladylike insults had been exchanged the two women grappled with each other, and blows were struck. Mme Riel fell down dead. Diblanc dragged the body down into the cellar. Later she decided to move it to the pantry, but found the task too difficult with the rope she had attached around the waist. She completed the task by putting the rope around the dead woman's neck and dragging her along.

Diblanc was not able to follow the legal procedure of the English court, nor was she able to understand much of the evidence. The point at issue was whether the charge against her could be reduced to manslaughter on the ground of provocation resulting from an exchange of verbal insults. The judge ruled that words alone were insufficient provocation to reduce the charge. The jury found Diblanc guilty of murder but made a recommendation to mercy. The convicted servant said in French, 'I never had the intention to cause death.' Sentence of death was passed on her, but on 21 June 1872 the Home Secretary announced a reprieve.

The servant's hatred for the master may find an escape in violence or murder against an individual, but there is another kind of vengeance which is forged in hatred of society as a whole. This sort of resentment was spawned by Charles Manson and his followers in their commune at Spahn Ranch near Los Angeles. He and his companions broke into the Hollywood home of film actress Sharon Tate in August 1969 and murdered her and four other people. The victims of the grudge killings were probably selected simply because they represented wealth, achievement and fame. Manson's followers, believing they had been discarded by society, expressed their hatred in brutal fashion.

Murder back at the ranch was an ordeal inflicted on Hope Masters, a 31-year-old mother of three and a native Californian who had spent most of her life in Beverly Hills. She had married twice, and was separated from her second husband, Tom Masters. She had the reputation of being a rich socialite, although in reality she qualified for food stamps for her children. In December 1972 Hope met Bill Ashlock, a rising star in the advertising world. The couple planned to marry, and in February 1973 went for a weekend to the ranch near Springfield in Tulare County which was owned by Hope's parents. They had arranged to meet there a photographer who was to take some publicity pictures in connection with Ashlock's work.

The photographer duly arrived, and announced himself as Taylor Wright. The atmosphere was relaxed until the night of 24 February, when an intruder disturbed the peace. Hope, who had been asleep, was threatened with a gun, and when she shouted out for Bill Ashlock was told by the intruder that he was dead. 'Look at all that blood — see all that blood. He's dead.' The man then

raped her and bound her hand and foot.

At this point Hope realized that her assailant was Taylor Wright. He told her, 'Someone wants you dead ... there's a contract out on you.' He explained that the underworld wanted her and her children killed, and added that instructions had been given by her husband.

Hope Masters later recounted an extraordinary sequence of events in which Taylor Wright behaved like a lover and spoke of marrying her. He drove her to a grassy meadow near the ranch where she thought he planned to kill her, but the moment passed and they drove first to Bill Ashlock's apartment in Los Angeles and then to her home in Beverly Hills. Wright moved in and met Hope's mother and step-father. He told them how he had arrived at the ranch and discovered Ashlock's body, and Hope tied up. 'The man who did this to your daughter has to be insane,' he confided.

After a family discussion it was decided that the police should be informed of what had occurred at the ranch. Wright went out of the house to use a pay-phone. He did not return, but police officers appeared at the house and Hope poured out a rambling account of what had happened, describing the intruder at the ranch in vague terms as possibly Mexican. In the meantime Ashlock's body was found with a bullet in the head and Taylor Wright had absconded. Hope was taken into custody, and in due course charged with murder; 'Socialite Booked for Murder' was one headline in the press.

Hope by this time had told her mother that Taylor Wright was the murderer. He kept his distance but maintained contact by means of telephone calls, and by sending tape-recorded messages through the mail. One of these included a statement which he said he would make to the authorities. In transcript form, it ran to fifty-one pages and told the story of how he became involved with the incident at the ranch by accident. 'I was inclined to believe her story of the intruder and the murder of the man on the sofa on the next room,' he said. He also stated, 'My identity is not to be known. My intent and purposes within the United States are definitely not to be known.'

Despite his pretensions to anonymity the police were already closing on Taylor Wright's trail, and he was arrested in a Hollywood motel. His real name was G. Daniel Walker and when apprehended he had on him credit cards belonging to Taylor Ortho Wright, a jewellery salesman, who had been beaten up and robbed in an Ann Arbor hotel room early in February. A copy of the novel *Day of the Jackal* was found in Walker's car, and a gun in his possession was proved to be the weapon used to kill Bill Ashlock.

On 18 April Walker and Hope Masters were bound over to a superior court to be tried for murder. At their trial in November all charges against Hope were dismissed, and the case proceeded solely against Walker. The trial lasted nearly two months, and over ninety witnesses, including Hope, were called. She told the court that Walker had discussed his preferred method of killing — which was by poisoning or by means of an ice-pick driven through the ear — but that her husband demanded a blood-bath. Tom Masters also testified, and was exonerated from any allegation that he had hired Walker to kill his wife.

Walker confirmed that Hope had not killed Ashlock, but denied committing the murder himself. 'My name is Daniel Walker,' he said, 'more commonly known as G. Daniel Walker … I have used approximately ninety names in the past twenty-three years.' He was well known to the police on account of convictions for armed robbery and attempted murder, and at the time of the ranch murder was a prison escapee. The jury found little difficulty in convicting Walker of first-degree murder, and he was sentenced to life imprisonment.

The danger of the offspring of wealthy parents putting their idle minds and hands to violent use was exemplified by the famous Leopold and Loeb case in the USA in 1924. These sons of respected Chicago families killed a fourteen-year-old boy for excitement, and only the brilliance of their defence lawyer saved them from the death penalty. This case had its echoes in a Dutch murder which occurred thirty-six years later.

The teenage brothers, Boudewijn and Evout, lived with their parents at Baarn, a Dutch town close to Hilversum. Their father was a company executive, and they lived in a thirty-roomed mansion set in five acres of land. Some of the rooms were used as offices and the remainder as family accommodation, but the house was so extensive that some of the cellars and attics were unused. A feature of the flat roof was a sizeable cupola entered through an attic.

The brothers' inseparable companion was another teenager called Hendrick who lived in Baarn. This trio were somewhat wayward, and decided that it would be exciting to steal. They planned various escapades in a snack bar in the near-by town of Soest. On the fringe of this tight group of friends was fourteen-year-old Theo Mastwijk, an unhappy lad who was regarded as difficult at school, and who soon landed in trouble through theft. When Theo let it be known that in order to take the pressure off himself he might have to widen the circle of suspicion by reference to his friends, Hendrick and his companions decided to help. On 23 June 1960 Theo was taken in secret to the mansion at Baarn and smuggled into the cupola on the roof, which had been fitted out with the bare essentials to accommodate him. The idea was that he should stay out of harm's way for ten days or so while a plan could be worked out to sneak him across the border to Belgium or France.

Boudewijn and Evout took their roof-top guest plates of food twice a day, and generally looked after him. But the days and weeks dragged on and no plan emerged. With the summer holidays fast approaching it was clear that something would have to be done. The two brothers were due to leave on 2 August to accompany their parents on a trip to Switzerland. When the suggestion that another boy might be allowed to join them on holiday was turned down by their parents Boudewijn and Evout took council with Hendrick.

The trio decided that Theo should be killed, and various methods were discussed. They elected to use an overdose of sleeping-pills, and planned to bury the body in the garden rubbish-pit. The drug was administered to Theo via a bottle of beer, but the plot was foiled when his stomach rebelled and he vomited.

A further council of war ensued, and an alternative plan was devised. A hole had already been dug in the garden, and a bag of quicklime had been purchased from a local builders' supply merchant. At about midnight on 1 August 1960 the trio appeared in the cupola and told Theo the time had come to smuggle him out of the country. He was led quietly downstairs and out into the garden shed. There he was partially strangled, and beaten about the head with an axe. His body — possibly still conscious — was thrown into the hole prepared to receive it and covered with quicklime, which was first watered and then covered with soil. The following day Boudewijn and Evout went on holiday with their parents and Hendrick returned to his home.

In the summer of the following year Boudewijn uncovered the corpse, with the intention of disposing of the bones. The task proved so daunting that he covered the grave over again. Then in October 1961 a workman engaged at the mansion to dig a channel for a water-pipe accidentally uncovered the body. The quicklime had done its work exceptionally well, for the body had been reduced to skeleton and rags. A forensic expert called in from The Hague believed the body was that of a young man, and he thought it had lain buried for about fifteen years. The theory was that the body might have been that of a person killed at the end of the war by the Dutch Resistance.

Detailed examination of the remains resulted in a different opinion. Remnants of a nylon shirt on the skeleton suggested that the body had been buried after 1955, as nylon materials were not widely used before then. When the police reviewed their missing-persons files the name of Theo Mastwijk came to the fore. Moreover, a police photograph showed the lad wearing a shirt with a pattern identical to the shirt remnant found clinging to the skeleton. As Hendrick was known to have been one of the last persons to see Theo alive, he was immediately sought for questioning.

On 2 November 1961 Hendrick made a full confession in which he implicated his two companions. Boudewijn was arrested in Amsterdam and denied everything; Evout was arrested in The Hague and admitted involvement in preparations for murder but nothing more. Boudewijn managed to escape from custody but when he was recaptured he broke down, admitting his part in the murder but putting the blame on Hendrick; 'I was an automaton, an automaton ....' he said.

Theo Mastwijk was buried on 15 November 1961. A pathological examination of his remains showed injuries to the skull caused by axe wounds. It was not possible to determine the exact cause of death, but it was likely the boy had been rendered senseless by a combination of strangulation and blows to the head. If he was still alive when covered up in the pit he would have died from suffocation and shock as a result of the sudden increase in temperature (to about 100°C) brought about by the action of the quicklime.

The three lads were examined by psychiatrists before being separately tried for their part in killing Theo Mastwijk. Hendrick and Boudewijn were regarded as having acted together, with Evout playing a more minor role as look-out. The two senior partners each accused the other of being the prime instigator. Boudewijn said that he was instructed to hold Theo's wrists while Hendrick strangled the boy and then hit him with the axe. Hendrick testified that it was Boudewijn who first suggested that Theo be murdered and Evout who came up with the idea of using quicklime to destroy the body.

The court found the indictment proved, and sentenced Boudewijn and Hendrick to nine years' detention at Her Majesty's pleasure and Evout to six years. Reference was made in court to the famous Leopold and Loeb case in Chicago in 1924. There were certain similarities; in each case the victim was a young boy and the killers were youths from distinguished families. The difference was one of motive. Leopold and Loeb killed for the excitement of experiment, whereas the Baarn murder was committed to eliminate someone who represented a threat.

(49, 85, 132, 416, 603, 750, 827, 837, 884, 1048, 1057, mw)

MARSHES AND MOORS

'I am indeed thankful I have got rid of you so easily.'

George Woolfe (1902)

Tottenham Marshes, an area of waterlogged wasteland in North London, had a reputation for attracting violence. In the eighteenth and nineteenth centuries it was bandit country where robbers lurked and innocent people feared to tread. It was the place where Thomas Orrock went in 1881 to practise shooting his revolver before murdering PC George Cole. The evil reputation of the place seemed to soak up the noise of violence and cloak the escape of the criminal.

On 26 January 1902 some boys playing football in the marshes kicked their ball into a ditch. When they retrieved it they discovered the body of a girl. She was dead but still warm, and there were several severe injuries to the face and head. It did not take the police long to establish that the dead girl was Charlotte Cheeseman, a worker from a cigar factory in Hoxton. Letters found in her possession suggested a possible motive for her death. Charlotte, it seemed, was courting a man by the name of George Woolfe who was behaving less than honourably towards her. One of his letters informed her, 'I made the acquaintance of a young lady I admire much better than you; therefore you had better do the same and think no more of me.' Not content with this abrupt dismissal, Woolfe added a touch of menace in a PS, 'I am indeed thankful I have got rid of you so easily. I have got the date I went to see you, so if you find yourself in any trouble, or I mean a certain condition, it will be no good to put the blame on me ... I pity the man who ever gets tied up to you.'

Inquiries made at the offices of Charlotte's employers revealed that three weeks before the girl's death they had received a letter from 'Alfred Dixon' which set out to impugn her character. The writer accused her of theft and drunkenness, and offered to provide 'further information'. The police proved to their satisfaction that neither Alfred Dixon nor the address from which he allegedly wrote the letter existed except in someone's malicious mind.

Charlotte, in the best manner of victims of tragedy, wrote to Woolfe telling him, 'You don't know how much I love you.' The result was a meeting on 25 January 1902, and the couple were seen together in Southgate Road at the 'Rosemary Branch' public house. Both Woolfe and the girl were positively identified. After the girl's death Woolfe enlisted in the Surrey Regiment, from whose ranks he was seized by police on 6 February and charged with murder. He admitted meeting Charlotte, but said she left his company and he never saw her again. He found it difficult to explain how he sustained scratches on his face, and his admission that he was responsible for the letter sent to her employers did little to endear him to the jury at his trial. It was clear that Charlotte had become an encumbrance, so he lured her out into the marshes, where he battered her to death and hoped to escape by enlisting in the Army. George Woolfe was convicted of murder and sentenced to death.

Sidney Tiffin, a farm labourer with a love of wild-fowling, had the misfortune to discover part of the mortal remains of Stanley Setty in the Essex Marshes on an autumn morning in 1949. Lying north of the Thames Estuary, the marshes are a deserted area of mud flats and reeds populated mainly by birds. On this particular morning Tiffin saw an odd-looking bundle floating in the water. Thinking it might be a drogue parachute from an RAF trainer plane, and therefore worth recovering, he pulled it out of the water. He cut through the rope holding the water-sodden bundle together and, to his horror, found himself looking at a human male torso.

The headless remains were clothed in shirt and pants and the hands were tied together. Fingerprint examination established the man's identity as Stanley Setty, who was known to the police as a dealer on the black market. Setty's murder was eventually laid at the door of Brian Hume, who had decided on a novel method for disposing of his victim's body. Hume hired a light aircraft at Elstree and flew out over the English Channel. He made two trips, and from a position close to the Channel Islands he dropped out his parcels containing Setty's dismembered corpse. In time-honoured fashion the workings of the currents and tides contrived to wash up the bundle containing the torso in the Essex Marshes. Two further parcels containing the head and legs were consumed by the deep.

The isolation of the marshy landscape is surpassed by the desolation of the moor. The inhospitable, trackless and often boggy terrain of Dartmoor was given to the crime reader by Sir Arthur Conan Doyle as the sinister backdrop to *The Hound of the Baskervilles*. Dartmoor, described as 'a barren and soul-destroying spot', has long been associated with crime — or rather its punishment — because of the prison built on its bleak, windswept landscape in 1806. Originally constructed to house French prisoners of war, Dartmoor Prison in due course served as a maximum-security gaol for the worst murderers. Its situation in hostile moorland defeated many prison escapes.

But it is the moors north of Manchester with the gentle-sounding names — Hollin Brow Knoll and Sail Bark Moss — that gave rise to chilling headlines in the English newspapers of 1966 describing the infamous Moors Murders. Ian Brady and Myra Hindley worked together in the same office. After hours they developed an appetite for sadism, Nazism and pornography which resulted in brutal murder.

In September 1964 the couple moved into a house near Manchester where they lived with Hindley's grandmother. They were on friendly terms with Hindley's sister Maureen and her husband, and Brady sought to impress the young man with his books on sadism, torture and guns. There was talk of robbing banks and of murder. To prove that he was no idle boaster, Brady picked up a seventeen-year-old homosexual youth in Manchester on 6 October 1965 and took him home. Late that night Hindley was dispatched to fetch her brother-in-law to witness a grisly scene. On the sofa in the living room lay the youth Brady had picked up earlier. He was alive, but Brady, wielding an axe, proceeded to bludgeon him to death. 'It's done,' he said. 'It's the messiest yet. It normally only takes one blow.'

Terrified by what he had seen, Brady's brother-in-law telephoned the police the next morning. Police called at the house and found the youth's dead body in a bedroom. In response to questions Brady and Hindley were evasive and unhelpful. A search of the house produced two left-luggage tickets which related to two suitcases at Manchester Central Railway Station. The cases contained coshes, wigs, photographs and two tape-recordings.

Some of the photographs were of a girl in obscene poses. She was identified as ten-year-old Lesley Ann Downey who had been missing from home since December 1964. Other photographs were separate prints of Brady and Hindley standing on the moors at a spot later determined to be within feet of Lesley Ann Downey's grave. One of the tape-recordings carried the child's piping voice pleading to be allowed to go home. Another child, twelve-year-old John Kilbride, who had been missing from home since November 1963, featured in some of Brady's notes which were a plan of murder. By making painstaking comparisons, police were able to identify the moorland grave of the missing boy. Again the photographs were of help. In her book on the Moors Murders called *On Iniquity* Pamela Hansford Johnson wrote, 'Hindley on the moors, crouching down with her dog in her arms and gazing at a disturbed patch of earth. She was, in fact, staring like a pointer at the grave of John Kilbride.'

Brady and Hindley were tried in 1966 for the murder of a teenage youth and two children. The tape-recording was played in court, and the voice of the frightened victim at the mercy of her captors shocked the jury. The Moors Murderers were convicted and sentenced to life imprisonment.

An earlier moors murder in England's west country focused similar hostility on the murderer. William Burgess, a labourer, lived with his wife and three children at Simonsbath on Exmoor. He was recognized in the village as a rogue, and was strongly suspected of sheep-stealing. On one occasion he claimed to have lost some of his livestock, and solicited sympathy from fellow-villagers, who responded in the traditional manner with gifts of money intended to help him buy fresh animals. The fact that Burgess spent this money in the public house did little to endear him to his neighbours.

In 1858 genuine misfortune struck when Mrs Burgess died and their home was sold up. Two of the children were given a home by a family in another village, but Anna stayed with her father in lodgings. In the summer of that year several local people observed that Anna appeared to be missing, although she had not been reported as such. Rumours were current that 'Her father 'av done 'er in!'

When these rumours reached the ears of the parson, William Thornton, proper inquiries were made. It was established that Burgess had left his lodgings several days earlier, saying that he was taking Anna to stay with her grandmother at Porlock. He had the child's spare clothes wrapped up in a bundle under his own. He returned later, but after a few days left again, saying he too was going to live at Porlock. Mr Thornton's discreet inquiries established that Anna was not residing with her grandmother. Moreover, examination of the remnants of a fire found near Burgess's last lodgings turned up traces of burnt clothing identified as the missing child's. The police were now informed of the suspicions regarding William Burgess and his missing child. His movements were traced to Swansea, and the police set out to locate him. In the meantime a search was mounted for Anna.

Burgess was soon found and brought back to Simonsbath, where he was confronted by Parson Thornton, who, rather ill-advisedly, accused the man of murder. Burgess remained silent when asked to say where Anna was.

Searchers on Exmoor found what they thought was an empty grave in an area of mining spoil. It was the practice for sheep-thieves to bury an animal carcass in a temporary grave before returning at night to retrieve it for butchering. It was suspected that Burgess, who was known to indulge in sheep-stealing, had done something of this kind to his daughter. Suspicion as to the final resting-place of the girl focused on the near-by Wheal Eliza, a derelict mine. The main shaft was flooded, but when it was pumped out the body of Anna, sewn into a tarpaulin sheet, was soon recovered. In the aftermath of this discovery a number of locals maintained that they had seen a mysterious blue light over the Wheal Eliza which disappeared the night Anna's body was found.

William Burgess stood trial for murder at Taunton, where he was speedily convicted and sentenced to death. He told Parson Thornton regarding his daughter's death, 'I thought she would be better out of the way.' Burgess was executed on 4 January 1859, and there were those who thought he had been responsible for starting a fire in January of the previous year which cost the lives of three people. This was allegedly an act of revenge against a family that had declined to help him.
(4, 27, 78, 279, 320, 408, 414, 478, 489, 601, 632, 756, 940, 985, 992, 1015, 1018, 1026, MWW)

MOUNTAINS

'It might be six weeks before you hear from us.'

Frank Butler (1896)

Mountain areas have been traditional territory for robbers and brigands of all kinds. The remote, rugged and least accessible parts of the world offer special advantages to those who prey on innocent travellers. Ambush is made easier in difficult, rocky terrain, which also aids escape and hinders detection. Remoteness adds delay to discovery of a crime, and bad weather may obscure tracks altogether.

Disposal of the victims of murder in mountainous regions is assisted by geography. Combing a mountainside for a body which may be hidden under rocks or a crevasse requires intensive search procedures. The forces of nature also accelerate the destruction of a corpse, which deteriorates quickly due to the ravages of climate and attacks by animals. The likelihood of discovery diminishes as a corpse is reduced to its elements, and identification becomes a forensic challenge.

Norma Carty Bell Wilson, an ageing American millionairess, disappeared from Los Angeles in 1968. The search for her took investigator Bill Burnett to Europe, and in particular to the Swiss Alps. Here the trail went cold, and as he surveyed the thousands of square miles of unbroken mountains, many of them permanently snow-covered, he realized that a buried body could be undiscovered for centuries.

Mrs Wilson had indeed been murdered, and her dismembered body buried in the mountains. This was proved in January 1974, when a man picking mushrooms in the Alps found some human remains. The teeth remaining in a jawbone were sufficient to prove identification. This wealthy woman had been defrauded and then murdered, allegedly by her financial adviser, who was convicted of the crime and subsequently freed on appeal.

Jeannette May was another woman with a wealthy background whose body, together with that of her companion, Gabriella Guerin, was found in the mountains. the two women vanished from their hotel in the Italian town of Sarnano on 29 November 1980. The first explanation for Mrs May's disappearance was that she had been kidnapped, a theory apparently strengthened by the knowledge that she had formerly been married to banker Evelyn de Rothschild.

No ransom notes appeared, but two weeks after Mr May offered a reward of £125,000 for information leading to the recovery of the two women alive, their bodies were found. On 27 January 1982, fourteen months after they were last seen alive, the remains of Jeannette May and Gabriella Guerin were found by boar-hunters in the mountains of Central Italy near the village of Podalla. The dead women's car was found abandoned some seven miles away from the spot where their bodies were discovered.

The explanation offered by the Italian police was that the women went sightseeing in the mountains and ran into bad weather. The region saw some of its worst snow-storms for fifty years, producing raging blizzards and

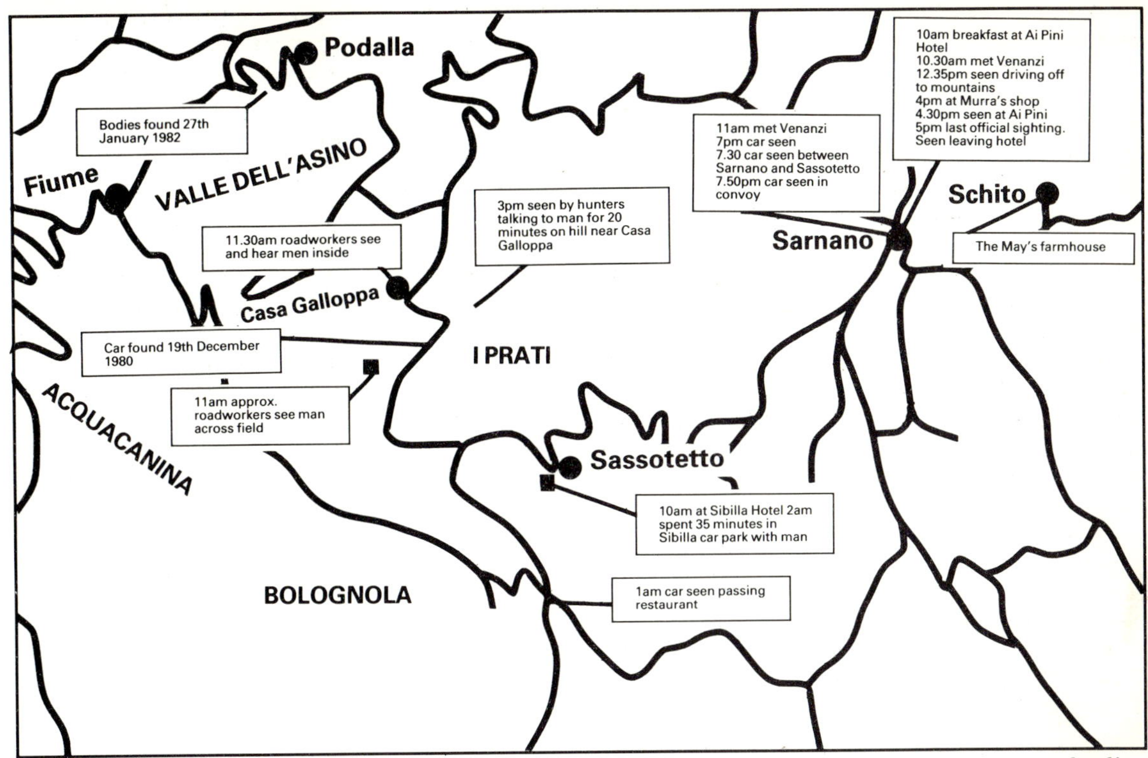

Jeanette May and her companion disappeared in the Italian mountains of the Marche

six-foot-high snow-drifts. Unable to continue their journey by road, Jeannette May and her companion left the car and perished while trying to reach shelter on foot.

This account of accidental death left several mysteries unexplained. Some 250 yards from the spot where the bodies were found stood a shepherd's summer cottage which had been broken into and showed signs of seven persons having eaten a meal there. A fork from the cottage was found in Gabriella's handbag — an indication, according to local gossip, that she was preparing to defend herself. Another link with the cottage was the discovery in the bathtub of hair which matched that of Mrs May.

Local opinion was that the snowstorm on the day the women disappeared was so fierce that it would have been impossible for them to have walked seven miles. The argument was that they had been victims of a bungled kidnap attempt. When things went wrong their captors murdered them and later dumped their bodies near Podalla. The spot where they were found was near a farm road in regular use,

which made it inconceivable that two bodies had lain there unnoticed for over a year.

Post-mortem examination of the bodies showed no signs of bullet-wounds, but the state of the remains was such that strangulation need not be ruled out. It was also alleged that the hands had been severed from the corpses. This is a well-known practice in Italian kidnapping cases and is designed to thwart identification — without realizing the importance of the teeth in such matters. The strong suspicion remains that Jeannette May and Gabriella Guerin were murdered.

The lure of gold has drawn both prospectors and robbers to the mountains and, like human society everywhere, has produced victims and felons. New Zealand's gold-rush in the 1860s attracted men of vastly differing character on a trek to the northern mountains of South Island in search of a fortune. In June 1866 two groups of four men were destined to meet in an act of violence on Maunga Tapu, 'the sacred mountain', which lay south-east of Nelson in gold-mining territory.

Richard Burgess, a convicted criminal who used several aliases, was a Londoner who had been sentenced to transportation by a British court and shipped to Australia. After serving his time he became an influential figure in Melbourne's underworld, and in 1861 moved to New Zealand to try his hand at gold-mining. He soon decided that prospecting was hard work, and less rewarding than robbing miners who had succeeded. He gathered round him three other former Londoners with shady backgrounds, and they decided to arm themselves and roam the miners' highways looking for easy victims.

On 12 June 1866 four honest men set out from Deep Creek bound for Nelson, where they planned to go to work in the Wakamarina gold-diggings. They were led by John Kempthorne, a storekeeper, and the party included Felix Matthieu, a hotel-keeper, James Dudley, another storekeeper, and James de Pontius, a miner. They carried their joint assets of £300 with them, and a packhorse bore their equipment. Matthieu, who owned the packhorse, had arranged for a man called Heinrich Moller to set out after them in order to retrieve the animal at Nelson, from where they would proceed entirely on foot.

Moller proved to be a good walker, and soon began to gain ground on the main party. Several travellers going in the opposite direction told him they had passed his party. His surprise can only be imagined when he arrived at Nelson to find that his companions had not yet reached the town. Moller backtracked to Canvas Town and made inquiries of the storekeeper there. This rather pessimistic individual told him that four strangers had been seen in the neighbourhood, and mentioned the possibility of foul play. The police were informed that a party of men were missing, and they had no hesitation in rounding up Burgess and his companions, who they suspected had criminal intentions. Unfortunately, as it turned out for them, they were forced to remain several days in Nelson waiting for a boat to take them to North Island. They also drew attention to themselves by their free spending in the hotels, shops and bars. On 18 June Phil Levy, Burgess's right-hand man, was arrested, and the following day Burgess himself and the other two, Joseph Sullivan and Joseph Kelly, were locked up in Nelson's gaol.

Meanwhile a search was organized for the missing men, and Maori trackers were brought in to help. They found a dead pack-horse, but their efforts were hampered by bad weather. Various rewards were offered for information

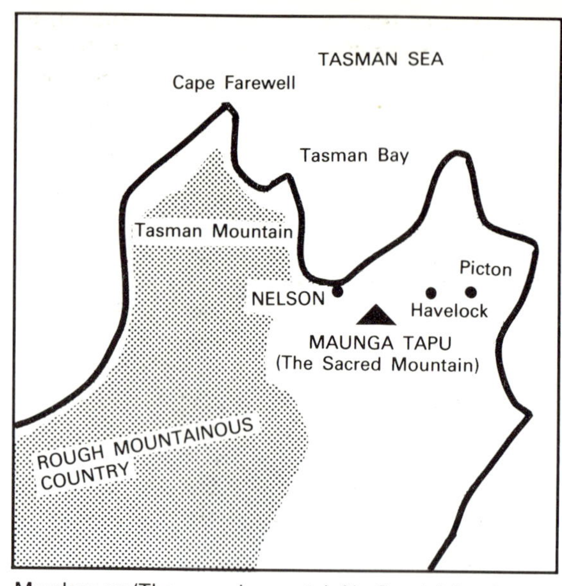

Murders on 'The sacred mountain' in South Island, New Zealand

leading to the discovery of the missing men, including one which guaranteed a free pardon for an accomplice. These announcements stimulated Joseph Sullivan to make a confession. He said that his companions had murdered the four men from Deep Creek, while his part in the incident was to act as look-out. He also mentioned the killing of another man, an old sailor called James Battle, whose murder came as a surprise to the police. Sullivan also told the search party where to find the bodies. The victims were found near a shallow creek where they had been strangled or knifed before being robbed and hidden under bracken.

The murders had occurred on 13 June on Franklyn's Flat, an area near the rugged 3000-ft summit of Maunga Tapu where the track across the mountain ran between dense banks of undergrowth. Burgess and his gang had lain in wait and ambushed the Deep Creek men when they entered this corridor from which they could not escape. Almost the entire population of Nelson — some 3,000 people — attended the funeral of the dead prospectors.

Sullivan, an ex-prize fighter, informed against his companions, no doubt to reduce his sentence. Burgess retaliated with his own confession, which plainly implicated Sullivan in both the planning of the ambush and the subsequent murders. Burgess's lengthy statement was a remarkable contribution to the literature of murder. It began, 'Written in my dungeon drear this 7th of August in the year of Grace, 1866. To God be ascribed all power and glory in subduing the spirit of a most guilty wretch, who has been brought, through the instrumentality of a faithful follower of Christ, to see his wretched and guilty state ....' Thus humbled, Burgess spoke of the 'heinous sins' committed by Sullivan, but attempted to absolve Levy and Kelly.

Not that this statement deflected the Nelson murder trial jury from its duty. Burgess, Levy and Kelly were found guilty and sentenced to death, and the following day Sullivan was tried and found guilty of murdering James Battle. On 5 October the murderers of the Deep Creek prospectors were hanged after each harangued the spectators at the scaffold. Sullivan's sentence was commuted to life imprisonment, and he was removed to Dunedin to prevent a possible lynching.

Another criminal who saw the profit to be made from other men's greed was Frank Butler, one of Australia's most notorious murderers. This restless adventurer was born in England in 1858, and before he took to crime joined and deserted from the uniformed services of several countries. The Royal Navy, the United States Army, and the Canadian North-West Mounted Police all counted Butler in their ranks at one time or another.

He arrived in Australia in 1893, and was quickly in trouble with the police on charges of theft. After several short terms of imprisonment, he adopted the alias of Frank Butler Harwood, a professional mining engineer whose papers he had stolen. Using this identity, he established himself in Sydney and set about looking for victims whom he could lure into his murder-for-profit scheme. Like George Nichols and Alfred Lester (see under RIVERS AND LAKES), he realized the power of advertising. Accordingly he placed advertisements in the *Sydney Morning Herald* for partners to take up equal shares in a gold-prospecting trip. The first reply was from a young Scandinavian only recently arrived in Australia, known only as Burgess.

On 13 August 1896 the pair set out from Gilham's Hotel — which Butler used as a base — in Burgess's wagonette bound for the Blue Mountains. Butler returned alone and sold the wagonette and horses for fifteen pounds. Settling back into Gilham's, he awaited the response to his next advertisement for a partner to prospect in the mountains. It came in the form of twenty-year-old geology student Arthur Preston, who no doubt hoped to acquire some useful mining experience. They were waved off by Preston's friends when they travelled by train from Sydney to Emu Plains; 'it might be six weeks before you hear from us', Butler advised.

Again Butler returned alone, earlier than expected and giving the excuse that Preston 'got knocked up' and he had to come back to find another partner. An advertisement in the *Herald* attracted Lee Mellington Weller, a sea captain recently widowed, who was looking for something to take his mind off his sorrow. A gold-prospecting trip in the company of an experienced engineer sounded a good opportunity. On 29 October, Butler and Weller set out by train for Glenbrook in the mountains. Butler returned unaccompanied a few weeks later and busied himself selling Weller's possessions. He also began masquerading as Captain Lee Weller, and decided that it was time to shake Australia's dust from his feet. He signed up as a seaman on the *Swanhilde*, a sailing-vessel bound for San Francisco. On 21 November Captain Lee Weller was reported to the police as a missing person, and two days later the *Swanhilde*, carrying Butler among her crew, slipped anchor.

Police inquiries into Weller's disappearance soon came up with Butler's name, and the likelihood that the Blue Mountains would provide answers to the mystery. Using black trackers, the police came across some of Weller's clothes and personal effects, but they were frustrated by not finding a body. The search continued around Glenwood's deep mountain gullies and ravines and on 3 December an area of disturbed soil under an overhanging rock was found to be a shallow grave. The body it contained was not that of Weller but of Preston, who had been shot through the head. Two days later Weller's corpse was found in a similar shallow grave.

A warrant was issued for Butler's arrest on 9 December, by which time he had been at sea for sixteen days. What followed had later echoes in the arrest of Dr Crippen, when wireless telegraphy was first used in the apprehension of a murderer. To begin with, the *Swanhilde* was intercepted by a New Zealand vessel from Auckland with news of the search for Butler following Captain Weller's murder. The captain of the *Swanhilde* knew he had a murderer on board, but shared the secret only with his first officer. Secondly, the Attorney General of New South Wales, ignoring the constitutional problems posed by requesting the extradition of a fugitive, cabled the police department at San Francisco requesting the arrest of Frank Butler when the *Swanhilde* docked.

When, on 2 February 1897, the vessel tied up at her berth, police officers went on board immediately. Putting a hand on Butler's shoulder, the *Swanhilde's* captain said, 'Officer, this is your man.' Butler, taken completely by surprise, was led away to gaol to await the outcome of the extradition proceedings. While in San Francisco's City Prison, Butler became the subject of considerable notoriety, and kept himself occupied by posing for sketches and selling his autograph.

In the meantime the body of Burgess had been found, and the New South Wales police now had three good reasons for getting their hands on Butler. His extradition from the USA was granted in March, and he was

Frank Butler sits it out in a San Francisco Prison

shipped to Australia in chains. He had already virtually been tried by the newspapers, but his formal trial for murder began in Sydney's Central Criminal Court in June 1897. He was convicted on largely circumstantial evidence, but confessed to the three murders on the eve of his execution. 'Let go! Let go!' he demanded of the hangman, urging him to release the drop.

The possibilities that mountains offer to cloak murder in the guise of accident were exploited by one Count Henri de Tourville, although, as it turned out, not too successfully. De Tourville, a good-looking Frenchman, fluent in several languages and trained as a barrister-at-law in England, arrived at the village of Trafoi in the Austrian Tyrol in July 1876. He was accompanied by his wife, a wealthy English widow whom he had married the previous year. They were on their honeymoon, having recently visited France, Italy and Switzerland, and the Countess was attended by her maid, an English girl called Sarah Clappinson.

The Count told the proprietor of the hotel where they were staying that he wanted to take his wife to see the beautiful Stelvio Pass. He was advised that Ferdinandhöhe was the best place from which to appreciate the scenic countryside. A carriage and driver were hired and the couple set out for their sight-seeing trip, leaving Sarah Clappinson behind. Some distance from the pass de Tourville stopped the carriage and dismissed the driver, saying that he and his wife would proceed on foot.

When the couple did not return to their hotel for dinner that evening fears were expressed for their safety. A search party was about to be assembled when de Tourville, in an agitated state, returned alone. He explained that there had been an accident, and while walking close to the edge of the mountain his wife had fallen and plunged into the ravine below. Police were called, and the Countess's body was found lying in the rock-strewn river Klambach.

Count de Tourville wanted his wife's body brought up immediately to the village, but the local police refused to do this until senior officers had viewed the circumstances of death. Several aspects of the woman's fatal fall were difficult to explain. For one thing, the body had been found at some distance from the base of the precipice, and for another it was surprising that she fell so far without being checked by the outcrops of rock and vegetation which covered the side of the mountain. The grieving widower was therefore held in Austria while further inquiries were made. Despite the controversial nature of the evidence, a coroner's inquiry delivered a verdict of accidental death, and Count de Tourville was free to return to England.

Safely back in England, de Tourville wrote to one executor of his wife's will — he stood to inherit £40,000 — giving an account of her death which was at variance with what was already known. He now said his wife had committed suicide for health reasons and because of a scandal resulting from her previous marriage. Suspicions were aroused, and further inquiries were begun, in England and also in Austria.

Count Henri de Tourville's title was self-bestowed — his real name was Henri Perreau, and in 1867 he had been working as a waiter in Paris. Subsequently, on account of his linguistic ability, he was employed as a travelling companion by a wealthy Englishman, William Cotton. Master and servant visited Istanbul, where after three days Mr Cotton mysteriously disappeared and the servant — now calling himself Count de Tourville — travelled to England. In Scarborough in 1868 he met and married Henrietta Brigham, who would come into an inheritance on the death of her widowed mother.

Following a whirlwind romance and a honeymoon in Paris, de Tourville began to borrow money from his mother-in-law. A dramatic encounter ensued when he visited Mrs Brigham at his own request to repay the loan. He arrived carrying a revolver which he later alleged his mother-in-law had asked for to deter burglars. At any rate, a shot was fired and Mrs Brigham fell dead from a wound in the head, ostensibly while handling the revolver. A verdict of death by misadventure followed, and within a year Mrs Brigham's daughter had also died — in her case, from natural causes — and de Tourville thus became a widower for the first time.

His next move was to insure the house at Scarborough for a large sum of money. His small son nearly lost his life when it was accidentally burned to the ground, and when the insurance company refused to pay out de Tourville took himself off to London. In the

capital he took up law and became a barrister (although he never practised), and in 1871 became a naturalized British subject. He lived in style with a large house, a boat on the river and a box at the opera; he was regularly seen at such fashionable events as Ascot, Goodwood and Cowes. Then in 1875 he married again, taking as his bride Madeleine Miller, a widow with a healthy income of £7,000 a year. After a quick trip round Europe she fell down an Austrian mountainside to become another 'death by misadventure' in her husband's life.

Having reconsidered the evidence, the Austrian authorities decided to bring a murder charge against de Tourville and secured his extradition from England. He stood trial at Bötzen before two judges, and the proceedings were something of an attraction, with many tourists and several high-ranking aristocrats in the court. Henri de Tourville pleaded not guilty, and launched into a long speech for which he was rebuked by one of the judges who told him, 'You talk too much.' The prosecution presented a strong case indicating that there had been signs of a struggle at the scene of the crime, and every indication that the victim had been first murdered and then dumped where she was found. A telling blow was provided by the Rev. Albert Glynn, who had met de Tourville in Scarborough. He recalled how the Count had told him of an infallible method he had for getting rid of inconvenient mothers-in-law and wives. The jury had no hesitation in finding Henri de Tourville guilty and he was sentenced to death although on appeal this was reduced to life imprisonment.

Perhaps the most renowned mountain murderer was Alfred Packer, who combined killing with cannibalism. Denver, Colorado, was the scene of an unusual ceremony in August 1982 when the State Governor unveiled a bust of Packer which stands in the Boulder University campus. The bust honours a man reviled in his day, and for whom recent petitions to grant an unconditional pardon have been refused.

Alfred Packer's rise to infamy began in the autumn of 1873 when he set out as guide from Salt Lake City leading twenty gold-prospectors. This party, bound for the San Juan Mountains, was comprised entirely of novices except for Packer. As they progressed along the Gunnison river winter set in with a vengeance, and knowledgeable men advised them to turn back as the mountains would prove impassable. Ten members of the party decided to return to Salt Lake City, but the remainder were persuaded by Packer to press on.

Within weeks Packer's group was running desperately short of food, and four of them elected to make for shelter at the Los Pinos Indian Agency. Packer and the five who remained pushed on, groping their way through blinding blizzards and biting cold. At the point of starvation and fatigue they stumbled into a lonely mountain hut where they consumed what was left of their food and resigned themselves to the end.

Packer saw a way out of this desperate situation — at least for himself. While his five companions slept he shot each in the back of the head and stole their money and valuable possessions. Packer, perhaps unhinged by starvation, cut some slivers of flesh from one of the corpses, which he took with him for sustenance on his journey to the Los Pinos Agency. He arrived there in February 1874, an exhausted wreck.

The story he told about the fate of his companions was vague, but when he recovered from his ordeal he created suspicion by his profligate spending. When some strips of human flesh were found in the snow at the entry to the Agency he was asked some straight questions. He then said that his companions had killed one of their number for food, and at the finish only he and one other was left. Crazed with starvation and deprivation, this man attacked him and he was forced to kill in self-defence. He admitted cutting strips of flesh from one of the bodies to sustain himself, adding, 'I had grown fond of human flesh, especially that portion around the breast.'

Packer agreed to lead a party to locate the bodies of the ill-fated prospectors, but in reality he led them in circles and tried to escape. In due course when the bodies were found in the lonely San Juan mountains, it was clear that they had been murdered. At his next attempt Packer did manage to escape, and it was not until ten years had passed that he was recaptured. He was tried for murder in Salt Lake City in 1883, when he pleaded that he had killed only in self-defence. He was nevertheless convicted of murder and sentenced to death.

Following a successful appeal, the charge against Packer was reduced to manslaughter and he was sentenced to forty years imprisonment. He served only sixteen years, being discharged in 1901 as a model prisoner. He went to work on a ranch in Denver where he died in 1907. Seventy-five years later the campaign to rehabilitate the memory of Alfred Packer, supposed cannibal and murderer, of whom it was now said that he really did kill only in self-defence, culminated in the unveiling of his bust. The State Governor was reported to have told onlookers, 'I must admit to you that I have little appetite to appear before you today ... I have better things to do than come over and chew the fat with a pack of cannibal lovers.'

America's so-called 'Laughing Killer', Ralph Jerome von Brown Selz, also chose the Santa Cruz Mountains for his murderous exploit. In December 1935 58-year-old Ada Franch Rice, a wealthy San Franciscan, was reported missing. In the following February a man picked up by the police on a car-theft charge was found to have been forging Mrs Rice's cheques. Ralph Selz, aged twenty-eight, broke down under questioning and confessed to killing Mrs Rice and burying her body in the Santa Cruz Mountains.

He led a police team and a party of newspaper reporters to a remote mountain ridge, and laughed and joked as his victim's body was disinterred. 'If you guys want a sensation,' he declared, 'try hauling a corpse around in a car with the hoot owls hooting at night.' Selz pranced around the grave like a man possessed and earned the nickname 'The Laughing Killer'.

Selz was sent for trial, and pleaded guilty; he was convicted and sentenced to life imprisonment. But the authorities had difficulty confining 'The Laughing Killer', for he escaped in 1945 and again in 1962. He complained that his erratic behaviour when he was arrested in 1936 was due to being starved by the police, which induced an hallucinatory condition. He was paroled in 1966, but again ended up in prison following conviction for fraud.

Whatever else may be said of those murderers who chose mountain locations for their crimes, they cannot be faulted for lack of criminal virtuosity.
(120, 179, 250, 287, 795, 922, 944, 945, 1045)

MURDER BY POST

'Please accept this fine old whiskey from your friend.'

Thomas Graves (1892)

The idea of using the postal service to deliver the killer's lethal blow to the victim by remote means surely ranks as the most cowardly method of murder. It is murder by proxy which allows the perpetrator to keep his distance while an unwitting third party is used to complete the plot. Such murders usually involve poison, but the letter bomb which has become part of the terrorists' arsenal in recent years has earlier origins.

On Good Friday 1936 the US postal service delivered a packet to Tom Maloney, an official of the mine workers' union, who lived in Wilkes-Barre, Pennsylvania. When he opened the packet it exploded, killing him and his young son. Another union official was killed in his home by a similar device, but a third package sent to Luther Kniffen failed to explode because he opened it in an unorthodox way. The packet contained a cigar-box, which by a fortunate mistake he opened from the back, to find himself looking at two sticks of dynamite. The trigger mechanism which was attached to the front of the lid remained intact.

As the result of a police alert, three unopened letter bombs were found — each had been mailed to a mine workers' union official. The likely perpetrator of the grudge killings was thought to be Michael Fugmann, who was known for his anti-union views. A search of his home produced pieces of wood similar to those used to construct the cigar-box bombs. Arthur Koehler, the forestry expert who had so distinguished himself in tracing the materials used to construct the ladder which featured in the Lindbergh kidnapping in 1932, examined the fragments of wood. He found that they matched the wood used in the bomb kits. This was sufficient to convict Michael Fugmann, who died in the electric chair in 1937.

Roland Molineux, a member of New York's famous Knickerbocker Athletic Club, tried to get his own back on a fellow-member in 1898 after an argument by sending him a bottle of Bromo salts through the post. His action

Major Armstrong attempted murder by post using poisoned chocolates

demonstrated the chief deficiency of attempting to commit murder by post, because the salts which he had laced with cyanide were taken not by the intended victim but by his landlady, who promptly collapsed and died.

Major Herbert Rowse Armstrong who successfully poisoned his wife in February 1921 failed in his attempt on the life of rival solicitor Oswald Martin. He made two attempts to poison Martin, one of them by means of a box of poisoned chocolates addressed to him by name and delivered to his home at Hay-on-Wye by Royal Mail.

At the time he received the chocolates Martin was entertaining guests, and, playing the attentive host, offered them round. His sister was violently ill as a result of eating one, and it was discovered afterwards that several of the chocolates had been doctored with arsenic. The intended victim escaped this attempt at murder by proxy, although he was subjected to a second attempt which also failed, but led to the Major's arrest. Another military man, Lieutenant Hofrichter (see under BARRACKS) became a successful exponent of murder by post by disguising his poison as an aphrodisiac.

Poisoned chocolates were the vehicle for a murder attempt in a celebrated Scandinavian case. Odvar Eiken and Anders Muren had served together in the Norwegian Air Force during the Second World War. The two men maintained their friendship after the war when they trained as doctors, and in the summer of 1948 Muren invited Eiken to visit his family at their home in Vraadal, Southern Norway. There Eiken met his friend's sister Randi, and they were immediately attracted to each other.

Randi Muren was studying at a Teacher Training College in Kristiansand, and it was decided, after a whirlwind courtship, that she and Eiken would announce their engagement the following Easter. Meanwhile the couple went their separate ways, Randi to Kristiansand and Odvar Eiken to Lund, where he had lodgings. While he was staying with the Svendson family in Lund, Eiken received two anonymous letters. The first set out to denigrate Randi, and the second contained a press cutting announcing her engagement to Carsten Brekke, a fellow student teacher.

The letters were followed by two parcels. The first, purporting to come from Kari Straume, contained a bottle of spirits which Eiken shared with Muren, with the result that both men were mildly sick. Then came the second parcel, posted from Kristiansand, enclosing some chocolates and a note in Randi's handwriting. The chocolates were put to one side for a week, when Eiken shared them with Muren, his landlady's eight-year-old daughter Marianne, and one of her friends. All four were taken seriously ill, retching and vomiting, and had to be treated in hospital. Marianne, who had eaten the most chocolates, never recovered and died in hospital.

Randi Muren, the apparent sender of the chocolates, was interviewed by the police in what now amounted to a murder inquiry. She revealed that she too had been receiving unsolicited mail posted in Oslo by Signe Lundgren. The gist of the letter was that Eiken was the father of the writer's child. Both Signe Lundgren and Eiken's correspondent Kari Straume were perfectly respectable people whose names had been taken from a directory to further someone's malice.

Then, out of the blue, another name joined the inquiry, that of Carsten Brekke, a fellow-student of Randi's at Kristiansand to whom, according to an earlier newspaper cutting, she was engaged. Brekke told police that he too had been sent poisoned chocolates, and that in view of press reports regarding the death of Marianne Svendson he thought he should report the matter, although he believed it was a joke. It was a grim piece of humour, for the chocolates were found to contain arsenic.

The breakthrough in the investigation came when Randi Muren was shown all the containers and wrappings involved in the various anonymous letters and parcels. Straight away she recognized the box which had contained the poisoned chocolates sent to Eiken as belonging to Carsten Brekke. He was closely questioned, and despite early denials suspicion hardened when one of his college notebooks was found to contain samples of Randi's handwriting and signature. Brekke eventually admitted sending the poisoned chocolates to Eiken in order to warn off his rival for Randi's affections. He then wrote out a detailed confession.

Brekke was tried for murder at Kristiansand in October 1949. He promptly withdrew his confession, which he said had been made under duress. He also set up a wild-goose chase by claiming that the poison had been obtained from the chemistry teacher at a French college where he had studied briefly in 1947. The teacher was traced, and he said that while the college had a medicine cupboard, it contained nothing that was poisonous. Carsten Brekke was found guilty of the attempted murder of Eiken and guilty of the manslaughter of Marianne Svendson. He was sentenced to twelve years in prison, and this was increased to fifteen years when his appeal to the Norwegian Supreme Court was rejected.

If poison sent through the post is concealed in an attractive gift, such as a box of chocolates, there is a greater likelihood that it will find its target. Dr Thomas Graves chose whiskey as the vehicle for his poison draught, and the unsolicited gift of a bottle of spirits was eagerly accepted by his victim.

Josephine Burnaby was the estranged wife of a clothing-store owner. She was rich and elderly and lived in Providence, Rhode Island, where she was treated for a number of minor ailments by Dr Graves. When her husband died Mrs Burnaby was persuaded by her doctor to give him power of attorney. Dr Graves prescribed long visits to California for his patient, which he advised would improve her health.

On returning from California at the end of 1892 Mrs Burnaby announced that she would stop over in Denver, Colorado, to visit a friend. When she arrived at her friend's house she found waiting for her a postal packet addressed to Mrs Josephine Burnaby. She opened it to find a bottle of whiskey with a handwritten note attached to it: 'Wish you a Happy New Year's. Please accept this fine old whiskey from your friend in the woods.' The two women drank some of the whiskey, declaring it to be 'vile stuff', with the result that within six days both lay dead from poisoning.

One of Mrs Burnaby's daughters arranged for a private autopsy, and poisoning was confirmed as the cause of death, with the whiskey being the most likely agent. Suspicion immediately fell on Dr Graves on account of his attempts to profit from the widow's wealth. In the face of trial by newspaper, Graves strongly denied the allegations. There was no evidence linking him with the unsolicited gift sent through the mail, and his patients loyally rallied round in support.

Dr Graves was nevertheless charged with murder, and the prosecution appeared to falter until a surprise witness was produced. This was a young man who testified that he had been approached by Dr Graves at Boston Railway Station with a request for help. The defendant, claiming that he could not write, asked the man to pen a note for him containing wording which he dictated. This was the note attached to the whiskey bottle and the means by which the wily doctor made sure he could not be traced through the handwriting. Furthermore, this piece of artful planning took place five months before the whiskey package was posted.

Dr Graves was duly convicted of murder and sentenced to death. In April 1893, while awaiting retrial after successfully appealing against his sentence, he committed suicide in his cell by taking poison.
(1, 45, 100, 103, 126, 192, 204, 355, 381, 687, 715, 765, 767, 770, 881, 914, 1013, MWW)

MURDER HOUSES

'It was a crazy house. I couldn't take it.'
Donald DeFeo (1974)

When murder houses are mentioned No.10 Rillington Place often springs to mind. This house in West London made sinister by the murders committed in it by John Christie, and made famous by Ludovic Kennedy's account of them in his book, *Ten Rillington Place*, is perhaps the most celebrated of all murder houses. Most cities have such addresses which have been besmirched by violence, leaving property-dealers with houses which tend to attract more curiosity-seekers than buyers.

No.29 Hanbury Street in London's East End was one of Jack the Ripper's haunts, and Dr Crippen left his mark on 39 Hilldrop Crescent in North London. Dr Marcel Petiot, the French mass murderer, burned his victims' bodies in the basement stove at 21 rue Lesueur, Paris, and H.H. Holmes turned his Chicago hotel into a special murder house.

Holmes and Petiot converted their houses into murder factories. Holmes, possibly the greatest mass murderer of all time, installed various pieces of death-dealing apparatus in the rooms of the Gothic-style hotel he built in Chicago to attract visitors to the World Fair in 1893. Supervision of the building works was entrusted to Benjamin F. Pitzel, who like many others associated with Holmes, disappeared. 'Holmes's Castle', as the building was known, was situated on Chicago's 63rd Street. It had a basement and three floors; Holmes used an office on the third floor from which he controlled his murderous operations.

The second floor of the 'Castle' contained thirty-six rooms connected by a labyrinth of secret passages and doors. Several rooms were windowless; one was fitted out as a bank vault with a gas inlet, and another was lined with sheets of metal and asbestos. Many of the rooms had gas inlets, with the supply being monitored from valves in Holmes's office. The main equipment in his office was a 6-foot-high stove, several feet in diameter, in which there were found remnants of human bodies and clothing.

Human remains were also found in the basement, which was connected to the third floor by an elevator. There were quicklime pits and barrels of acid, and also a huge, double-skinned oil-burning furnace capable of producing high temperatures which served as a crematory. The basement also contained a dissecting table with trays of surgical instruments and numerous torture devices, including a rack. A number of skeletons lying about spoke eloquently of the nature of Holmes's grim business. The police believed that, among other ghoulish practices, he locked his victims in the asbestos-lined room and turned on the gas supply. He had perfected a means of igniting the gas from outside the room which turned the gas jet into a virtual flame-thrower with the poor victim hopelessly trapped. Blood traces in numerous of the rooms suggested that would-be hotel guests met a violent end and were then spirited down through secret passages and trap-doors to the basement where the evil genius conducted his experiments.

At least fifty people were reported missing in the Chicago area at the time Holmes was proprietor of the 'Castle'. Holmes was found guilty at his trial for murder in 1895. Before he was hanged he confessed to killing twenty-seven people, but the real figure was thought to be considerably higher. The 'Castle' was mysteriously burned down after Holmes's arrest, so that ultimately both he and his works were destroyed.

Dr Petiot's murder house in Paris, where perished the same number of victims as in 'Holmes's Castle', was less elaborately fitted out for its work. It nevertheless contained an intriguing, triangular-shaped chamber next to the doctor's consulting-room. The room was empty, and its only fittings consisted of a door with no handle on the inside, a single, naked electric-light bulb in the ceiling and eight metal rings fixed to one wall. One of the walls also contained a magnifying spy-glass which permitted a viewer outside the room to observe the wall fitted with the metal rings.

Human remains stuffed into a roaring basement furnace produced filthy clouds of polluting smoke from the chimney of 21 rue Lesueur. The fire brigade answered a neighbour's call, and the discovery of Petiot's human fuel and rotting remains in his quicklime pits soon brought the doctor to justice. He went to the guillotine in 1946.

Another infamous Frenchman, Henri Landru, had perfected the use of the well-flued kitchen stove as a means of disposing of his victims' remains. When fuelled with ordinary house coal the stove in his villa at Gambais produced a formidable draught which in a police experiment totally consumed a sheep's head, save for its teeth, inside fifteen minutes. At least eight women had perished in this infernal apparatus, but like Petiot, Monsieur Landru was eventually trapped by his own smoke signals.

Dr Marcel Petiot with police at 21 rue Lesueur, Paris

Another class of murderer – those with homosexual leanings — go in for storage rather than disposal of their victims. This puts pressure on the available accommodation, and murderers with such inclinations resort to weird solutions. Dean Corll, the Houston electrician who murdered at least twenty-seven boys, rented a boat-shed under the floor of which he stored his bodies wrapped in plastic sacks. Corll was shot dead by an accomplice in 1973. Wayne Gacy topped Corll with thirty-two homosexual murders laid literally at his door. The crawl space under his ranch-style house at Norwood near Chicago contained the shallow graves of twenty-seven victims. Gacy, the genial man who dressed up to entertain children at the local hospital, was convicted of murder at his trial in 1980.

Dennis Nilsen's appetites were cast in a similar mould to those of Corll and Gacy. He too was destined to create a murder house and to fill it with corpses which his evil work created. When the drain-cleaning specialist

Henri Landru's house at Gambais, France, had a
powerful kitchen stove

was called out on the evening of 6 February
1983 to a house in North London, he probably
thought he was making a routine call. There
was no reason why he should have been
suspicious, but he was about to stumble on the
awful secret of 23 Cranley Gardens — it was a
murder house where human remains had been
flushed down the drains, causing the system to
become blocked. Descending into the manhole
outside the house and braving the smell, the
drain specialist found several pieces of rotting
flesh blocking the pipe. He made inquiries of
some of the tenants as to whether they had
flushed away any dog meat or meat from the
deep-freeze. No one admitted to such a practice, and he decided to return the next day
with his boss.

Inspection of the drains the following day
produced a surprise — the offending material
had disappeared. One of the tenants said that
late the previous evening the civil servant who
occupied the top flat had been seen entering
the manhole. The drain men retrieved a
remnant of flesh that was still lodged in the
pipe and called the police. Forensic examination quickly confirmed that the flesh was
human, and early that evening police officers
arrested Dennis Nilsen, the tenant who occupied the top flat.

The room occupied by the 37-year-old civil
servant stank, and he admitted that the ward-
robe contained horrors that had not been
consigned to the drains. Nilsen told the police,
'There are sixteen bodies,' and when forensic
experts examined the contents of the ward-
robe they found plastic bags containing three
severed heads and a tea chest full of other
disjecta membra.

Mild-mannered, bespectacled Nilsen, who
worked for the Manpower Service Commission
at one of their Job Centres, made a full
statement. In addition to the remains of three
bodies at 23 Cranley Gardens, he said thirteen
others had been buried in the back garden of
the house he formerly lived in a few miles away
at 195 Melrose Avenue, Cricklewood. He later
amended his total of sixteen victims to fifteen;
'I didn't keep a body count,' he remarked. He
was not sure of the identity of his victims
either, but he was calm and co-operative in his
response to police questioning. His victims
were all male — students, down-and-outs or
drifters whom he had picked up in bars and
taken home with the promise of drinks and
accommodation. He reported in a matter-of-
fact tone that he strangled them all except one,
whom he drowned.

Nilsen began his trail of destruction in
December 1978 after the man who had been
his flat-mate for three years in a relationship
remarkable only for its dullness moved away
from Melrose Avenue. Left alone with his cat
and dog, Nilsen's mind yielded to the forces of
destruction which lurked within. He was a
veritable Jekyll and Hyde — by day the dull
civil servant, and by night a drunken murderer. During the five years beginning December 1978, until he was arrested in February
1983, he killed or attempted to kill twenty-two
men. He was often so insensible with drink that
he could not remember their names, or even
for sure whom he had killed.

Whether it was fifteen or sixteen, he knew
he had taken many lives, and he remarked, 'If
I had been arrested at sixty-five years of age
there might have been thousands of bodies

Dennis Nilsen concealed his victims' bodies under the floor

behind me.' As it was he had problems enough over disposal of bodies — at times there were as many as four or five corpses under the floorboards of his flat at Melrose Avenue, and suitcases of dismembered portions in the garden shed. Nilsen's crises were created by disposal problems, and when he was bought out of his tenancy at Melrose Avenue he had a big garden bonfire to commit the results of his carnage to the flames.

Three young men escaped Nilsen's web after he had attempted to strangle them. After surviving an attack at Nilsen's hands in November 1980 one of these intended victims reported the episode to the police. The mild-looking civil servant told inquiring officers that he had had a misunderstanding with his friend. The explanation sounded quite plausible and no further questions were asked until the mass-murderer was arrested and the reaction was: 'If only ....'

Dennis Nilsen was born in Fraserburgh, Scotland. He was a child of average talents, if somewhat shy and introverted. He joined the army cadets, and in 1961 enlisted in the regular army. He trained as a cook and served in Aden, Cyprus and Germany before being discharged in 1972. Uniforms seemed to be to his liking, for he then joined the Metropolitan Police, and later became a security guard. Nilsen gave up this job in 1974 when he took a civil service post with the Manpower Services Commission and worked in a Job Centre. This position provided him with contacts in the form of young drifters seeking employment, and with the addition of his police experience and knowledge of London's bars and pubs, he was well equipped to carry out his plan of mass murder.

Dennis Nilsen's trial for murder began at the Old Bailey in October 1983. The 'Murderer of the Century', as he was called by some of the newspapers, sat impassively in the court as the catalogue of his strangulation and disposal by dismemberment, burning and burying was unfolded. His defence counsel pleaded that Nilsen acted with diminished responsibility, and was guilty only of manslaughter. The state of Dennis Nilsen's mind produced heated exchanges between the defence psychiatrist and prosecuting counsel. It was agreed that the accused man's behaviour was abnormal, but it was a matter of deciding whether he was responsible for his actions at the time of the killings.

Nilsen, who once described himself as a 'creative psychopath', enjoyed the sense of power that killing gave him, and he admitted performing sexual acts on the corpses of some of his victims. He expressed no remorse, but rather gloried in the prominence he had achieved through his actions. He described the killings as 'fifty per cent thrill and fifty per cent fear — like Russian roulette'. The jury found him guilty on all murder charges on a majority verdict, and he was sentenced to life imprisonment.

While in prison at Wormwood Scrubs, Nilsen was attacked by a fellow-inmate and slashed across the face with a razor. The property which was the scene of his last murders was put up for sale in November 1983, and attracted many curiosity-seekers and only a few would-be buyers. The 'House of Horrors', as some called it, was bought by a developer for conversion into flats.

Some homes become the scene of terrible domestic violence which creates a murder house by overnight sensation. One such was the house at Amityville in which Ronald DeFeo (aged twenty-two) wrought a few minutes of deadly slaughter. 'I was God when I had a gun in my hand,' declared DeFeo when he was interviewed by a psychiatrist after killing six members of his family.

The DeFeo house at 112 Ocean Drive, Amityville, Long Island, was named 'High Hopes'. During the early hours of 13 November 1974 the house was ablaze with lights and neighbours heard the dog barking continuously. Lying dead on the beds in their separate rooms were Ronald DeFeo senior and his wife Louise, their two daughters, Allison and Dawn, and two of their three sons, Mark and John. All had been shot in the back or in the head at close range with a .35 Marlin rifle.

At 6.30 a.m. Ronald DeFeo junior told a friend, 'Someone shot my father and mother.' When the police arrived at the scene DeFeo told them his father had connections in the criminal underworld and that the killings had been the work of two hit-men; DeFeo changed this story several times. First he said the underworld assassins had used his rifle in order to implicate him in the murders. Then

he alleged that his sister Dawn had shot his brothers, and claimed that he had taken the gun from her because he was afraid she would turn it on him. But slowly the hate which DeFeo had for his family came to the surface, and eventually he admitted carrying out the murders himself. 'Once I got started,' he told the police, 'I just couldn't stop. I went so fast.'

DeFeo's psychiatric history showed that he had a miserable childhood and was constantly involved in fights and rows, both at school and at home. He was first examined by a psychiatrist when he was fifteen years of age. He took to drugs as a means of escaping from his unhappy home life, and he once told his family in a prophetic statement that he could not live at home any longer or he would end up killing them all.

When he killed the six members of his family as they lay sleeping he fired eight shots at close range. Each bullet found its target and he reloaded his seven-shot Marlin rifle in order to fire the last shot. After he had finished the killings he collected the spent cartridge cases, which, together with his bloodstained clothes, he hid in a sewer. The rifle was thrown into the sea. This evidence was used at his trial to show the cold-blooded execution and concealment of his crimes.

During his psychiatric examination while in custody DeFeo said, 'I honestly believe — you might laugh about it — I honestly believe sometimes that I'm a secret agent for God.' Of his home he said, 'It was a crazy house. I couldn't take it.' He spoke of his parents with unconcealed hatred, and at his trial, after being shown a photograph of his dead father's body and asked the question, 'Did you kill your father?' he replied, 'Did I kill him? I killed them all. Yes, sir. I killed them all in self-defence.' He persistently tried to implicate his dead sister in the shooting, but openly admitted his guilt in court: 'When I get a gun in my hand, there's no doubt in my mind who I am. I am God.' As if to drive home his overflowing malice for the benefit of the jury, he threatened to kill the District Attorney.

Despite defence arguments that he was insane, DeFeo was found guilty and sentenced to twenty-five years to life on each of the six counts of second-degree murder with which he had been charged. 'High Hopes', the three-storey Dutch Colonial style house in which six members of the DeFeo family were gunned to

DENNIS NILSEN'S CALENDAR OF MURDER

1975   **Moved into flat at 195 Melrose Avenue**

December 1978	His flat-mate moved away	
December 1978	MURDER VICTIM No.1; a teenager	Body burnt in Aug. 1979
October 1979	Attempted murder of a young Chinese	
End of 1979	MURDER VICTIM No.2; a Canadian	Body put under floor
Summer 1980	MURDER VICTIM No.3; a teenager	Dismembered the body
Autumn 1980	MURDER VICTIM No.4; a young Scot	Body put under floor
Autumn 1980	MURDER VICTIM No.5; a Mexican or Filipino	Dismembered the body
Autumn 1980	MURDER VICTIM No.6; an Irishman	Body put under floor
Autumn 1980	MURDER VICTIM No.7; a down-and-out	Body put under floor
Autumn 1980	Bonfire in garden to burn up some of the remains	
Winter 1980	MURDER VICTIM No.8; a young man killed after a drinking-bout	Corpse burnt in Sept. 1982
Early 1981	MURDER VICTIM No.9; a young Scot	Dismembered the body
Early 1981	MURDER VICTIM No.10; a young Irishman	Body put under floor
Early 1981	MURDER VICTIM No.11; a skinhead	Body put under floor
Summer 1981	Disposal problem; major reorganization of corpses under floor	
September 1981	MURDER VICTIM No.12; a man who collapsed outside the house	Body hidden under the kitchen sink
September 1981	Bonfire in garden to burn up remains prior to leaving Melrose Avenue	
October 1981	Attempted murder	
October 1981	Moved to 23 Cranley Gardens	
March 1982	MURDER VICTIM No.13; a young Guardsman	Body dismembered and portions flushed down the WC
September 1982	MURDER VICTIM No.14; a drunk	Body dissected in bath
February 1983	MURDER VICTIM No.15; a young drug-addict	Dismembered the body

death to the accompaniment of a barking dog, has twice been sold. The property was sold for a fraction of its true value in 1975 after being on the market for nearly a year. The purchasers abandoned the house after only one month following disturbing phenomena which led to claims that the house was permeated with evil forces. A book relating to these experiences was subsequently made into the film *The Amityville Horror.*

In previous eras notorious houses of murder were often burned down by fearful neighbours who wished to erase the taint of killing. In the twentieth century it is perhaps the fate of such houses to become film sets for the perpetuation of horror on celluloid.

(1, 24, 66, 149, 150, 234, 235, 298, 312, 315, 369, 449, 524, 526, 568, 583, 609, 639, 654, 708, 787, 809, 851, 871, 943, MWW)

NEXT DOOR

'I wanted to do something big.'
Robert Morton (1973)

Despite the natural inquisitiveness displayed by most human beings over their neighbours' activities, curiosity often fails when it comes to murder. Happily, murder is not so commonplace that it readily springs to mind as an explanation of strange events that happen next door. However, it is remarkable how persons living in close proximity to a murder scene hear nothing and see nothing, even when the most ghastly deeds are being performed with gun or bludgeon.

Even when an unusual occurrence is noted, and later associated with the commission of a crime, neighbourhood witnesses are often unreliable in their recollections. They might vaguely remember hearing a dog barking, or a car backfiring, or seeing a shadowy glimpse of a stranger in the district. Such was the gist of neighbours' statements in a murder case which rocked Hollywood in 1922.

William Leonard Taylor was an Irishman who emigrated to Canada to try his luck as an engineer, gold-prospector and antique dealer before becoming a successful Hollywood silent-movie director in the 1920s. His life ended in tragedy on 1 February 1922 when he was murdered in his home, and in the ensuing scandal several movie stars' careers were shattered.

Taylor was a handsome man with charm and a polished style. He had what is known today as charisma. After he had graduated from bit parts to star roles he crowned his achievements in Hollywood by becoming chief director for one of Paramount's subsidiary studios with an enormous salary (for the time) of $40,000 a year. He lived in a Spanish-style house on South Alvarado Street, Hollywood, near Wilshire Boulevard. His home was furnished with distinction, and included a large library, as befitted a man of cultural tastes.

This man of culture was also said to have considerable sexual appetites, and it was well known that many of Hollywood's star actresses had been entertained at his home. One of these was Mabel Normand, a popular comedienne who had been one of Taylor's regular companions for two years. On 1 February 1922 he telephoned her, asking her to call in and pick up some books that evening. She arrived in her chauffeur-driven car at about 6.45 p.m. and was received by Taylor's butler. She waited while Taylor finished a telephone conversation which included some angry exchanges. Mabel declined an invitation to dinner, but accepted a drink while the books were discussed. After leaving a cold meal for his master the butler went home at about 7.15 p.m.

Taylor complained to Mabel about the state of his income-tax affairs, which he said were in disarray because his former butler, Edward Sands, had mismanaged his finances and stolen from him. At 7.45 p.m. Mabel Normand left, and neighbours observed Taylor walking her to her car. About 8.15 p.m. the same neighbours heard what they thought was a car backfiring, and noticed a man leaving Taylor's house. Several hours later Edna Purviance, an actress who lived next door, knocked on Taylor's door but received no reply. The chauffeur received the same negative response when he returned with the car, although the house lights were on. Both Taylor's friend and his employee were aware of his diversions, so they decided not to disturb him and simply went on their way.

At 7.30 next morning the butler arrived to start work and discovered Desmond Taylor lying sprawled on the living-room floor with a trickle of blood issuing from his mouth. Pandemonium ensued as friends, neighbours and film people arrived on the scene. A doctor pronounced Taylor dead, the suggested cause being gastric haemorrhage. With the dead man still lying where he was found, his erstwhile friends rushed about the house collecting up bottles of liquor (prohibition was in effect at the time) and destroying clothes and papers that might damage reputations. Bundles of letters were burned in the living-room fireplace. Only after this wave of hysteria subsided did anyone think of calling the police. When detectives arrived to examine the body it became apparent that Taylor was a murder victim, with two bullet-wounds in the back. A second wave of hysteria was triggered off by the news, but by this time clues which might have existed at the scene of the crime had been irretrievably trampled under foot.

Detectives systematically searching Taylor's house discovered hundreds of letters, including amorous correspondence from Mabel Normand and Mary Miles Minter, a twenty-year-old up-and-coming movie star. 'I'd go to my room and put on something scant and flowing; then I'd lie on the couch and wait for you ... then I'd wake to find two strong arms around me and two dear lips pressed on mine in a long, sweet kiss ....' This was a casting couch with a difference, and the newspapers squeezed it for all it was worth. The scandals which followed Taylor's murder dented several reputations, and the careers of both Mabel Normand and Mary Miles Minter were ruined.

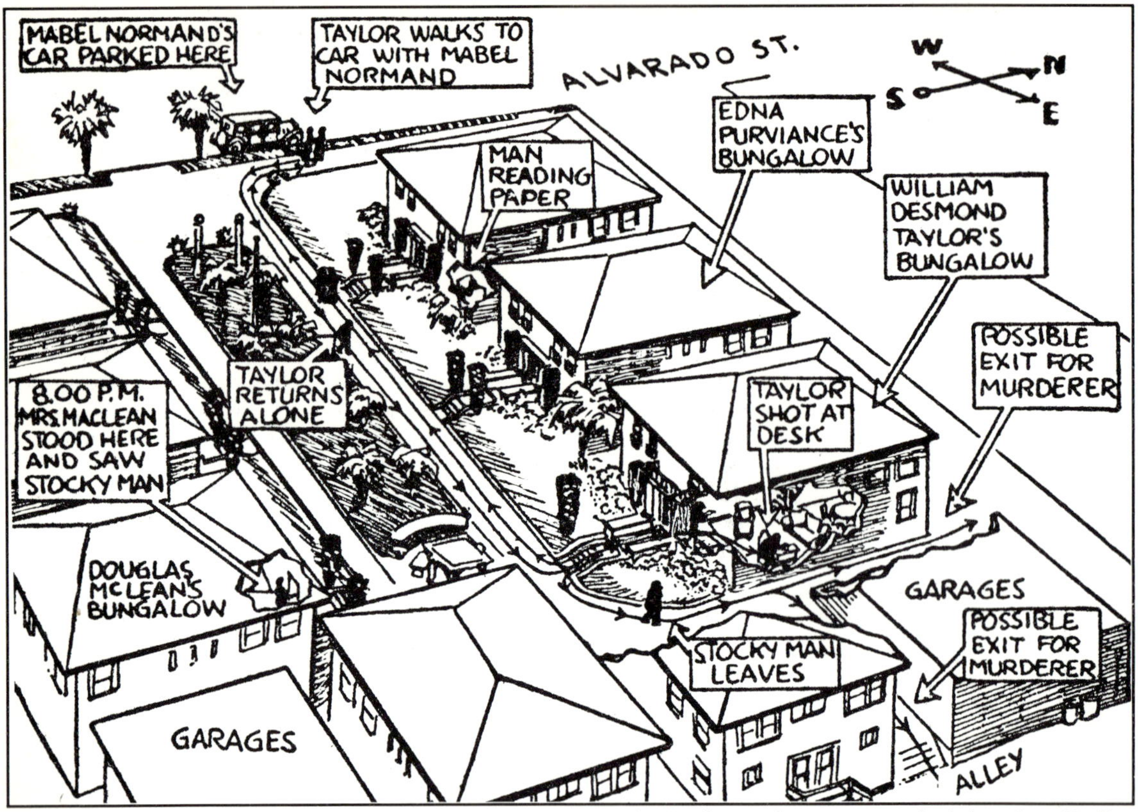

Murder scene at the Hollywood home of Desmond Taylor

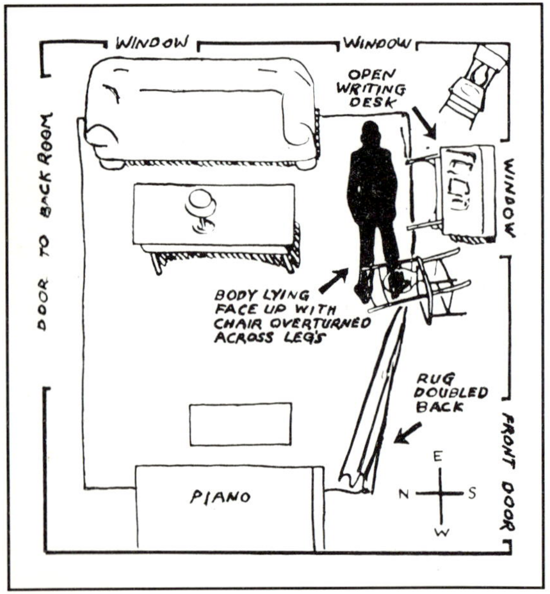

Taylor's funeral was attended by the Hollywood faithful, and Mary, after kissing the lips of the corpse, declared, 'He spoke to me just now; it sounded like "I shall love you always, Mary!"' Once again the newspapers had a field day.

The police had less success in finding the murderer. The mysterious person seen leaving Taylor's house on the night of the murder was never identified, although there were plenty of theories. One was that Edward Sands, the former butler, was in fact Taylor's brother, who blamed Desmond for ruining him financially during their early days together in New York. It was suggested that in addition to messing up Taylor's finances, he also sought the ultimate revenge. Another theory was that Mary Miles Minter's mother was in love with Taylor herself, and resented her daughter's relationship with him. She was known to possess a .38 calibre revolver and to have had lessons in marksmanship. It was also known that Mabel Normand's use of drugs so incensed Taylor that he collected information about drug-dealing which he handed over to the police. The idea that Taylor was murdered by drug-traffickers was about as credible as the other theories regarding his death.

The death of Desmond Taylor therefore remains Hollywood's greatest murder mystery. The murderer certainly had luck, for Taylor's house was readily observed by his next-door neighbours, and a great deal was known about his movements to within a few hours of his death. In the event his friends, out of blind selfishness, deprived the police of evidence which might have aided their investigation. There was certainly no doubt about the tragedy which followed in the wake of his death. His butler went insane, Mabel Normand's career was finished and she died of tuberculosis at the age of thirty-three, and Mary Miles Minter, the screen virgin idolized by millions, went into early retirement.

When the attention of neighbours or passers-by is attracted by some strange noise or sight associated with another person's home they are usually inclined to put suspicion out of mind in favour of some simple explanation. Thus when people passing the doctor's house in Marlowe Avenue, Detroit, about 9.00 p.m. on 22 February 1929 heard moaning noises, they attributed them to the painful reaction of a patient undergoing medical treatment. Knowing glances were exchanged as people walked by. But forty-five minutes later Dr Frank Loomis called out to his next-door neighbour, Mrs Mildred Twork, 'My wife has been murdered.' The neighbour went into the house with the doctor and saw Grace Loomis sprawled on the floor of the sun-parlour in a pool of blood.

The room was a shambles — the furniture was overturned, a window had been broken and the violence of the assault was evident from the blood splattered on the walls and ceiling. The two Loomis children were still asleep upstairs. Dr Loomis told the police that he had gone straight home from his office and had given his wife $100 in order to buy clothes for the children. Then at about 9.00 p.m., as was his custom, he left the house for a constitutional walk. When he returned forty-five minutes later he found his wife's body, and while examining her to see if she was still breathing stained his clothes with blood.

Robbery did not appear to be the motive for this brutal killing, for the dead woman still had jewellery on her body. There were no strange fingerprints, no signs of an intruder and no indication of forcible entry to the house. The obvious conclusion drawn by the police was that Dr Loomis had murdered his wife. Despite his reputation as a good doctor and a devoted family man, he was known to have a fiery temper. The theory was that his temper had flared after some disagreement and he had gone berserk.

The doctor was held on suspicion of murder, but he was released from custody after his wife's funeral. Detectives believed that Loomis was having an affair with another woman, and they decided to shadow him in the hope that a love triangle would be exposed to give a motive for killing his wife. This time the inquiry quickly bore fruit, when Loomis was known to have visited a woman friend at her apartment in Wabash Avenue. He was rearrested in April and sent for trial.

Public opinion believed the 36-year-old doctor innocent, and while the prosecution case was mainly circumstantial it was hoped that sensational developments would emerge regarding his love-life. The case against Loomis was simply that he had killed his wife in a fit of anger — probably following an argument about another woman — and that he had then carefully arranged an alibi. The defence argument was that a peeping tom or intending intruder saw the doctor return home and give his wife some money. This person then entered the house, robbing and killing Mrs Loomis. There were no muck-raking developments at the trial, and the prosecution did not produce the 'other woman' who was believed to be a hostile witness. The jury found Frank Loomis not guilty and he was set free.

The doctor found it difficult to pick up the threads of a normal life again. He neglected his medical practice and fell into debt. Worse still, he developed a persecution complex and moved house several times. On 19 May 1928, almost a year after his wife was murdered, he drove home late after a dinner party with friends and gassed himself.

Dr Loomis left three suicide notes, two addressed to friends and one to the press. He wrote to a friend, 'The mystery of my wife's death will be cleared up in the newspapers within twenty-four hours,' and to the press he wrote, 'I am not guilty of murder. My conscience is clear.' Critics were quick to point out that he did not say he had not killed his wife, only that he had not murdered her. Officially the case remains unsolved, but the police were convinced of Loomis's guilt. It was certainly amazing, in view of the violent manner of Grace Loomis's death, that the neighbours had no suspicion of anything wrong.

Greater alertness on the part of the neighbours might have helped both the police and the judiciary in an unusual Australian murder case. Most importantly, it might have aided the deaf-mute who was imprisoned for the crime in face of another man's uncorroborated confession.

At some time during the night of 19 December 1959 22-year-old Jillian McPherson Brewer was murdered in the bedroom of her flat. She lived at No.18 Brookwood Flats in Cottesloe, Western Australia, and her mother lived in the next-door apartment. Jillian was engaged to be married, and her fiancé had been in the flat with her until about midnight, when he returned home. Her body was found the following morning at about 9.00 a.m. and it was clear that she had been brutally attacked. There were several wounds in the head, the windpipe had been severed and there were multiple stab-wounds in the abdomen.

The wounds had been inflicted with a tomahawk, which was found in the close vicinity of the flats, and a pair of scissors which belonged to the victim. The tomahawk was the property of a neighbour, which he kept in his garage along with a number of tools. He noticed that it was missing when he went to use it on the afternoon of the murder. There were no signs of a struggle in the bedroom, nor was there any indication of forced entry to the flat. Despite a careful search, no strange fingerprints were discovered and neighbours could offer little information regarding any prowlers in the district. One witness heard a dog bark at about 1.00 a.m. on the night of the murder, and she also thought that she saw a stranger around the flats some two hours previously.

In February 1960 Eric Edgar Cooke was arrested on a charge of loitering with intent, and as a routine procedure the police questioned him about the Brewer murder. Cooke denied all knowledge of the incident. Over a year later, in April 1961, another man arrested on charges involving sexual assault on small girls was similarly questioned. Twenty-year-old Darryl Raymond Beamish, a deaf-

mute, was charged with four assaults during the preceding six months in the Perth area.

Because of his disability, communicating with Beamish was by way of sign language, although he could write a little. In June, after admitting, 'I killed lady,' he was charged with murdering Jillian Brewer. During his trial at Perth he claimed that he had made admissions to the police because they had threatened him. He was nevertheless found guilty, with the jury making a strong recommendation to mercy. Sentence of death was commuted to life imprisonment, and his appeal was subsequently rejected.

In 1963 a series of sadistic murders in the Perth area culminated in the arrest of Eric Edgar Cooke, who admitted to five of the killings. He was known to be a night prowler, and the police questioned him for the second time about the Brewer murder of which he had previously denied all knowledge. Now he admitted to two futher murders, including that of Jillian Brewer, for which Beamish had been convicted.

Cooke was tried in November 1963 for one of the five murders to which he had originally confessed, and he was duly convicted and sentenced to death. No action was taken regarding Cooke's admission of the Brewer killing, and the police view was that his statement was inconsistent with the known facts. He then withdrew his statement, but reconfirmed it a short while later when he swore an affidavit in December 1963 to the effect that he was sure he had killed the Brewer girl.

Beamish appealed a second time against his conviction of the crime which Cooke claimed to have committed. The Court of Criminal Appeal heard in March 1964 that Cooke had retracted confessions made to detectives in September 1963. Beamish's appeal was dismissed on the grounds that Cooke's confession was fabricated, and the judge referred to his 'perjurous machinations'.

Cooke was hanged on 26 October 1964, allegedly repeating on the scaffold his claim to have committed the Brewer murder. He was also said to have claimed, 'Nobody in Australia has committed as many murders as I have.' Cooke's death meant that if a retrial were ordered in the Beamish case his confession would be inadmissible as evidence.

By 1971 five courts had heard Beamish's

case in one form or another. His conviction and subsequent appeals created the greatest controversy in Australian criminal history. On 26 March 1971, aged thirty, Darryl Beamish was released from prison on parole.

'The Great Billik, Card-reader and Seer' moved into 19th Street, Chicago, because he had selected a victim for his particular evil designs who was now his neighbour. Herman Billik's origins were in Central Europe, and he boasted that his mother was a witch and he himself a wizard. 'The Great Billik' sold charms and peddled potions to the gullible, which was a relatively harmless pursuit, but he also had grander notions.

One of his neighbours in Chicago's Bohemian quarter was Martin Vzral, a hard-working man whose prosperous milk-delivery business provided an adequate living for his family of seven children. Billik began a campaign of intimidating the Vzrals with his evil, Svengali-like influence. He told Martin Vzral, 'You have an enemy. I see him. He is trying to destroy you.' Understandably alarmed, Vzral accepted Billik's offer to name the enemy and to provide him with a potion which would nullify the threat. The enemy turned out to be a rival milk-dealer who had one of The Great Billik's foul-smelling potions spread on his doorstep. Vzral was so pleased when the threat against him had been removed that he showered gratitude upon Billik and pressed him to accept some kind of payment. The wizard declined all such offers, but he now had Vzral firmly caught in his web.

Slowly and deliberately Billik strengthened his hold on Martin Vzral's family. He slept with his wife and seduced his daughters, turning them into slaves who responded to his every whim and command. The sons of the family were made to work for him and the profits of the milk business were siphoned off into his own funds. Soon Billik's control was absolute, and the once proud family sank into poverty and despondency. The milkman had been completely milked of everything he possessed.

The wizard's next move was to tell Mrs Vzral to insure the lives of her husband and her four daughters, which she did without question. At this point Martin Vzral, humbled but not entirely beaten, decided to rebel, but he had left it too late. He died on 27 March 1905, and the $2,000 collected on his life insurance by his widow found its way into Billik's pocket. Then,

in the course of the next eighteen months, Vzral's four daughters died. The milk business, already in ruins, was sold on Billik's instructions and his campaign of destruction was nearly at an end. Using the proceeds of the business sale to finance a holiday at Niagara Falls, he returned to Chicago to be present when Mrs Vzral died.

The hardships of the Vzral family and the succession of deaths — there were three survivors out of nine — started tongues wagging and there were accusations of murder against Billik. Detectives began an investigation, but were hampered by lack of concern on the part of the insurance companies and by the reluctance of witnesses to come forward. Perhaps the wizard's power had influence beyond the poor Vzral family.

Despite an impressive defence fund, Herman Billik was convicted of murder and sentenced to death. There was a great outcry to save his life and in January 1909 his sentence was commuted to life imprisonment. Sympathy for Billik's victims had proved short-lived, and the wizard served only a few years in prison before being inexplicably set free in 1917 with a full pardon.

Neighbours occasionally take correct stock of what is happening around them, and when Edgar Edwards began intensively digging the garden of his house in London, he aroused considerable curiosity. In 1902 he acquired a house in Church Road, Leyton, and when he went out in his shirt-sleeves to dig the garden he was unaware that the lady living next door was watching him from behind her curtains. She wondered why he was digging such a deep trench, and her inquisitiveness increased the following morning when she saw that the trench had been filled in.

Thanks to this lady's curious observation the dismembered corpse of Edwards's three murder victims were found in their garden grave. He had murdered them in a house in another London borough, six miles away, and transported them in packing cases to what he doubtless thought was a secret burial.

Neighbours frequently have their quarrels and disputes, and while these may occasionally result in violent assault, cold-blooded murder is not usually the outcome. But when the murderer's mind snaps and he is looking for a victim — any victim — his next-door neighbour is vulnerable. A young teenage girl became such a victim in a Cape Town murder for no better reason than that the intended killer who lived in the house next to hers decided he would kill the next girl he saw.

Robert Victor Morton, aged twenty-two, was employed as caretaker and handyman by a surgeon who worked at Cape Town's Groote Schuur Hospital. He was a drifter with no apparent ambition, and seemed quite content with his life at 13 Kensington Gardens, where he had his own living-in quarters.

On 28 January 1973 he entertained his fifteen-year-old girl-friend in his room, and there was an argument about another girl with whom he was supposed to be corresponding. His girl went off in a temper and when she reached home wrote Morton a letter in which she said, 'I want nothing more to do with you. You are bad, I hate you.' When they next met, on 1 February, the row continued — harsh words were spoken, and after calling him a liar Morton's girl-friend left him.

Later that same afternoon the house next door, 11 Kensington Gardens, became the scene of a murder. When Mrs Ashford returned home at about 5.00 p.m. she expected to find her fourteen-year-old daughter Sharon home from school. School books strewn about the hall and patches of blood on the floor led Mrs Ashford to a ground-floor toilet. There, bundled inside, she found the blood-smeared body of her daughter, dead from thirty-seven stab wounds in the chest and neck.

The neighbours, Morton among them, were questioned by the police; he proved eager to assist. The murder scene contained the sort of clues that encourage detectives. There was a bloody fingerprint impression on the door of the toilet, and on the floor of the hall was the clear outline of a footprint. Both impressions matched prints taken from Robert Morton, who was arrested and charged with murder.

He first denied the accusation but then confessed. 'I wanted to do something big. I opened a bottle of beer and the first thing that came into my head was murder. So the only girl I saw that day I decided I would kill her for the fun of it .... I just pushed her into the house and killed her without thinking whether I was doing the right thing or not.' Sharon Ashford had the misfortune to be the girl next door at the time Morton's mind turned to murder. He was found guilty of murder without extenuating circumstances and sentenced to death.

Morton was hanged on 27 February 1974. (*70, 113, 579, 590, 792, 793, 914*)

PARKS AND COMMONS

'Here you go!'
Fitzhugh Coyle Goldsborough (1911)

Parks and common land are oases in built-up areas; their greenery acts as lungs for city dwellers. Open spaces with grassed areas and trees are miniature woodlands offering scope for recreation and leisure. They also provide suitable territory for human vultures bent on robbery and violence. There is the chance of lurking unseen in protective shrubbery and of ambushing the unwary; the innocent stroller at night is especially cast in the role of prey for the vulture.

Parks and commons are often quite large areas with networks of pathways weaving in and out of open spaces and trees. Privacy is afforded to courting couples and concealment given to the criminal who can strike and within minutes escape unnoticed into the surrounding city life. A number of park murders have remained unsolved for this reason.

Perhaps the best-known park murder was that of Leon Beron in 1911. The battered body of the East End property dealer was found among furze bushes on Clapham Common by a policeman on early morning patrol on New Year's Day. The possible implication of Peter the Painter and the anarchist movement lent the case an air of mystery, although Stinie Morrison was eventually convicted of the murder. Ten years later he protested his innocence to the point of starving himself to death at the age of forty-one in his prison cell.

Eighteen-year-old Louisa Maud Steel worked as a domestic servant in the home of a music teacher in Lee Road, Blackheath. The common land which gives the area its name is famous as the place where James I introduced the game of golf to England in the seventeenth century. Blackheath is crossed by many roads and paths, and is known for being a windswept open space.

On the evening of 23 January 1931 Louisa Steel was sent on some errands to Blackheath Village. When she had not returned by 11.00 p.m. her employer called the police and reported the girl missing. Early next morning a lamp-lighter walking across Blackheath to Shooters Hill Road found the missing girl's naked body. She had been strangled and badly mutilated in a sexual attack. Police believed the murderer surprised the girl from behind while she was walking along one of Blackheath's paths in the dark. She had been dragged some ninety yards away from the path to a quiet spot, where the attacker tore off her clothes and killed her. The girl had been subjected to a brutal assault and her injuries — some of which had been inflicted after death — included several kicks in the face. The violence of the attack led to comments about a Ripper-style murder.

Detectives working on the case discovered that two other women walking in near-by public parks at Lee and Lewisham had been attacked on the same night. Both had ben surprised from behind, and there was reason to suppose that the assailant was the same man as Maud Steel's murderer. These women who had escaped the attacker's clutches helped the police to issue a description of a man they wanted to interview. The public were asked to keep a look-out and the police maintained a careful surveillance on public parks and open spaces.

This vigilance resulted in the apprehension of the murderer, although officially the case is regarded as unsolved. Superintendent Charles Cooper, writing about the murder inquiry in a book of unsolved crimes, said that he knew the identity of the murderer but was not at liberty to divulge it. 'The man responsible for this terrible crime', he wrote, 'is now in a State institution.' The Superintendent went on to inveigh against the practice of discharging from mental institutions persons who were regarded as cured but who progressd to further crimes after their release.

While parks can be dangerous places for the lone girl at night, they can also be hazardous locations for the girl hoping to be courted by a new acquaintance. Constance Gertrude Oliver, a 21-year-old typist who lived in Battersea, met a young motor mechanic who she thought would lighten her otherwise dull life. They arranged to meet at Putney Railway Station on 2 October 1927, and then made their way to Richmond Park. It is sometimes the fate of those who start their work early in the morning to 'meet Murder on the way'. This was the

destiny in store for the park-keeper setting about his routine patrol of Richmond Park on 5 October 1927. Lying on her back amid bracken and bushes in a secluded corner of the park was the body of Constance Oliver — she had been strangled by a piece of cloth tightly knotted around her neck. There was evidence of a violent struggle, and a broken umbrella lay close by in the bracken. The girl had bruises on the face and a wound on the back of the head; there was also a mysterious superficial burn-mark on her thigh. Although her clothing was disarranged she had not been sexually assaulted.

The police ascertained that Constance Oliver had left her home at Battersea on the evening of 2 October indicating that she planned to meet her latest boy-friend. Sidney Goulter, the son of a retired police officer, who lived with his parents at Kingston-upon-Thames, was quickly arrested and was duly charged with murder. During his trial at Guildford, Goulter related his account of what happened in Richmond Park. He claimed that a quarrel broke out after Constance told him of arrangements she had made to visit the theatre the next evening with two girl-friends and their male companions. In what was meant to be construed as jealous rage, Goulter hit the girl several times with the umbrella in order to subdue her. He then tore strips from her clothing to make a ligature which he put round her neck. He said he had not intended to kill her, merely to render her unconscious so that he could get away.

There was considerable debate in court over the burn on the dead girl's thigh. Goulter's explanation was that before leaving the scene he lit a cigarette and threw away the still burning match which must have pitched on her clothing and burnt through before becoming extinguished. If Goulter had not the intention to strangle the girl he would not be guilty of murder. His defence was that he had only tied the ligature loosely with the aim of making her senseless. The fact that she died from strangulation must have been due to her own struggles to free herself. The jury was inclined to believe that the evidence of how deeply the strangulation cord had been pulled into the flesh of the neck was sufficient to indicate Goulter's true intentions, and after an absence of a mere ten minutes it returned to find Goulter guilty of murder. It appeared that the friend Constance Oliver introduced to her parents as 'a delightful young man' was known for his erratic and often violent behaviour, which had made his own family fearful of him. Goulter was hanged at Wandsworth in January 1928 and it fell to Sir Bernard Spilsbury to conduct the post-mortem after the execution. Spilsbury's biographers remarked that it was a pity Goulter had not introduced his new girl-friend to his parents, who might have warned her off.

While murdering in the park frequently has the stamp of sexual frenzy, elimination was the motive which drove Fitzhugh Coyle Goldsborough. On 23 January 1911 David Graham Phillips, the popular novelist, walked out of his New York apartment for his morning stroll in Gramercy Park. Suddenly, while following his customary circuit, he was accosted by Goldsborough who appeared from the bushes and menacingly pointed a pistol at him. Shouting, 'Here you go!' he fired several times at Phillips, who fell dying to the ground. As passers-by gathered at the scene Goldsborough put the

Fitzhugh Coyle Goldsborough jealously murdered his sister's boyfriend in Gramercy Park, New York City

gun to his own head and shouting, 'Here I go!' pulled the trigger. He also fell to the ground, so that victim and murderer lay dead together.

Subsequent inquiry suggested that Goldsborough murdered Phillips because he believed the novelist had wronged his sister. The murderer, a neurotic, spoiled young man aged twenty-one, had wealthy parents and little inclination to work. He spent his days reading popular novels and idolizing his sister who played the socialite. He guarded her with a bizarre protective jealousy even to the extent of being angry with his father if he dared to criticize her.

During his reading the indolent young Goldsborough came across *The Fashionable Adventures of Joshua Craig*, a novel by David Graham Phillips. One of the chief characters in the story was a self-centred girl who moved in high social circles. Goldsborough interpreted the author's treatment of his character as a slur against his sister, and decided to exact a bitter revenge. At the age of forty-three, Phillips's promising creative life was terminated by a jealous neurotic.

The Zodiac murderer, who killed five people and wounded two others during a nine months' reign of fear in California in 1969, had a grudge against courting couples. His attacks were made against couples sitting in their parked cars, usually in a quiet spot such as a lovers' lane or a public park. He earned the name of Zodiac murderer because of two letters sent to San Francisco newspapers describing details of the killings which he signed with a cross and a circle.

The first murders occurred on 20 December 1968 when he shot dead a student couple sitting in their parked car. This was followed by two further attacks in July and September of the following year, when the man in both incidents survived his injuries. The last murder was in October 1969 when he shot dead a taxi-driver in San Francisco. Apart from sending letters to the newspapers, the Zodiac murderer made direct telephone calls to the police and others. In July 1969 he reported the double murder attempt which had taken place in a public park, and added, 'I also killed those kids last year.' Several days after what proved to be the last Zodiac killing he talked briefly on several occasions with Melvin Belli, the famous criminal lawyer. On 22 October 1969 thousands of breakfast-time TV viewers in the

San Francisco area saw Belli on his regular morning talk show answering the telephone to a soft-voiced caller who complained of headaches. 'I don't want to go to the gas chamber. I have headaches,' he said. On another occasion, still complaining of headaches, he said, 'I've got to kill! I've got to kill!'

Belli arranged to meet his caller privately in Daly City — he waited forty-five minutes, but the Zodiac murderer did not turn up. He received a note in December wishing him a happy Christmas. After that there was silence, but letters purporting to come from the mysterious killer were sent to the *Los Angeles Times* in 1971 and to the San Francisco police in 1974. The handwriting was the same as in previous letters.

Survivors of the 1969 attacks described their assailant as aged between twenty-five and thirty. One said that he wore a hood, decorated with zodiacal signs, over his head. The killer verified his crimes by telephoning the police afterwards with details known only to them and to the murderer.He left characteristic signs of the zodiac at the crime scene and sent part of a victim's shirt to one of the newspapers.

Janie Shepherd, 24-year-old stepdaughter of an Australian petrol company executive, disappeared from her home in St John's Wood, London, on 4 February 1977. She left her flat that evening intending to drive to Knightsbridge to spend the weekend with her boy-friend. She never arrived and fears for her safety mounted when her car was found four days later parked in a restricted area of Notting Hill Gate. The vehicle was splashed with mud and the interior showed evidence of a struggle having taken place.

Ten weeks after she went missing Janie Shepherd's body was found some twenty miles north of London on a piece of common land known as Nomansland. Her body was discovered by two boys playing on the lonely common, lying in thick bushes close to the B651, the St Albans-Wheathampstead road. The girl had been raped and strangled, and there was evidence that at some stage in her abduction she had been bound. The conclusion was that she had been raped in the back of her car, which was then driven to Nomansland, where her body was dumped.

The police interviewed a number of known sex offenders, but the case remains officially unsolved. In 1981, in his book *Clues to the Unknown*, the psychic Robert Cracknell claimed to know that the murderer of Janie Shepherd was a man serving a prison sentence for rape and attempted murder.
(6, 58, 201, 868, 941, 1028)

PARLOURS

'I went to the living room ... and waited for my father to come out ...'
Wayne Dresbach (1961)

To a casual observer of the Victorian era, murder in the parlour might appear to have been a popular pastime. Perhaps murder was an inevitable outlet for the suppressed emotions which lay beneath the outward show of respectability. The philosophy of everyone to their station and everything in its place made no allowance for deviation, least of all for Victorian women. Swaddled in black satin, they held the home front while their husbands pursued the challenges of industry and empire.

The parlour was the seat of domesticity. Its velvet-draped windows, the favourite armchair by the hearth, the cat on the mat and the aspidistra in the corner comprised a scene which reflected the stability of the age. But some of the foundations of the structure were not too secure, and the very fabric of the parlour was in many ways permeated with the heavy odour of repressed feelings and the bitterness of family strife. Certainly the barriers of moral rectitude built by the Victorians were breached countless times, not least by errant husbands who practised a different code to the one they preached.

When the women reached for excitement beyond the stuffy confines of restricted family life they sometimes found it in murder. Dorothy Dunbar in her excellent book *Blood in the Parlour* described the feeling of Victorian murder as 'the act of removing an ugly fact to maintain a pleasant fiction, the grim reality of a dead body, or bodies, contradicting the fantasy of high-flown or obscure motives.'

The parlour as a focus for this grim reality was epitomized by Lizzie Borden, who although not proved a murderess, is widely regarded as having meted out the 'forty whacks' which dispatched her father and step-mother to bloody axe-deaths in their Fall River home in 1892. The grim reality was also confronted by Madeleine Smith, whose passionate character shocked her trial judge when she won a Not Proven verdict in an Edinburgh court in 1857 against the charge of murdering her lover. Florence Bravo survived an accusatorial inquest in 1876 over her husband's death by poisoning, and in 1886 Adelaide Bartlett stood her ground at the Old Bailey to win an acquittal on a murder charge. Florence Maybrick in 1889 was convicted of murdering her husband with arsenic, and served fifteen years of a life sentence.

All these cases had strong undercurrents of repressed sexual feelings and in each incident, regardless of the outcome, the woman proved capable and of firm resolve. However they judged their ordeals, two of them, Smith and Maybrick, lived to enjoy their old age.

As a place of murder it is the parlour's intimacy that always disarms the victim and aids the murderer. The comfort and serenity of pleasant surroundings cloak the murderer's intention as poison is administered. Marie Lafarge secured her husband's demise in 1839 with some specially made arsenic-laden cakes, and Florence Maybrick fed her weakened husband with poisoned meat-extract. Not that all the villains of the parlour have been women, or all such murders committed in Victorian times. Doctors Pritchard and Lamson administered poison in congenial surroundings and the parlour (translated into the modern living-room) remains a popular location for domestic murder.

Louis Bertrand, though, belonged to the classic school. He practised as a dentist in Sydney, Australia. Aged thirty-five, married with two children, he had by 1865 prospered sufficiently to move to a house in Wynyard Square, one of the city's fashionable areas. In January of that year Louis and Jane Bertrand met the Kinders, a New Zealand couple with two children who lived at St Leonards, a Sydney suburb. The two families became close friends.

Henry Kinder was a teller at a branch of the City Bank in Sydney. His wife Ellen was a passionate woman who had taken a lover before they moved to Australia. Within days of their first meeting Ellen Kinder and Louis Bertrand were madly in love. Their affair

blossomed as their respective spouses stood on the sidelines. In June 1865 a potential embarrassment arrived in the form of Frank Jackson, Ellen's former lover, who had turned up from New Zealand.

The passionate lady and mother of two now had two lovers with whom to contend. The dilemma was solved when she chose Bertrand as her favourite, and magnanimous in victory, the dentist offered his rival accommodation in his home. This generous gesture was not entirely unselfish, for Bertrand rather hoped that he would be able to pair off Jackson with his wife. No doubt this would have relieved the pressure on his own emotional life, but Jane Bertrand would have none of it.

Despite the outward show of courtesies, Bertrand was burning with jealousy. It was not enough for him to have seen off his rival; his need was for Ellen's exclusive favours, which meant that her husband was an obstacle. The scheming dentist confided in Jackson that he was planning to murder Henry Kinder, and he advised the vanquished lover to return to New Zealand. Frank Jackson left, but only moved a hundred miles away to Maitland. Louis Bertrand now involved his young dental assistant, Alfred Burne, in several bizarre nocturnal attempts on Kinder's life. 'I intend to knock his brains out,' he told the wide-eyed Burne as he brandished a hatchet. These efforts failed, through loss of nerve or for other reasons, and Bertrand was forced to think again. Meanwhile the acquiescent Henry Kinder — not surprisingly, in view of all that was going on around him — took to drink.

In October 1865 the Bertrands visited the Kinders at the latter's home, Burbank Cottage, Falconer Street, St Leonards. Louis took Henry to near-by Dind's Hotel for a drink, and they returned to the cottage to spend the evening with their wives. The two men played cards in the parlour and the women chatted. Suddenly this blissful scene was shattered by the noise of a gun, and Henry Kinder collapsed on the floor bleeding from a head wound — a pistol lay beside him. While Jane Bertrand tended to the wounded man, Louis and Ellen walked out to the verandah, where they grasped each other in a fond embrace.

Several hours went by before a doctor arrived at the cottage, to be told by Bertrand that Kinder had shot himself. It was two days before the police were called and Kinder told them, 'What lies to say that I shot myself!' Although he was badly wounded in the side of the face, it was several days before he died, allegedly assisted by poison administered by Jane Bertrand on her husband's instructions.

At the coroner's inquest Louis Bertrand said, 'I saw Kinder place the pistol to the side of his head,' and added, 'Kinder was jealous of his wife; but, for the last six months, she gave him no cause for his unkind treatment of her.' The inquest's verdict was that Kinder had committed suicide while emotionally insane by discharging a pistol loaded with powder. As no bullet had been found at the scene of the shooting or in the wound, it was assumed that none had been fired, and that the fatal wound had been caused solely by a powder discharge. The spent bullet had in fact been retrieved by Jane Bertrand, who gave it to her husband.

On 21 October Ellen Kinder left Sydney with her two fatherless children and went to stay at her parents' home in Bathurst. Several revelations followed. On reading the news of Henry Kinder's death, Ellen's former lover,

Henry Kinder was shot dead in the parlour by his wife's lover

Frank Jackson, decided to write to Bertrand. He threatened to tell what he knew to the police unless Bertrand gave him money to help him leave Australia. Coolly, Bertrand informed the police that he was being blackmailed, and Jackson ended up with twelve months in prison.

To add to Bertrand's troubles, his sister Harriet Kerr, who stayed for a while at Wynyard Square, let it be known that she was appalled to discover her brother ill-treated his wife. He often beat her and Harriet Kerr was present when he demanded that Jane write a note explaining why she intended to end her life. For his part, Louis Bertrand began complaining that he was being haunted by Henry Kinder's ghost.

Meanwhile the grieving widow started writing letters to Bertrand in which she poured out her passion. 'Dear, dear love, your kind loving words seemed to have filled a void in my heart.' And again, 'Love you? Oh yes, better than anything in this wide, wide world — not only love, but respect. I look up to you as through nature.' Ellen's lover, like Madeleine Smith's, kept all her letters but few of his replies survived.

Matters came to a head when Louis Bertrand found himself serving fourteen days' imprisonment for threatening with a knife a friend who dared to comment on his affairs. During that time Frank Jackson talked to the police, as did Harriet Kerr, and both Ellen Kinder and Jane Bertrand were arrested. Charges of murder were brought, and when those against the two women were dropped, Louis Bertrand stood trial. He faced Sir Alfred Stephen, the Chief Justice, in Darlinghurst Court House in February 1866. Like the judge who tried Madeleine Smith eight years earlier in Edinburgh, Stephen was fired by moral indignation at the abandoned sexual behaviour of Louis Bertrand and Ellen Kinder. Nevertheless, the jury failed to reach a verdict, and a second trial was called. The jury at the second trial brought in a Guilty verdict, and in passing sentence of death on Bertrand, Sir Alfred Stephen (who again presided) spoke of the 'passion eating into your vitals; and you would have committed any crime to have her as your own'. The amorous dentist declared from the dock, 'I defy the world to say that I am guilty .... If I die, I am murdered.'

Although there was no Court of Criminal Appeal in Australia in the 1860s the sentence was contested by Bertrand's uncle supported by the Jewish community. It was eventually referred to the Privy Council, and in July 1867 sentence of death was commuted to one of life imprisonment with hard labour and three years in irons. Louis Bertrand served twenty-eight years, being released in 1894 at the age of sixty-five.

Resentment in the confined atmosphere of the home can build up to such an extent that explosive release of pressure is inevitable. This is what happened to fifteen-year-old Wayne Dresbach, who came home late from a school basketball game on 6 January 1961. He was severely reprimanded by his parents before going to bed. The following morning he took his father's .22 rifle and waited for his parents to rise from bed. First his father appeared and the boy shot him as he was making his way to the kitchen, then his mother emerged from the bedroom and he shot her too.

Harold Dresbach practised as an attorney in Washington, D.C. He lived with his wife Shirley and two boys, Wayne and Lee, in Anne Arundel County, Maryland. He travelled thirty miles to the office every day, but took great pride in his exclusive house which commanded a view across Chesapeake Bay. When the early-morning calm was shattered by the sound of gun-shots, young Lee ran to a neighbour's house shouting, 'Wayne killed them! Wayne killed them!' Harold and Shirley Dresbach were found dead in their home — Harold had been shot six times and his wife four times.

Wayne had fled from the scene in his father's car but was soon picked up. 'I shot my parents,' he told the arresting officer, and a loaded .22 rifle was found in his car. In a statement to the police the teenage boy described how he carried out the killings: 'I went to the living-room and stood behind the television so that I would not be seen easily and waited for my father to come out of the bedroom ... I shot him in the back ... my mother came out of the bedroom ... I shot her about three times.' His brother Lee was in the kitchen when the shooting took place. Wayne's reason for shooting his parents was that 'they were yelling at me'.

Inquiries by social workers and psychiatrists began to unravel the tangled skein of circumstances which provided the background to the deaths of the Dresbachs. Firstly, Wayne and Lee were adopted children, and while Harold Dresbach treated both boys strictly, he singled out Wayne for continuous harassment. He seemed to enjoy humiliating the boy in front of guests, and he often beat him for trivial offences. Wayne ran away from home several times and told friends that he wished his father were dead.

Dresbach drank heavily and beat his wife, and in addition to the domestic violence which he perpetuated, also engaged in bizarre sexual pursuits. He and Shirley were nudists, and some of their house guests were sexual deviants. Dresbach liked to perform sexual manœuvres on the white rug in front of the fire, and late one night Wayne witnessed his parents performing with different partners in the living-room of his home. The boy also found a collection of pornographic pictures which his father had kept hidden in a desk drawer. Finally, Dresbach's cruel taunts and physical violence towards his teenage son exploded in his face and the boy killed the tyrant.

Wayne was indicted on a charge of first

degree murder in 1961 and was sent for trial. The judge ruled that he should be tried separately for the two killings, starting with the death of his father. The defence was prevented from introducing evidence of events not directly relating to the shooting incident, so that the court was not told how Dresbach had tormented his son. Dr Manfred S. Guttmacher, the eminent forensic psychiatrist, had examined Wayne, and gave it as his opinion that although the boy was 'a very disordered individual' he was not technically insane.

The jury deliberated for only twelve minutes before reaching its verdict. This was delivered by the foreman, who declared that a verdict of insanity had been reached. Amid uproar, he corrected himself by delivering a verdict of guilty of murder in the first degree. Wayne Dresbach was sentenced to life imprisonment.

The outcome was widely regarded as a miscarriage of justice, and the knowledge that one member of the jury was illiterate made it difficult to believe that the complex psychiatric evidence given at the trial was fully understood. Nevertheless, Wayne Dresbach served ten years at the Patuxent Institute before being paroled in 1971.

Elimination of an unwanted spouse is a time-honoured motive for domestic murder, and one that Dietrich Nel felt obliged to pursue. He was an ambitious young man, especially when it came to dealing with the opposite sex. Although married he vigorously courted a girl, telling her that he was a widower.

On 29 January 1934 Nel, who worked as a train driver in the Orange Free State, told the General Secretary of his Trade Union that his wife had committed suicide by hanging herself. Having visited the trade union's offices in Johannesburg to report the matter, and to discuss funeral expenses, Nel returned home to Krugersdorf. Two days later during the early hours of 31 January neighbours thought they heard screams coming from the Nel residence. At about 6.30 that morning Nel called his next-door neighbour and said, 'My wife has hanged herself.'

Mrs Nel, dressed in pyjamas, was suspended against the sitting-room door by means of a length of electric flex tied round her neck, passing over the top of the door and secured to the handle on the other side. A chair stood about two feet away from the limp but still warm body. Assisted by Nel, the neighbour took the body down, and fought to remove the ligature which bit deeply into the woman's neck. The noose had been fastened with three knots and there was no hope of reviving her.

There was a great deal of local gossip about Mrs Nel's tragic death, and the significance of the screams was the subject of intense speculation. Nel moved away from the neighbourhood, and with money borrowed ostensibly to pay his wife's funeral expenses, bought an engagement ring for his new girl-friend. Their official engagement was announced on 3 February.

At the inquest on his wife's death Nel admitted that they had quarrelled and said she had threatened to take her own life with a gun which he seized from her. When it was revealed that he had spoken about her having committed suicide two days before she died suspicions of murder began to harden. Mrs Nel's body was exhumed, and the pathologist established from the bruises on the neck that she was already dead before her body was suspended from the door.

Nel was tried for murder in May 1934, when the evidence against him proved overwhelming. Letters he had written to his girl-friend proved his motive: 'I would rather shoot myself than make love to you if I were married to a woman who is still alive,' he wrote. He strangled his wife, producing the screams heard by neighbours, and then secured a cord around her neck with three knots — an unlikely act for a suicide — before suspending her body to simulate hanging. Dietrich Nel was convicted, and unlike his wife, really was hanged. He confessed his crime in the condemned cell.

(1, 66, 103, 253, 375, 417, 467, 497, 578, 610, 612, 622, 645, 670, 689, 690, 739, 911, 914, MWW)

PUBLIC BUILDINGS

'I did it because I had a grudge against him and he deserved it.'

Udham Singh (1940)

Public buildings attract the lurking assassin and terrorist who kill for political motives. Well-publicized engagements place great personages in vulnerable circumstances, giving an intending killer advance notice of where and when his target will appear. Consequently, travelling in cars and making public appearances are dangerous assignments for kings and presidents. Archduke Ferdinand (1914), King Alexander I of Yugoslavia (1934) and President John F. Kennedy (1963) all fell victim while journeying in cars, and President William McKinley (1901), Dr Martin Luther King (1968) and President Park Chung-Hee of South Korea (1974) were murdered in public places.

These crimes occurred in times when it was easy for anyone to gain admission to a public building during a visit by a VIP. The increasing activities of terrorist groups around the world have led to heightened security surveillance of the buildings and facilities used by potential assassination targets. While the chances of planting explosive devices and smuggling firearms into public buildings have been reduced, they have not been completely eradicated. This was savagely demonstrated by the bomb, intended to obliterate the British Prime Minister and her Cabinet, which exploded in the Grand Hotel, Brighton, in October 1984.

Timing devices and remotely operated detonation make it possible for the modern assassin to commit his crime at a safe distance. Earlier murderers who chose to kill their target in a public building, even with the use of a firearm, still had to go in close and thereby endanger their chances of escape.

Not surprisingly, British rule in India produced a crop of politically motivated murders, and hate-filled assassins followed some of their former masters to England. Madar Lal Dhingra, a 25-year-old student in London in 1909, obtained a firearms licence and practised shooting three days a week in readiness for his big moment. On 1 July he went to a concert to which he had been invited at the Imperial Institute. In the audience was Sir William Hutt Curzon Wylie, who for many years had served in India, and at that time was Honorary Treasurer of the National Indian Association.

The concert ended at about 11.00 p.m. and the audience began to stream out of the building in South Kensington. Dhingra followed Sir William and engaged him in conversation. After a few minutes the Indian produced a revolver and fired five shots at point-blank range. Sir William fell dead to the

ground, and a member of the public who made a valiant attempt to disarm the assassin was also shot dead by Dhingra. The revolver misfired when the Indian turned it on himself, and he was thus spared for the executioner. At his trial Dhingra, far from seeking sympathy, told the court, 'It is perfectly justifiable on our part to kill the Englishman who is polluting our sacred soil.' Madar Lal Dhingra was hanged for his crime in August 1909.

Another Indian — a Sikh on this occasion — was present in Caxton Hall, Westminster, London for a joint meeting of the Royal Central Asian Society and the East India Association on 15 March 1940. Three hundred people were gathered to hear Sir Percy Sykes lecture on Afghanistan. A distinguished platform party included the Marquess of Zetland, Secretary of State for India, who chaired the meeting, Lord Lamington, Sir Louis Dane and Sir Michael O'Dwyer, all of whom had close connections with the sub-continent. The meeting had concluded and people were beginning to leave when a Sikh who had worked his way up to the platform produced a revolver and fired six shots at point-blank range at the dignitaries and then rushed towards one of the exits. A man in the audience brought the gunman down with a flying tackle as the hall erupted in panic.

Sir Michael O'Dwyer was struck by two bullets and died instantly. Three of the others were wounded, but none seriously. Each of the six shots fired found a target. The murderer was a fanatical Sikh, Udham Singh, who nursed feelings of bitter hatred against the British on account of the death of his brother in the Amritsar riots in 1919 at a time when Sir Michael O'Dwyer was Governor of the Punjab.

Singh was carrying twenty-five rounds of ammunition on him, and when arrested he expressed disappointment at only having caused one death. 'I did it', he said, 'because I had a grudge against him and he deserved it.' His words were those of the fanatic: 'You want to die when you are young. That is good. That is what I am doing. I am dying for my country.' While in prison awaiting trial he went on a hunger strike and had to be forcibly fed. The Sikh proved to be much travelled. After serving in the Indian Army he had voyaged to England, Mexico and the United States, returning to India in 1931, where he was sentenced to five years' imprisonment for illicit possession of firearms. Doubtless this did little to alleviate the grievance against the British which he already had, and he returned to Britain in 1938 by way of Russia.

He also continued to be vocal at his trial, which was held at the time of the Dunkirk evacuation. At the Old Bailey Singh claimed that the killing was accidental — he had planned only to fire protest shots in the air, but someone had knocked his hand, with the result that the gun discharged into the platform party. This unlikely explanation of events carried little weight and Robert Churchill, the gun expert, pointed out that the death toll could have been greater. The Sikh had used a .45 Smith and Wesson revolver with ill-fitting ammunition and lack of penetration of the bullets, even when fired at close range, probably saved the lives of the unfortunate Sir Michael O'Dwyer's companions.

The jury found Udham Singh guilty, and he constantly interrupted the judge during his passing of sentence of death. He referred to notes written on a piece of paper and used a torrent of words to damn British imperialism and all its works. The judge tried valiantly to stem the flow, but was spat at for his pains while Singh ranted on, 'I do not care about sentence of death. It means nothing at all. I do not care about death or anything.' Udham Singh was hanged on 25 June.

Causing death by explosion is not a common form of murder except when used by terrorists and assassins. When Huibrecht Jacob de Leeuw blew up the town hall at Dewetsdorp, killing three people, his motive was not one rooted in terrorism but in the deep desire to avoid the consequences of another crime. At the age of twenty-six de Leeuw was a young appointee to the office of Town Clerk in Dewetsdorp, a small town in South Africa's Orange Free State. He was well known and popular, and looked set for a respectable career when he married and began to settle down. The responsibilities of marriage and bringing up a family, far from settling him down, seemed to bring out the wild side in de Leeuw, who began to live beyond his means and fell into debt.

Soon his financial problems became so severe, and his opportunities to borrow money from his friends so exhausted, that he began to dip into the town exchequer of which he was guardian. His deputy was aware that the Town Clerk took money from the office safe and protected himself by keeping the books in arrears so that the true state of affairs was concealed. In due course rumours began to gain currency that de Leeuw was in financial difficulty. The Mayor, P. J. von Maltitz, decided it would be prudent to cast an eye over the town's financial records. He found them in a mess with many receipts missing, and accused de Leeuw of negligence. The young Town Clerk pretended indignation, saying that affairs were only in arrears because he was overworked. He promised to bring the books up to date, and to demonstrate that everything was in order.

De Leeuw was in a dilemma. He tried and failed in every attempt to borrow money to put right the thefts he had made. Consequently, when the time came to fulfil his claim that the town's finances were in good order he failed miserably. He was given a week to put matters right or face dismissal. Desperation now set in — there was no way left to make up the losses, and he could not bear to contemplate the loss of his job with his wife expecting a child. His thoughts then turned to murder. He contemplated strychnine poisoning, and made inquiries about the combined explosive effect of petrol and dynamite. He even carried out some experiments with explosives on open land outside the town.

On 8 April 1927, the day set for de Leeuw to give account to von Maltitz and his two-member Finance Committee, the Town Clerk's assistant noticed two tins of petrol in the office. De Leeuw had earlier made some reference to a smell of petrol coming from the generator used to supply the office lighting. During the course of inspecting the ledgers von Maltitz was heard to accuse de Leeuw of misusing municipal funds. The meeting broke up at lunch-time and was due to recommence at 3.00 p.m. for a final session in de Leeuw's office.

The members of the Finance Committee duly arrived for what would certainly have led to de Leeuw's dismissal from office when there was a tremendous explosion. The roof was blown off the Town Hall, every window was shattered and flames belched from the building. Von Maltitz died almost immediately, and his two colleagues died in hospital of severe burns — but not before making dying declarations implicating de Leeuw in theft. The Town Clerk, who had suffered minor injuries and dispatched his assistant on an errand at the crucial time, contemplated the wreckage of his office and the destruction of the odious ledgers, but his satisfaction was short-lived, for he was quickly arrested after police found firearms and poisonous substances in his home. He was charged with murder, and sent for trial at Bloemfontein in August 1927.

The assistant whom de Leeuw had thought to spare from his plan of destruction now gave the court the benefit of all his silent observations. His evidence was damning, as was that of a local shopkeeper who recounted how de Leeuw had rushed into her shop in a trembling and agitated state on the afternoon of the explosion. 'I only want some matches,' he explained. It appeared that having set up his petrol and dynamite bomb he had forgotten to provide any means of ignition.

De Leeuw, as South African law allowed, opted not for trial by jury but by a judge sitting with two assessors. The defence put up by his counsel was thought by many to have had the power to win over a jury, but the judge found the accused guilty. The condemned man protested his innocence, claiming — as have many murderers, both before and since — that he was the victim of circumstantial evidence. The tragedy was that de Leeuw was prepared to murder three men, apparently to save his reputation and his job, when information which subsequently came to light showed that he could easily have paid off his debts. As it was, he told the judge, 'I am prepared to go to meet my Creator,' and he was hanged on 30 September 1927.

(69, 419, 487, 864)

RAILWAY MURDERS

'Everything undesigned or unexpected is not an accident.'

C.A. Russell KC (1910)

In common with many other innovations, the introduction of the passenger railway train in the early part of the nineteenth century soon led to a connection with murder. 'The isolation of a passenger in an old-fashioned railway carriage, the difficulty of obtaining assistance and the want of proper communication have led to terrible crimes on the line', wrote Major Arthur Griffiths in his *Mysteries of Police and*

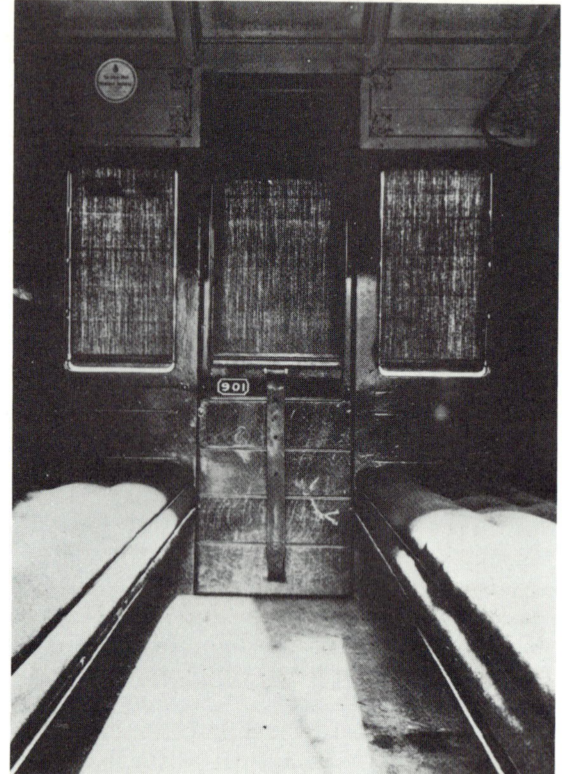

Trains without corridors afforded protection to murderers

Crime in 1902. Trains certainly offered possibilities as mobile scenes of crime rather than as instruments of murder — the victim tied to the line in the path of the oncoming train belonged to the silent movie rather than to reality.

As a location for crime the trains provided the murderer with some distinct advantages. Passengers carrying money and jewellery became easy victims once isolated in a closed compartment with their potential attacker. Murder could occur in privacy with no means of escape from a corridorless train moving quickly between stations. Moreover, sounds of violence were conveniently drowned by the noise of the train. Trains also moved between the centres of large towns and cities, so that once the deed was done the murderer could alight at his destination and melt away into the population of some vast metropolis before his crime was discovered.

The possibilities for railway murder have all been exploited in fiction, and most skilfully by Agatha Christie in her classic *Murder on the*

Orient Express. Real railway murders, however, have tended to occur on less glamorous trains, such as the North London Railway's Bow to Hackney service which provided the setting for the world's first train murder in 1864, when Franz Müller, a German tailor working in England, killed and robbed a London jeweller. Two other notorious railway murderers were Percy Lefroy, who robbed and killed a man on a London to Brighton train in 1881, and John Dickman, a bookmaker who shot and robbed a colliery wages clerk on the Newcastle to Alnmouth service in 1910.

Müller, Lefroy and Dickman did not prosper from the benefits offered by trains as places of murder — each was convicted, and suffered the penalty of hanging. But as Arthur Lambton pointed out in an account of the murders in his book *Thou Shalt Do No Murder*, 'the main reflection after all is this ... if all trains were compulsorily corridor trains neither Mr Gold, Mr Briggs (victims of Lefroy and Müller) nor anybody else, either man or woman, would have met with a violent death.' Not that the isolation of the railway compartment was given even passing consideration by George Henry Parker, who murdered his victim in full view of a witness. On 17 January 1901 Parker boarded a London-bound train at Eastleigh in Hampshire and took a seat in a third-class compartment in which the only other occupant was Mrs Rhoda King. The train stopped at Winchester before entering the non-stop phase of its journey to Vauxhall. A third person entered the compartment occupied by Parker and Mrs King in the form of William Pearson, a farmer whose appearance of prosperity marked him down for robbery.

As the train approached Surbiton, Parker produced a revolver and, levelling it at Pearson, shot him dead. He then fired at Mrs King, wounding her slightly in the face. 'My God', she cried, 'what have you done?' 'I did it for money' was Parker's prompt reply. 'I want some money. Have you got any?' Mrs King, fearing for her life, offered him a coin from her handbag, but the murderer had already seized a handful of sovereigns from the dead man's purse. 'What shall I do with the bloody thing?' asked Parker, referring to the revolver. 'How would it do to put it in the old bloke's hand so that people will think he killed himself?' With great presence of mind, and

with the hope of lessening the danger to herself, Mrs King advised him to throw the weapon out of the window of the train, which he did.

As the train slowed on its approach to Vauxhall station, Parker jumped out on to the platform and dashed through the ticket barrier and out into the street. When the train drew to a halt, Mrs King, blood streaming down her face, raised the alarm, and within minutes, following a chase, Parker was captured. Desite a defence plea of temporary insanity, he was found guilty and sentenced to death.

As against Parker's foolhardy behaviour, at least two other railway murderers exercised sufficient guile to remain undetected. The first victim was a young woman who was bludgeoned to death with robbery as a motive and the second was a child strangled for no apparent purpose. On 11 February 1897, Elizabeth Camp, an East End barmaid, arranged to meet her fiancé at Waterloo Station. She boarded the 7.42 p.m. train at Hounslow, and was seen off by her sister whom she had been visiting. Miss Camp remarked that she preferred to travel second class because she met a better type of passenger. Her sister — wisely, as it turned out — replied, 'That may be so, but the third is safer for women.'

At 8.25 p.m., after the train had disembarked its passengers at Waterloo, a cleaner discovered Elizabeth Camp's body lying on the floor of her compartment. She had been brutally battered to death, and had evidently put up a fierce struggle. Her handbag containing £16 was missing. The murder weapon — and an unusual one at that — turned out to be a five-pound Wedgwood pestle of a type used for gold-beating. This was found beside the railway line at Wandsworth Station. Blood and hair still clinging to it marked it — at least circumstantially — as the murder weapon, and its location indicated that it had been used to kill Elizabeth Camp before the train made its stop at Vauxhall.

The police naturally hoped that recovery of the blood-stained pestle would lead them to the murderer. Indeed, a second-hand dealer quickly came forward and tentatively identified the implement as one that he had sold a few days before the murder to an American who had been lodging at his house for several months. He volunteered the information that the article he had sold had been used for gold-beating. It also transpired that the American had on one occasion returned to his lodging accompanied by Miss Camp, whom he said he had married three weeks previously. Any chance of solving the mystery attached to Elizabeth Camp's affairs or of her tragic end disappeared with the American, who had absconded. Despite a reward of £200 offered by the London and South Western Railway Company for information leading to an arrest, the case of the first woman to be murdered on a train in Britain remained unsolved.

The police were similarly frustrated in their efforts to find the murderer of five-year-old Willie Starchfield, whose body was found under the seat of a compartment of a North London Railway Chalk Farm to Broad Street train on 8 January 1914. The boy had been strangled, and the doctor who examined him at 4.30 p.m. thought he had been dead for about two hours. There was no evidence of a struggle having taken place.

Willie's parents were separated, and the boy stayed with his mother. During the early part of the afternoon on which he met his death, the boy was seen running errands in Kentish Town. The *Daily Sketch* offered £500 reward for information leading to the arrest and conviction of the murderer. As a result a witness came forward who identified Willie's father, John Starchfield, whom she had seen with the boy on the day of the murder. She remembered that the child was eating a piece of cake, and assumed it was coconut cake bought from a near-by shop. Dr Bernard Spilsbury's post-mortem findings tended to confirm this, for examination of the dead boy's stomach contents showed the presence of starchy foodstuff, raisins, sultanas and fragments of desiccated coconut.

Three witnesses in all testified that they had seen John Starchfield accompanied by a child on the day in question, and the coroner's inquest returned a verdict of wilful murder resulting in his committal for trial after appearing before the magistrates. The case against him was based on identification by the three persons who claimed to have seen him with young Willie, and there was also the linking evidence provided by the coconut cake. Motive, however, appeared to be completely lacking, and Mr Justice Atkin directed the jury to bring in a not guilty verdict on the grounds of there being insufficient evidence. John Starchfield left the court a free man, and his son's death on a train remained unsolved.

Train murder had its vogue in Europe during the nineteenth century, and the motive was usually robbery. This type of crime receded with the introduction of the corridor train which deprived the intending robber of the chance to isolate his victim. Writing of the London to Brighton rail service, which provided the locus for two railway murders, Gerald Sparrow in his book *Vintage Victorian and Edwardian Murder* remarked, 'There is today no real scope for murder. The Pullman coaches offer no privacy, the meals including the breakfast ... make each carriage a place of continual movement and chatter.'

In the USA, where trains travelled long distances and frequently carried bullion, large-scale robbery accompanied by murder was common. Jesse James and Cole Younger made rich pickings from train robbery in the mid-West during the 1870s, and set the pace for others. In 1886 the Rock Island Express travelling between Chicago and Davenport, Iowa, was robbed. The train's safe was smashed open and $22,000 looted from it as Express Messenger Kellogg Nicholls lay dying from head wounds. This crime was eventually brought home to two railway staff, Fred Schwartz and Newton Watt, who rather ill-advisedly had publicly discussed a windfall which would enable them to retire early. They were arrested by Pinkerton agents and subsequently convicted.

Perhaps the best-known American train murder was that involving the D'Autrement brothers. In 1923 the three brothers held up a Southern Pacific Express in the Siskiyou mountains in Oregon and dynamited the mail coach. In the course of robbery they killed four railway staff before making good their escape. The case was made famous by Dr Edward Heinrich, whose painstaking forensic investigation of a pair of overalls left at the scene of the crime led to the capture of the brothers, and assisted in their conviction.

Probably the most unusual train murders are those attributed to Hungarian-born Sylvestre Matushka. On 12 September 1931 the Budapest-Vienna express exploded as it was crossing a viaduct at Torbagy in Austria. The train dropped into the gorge beneath, resulting in a death toll of twenty-two. After the disaster Matushka, claiming to be a company director from Vienna, sued the railway authorities for injuries allegedly sustained in the crash. It was while his claim was being investigated that doubt arose as to whether he had been a passenger on the train at all. This evoked an inquiry into his background, and it was discovered that he had become involved in swindling and black-market activities following the First World War and, more importantly, that he had made recent purchases of dynamite.

Matushka was arrested and questioned about his movements and activities. He finally confessed to blowing up the express train, using an electrical detonating device. He also claimed responsibility for attempting to derail

SOME TRAIN MURDERS IN BRIEF

Date	Victim	Murderer	Location	Motive
9 July 1864	Thomas BRIGGS	Franz MÜLLER	North London Railway Company; compartment on a Bow to Hackney train	Robbery
27 June 1881	Isaac Frederick GOLD	Percy LEFROY	Southern Railway Company; London to Brighton line, entrance to Balcombe tunnel	Robbery
12 March 1886	Kellogg NICHOLLS	Fred SCHWARTZ and Newton WATT	Rock Island Express; mail van on Chicago to Davenport, Iowa, service	Robbery
11 February 1897	Elizabeth CAMP	Undetected	South Western Railway Company; compartment on a Hounslow to Waterloo train	Robbery
17 January 1901	William PEARSON	George Henry PARKER	Southern Railway Company; Winchester to London service	Robbery
24 September 1905	Mary Sophia MONEY	Undetected	Southern Railway Company; London to Brighton service, Merstham tunnel	Suspected rape
18 March 1910	John Innes NISBET	John DICKMAN	North Eastern Railway Company; Newcastle to Alnmouth service	Robbery
8 January 1914	Willie STARCHFIELD	Undetected	North London Railway Company; Chalk Farm to Broad Street service	Not apparent
11 October 1923	Charles Owen JOHNSON Sidney BATES Marvin SENG Edwin DAUGHERTY	D'AUTREMENT brothers (Hugh, Roy & Ray)	Southern Pacific Express; Portland to San Francisco, California; held up in the Siskiyou Mountains, Oregon	Robbery
12 September 1931	twenty-two deaths	Sylvestre MATUSHKA	Budapest-Vienna express; dynamited at Bia-Torbagy in Austria	Sadism

the Vienna-Passau express near Ansbach on 1 January 1931, and the successful derailment of the Vienna-Berlin express at Jueterberg on 8 August 1931 which resulted in injuries to sixteen passengers. Matushka claimed a boyhood fascination with train disasters which became evident after a visit to a hypnotist. These latent sadistic urges came to the fore after his failure in business, and in addition to fulfilling his fantasies, he possibly saw train-wrecking as a means of hitting back at society. He set a precedent for later murderers by claiming that he was urged on by voices, in his case by a spirit called 'Leo'.

At his trial in 1931 psychiatric evidence was given suggesting that Matushka was driven by lust for power and sensation. In court he gave his profession as 'train wrecker', and spent a great deal of time openly weeping. The jury could not reach a conclusion at the first trial but at subsequent proceedings he was convicted of murder and sentenced to death. A deciding factor may have been the discovery of a map at Matushka's home in Vienna on which future train disaster sites had been marked. These included Amsterdam, Marseilles and Paris. Sentence of death was commuted to life imprisonment, and the train-wrecker had ample time to dream of disasters which might have been.
(1, 16, 90, 112, 372, 384, 554, 589, 594, 646, 734, 849, 864, 865, 893, 995, 1027, MWW)

REMOTE PLACES

'I have never been guilty of a crime that has never been committed!'
'Snowy' Rowles (1930)

Murder stalks human footsteps wherever they lead, even to some of the world's most remote regions — desert, bush and frozen wastes. Remoteness in itself offers advantages to the murderer, lessening discovery by the chance observations of witnesses and aiding concealment of the crime.

The extremes of tropical climate may accelerate the destruction of the victim's body, aided perhaps by the predations of animals and insects. On the other hand, the dry heat of the desert often promotes mummification rather than decomposition, and extremes of cold also preserve rather than destroy.

The latter phenomenon enabled the mysterious death of the American explorer Charles Francis Hall to be explained long after the event. Hall took an expedition to the North Pole in 1871, and remained out of contact with the rest of the world for two years. When survivors of the party returned home they were without their leader. Hall had been taken ill with a gastric disorder and had died on 9 November 1871; he was buried in the frozen soil of north-west Greenland. It appeared that during his illness Hall had accused his fellow-explorers of poisoning him. The exact cause of his death remained a mystery until 1968, when his body was exhumed. The permafrost had preserved his remains in excellent condition, and tests showed that he had died of arsenic poisoning. Thus the cause of his death (although not the perpetrator) became known ninety-seven years later.

Despite the huge tracts of uninhabited or sparsely populated territory in North America, Southern Africa and Australia, which might be expected to work entirely in favour of the criminal, the forces of law and order have developed a canny persistence in their investigations. This is exemplified by the Royal Canadian Mounted Police who, as the world knows, 'always get their man'.

The European tradition of prosecuting the wrong-doer has been perpetuated in the colonized parts of the world, and the combination of white lawman and native tracker has led to some remarkably successful manhunts in outlandish places. In his book *Dreamtime Justice* Victor Hall, a trooper in Australia's Northern Territory Mounted Police in the 1920s, spoke highly of his aboriginal trackers, whom he called the 'Black Watch'.

These trackers formed close one-to-one relationships with the white men they served, to the extent that they were effectively blood-brothers. Combining physical prowess with such gifts as precognition and bone-pointing, they combed vast areas of untamed land for fugitives. Victor Hall recounted the extraordinary sequel to a mass murder which occurred in Arnhem Land in September 1932. Six Japanese fishermen who had landed in Caledon Bay from their boat were butchered with spears by Balamumu tribesmen. The Balamumu were a renegade tribe feared for their criminal activities even among their own people.

The Japanese Government registered loud protests over the massacre of the fishermen and demanded that those responsible be brought to justice. The Northern Territory Mounted Police responded by ordering four troopers and six black trackers to investigate the murders. They set out from Roper River Police Station heading north into the 32,000 square mile Aboriginal Reserve of Arnhem Land. Several weeks later contact was made with the killers on Woodah Island in the Gulf of Carpentaria. Constable Albert McColl was killed in the ensuing skirmish, and the attackers escaped into the jungle. In due course an Aborigine called Tuckiar was arrested, and readily confessed to killing the police officer. He was sent for trial to Darwin, where the court duly found him guilty and he was sentenced to death. Various appeals were raised, as a result of which sentence was quashed and Tuckiar was allowed to return home.

It was at this point that the murdered constable's tracker, 'Big Pat', decided to take a hand. He swore vengeance on his boss's killer and trailed him across three hundred miles of mostly inhospitable country. With the prescience known only to the Aborigine, each knew his role as hunter and hunted. Tuckiar employed all the bushcraft he knew to conceal his tracks, but found the avenging Big Pat lying in wait for him at a place called the Pool of Yark. After a bitter struggle Tuckiar was killed and honour was served.

The massacre of the Japanese fishermen paled to insignificance in the light of the murder of the policeman and the remarkable kind of rough justice which followed. An interesting sidelight was that the Balamumu tribe of which Tuckiar was a member were the product of racial mixing between Aborigine

Australia's Northern Territory where 'Big Pat' revenged the murder of Constable McColl

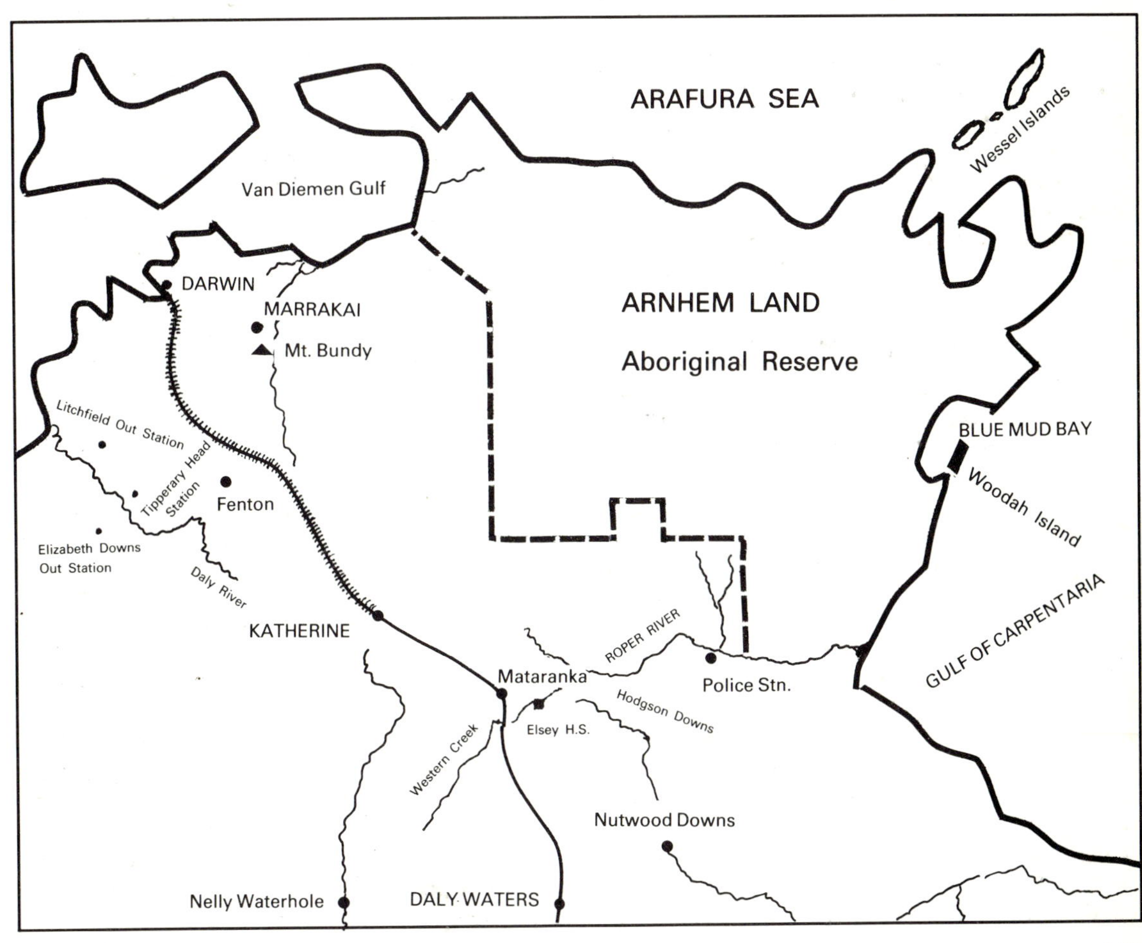

and Malay sailors which, it was thought, engendered a criminal mentality.

Harshness of climate fosters unrelenting attitudes to survival. For example, among some of the Eskimo tribes in Northern Canada's Arctic region it was the custom to kill unwanted female children at birth. Infanticide was practised as one of the realities of life in this most inhospitable part of the world. This cruel solution of one problem created other difficulties, for there were frequently too few women to partner the male hunters. The result was outbreaks of lawlessness and blood feuds between tribes which ended in savage killings.

The Cogmollocks, an Eskimo tribe living inside the Arctic Circle on Herschel Island in the Coronation Gulf, were adept hunters with both knife and gun. They also had a reputation for violence and in the early 1920s several white traders and missionaries had been murdered in this bleak area. In the summer of 1922 a local Cogmollock chief was killed on Herschel Island in one of the periodic fights over ownership of a wife. The dead chief's wife was taken by Pugnana, one of his main rivals, which left fellow-conspirator Tatamagama out in the cold. Tatamagama sought the help of his eighteen-year-old nephew, Aligoomiak, to acquire the late chief's wife for himself. The two men conspired to kill Pugnana when they were out together on a hunting trip.

Their opportunity came during a caribou hunt. When they sighted a group of animals Aligoomiak hung back, allowing his two companions to shoot their selected prey. With Pugnana absorbed in killing caribou the teenage Eskimo lined up his target in his rifle sights and killed him with a single shot. Pugnana's body was left in the snow to be finished off by wolves, while his murderers returned to the village to report his death by accident. In time-honoured fashion Tatamagama seized the dead man's wife and possessions and moved into his igloo. Aligoomiak's reward was a new rifle. Tatamagama had also acquired a nine-month-old daughter whose cries so disturbed his sleep that he called on his nephew to perform another service for him. For the price of a box of ammunition for his new rifle, Aligoomiak killed the child so that silence reigned in his uncle's igloo.

News of a fresh round of killings reached the Royal Canadian Mounted Police, and a corporal was sent up to Herschel Island to

Aligoomiak, the Eskimo murderer, awaits 'Neck-Tie Bill'

investigate. With the help of a little bribery he persuaded a few Eskimos to talk, and he soon found Tatamagama and Aligoomiak, who made no attempt to escape. The two suspects were put under arrest and the policeman prepared to take them down to Tree River, where there was a police post. During this long and hazardous journey, travelling through Arctic blizzards and living off fish and seal meat, it was inevitable that the policeman should draw close to his fellows in adversity. Aligoomiak's response to this generosity was to bide his time before killing the friendly corporal. When they reached the shelter of the trading post he shot the policeman and the sole occupant of the trading post. He went completely off the rails, declaring his intention to kill any white men he came across.

Months later, in a tale reminiscent of the *Boy's Own Paper* and stories in which the 'Mounties always get their man', the fugitives,

Tatamagama and Aligoomiak, were arrested and brought to justice. At the end of 1923 a party consisting of a judge and court officials travelled four thousand miles from Edmonton to Herschel Island to conduct a trial for murder. The party also included William Brown, the public hangman, who was known to Eskimos as 'Neck-tie Bill'. Aligoomiak put up a spirited defence, claiming that the RCMP corporal planned to kill him rather than bring him to justice. He decided therefore to pre-empt matters by wounding the policeman in the leg. He had not wished to kill him. He found it a little more difficult to defend his killing of the trader, and the jury had no hesitation in bringing in a guilty verdict. The two Eskimos were sentenced to death, and Aligoomiak, thoroughly corrupted by his association with white men, offered the judge a cigarette! 'Neck-tie Bill' hanged Tatamagama and Aligoomiak on 1 February 1924.

While survival is a way of life among the Eskimos and others, it is practised as a form of escape by some who become bored with the comforts of city life. Canada's Gaspé Peninsula at the mouth of the St Lawrence river is a remote area of Quebec Province. It is hilly and mountanous country with thick forested slopes which attract tourists looking for adventure in a rugged landscape. It is also bear country, and each summer beckons hunters who travel up from the USA to answer the call of the wild. The area is sparsely populated with widely separated villages on the coast and prospectors' camps dotted about inland.

On 5 June 1953 three Americans left their homes in Hollidaysburg, Pennsylvania, in a truck loaded with equipment to spend two weeks hunting in the Gaspé region — they never returned. Eugene Lindsay, his son Richard and Frederick Claar were reported missing on 5 July, and the Canadian authorities were asked to mount a search. Their truck was found abandoned near some unoccupied prospectors' camps on the St John River. The search was aided by a mining prospector, 43-year-old Wilbert Coffin, who said he had encountered the three Americans on 10 June, and helped them move their truck, which had broken down. By the time Coffin had joined the search party the body of Eugene Lindsay had already been found lying near a stream at a spot known as Camp 24. Part of his scalp was found on one side of the stream, and his

decapitated, badly mauled body on the other. It appeared that the body had been attacked by bears, and judging from the shredded clothes, had been dragged across the stream. Close examination showed that his clothing bore bullet-holes and his rifle, found near-by, had some of his own head hair on the butt. Lindsay was known to carry large sums of money with him, and when his empty wallet was retrieved the most likely explanation for his death seemed to be that he was robbed and murdered before the bears attacked the corpse.

The bodies of Lindsay's two companions were found about two miles away at Camp 26. They too had been shot and subsequently mangled by marauding bears. The authorities believed that Lindsay had been killed for his money and his companions suffered the same fate because they were dangerous witnesses. Wilbert Coffin, who had admitted meeting the three hunters, was arrested and charged with their murder in what was to become one of the most sensational criminal cases in Canadian history.

The evidence against Coffin was circumstantial, and there were several unexplained irregularities which led to strong views that an innocent man was convicted. Despite his pleas of innocence, Coffin's counsel would not allow him to testify in court, and the only account he was able to make was a statement written in prison after he had been sentenced to death. According to this, he had seen two other American hunters travelling in a jeep in the vicinity of Lindsay's party. He had referred this to the police before being arrested, and independent witnesses had reported seeing a similar vehicle. None of this was followed up, and indeed after the trial a jeep matching this description was recovered near the town of Bathurst.

Two other remarkable incidents were associated with the Coffin affair, one occurring before his execution and the other afterwards. Having been refused permission to plead before the Supreme Court, Coffin broke out of Quebec City Prison on 6 September 1955 using a revolver fashioned from a piece of soap. He went straight to his lawyer, who advised him to return to prison — which he did. Coffin was refused appeals for a new trial, and not allowed to marry his common-law wife. He was hanged on 10 February 1956 after seven stays of execution.

On 2 November 1958 Miami police arrested Francis Gilbert Thompson, a Canadian Indian who confessed to the murder of the three American hunters five years previously. Thompson had been arrested on a vagrancy charge when he made this revelation, and implicated a second man called Johnny Green. The Quebec police were notified, but despite Thompson's detailed account of killing the hunters and dismembering their bodies, they declared him an impostor and refused to believe him. Thompson stuck to his confession for several days and then withdrew it.

It became known that Eugene Lindsay had a reputation as a money-lender who exacted tough terms from his customers. He frequently carried a large bankroll consisting of $2,000 or more, and was a man with enemies. Whoever murdered him and his companions, the lonely location was well chosen for the scope it offered to delay the discovery of the bodies and enhance the chances of escape. Nature played its part, in the form of the marauding bears tearing at the dead bodies, making identification and cause of death more difficult to ascertain. An abiding mystery lay in the fact that Lindsay's head was never discovered.

Because of its vastness and sparse population, the bush has qualities that should work to the advantage of the careful murderer. The camel-breeding station at Dromedary, north of Kalgoorlie in Western Australia, was the unlikely venue for a discussion of the 'perfect murder'. In October 1929 Arthur William Upfield, a boundary rider and author of detective novels, stopped off at Dromedary and joined a group of men sitting round the station manager's fireside. During the ensuing chatter conversation lighted on Upfield's crime-writing hobby, and the idea of the 'perfect murder' was discussed.

One of those present was a young man from Perth, Snowy Rowles. He took a particular interest in Upfield's offer of a pound to anyone who could provide him with a plot to commit the perfect murder in the bush which he would use in his next book. But it was George Ritchie, the station manager, who won the prize after an entertaining debate. His suggestion was to shoot the victim in the back of the head and burn the corpse on a wood fire together with an animal carcass which would disguise the nature of any remains. The ashes would be sieved for any metal remnants such as buttons or boot eyelets, which would be destroyed in sulphuric acid. Any remaining bones and teeth would be crushed and scattered to the four winds.

This plot to commit murder and destroy the victim's body was used by Upfield in a novel called *The Sands of Windee* which was published in 1932. By that time the fictional plot had already been enacted and Snowy Rowles stood in the dock at Perth accused of murder. Since their fireside conversation at the camel station, Upfield had seen Rowles occasionally, and had recommended him to James Ryan, who was looking for a helper in his fencing business. Large stretches of Western Australia were fenced in order to keep bush animals out of the cultivated areas. Patrolling the fences and keeping them in an effective state of repair was thus an important job. When last heard of Rowles had joined Ryan's working party at a place called Mount Magnet, north-west of Dromedary.

Towards the end of 1930 Mount Magnet police received an inquiry from a woman in New Zealand who was trying to trace her former husband, whom she knew had been working in the area. It appeared that Leslie John Brown had last been seen in May of that year in the company of Snowy Rowles. Police questioned Rowles, who readily admitted working with Brown, but said they had parted company and his companion had travelled up to the north. The police were tenacious in their inquiries regarding the missing man, and followed up a report that some human remains had been found out in the bush. At a deserted encampment close to a fence location known as 183 Mile Gate the ashes of three separate fires were closely examined. Careful sifting revealed charred fragments of bone, a few shirt-buttons, a gold ring and some false teeth. Rowles was held for questioning, and twice attempted to commit suicide. When Upfield's book was published the similarity between his fictional crime and the discoveries made in the bush was so close that he was questioned by the police. He recalled that a year earlier Rowles had been present when the idea of a perfect murder had been discussed.

Snowy Rowles was tried for the murder of Brown, but the lack of a body made the evidence purely circumstantial. The gold ring and the dentures were unquestionably identified as belonging to Brown, and it was virtually certain that he had perished as a murder victim. Snowy Rowles, who had failed to carry out the perfect murder plan in all the details discussed, left just sufficient evidence to secure his conviction. He told the court, 'I have never been guilty of a crime that has never been committed.' He was nevertheless found guilty, and was hanged at Fremantle Prison.

In contrast to the open wastes of bushland, jungle terrain is a dense, impenetrable maze. Jungle is an inhospitable environment which poses its own kind of survival problems. Energy-sapping heat and the perils of poisonous wild life make it an unattractive place in which to be abandoned. But this was the fate meted out to a robbery victim in Ceylon (now Sri Lanka), for whom the experience proved fatal. On 27 January 1947 a car drew up outside the offices of the Turf Club in Colombo. It excited no particular attention, as it was assumed to be the hired car routinely arranged to call on Monday mornings to convey the weekend takings to the bank. A stranger was at the wheel rather than the usual driver, but his companion, a police-officer escort, appeared perfectly genuine.

The Turf Club cashier and his assistants loaded the car and the club van with locked satchels containing £40,000. The three men then got into the car, which drove away at speed and quickly lost the van which was supposed to follow. The car did not take the normal route to the bank, and when it slowed down in a quiet suburb two armed men leapt into the vehicle. The cashier and his assistants were roughed up and thrown into the street before the car roared away with the Turf Club takings. It soon became clear that the regular hired car driver, a reliable man named John Silva, had been abducted before the robbery. He had been hired the previous day to drive two men to Puttalam, some eighty miles from Colombo, and had not reported for work since.

Inquiries at Puttalam produced a witness who had seen a car and four men in the town on the day before the robbery. They had stopped at his café to eat, and he noticed that the driver was bought several drinks — in fact, his glass was never empty. Later the party drove off in a northerly direction towards the jungle. The witness identified the driver as John Silva from a photograph. The police at Puttalam received a postcard from an anonymous sender informing them that Silva had gone into hiding with the stolen money. Despite the poor chance of finding the man in the dense jungle and elephant country which characterized the area, the police decided to mount a search for the missing man. Their endeavours were rewarded by success, but only by chance when two of the search party became temporarily lost and stumbled into a track where they found John Silva. The driver was securely fastened with ropes to a tree with his arms drawn back and bound behind him. He hung limply in a crucifixion pose with a gas mask fastened over his head and face. The breathing tube of the mask was blocked and he had evidently suffocated in a most cruel manner. A doctor who viewed the body thought that suffocation would have occurred within thirty minutes, and that in any case left alone trussed up in the jungle the unfortunate man would have died in ten to twelve hours.

The search for the Turf Club robbers had now become a murder hunt. A breakthrough came quickly when one of the gang decided to confess in the hope of obtaining leniency. He made a full confession, naming eight men who were involved in the robbery. He related how Silva had been abducted and taken out into the jungle and left helpless with the gas mask covering his face. All eight men were arrested, and three were discharged at a preliminary hearing. Of the remainder, one was an ex-policeman and another an ex-soldier: both were men who would be familiar with gas mask drill. In their defence it was stated that the aim of sending the postcard to the police was to alert them to Silva's whereabouts so that he could be released. The jury was not impressed by this argument and found all five guilty — they were sentenced to death. Wijdedasa Perera, Warlis Munasinghe, Don James Senivaratne and R.L. Premalal were executed. The fifth man's sentence was commuted to ten years' imprisonment.

(340, 403, 429, 854, 873)

RIVERS AND LAKES

'The dark waters of ocean and river shall give up their coffined millions.'
Mr Justice Hargreaves (1872)

Water is regarded by many murderers as an ideal medium, both to cause death by drowning and also to dispose of the victim's body. Rivers and canals are frequently used in attempts to conceal the consequences of murder, but like the sea (see under BEACHES), they have the uncanny habit of eventually giving up their dead.

Frederick Nodder discovered this to his misfortune in 1937 when the body of his young victim turned up in the river Idle at a point some twenty miles distant from the place where he murdered her. Moreover, five months elapsed between the crime and the recovery of the victim. The sacked-up body of their employer was thrown into the Leeds and Liverpool Canal by George Ball and Samuel Elltoft in 1913. They went home to bed unaware that their victim's body had been swept downstream and become an obstruction to the effective operation of a set of lock gates.

River banks and towpaths are used by people going about their business or leisure pursuits. The lone walker or cyclist, or teenagers innocent of the threat of danger, all too easily become the prey of the prowling miscreant, for whom opportunity may incite murder. One such prowler was Alfred Whiteway, the so-called 'Towpath Murderer', who raped and murdered two young women cyclists on the Thames towpath near Teddington in 1953. He threw their ravished bodies into the river after stabbing them to death.

Another towpath prowler was John Joseph Power, a 36-year-old former policeman. He took pleasure by spying on courting couples who used the grassy banks of the Winson Canal at Birmingham. Posing as a plain-clothes police officer, he would bear down on these couples and upbraid them for trespassing on private property. His ploy was to let it be known that for a monetary consideration he would drop the charge. Covered in embarrassment, most 'offenders' paid what he asked. On 2 July 1927 Power accosted Olive Turner and her boy-friend, Charles Bromhead, accusing them of trespassing. The girl's inclination was to run away, but when Power forcibly restrained her Bromhead intervened, only to be easily knocked to the ground and temporarily disabled by the ex-police constable.

The following day Olive Turner's body was recovered from the canal. That she was dead was beyond dispute, but whether she had been pushed into the water or had jumped in of her own accord to avoid her assailant was unclear.

Power was charged with a variety of offences, including rape and murder. He denied the charges, and maintained that he had spent the evening drinking in a public house with a friend, after which he had gone straight home. Witnesses disproved his alibi to the satisfaction of the jury, who convicted him of murder. Power abused the judge, telling him he did not want any sympathy. The hangman might have been gentle in his task, but that was the only consideration which Power received on the scaffold.

An elaborate murder for profit plan was that devised by Alfred Lester and George Nichols, who selected watery graves for their victims. The Parramatta River Murders caused a sensation in Sydney, Australia, in 1872. Although there were only two victims, the brutal manner of their deaths and the callousness of the murderers created the feeling that an outbreak of mass murder had only just been averted.

On 12 March a man's body was found floating in the river near Ryde. Once it was pulled ashore it became apparent that a savage murder had been committed. The head had been fiercely battered, with at least one wound penetrating the brain, and the body was trussed up and weighted with a heavy stone tied to the ankles. Identification was easy, for the inside pocket of the man's jacket contained a naval discharge document in the name of John Bridger. Bridger, a 26-year-old wardroom steward on HMS *Rosario*, had been discharged from the Navy five days before he was found dead. A week later, on 19 March, a fisherman rowing near Five Dock Bay saw a body in the water about three hundred yards from shore. It was floating, feet uppermost, having been weighted with a stone tied by a cord around the neck. There were several wounds to the head, and the contents of the pockets appeared to be intact. This victim of violence was identified as William Percy Walker, a newly arrived immigrant. Within forty-eight hours of the body being discovered, Alfred Lester was arrested attempting to sell the dead man's watch, and his accomplice, George Robert Nichols, was already in police custody.

A letter found among Walker's personal effects demonstrated how he and Bridger had been lured to their deaths. The letter, signed by 'Arthur T. Norton', offered Walker the post

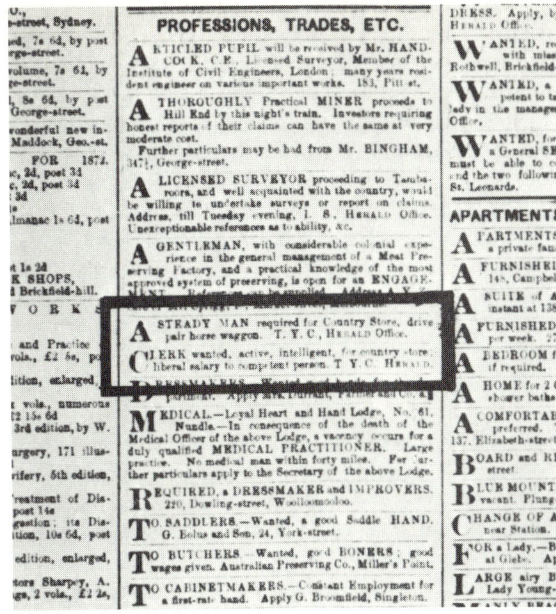

Advertising for murder victims

'of clerkship advertised in the *Herald* .... The salary will be thirty shillings a week and you will reside with us.' The signatory was George Nichols, who had placed two advertisements in the 4 March 1872 edition of the *Sydney Morning Herald,* to which he was said to have received two hundred replies. Nichols sported a distinctive beard (even for those days), and was readily identifiable by a newspaper office clerk and also by a boatman who saw him in company with John Bridger.

Following the accumulation of considerable circumstantial evidence, Nichols and Lester were tried for murder at Sydney's Central Criminal Court. Nichols, aged thirty, and Lester, aged twenty, both had criminal records, and had only recently been released from prison after serving sentences for acting under false pretences. Nichols used several aliases, and spoke a number of languages fluently. His partner had fled from England after he had embezzled money from his employer. Both men had been seen by several witnesses in the company of the second of the victims, whom they had escorted to Blow's Hotel where his trunk was left for safe-keeping. The two men alone were seen on their return from a night-time trip up the Parramatta river when Nichols said they had 'killed several fish'.

The jury was out for thirty minutes, and when it returned the prisoners were found guilty. Four policemen were required to keep Nichols and Lester upright in the dock when sentence was passed. Mr Justice Hargreaves referred to the time 'when the dark waters of ocean and river shall give up their coffined millions to the voice of God', and condemned the two accused to death. Sentences were carried out at Darlinghurst Gaol on 18 June 1872.

Police map showing where the bodies were found in the Parramatta River

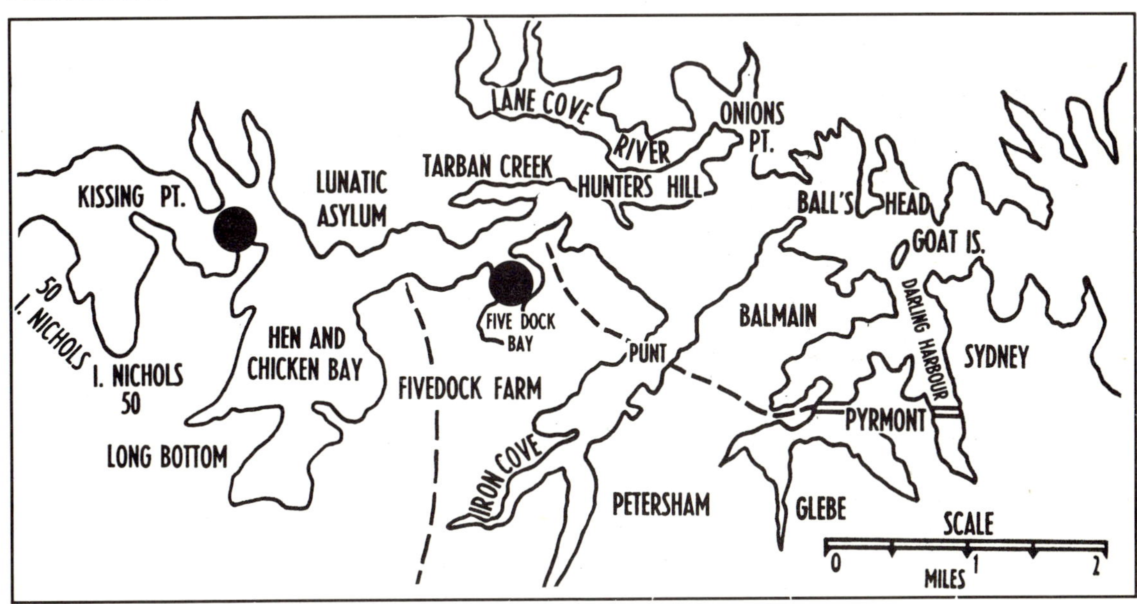

Both men made confessions after they had been convicted. Their scheme was to profit by murder, as borne out by the haste with which they retrieved Walker's belongings from Blow's Hotel and attempted to sell his watch. Advertising in the newspapers for potential victims proved to be only too easy, and it was this revelation perhaps as much as the violence of the crimes which sent shivers down the spines of Sydney's population. Indeed, had the villains been more careful with their elected method of killing, and a little more circumspect in their comings and goings, they might well have gone on to mass murder.

The young man who signed the register at an Adirondack hotel as 'Charles George and wife' asked the proprietor about the local scenery. He particularly wanted to know if 'there were any lakes around'. On 11 July 1906 the couple arrived at Big Moose Lake and made inquiries about the timetable of the lake steamer. The timings did not appear to be convenient, so the man hired a rowing-boat. The boat-hirer wore a straw boater, and carried a heavy suitcase with a tennis racket strapped to the side.

The boat was not returned to the landing stage by nightfall, and the following day a girl's body was washed up on the shore. The men who carried the body ashore noticed that the girl had been badly injured about the face. The missing rowing-boat was found later, floating upside down in the water, and near-by was a man's straw boater.

The immediate reaction was that the resort town had suffered the first fatal boating accident of the season, and a search was made to find the girl's companion, who was also presumed to have drowned. A different construction was put on the incident when the girl's body was medically examined. Twenty-year-old Grace Brown was five months pregnant, and the injuries she had received to her face were not of a type likely to have been caused in a drowning accident. Moreover, a search of Big Moose Lake had failed to locate the girl's companion. Inquiries revealed that Grace Brown's boy-friend was Chester Gillette, who was employed by his uncle as superintendent of the wealthy family's skirt factory at Cortland, New York. Grace Brown was a worker at the factory, and her friends were well acquainted with her love for the boss's nephew.

News of the tragic drowning at Big Moose drew in many reports from hoteliers in the Adirondack lake resorts. Many of them recalled a young couple who stayed for a brief period — the man appeared surly, and the girl frightened. A common thread was that the couple registered as man and wife under the name of Carl Graham or Charles George. Could this 'C.G.' be Chester Gillette? wondered the police. Police officers called at Gillette's lodgings in Cortland, where they found a bundle of love letters from Grace Brown. These letters painted a poignant scene, and provided a motive for murder. The desperate girl was trying to hide her pregnancy from her parents. 'Please come and take me away some place,' she begged Gillette, adding, 'I am so frightened.' On 21 June she wrote miserably, 'I hope I can die. Then you can do just as you like', and on 6 July, a few days before she disappeared beneath the waters of Big Moose Lake, she wrote, 'I wish I could die. You will never know what you made me suffer.'

Believing that Chester Gillette had granted her wish, the police set out to find him. He was located at Arrowhead on Fourth Lake and arrested on a charge of murder. He told detectives that he had gone on to the lake in a boat with Grace Brown, and that while he was leaning over the side to pluck a water lily for her the boat had overturned, pitching them both into the lake. He had tried to save Grace, but she drowned before he could help her.

Gillette, twenty-three, was tried for murder in November 1906, and as often proves the case, public sympathy switched from the victim to the accused. His family, avoiding unwelcome publicity, shunned him, but their desertion was compensated in some small measure by the hundreds of letters he received from women who promised him their undying love. It was reported that the two cells which he had been allocated were decorated with pictures of women cut from the fashionable magazines of the day.

Medical evidence at the trial clearly showed that Grace Brown had been beaten unconscious, probably with Gillette's tennis racket, before being thrown into the lake to drown. Several strands of the girl's hair had been caught in one of the oarlocks, and the name band had been wrenched from the straw boater left as part of the decoy evidence. In his testimony at the trial Gillette said that he and Grace had discussed their circumstances, and she said she would end it all by throwing herself into the lake, which she did despite his efforts to prevent it. The jury found Gillette guilty of first-degree murder, and he was sentenced to death in the electric chair. Various appeals were heard during the next year, but finally, in January 1908, the New York State Court of Appeals upheld the trial verdict and he was executed in March.

Theodore Dreiser, the great American novelist, based his book *An American Tragedy* on the Charles Gillette story. The central character of the novel is pictured as a victim of a social background which provided him with a pampered childhood and little sense of responsibility. The young man who dragged a pregnant girl from place to place until he found a way of eliminating his burden showed complete indifference when he first learned that her body had been found.

Poisoning, assault and drowning in a lake was the fate of ten-year-old Leona O'Loughlin. Leona was the daughter of Leo O'Loughlin, a police detective, who lived at 2320 Trement Street, Denver, with his second wife, Pearl. Early in the morning of 15 October 1930 Pearl asked her husband, who had just come off night duty, if he had seen Leona, as it appeared she had left the house before breakfast. He had not seen the girl, and thought it out of character that she would leave for school without saying goodbye.

After a round of anxious telephone calls to friends and neighbours and finally to Leona's school he reported her officially missing. A neighbour stated that she had heard a muffled cry during the night, and there were numerous stories from people who claimed to have seen the missing child with strange men. Bearing in mind Leo O'Loughlin's service with Denver Police Department, detectives did not rule out a grudge abduction of his child. The last time Leona was seen alive was at about midnight when her stepmother looked into her bedroom and saw her sleeping. Her father was on duty at the time.

As the inquiry got under way both Leo and Pearl O'Loughlin were taken ill and were unable to answer questions. Then on 18 October a body was sighted floating in Berkeley Park Lake. The fully clothed body of

Leona O'Loughlin was brought ashore, and abrasions on her head suggested she had been assaulted. The autopsy showed that she had died from drowning, and an analysis of the stomach contents showed the presence of powdered glass. Hardly had this piece of information been announced before it was revealed that Leo O'Loughlin, now recovering in hospital, had been subjected to a stomach pump, and that ground glass had been found.*

Careful examination of the O'Loughlins' home turned up a blood-stained tyre lever in the car and traces of powdered glass in the kitchen sink and on the kitchen floor. Furthermore, the basement washing-machine contained vestiges of fine sand similar to that on the sandy shore of Berkeley Park Lake. Suspicion immediately focused on Pearl O'Loughlin, who maintained a convincing attitude of innocence in respect of any crime against her stepdaughter. Then came a further sensation in the form of a statement made by the dead girl's grandfather, Dennis O'Loughlin. He claimed that after a visit to his home by Leo and Pearl and young Leona he found ground glass in his sugar bowl. It was also alleged that pet animals belonging to a relative had died after eating food scraps from the O'Loughlin home. Pearl O'Loughlin treated all these revelations with smiling disbelief.

The breakthrough in their inquiries which the police hoped for came when one of Pearl's acquaintances said she had lied in her statement. It seemed that Pearl had asked her to help establish an alibi for the night of 14 October, and this she foolishly agreed to do. Pearl O'Loughlin was now charged with murder, and she stood trial in November 1930. The prosecution argued its case with all the force of some commanding circumstantial evidence which included the numerous ground-glass incidents and the broken alibi. It was alleged that Pearl had told her police interrogators, 'You can't hang me if I don't confess. You don't think I've been a detective's wife for two years for nothing?' She did not testify on her own behalf and her defence lawyer made much of prejudice directed at a stepmother. Nevertheless, the jury found her guilty of first-degree murder and she was

---

*Ordinary ground glass is ineffective as a poison, as Edith Thompson discovered in 1922 when she was alleged to have repeatedly used it on her husband.

sentenced to life imprisonment. Pearl continued to maintain her innocence and there was considerable public disquiet about the verdict.

(1, 136, 186, 199, 221, 252, 269, 286, 473, 492, 601, 702, 788, 831, 1039, MWW)

SHOPS AND OFFICES

'One of these days I'm going to rob a Hi-Fi shop ...'

Dale Pierre (1974)

The murder of shopkeepers, usually in the course of theft or as the result of a disputed purchase, is common in the criminal records of most countries. The shopkeeper maintains both goods and a ready supply of cash; he is also easily put at a disadvantage. The cunning would-be robber easily presents himself in the guise of potential purchaser, and while the small shop has its regular customers, the appearance of a stranger at the counter is not a matter to cause excitement. Moreover, in the small shop the proprietor's attention is readily diverted, or his back turned, by a request for an item on a high or distant shelf. This was the ploy used by John Williams, who has been turned into something of the archetypal murderer by the writings of Thomas de Quincey.

In the postscript to his essay 'On Murder as a Fine Art' de Quincey gave a masterful account of the murders committed in London by John Williams in 1811. Graphically described as having hair 'something between orange and a lemon colour' and possessing a ghostly pallor as if his veins were filled with 'a green sap that welled from no human heart', Williams conjures up a terrible apparition.

Perhaps it was the feelings of revenge which he harboured that had curdled his blood. Having been bested by his friend Timothy Marr for the affection of one Cecilia, Williams decided to destroy the newly wedded couple and their young baby. On the night of 7 December 1811 he lurked in the shadows of Ratcliff Highway, where at Number 29 Marr ran a small hosiery shop. Many of the shops were still open at midnight, their owners completing the labours of a sixteen-hour day. Marr, no exception to the general rule, was putting up his shutters when Williams stealthily glided past him and, unnoticed, entered the shop.

When Marr returned and closed the door behind him Williams appeared from the shadows and asked to buy a pair of socks. The particular item requested, he knew from earlier reconnaissance, was located on a low shelf behind the counter. As soon as Marr turned and bent down Williams delivered a crushing blow to the back of his head with a mallet. He then cut his victim's throat and inflicted the same brutal injuries on Mrs Marr and her child; he did not even spare the thirteen-year-old apprentice who lived with the Marrs. Leaving four dead behind him, Williams escaped into the night through a rear door.

Twelve days later Williams struck again, this time annihilating three members of the Williamson household, who ran a tavern at 81 New Gravel Lane. He escaped with a large sum of money, but was quickly apprehended. The man who bore a heavy grudge against his fellow human beings committed suicide in prison. Williams had confided to a room-mate, 'I am unhappy, and can't remain easy,' adding 'the gallows will get hold of me soon.' His fate was to receive the treatment routinely accorded to suicides at that time. His body was paraded through the streets of the East End on a cart and he was buried in quicklime at the point where Cannon Street crossed New Road — a stake was driven through his heart to still his vampire-like soul.

In another time and in another place, an American shop echoed Williams's violence. All was quiet in the Hi-Fi shop at 2323 Washington Boulevard, Ogden, Utah, when sixteen-year-old Courtney Naisbitt walked in at around closing time on 22 April 1974. He was looking for his friends, Stan Walker and Michelle Ansley, who were running the shop while the proprietor was away for the day. Naisbitt guessed that his friends were in the basement, and he quickly joined them when he was unceremoniously pushed downstairs by three intruders whom he had disturbed in the course of robbery.

Naisbitt was tied up and forced to lie down next to the two shop assistants who had been similarly treated. Two other innocent parties were to interrupt the progress of the Hi-Fi shop robbery. First, Carol Naisbitt, who arrived looking for Courtney (who was late from school) and then Orren Walker calling for his son. Soon there were five victims tied up on the basement floor and at the mercy of the robbers.

The intruders seized wallets, purses, jewellery and rings from their captives and then embarked on a bout of unbelievably savage violence. Taking a bottle from a brown paper bag, one of the assailants declared, 'It's a mixture of Vodka and a German drug. We're going to have a little cocktail party.' He poured out a cupful of thick blue liquid which he forced down the throat of one of the helpless victim. As the liquid burned his mouth and throat the captive gagged and vomited. This operation was repeated on the remaining victims in the basement, and with the same horrible results. They had been forced to drink liquid Drano, a caustic compound used to unblock drains. The label on the bottle read, 'Tough on Clogs, Won't hurt Pipes!'

Next the assailants systematically shot each of their bound captives in the back of the head, leaving nineteen-year-old Michelle Ansley until last. She was first raped, then dispatched with a bullet in the head. Three lay dead in the basement of the shop. Courtney Naisbitt was alive but badly wounded in the head, and Orren Walker — mercifully only superficially wounded — was subjected to two further barbaric acts. An attempt was made to strangle him with a piece of cord, and a ballpoint pen was forced through his ear until it protruded into his throat.

The discovery of the carnage in the Hi-Fi shop shocked the citizens of Ogden, whose doctors fought to save the life of Courtney Naisbitt. Both he and Orren Walker survived their ordeal. From descriptions given by Walker, the police quickly formed a view as to one of the men they were looking for. Officers recalled a murder the previous year at the near-by USAF base at Hill Field when they had interviewed an airman named Dale Pierre. No charges had been brought home on that occasion, but Pierre's demeanour coincided remarkably with that of one of the Hi-Fi shop killers.

The police also received help from an informant, who said he had overheard the killers talking about a proposed crime and of their intention not to leave any witnesses. One of the men was Dale Pierre, who had remarked, 'One of these days I'm going to rob a Hi-Fi shop and if anybody gets in my way I'm going to kill 'em.' Children searching for returnable bottles at a garbage dump near the air base found a wallet and a purse belonging to two of the Hi-Fi shop victims. The garbage dump was on ground opposite barracks No.351 which accommodated Dale Pierre. A search of Pierre's quarters produced a rental agreement which he had signed the day before the murders for a garage store situated a few blocks away from the Hi-Fi shop. Detectives broke into the locked store and found it stacked high with $24,000 worth of stolen Hi-Fi and stereo equipment. Standing incongruously among the gleaming electronic units was a half-empty bottle of Drano. Dale Pierre, William Andrews and Keith Robert, all airmen at Hill Field Base, were arrested and charged with first-degree murder.

Their trial was held at Farmington, Utah, and lasted a month. Pierre and Andrews were found guilty on all counts and sentenced to death. Roberts was acquitted of the murder charges but convicted of aggravated robbery. An execution date was set on five different occasions, but sentence was not carried out while appeal procedures were in hand. Pierre and Andrews remain under maximum security at Utah State Prison, where Dale Pierre, the frustrated executive, founded a company called Poboi Enterprises of which he is the president and sole member.

It is an unfortunate aspect of business life that proprietors sometimes have creditors who press their claims hard. When the pressure becomes too great, elimination of the threat is a tempting proposition. But when murder springs to mind there is always the problem of disposing of the body.

Professor John Webster discovered the magnitude of this task when he murdered Dr Parkman, who was hounding him for repayment of a loan. He decided to burn his victim's corpse, and although sufficient evidence remained to secure his eventual conviction, he made a better job of it than did James Cook. Like the professor, Cook was in debt and suffered the embarrassment of being pressed for repayment. He was a 21-year-old bookbinder from Leicester who achieved the dubious distinction of being the last man in England to be gibbeted. Gibbeting was provided for by the 1752 Act For the Better Preventing the Horrid Crimes of Murder, and could be ordered by a judge as a form of further punishment after death.

The crime which resulted in James Cook's

body being hung in chains was that of murder and dismemberment. On 30 May 1832 the bookbinder received a visitor at his shop in Wellington Street, Leicester. John Paas, a London tool-cutter and engraver, had called to collect a sum of money owed to him by Cook. The bookbinder took exception to this and attacked his creditor, bludgeoning him to death.

Faced with disposing of his victim's body, Cook decided on dismemberment and destruction of the pieces by burning them in the shop's grate. The task of cleaning up the mess and consuming the human flesh and bone by fire took many hours' labour. At last the exhausted murderer consigned the final portion of his victim to the flames and went home to his lodgings to recover.

The following morning neighbouring shopkeepers were attracted by the smoke belching from the unoccupied bookbindery and thought the chimney was on fire. Looking through the window, they saw the grate containing a roaring fire, and what appeared to be a large piece of meat cooking on it. Cook was fetched to his shop, and he explained that he was burning some bad dog-meat.

His explanation did not satisfy some suspicious minds, and the curious anatomy of the charred flesh was examined by three surgeons. They declared it to be the pelvic area of a human body. By this time Cook had absconded by coach to Liverpool. He was captured while being rowed out to a ship bound for America.

James Cook confessed to his crime, and the result of his trial was a foregone conclusion. Sentence of death was carried out on 10 August 1832 before a crowd of 30,000 people. Afterwards his body was hung in an iron gibbet high above the junction of Saffron Lane and Aylestone Road. Such was the commotion caused by the thousands of people who went to view the body that after three days Cook's mortal remains were taken down and the practice of gibbeting was stopped.

The idea of using popular medicine available from thousands of drugstores and supermarkets as a vehicle for mass murder occurred to an unidentified poisoner in Chicago. Between 29 September and 10 October 1982 seven people died in the Chicago area after taking Tylenol painkiller capsules which had been doctored with cyanide. This form of self-service murder created a nationwide alert

COOK, THE MURDERER,

OR THE

LEICESTER TRAGEDY:

Being a Full and Faithful Account of the

HORRIBLE ASSASSINATION

OF

MR. JOHN PAAS, OF LONDON,

On the 30th of May, 1832,

PERPETRATED BY

JAMES COOK, OF LEICESTER;

WITH

An authentic detail of the cruel means adopted by the murderer to accomplish the

BLOODY DEED,

And of the Inhuman Method which he used to dispose of the

BODY OF HIS MURDERED VICTIM;

TO WHICH IS ADDED,

THE SINGULAR MANNER

In which the Melancholy Fate of the Deceased Gentleman was discovered;

THE FLIGHT OF THE CULPRIT, HIS SUBSEQUENT APPREHENSION AT LIVERPOOL, AND

His Confession of the Barbarous Fact,

WITH HIS

TRIAL, CONVICTION, SENTENCE, AND EXECUTION.

WRITTEN FROM THE MOST ACCURATE INFORMATION,

BY C. J. WILLIAMS.

DERBY:

PUBLISHED BY THOMAS RICHARDSON;

SIMPKIN, MARSHALL, AND CO., LONDON.

Contemporary account of the murder committed in Leicester by James Cook

in America, and the Governor of Illinois spoke of the 'madman out there' whom it was supposed was enjoying the mayhem he had created.

The manufacturers of the best-selling capsules took immediate action at an estimated cost of $100 million by withdrawing millions of bottles from shop and pharmacy shelves throughout the USA and elsewhere. Eight million individual capsules were tested, but only seventy-five, from one manufactured batch, proved to be laced with cyanide. The two halves of the capsules had been pulled apart so that the poison could be introduced. Then the doctored capsules were reassembled and the packaging restored. These deadly bottles were traced to a handful of retail shops in the Chicago area.

A team of a hundred police officers dealt with over two thousand inquiries. Various motives were suggested, including industrial sabotage, stock-market manipulation and a grudge background. Two dozen suspects were questioned and later released. One of these was an unemployed Chicago man who was alleged to have tried to extort one million dollars from the manufacturers of Tylenol against the threat that he would kill more people. He was charged with extortion, but there was no evidence to link him with the doctored bottles of capsules.

If the motive was to harm the manufacturers it failed, because by taking prompt and responsible action they quickly regained public confidence and restored their sales. The deaths forced the introduction of new tamper-resistant packaging for medicines, the need for which was underlined by several 'copycat' incidents. Acid-laced mouthwash and eye-drops and strychnine-tainted aspirin appeared in shops in different shops in different parts of the USA. Any direct connection with the deaths in Chicago was discounted.*

Lethal tampering with medicine available to the general public over the shop counter, like murder by post, is a form of dealing out death by proxy. Those who died by taking cyanide-laced capsules became murder victims purely by chance. As a relative of one of the deceased remarked, 'The killer is probably sitting somewhere watching TV and laughing about this.'

The idea of poisoning consumer products available to the general public through supermarket chains for the purpose of extortion was taken up by Japanese gangsters in October 1984. A group calling itself 'The Man With 21 Faces' put boxes of cyanide-laced sweets on to supermarket shelves in Tokyo. The confectionery company whose products had been tampered with was sent a note demanding 100 million yen (£300,000).

The boxes of doctored sweets had been labelled 'Danger — eat this and you die — Poison', thus giving a warning which the Tylenol killer had failed to do. The gang nevertheless threatened to distribute another thirty boxes of poisoned sweets unless their deadline for payment of the extortion money was met. They taunted the police, telling them 'It is going to be like treasure-hunting.'

After the confectionery company announced that it would not 'bow down to crime', extra police were drafted into the city to patrol the supermarkets, and mothers forbade their children to buy sweets with their pocket-money. A cat and mouse game ensued with 'The Man With 21 Faces' — a villainous character taken from a 1930s Japanese novel — whose activities tied up huge police resources and introduced the word 'sweetmailing' into the language.

In his *Casebook of Crime* Alan Brock wrote, 'With the exception of the women of the street, no class of individuals has provided more victims for unsolved murder mysteries than the small shop-keeper.' This is borne out by a string of English murders-over-the-counter, some of which have been solved but others remain mysteries. The killers of Alfred Oliver, a Reading tobacconist, in June 1929 and of Margery Wren, who ran a confectionery shop in Ramsgate, in September 1930, were never found. George Armstrong perished in his Manchester hosiery shop in May 1929, and elderly Frederick Gosling was asphyxiated in his corner shop at Chertsey in January 1951; the murderers in both cases were brought to justice.

A shop mystery and supposed murder in 1870 had as its victim a man with an unusual name — Urban Napoleon Stanger. He came to England with his wife from Germany and set up a bakery at 136 Lever Street in Whitechapel, London. The Stangers' business prospered with its mainly Jewish customers and the proprietor was regarded as industrious and uncomplaining, bearing in mind the manner in which his wife behaved. Elizabeth Stanger, an unprepossessing woman who liked to adorn herself with cheap jewellery and garish clothes, was the subject of considerable gossip, and it was rumoured that she browbeat her husband.

The Stangers kept a maid, an errand boy and an apprentice, Christian Zentler. A friend of Stanger's and a fellow-countryman, one Franz Felix Stumm, lived nearby and often assisted in the bakery. Stumm was married but it was no secret that he was on especially good terms with Mrs Stanger.

When the bakery opened for business on the

---

*In February 1986, a woman died near New York City after taking two pain-killing capsules which had been doctored with cyanide. A second bottle of poisoned capsules was found on the shelves of a supermarket in Bronxville.

morning of 13 November 1881 Stanger did not put in an appearance. In answer to customers' inquiries, Mrs Stanger said that her husband had been called to Germany on urgent business. Young Zentler reported that at about midnight on the previous day on his way home he had seen his employer standing outside the shop with three other men, one of whom was Stumm.

Mrs Stanger seemed unconcerned that her spouse was missing, and Stumm appeared daily to help keep the bakery functioning. After a couple of weeks he took up permanent residence, and was seen one Sunday afternoon walking arm-in-arm with Mrs Stanger. The baker's wife seemed to flaunt the relationship, and it was not long before the name 'U.N. Stanger' disappeared from the shop-front, to be replaced with that of 'F. F. Stumm'.

At this point what had been disapproving gossip of a fairly quiet kind now erupted into something more voluble. It was rumoured that Stanger had been murdered and his corpse

Urban Napoleon Stanger disappeared from his East End shop: was he murdered?

converted into meat pies prepared by his wife. Crowds formed outside the shop, pointedly directing their gossip at the occupants. The police moved the spectators on but took no other action.

In April 1882 a notice published by a private inquiry agent offered fifty pounds reward for information leading to the whereabouts of Urban Napoleon Stanger, who was described as having 'mysteriously disappeared'. In October Stumm and Mrs Stanger were arrested on a charge of conspiring to defraud, and Stumm was charged with forging a cheque. These charges were brought by the executors of Stanger's will, who believed that the baker's property was being fraudulently handled.

When it became known that Stanger left everything to his wife on condition that she did not remarry, suspicion hardened still further. The couple were sent for trial, when Mrs Stanger did her best to blacken her husband's character. She maintained that after a quarrel

he left the house with nothing more than the clothes he stood up in and she had not seen him since. She alleged that Stumm had lent money to her husband, and described him as a good friend. Following her evidence, Mrs Stanger was hissed from the court. Stumm was found guilty of what the judge called 'a very wicked forgery' and was sentenced to ten years' penal servitude.

The case against Mrs Stanger was dropped, and Stumm — who proved to be a tiresome prisoner — served his full sentence. When he was released he took his wife and Mrs Stanger to Germany. Their former neighbours in Whitechapel strongly believed that Mrs Stanger had murdered her husband, and that Stumm had helped her dispose of the body.

Offices and other places of work form natural extensions to the environment for domestic violence. The victim can be pursued to a known location at times when it is likely he will be present. At his place of work the victim is also something of a sitting target, in that he will want to hush up any quarrel or incident in order not to be embarrassed in front of his colleagues.

Gaston Calmette, Editor of *Le Figaro*, was shot dead at this desk

Henriette Caillaux, wife of the French Finance Minister, was distressed to find the newspaper *Le Figaro* in the issue of 16 March 1914 had published a politically damaging letter written by her husband to his former wife. Her husband, an unpopular Minister on account of his pacifist leanings, had attracted considerable criticism from *Le Figaro,* in whose pages he had been regularly lampooned. There was no love lost between Caillaux and the paper's chief columnist, Gaston Calmette, whom he had exposed by unearthing unsavoury details of his background.

The situation was well primed to explode, and Madame Caillaux bought a gun, rushed round to the newspaper office and killed Calmette with five shots. During a trial conducted in Paris at the height of war fervour the proceedings were distinguished by prejudice, scandal and claims of unpatriotic behaviour. Mme Caillaux was eventually acquitted of the charge of murder when it was shown that the dead editor had been implicated in anti-French propaganda.

Horace George Rayner took similarly decisive action to settle his grievance. On 24 January 1907 he walked into the office of William Whiteley, the London department-store owner, and fired two shots into his head at point-blank range. The 27-year-old Rayner claimed that Whiteley was his father but refused to accept his son. The public demonstrated considerable sympathy for Rayner, inasmuch as his supposed father, George Rayner, repudiated paternity, alleging that his mistress Emily Turner had incorrectly registered the birth. Emily's sister, Louisa, let it be known that she had been Whiteley's mistress for years, and together with George Rayner and her sister Emily, the two had made a foursome for frequent weekends to Brighton. These liaisons had produced three illegitimate children, two for Emily by Rayner and one for Louisa by Whiteley.

Although Horace Rayner was sentenced to death for committing murder, he was reprieved after a public petition of 200,000 signatures was put before the Home Secretary. He was released from prison in 1919 after serving twelve years.

The routine environment of a busy office is the ideal place to commit murder if the object is to have the act witnessed. This appeared to be the intention of Frederick Cox when, on 21 February 1924, he entered the Cape of Good Hope Savings Bank Building in Cape Town with his cousin Annie Cox. Eighteen-year-old Annie worked for a firm of accountants whose offices were in the Savings Bank Building. On that morning she commuted into the city from her parents' home in Wynberg and met her cousin, Frederick Cox, at the railway station. They walked to the building in St George's Street and were seen entering the second-floor office by a painter working in the corridor.

Shortly after 9.00 a.m. screams were heard and shouts of 'Murder! Murder!' brought people running to the office. There several eye-witnesses saw Annie Cox sink to the floor under a flurry of stab wounds inflicted by her cousin. Cox, smothered in blood, made no attempt to escape, and said that if he had had the chance he would have killed himself too. The girl died as the result of the attack, in which she sustained twenty knife-wounds, and Cox was charged with her murder.

Frederick Cox had a wife whom he left behind in England when he travelled to South Africa in 1922. He stayed with an uncle at Wynberg, and quickly fell for his teenage cousin. Their mutual attraction and demonstrations of affection were a source of embarrassment to Annie's father, who eventually asked Cox to find lodgings elsewhere. The couple's *grande passion* was also manifested in the office at lunch-times, frequently in the presence of Annie's colleagues.

After Frederick moved they wrote letters to each other every day. Six hundred letters from Annie were found in Cox's room, and three hundred from him turned up in filing cabinets at the office where the dead girl had worked. This correspondence was mostly taken up with expressions of endearment, but there were occasional hints of argument laced with chastisement and apology. A particularly brutal letter from Cox told Annie that she was 'merely a plaything' and added a catalogue of his love affairs with other women. The reason he later gave for writing this letter was that he wanted to test her love for him.

The affair came to a crisis following the breakdown of a business deal. In 1923 Cox, on the pretence of inheriting some money from England, took on a business partner. When the money did not materialize Cox's partner demanded an explanation, and a meeting was arranged at a Cape Town bank on 21 February

1924 to sort out the problems. Cox failed to keep the appointment, and instead murdered his cousin. He alleged that he and Annie had made a pact such that they agreed to die together if things went against them. This was the plan which Cox put into effect, except that he spared himself.

He was tried for murder in May 1924, and his defence wanted to plead insanity. He refused to consider any move that would avoid the death sentence, and the prosecution had no difficulty in proving the case against him. After all, he had committed murder in front of several witnesses and openly confessed his guilt. Equally, the jury had no difficulty in finding him guilty, and in a written statement read out to the court Cox made it clear that his motive was one of carrying out the solemn pact which he had made with Annie. On 1 July 1924 the hangman sealed the pact for him.

An office with a difference was that used by the Sailors' Union in Aberdeen, Washington State. It was situated in a building constructed on piles over the Wishkah river. The official in charge was Billy Gohl, and his office was the first place that sailors returning to the port made for as soon as they landed. They collected their mail and left valuables and sea pay for safe-keeping, in addition to catching up on all the news and gossip.

In the early 1900s Aberdeen began to gain a reputation as the port to which sailors called and then went missing. Between 1909 and 1912 over forty bodies were recovered from the Wishkah river, but all had been stripped of articles which could identify them. However, a 'floater' eventually turned up who was identified by an engraved pocket watch as a missing German seaman. The trail led back to the Seamen's Union building and to the office used by Billy Gohl, which was equipped with a trap-door in the floor giving way to the fast-flowing river beneath. This Sweeney Todd of the Union Office shot his seamen visitors, robbed them and removed all identification before tipping them through the trap-door into a watery grave. Gohl was convicted of two murders, although the real tally was thought to be much greater. He escaped the death penalty (which at that time was suspended in Washington State) and he died in 1928 in prison.

The Consorcio Italiano building situated in the commercial heart of Valparaiso in Chile contained the offices of many small businesses and a number of professional men such as accountants and lawyers. When the night watchman came on duty on 7 May 1962 he set out on his usual security check, making sure that all the offices were unoccupied and their doors locked.

As soon as he stepped out of the lift on the fourth floor he noticed that the light was on in one of the offices, and the door leading in to it was open. He entered the office — which was used by a well-known lawyer — and saw an elderly man clad only in his shirt and wearing shoes and socks lying sprawled on the floor. He had been battered about the head, and was barely conscious. Near the body was a blood-stained piece of brown paper wrapped around a stone which weighed five pounds.

The victim of the assault was Enrique Mercier, a respected lawyer, who died soon after he was found injured. His clothes were scattered about the office, although there did not appear to have been a struggle. The office safe was open and the dead man's wallet was missing from his jacket. As befitted a prominent citizen, Mercier's funeral at Valparaiso Cathedral was conducted by the Archbishop. But once the ceremony was over questions were asked which probed at less than admirable facets of the dead man's character.

The duty lift man in the Consorcio Italiano building on 7 May said he had taken Mercier up to the fourth floor at about 6.45 p.m. The lawyer was accompanied by a young man in shabby clothes. It appeared that Mercier had been in the habit of taking male prostitutes up to his office in the evenings and paying them for sexual favours. There had been complaints about his choice of companions, and considerable gossip about his activities.

The lift operator provided a detailed description of the young man seen with Mercier, and the police issued an Identikit picture. The theory was that the gay lawyer had been the victim of a homosexual murder motivated by jealousy. The hunt for the murderer had a break-through with a forged cheque which had originated from Mercier's stolen cheque book. This was presented for payment at a bank, which immediately alerted the police. The bearer of the cheque said he had been given it by a friend, seventeen-year-old Manuel Garcés.

Garcés was arrested at his lodgings, where Mercier's wallet and cheque book were found among his possessions. He immediately confessed, saying that he realized the lawyer was stringing him along with promises about money and a job. He had picked up a large stone on the sea-shore at San Mateo which he intended to use as a weapon. When he reached Mercier's office for their pre-arranged meeting he hit the lawyer, who had partially undressed in expectation of performing sex. 'I took the stone in both hands', said Garcés, 'and hit him twice with it on the back of the head.'

Despite the confession, there were those who believed that Garcés had been made a scapegoat for a group of homosexuals who had arranged a revenge killing. It was odd that Garcés had made no attempt to benefit from the money stolen from the victim, and he had made no effort to hide the incriminating evidence. Perhaps the suggestion that he had been made a scapegoat reached Garcés in prison, for on 30 July he made a new statement. He now claimed that he was covering up for others, and that he was not guilty of murder. But on 4 August he retracted this statement and reverted to his original confession, in which he accepted responsibility for the murder and robbery.

A professor at the University of Chile at the time of the murder, Christopher Jackson, visited Garcés while he was awaiting trial. The results of his interviews were published in a book called *Manuel* which set out a sympathetic portrayal of a boy born in the slums who gradually became institutionalized after a life of delinquency. Garcés admitted committing homosexual acts, at which he was inexperienced and which he said disgusted him. Lured to the prospect of better things through male prostitution, he suffered one indignity too many and decided to retaliate. 'I really don't know why I went there,' he said in reference to his appearance at Mercier's office, 'I don't know why I did it.' A Chilean court sentenced him to ten years' imprisonment for murder and another five years for robbery.

(27, 60, 120, 229, 434, 485, 526, 535, 579, 772, 919, 1002)

STREETS

'A Night of Killing in S F: — 4 Slain on City Streets'

San Francisco Examiner (1974)

The well-lit, busy thoroughfares of large towns and cities can be just as menacing places of murder as alleyways which cloak killing with darkness and privacy. The streets and byways of the world's great political centres have been the traditional territories of the assassin. President John F. Kennedy succumbed to the marksman's bullet in Elm Street, Dallas, in 1963 while President Ronald Reagan survived an attempt on his life in the street outside the Washington Hilton Hotel in 1981. In other parts of the world kings and presidents, archdukes and ministers have all been laid low by assassins projecting their bombs and bullets from the kerbside — some with catastrophic results for mankind, such as the assassination of Franz Ferdinand, heir to the Austrian throne, at Sarajevo in 1914.

Killing in the streets has also been a hallmark of gangland violence. Chicago gangster-style elimination of rivals by gunning them down from moving cars has been depicted more or less accurately in countless films. Al Capone is said to have been responsible for the deaths of some fifteen hundred opponents in Chicago during the Prohibition era.

Victims of assassination and gangland violence are in a special category, in as much as they are usually aware of their habitual danger. But the advent of so-called stranger-to-stranger murders in the 1970s meant that the victims were murdered simply because they were people in the wrong place at the wrong time. David Berkowitz, for example, New York City's 'Son of Sam' murderer, shot dead six persons selected at random on the streets of the metropolis in 1976–7.

Berkowitz's victims had no inkling that they were in mortal danger — they were simply getting on with their lives when confronted by the demented murderer, urged on (so he claimed) by voices in his head. Voices of another kind had stimulated an earlier series of stranger-to-stranger murders in San Francisco in 1973–4, known as the Zebra killings. Fifteen persons were shot dead and eight others wounded during a six-month period of violence. The police gave the episode the codename 'Zebra' because all the victims were White and the killers Black.

Completely unsuspecting, the victims were shot in the back and usually at close range as they walked the streets going about their ordinary affairs. The killers claimed five victims on 28 January 1974 — which became known as the 'Night of the Five' — and caused a public outcry in San Francisco. The victims, three women and two men, varied in ages from twenty-three to eighty-four, and in occupation from bank employee to down-and-out. All were shot with a .32 calibre weapon, and the escaping killers were identified as Black by shocked eye-witnesses.

The police suspected a possible Black Muslim influence connecting the series of violent murders. Following press announcements of rewards amounting to $30,000 for information leading to the arrest and conviction of the killers, an informant came forward to assist the police. Anthony Cornelius Harris made a full confession of his part in the crimes, and named his fellow-assailants. As a result a force of a hundred police officers gathered on 1 May 1974 to storm the apartment blocks housing seven of the named men. The arrests were made without resistance, and J.C. Simon, Manuel Moore, Larry Green and Jesse Cook were eventually indicted. Their trial for murder, the longest in Californian history, lasted a year. Anthony Harris testified for twelve days, and over a hundred and fifty witnesses unfolded a story of terror and violence.

The men were attracted to the ideas of the Black Muslims, and attended meetings held in the loft of a San Francisco warehouse. There they were fed a diet of hatred against Whites who, they were told, were the enemies of Allah. Christians and Jews alike were accused of the crime of setting up as rivals to Allah and of being dedicated to the destruction of Black people. As 'white devils' were incapable of being reformed, the solution was to eliminate them by murder. The doctrine was that the use of evil to fight evil made evil into good.

'Death Angels' were recruited to carry out this task, and the killing was supposed to be indiscriminate and unaccompanied by rape or theft. To qualify as a 'Death Angel' a Black Muslim had to kill nine white men, five white women or four white children. The feeling was that 'offing' children (as their elimination was termed) was the most difficult. As an intermediate reward, each Muslim who killed four 'white devils' was given a lapel badge and promised free transportation to the Holy City to meet Brother Mohammed.

Sated with this violent doctrine, Harris and Simon and their friends roamed the streets looking for quick kills and goading each other to fresh horrors. Their victims were selected completely at random, and were then shot from behind in the most cowardly fashion. The infamous 'Night of the Five', inspired by Simon, followed a viewing of the television transmission of the Mohammed Ali versus Joe Frazier heavyweight fight. Ali's win prompted the would-be 'Death Angels' to their worst excesses. The phenomenon of killings linked to prize-fights has since been commented on by a Californian sociologist. David Phillips writing in the American Sociology Association's journal remarked on evidence suggesting that heavyweight fights stimulated fatally aggressive behaviour in some Americans. Throughout the USA the murder rate is reckoned to increase by over 12 per cent for every big fight.

In the case of the Zebra killings, the trial judge brought in unanimous verdicts of guilty against the four principal defendants, who were sentenced to life imprisonment. Public horror over the episode was vented in the media, and a group of San Franciscan women campaigned against the use of their city as the location for such crime films and TV programmes as *Dirty Harry* and *The Streets of San Francisco*.

Another American street murder case which had stimulated a debate about the roots of violence occurred in 1951 and involved three teenagers. Ann Arbor is a quiet town. Its environs incorporate a University of Michigan campus and a teaching hospital. Its population naturally comprises a large number of young people, including nurses working at St Joseph's Mercy Hospital. At about midnight on 15 September 1951 Pauline Campbell was walking home to her lodgings after work at St Joseph's. She turned into Washington Heights, a rather narrow and badly lit street which led down to the Observatory. Out of the shadows leapt an attacker who felled her with crushing blows to the head.

A medical student driving along Washington Heights saw her body in the road lying near a parked car. She died in hospital from a severe compound fracture of the skull which had caused damage to the brain — blood and brain-matter spattered over the near-by car testified to the ferocity of the attack on the girl. News of the murder created considerable anxiety in Ann Arbor, especially as there had been two attacks on nurses in recent months.

A few days after the murder twenty-year-old preacher's son Dan Baughey, who lived in Ypsilanti, went to his father for advice. The young man thought he knew the identity of the killers of Pauline Campbell. His father told him to report his views to the police, which he did on 19 September. Within hours the police had taken three eighteen-year-old youths into custody. They were Bill Morey, Max Pell and Dave Royal, all sons of respected families. The basis of Baughey's suspicion was that Bill Morey and Max Pell had told him of their attack on a nurse a few days before the murder occurred.

Max Pell was the first to break. He was a car fanatic, and when police threatened to take his car to pieces in a search for bloodstains he said, 'You don't need to tear my car apart — I'll tell you. It's blood.' His confession was followed by admissions from his companions, and all three were charged with murder. Public anger was such that there were mutterings of lynching.

The three teenagers were tried for murder at Ann Arbor, and despite the contention that he was drunk at the time, Bill Morey was found guilty of first-degree murder together with Max Pell. They received life sentences. Royal was convicted of second-degree murder and was sentenced to twenty-two years to life.

In the aftermath to the murder trial there was a great deal of discussion as to the motives of the teenage murderers. One newspaper referred to the 'whining alibis' of the young delinquents, and others made reference to the 'rootless and materialistic environment' in which they lived. 'Poor, misguided children' was another sympathetic assessment.

Morey was regarded as a good scholar although rather immature. He had experimented with marijuana and glue-sniffing before lapsing into delinquency. He had a reputation for starting fights, and his parents spoke of his being depressed in the week before the murder. Pell, the car fanatic, had left home on two occasions and had been recommended for psychiatric treatment.

Royal, whose father was dead and his mother in a mental institution, was completely without parental guidance. What became evident was that this trio roamed around in Pell's car looking for mischief by stealing accessories from cars or snatching nurses' handbags, daring each other with taunts of 'chicken'. The trial prosecutor believed the youths were part of a teenage group among whom delinquency was normal and murder perhaps inevitable.

Occasionally the murder victim almost courts disaster by placing himself within reach of his killer's venom. One such unwitting victim was Philip Barton Key, the son of Francis Scott Key who wrote *The Star-Spangled Banner*, and who in 1859 was District Attorney for the District of Columbia. On 27 February of that year this handsome and famous man was walking along Monroe Place bordering Lafayette Square in Washington DC. As he approached the house of Congressman Daniel E. Sickles he stopped, and looking towards the upper windows, waved his handkerchief.

Daniel Sickles at that very moment was contemplating reports of his wife's seduction by this man, who had the audacity to stand in front of his house signalling to her. Washington was alive with rumour about Key and Teresa Sickles, and the fact that they had rented a small house just a few blocks from Lafayette Square was a badly kept secret.

Sickles had confronted Teresa, who had confessed everything, and he had consulted his friends on the question of whether he should challenge Key to a duel. Suddenly he spotted his wife's seducer outside his house making signals to attract her attention. He rushed from the house and pursued Key to Madison Avenue where, gun in hand, he accused him: 'Key, you scoundrel, you have dishonoured my bed — you must die.' The District Attorney tried to evade the irate Congressman by dodging behind a tree and shouting, 'Don't shoot!'

Blinded with rage, Sickles shot at his quarry and missed. He shot again and Key fell to the ground. He fired at him repeatedly until with the gun pointed at his head the weapon jammed. Several spectators witnessed the shooting, and eventually Key was carried to the National Club, where he died before the doctor arrived.

Daniel Sickles stood trial for the murder of Philip Barton Key in April 1859 in Washington

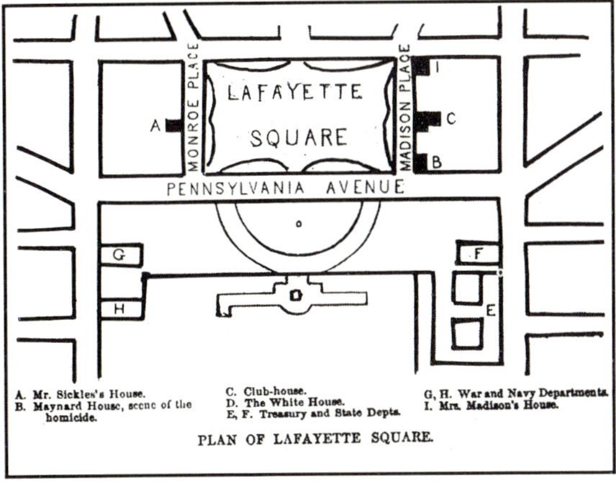

Daniel Sickles guns down his rival in a Washington DC street

City Hall. Robert Ould, Key's successor as District Attorney, led the prosecution and pointed out that the accused had chosen the Sabbath on which to commit his 'deed of blood'. The deliberate nature of the killing was emphasized, and several eye-witnesses added their endorsement. The defence denied that Sickles had acted with malice and turned the proceedings into a defence of morality: the unwritten law of a husband's right to 'vindicate his marriage bed by slaying the man who dares to defile it'. Biblical references were pulled into the argument and the case was made out that Sickles's provocation was so great as to unbalance his mind and exonerate him from the legal consequences of his act.

References to both the Old and New Testaments, bolstering counter-arguments for charity and retribution, were bandied about the courtroom. Daniel Sickles broke down and sobbed in the dock, and a statement from Teresa was read out in which she admitted, 'I did what is usual for a wicked woman to do.' The jury was out for just over an hour and returned with a verdict of Not Guilty. The acquittal was given a mixed reception in Washington — many were shocked at the cold-blooded way in which Key had been killed. Daniel Sickles's career was wrecked, although he found modest fame as a major-general in the Civil War. Teresa, broken by the ordeal, died eight years after the trial.

The murder of pop star John Lennon outside his New York apartment by Mark David Chapman in 1980 was an example of the premeditated street murder. Chapman, a one-time Jesus freak, was driven by idolatry turned to hatred. He sought out his former idol and asked him for his autograph. At that moment, with his victim concentrating on signing his name, he pulled out a gun and fired five shots into Lennon's body. Whether one is signing autographs, waiting at a bus stop or climbing into a car, the street is a place where people can be vulnerable because they are absorbed with the ordinary routines of life.

The full potential of the street as a place of murder was exploited by Karl Hau, a handsome young German student of law. He had a reputation as a bully and braggart, but did well in his studies and qualified in America as a barrister. He met Lina Molitor in Baden-Baden, and when he could not secure her parents' acceptance of his marriage proposal, eloped with her. In 1901, after Lina had attempted to commit suicide, her parents relented and the couple were married.

Hau travelled a great deal in his capacity as private secretary to the Turkish Consul-General in Washington DC. In October 1906 he was in Paris with his wife and her sister Olga when Frau Molitor received a mysterious telegram at her home in Baden-Baden urging her to travel to Paris because Olga was ill. Elderly Frau Molitor, already frail with a weak heart, was understandably upset when she arrived in Paris to find Olga perfectly well, and everyone expressing ignorance about the telegram.

Karl Hau: sophisticated street murderer

Frau Molitor returned home with Olga on 31 October, and Hau and his wife moved on to London. In the early evening of 6 November Frau Molitor received an urgent message to call at her district Post Office, where an important message from Paris was waiting for her. Accompanied by Olga, she hurried down Kaiser-Wilhelm Strasse to the Post Office when, reaching a poorly lit section of the street, a shot rang out and the old lady collapsed and died. Olga caught sight of a man emerging from the shadows and hurrying down the street.

Again it was not known who had sent the message, but family suspicion began to centre on Karl Hau. He stood to gain financially through his mother-in-law's death, and it was known that he had money problems. It was learned that he had made several crude attempts to gain money, including defrauding his own bank. Hau was arrested in London and returned to Germany. He admitted sending the false messages to Frau Molitor and to being in Baden-Baden at the time of the murder, although he denied shooting her.

Hau was charged with murder and sent for trial at Karlsruhe — his wife Lina committed suicide before the trial began. He played the part of the cool barrister in facing the charge against him and admitted everything except the actual murder. He said his actions were governed by his secret passion for his sister-in-law, and managed to imply that she was the real murderer. Hau was nevertheless convicted and sentenced to death — a verdict which did not meet with popular acclaim, for the public by now had branded Olga as a murderess. Eventually she was forced to bring libel actions against her accusers in order to clear her name.

Karl Hau's sentence was commuted to life imprisonment. He served only seventeen years before being pardoned in 1924. He wrote two books — *For Life* and *The Death Sentence* — in an attempt to refute the evidence on which he had been convicted. He repeated his previous thesis that he was shielding a woman's honour. However, while he had been in prison his country had suffered the ravages of a world war, and no one was really interested in the explanations of a pardoned murderer. On 4 February 1926 Hau was found dead in Rome where he chose to commit suicide.

The murderer's ploy of drawing his victim

away from the safety of her home and into the darkness of the street was carefully thought out. He knew that the urgent call from the Post Office would bring her hurrying from her house along Kaiser-Wilhelm Strasse. He knew also that her daughter might be with her, so a disguise was necessary to prevent recognition. Once the shot was fired, he readily scurried to safety through the shadows of the night. The fact that the old lady was killed so deliberately and not in the course of robbery, for instance, suggested a motive closer to home: Karl Hau had that motive in his desire to obtain money through his wife's inheritance.

(79, 394, 458, 520, 538, 637, 692, 886, 969, mw)

TAXIS

'I seemed to lose control.'
George Iggulden (1923)

Taxi-cabs and their forerunners, the hansom cabs, have played a regular role in countless human dramas. Their drivers have assisted mothers in delivering their babies and helped to ease the last moments of passengers who die in transit. The job of a cabbie may be exciting, dealing with all the passions between birth and death, but there is also danger. The greatest hazard is of being made the victim of robbery, occasionally accompanied by murder.

Two taxi-cab murders in London in 1983 and 1984, thought to have been motivated by robbery, remain unsolved. In November 1983 Stephen Sylvester, a West Indian mini-cab driver, was found dead in the boot of his cab, which had been parked at London Airport. A few months later, in April 1984, Pradeep Singh Sangha, a Sikh mini-cab driver, was found by an airport security guard at Hatton Cross underground station. He had been stabbed several times. The police believed these two crimes were linked, and that robbery was the motive.

The urge 'to do something exciting' led 22-year-old Gustav Hulten to rob and murder a taxi-driver in London in 1944. On 7 October George Heath was found dead from bullet-wounds on a grass verge near Staines, Middlesex. Tyre tracks in the soft ground

The taxi which featured in the murder for excitement case

enabled the police to trace the stolen taxi-cab which they found in Fulham Palace Road. Waiting detectives arrested Gustav Hulten, an armed American GI, who was absent without leave from his army base. He denied the shooting, and claimed that he had spent the night in question with his girl-friend, Elizabeth Marina Jones, an eighteen-year-old strip-tease dancer. The girl eventually revealed that Hulten had shot the cab-driver and made her go through the dying man's pockets. The American had told her that he was a Chicago gangster, but when Hulten finally confessed to the killing he said he had been incited by the girl.

Hulten and Jones were tried in January 1945. Both were found guilty of murder, although a recommendation to mercy was made in the case of the girl. She was eventually reprieved, but her would-be gangster boy-friend was hanged.

The Brixton Taxi-Cab Murder of 1923 had already illustrated the vulnerability of the cab-driver. At about 9.00 p.m. on 9 May, Jacob Dickey was hired in the West End of London and instructed by his fare to drive to Brixton, south of the river Thames. About 9.30 p.m. passers-by in Baytree Road, Brixton, saw two men struggling near a taxi-cab. Shots rang out, and one of the men fell dying to the ground while the other made his escape.

Jacob Dickey had been shot dead by his passenger who left behind a gold-knobbed ebony stick, a jemmy and a pair of gloves. A photograph of the stick appeared in the newspapers, and information received directed police inquiries to a young American, James Vivian, who lived in Pimlico. Vivian, a convicted criminal, admitted ownership of the stick but said he had loaned it to Alexander 'Scottie' Mason. Vivian's story was that he and Mason had been planning house robbery, for which they had assembled some appropriate tools including a revolver which he claimed was Mason's. When the time came to carry out their plan Vivian was ill with food poisoning and unable to accompany Mason. Consequently, Mason went on his own, taking the gold-topped stick with him. Later that evening Mason allegedly returned to Vivian's flat in a highly excited state saying that he had shot a taxi-driver.

Mason was arrested, but he told a different story. He maintained that Vivian shot the cabbie, and when he realized what had happened fled to safety through the gardens of near-by houses. Mason was tried for murder at the Old Bailey, and Vivian was the principal witness for the prosecution. The accused man refuted his companion's account, claiming that Vivian's illness was a pretence to calm his girl-friend's fears over their plan. When the girl left the house Vivian leapt from his bed and the pair set out together to fulfil their robbery plan. Mason was found guilty, but sentence of death was later commuted to one of life imprisonment. Released, he died as a merchant seaman in a torpedoed ship in the Second World War.

An unsolved murder of a taxi-driver who was also robbed occurred in South Africa on 21 September 1931. At about 7.20 p.m. Arthur Kimber picked up a fare from the taxi rank outside Maritzburg Town Hall. His passengers, a man and a woman, were seen entering his cab by fellow-drivers in the rank. Just after 8.00 p.m. Kimber's cab was seen on the Durban Road by two other drivers. At about 9.00 p.m. a tram-driver in King Edward Avenue on the outskirts of Maritzburg noticed an abandoned taxi with its lights full on. Examination of the empty cab revealed blood on the front seat and a spent cartridge case on the floor.

Kimber's body was found next morning lying on a railway embankment about seven miles out of town. He had been shot in the head and from the fact that his wallet was missing the police presumed robbery was the motive for his killing. Numerous fingerprints were found in the taxi, but they were mostly Kimber's. A packet of cigarettes, a cheap novel and a cheque book also belonged to the driver, but a blue handkerchief of superior quality was thought to have been left behind by one of his missing passengers. It was determined from a reconstruction of the crime that Kimber was shot from behind while seated in the driving position. His body was carried to the embankment by the side of the road where it was later found, and his taxi was driven back to Maritzburg and abandoned.

Several people had seen Kimber driving a man and a woman in his cab and the search for them began to focus on the criminal underworld following a letter published by a Durban newspaper. 'The man who was shot on Monday deserved all he got. He was a scab,' ran the letter, signed 'The Bat'. This was a reference to an industrial dispute then current in South Africa, but another theory which gained ground was that Kimber had been driving two gunmen to a job when he refused to go any farther and was killed for not co-operating.

The missing passengers were traced without much difficulty and turned out to be less sinister than underworld hitmen. Richard Louis Mallalieu and Gwendoline Mary Tolputt proved to be a pair of swindlers who were in possession of a gun and a forged passport when arrested in their hotel room in Cape Town on 10 October. Mallalieu was an English ex-public schoolboy and Tolputt was a doctor's daughter from Eastern Province. The couple wished to be married but the girl's parents refused permission because she was under age. They nevertheless regarded themselves as privately engaged and eloped following an incident with a gun in which Mallalieu's room-mate was shot dead. This was in May 1931, and after the official verdict of suicide was given Mallalieu and Tolputt travelled from place to place setting up fraudulent bank accounts and running up large hotel bills.

Ballistic evidence proved that the shots which killed Kimber had been fired from Mallalieu's gun. In addition there was the crime scene evidence provided by the blue monogrammed handkerchief which a hotel laundry woman said belonged to Mallalieu. When the couple appeared before magistrates at Maritzburg a serving prisoner from the town's gaol related that Tolputt while in custody had told her, 'We murdered a taxi-driver .... Dick shot him ... we thought he would have some money on him.'

The pair were sent for trial separately, and Mallalieu was the first to face the charge of murder. The firearms evidence was crucial, and the exhaustive cross-examination of the ballistics expert lasted nine hours. In the course of this rigorous questioning the expert changed his mind when it was pointed out that he had confused some of the exhibits. Mallalieu won an acquittal, and Tolputt never stood trial.

The couple drew apart after the trial because of Tolputt's confession, and she sued Mallalieu for breach of promise. Mallalieu was rearrested to face numerous fraud charges to which he pleaded guilty. They were deported from South Africa in August 1932, and the murder of taxi-driver Arthur Kimber remains officially unsolved.

Cab-drivers sometimes become party to other people's affairs when their passengers allow their passions to spill over. The man in the cab may inadvertently be cast in the role of eavesdropper or he may become eyewitness to an act of violence. The New York cabbie who picked up chorus-girl Nan Patterson and her escort, Caesar Young, on Broadway on 4 June 1906 embarked on an eventful journey. During the course of their short ride Nan Patterson shot her companion and the cabbie was privy to one of the city's most famous homicides. The chorus-girl was tried three times for murdering her lover, and to great public acclaim was eventually acquitted.

A taxi death of equal tragedy occurred in New York thirteen years later when Ernest Fritz, a cabbie from Tuckahoe, met his girl-friend and embarked on a passionate spell of back-seat love-making. After drinking in several bars the couple drove out to the Bronx, where they stopped the taxi at about midnight in Rosedale Avenue to satisfy their passions. A violent sexual encounter followed during which Florence Coyne suffered an internal haemorrhage which was so severe that she fainted from loss of blood. A passing police motor-cyclist saw the parked car and stopped to make inquiries. When he directed his flashlight into the rear and saw the badly bleeding girl he ordered Fritz to drive to Fordham Hospital. Fritz, explaining, 'She often faints and bleeds,' did as he was told. Shortly after arrival at the hospital Florence Coyne died from the severe internal bleeding. Doctors at the post-mortem examination of the dead woman described abdominal tearing injuries, bruises to the face and chest and fractures of the nose and jaw. The word 'ripper' was used to characterize the principal injuries, and Fritz was charged with murder.

Ernest Fritz came to trial in February 1920. His defence counsel, William J. Fallon, who was known as 'The Great Mouthpiece', made out a case for accidental death. This thesis was based on the gynaecological history of the dead woman, which made fatal haemorrhage possible given the cramped conditons in which sex was performed in the back of the taxi. After being out for three and a half hours, the jury found Fritz not guilty.

Another taxi-cab love affair with fatal consequences was pursued by Edward Hopwood. He saw Florence Dudley perform at the Tivoli Theatre in Manchester in May 1912, and immediately fell in love with her. Their subsequent relationship proved to be riven with jealousy on the part of Hopwood. Many violent encounters ensued from his suspicion that Florence was seeing other men; he even had her watched. This intense relationship was too much for Florence, who tried to disentangle herself, especially when she learned that her ardent lover was already married and was wanted by the police for fraud. On 28 September 1912 she met Hopwood in London and told him she intended to make the break. They talked and argued about her decision until midnight, when they left the Holborn Viaduct Hotel in a taxi whose driver was instructed to take them to Fenchurch Street Station.

As the taxi approached the station a shot rang out and the driver immediately stopped the cab. He opened the rear door and Florence Dudley fell dying to the ground. There was a second shot which Hopwood directed at himself but which failed to end his misery. Having recovered from his suicide attempt, Hopwood was tried for murder at the Old Bailey. He conducted his own defence, claiming that he had taken the revolver intending to kill himself. When he produced the weapon in the taxi Florence tried to disarm him, and was accidentally shot. He made an impassioned plea to the jury, saying that Florence Dudley was the only woman he had ever loved. The sobbing conclusion to his defence did not deter the jury from finding him guilty, and he was subsequently hanged.

The extraordinary way in which emotion can erupt between two people being driven on a short journey was demonstrated in a London taxi in 1923. George William Iggulden, a portrait-painter, sought to overcome his loneliness by advertising for a companion: 'Lonely bachelor desires marriage with homely person.' Ethel Eliza Howard, a divorcée with two children, replied and Iggulden quickly proposed marriage despite the woman's suicidal tendencies.

On 15 November 1923 Iggulden flagged down a taxi outside the Regent Palace Hotel, Piccadilly. He sat in the cab with his female companion and told the driver to take them to an address in Brompton Road. During the course of this journey Iggulden drew a razor

from his pocket and cut the woman's throat. He then told the taxi-driver to take him to the nearest police station. At Walton Road Police Station, Iggulden stepped out of the taxi and told the duty officer, 'I did it with a razor.'

Iggulden said that he had suffered from depression for two or three years and had thought of committing suicide. He met Mrs Howard, who seemed to share his melancholy disposition and, he claimed, she constantly talked of suicide. The subject of self-destruction came up while they were riding in the taxi, and, said Iggulden, 'I seemed to lose control. I took my razor from my pocket and cut her throat with one slash.' He said he believed he was doing Mrs Howard a service by killing her — 'putting her out of her misery', as he described it.

The Medical Officer of Brixton Prison, Dr (later Sir) William Norwood East, believed that Iggulden was unfit to plead, although he thought the prisoner was able to follow the proceedings. The jury decided that the prisoner *was* fit to plead, and despite a defence which demonstrated a strong streak of insanity in Iggulden's family, also found him guilty of murder. Sentence of death was not carried out, though, and in due course Iggulden was transferred to Broadmoor.
(2, 3, 45, 64, 76, 112, 160, 167, 279, 294, 355, 558, 576, 610, 720, 786, 985, MWW)

TRUNK MURDERS

'I know nothing about a trunk. You have made a mistake.'

Arthur Devereux (1905)

Disposal of murder victims' bodies by putting them in trunks, boxes and suitcases is an 'out of sight — out of mind' policy often associated with dispatch of the *disjecta membra* by train. Evil-smelling trunks awaiting collection have been an occupational hazard for railway left-luggage officials since trains came into use (see also RAILWAY MURDERS).

The practice in Britain reached a high point in 1934 when two such phenomena, apparently unconnected, occurred within the space of four weeks at Brighton. On 17 June a plywood trunk left in the cloakroom at the railway station eleven days earlier produced such an offensive smell that the police were called. The trunk was found to contain the body of a woman minus head and legs. This sensational discovery was to become known as 'Brighton Trunk Crime No.1'. Sir Bernard Spilsbury was called in to examine the remains. He calculated the woman's age at twenty-five or more, and established that she was several months pregnant. As a result of increased police activities a suitcase was found at King's Cross railway station in London which contained a pair of legs severed at the knees. Spilsbury was confident they belonged to the torso found at Brighton. Despite a massive search — which involved a check on seven hundred women reported as missing persons — the identity of the victim was never established, and the incident remains an unsolved murder.

On 15 July 1934 Spilsbury was again called to Brighton to examine the contents of another trunk. An evil-smelling box was found in a cupboard at a house in Kemp Street close to the railway station. It contained the body of a woman who had died from head injuries. The corpse had not been dismembered, and was quickly identified. The victim of 'Brighton Trunk Crime No.2' was ex-dancer Violette Kaye, whose real name was Violet Saunders. Not surprisingly, the police were inclined to link the two cases, and the person they wanted to question urgently was the last occupant of the rented room in Kemp Street. He was known as Tony Mancini, an ex-thief who worked as a waiter and had few qualms about living off the immoral earnings of his mistress.

Mancini was arrested in London on 17 July and he told the police, 'Yes, I'm the man. I didn't murder her, though.' Despite his denial he was charged with Violette Kaye's murder and appeared on trial at Lewes. His story was that he had found his mistress lying dead on the bed at their lodgings in Park Crescent and, in a state of panic, decided to hide the body. When asked why he did not call the police Mancini replied that a man with previous convictions 'never gets a square deal'. Norman Birkett, defending counsel, argued brilliantly that Mancini had been caught up in a chain reaction of concealment, and lied as a result of his panic and of finding the body. Tony Mancini, whose real name was Lois England, was acquitted at his trial, but over forty years later he stated in a Sunday newspaper that he was responsible for Violette Kaye's death.

Murder victims have been bundled into trunks for straightforward concealment and to win the murderer longer getaway time. The time secured depends on the progress of decomposition, especially when the trunk is left in a more or less public place. Another reason for the use of trunks is to transport bodies to another place some distance from the scene of the crime. The history of trunk murders shows a close association with rail transport. While the murderer may not feel decomposition merits consideration, he may be faced with the technical problem of putting a body into a trunk that is too small. Dismember-

Brighton Trunk Crime No. 1

ment is therefore a common element in trunk murders.

Two train drivers going off duty at Wolverhampton Railway Station on 5 April 1968 noticed a suitcase in an empty compartment of a train which had arrived from London. They picked it up and took it to the left-luggage office, where it was opened and found to contain the upper part of a young woman's body. The head and legs were missing, and the clothing on the torso suggested that the remains were those of a young Asian woman. Inquiries confirmed that the suitcase had been put on the train at Euston, and a description was issued of a man of Indian origin who had been seen carrying the case. A few days later another suitcase was found abandoned in the river Roding where it passed under a bridge carrying the Romford Road in Ilford, Essex. This case contained the lower torso and legs of a young woman, and a pathologist confirmed that the remains in the two suitcases belonged to the same individual.

In the hope of finding the missing head in order to establish identity, police searched the railway line between Euston and Wolverhampton, but to no avail.

The head was found on 8 May by a man cycling home from work near Wanstead Flats. He spotted a duffel bag which had been thrown down near the roadside, and as it appeared to be in too good condition to throw away, thought he would investigate. To his horror he found it contained a human head bearing two severe injuries to the skull.

Patient inquiries led to the identification of the dismembered corpse as Sarabijit Kaur, a teenage Asian girl who was pregnant. She had lodged at an Ilford address, and had been missing for several weeks. It transpired that she was the eldest daughter of Suchnam Singh Sandhr and left the family home in Barking in February 1968 following an argument over her decision to continue an affair with a married man. She had threatened to commit suicide unless she had her own way.

Sandhr eventually confessed to killing his daughter following a heated argument over the disgrace her pregnancy would bring to the

One of the suitcases containing human remains found at Wolverhampton Railway Station

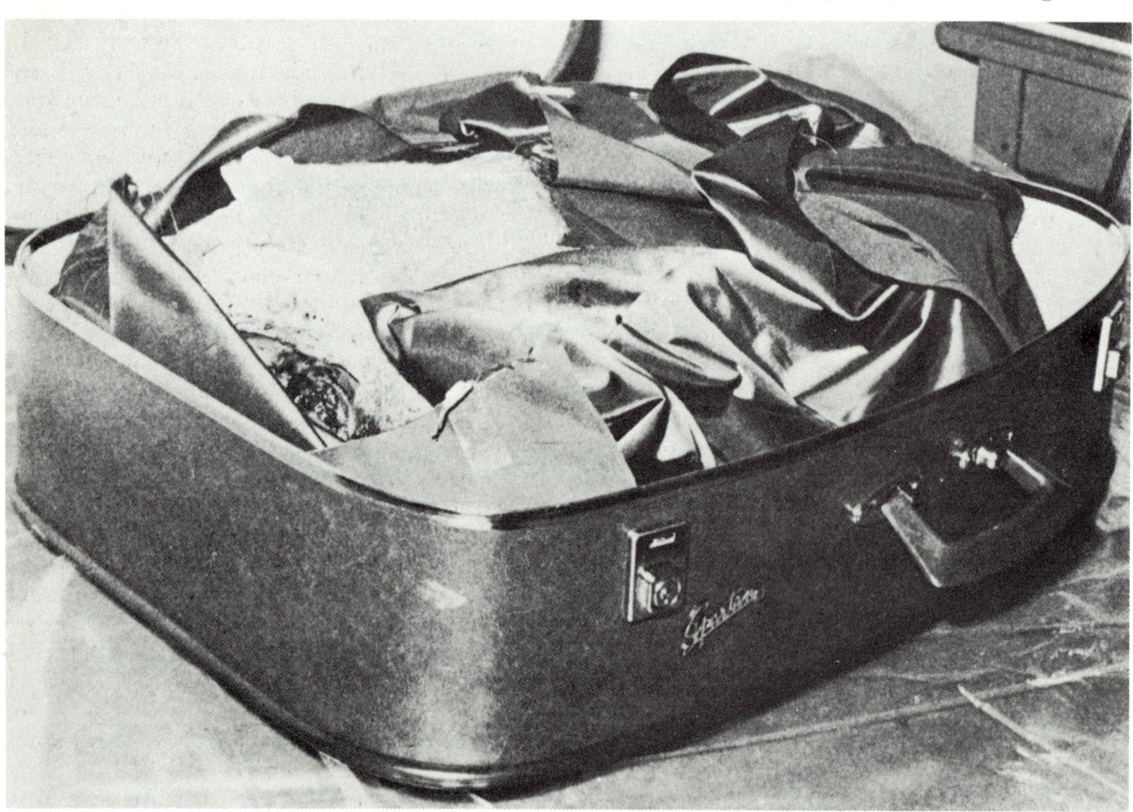

family. He felled her with a coal hammer and then cut up the body on a large plastic sheet from which he drained the blood into the bath. Sandhr packed the remains into the two suitcases and duffel bag for disposal. He was convicted of murder, and was sentenced to life imprisonment.

Trunk murders usually come to light when the receptacle either leaks or starts to smell, by which time the murderer has put some distance between himself and the crime. London's Charing Cross Trunk Murder came to light in May 1927 when the left-luggage attendant was disturbed by the offensive smell issuing from a large black trunk which had been deposited five days earlier. When it was opened the trunk's reeking contents were found to consist of the remains of an unidentified female corpse. Sir Bernard Spilsbury believed the victim had died of asphyxia about a week previously. Clothing found with the remains led to the dead woman being identified as Minnie Bonati, the wife of an Italian waiter in London.

As a result of police inquiries a taxi-driver was located who reported having driven a man with a heavy trunk to Charing Cross from an address in Rochester Row on 6 May. This man was soon identified as John Robinson, an estate agent, who was promptly arrested. His first reaction was a blunt denial, but then came a confession. He claimed that Mrs Bonati went to his office asking for money in terms which he claimed were abusive. He pushed her aside, and in falling she struck her head and died. In the time-honoured manner of the panic-stricken murderer, he resorted to dismemberment and concealment of the body in a trunk, leaving a left-luggage attendant at Charing Cross Railway Station to deal with the inevitable outcome. Robinson was tried and convicted of murder, for which he suffered the death penalty.

It is uncommon for murderers to accompany their luggage, but Winnie Ruth Judd did so on a journey from Phoenix to Los Angeles in 1931. After killing two female acquaintances the 'Tiger Woman' (as she later became known) put her victims' bodies into two trunks. One was too small, so the victim was dismembered to fill the space. She then called a delivery company to move the trunks to Phoenix railway station, where they were put on board for Los Angeles. Winnie accompanied her luggage, and on arrival at her destination was questioned about fluid escaping from one of the trunks. Her answer was to disappear promptly from the scene, the reason being apparent when the trunks were eventually opened. Winnie Ruth Judd gave herself up in due course and was tried for murder. She was sentenced to death but later, at a retrial, was judged to be insane.

Another female trunk murderer was Maria Vere Goold, whose frivolous antics in a Monaco court in 1907 earned her the title *une grande comédienne*. Not that her crime was particularly comical, for with her husband she had killed a wealthy widow in Monte Carlo and dismembered the body for disposal in a trunk. They took their cargo to Marseilles, intending to ship it to London in order 'to avoid trouble with the police'. Not only did the luggage clerk complain of the smell, but he was also appalled at the sight of blood dripping from the trunk. Maria Goold and her husband were found guilty of murder, but both died of causes connected only indirectly with judicial punishment, she of typhoid and he by suicide.

Like Winnie Ruth Judd, George Crossman had a strange compulsion to stay close to his murder victim. When one of the tenants at his house in Ladysmith Road, Kensal Rise, North London, complained about an offensive smell which appeared to originate from the cupboard beneath the stairs, all the alarm bells should have been ringing. Instead of taking immediate action to deal with the complaint, he made excuses, saying that the smell was caused by some size which he had stored away. It took several more complaints for him to be stirred into action, and in March 1904 he said he would dispose of the box. While a firm of carters was in the process of removing a tin trunk from the house, police arrived at the instigation of a suspicious tenant. Crossman took flight and the police gave chase. When he realized that he would be caught he took a razor from his pocket and cut his throat.

The offensive trunk contained the remains of Crossman's fifth wife embedded in cement. Crossman, a bigamist in the mould of George Joseph Smith, was a man who embroidered his life with incredibly complex affairs. He had undergone a form of marriage with seven women, using different names, and resorted to complicated measures to keep the affairs separate. At one time he was living with three different 'wives' whom he had set up in accommodation in various parts of London. At the coroner's inquest on the incident of the tin trunk, a verdict of suicide and murder was given against Crossman.

Cabin trunks are a customary part of a voyage by sea, but not when they contain human remains. The *Shanghai Maru* docked at Kobe, Japan, on 7 August 1933. After the passengers' baggage had been cleared from the dockside a customs officer noticed an unattended cabin trunk. It was labelled 'Q.T. Man — destination Yokohama', but reference to the passenger list showed that no person of that name had sailed from Shanghai.

When the trunk was opened the dead body of a young Chinese girl, bound hand and foot, was revealed. Japanese police referred inquiries to Shanghai and a description was obtained of a man who had delivered the trunk to dockside baggage clerks. When news of the trunk and its grim contents appeared in the press a lodging-house owner came forward to report her suspicions. She said that she had rented a room to a Eurasian and his Chinese girl-friend in July, and had been disturbed by their violent quarrels. The lodging-house owner told the couple to mind their behaviour, and after several nights of heated quarrelling — during which the girl was severely beaten — told them to leave. The girl had been heard pleading, 'Don't hit me any more.' After leaving, the man returned with a friend and removed a trunk from the room. It was so heavy that the men staggered under its weight.

The Eurasian was identified as Patrick Remedios and his girl-friend as Mary Chin. When the trunk and its contents were returned to Shanghai on 13 August police were able to make a positive identification — the girl shipped to Japan in the trunk was Mary Chin. A search of Patrick Remedios's present lodgings produced a blotter on which had been jotted the name 'Q.T. Man'.

Patrick Remedios and his brother Joseph were tried for murder. Patrick accepted full responsibility for the crime, completely absolving his brother, who he said helped him to carry the trunk without knowing what it contained. Remedios was convicted of murder and sentenced to twenty years' imprisonment in the Dutch East Indies penal settlement.

Arthur Devereux, a chemist's assistant with rather grand ideas of his status, found himself restrained by the need to maintain his wife and their twin daughters. He therefore decided to rid himself of these encumbrances by poisoning them with a chloroform mixture. Having

SOME TRUNK CRIMES

1889	Michel EYRAUD and Gabrielle BOMPARD	Riverside	Near Lyons, France
1904	George CROSSMAN	Ladysmith Road	Kensal Rise, London, England
1905	Arthur DEVEREUX	Warehouse	Harrow, England
1907	Maria GOOLD	Railway Station	Marseilles, France
1914	Hera BESSARABO	House in Paris	Nancy, France
1927	John ROBINSON	Railway Station	Charing Cross, London
1931	Winnie Ruth JUDD	Railway Station	Los Angeles, USA
1933	Patrick REMEDIOS	Dockside	Kobe, Japan
1934	Brighton Trunk Crime No.1	Railway Station	Brighton, England
1934	Brighton Trunk Crime No.2	Kemp Road	Brighton, England
1968	Suchnam Singh SANDR	Railway Station	Wolverhampton, England

administered this in the guise of cough medicine, he sealed their bodies in a trunk which he deposited in a warehouse at Harrow, Middlesex. With his crime out of sight and out of mind he moved to Coventry with his seven-year-old son in 1905 to start a new life.

Among his varous miscalculations, Devereux had reckoned without the determination of his mother-in-law, who refused to accept his lame reasons for explaining her daughter's disappearance. Eventually, this shrewd lady ascertained the name of the removals firm which had taken a trunk from the Devereuxs' home and traced them to Harrow. The moment he was confronted by a police officer, Devereux sealed his fate by blurting out, 'I know nothing about a trunk.'
(42. 107, 126, 186, 238, 242, 268, 278, 364, 397, 405, 435, 440, 530, 531, 540, 554, 577, 584, 608, 610, 717, 714, 765, 770, 792, 810, 826, 836, 865, 954, 990, 1005, MWW)

WASTELAND

'I can't say why I did this.'
Arnold Sodeman (1936)

Areas of wasteland in the heart of big cities provide scope for various fringe activities. Such places attract the unwanted debris of city-dwellers, including both their refuse and murder victims. The partially burned body of Jack Tupper (see under APARTMENTS AND PENTHOUSES) turned up on a vacant lot in New York's Bronx district in August 1978. He had not been killed there, but had been taken to the plot of waste ground where an attempt was made to cremate the body.

Railway yards and sidings have all the bleak characteristic which attract the hoboes, down-and-outs and winos. They scavenge off other people's junk, and often set themselves up in small communities. One such community existed at Scratchwood Sidings on the Southern Railway near Elstree in 1931. A group of labourers, including two characters nicknamed 'Tiggy' and 'Moosh', lived there in makeshift huts. After an argument with a fellow-labourer this pair, whose real names were William Shelley and Oliver Newman, killed him with an axe and buried his body in a heap of smouldering refuse. The badly charred body was discovered by chance when the ash subsided, and

the murderous pair were later convicted.

War-torn Britain, and especially the aftermath of the blitz, left numerous bomb sites and empty plots of ground which in one notable case revealed a murder and in another provided an opportunity for murder. Workmen clearing a bomb site in South London in 1942 discovered the body of Mrs Rachel Dobkin. It took a remarkable feat of forensic detection to identify the murdered remains, which would probably have remained undisturbed but for the work of the German Luftwaffe. In due course Harry Dobkin was convicted for the crime of murdering his wife. In 1946, in another remarkable case, the body of Olive Balchin was found on a bomb site in Manchester — she had been killed by hammer blows to the head. Walter Rowland a convicted child-murderer, was eventually hanged for this crime. But while he was in the condemned cell awaiting execution another man claimed that he had killed the woman. An appeal was heard and dismissed and the surprise confession was later withdrawn.

The twilight world of the wastelands may be shunned by most people, but children find illicit adventure in exploring their mysteries, and seek treasure among their junk. Kingsbury Run, a tract of wasteland in an industrial valley which leads out of the city of Cleveland and runs down to Lake Erie, is such a hunting-ground. It carries the railway lines to Pittsburgh, and in several places is bounded by steep embankments. The unkempt wasteland which borders the tracks nurtures scruffy vegetation and weeds. In the 1930s this somewhat desolate valley which ran alongside Cleveland's Third Precinct (noted for its shady activities and high crime-rate) occasionally provided a home for down-and-outs and hoboes riding America's rail tracks. Kingsbury Run, because it was a place where people abandoned their rubbish, was also a tempting children's playground.

It was there on 23 September 1935 that two boys playing and exploring stumbled on the beginnings of a noted murder mystery. They found two headless bodies lying in a clearing among tall weeds. The bodies were both male; they were naked, and had been castrated. A police search of the area turned up a bucket containing a revolting mixture of oil, blood and hair, and the missing genital organs were also retrieved from the undergrowth. The missing heads were recovered near by where they had been planted in the soil of the embankment.

Post-mortem examination of the bodies established that one of the victims was aged about twenty-eight and the other about forty-five. The first had been dead for two or three days, but the advanced state of decomposition in the other indicated an earlier death. Decapitation had been carried out skilfully, and possibly while the victims were still alive, or at least immediately after death. This conclusion was reached because the neck muscles had retracted at the point of severance, indicating that the nervous reflexes were still functioning.

Decomposition in the older body was too far advanced to permit identification, but fingerprints taken from the younger one enabled it to be identified as Edward Andrassy. He had a

The killing territory of Cleveland's 'Mad Butcher'

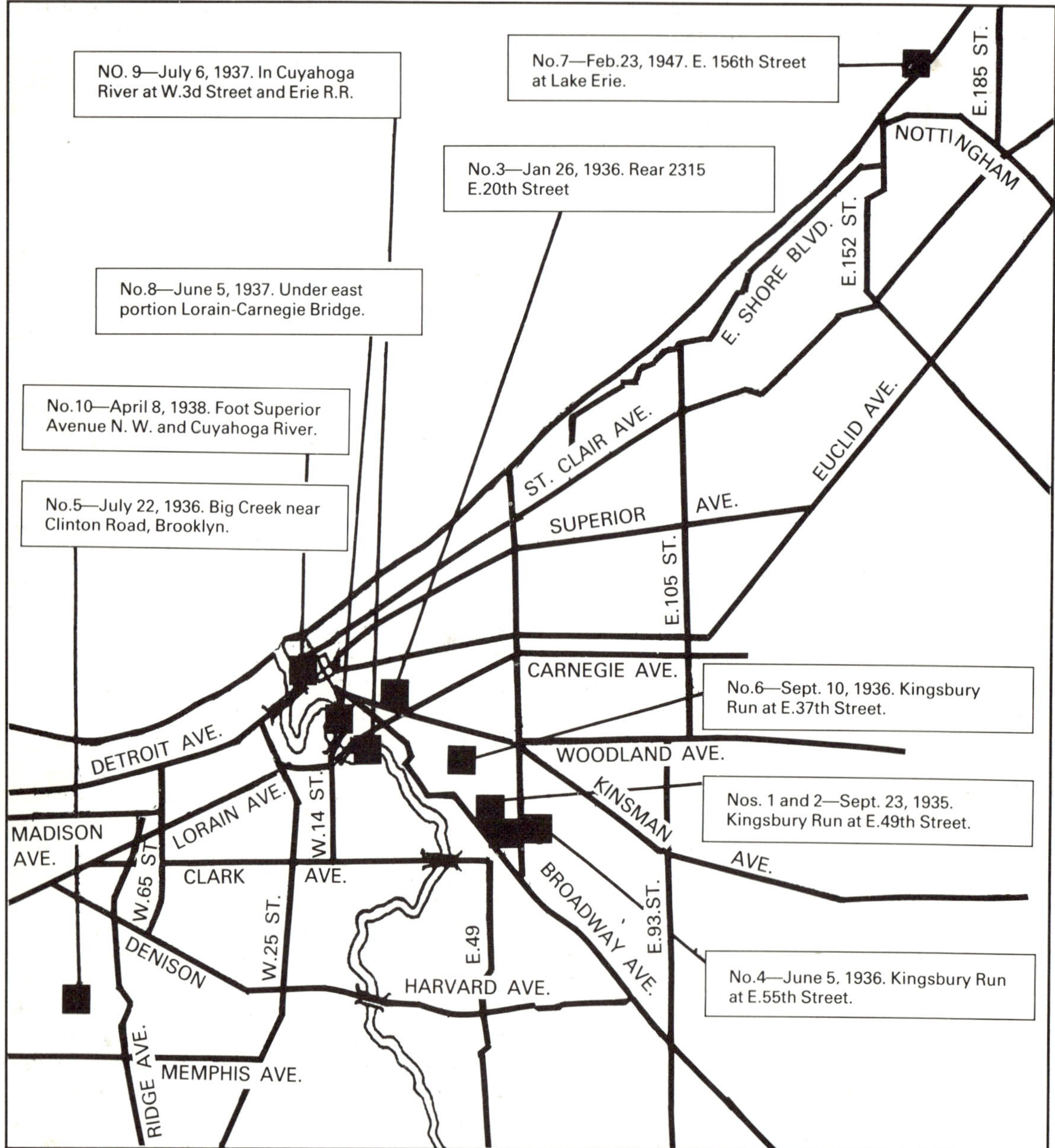

reputation as a petty criminal with a tendency towards perverse sexual behaviour. He was living apart from his wife and child, but little more was known about him. The police investigation quickly ran out of leads and the broad conclusion was that the two bizarre deaths had been the result of some private vendetta.

Four months later, on 25 January 1936, another mutilated body was discovered in Cleveland. A butcher in the neighbourhood of Kingsbury Run found parts of a dismembered corpse in some baskets left in an alleyway. Several days later the rest of the body, with the exception of the head, was found in a near-by vacant house. The nature of the surgical handiwork showed the same touches as in the previous murders. On this occasion the victim was female, and was quickly identified as 36-year-old Florence Polillo, a local prostitute. Apart from being well known in the local bars and dives, where she was frequently drunk, her life gave the police little to go on.

As public unrest began to mount police recalled that about a year before Andrassy's killing parts of a dismembered woman's body had been found on the shores of Lake Erie at Cleveland. The head was never found, and no identification had been made. If this woman had been a victim of the same killer the authorities were confronted by a series of four unsolved murders. But the 'Mad Butcher of Kingsbury Run', as the mysterious killer came to be known, had not yet finished. On 6 June 1936 two schoolboys amusing themselves at the lake end of the Run spotted a pair of trousers lying by a tree. Their curiosity was rewarded by the awful discovery that the garment contained a severed head. The rest of the body was found a short distance away. This latest victim was a young man whose corpse bore the same signs of surgery as the previous victims. There were no marks on the body save for a number of tattoos. When fingerprint examination failed to confirm identification it was thought that publicity regarding the tattoos would generate a name. Despite vigorous attempts to stimulate public recognition of this latest victim's facial features and tattoos at the Cleveland Exposition, identification was never achieved.

By this time the public had grown frightened of the terror in its midst. People were afraid to venture out to the shops, and the city's business life suffered accordingly. Railway workers were particularly sensitive, especially the track inspectors whose duties took them to Kingbury Run; they would not work singly on that section but only as a team. The police were offered both abuse and advice by the public, and chased up many cranky stories. What was beyond doubt was that the killer usually selected his victims from the poorer echelons of society, both sexes were at risk and some of the male victims had been castrated. The clean knife-work on the bodies led to the belief that the killer possessed some practical knowledge of anatomy or butchery.

The trail of corpses continued, and during the next twenty-two months up to April 1938 a further six victims fell to the 'Mad Butcher of Kingsbury Run'. Part of a woman's body was found on the shore of Lake Erie, and other bodies were retrieved from Cuyahoga river. The one characteristic they had in common was the distinctive neatness of the cutting inflicted on them. Public outrage reached a crescendo, and exasperation with the police was hysterical. Mercifully for the authorities, the victim found on 8 April 1938 was the last in Cleveland's spate of mass murder.

Like Jack the Ripper, the Cleveland killer stopped for reasons which could only be speculated about. Perhaps he was killed in an accident, his identity remaining unknown for ever, or possibly he had simply had enough. There were rumours that 'he' was in reality a woman, or that he was a hobo who rode the tracks to find ready victims. There were fears that he had appeared ten years previously in New Castle, Pennsylvania, and committed thirteen murders there which had remained unsolved. Five murders which occurred in Pittsburgh between 1939 and 1942 were also laid at the 'Mad Butcher's' door, as indeed were almost any unsolved killings involving headless bodies. The speculation was inventive but did not elucidate the identity of the Kingsbury Run murderer — he remained anonymous, as did all but two of his victims.

The Cleveland murderer knew his killing-grounds well, and remained unidentified and uncaught. Arnold Karl Sodeman was another murderer who killed and blandly smiled his way through an intense police investigation for five years in Australia. He was a child-strangler who cunningly spirited his young victims away to some quiet spot where he killed them without fear of interruption.

On 9 November 1930 a tallish man with gentle manners stopped to watch some children playing on the swings at Fawkner Park, South Yarra, Melbourne. He gave the children money to buy sweets, and thereby isolated twelve-year-old Mena Griffiths from her playmates. He told the girl he would like her to run an errand for him, and quietly won her confidence. It was the classic situation that mothers warn their children about: not to talk to strangers or to go off with them. Two days later some boys playing in an empty house in Wheatley Road found Mena Griffiths's body — she had been bound and strangled. Police inquiries led to the arrest of a man in Sydney who was charged with murder. His strong denials were undercut when three witnesses identified him as a person they had seen in Fawkner Park on the day of the murder. This man was committed for trial, but successfully proved an alibi which placed him in another town at the time of the murder. To put the matter beyond doubt, another victim fell to the strangler while this now cleared suspect was still in police custody.

The body of sixteen-year-old Hazel Wilson was found on a disused allotment on 10 January 1931. She had been bound and gagged; death was caused by strangulation. Police investigation of the two murders slowly ground to a halt as the months went by. Indeed, the files had probably begun to collect dust by the time interest in the unsolved killings was rekindled. On 1 January 1935 twelve-year-old Ethyl Belshaw disappeared at Inverloch, a seaside holiday resort some eighty miles from Melbourne.

The girl's body was found the next day lying in bracken on waste ground between the beach and the main road. She had been bound hand and foot, and her face was battered. Death had been caused by strangulation. Thousands of holiday-makers were questioned by the police, including Arnold Sodeman, but once again an innocent man was charged with murder. An eighteen-year-old youth suffered the ordeal of being accused before it became obvious that the charge had no foundation.

The fourth victim of the strangler was a six-year-old girl whose body was found at Leongatha on 1 December 1936. She had been strangled at a location just half a mile from her home. Again the police mounted a manhunt and began intensive inquiries regarding a man on a bicycle seen talking to the victim on the day she was murdered. A few days later a labourer working at a near-by construction camp reported to the police. He recounted the odd behaviour of one of his colleagues, a man named Arnold Sodeman. One evening while a group of men at the camp were seated together round a fire discussing the murder — the topic which was on everyone's lips — a jibe was made at Sodeman to the effect that he had been seen riding his bicycle in the place where the girl had been killed. The reaction of the normally mild-mannered Sodeman was so violent that one of his workmates thought the man had something to hide.

Sodeman was arrested, and after trying to talk his way round the police questions he broke down and made a confession. He explained in detail how he had killed the girl at Leongatha, but said, 'I can't say why I did this.' He then told the police that he had killed three times before. Officers were reluctant to believe him at first, but were convinced when he demonstrated the way in which he locked his thumbs together in order to reinforce his strangler's grip. Sodeman appeared to have led a normal family life, and was devoted to his wife and young daughter. After he had confessed to the police he confessed to his wife in a written message in which he spoke of 'my mania'. He told her, 'Please don't make any effort to obtain counsel for me as I will plead guilty .... May God be always with you and forgive the harm I have done.' The mania of which he spoke was his knowledge that his father, grandfather and great-uncle had all died insane, and the realization that he developed uncontrollable murderous impulses after he had been drinking. It was later confirmed that he was suffering from leptomeningitis, a chronic inflammation of the brain-covering which was triggered off by consuming alcohol.

Arnold Sodeman was convicted of murder, and was sentenced to death. The child-killer, that most despised of all murderers, was hanged at Pentridge Prison on 1 June 1936. *(3, 126, 247, 363, 367, 453, 499, 500, 576, 602, 761, 773, 791, 871, MWW)*

WOODS AND FORESTS

'She's gone off with a damned circus fellow.'

Jim Lowell (1870)

Being off the beaten track, woods and forests offer the murderer good prospects for privacy and concealment. Trees and open spaces easily absorb the sounds of violence, and the loose earth of the leaf-strewn forest floor makes grave-digging a simple matter. Observed only by the wild life he has disturbed, the murderer entices his victim into the forest's silent embrace, commits his violence, disposes of the body and quietly steals away.

William Burton devised a plan which made effective use of these advantages. He worked as odd-job man for the squire of Manor Farm in the small Dorsetshire village of Gussage St Michael. Burton, aged twenty-nine, was married to the village post-mistress, who was some twelve years his senior. In October 1912 Manor Farm took on a new cook in the attractive form of 24-year-old Winifred Mitchell. Burton (who liked to boast of his amorous conquests) made immediate advances to the new girl. Winifred became Burton's mistress, and he talked of deserting his wife and child to elope with her to Canada. When he learned that the girl was pregnant his ardour cooled, and by March 1913 he began to regard her as an encumbrance. He therefore devised a plan to get rid of her. He persuaded Winifred to tell her mother that she was going to take a job in London. Then he arranged to meet her in the woods near Manor Farm, ostensibly to discuss their future together.

Unfortunately for Burton, she had to call off their meeting at the last moment, and they agreed to see each other in the same place two days hence. Meanwhile, children picking flowers in the woods came across a freshly dug trench in the loose soil. They told their parents of this curious discovery, but their elders paid scant regard.

On 31 March, her head full of elopement to Canada, Winifred set out from Manor Farm for her postponed appointment with Burton. When she did not return the villagers of Gussage St Michael assumed she had gone to London. The chidren who had found the strange trench in the woods now reported that it had been filled in, but still no one listened. On 6 April a dairyman walking through the woods found some false teeth lying among the leaves. He was mildly curious, but did not report his discovery. It was only when the rector's wife heard about the teeth on 29 April that the matter was reported to the police.

On 2 May Winifred Mitchell's body was found in the grave in the woods which the children had seen freshly prepared to receive its victim and then covered over. The girl had been shot dead by Burton, who had borrowed a gun and cartridges in order to rid himself of an unwanted attachment. He was convicted of murder, and made a full confession before achieving the distinction of being the last man to be hanged at Dorchester.

Wooded areas are the traditional meeting-grounds for lovers. The protection which they afford against intrusion permits the exercise of passion, and also disarms the unwanted lover who has been earmarked for murder. This was the fate of Winifred Mitchell, and it is a plan that works equally well against a spouse.

The weekend of 11 and 12 June 1870 was an eventful one in the town of Lewiston in Maine, New England. On the Saturday the visiting Great Australian Circus gave a gala performance and on Sunday the town's Central Hall burned down. Jim and Lizzie Lowell were spectators at both events, and for Lizzie it proved to be her last entertainment, whether paid for or provided free of charge. Jim and Lizzie were married but were living apart — quite amicably, or so it seemed — following a marital dispute. Jim was a teamster, and Lizzie was the living-in-help at Mrs Sophronia Blood's house in Lewiston. After supper on Sunday, Jim collected Lizzie from Mrs Blood's to take her for a drive in his horse and trap. They headed out of town along Switzerland Road and into wooded country that was a popular haunt in the summer with courting couples.

Mrs Blood locked up at 10.00 p.m. aware that Lizzie had not returned, and assuming that she had decided to stay the night with her husband. She saw Jim the following afternoon and asked after Lizzie. 'I left her at your door at ten o'clock last night' was Lowell's reply, adding that she had gone off with a 'damned circus fellow'. This explanation for Lizzie's disappearance seemed to be accepted, and few inquiries were made. About a month later,

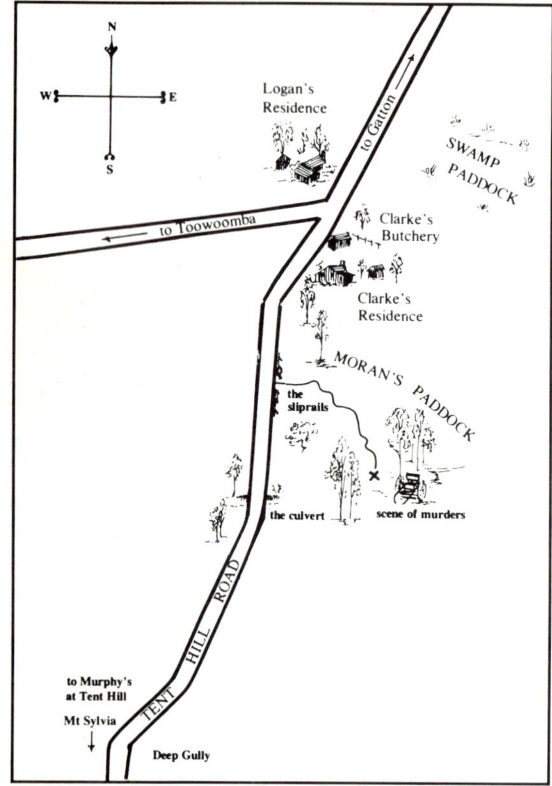

Scene of the Gatton murders in Queensland, Australia

Lizzie's mother, Sarah Burton, who lived at near-by Dedham, arrived in Lewiston and confronted Jim Lowell.

In answer to earlier inquiries, he had written her a letter dated 4 August which was distinguished by its illiteracy and nonchalance. He repeated his story about Lizzie going off with another man, but seemed unable or unwilling to answer any questions. With growing unease, Mrs Burton went to the City Marshal, who proved less than helpful. She then visited Mrs Blood who showed her a curious letter, addressed to 'Miss blood' and purporting to come from Lizzie which she had received two weeks after the girl's disappearance.

> Dear friend
> Tell my Dear beloved husbun that he will never see me again i hav don wrong i have Lied a bout him he never used me bad but once i want you to see him and tell him i want you to giv him all my clothes tell that girl that goes with Savage that i want her to cort Jimy and have him She can never get a beter one (tell Jennie to kiss Jimmy three times for me)
>
> Lizzie

Georgia, Lizzie's sister, also produced a letter received on 1 August.

> Dear Sister, [it read] I take the pen in hand to let you no i am not ded [concluding] dont let aney wone no that you have heard from me Good by from your sister Lizzie M Lowell.

Thoroughly perplexed, Mrs Burton returned to Dedham, where she wrote to a friend about a dream she had had around the time Lizzie disappeared. She saw Jim and Lizzie together in a pine thicket, and then her daughter was on the ground with her husband standing over her as she pleaded for her life — 'Don't murder me,' she cried. Bearing in mind the old maxim 'Dream Sunday night and tell it Monday morning it will surely come to pass', Mrs Burton committed her dream recollections to paper.

Time passed, and in the autumn of 1872 Jim Lowell married again and went to live in Lawrence, Massachussetts. The following year a farmer who had bought a piece of ground near Switzerland Road outside Lewiston, decided to fell some timber. While cutting down a stand of pine trees he stumbled across a shallow grave containing a skeleton. There was no head with the remains, but sufficient of the rotting clothing was intact to identify the body of Lizzie Lowell.

A coroner's inquest confirmed the identification and brought in a verdict of murder by person or persons unknown. Two days later Jim Lowell was arrested and charged with murdering his wife. On the day that he was brought back to Lewiston the town's newspaper published Mrs Burton's letter which she had written nearly three years previous relating her dream about Lizzie's murder.

While the evidence against Lowell was purely circumstantial, the effect of his mother-in-law's insight was electrifying. Public opinion had no doubt that Lowell was the murderer, and the letters brought in evidence clearly showed the same hand and mind at work. Mrs

Burton's dream aside, he had committed a carefully concealed murder, but chose to excite suspicion with his ill-conceived letters.

Lowell strongly believed he would leave the court a free man, but his trial jury had other ideas and convicted him of murder in the first degree. Although he was sentenced to death, Maine law required a year to pass before execution could be carried out. After that period had lapsed Lowell's sentence was commuted to gaol for life.

The advantages of a wooded area for the commission of murder were amply demonstrated by the unknown perpetrator of the Gatton killings in Queensland, Australia. Daniel and Mary Murphy had ten children: six boys and four girls with ages ranging between thirty-three and thirteen. Dan Murphy was a highly respected farmer, and two of his sons were Queensland policemen. His farm was at Blackfellow's Creek near the little town of Gatton. Tragedy struck this household on Boxing Day 1898. On that day Michael Murphy drove his sisters Norah and Ellen to the races at Mount Sylvia, and later into Gatton where they spent the evening.

The trio did not return that night as expected, and the following morning their brother-in-law, William McNeil, set out on horseback to search for them. He rode into Gatton, where he ascertained that they had left for home at about 10 p.m. the previous evening. By retracing their likely journey to Blackfellow's Creek he found wheeled tracks leading off the road and towards Moran's paddock. There, by a clump of wattle-trees, he found his missing relatives. All three were lying dead. Michael's hands were tied behind his back and he had been shot through the head. The two women had been raped. Their hands were also bound and their heads had been savagely battered. The horse had been shot and lay in the shafts of the dog-cart.

The police were sent for, but before they arrived news of the tragedy had spread like wildfire and many curiosity-seekers had visited Moran's paddock, trampling underfoot much valuable scene-of-crime evidence. Aborigine trackers were called in to help, and a large-scale murder investigation was mounted. There was an overwhelming attendance at a

Scene of the Lowell murder in Massachusetts, USA

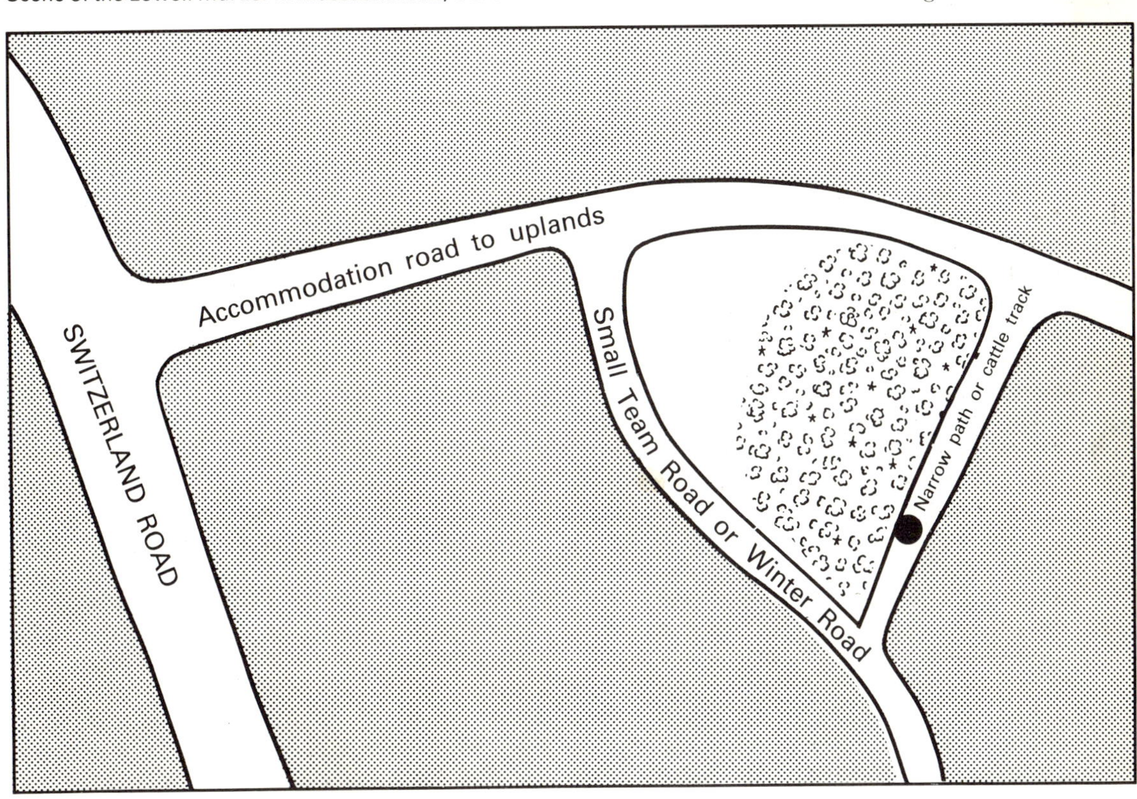

special church service in memory of the victims which included a mile-long procession.

As the murder hunt dragged on without producing results the Queensland police came in for a fair amount of criticism, and £1,000 was offered as a reward for information leading to the arrest of the murderer. There were several curious aspects to the murders, not least of which was that the bodies appeared to have been carefully laid out after death with their feet pointing due west. There were no signs of a struggle having taken place, and the wheel-tracks of the dog-cart which bore the trio to their deaths did not stop before turning off the main road, but rolled on purposefully to the spot in Moran's paddock where the carnage took place. Furthermore, there were no bloodstains in the dog-cart, which supported the suggestion that Michael Murphy and his two companions had been lured unknowingly to their doom. Certainly it did not seem that they had been murdered elsewhere than Moran's paddock.

This was borne out by statements from two witnesses at different locations who heard the sound of two shots at about 10 p.m. The shots were followed by screams from the direction of Moran's paddock, and one of the witnesses thought she distinguished the cry 'Father! Father!'

Perhaps the most intriguing facet of the case was that five persons had seen a man standing at the railed entrance to the paddock at different times between 7.45 and 9.15 p.m. on the night of the murder. The theory was that this man was looking for Michael Murphy with a view to forcing or coaxing him off the road. From the description given of this individual — who was judged to be a stranger to the district — the police picked up an itinerant named Richard Burgess. He was something of an outlaw, and had a criminal record for sexual assault. Despite being picked out on an identification parade, Burgess satisfactorily proved an alibi to the police. Later he boasted that he was the Gatton murderer, but he was never tried for the crimes, and the authorities seemed satisfied that he was not the culprit.

At the close of the inquiry into the murders in 1899 the magistrate felt obliged to remark on the apathy of the Murphy family to the tragedy which had overtaken three of their number. He suggested that they had given their evidence reluctantly and in a contradic-tory manner. These remarks led to unsubstantiated rumours that the desire to keep something hidden lay behind the Murphys' apparent indifference.

The Gatton murders remain unsolved, but it is clear that their perpetrator, bent on lust, planned them with cunning and with due regard for location.

Driving out into the country to commit murder might seem a good idea to a city-dweller anxious to avoid observation by a chance witness. This does not mean that he should throw all caution to the winds, as Guy Davin did after he had decided to kill and rob. An abandoned car was found by French police near Vincennes racecourse on 17 December 1931. Bloodstains on the car's interior and several items of discarded clothing suggested foul play. The separate discovery of partially burnt bloodstained clothing at near-by Triel, and of the car's folding seat at another spot, added to the mystery.

The car — registration 7119–RF3 — had been stolen in Paris on 14 December. The garage-owner at Triel said he had filled its petrol tank on 15 December, and gave a brief description of the driver, who was a well-dressed young man. The car had also been seen by a woman at Garches, near Versailles. She had heard the sound of shots coming from the direction of the woods at Garches and saw a man disappearing in a car, the number of which she noted in order to report the incident.

Examination of the burnt clothing revealed a button bearing the words 'Lividal – Paris'. By scrutinizing the button and the charred cloth to which it was attached the tailor concluded that these were remnants of a suit he had made for an American customer, Richard Wall, who was living in a Paris hotel at the time. Wall was known to the French police on account of a report he had made regarding a theft from his home of $10,000 in banknotes. He was a lavish spender, and lived at Bougival near Paris with Emily Verbeech, an American dancer. There were strong suspicions about Wall's activities, not the least of which was that he was involved in large-scale car-theft.

The police were able to reconstruct Wall's movements from various information sources, and it appeared that he had stolen the car found crashed at Vincennes. An acquaintance told the police that on 16 December Wall

Crowds gather round Guy Davin during a police reconstruction of the crime

mentioned that he had arranged to meet a friend at a bar near the Arc de Triomphe. That friend was Guy Davin, a young man about town, who offered to drive Wall out to the country.

Davin broke down the instant police started to question him. He said the idea of murdering the American came to him when Wall asked him to change $300 into French currency. He saw an opportunity to make some money, and bought a gun in order to kill Wall — he first used it for practice shooting in the Bois de Boulogne. His victim readily agreed to the idea of taking a ride in the country, and when they reached a secluded road in the woods at Garches he stopped the car on a pretext and shot Wall three times in the head. Taking an enormous risk, Davin had stopped at a shop to buy a pair of scissors with the dead man still in the car. He used the scissors to cut up the clothes before burning them with petrol and dumping the body into the river Seine. Davin then drove back to Paris, and the following day crashed the car at Vincennes to fake an accident. He killed Richard Wall for a mere 5,000 francs, for which he was convicted of murder and sentenced to life imprisonment in the penal settlements.
(56, 79, 140, 286, 331)

ZOOS

'They come, they go.'

Joe Ball (1937)

The possibility of using the deadly and destructive capabilities of animals normally found in zoos for criminal ends has not escaped the human mind. Robert James (see under BATHROOMS) used rattlesnakes as a poisonous murder weapon and Joe Ball found a novel use for the alligators which he kept in the pool of his tavern, The Sociable Inn, at Elmendorf, Texas. He liked to make feeding-time an entertaining feature for his guests, but a less rewarding aspect of life at The Sociable Inn was the high turnover of staff, especially of waitresses. When this was remarked on, Joe's comment was 'They come, they go.'

In 1937, the family of one of these waitresses

reported her missing and called in the police. Inquiries produced the startling information that the whereabouts of over a dozen girls could not be accounted for. In due course the tavern's handy-man confessed that he had helped Joe Ball kill some of the girls with an axe and feed their dismembered bodies to the alligators. Ball thwarted detectives intent on arresting him for murder by shooting himself. His well-fed alligators were taken to a new home at San Antonio Zoo.

While piranha fish and Black Widow spiders often feature in detective and spy fiction as the tools of villainy, they are rarely encountered in real murder. Animals in captivity have frequently taken a toll of their masters, and Victorian newspapers liked to imbue their monsters with human instincts; hence a headline in 1876 'Murderous Attack by Gorilla'. The newspapers of that era were fascinated by the idea of young women attacked by gorillas and snakes.

The readiness of some wild animals to attack human beings is well recorded, from the tales of man-eating tigers to those of ravenous sharks. A more unusual claim was that of Lindy Chamberlain in August 1980, who said that a dingo had seized her nine-week-old child from the family camp site in the Australian desert (see under CAMPS AND CARAVANS).

The ability of animals to destroy a corpse is a more common phenomenon, although this usually occurs more by accident than by design on the part of the killer. Bears nearly destroyed the corpses of the three American hunters whose murders in 1953 were attributed to Wilbert Coffin (see REMOTE PLACES), while the capacity of farmyard pigs to consume a human body without leaving a trace was judged to have accounted for the disappearance of the Hosein brothers' murder victim in 1968, and also the body of farmer Stanislaw Sykut, who vanished in Carmarthenshire in 1953.

There have been a number of so-called Zoo Murders, but for the most part they have been crimes where the location was chosen because of the opportunities for concealment and escape. This was so in the Lainz Zoo and Johannesburg Zoo Murders, but London Zoo provided the locus in 1928 for an incident fomented by rivalry between two keepers over profits gleaned from the

elephants. The zoo received a newcomer in 1927 in the shape of a white Burmese elephant which arrived from Rangoon with its young attendant San Dwe, and the prophecy was that removal of the sacred beast from its native land would invite disaster. The first misfortune was that the animal found the climate in London so disagreeable that after a few months it was shipped back to Burma. The real disaster, though, was yet to come.

San Dwe decided not to accompany his charge back to Burma but to stay on at London Zoo. The head elephant-keeper was an Indian, Sayed Ali, who was so well regarded by his employers that he was allowed to return each year to Calcutta. During Ali's absence in 1927–8 San Dwe stood in and made a successful job of looking after the elephants. He also enjoyed a useful perk in the form of tips given by parents whose children enjoyed rides on the elephants. These extra earnings often amounted to thirty shillings a week, which was no mean sum at that time. This happy arrangement came to an end in June 1927 when Sayed Ali returned to his duties and San Dwe was relegated to more menial tasks. The two men shared accommodation above the Tapir House, which was situated close to the Outer Circle of Regent's Park. They appeared to be on amicable terms, but in August the 'prophecy of doom' was fulfilled.

During the night of 24 August two policemen patrolling the Regent's Park area heard sounds of distress coming from the direction of the railings which fenced off the Tapir House from the road. They found San Dwe lying on the ground with an injured foot, and babbling about four men who had tried to kill him and his fellow-keeper. Sayed Ali was discovered dead in his room from severe head-wounds. The accommodation had been ransacked and a bloodstained pick-axe and sledge-hammer lay discarded near-by. San Dwe's story of an attack by intruders was not believed, and he was charged with murdering his rival.

Sir Henry Curtis-Bennett defended the Burmese at his trial but called no evidence to counter the prosecution's claim that San Dwe had meted out blows to his friend with 'a ferocity that was beyond belief'. He submitted that the prosecution had not proved their case.

Murder among the elephant keepers at London Zoo

Nevertheless, San Dwe was convicted of murder and sentenced to death. Curtis-Bennett worked hard for a reprieve, and this was signed by Queen Mary, acting for the King, who was ill. In 1932 San Dwe was released from prison and returned to his native land, perhaps to be reunited with his white elephant.

An opportunist zoo murder which remained unsolved despite the attentions of Sir Arthur Conan Doyle, the creator of Sherlock Holmes, was that which occurred in Johannesburg in 1927.

Irene Kanthack was an eighteen-year-old student at Witwatersrand University. She lived with her parents in Oxford Road, Forest Town, an exclusive residential area bordering on Johannesburg's Zoological Gardens. It was her habit after a day's studies to take the dog for a walk through the Gardens, around the lake.

On 24 November 1927 Irene went out for her walk as usual, and was seen at about 6.15 p.m. apparently heading for home. When the dog returned on its own her parents became concerned and called the police. The area around the zoo was thoroughly searched, the lake was dragged and aerial surveillance was carried out. Her body was found by a Boy Scout who was aiding the search teams when he disturbed a pile of leaves near the zoo entrance.

The girl had been stabbed, and there was ample evidence of a running struggle having taken place over a considerable distance. Irene had obviously put up a fight, for the two halves of her walking-stick were found in different places. The nature of the attack was sexual, and the time of the assault was fixed at 6.35 p.m. by her wristwatch, the glass of which had been damaged in such a way as to prevent the hands moving.

Several apparently promising leads came to nothing and the police, frustrated by lack of progress, were drawn into further dead ends by amateur detectives. The first of these was a spiritualist who confused the issue with a story which ran completely counter to the police's own reconstruction of the crime. Other spiritualists came forward, and an ex-policeman reported on a seance at which the medium produced the 'spirit' of Irene Kanthack. The dead girl was supposed to have said that she had been attacked by two men, one of whom was an employee at the zoo.

These supernatural claims added nothing to the inquiry, which was rapidly losing its way. The next development, while not exactly supernatural, was somewhat fanciful. A young woman who lived in Johannesburg began to discuss what she claimed to be information which would lead to conviction of the zoo murderer. A reward of £500 had been posted for such information so that her claim was not without incentive. The essence of her story was that she possessed letters written to her by her boy-friend 'Billy' in which he confessed to the murder. Willing to try almost anything to solve the crime, the police took charge of the letters, which had been written between February and September 1928. She claimed that 'Billy' had visited her on the night of the murder, and she noticed that he had blood on his clothes. Her story was partly corroborated by her father, and also by 'Billy's' landlady.

The stumbling-block was the handwriting in the letters appeared to be remarkably similar to that of Miss 'X' (whose anonymity was preserved). Meanwhile Miss 'X' created a further sensation by drinking some caustic soda and being rushed to hospital in a critical condition. She repeated her story to detectives at her bedside, and the retelling seemed to be given more credence as a dying declaration.

Miss 'X' recovered from her ordeal, and 'Billy' was arrested in Rhodesia and sent to Johannesburg amid wild public speculation. Miss 'X' gave evidence at 'Billy's' trial, which merely heightened the view that the letters were specious and that the whole affair was a fantasy. 'Billy' was acquitted, and the zoo murder remained unsolved after a police inquiry distinguished more for its reliance on the supernatural than on criminal procedure. The police did, however, have the foresight to consult Sir Arthur Conan Doyle, who was visiting Johannesburg at the time, but the great man was unable to plumb the mystery.

The Lainz Zoo Murder, as it was known, was a case which kept Vienna alive with sensation for nearly four years. The irony was that the Lainz Zoo was a zoological garden with no animals — the zoo population had been destroyed during the First World War, and up to 1928 had not been replaced. Nevertheless, the nine square miles of parkland remained, and the gardens were kept up as a public amenity.

The zoo was closed to the public on 17 July 1928, which was a warm, thundery day. At about 3.30 in the afternoon two gardeners tending their shrubs heard a succession of shots. With questionable restraint, they contained their curiosity until they had finished work and then went to investigate. They came to a wooded area where the parched grass was burning, and as they set about extinguishing the flames they noticed a blackened bundle lying under one of the trees. To their horror they discovered the body of a woman which had been severely burned in the fire. One of the gardeners looked up at that moment and got a fleeting glimpse of a dark-haired man who was standing some 300 yards away watching them. The storm which had been threatening all afternoon then broke, and lashing rain completely quenched the fire.

The body was not immediately identifiable. There were six bullet-wounds including one in the head which had been caused by a 6.35 mm weapon. The woman had been robbed; on and around her body were the materials of combustion — newspapers, sticks of metaldehyde

and traces of benzine. The straw hat she had been wearing, singed by the flames, lay near-by.

Pictures of the face of the murdered woman were widely circulated, but identification was not made for a year. The head of the Vienna Police Identification Department on a visit to his dentist mentioned the case, and invited him to take a look at the teeth of the murder victim. The dentist immediately recognized his own handiwork, and quickly identified the dead woman as a former patient named Katharina Kellner.

Katharina, aged thirty-one, was a person who liked high living and did not mind how she sold her favours. For nearly ten years she had lived with a wealthy banker. When he grew too infirm to support her she married Hungarian entrepreneur Andreas Kellner. The marriage was short-lived, and after the couple separated in 1928 Katharina had wandered round Europe, finally ending up in Vienna. The police strongly suspected Kellner of murdering his wife, but his alibi proved too strong. He advised the detectives to look for a man called Gustav Bauer, whom he openly accused of murder.

Bauer, an ex-army lieutenant, was a traveller for an Austrian pencil-manufacturer. He was also a ladies' man, and at the time of his arrest in Berlin to answer a murder charge in Vienna he was escorting the head of one of the foremost fashion houses. The evidence against Bauer began to build up. Letters were found among Katharina's possessions signed by 'Gustl', and he was identified by the proprietor of a pawn-shop as having pledged two fur coats belonging to the victim. He was also identified by a taxi-driver, who remembered picking him up outside the Opera with his lady friend who was wearing a straw hat. They were driven to the Lainz Zoo where the driver waited, and then later picked up Bauer, who returned on his own. Furthermore, Bauer owned a Steyr pistol and had bought ammunition for it just before the murder.

Gustav Bauer was put on trial for murder in October 1930. The mainly circumstantial evidence against him was countered by his alibi, which at the material time placed him an hour's journey from the Zoo at his brother's hospital bedside. Two witnesses claimed to have seen Bauer in the Zoological Gardens on the afternoon of the murder. The circumstances of these observations were put to the test when the judge decided to take the jury, the accused and the witnesses to the scene of the murder. There one of the witnesses picked out another man in mistake for Bauer. The judge decided to adjourn the trial and submit the papers for a further examination of the evidence.

The second trial began in March 1931 when all the previous witnesses were re-examined and all the evidence was resubmitted. The jury could not agree on a verdict, and came out with seven in favour of conviction and five against. As Austrian law required eight votes to secure conviction, this result amounted to an acquittal, and Gustav Bauer was a free man. There was widespread feeling that justice had not been done, but sixteen months after his acquittal Bauer set the matter straight himself. On 17 July 1932, four years to the exact day of the Lainz Zoo murder, he hanged himself in his apartment. This act was generally regarded as an expression of guilt.

Gustav Bauer chose his location for murder with some thought. The zoological gardens were vast, and only the occasional gardener would be expected there, as on the day he chose they were closed to the public. It also became clear that he had made several reconnaissance trips to the Zoo. At least five visits were made in the company of different women, and it was alleged that he had rehearsed the crime by persuading one of his companions to lie down on the spot where he later killed Katharina Kellner.
(64, 71, 126, 232, 381, 394, 429, 764, 859, 868)

Bibliography

1   **Notable British Trials** (eighty-three titles)

2   **Famous Trials** (sixteen titles)

3   **Old Bailey Trials** (seven titles)

4   **Celebrated Trials** (six titles)

5   **Abbott, J H :** *In the Belly of the Beast*, London (1982)

6   **Abinger, Edward :** *Forty Years at the Bar*, London (1930)

7   **Abrahams, Gerald :** *According to the Evidence*, London (1958)

8   **Adam, H.L. :** *Police Work from Within*, London (1914)

9   —: *Murder Most Mysterious*, London (1932)

10   —: *Murder by Persons Unknown*, London (1931)

11   —: *Old Days at the Old Bailey*, London (n.d.)

12   **Adams, N. :** *Dead and Buried?*, Aberdeen (1972)

13   **Adams, Virginia :** *Human Behaviour-Crime*, Amsterdam (1976)

14   **Adamson, Iain :** *A Man of Quality*, London (1964)

15   **Adleman, Robert H :** *The Bloody Benders*, London (1971)

16   **Alan, A J et al :** *Great Unsolved Crimes*, London (n.d.)

17   **Allen, William :** *Starkweather*, Boston (1976)

18   **Altick, Richard T :** *Victorian Studies in Scarlet*, London (1970)

19   **Altman, Jack** *and* **Ziporyn, Marvin :** *Born to Raise Hell*, New York (1967)

20   **Ambler, Eric :** *The Ability to Kill*, London (1963)

21   **Andrew, Kenneth :** *Hong Kong Detective*, London (1962)

22   **Andrews, Allen :** *Intensive Inquiries*, London (1973)

23   **Angelella, Michael :** *Trail of Blood*, New York (1979)

24   **Anson, Jay :** *The Amityville Horror*, London (1978)

25   **Anspacher, Carolyn :** *The Acid Test*, London (1965)

26   **Appleton, Arthur :** *Mary Ann Cotton*, London (1973)

27   **Archer, Fred :** *Killers in the Clear*, London (1971)

28   **Armbrister, Trevor :** *Act of Vengeance*, London (1976)

29   **Arthur, Herbert :** *All the Sinners*, London (1931)

30   **Aston-Wolfe, H :** *The Underworld*, London (1926)

31   —: *Strange Crimes*, London (1932)

32   —: *The Forgotten Clue*, London (n.d.)

33   **Atholl, Justin :** *The Reluctant Hangman*, London (1956)

34   **Atlay, J B :** *Famous Trials*, London (1899)

35   **Bailey, F Lee :** *The Defence Never Rests*, London (1972)

36   **Bailey, Guy :** *The Fatal Chance*, London (1969)

37   **Balchin, Nigel :** *The Anatomy of Villainy*, London (1950)

38   **Ball, J M :** *The Sack-'em-up Men*, London (1928)

39 **Ballantine, Serjeant :** *Some Experiences of a Barrister's Life*, London (1883)

40 **Banks, Harold K :** *The Strangler!*, New York (1967)

41 **Bardens, Dennis :** *The Ladykillers*, London (1972)

42 —: *Lord Justice Birkett*, London (1962)

43 —: *Famous Cases of Norman Birkett KC*, London (1963)

44 **Barker, Dudley :** *Palmer : The Rugeley Poisoner*, London (1935)

45 —: *Lord Darling's Famous Cases*, London (1936)

46 **Barker, Ralph :** *Verdict on a Lost Flyer*, London (1969)

47 **Barnard, A :** *The Harlot Killer*, London (1953)

48 **Barthel, Joan :** *A Death in Canaan*, New York (1976)

49 —: *A Death in California*, New York (1981)

50 **Barzun, J :** *Burke and Hare:The Resurrection Men*, New Jersey (1974)

51 **Beal, E (Ed) :** *The Trial of Adelaide Bartlett*, London (1886)

52 **Beattie, John :** *The Yorkshire Ripper Story*, London (1981)

53 **Beaver, Ninette, Ripley, B K** and **Trese, Patrick :** *Caril*, Philadelphia (1974)

54 **Bechhofer Roberts, C E :** *Famous American Trials*, London (1974)

55 —: *Sir Travers Humphreys:His Career and Cases*, London (1936)

56 **Belin, Jean :** *My Work at the Sûreté*, London (1950)

57 **Bell, Terry :** *Bitter Hill*, Manurema NZ (1972)

58 **Belli, Melvin :** *My Life on Trial*, New York (1976)

59 **Benedetti, Jean :** *Gilles de Rais:The Authentic Bluebeard*, London (1971)

60 **Bennett, Benjamin :** *Too Late for Tears*, Cape Town (1950)

61 —: *The Amazing Case of the Baron von Schauroth*, Cape Town (1966)

62 —: *Freedom of the Gallows*, Cape Town (1956)

63 —: *Genius for the Defence*, Cape Town (1967)

64 —: *Some Don't Hang*, Cape Town (1973)

65 —: *Murder Will Speak*, Cape Town (1972)

66 —: *Why Did They Do It?*, Cape Town (1953)

67 —: *Famous South African Murders*, London (1938)

68 —: *The Cohen Case*, Cape Town (1971)

69 —: *The Evil That Men Do*, Cape Town (1950)

70 —: *The Noose Tightens*, Cape Town (1974)

71 —: *Up for Murder*, London (1934)

72 —: *Murder is My Business*, Cape Town (1951)

73 —: *Was Justice Done?*, Cape Town (1975)

74 **Bentley W.G. :** *My Son's Execution*, London (1957)

75 **Berg, Karl :** *The Sadist*, London (1945)

76 **Berrett, James :** *When I was at Scotland Yard*, London (1932)

77 **Berry, James :** *My Experiences as an Executioner*, Newton Abbot 1972)

78 **Beveridge, Peter :** *Inside the CID*, London (1957)

79 **Bierstadt, Edward Hale :** *Enter Murderers*, New York (1937)

80 **Bingham, John :** *The Hunting Down of Peter Manuel*, London (1973)

81 **Birkenhead, Earl of :** *Famous Trials*, London (1926)

82 —: *More Famous Trials*, London (1938)

83 **Birmingham, George :** *Murder Most Foul*, London (1929)

84 **Bishop, Cecil :** *From Information Received*, London (1932)

85 **Bishop, George :** *Witness to Evil*, Los Angeles (1971)

86 **Bishop, Jim :** *The Murder Trial of Judge Peel*, New York (1963)

87 **Bixley, William :** *The Guilty and the Innocent*, London (1957)

88 **Blackham, Robert J :** *Sir Ernest Wild KC*, London (1935)

89 **Bloch, I :** *Marquis de Sade*, New York (1958)

90 **Block, Eugene :** *Chemist of Crime*, London (1975)

91 **Blom-Cooper, Louis :** *The Law as Literature*, London (1961)

92 **Blyth, H :** *Madeleine Smith*, London (1975)

93 **Boar, Roger** and **Blundell, Nigel :** *The World's Most Infamous Murders*, London

(1983)

94 Bocca, Geoffrey : *The Life and Death of Sir Harry Oakes*, London (1959)

95 Bohannan, Paul (Ed) : *African Homicide and Suicide*, Princeton (1960)

96 Bolitho, William : *Murder for Profit*, London (1926)

97 Borniche, Roger : *Flic Story*, London (1976)

98 Borowitz, Albert : *The Woman Who Murdered Black Satin*, Ohio (1981)

99 Borrell, Clive and **Cashinella, Brian :** *Crime in Britain Today*, London (1975)

100 Bosanquet, Sir Ronald : *The Oxford Circuit*, London (1951)

101 Boswell, Charles and **Thompson, Lewis :** *The Carlyle Harris Case*, New York (1961)

102 —: *The Girl with the Scarlet Brand*, London (n.d.)

103 Boucher, Anthony : *The Quality of Murder*, New York (1962)

104 Bowen-Rowlands, Ernest : *In the Light of the Law*, London (1931)

105 —: *Seventy-two years at the Bar*, London (1924)

106 Bowker, A E : *Behind the Bar*, London (1947)

107 —: *A Lifetime with the Law*, London (1961)

108 Bowers, William J : *Executions in America*, Lexington (1974)

109 Brennan, T C : *The Gun Alley Tragedy*, Melbourne (1922)

110 Bresler, Fenton : *Lord Goddard*, London (1977)

111 —: *Reprieve*, London (1965)

112 —: *Scales of Justice*, London (1973)

113 Brett, Peter : *The Beamish Case*, Melbourne (1966)

114 Brice, A H M : *Look Upon the Prisoner*, London (1926)

115 Bridges, Yseult : *Two Studies in Crime*, London (1959)

116 —: *How Charles Bravo Died*, London (1956)

117 —: *Poison and Adelaide Bartlett*, London (1962)

118 —: *Saint with Red Hands*, London (1954)

119 Broad, Lewis : *The Innocence of Edith Thompson*, London (1952)

120 Brock, Alan : *Casebook of Crime*, London (1948)

121 Brome, Vincent : *Reverse Your Verdict*, London (1971)

122 Brookes, Canon J A R : *Murder in Fact and Fiction*, London (1926)

123 Brophy, John : *The Meaning of Murder*, London (1966)

124 Brown, Wenzell : *Introduction to Murder*, London (1953)

125 Browne, Douglas G : *Sir Travers Humphreys*, London (1953)

126 Browne, Douglas G and **Tullett E V :** *Sir Bernard Spilsbury:His Life and Cases*, London (1951)

127 Browne, G Lathom and **Stewart C G :** *Trials for Murder by Poisoning*, London (1883)

128 Browning, Norma Lee : *The Psychic World of Peter Hurkos*, London (1972)

129 Brussel, James A : *Casebook of a Crime Psychiatrist*, New York (1968)

130 Buchanan, A J (Ed) : *The Trial of Ronald Geeves Griggs*, Sydney (1930

131 Buchanan, Edna : *Carr: Five Years of Rape and Murder*, New York (1969)

132 Bugliosi, Vincent : *The Manson Murders*, London (1974)

133 Bugliosi, Vincent with **Hurwitz, Ken :** *Till Death Us Do Part*, New York (1978)

134 Burn, Gordon : *Somebody's Husband, Somebody's Son*, London (1984)

135 Burnaby, Evelyn : *Memories of Famous Trials*, London (1907)

136 Burt, Leonard : *Commander Burt of Scotland Yard*, London (1959)

137 Busch, Francis X : *Guilty or Not Guilty?*, London (1967)

138 —: *They Escaped the Hangman*, London (1957)

139 Butler, Geoffrey L : *Madeleine Smith*, London (1935)

140 Butler, Ivan : *Murderers' England*, London (1973)

141 —: *Murderers' London*, 1973)

142 Byrne, Gerald : *Borstal Boy*, London (n.d.)

143 —: *J.G Haigh:Acid Bath Killer*, London (n.d.)

144 Byrnes, Thomas : *Professional Criminals of America*, New York (1886)

145 Camp, John : *One Hundred Years of Medical Murder*, London (1982)

146 —: *Holloway Prison*, Newton Abbot (1974)

147 Campbell, Marjorie Freeman : *A*

Century of Crime, Toronto (1970)

148 —: *Torso*, Toronto (1974)

149 **Camps, Francis E :** *Camps on Crime*, London (1973)

150 —: *Medical and Scientific Investigations on the Christie Case*, London (1953)

151 —: *The Investigation of Murder*, London (1966)

152 **Cannell, J C :** *New Light on the Rouse Case*, London (1932)

153 —: *When Fleet Street Calls*, London (1932)

154 **Cantillon, Richard H :** *In Defence of the Fox*, Atlanta (1972)

155 **Capon, P :** *The Great Yarmouth Mystery*, London (1965)

156 **Capote, Truman :** *In Cold Blood*, London (1966)

157 **Capstick, J :** *Given in Evidence*, London (1960)

158 **Carey, Arthur A :** *On the Track of Murder*, London (1930)

159 **Cargill, David** *and* **Holland, Julian :** *Scenes of Murder – A London Guide*, London (1964)

160 **Carlin, Francis :** *Reminiscences of an ex-Detective*, London (n.d.)

161 **Carpozi, George :** *Ordeal by Trial*, New York (1972)

162 **Carroll, Brian :** *Ned Kelly – Bushranger*, West Australia (1976)

163 **Cartwright, Gary :** *Blood Will Tell*, London (1979)

164 **Carvalho, C** *and* **Sparks, B :** *Crime in Ink*, New York (1929)

165 **Cassellari, René :** *Dramas of French Crime*, London (1930)

166 **Cassity, John Holland :** *The Quality of Murder*, New York (1958)

167 **Casswell, J D :** *A Lance for Liberty*, London (1961)

168 **Cave, Colin F (Intro) :** *Ned Kelly – Man and Myth*, Sydney (1968)

169 **Chamberlain, Sir Roderic :** *Stuart Affair*, London (1973)

170 **Chandler, Geoffrey :** *So You Think I Did It?*, Melbourne (1969)

171 **Cheney, Margaret :** *The Co-Ed Killer*, New York (1976)

172 **Cherrill, Fred :** *Cherrill of the Yard*, London (1954)

173 **Christie, Trevor L :** *Etched in Arsenic*, London (1968)

174 **Churchill, Allen :** *A Pictorial History of American Crime*, New York (1964)

175 **Clark, Ramsey :** *Crime in America*, New York)1970

176 **Clark, Tim** *and* **Penycate, John :** *Psychopath*, London (1976)

177 **Clarke, Sir Edward :** *The Story of My Life*, London (1918)

178 **Clegg, Eric :** *Return Your Verdict*, Sydney (1965)

179 **Clune, Frank :** *Murders on Maunga-tapu*, Sydney (1959)

180 **Cobb, Belton :** *Critical Years at the Yard*, London (1956)

181 —: *Murdered on Duty*, London (1961)

182 —: *The First Detectives*, London (1957)

183 —: *Trials – and Errors*, London (1962)

184 **Cochran, M :** *Texas vs Davis*, Indianapolis (1980)

185 **Cochrane, Louis :** *FBI Man*, London (1967)

186 **Cohen, Sam D :** *One Hundred True Crime Stories*, Cleveland (1946)

187 **Cole, Peter** *and* **Pringle, Peter :** *Can You Positively Identify This Man?*, London (1974)

188 **Cole, Hubert :** *Things for the Surgeon*, London (1964)

189 **Collis, Maurice :** *Trials in Burma*, London (1938)

190 **Condon, John F :** *Jafsie Tells All!*, New York (1936)

191 **Connery, Donald S :** *Guilty Until Proven Innocent*, New York (1977)

192 **Conrad, Barnaby :** *A Revolting Transaction*, New York (1983)

193 **Cook, Fred J :** *The Girl on the Lonely Beach*, New York (1956)

194 **Cooper, David D :** *The Lesson of the Scaffold*, London (1974)

195 **Cooper, William :** *Shall We Ever Know?*, London (1971)

196 **Copeland, James :** *The Butler*, London (1981)

197 **Cornish, G W :** *Cornish of the Yard*, London (1935)

198 **Cornwall, Rupert :** *God's Banker*, London (1984)

199 **Cotton, Leicester :** *The Sydney Assassins*, London (1965)

200 **Coulter, Jack :** *With Malice Aforethought*, Perth (1982)

201 **Cracknell, Robert :** *Clues to the Unknown*, London (1981)

202 **Cray, Ed :** *Burden of Proof*, New York

(1973)

203 Crew, Albert : *The Old Bailey*, London (1933)

204 Criminological Studies No 3 : *The Case of Major Armstrong*, London (n.d.)

205 Crocker, W C : *Far From Humdrum*, London (1967)

206 Cross, Roger : *The Yorkshire Ripper*, London (1981)

207 Crouse, Russel : *Murder Won't Out*, New York (1932)

208 Cullen, Tom : *Autumn of Terror*, London (1965)

209 —: *Crippen:The Mild Murderer*, Boston (1977)

210 —: *Maundy Gregory*, London (1974)

211 Curling, Jonathan : *Janus Weathercock*, London (1938)

212 Curtin, Philip : *Noted Murder Mysteries*, London (1974)

213 Damore, Leo : *In His Garden*, New York (1981)

214 Darrow, Clarence : *The Story of my Life*, New York (1932)

215 David, Andrew : *Famous Criminal Tales*, Minneapolis (1979)

216 David, Christopher : *Waiting For It*, New York (1980)

217 David, Jay : *The Scarsdale Murder*, New York (1980)

218 Davis, Bernice Freeman and **Hirschberg, Al :** *Assignment San Quentin* London (1961)

219 Deale, Kenneth E L : *Memorable Irish Trials*, London (1960)

220 —: *Beyond Any Reasonable Doubt*, Dublin (1971)

221 Deans, R Storry : *Notable Trials:Difficult Cases*, London (1932)

222 Dearden, Harold : *Death Under the Microscope*, London (1934)

223 —: *Queer People*, London (1922)

224 Deeley, Peter : *The Manhunters*, London (1970)

225 Deeley, Peter and **Walker, C :** *Murder in the Fourth Estate*, London (1971)

226 DeFord, Miriam Allen : *Murderers Sane and Mad*, London (1966)

227 De La Torre, Lilian : *The Truth about Belle Gunness*, New York (1955)

228 De Marigny, Alfred : *More Devil Than Saint*, New York (1946)

229 De Quincey, Thomas : *On Murder Considered as one of the Fine Arts*, London (1827)

230 Derleth, August : *Wisconsin Murders*, Sauk City (1968)

231 Devitt, Napier : *Memories of a Magistrate*, London (1934)

232 De Vries, Leonard : *'Orrible Murder*, London (1974)

233 Dew, Walter : *I Caught Crippen*, London (1938)

234 Dewes, Simon : *Doctors of Murder*, London (1962)

235 Dickson, Grierson : *Murder by Numbers*, London (1925)

236 Dilnot, George : *Celebrated Crimes*, London (1925)

237 —: *Man Hunters*, London (1937)

238 —: *Rogue's March*, London (1934)

239 —: *The Real Detective*, London (1933)

240 —: *Triumphs of Detection*, London (1929)

241 Dinnerstein, Leonard : *The Leo Frank Case*, New York (1968)

242 Dobkins, Dwight J and **Hendricks J :** *Winnie Ruth Judd:The Trunk Murders*, New York (1973)

243 Donovan, Robert J : *The Assassins*, London (1956)

244 Douglas, Arthur : *Will the Real Jack the Ripper*, Lancashire (1979)

245 Douglas, H : *Burke and Hare:The True Story*, London (1973)

246 Douthwaite, L C : *Mass Murder*, London (1928)

247 Dower, Alan : *Crime Chemist*, London (1965)

248 Downie, R Angus : *Murder in London*, London (1973)

249 Duffy, C : *88 Men and 2 Women*, New York (1962)

250 Duke, Thomas : *Celebrated Criminal Cases of America*, San Franicso (1910)

251 Duke, Winifred : *Six Trials*, London (1934)

252 —: *The Stroke of Murder*, London (1937)

253 Dunbar, Dorothy : *Blood in the Parlour*, New York (1964)

254 Duncan, Ronald (Ed) : *Facets of Crime*, Cornwall (1975)

255 Dunning, John : *Truly Murderous*, London (1977)

256 —: *Strange Deaths*, London (1981)

257 —: *Murderous Women*, London (1983)

258 Du Parcq, Georges : *Secrets of the French*

Police, London (1934)

259 Du Preez, Peter : *The Vontsteen Case*, Cape Town (1972)

260 Du Rose, John : *Murder was my Business*, London (1971)

261 Dyne, D G : *Famous New Zealand Murders*, Auckland (1969)

262 Eaton, Harold : *Famous Poison Trials*, London (1923)

263 Eddowes, M : *The Man on your Conscience*, London (1965)

264 Eddy, J P : *Scarlet and Ermine*, London (1960)

265 Edgington, Harry : *The Borgias*, London (1981)

266 Ehrmann, Herbert R : *The Case That Will Not Die*, London (1970)

267 Elliott, Robert G *with* **Beatty, Albert R :** *Agent of Death*, New York (1940)

268 Ellis, Anthony : *Prisoner at the Bar*, London (1934)

269 Ellis, J C : *Black Fame*, London (n.d.)

270 —: *Blackmailers and Co.*, London (1928)

271 Eshelman, B : *Death Row Chaplain*, New Jersey (1962)

272 Fabian Robert : *Fabian of the Yard*, London (1950)

273 Fairlie, Gerard : *The Reluctant Cop*, London (1958)

274 Faralicq, René : *The French Police from Within*, London (1933)

275 Farson, Daniel : *Jack the Ripper*, London (1972)

276 Fast, Howard : *The Passion of Sacco and Vanzetti*, London (1954)

277 Fawkes, Sandy : *Killing Time*, London (1978)

278 Fay, E S : *The Life of Mr Justice Swift*, London (1939)

279 Felstead, S T : *Sir Richard Muir*, London (1927)

280 Ferrier, J K : *Crooks and Crime*, London (1928)

281 Fielder, Peter and **Steele, Peter :** *Alibi at Midnight*, London (1974)

282 Finney, Jack : *Forgotten News:The Crime of the Century and Other Lost Stories*, New York (1983)

283 Firmin, Stanley : *Murderers in our Midst*, London (1955)

284 —: *Crime Man*, London (1950)

285 Firth, J B : *A Scientist Turns to Crime*, London (1960)

286 Fitzgerald, John D : *Studies in Australian Crime*, Syndey (1924)

287 —: *Studies in Australian Crime-Second Series* Sydney (1924)

288 Fletcher, G : *The Life and Career of Dr William Palmer of Rugeley*, London (1925)

289 Floriot, René : *When Justice Falters*, London (1968)

290 Foot, Paul : *Who Killed Hanratty?*, London (1971)

291 Forbes, Ian : *Squad Man*, London (1973)

292 Forrest, A J : *Interpol*, London (1955)

293 Forster, Joseph : *Studies in Black and Red*, London (1896)

294 Fowler, Gene : *The Great Mouthpiece*, New York (1931)

295 Fox, James : *White Mischief*, London (1982)

296 Fraenkel, Osmand : *Sacco-Vanzetti Case*, London (1931)

297 Frank, Gerold : *The Boston Strangler*, London (1967)

298 Franke, David : *Torture Doctor*, New York (1975)

299 Franklin, Charles : *The Woman in the Case*, London (1967)

300 —: *A Mirror of Murder*, London (1964)

301 —: *The World's Worst Murderers*, London (1965)

302 Freeman, Lucy : *Before I Kill More*, New York (1955)

303 French, Stanley : *Crime Every Day*, London (1976)

304 Friedland, Martin L : *The Trials of Israel Lipski*, London (1984)

305 Frost, George : *Flying Squad*, London (1949)

306 Furneaux, Rupert : *Michael John Davies*, London (1962)

307 —: *Robert Hoolhouse*, London (1960)

308 —: *Guenther Podola*, London (1960)

309 —: *The Medical Murderer*, London (1957)

310 —: *The Murder of Lord Erroll*, London (1961)

311 —: *They Died by the Gun*, London (1962)

312 —: *The Two Stranglers of Rillington Place*, London (1961)

313 —: *Courtroom USA — 1*, London (1962)

314 —: *Courtroom USA — 2*, London (1963)

315 —: *Famous Criminal Cases–1*, London (1954)

316 —: *Famous Criminal Cases–2*, London (1955)

317 —: *Famous Criminal Cases–3*, London (1956)

318 —: *Famous Criminal Cases–4*, London (1957)

319 —: *Famous Criminal Cases–5*, London (1958)

320 —: *Famous Criminal Cases–6*, London (1960)

321 —: *Famous Criminal Cases–7*, London (1962)

322 **Gaddis, Thomas E** and **Long, James O** : *Killer;A Journal of Murder*, New York (1970)

323 **Gaddis, Thomas E** : *Birdman of Alcatraz*, New York (1955)

324 **Galtier-Boissière, Jean** : *Mysteries of the French Police*, London (1938)

325 **Garvie, Sheila** : *Marriage to Murder*, Edinburgh (1980)

326 **Gaute, J H H** and **Odell, Robin** : *Lady Killers*, London (1980)

327 —: *Lady Killers–2*, London (1981)

328 **Gaylin, Willard** : *The Killing of Bonnie Garland*, New York (1982)

329 **Gettinger, S H** : *Sentenced to Die*, New York (1979)

330 **Gibbs, Dorothy** and **Maltby, Herbert** : *The True Story of Maria Marten*, London (1949)

331 **Gibney, J and D** : *The Gatton Mystery*, Sydney (1977)

332 **Gilmore, John** : *The Tucson Murders*, New York (1970)

333 **Giono, Jean** : *The Dominici Affair*, London (1956)

334 **Gilbert, Michael** : *Doctor Crippen*, London (1953)

335 **Gladstone-Smith, Peter** : *The Crime Explosion*, London (1970)

336 **Glaister, John** : *Final Diagnosis*, London (1964)

337 —: *The Power of Poison*, London (1954)

338 **Glaister, John** and **Brash, James Couper** : *Medico-Legal Aspects of the Ruxton Case*, Edinburgh (1937)

339 **Glaser, H** : *Poison*, London (1937)

340 **Godsell, Philip A** : *They Got Their Man*, London (1932)

341 **Godwin, George** : *Peter Kürten–A Study in Sadism*, London (1938)

342 **Godwin, John** : *Murder USA*, New York (1978)

343 **Godwin, John** : *Killers in Paradise*, London (1962)

344 —: *Killers Unknown*, London (1960)

345 **Golden, Harry** : *The Lynching of Leo Frank*, London (1965)

346 **Gollomb, Joseph** : *Crimes of the Year*, New York (1931)

347 **Goodman, Derrick** : *Crime of Passion*, London (1958)

348 **Goodman,** Jonathan : *Posts Mortem*, Newton Abbot (1971)

349 —: *The Killing of Julia Wallace*, London (1969)

350 —: *The Stabbing of George Harry Storrs*, Newton Abbot (1983)

351 —: *The Burning of Evelyn Foster*, London (1983)

352 —: *The Pleasures of Murder*, London (1983)

353 **Gough, W C** : *From Kew Observatory to Scotland Yard*, London (1927)

354 **Graham, Evelyn** : *Fifty Years of Famous Judges*, London (1930)

355 —: *Lord Darling and his Famous Trials*, London (1929)

356 **Graves, Robert** : *They Hanged my Saintly Billy*, London (1957)

357 **Green, Jonathon** : *The Directory of Infamy*, London (1980)

358 **Greeno, Edward** : *War on the Underworld*, London (1960)

359 **Greenwall, Harry** : *They Were Murdered in France*, London (1957)

360 **Gribble, Leonard** : *Famous Judges and Their Trials*, London (1957)

361 —: *Great Detective Exploits*, London (1958)

362 —: *Adventures in Murder*, London (1954)

363 —: *Clues That Spelled Guilty*, London (1961)

364 —: *Famous Feats of Detection and Deduction*, London (1933)

365 —: *Famous Manhunts*, London (1953)

366 —: *Famous Stories of the Murder Squad*, London (1966)

367 —: *Great Manhunters of the Yard*, London (1966)

368 —: *Hallmark of Horror*, London

369 —: *Murders Most Strange*, London (1959)

370 —: *Queens of Crime*, London (1932)

371 —: *Sisters of Cain*, London (1972)

372 —: *Stories of Famous Detectives*, London (1963)

373 —: *Strange Crimes of Passion*, London (1970)

374 —: *Such Was Their Guilt*, London (1974)

375 —: *Such Women Are Deadly*, London (1965)

376 —: *When Killers Err*, London (1962)

377 —: *They Got Away With Murder*, London (1971)

378 —: *They Challenged Scotland Yard*, London (1963)

379 —: *They Had a Way With Women*, London (1967)

380 —: *Triumphs of Scotland Yard*, London (1955)

381 **Grice, Edward** : *Great Cases of Sir Henry Curtis-Bennett*, London (1937)

382 **Grierson, Francis** : *Famous French Crimes*, London (1959)

383 —: *The Complete Crook–in France*, London (1934)

384 **Griffiths, Major Arthur** : *Mysteries of Police and Crime*, London (1898)

385 **Grimshaw, Eric** and **Jones, Glyn** : *Lord Goddard:His Career and Cases*, London (1958)

386 **Grombach, John V** : *The Great Liquidator*, New York (1980)

387 **Gross, Kenneth** : *The Alice Crimmins Case*, New York (1975)

388 **Grosso, Sonny** and **Devaney, John** : *Murder at the Harlem Mosque*, New York (1977)

389 **Gurr, Tom and Cox, H H** : *Famous Australasian Crimes*, London (1957)

390 —: *Obsession*, London (1958)

391 **Gurwell, John K** : *Mass Murder in Houston*, Houston (1974)

392 **Gurwin, Larry** : *The Calvi Affair*, London (1984)

393 **Gwynn, Gordon** : *Did Adelaide Bartlett ...?* London (1950)

394 **Habe, Hans** : *Gentlemen of the Jury*, London (1967)

395 **Haden-Guest, Anthony** : *Bad Dreams*, New York (1981)

396 **Haestier, Richard** : *Dead Men Tell Tales*, London (1934)

397 **Haines, Max** : *Bothersome Bodies*, Toronto (1977)

398 —: *Crime Flashback*, Toronto (1980)

399 —: *Crime Flashback 2*, Toronto (1981)

400 **Halbert, Sara** : *Call Me Counselor*, Philadelphia (1977)

401 **Hale, Leslie** : *Hanged in Error*, London (1961)

402 **Hall, Sir John** : *The Bravo Mystery and Other Cases*, London (1923)

403 **Hall, Victor C** : *Dreamtime Justice*, Adelaide (1962)

404 **Halper, Albert (Ed)** : *The Chicago Crime Book*, Cleveland (1967)

405 **Hambrook, Walter** : *Hambrook of the Yard*, London (1937)

406 **Hammer, Richard** : *Illustrated History of Organised Crime*, New York (1975)

407 **Hancock, R** : *Ruth Ellis*, London (1963)

408 **Hansford Johnson, P** : *On Iniquity*, London (1967)

409 **Hardwick, M** : *Doctors on Trial*, London (1961)

410 **Harlow, Alvin F** : *Murders Not Quite Solved*, New York (1938)

411 **Harris, Paul** : *The Garvie Trial*, Aberdeen (1969)

412 **Harris, Richard (Ed)** : *The Reminiscences of Sir Henry Hawkins*, London (1904)

413 **Harrison, Michael** : *Clarence*, London (1972)

414 **Harrison, Richard** : *Criminal Calendar*, London (1951)

415 —: *Criminal Calendar II*, London (1952)

416 **Hart, Dennis** : *Hendrick The Axe Collector*, London (1964)

417 **Hartman, Mary S** : *Victorian Murderesses*, New York (1976)

418 **Harvey, John R** : *Hangman's Clients*, Sydney (1948)

419 **Hastings, Macdonald** : *The Other Mr Churchill*, London (1963)

420 **Hastings, Sir Patrick** : *Autobiography*, London (1948)

421 —: *Cases in Court*, London (1949)

422 **Hastings, Patricia** : *The Life of Sir Patrick Hastings*, London (1959)

423 **Hatherill, George** : *A Detective's Story*, London (1971)

424 **Hattersley, Alan F** : *The First South African Detectives*, Cape Town (1960)

425 **Havers, Sir Michael, Shankland, P** and

Barrett, A : *A Tragedy in Three Voices*, London (1980)

426 Hawkes, George H : *Hand in Glove*, Sydney (n.d.)

427 Hawkes, Harry : *Murder on the A34*, London (1970)

428 —: *Capture of the Black Panther*, London (1978)

429 Hébert, Jacques : *The Coffin Affair*, Toronto (1982)

430 Heimer, Mel : *The Cannibal*, New York (1971)

431 Helpern, Milton *with* Knight, Bernard : *Autopsy*, New York (1977)

432 Henderson, Bruce *and* Summerlin, Sam : *The Super Sleuths*, London (1976)

433 Henry, J : *Detective Inspector Henry's Famous Cases*, London (n.d.)

434 Heppenstall, Rayner : *A Little Pattern of French Crime*, London (1969)

435 —: *Bluebeard and After*, London (1972)

436 —: *French Crime in the Romantic Age*, London (1970)

437 —: *The Sex War and Others*, London (1973)

438 Hervey, H : *Cameos of Indian Crime*, London (n.d.)

439 Hibbert, C : *The Roots of Evil*, London (1963)

440 Hicks, Seymour : *Not Guilty M'Lord*, London (1939)

441 Higdon, Hal : *The Crime of the Century*, New York (1975)

442 Higgins, Robert : *In The Name of the Law*, London (1958)

443 Hill, Paull : *Portrait of a Sadist*, London (1960)

444 Hodge, Harry : *The Black Maria*, London (1935)

445 Holden, Anthony : *The St Albans Poisoner*, London (1974)

446 Holmes, Paul : *The Trials of Dr Coppolino*, New York (1968)

447 —: *The Sheppard Murder Case*, New York (1961)

448 Holroyd, J E : *The Gaslight Murders*, London (1960)

449 Holzer, Hans : *Murder in Amityville*, London (1980)

450 Honeycombe, Gordon : *The Murders of the Black Museum*, London (1982)

451 Hoover, J Edgar : *Persons in Hiding*, Boston (1938)

452 Horwell, John E : *Horwell of the Yard*, London (1947)

453 Hoskins, Percy : *The Sound of Murder*, London (1973)

454 —: *They Almost Escaped*, London (1937)

455 House, Jack : *Square Mile of Murder*, Edinburgh (1961)

456 —: *Murder Not Proven*, Glasgow (1984)

457 Houts, Marshall : *Kings X*, New York (1972)

458 Howard, Clark : *The Zebra Killings*, New York (1979)

459 —: *Brothers in Blood*, New York (1983)

460 Huggett, R *and* Berry, P : *Daughters of Cain*, London (1956)

461 Hughes, Rupert : *The Complete Detective*, New York (1950)

462 Humphreys, Christmas : *Seven Murders*, London (1931)

463 —: *Both Sides of the Circle*, London (1978)

464 Humphreys, Sir Travers : *A Book of Trials*, London (1953)

465 —: *Criminal Days*, London (1946)

466 Hunt, Peter : *Oscar Slater:The Great Suspect*, London (1951)

467 —: *The Madeleine Smith Affair*, London (1950)

468 Huntley, B : *Bomb Squad*, London (1977)

469 Huson, Richard (Ed) : *Sixty Famous Trials*, London (1938)

470 Hussey, R F : *Murderer Scot-Free*, Newton Abbot (1973)

471 Hyde, H Montgomery : *Carson*, London (1953)

472 —: *Crime Has its Heroes*, London (1976)

473 —: *Norman Birkett:The Life of Lord Birkett of Ulverston*, London (1964)

474 —: *Sir Patrick Hastings:His Life and Cases*, London (1960)

475 —: *Cases That Changed the Law*, London (1951)

476 —: *Lord Reading*, London (1967)

477 —: *United in Crime*, London (1955)

478 Hyde, H Montgomery *and* Kisch, John H : *An International Casebook of Crime*, London (1962)

479 Hynd, Alan : *Violence in the Night*, London (1955)

480 Idriess, Ion L : *Man Tracks*, Sydney

(1935)

481 **Inglis, K S :** *The Stuart Case*, Melbourne (1961)

482 **Irving, H B :** *A Book of Remarkable Criminals*, London (1918)

483 —: *Studies of French Criminals in the Nineteenth Century*, London (1901)

484 **Jackson, Brian :** *The Black Flag*, London (1981)

485 **Jackson, Christopher :** *Manuel*, London (1965)

486 **Jackson, J H :** *Murder Book*, New York (1945)

487 **Jackson, Sir Richard :** *Occupied With Crime*, London (1967)

488 **Jackson, Robert :** *Coroner:The Biography of Sir Bentley Purchase*, London (1963)

489 —: *Francis Camps*, London (1975)

490 —: *Case for the Prosecution: A Biography of Sir Archibald Bodkin*, London (1962)

491 —: *The Chief:The Biography of Gordon Hewart, Lord Chief Justice of England 1922–1940*, London (1959)

492 —: *The Crime Doctors*, London (1966)

493 **Jackson, Stanley :** *Mr Justice Avory*, London (1935)

494 —: *The Life and Cases of Mr Justice Humphreys*, London (1955)

495 —: *John George Haigh*, London (1953)

496 —: *The Old Bailey*, London (1978)

497 **Jacobs, Philip A :** *Famous Australian Trials and Memories of the Law*, Melbourne (1943)

498 **Jacobs, T C H :** *Aspects of Murder*, London (1955)

499 —: *Cavalcade of Murder*, London (1955)

500 —: *Pageant of Murder*, London (1956)

501 **Jenkins, Romilly :** *The Dilessi Murders*, Londono (1961)

502 **Jesse, F Tennyson :** *Comments on Cain*, London (1948)

503 —: *Murder and its Motives*, London (1924)

504 **Johnson, W Branch :** *The Arsenic Age*, London (n.d.)

505 **Jonas, George** and **Amiel, Barbara :** *By Persons Unknown*, Toronto (1977)

506 **Jones, Ann :** *Women Who Kill*, New York (1980)

507 **Jones, Elwyn :** *On Trial*, London (1978)

508 —: *The Last Two to Hang*, London (1966)

509 **Jones, Elwyn** and **Lloyd, John :** *The Ripper File*, London (2975)

510 **Jones, Ken :** *Etched in Murder*, New York (1959)

511 **Jones, Walter :** *My Own Case*, London (1966)

512 **Jowitt, Earl :** *Some Were Spies*, London (1954)

513 **Joyner, William :** *Murder Squad*, Johannesburg (1968)

514 **Justice, Jean :** *Murder v Murder*, Paris (1964)

515 **Kaplan, John** and **Waltz, Jon R :** *The Trial of Jack Ruby*, New York (1965)

516 **Keeton, G W :** *Guilty but Insane*, London (1961)

517 **Kefauver, Estes :** *Crime in America*, London (1952)

518 **Kelly, Alexander :** *Jack the Ripper:A Bibliography and Review of the Literature*, London (1973)

519 **Kelly, G G :** *The Gun in the Case*, Auckland (1963)

520 **Kelly, Tom :** *Murders:Washington's Most Famous Murder Stories*, Washington (1976)

521 **Kelly, Vince :** *The Shark Arm Case*, Sydney (1963)

522 —: *The Charge is Murder*, London (1965)

523 **Kennaugh, Robert Charles :** *Contemporary Murder*, Johannesburg (1968)

524 **Kennedy, Ludovic :** *Ten Rillington Place*, London (1961)

525 **Kent, Arthur :** *Death Doctors*, London (1974)

526 **Kershaw, Alister :** *Murder in France*, London (1955)

527 **Keyes, Edward :** *The Michigan Murders*, London (1978)

528 **Keylin, Aileen** and **Demirnian, Arto Jr :** *Crime as Reported by the New York Times*, New York (1976)

529 **Kilgallen, Dorothy :** *Murder One*, New York (1967)

530 **Kingston, Charles :** *Enemies of Society*, London (1927)

531 —: *Remarkable Rogues*, London (1921)

532 —: *Rogues and Adventuresses*, London (1928)

533 —: *Dramatic Days at the Old Bailey*, London (1923)

534 —: *Law-Breakers*, London (1930)

535 **Kinder, Gary :** *Victim*, New York (1982)

536 **Kinsley, Peter** and **Smyth, Frank** : *I'm Jack*, London (1980)

537 **Klaus, Samuel** : *The Molineux Case*, London (1929)

538 **Klausner, L D** : *Son of Sam*, New York (1981)

539 **Knight, Stephen** : *Jack the Ripper:The Final Solution*, London (1976)

540 **Knowles, Leonard** : *Court of Drama*, London (1966)

541 **Knox, Bill** : *Court of Murder*, London (1968)

542 **Kobler, John** : *The Trial of Ruth Snyder and Judd Gray*, New York (1938)

543 **Krafft-Ebing, Richard von** : *Psychopathia Sexualis*, London (1959)

544 **Kunstler, William A** : *The Minister and the Choir Singer*, London (1964)

545 —: *Beyond a Reasonable Doubt*, New York (1961)

546 **Kurth, Ann** : *Prescription Murder*, New York (1976)

547 **Kwitny, Jonathan** : *The Mullendore Murder Case*, New York (1974)

548 **La Bern, A** : *Haigh:The Mind of a Murderer*, London (1973)

549 —: *The Life and Death of a Ladykiller*, London (1967)

550 **Laborde, Jean** : *The Dominici Affair*, London (1974)

551 **Lambert, Richard S** : *When Justice Faltered*, London (1935)

552 —: *The Universal Provider*, London (1938)

553 **Lambton, Arthur** : *Echoes of Causes Célèbres*, London (n.d.)

554 —: *Thous Shalt Do No Murder*, London (n.d.)

555 **Lambourne, Gerald** : *The Fingerprint Story*, London (1984)

556 **Lamson, David** : *We Who are about to Die*, New York (1936)

557 **Lane, Mark** : *Rush to Judgement*, London (1966)

558 **Lang, Gordon** : *Mr Justice Avory*, London (1935)

559 **Langford, Gerald** : *The Murder of Stanford White*, Indianapolis (1962)

560 **Laurence, John** : *A History of Capital Punishment*, London (1950)

561 —: *Extraordinary Crimes*, London (1931)

562 —: *Seaside Crimes*, London (n.d.)

563 **Leach, Charles E** : *On Top of the Underworld*, London (1933)

564 **Leasor, James** : *Who Killed Sir Harry Oakes?*, London (1983)

565 **Lebourdais, Isabel** : *The Trial of Steven Truscott*, London (1966)

566 **Leeson, B** : *Lost London*, London (1934)

567 **Lefebure, Molly** : *Evidence for the Crown*, London (1955)

568 —: *Murder with a Difference*, London (1958)

569 **Lefkowitz, Bernard** and **Gross, Kenneth G** : *The Sting of Justice*, London (1970)

570 **Leighton, Isabel (Ed)** : *The Aspirin Age:1911–1941*, New York (1949)

571 **Lenotre, G** : *The Guillotine and its Servants*, London (n.d.)

572 **Leopold, Nathan F Jr** : *Life Plus 99 Years*, London (1958)

573 **Lesberg, Sandy (Ed)** : *Picture History of Crime*, New York (1976)

574 **Levitt, L** : *The Healer*, New York (1980)

575 **Levy, J G (Ed)** : *The Necessity for Criminal Appeal*, London (1899)

576 **Levy, Norman** : *The Nan Patterson Case*, New York (1959)

577 **Lewis, Leonard** : *Trunk Crimes Past and Present*, London (n.d.)

578 **Lincoln, Victoria** : *A Private Disgrace:Lizzie Borden by Daylight*, New York (1967)

579 **Lindsay, Philip** : *The Mainspring of Murder*, London (1958)

580 **Lindsey, J** : *Suburban Gentleman*, London (1942)

581 **Linedecker, Clifford L** : *The Man Who Killed Boys*, New York (1980)

582 **Linklater, Eric** : *The Corpse on Clapham Common*, London (1971)

583 **Lisners, John** : *House of Horrors*, London (1983)

584 **Liston, Robert** : *Great Detectives*, New York, 1966

585 **Livingston, Armstrong** and **Stein, John G** : *The Murdered and the Missing*, New York (1947)

586 **Lock, Joan** : *Marlborough Street:The Story of a London Court*, London (1980)

587 —: *The British Policewoman*, London (1979)

588 **Logan, Andy** : *Against the Evidence*, London (1970)

589 **Logan, Guy H B** : *Great Murder Mysteries*, London (1928)

590 —: *Masters of Crime*, London (1928)
591 —: *Rope, Knife and Chair*, London (1930)
592 —: *Verdict and Sentence*, London (1935)
593 —: *Wilful Murder*, London (1935)
594 —: *Guilty or Not Guilty?*, London (1928)
595 —: *Dramas of the Dock*, London (1930)
596 **Lombroso, C** : *Criminal Man*, New York (1911)
597 **Longoni, J C** : *Four Patients of Dr Deibler*, London (1970)
598 **Longworth, Frank** : *With Detectives Around the World*, London (1937)
599 **Lucas, Norman** : *Murder of Muriel McKay*, London (1971)
600 —: *Sex Killers*, London (1974)
601 —: *The Child Killers*, London (1970)
602 —: *The Laboratory Detectives*, London (1971)
603 —: *The Lucan Mystery*, London (1975)
604 —: *The Monster Butler*, London (1979)
605 **Lunde, Donald T** : *Murder and Madness*, San Francisco (1976)
606 **Lunde, Donald T** and **Morgan, Jefferson** : *The Die Song*, New York (1980)
607 **Lundsgaarde, Henry P** : *Murder in Space City*, New York (1977)
608 **Lustgarten, Edgar** : *Defender's Triumph*, London (1951)
609 —: *The Business of Murder*, London (1968)
610 —: *The Murder and the Trial*, London (1960)
611 —: *The Woman in the Case*, London (1955)
612 —: *Verdict in Dispute*, London (1949)
613 —: *The Chalkpit Murder*, London (1974)
614 —: *A Century of Murderers*, London (1978)
615 —: *The Illustrated History of Crime*, London (1976)
616 —: *The Judges and the Judged*, London (1961)
617 **Lynch, P P** : *No Remedy for Death*, London (1970)
618 **Lyons, Frederick J** : *George Joseph Smith*, London (1935)
619 **Lytton, Lord** : *Eugene Aram*, London (1831)
620 **MacDonald, John** : *The Murderer and his Victim*, Springfield (1961)
621 **MacDonald, John D** : *No Deadly Drug*, New York (1968)
622 **MacDougall, A W** : *The Maybrick Case*, London (1891)
623 **Macé, Gustave** : *My First Crime*, London (1886)
624 **MacGregor, G** : *The History of Burke and Hare*, Glasgow (1884)
625 **Machlin, Milt** : *Libby*, New York (1980)
626 **Mackaye, Milton** : *Dramatic Crimes of 1927*, New York (1928)
627 **MacKenzie, F A** : *World Famous Crimes*, London (1927)
628 **Maeder, Thomas** : *The Unspeakable Crimes of Dr Petiot*, Boston (1980)
629 **Magee, Doug** : *Slow Coming Dark*, London (1982)
630 **Mailer, Norman** : *The Executioner's Song*, London (1979)
631 **Manchester, William** : *Death of a President*, London (1967)
632 **Marchbanks, D** : *The Moors Murders*, London (1966)
633 **Marjoribanks, Edward** : *The Life of Lord Carson*, London (1963)
634 —: *The Life of Sir Edward Marshall Hall*, London (1930)
635 **Mark, Sir Robert** : *In the Office of Constable*, London (1973)
636 **Marks, L** and **Van Den Bergh, T** : *Ruth Ellis:A Case of Diminished Responsibility*, London (1977)
637 **Martin, John Bartlow** : *Why Did They Kill?*, New York (1952)
638 **Massie, Allen** : *Ill Met by Gaslight*, Edinburgh (1980)
639 **Masters, Brian** : *Killing for Company*, London (1985)
640 **Masters, R E L** and **Lea, Edward** : *Sex Crimes in History*, New York (1966)
641 **Matters, Leonard** : *The Mystery of Jack the Ripper*, London (1928)
642 **Matthews, David A** : *Crime Doctor*, London (1959)
643 **Maxwell, R** : *The Christie Case*, London (n.d.)
644 **May, H J** : *Murder by Consent*, London (1968)
645 **Maybrick, F E** : *Mrs Maybrick's Own Story*, London (1904)
646 **Maycock, Sir Willoughby** : *Celebrated Crimes and Criminals*, London (1890)
647 **Medley, Robert (Ed)** : *Classics in

Murder, London (1984)

648 McCafferty, John : *Mac, I've Got a Murder*, London (1975)

649 McClement, Fred : *The Strange Case of Ambrose Small*, Toronto (1974)

650 McClure, James : *Killers*, London (1976)

651 McComas, Francis : *Graveside Companion*, New York (1962)

652 McConnell Bodkin, M : *Famous Irish Trials*, London (1918)

653 McConnell, Brian : *Found Naked and Dead*, London (1974)

654 McConnell, Brian and **Bence, Douglas** : *The Nilsen File*, London (1983)

655 McConnell, Jean : *The Detectives*, London (1976)

656 McCormick, Donald : *Murder by Perfection*, London (1970)

657 —: *Murder by Witchcraft*, London (1968)

658 —: *The Identity of Jack the Ripper*, London (1959)

659 —: *The Red Barn Mystery*, London (1967)

660 McCurtin, Peter : *Murder in the Penthouse*, New York (1980)

661 McDade, Thomas M : *The Annals of Murder*, Oklahoma (1961)

662 McGinniss, Joe : *Fatal Vision*, New York (1983)

663 McKernan, M (Ed) : *The Crime and Trial of Leopold and Loeb*, New York (1957)

664 McKnight, Gerald : *The Murder Squad*, London (1967)

665 McLaughlin, Terence : *The Coward's Weapon*, London (1980)

666 McLendon, J : *Deathwork*, London (1978)

667 McNulty, Faith : *The Burning Bed*, New York (1980)

668 McVicar, John : *McVicar by Himself*, London (1974)

669 Mencken, A : *By the Neck*, New York (1942)

670 Mewshaw, Michael : *Life for Death*, New York (1983)

671 Millen, Ernest : *Specialist in Crime*, London (1972)

672 Meyer, Gerald : *The Memphis Murders*, New York (1974)

673 Meyer, Peter : *The Yale Murder*, New York (1982)

674 Miller, Orlo : *The Donnellys must Die*, Toronto (1962)

675 Miller, Webb : *I Found No Peace*, London (1936)

676 Mitchaud, Stephen G and **Aynesworth, Hugh** : *The Only Living Witness*, New York (1983)

677 Mitchell, C Ainsworth : *A Scientist in the Criminal Courts*, London (1945)

678 —: *Science and the Criminal*, London (1911)

679 —: *The Scientific Detective and the Expert Witness*, Cambridge (1931)

680 Moiseiwitsch, Maurice : *Five Famous Trials*, London (1962)

681 Mooney, M M : *Evelyn Nesbit and Stanford White*, New York (1976)

682 —: *The Hindenburg*, London (1972)

683 Morgan, Joan : *Mary Blandy*, London (1979)

684 Morland, Nigel : *An Outline of Scientific Criminology*, London (1950)

685 —: *Background to Murder*, London (1955)

686 —: *Hangman's Clutch*, London (1954)

687 —: *International Pattern of Murder*, London (1977)

688 —: *Pattern of Murder*, London (1966)

689 —: *That Friendless Lady*, London (1957)

690 —: *That Nice Miss Smith*, London (1957)

691 Morn, Frank : *The Eye That Never Sleeps*, Bloomington (1982)

692 Morris, Richard B : *Fair Trial*, New York (1952)

693 Morris, Terence and **Blom-Cooper, Louis** : *A Calendar of Murder*, London (1964)

694 —: *Murder in England and Wales since 1957*, London (1979)

695 Morshead, Ian : *The Life and Murder of Henry Morshead*, Cambridge (1982)

696 Mortimer, John : *Famous Trials*, London (1984)

697 Muncie, William : *Crime Pond*, Edinburgh (1979)

698 Murray, John Wilson : *Memoirs of a Great Detective*, London (1904)

699 Musmanno, Michael A : *Verdict!*, New York (1958)

700 Napley, Sir David : *Not Without Prejudice*, London (1982)

701 Nash, Jay Robert : *Among the Missing*, New York (1978)

702 —: *Bloodletters and Badmen*, New York (1973)

703 —: *Murder America*, London (1981)

704 —: *Compendium of World Crime*, London (1983)

705 **Nassau Daily Tribune** : *The Murder of Sir Harry Oakes Bt*, Nassau (1959)

706 **Neil, Arthur Fowler** : *Forty Years of Manhunting*, London (1932)

707 **Nesbit, Evelyn** : *The Untold Story* (1934)

708 **Neustatter, W Lindesay** : *The Mind of the Murderer*, London (1957)

709 **Neville, Richard** and **Clarke, Julie** : *Bad Blood*, London (1979)

710 **Nicholls, Ernest** : *Crime Within the Square Mile*, London (1935)

711 **Nicholson, Michael** : *The Yorkshire Ripper*, London (1979)

712 **Norman, C** : *The Genteel Murderer*, New York (1956)

713 **Noguchi, Thomas T** *with* **Dimona, Joseph** : *Coroner to the Stars*, London (1984)

714 **Oddie, S Ingelby** : *Inquest*, London (1941)

715 **Odell, Robin** : *Exhumation of a Murder*, London (1975)

716 —: *Jack the Ripper in Fact and Fiction*, London (1965)

717 **O'Donnell, Bernard** : *Crimes That Made News*, London (1954)

718 —: *Should Women Hang?*, London (1956)

719 —: *The World's Strangest Murders*, London (1957)

720 —: *The Trials of Mr Justice Avory*, London (1935)

721 **O'Flaherty, M** : *Have You Seen This Woman?*, London (1971)

722 **Olsen, Jack** : *The Man With the Candy*, New York (1974)

723 **Osborne, Charles** : *Ned Kelly*, London (1970)

724 **O'Sullivan, J S O** : *A Most Unique Ruffian*, Melbourne (1968)

725 **O'Sullivan, M** : *Cameos of Crime*, Sydney (1935)

726 **Oswald, H R** : *Memoirs of a London County Coroner*, London (1936)

727 **Packer, Edward** : *The Peasenhall Murder*, Oxford (1980)

728 **Park, W** : *The Truth About Oscar Slater*, London (1927)

729 **Parker, Tony** : *The Plough Boy*, London (1965)

730 **Parmiter, Geoffrey de C** : *Reasonable Doubt*, London (1928)

731 **Parrish, J M** and **Crossland, J R** : *The Fifty Most Amazing Crimes of the Last Hundred Years*, London (1936)

732 **Parry, Edward Abbott** : *The Drama of the Law*, London (1924)

733 **Parry, Leonard A** : *Some Famous Medical Trials*, London (1927)

734 **Pearce, Charles E** : *Unsolved Murder Mysteries*, London (1924)

735 **Pearson, Edmund** : *Murder at Smutty Nose and Other Murders*, London (1927)

736 —: *Instigation of the Devil*, New York (1930)

737 —: *Studies in Murder*, New York (1924)

738 —: *More Studies in Murder*, London (1953)

739 —: *Trial of Lizzie Borden*, London (1939)

740 —: *Five Murders*, New York (1928)

741 **Pearson, Francis** : *Memoirs of a KC's Clerk*, London (1935)

742 **Pearson, John** : *The Profession of Violence*, London (1972)

743 **Penrose, Valentine** : *The Bloody Countess*, London (1970)

744 **Perry, Hamilton Darby** : *A Chair for Wayne Lonergan*, London (1972)

745 **Peskett, S John** : *Grim, Gruesome and Grisly*, London (1974)

746 **Phillips, Conrad** : *Murderer's Moon*, London (1956)

747 **Phillips, D A** : *The Great Texas Murder Trials*, New York (1979)

748 **Pierrepoint, Albert** : *Executioner: Pierrepoint*, London (1974)

749 **Pitkin, J** : *The Prison Cell and its Lights and Shadows*, London (1918)

750 **Playfair, Giles** : *Crime in Our Century*, London (1977)

751 **Playfair, Giles** and **Sington, Derrick** : *The Offenders*, London (1957)

752 **Pollack, Jack Harrison** : *Dr Sam – An American Tragedy*, Chicago (1957)

753 **Pollock, George** : *Mr Justice McCardie*, London (1934)

754 **Porter, K A** : *The Never Ending Wrong*, London (1977)

755 **Postgate, Raymond** : *Murder, Piracy and Treason*, London (1925)

756 **Potter, J D** : *The Monsters of the Moors*,

London (1966)

757 Poynter, J W : *Forgotten Crimes*, London (1928)

758 Presley, James *and* **Getty, Gerald W** : *Public Defender*, New York (1974)

759 Proyer, Ronald : *Famous Stories of Assassination*, London (1973)

760 Pugh, John : *Goodbye for Ever*, London (1981)

761 Purvis, James : *Great Unsolved Mysteries*, New York (1978)

762 Quinn, M Constantine : *Doctor Crippen*, London (1935)

763 Radin, Edward R : *Twelve Against the Law*, New York (1953)

764 —: *Crimes of Passion*, New York (1953)

765 —: *Headline Crimes of the Year*, Boston (1952)

766 —: *Lizzie Borden:The Untold Story*, New York (1961)

767 —: *It's Time to Tell*, New York (1962)

768 Rae, George W : *Confessions of the Boston Strangler*, London (1957)

769 Rae, Isobel : *Knox the Anatomist*, Edinburgh (1964)

770 Randall, Leslie : *The Famous Cases of Sir Bernard Spilsbury*, London (1936)

771 Raper, A F : *The Tragedy of Lynching*, Chapel Hill (1933)

772 Raphael, John N : *The Caillaux Drama*, London (1914)

773 Rawlings, William A : *A Case for the Yard*, London (1961)

774 Reading, Marquess of : *Rufus Isaacs:First Marquess of Reading*, London (1942)

775 Reid, D *and* **Gurwell, J** : *Eyewitness*, Houston (1973)

776 Reinhardt, James Melvin : *The Murderous Trail of Charles Starkweather*, Springfield (1960)

777 Rentoul, Sir Gervaise : *Sometimes I Think*, London (1940)

778 —: *This is My Case*, London (1944)

779 Reuben, William A : *The Mark Fein Case*, New York (1967)

780 Rhodes, Henry T F : *Alphonse Bertillon*, London (1958)

781 —: *Clues and Crime*, London (1933)

782 —: *In the Tracks of Crime*, London (1952)

783 Rice, Craig : *Forty-Five Murderers*, New York (1952)

784 Roberts, G D : *Law and Life*, London (1964)

785 Robey, Edward : *The Jester and the Court*, London (1976)

786 Robinson, Edward : *Just Murder*, London (1947)

787 Rodell, Marie F (Ed) : *Chicago Murders*, New York (1945)

788 —: *Denver Murders*, New York (1946)

789 —: *Boston Murders*, New York (1948)

790 —: *Charleston Murders*, New York (1947)

791 —: *Cleveland Murders*, New York (1947)

792 —: *Los Angeles Murders*, New York (1947)

793 —: *Detroit Murders*, New York (1948)

794 —: *New York Murders*, New York (1944)

795 —: *San Francisco Murders*, New York (1947)

796 Roen, Samuel : *Murder of a Little Girl*, New York (1973)

797 Rolin, Jean : *Police Drugs*, London (1955)

798 Root, Jonathan : *The Life and Bad Times of Charlie Becker*, London (1962)

799 Roughead, William : *Classic Crimes*, London (1951)

800 —: *Famous Crimes*, London (1935)

801 —: *Tales of the Criminous*, London (1956)

802 —: *Malice Domestic*, London (1928)

803 —: *Rogues Walk Here*, London (1934)

804 —: *Mainly Murder*, London (1937)

805 —: *Neck or Nothing*, London (1939)

806 —: *Twelve Scots Trials*, London (1913)

807 Rovere, Richard H : *Howe and Hummel*, New York (1947)

808 Rowan, David : *Famous American Crimes*, London (1957)

809 —: *Famous European Crimes*, London (1955)

810 Rowland, John : *Criminal Files*, London (1957)

811 —: *More Criminal Files*, London (1958)

812 —: *The Peasenhall Mystery*, London (1962)

813 Rowland, John : *Murder Revisited*, London (1961)

814 —: *Poisoner in the Dock*, London (1960)

815 —: *Unfit to Plead?*, London (1965)

816   —: *The Wallace Case*, London (1949)

817   —: *A Century of Murder*, London (1950)

818   **Rule, Ann** : *The Stranger Beside Me*, New York (1980)

819   **Rumbelow, Donald** : *The Complete Jack the Ripper*, London (1975)

820   —: *The Triple Tree*, London (1982)

821   —: *The Houndsditch Murders*, London (1973)

822   **Runyon, Damon** : *Trials and Other Tribulations*, Philadephia (1926)

823   **Ruotolo, A K** : *Once Upon a Murder*, New York (1978)

824   **Russell, Donn** : *The Best Murder Cases*, London (1958)

825   **Russell, Francis** : *Tragedy in Dedham*, London (1963)

826   **Russell, Guy** : *Guilty or Not Guilty?*, London (1931)

827   **Russell, J D** : *A Chronicle of Death*, Woodbridge, USA (1971)

828   **Russell, Lord** : *Deadman's Hill:Was Hanratty Guilty?*, London (1965)

829   —: *Though the Heavens Fall*, London (1956)

830   **Ryan, B** *with* **Havers, Sir Michael** : *The Poisoned Life of Mrs Maybrick*, London (1977)

831   **Samuels, Charles** : *Death was the Bridegroom*, New York (1955)

832   **Sanders, Bruce** : *Murder Behind the Bright Lights*, London (1958)

833   —: *They Caught These Killers*, London (1968)

834   —: *Murder in Big Cities*, London (1962)

835   —: *Murder in Lonely Places*, London (1960)

836   —: *They Couldn't Lose the Body*, London (1966)

837   **Sanders, Ed** : *The Family*, New York (1970)

838   **Sanson, H (Ed)**: *Executioners All*, London (1962)

839   **Saunders, Edith** : *The Mystery of Marie Lafarge*, London (1951)

840   **Savage, Percy** : *Savage of Scotland Yard*, London (1934)

841   **Scaduto, Anthony** : *Scapegoat*, London (1976)

842   **Schofield, Carey** : *Mesrine*, London (1980)

843   **Schreiber, Flora Rheta** : *The Shoemaker*, New York (1983)

844   **Schwartz, Ted** : *The Hillside Strangler*, New York (1981)

845   **Scott, Sir Harold** : *Scotland Yard*, London (1954)

846   —: *Crime and Criminals*, London (1961)

847   **Seccombe, Thomas (Ed)** : *Twelve Bad Men*, London (1894)

848   **Seedman. A A** : *Chief!*, New York (1974)

849   **Sellwood, Arthur** *and* **Mary** : *Victorian Railway Murders*, London (1979)

850   **Sereny, Gitta** : *The Case of Mary Bell*, London (1972)

851   **Seth, Ronald** : *Petiot*, London (1962)

852   **Sharp, James** : *The Life and Death of Michael X*, Trinidad (1981)

853   **Sharpe, Alan** : *Australian Crimes*, Sydney (1979)

854   —: *Crimes That Shocked Australia*, NSW (1982)

855   **Sharpe, F D** : *Sharpe of the Flying Squad*, London (1938)

856   **Shapiro, Fred C** : *Whitmore*, London (1969)

857   **Shaw, Barry** : *Murderous Yorkshire*, Wakefield (1980)

858   **Shay, Frank** : *Judge Lynch*, New York (1938)

859   **Shears, Richard** : *The Dingo Baby Case*, London (1982)

860   **Shelman, Byron E** : *Death Row Chaplain*, New York (1962)

861   **Sheppard, Sam** : *Endure and Conquer*, Cleveland (1966)

862   **Sheppard, Stephen** : *My Brother's Keeper*, New York (1964)

863   **Sheridan, Leo W** : *I Killed for the Law*, New York (1938)

864   **Shew, E Spencer** : *Companion to Murder*, London (1960)

865   —: *Second Companion to Murder*, London (1962)

866   **Shore, W Teignmouth** : *Crime and its Detection*, London (1931)

867   **Short, Martin** : *Crime Inc.*, London (1984)

868   **Sifakis, Carl** : *Encyclopaedia of American Crime*, New York (1982)

869   **Silk, Stafford** : *The Bogle Mystery*, Sydney (1963)

870   **Simpson, Helen et al** : *The Anatomy of Murder*, New York (1937)

871 **Simpson, Keith** : *Forty Years of Murder*, London (1978)

872 **Singer, Kurt** : *My Greatest Crime Story*, London (1956)

873 —: *My Strangest Case*, New York (1958)

874 —: *Crime Omnibus*, London (1961)

875 **Singer, Kurt** and **Sherrod, Jane** : *Great Adventures in Crime*, Minneapolis (1962)

876 **Skelhorn, Sir Norman** : *Public Prosecutor*, London (1981)

877 **Slipper, Jack** : *Slipper of the Yard*, London (1981)

878 **Smith, Arthur** : *Lord Goddard*, London (1959)

879 **Smith, Edgar** : *Brief Against Death*, New York (1968)

880 —: *Getting Out*, New York (1972)

881 **Smith, Edward H** : *Famous American Poison Mysteries*, London (1926)

882 —: *Mysteries of the Missing*, New York (1927)

883 **Smith, Sir Sydney** : *Mostly Murder*, London (1959)

884 **Smith-Hughes, Jack** : *Unfair Comment Upon Some Victorian Murder Trials*, London (1951)

885 —: *Eight Studies in Justice*, London (1953)

886 **Smyth, Frank** and **Ludwig, Myles** : *The Detectives*, London (1978)

887 **Snow, Edward Rowe** : *Mutiny and Murder*, London (1961)

888 **Soderman, H** : *Policeman's Lot*, London (1957)

889 **Somerfield, Stafford** : *The Authentic Story of J G Haigh*, Manchester (1950)

890 **Soubiran, A** : *The Good Dr Guillotine*, Aberdeen (1962)

891 **Spain, David M** : *Post Mortem*, New York (1974)

892 **Sparrow, Gerald** : *Satan's Children*, London (1966)

893 —: *Vintage Victorian and Edwardian Murder*, London (1971)

894 **Speer, W H** : *The Secret History of Great Crimes*, London (1929)

895 **Spencer, Duncan** : *Love Gone Wrong*, New York (1981)

896 **Spiering, Frank** : *Prince Jack*, New York (1978)

897 **Stack, Andy** : *The I–5 Killer*, New York (1984)

898 —: *Lust Killer*, New York (1983)

899 —: *The Want Ad Killer*, New York (1983)

900 **Stapleton, J W** : *The Great Crime of 1860*, London (1861)

901 **St Aubyn, Giles** : *Infamous Victorians*, London (1971)

902 **Stead, Philip John** : *Vidocq:Picaroon of Crime*, London (1953)

903 —: *The Memoirs of Lacenaire*, London (1952)

904 **Steiger, Brad** : *Mass Murderer*, New York (1967)

905 **Stevens, McLure C L** : *Famous Crimes and Criminals*, London (1924)

906 **Stevens, William Randolph** : *Deadly Intentions*, New York (1982)

907 **Stewart, William** : *Jack the Ripper*, London (1939)

908 **Still, Charles E** : *Styles in Crime*, Philadelphia (1938)

909 **Still, Larry** : *The Limits of Sanity*, Toronto (1972)

910 **Stoddart, Charles** : *Bible John*, Edinburgh (1980)

911 **Sullivan, Robert** : *Goodbye Lizzie Borden*, London (1975)

912 —: *The Disappearance of Dr Parkman*, New York (1971)

913 **Sullivan, Gerald** and **Aronson, Harvey** : *High Hopes:The Amityville Murders*, New York (1981)

914 **Sutherland, Sidney** : *Ten Real Murder Mysteries Never Solved*, New York (1929)

915 **Sutton, Charles** : *The New York Tombs*, New York (1874)

916 **Symons, Julian** : *Beyond a Reasonable Doubt*, London (1960)

917 **Tallant, Robert** : *Murder in New Orleans*, London (1953)

918 **Tanenbaum, Robert** and **Rosenberg, Philip** : *Badge of the Assassin*, New York (1979)

919 **Tanner, Michael** : *Crime and Murder in Victorian Leicestershire*, Leicester (1981)

920 **Tawnahill, R** : *Flesh and Blood*, London (1976)

921 **Taylor, Bernard** : *Cruelly Murdered*, London (1979)

922 **Taylor, Lawrence** : *Trail of the Fox*, London (1981)

923 **Teeters, Negley** with **Hedblom, Jack H** : *"...Hang by the Neck..."*, Springfield (1967)

924 **Thaw, Harry K** : *The Traitor*, New York

(1926)

925 **Thomas, David** : *Seek Out The Guilty*, London (1960)

926 **Thompson, C J S** : *Poison and Poisoners*, London (1931)

927 —: *Poison Mysteries Unsolved*, London (1937)

928 —: *Poison Mysteries in History, Romance and Crime*, London (1925)

929 **Thompson, John** : *Crime Scientist*, London (1980)

930 **Thompson, Thomas** : *Blood and Money*, London (1976)

931 —: *Serpentine*, London (1981)

932 **Thomson, Basil** : *The Criminal*, London (1925)

933 **Thomson, Helen** : *Murder at Harvard*, Boston (1971)

934 **Thorp, Arthur** : *Calling Scotland Yard*, London (1954)

935 **Thorwald, Jurgen** : *Crime and Science*, New York (1967)

936 —: *The Century of the Detective*, New York (1965)

937 —: *Dead Men Tell Tales*, London (1966)

938 —: *Marks of Cain*, New York (1965)

939 —: *Proof of Poison*, London (1966)

940 **Totterdell, G H** : *Country Copper*, London (1956)

941 **Townsend, W** and **L** : *Black Cap*, London (1930)

942 **Train, Arthur** : *True Stories of Crime*, New York (1908)

943 **Traini, Robert** : *Murder for Sex*, London (1960)

944 **Travers, Robert** : *Murder in the Blue Mountains*, London (1972)

945 **Treadwell, C A L** : *Notable New Zealand Trials*, New Plymouth (1936)

946 **Treherne, John** : *The Galapagos Affair*, London (1983)

947 **Trent, Bill** *with* **Truscott, Steven** : *Who Killed Lynn Harper?*, Montreal (1979)

948 **Trillin, Calvin** : *Killings*, New York (1984)

949 **Trilling, Diana** : *Mrs Harris*, New York (1981)

950 **Tullett, Tom** : *No Answer from Foxtrot Eleven*, London (1967)

951 —: *Inside Dartmoor*, London (1966)

952 —: *Inside Interpol*, London (1963)

953 —: *Portrait of a Badman*, London (1956)

954 —: *Strictly Murder*, London (1979)

955 **Tully, Andrew** : *The FBI's Most Famous Cases*, New York (1965)

956 **Turner, C H** : *The Inhumanists*, London (1932)

957 **Twyman, H W** : *The Best Laid Schemes ....*, London (1931)

958 **Tyler, Froom** : *Gallows Parade*, London (1933)

959 **Valenti, Michael** : *Question of Guilt*, New York (1966)

960 **Valentine, Steven** : *The Black Panther Story*, London (1976)

961 **Van Every, Edward** : *Sins of New York*, New York (1930)

962 **Vanstone, Charles** : *A Man in Plain Clothes*, London (1961)

963 **Vassilyev, A T** : *The Ochrana*, London (1930)

964 **Veal, F J P** : *The Wallace Case*, Brighton (1950)

965 **Vidocq, Eugène-François** : *Memoirs of Vidocq*, London (1928)

966 **Villiers, Elizabeth** : *Riddles of Crime*, London (1928)

967 **Vincent, A (Ed)** : *Twelve Bad Women*, London (1897)

968 **Von Feuerbach, Anselm Ritter** : *Narratives of Remarkable Criminal Trials*, London (1846)

969 **Von Sonnenberg, E L** and **Trettin, O** : *Continental Crimes*, London (1935)

970 **Wagner, Margaret Seaton** : *The Monster of Düsseldorf*, London (1932)

971 **Wakefield, H R** : *Landru*, London (1936)

972 —: *The Green Bicycle Case*, London (1930)

973 **Walker-Smith, Derek** : *Lord Reading and his Cases*, London (1934)

974 —: *The Life of Mr Justice Darling*, London (1938)

975 **Walker-Smith, Derek** and **Clarke, Edward** : *The Life and Famous Cases of Sir Edward Clarke*, London (1939)

976 **Walling, George W** : *Recollections of a New York Chief of Police*, New York (1887)

977 **Waller, George** : *Kidnap*, London (1961)

978 **Walls, H J** : *Expert Witness*, London (1972)

979 **Walsh, Sir Cecil** : *The Agra Double Murder*, London (1929)

980 —: *Indian Village Crimes*, London (1929)

981 **Warden, R** and **Groves, M (Ed)** : *Murder Most Foul*, New York (1980)

982 **Warner-Hooke, Nina** and **Thomas, Gil** : *Marshall Hall*, London (1966)

983 **Watkins, Leslie** : *The Sleepwalk Killers*, London (1976)

984 **Watson, Dr** : *Dr Watson's Casebook*, Sydney (1944)

985 **Webb, Duncan** : *Crime is my Business*, London (1953)

986 —: *Deadline for Crime*, London (1955)

987 —: *Line-up for Crime*, London (1956)

988 **Weider, Ben** and **Hapgood, David** : *The Murder of Napoleon*, London (1982)

989 **Wellman, Manly Wade** : *Dead and Gone: Classic Crimes of North Carolina*, Chapel Hill (1954)

990 **Wensley, Frederick Porter** : *Detective Days*, London (1931)

991 **Wertham, Frederic** : *The Show of Violence*, New York (1949)

992 **West, Rebecca** : *A Train of Powder*, London (1955)

993 **Whipple, Sidney B** : *The Lindbergh Crime*, New York (1935)

994 —: *The Trial of Hauptmann*, London (n.d.)

995 **Whitbread, J R** : *The Railway Policemen*, London (1961)

996 **White, Henry A** : *Crimes and Criminals*, Ballarat (1851)

997 **White, W** : *Rope and Faggot: A Biography of Judge Lynch*, New York (1929)

998 **Whitehead, Don** : *The FBI Story*, New York (1956)

999 **Whitelaw, David** : *Corpus Delicti*, New York (1936)

1000 **Whiteley, Cecil** : *Brief Life*, London (1942)

1001 **Whittington-Egan, Richard** : *A Casebook of Jack the Ripper*, London (1975)

1002 —: *The Ordeal of Philip Yale Drew*, London (1972)

1003 —: *The Riddle of Birdhurst Rise*, London (1975)

1004 **Wild, Roland** : *Crimes and Cases of 1933*, London (1934)

1005 —: *Crimes and Cases of 1934*, London (1935)

1006 —: *The Jury Retires*, London (1937)

1007 **Wilkes, Roger** : *Wallace: The Final Verdict*, London (1984)

1008 **Wilkerson, Michael** and **Dick** : *Someone Cry for the Children*, New York (1981)

1009 **Wilkins, Philip A** : *Dramas of the French Courts*, London (n.d.)

1010 —: *Inside the French Courts*, London (n.d.)

1011 **Wilkinson, Lawrence** : *Behind the Face of Crime*, London (1957)

1012 **Willemse, Cornelius W** : *A Cop Remembers*, New York (1931)

1013 **Willcox, Philip H** : *The Detective-Physician*, London (1970)

1014 **Williams, Brad** : *Due Process*, London (1961)

1015 **Williams, E** : *Beyond Belief*, London (1967)

1016 **Williams, Guy** : *The Black Treasures of Scotland Yard*, London (1973)

1017 **Williams, John** : *Heyday for Assassins*, London (1958)

1018 —: *Hume: Portrait of a Double Murderer*, London (1960)

1019 —: *Suddenly at the Priory*, London (1957)

1020 **Williams, Montague** : *Leaves of a Life*, London (1891)

1021 **Williamson, W H** : *Annals of Crime*, London (1930)

1022 **Wilson, Colin** : *The Psychic Detective*, London (1984)

1023 —: *A Casebook of Murder*, London (1969)

1024 —: *Order of Assassins*, London (1972)

1025 —: *A Criminal History of Mankind*, London (1984)

1026 —: *(Intro) Murder in the West Country*, Cornwall (1975)

1027 **Wilson, Colin** and **Pitman, Pat** : *Encyclopaedia of Murder*, London (1961)

1028 **Wilson, Colin** and **Seaman, Donald** : *Encyclopaedia of Modern Murder, 1962–1982*, London (1983)

1029 **Wilson, H J (Ed)** : *The Bayly Case*, Wellington (1934)

1030 **Wilson, J G** : *The Trial of Peter Manuel*, London (1959)

1031 —: *Not Proven*, London (1960)

1032 **Wilson, Patrick** : *Children Who Kill*, London (1973)

1033 —: *Murderess*, London (1971)

1034 **Winslow, L Forbes** : *Recollections of Forty Years*, London (1910)

1035 **Wolfgang, Marvin** : *Patterns in Criminal*

Homicide, Pennsylvania (1958)

1036 Wood, Stuart : *Shades in the Prison House,* London (1932)

1037 Wood, Walter (Ed) : *Survivors' Tales of Famous Crimes,* London (1916)

1038 Woodhall, Edwin T : *Detective and Secret Service Days,* London (n.d.)

1039 —: *Secrets of Scotland Yard,* London (1936)

1040 Woodland, W Lloyd : *Assize Pageant,* London (1952)

1041 Wraxall, Sir Lascelles : *Criminal Celebrities,* London (1863)

1042 Wyden, Peter : *Hired Killers,* London (1964)

1043 Wyndham, Horace : *Famous Trials Retold,* London (n.d.)

1044 —: *Consider Your Verdict,* London (1946)

1045 —: *Crime on the Continent,* London (1928)

1046 —: *Dramas of the Law,* London (n.d.)

1047 —: *Feminine Frailty,* London (1929)

1048 Wyndham-Brown, W F : *The Trial of William Herbert Wallace,* London (1933)

1049 Yallop, David A : *To Encourage the Others,* London (1971)

1050 —: *Deliver Us From Evil,* London (1981)

1051 —: *Beyond Reasonable Doubt?,* Auckland (1978)

1052 —: *In God's Name,* London (1984)

1053 Young, Hugo : *My Forty Years at the Yard,* London (1955)

1054 Young, Gordon : *Valley of Silence,* London (1955)

1055 Young, Wayland : *The Montesi Scandal,* London (1957)

1056 Young, Winifred : *Obsessive Poisoner,* London (1973)

1057 Zamora, William : *Trial By Your Peers,* New York (1973)

Additions to the literature of crime

Bogdanovitch, Peter : *The Killing of a Unicorn,* London (1985)
Boyd, Guy : *Justice in Jeopardy,* Victoria (1984)
Clune, Frank : *The Demon Killer,* Sydney (1948)
Devlin, Patrick : *Easing the Passing,* London (1985)
Dower, Alan : *Deadline,* Victoria (1979)
Hallworth, Rodney *and* **Williams, Mark :** *Where There's a Will ...,*
    London (1983)
Mallon, Andrew : *Leonski: the Brown-out Murders,* Victoria (1979)
Miller, James William : *Don't Call me Killer,* Victoria (1984)
Molomboy, Tom : *Ratten: The Web of Circumstance,* Victoria (1978)
    —: *Who Killed Hannah Jane?,* Sydney (1981)
Schmalzbach, Oscar R : *Profiles of Murder,* Sydney (1971)
Simmonds, James : *Azaria:Wednesday's Child,* West Melbourne
    (1982)
Tennison, Patrick : *Cases in the Career of Philip Opas,* Melbourne
    (1975)

Specialist Booksellers

(Booksellers specializing in second-hand, non-fiction crime books)

Rod and Margot Armitage,
16 The Nook, Crookesmoor, Sheffield, S10 1EJ England.

Clifford Elmer,
8 Balmoral Avenue, Cheadle Hulme, Cheadle, Cheshire, SK8 5EQ, England.

W.H. Gillespie,
Tutt's Cottage, Manor Close, The Street, East Preston, Sussex, England.

Grey House Books,
12a Lawrence Street, Chelsea, London, SW3 5NE, England.

J.C.G. Hammond,
Crown Point, 33 Waterside, Ely, Cambridge, CB7 4AU, England.

Patterson Smith,
23 Prospect Terrace, Montclair, New Jersey 07042, USA.

Frank R. Thorold (Pty) Ltd.,
4th Floor, S.A. Fire House, 103 Fox Street, Johannesburg, South Africa.

Wildy & Sons Limited,
Lincoln's Inn Archway, Carey Street, London, WC2, England.

Richard Williams,
Unit C, 24 Dunstall Street, Scunthorpe, South Humberside, England.

Those who have enjoyed reading in this book about crimes past and present will also enjoy three monthly magazines : *True Detective*, *Master Detective*, and *True Crime*, all of which deal with murder throughout the world. They are published by Argus Consumer Publications Ltd, 12/18 Paul Street, London EC2A 4JS, England.

Y

Z

Index of Places

*N.B. Main entries only are given for the countries. Entries for London, Paris,
San Francisco or New York are omitted, as scattered through the text.*